LONG-RANGE PLANNING FOR MANAGEMENT

REVISED EDITION

EDITED BY

DAVID W. EWING

ASSOCIATE EDITOR,
Harvard Business Review

HARPER & ROW, PUBLISHERS
New York, Evanston, and London

LIBRARY OF CONGRESS CATALOG CARD NUMBER: 63–20320

C–T

Contents

Preface

When *Long-Range Planning for Management* was first published, in 1958, the field was new. There were no other books devoted exclusively to the subject, the number of articles on planning in business magazines was relatively small, and only a handful of companies had organized formally and systematically for long-range planning.

Today the picture is different. The literature covers the subject in far greater depth and detail, business meetings often feature discussions of planning, and many more companies have organized for planning. In fact, it is reported that while less than two hundred corporations had formal long-range planning departments (one or more men assigned to the task) five years ago, over seven hundred companies have such departments operating today. In addition, a great many smaller companies have taken pains to make long-range planning a part-time assignment for one or more executives.

The aim of this revised edition, therefore, is more to *select* from the literature than to bring together most of the available materials. The purpose of the selection is twofold: (1) to help executives think through the planning problems they face in managing operations; (2) to help business school students understand the most important aspects of the planning process. Because this can be only a sampling of the literature, I have had to leave out a good many deserving papers that, but for space limitations, would certainly have been included.

Those familiar with the 1958 edition will see that more than half of the material in this revision is new. Many more topics and issues are covered. Also, the parts and chapters are laid out in different order, with more emphasis in this volume on the strategic considerations and on the experience of organizations with planning. It will further be noted that the contributors represent a far wider range of backgrounds and interests.

As with the first edition, brief biographical notes on the contributors are included at the ends of the introductions. There is a short introduction at the beginning of each major part of the book.

In undertaking this revision I found the comments of Edward C. Bursk and H. Edward Wrapp, who studied the manuscript of the first edition, of continuing help; hence, I wish to thank them again. I am also grateful to many publishing organizations for permission to let me use their materials. Their responses to my requests were prompt, courteous, and helpful—clear evidence of their convictions about the educational mission of their publications.

D.W.E.

September 1963

I

NATURE AND PRINCIPLES

I find the real thing in this world is not so much where we stand, as in what direction we are moving.

—Oliver Wendell Holmes

Make no little plans; they have no magic to stir men's blood and probably themselves will not be realized. Make big plans: aim high in hope and work, remembering that a noble, logical diagram once recorded will never die, but long after we are gone will be a living thing, asserting itself with ever-growing insistency. Remember that our sons and grandsons are going to do things that would stagger us.

—Daniel H. Burnham

1 Introduction

Long-range planning is both a cause and a result of some of the great forces that are transforming business in this century. Numerous company achievements could not have taken place but for long-range planning, as we shall see later in this section. On the other hand, long-range planning itself could not have developed but for certain attitudes and conditions which would have had momentous effects even in its absence. What are these attitudes and conditions?

First, long-range planning is closely connected with the concept of the corporation as a long-living institution. Not so long ago we were accustomed to think of a business as a tool of short-term profit. A company was organized to meet a given need or serve a particular purpose, and when the need was met or the purpose served, the assets were sold and the proceeds divided up. There are still many businesses run on this basis, of course; but it is becoming more and more common to find a good deal of management time going into ways of perpetuating the firm—often at the expense of some immediate earnings to stockholders. In an airplane manufacturing concern, management is intent on finding out how to outlive the airplane business. A shoe manufacturer finds the going difficult at his end of the industry; so he branches out into retailing operations, too. A publishing firm turns to younger, greener fields in the communications industry. And so forth.

The more company executives look beyond current operations and short-term profits and worry about the prospects of the organization four, five, or ten years hence, the more likely they are to engage in some form of long-range planning.

Second, planning symbolizes the purposefulness of modern management. An increasing number of executives in business and government today are not content to go through the workday simply reacting to problems and crises. (Actually, I do not know that executives ever were; but histories and documents give the impression, at least, that they were more prone to this in the past.) They want to have a hand in molding the course of affairs. There are various and complicated explanations for this attitude, which I shall not go into here. Suffice it to say that the state of mind has a vital bearing on the acceptability of planning efforts.

Third, planning is connected with the concept of the corporation as an agent of change. As Peter Drucker points out in his chapter, people have not always regarded business in this way. "Up to the seventeenth century it was the purpose of all human institutions to prevent change," he states. "The business enterprise is a significant and rather amazing novelty in that it is the first human institution having the purpose of bringing about change."

Now, some may argue that Drucker overstates the contrast here, but nevertheless the fact stands that planning does increase a company's capacity to change. Managers tied to current operations *can* make important changes in goals and policies—but they are *more likely* to formulate change if they stand back from operations now and then and think ahead. In fact, in the minds of some observers I know, long-range planning stands for change almost by definition. This is because wherever they have seen good planning programs in operation, they have seen intelligent, aggressive interest in change grow.

Fourth, long-range planning owes part of its rise to increasing research and development. As research and development outlays have multiplied, so has the number of new products and processes—and the investments of companies in the future. At the same time, technology has become more complicated and payoff times for new investments have lengthened. This all-too-familiar picture has been a strong practical incentive to plan farther ahead.

Fifth, planning represents the "intellectual movement" in management. Ever since administration became a subject of teaching and analytical writing, scholars have emphasized the need (which many thoughtful managers saw, too) to break away from "managing by the seat of the pants." So long as administrative decisions were made by instinct, impulse, or rote, there was little hope for the kind of probing, reflective thinking that characterized older fields of learning. Now, few management activities are so immediately and intimately related to the intellectual approach as planning is. As Professors Koontz and O'Donnell remark in their chapter, planning is "an intellectual process, the conscious determination of courses of action, the basing of decision on purpose, facts, and considered estimates."

Sixth, long-range planning reflects the strategic approach (as opposed to the tactical approach) to organizational behavior. As managers have become more conscious of the importance of goals, and of the discussion of goals, in employee behavior, the conditions for planning have become more favorable. Planning has become a valuable educational tool for managers and managed alike, helping the former to see the folly of exploiting trust and good will for short-term gain, helping the latter to relate their interests as individuals to the long-term prospects of the organization.

Seventh, long-range planning is evidence of confidence in the economic and political stability of our society. Leaders in business and government may clamor against "dangerous" trends in taxation, government spending, public responsibility, and so forth; yet they accept the probability of long-term safety and prosperity. Their time horizons may reach well into the future. Needless to say, this state of mind is indispensable to planning. In an organization where managers cannot take this attitude because of political uncertainty, poverty, or warfare, long-range thinking must be limited to idealists and visionaries.

All in all, the rise of long-range planning cannot be understood out of context, and the context is the whole industrial scene. Yet it would be a mistake to think of planning as being purely a result of large forces and trends. It is sometimes implied, for instance, that it has been "forced" on management because of changed technology, longer manufacturing and marketing lead times, and competitive necessities. I think this view overlooks something important. I am quite sure that if there were hundreds of societies just like those of the West today, with exactly the same economic, social, and political conditions, there would still be no aggressive long-range planning in any of them if one crucial, priceless ingredient were missing.

That precious ingredient is the personal interest of top management. Because planning appeals to and entices managers, they have worked on it, formulated it, and sold it. Without this push it could not have succeeded as it has.

The growing popularity of planning at the top-management level should come as no surprise. After all, the men who guide business destinies today are on the whole an adventurous lot. They are risk-takers. They love challenge. They blaze trails rather than follow them. They create wealth where there was nothing. They are the present-day descendents of the nineteenth-century "captains of industry," the great merchants of the Renaissance, and the famous traders of ancient Phoenicia. Is it any wonder that they are seizing on long-range planning? It is one of the most potent tools for expansion ever developed.

CONTRIBUTORS TO THIS SECTION

Peter F. Drucker is the famous author of *Landmarks of Tomorrow* (Harper & Row, 1959), *The Practice of Management* (Harper & Row, 1954), and other books. He has also written numerous articles in professional journals, and has received some of the highest awards for business journalism, including the Wallace Clark International Medal of the American Management Societies and the McKinsey Foundation's "best article" prize.

Harold Koontz is Professor of Business Policy and Transportation and *Cyril O'Donnell* is Professor of Business Organization and Policy, both at the School of Business Administration, University of California at Los Angeles. They draw upon a good deal of original research data as well as personal experience in management.

Henri Fayol, the noted French industrialist, lived from 1841 to 1925. The story of how he took a mining and metallurgical concern that was collapsing and turned it into a large strong combine is regarded as one of the romances of French industrial history. His book, *General and Industrial Management* (London, Sir Isaac Pitman & Sons, Ltd., 1949), has become a business classic.

George A. Steiner is director of the Division of Research and Professor of Business Administration at the University of California, Los Angeles. He has written extensively on long-range planning and business forecasting, is managing editor of *California Management Review,* and has served as a consultant to industry.

2

Long-Range Planning Means Risk-Taking[1]

Peter F. Drucker

I

It is easier to define long-range planning by what it is not than by what it is. Three things in particular, which it is commonly believed to be, it emphatically is not.

1. *It is not "forecasting."* It is not masterminding the future, in other words. Any attempt to do so is foolish; human beings can neither predict nor control the future.

If anyone still suffers from the delusion that the ability to forecast beyond the shortest time span is given to us, let him look at the headlines in yesterday's paper, and then ask himself which of them he could possibly have predicted ten years ago. Could he have forecast that by today the Russians would have drawn even with us in the most advanced branches of physical sciences and of engineering? Could he have forecast that West Germany, in complete ruins and chaos then, would have become the most conservative country in the world and one of the most productive ones, let alone that it would become very stable politically? Could he have forecast that the Near East would become a central trouble spot, or would he have had to assume that the oil revenues there would take care of all problems?

[1] From *Management Science,* April 1959. The original title was "Long-Range Planning." Used by permission.

This is the way the future always behaves. To try to mastermind it is therefore childish; we can only discredit what we are doing by attempting it. We must start out with the premise that forecasting is not respectable and not worthwhile beyond the shortest of periods. *Long-range planning is necessary precisely because we cannot forecast.*

But there is another, and even more compelling, reason why forecasting is not long-range planning. Forecasting attempts to find the most probable course of events, or at best, a range of probabilities. But the entrepreneurial problem is to know the unique event that will change the possibilities, for the entrepreneurial universe is not a physical but a value universe. Indeed, the central entrepreneurial contribution, and the one which alone is rewarded with a profit, is to bring about the unique event, the *innovation* that changes the probabilities.

Let me give an example—a very elementary one which has nothing to do with innovation but which illustrates the importance of the improbable even for purely adaptive business behavior:

A large coffee distributor has for many years struggled with the problem of the location and capacity of its processing plants throughout the country. It had long been known that coffee prices were as important a factor in this as location of market, volume, or transportation and delivery strategy. Now if we can forecast anything, it is single-commodity prices; and the price forecasts of the company economists have been remarkably accurate. Yet the decisions on plant location and capacity based on these forecasts have again and again proven costly blunders. Extreme pricing events, the probability of which at any one time was exceedingly low, had, even if they lasted only for a week at a time, impact on the economics of the system that were vastly greater than that of the accurately forecast "average." Forecasting, in other words, obscured economic reality. What was needed (as the Theory of Games could have proven) was to look at the extreme possibilities, and to ask, "which of these can we not afford to disregard?"

The only thing atypical in this example is that it is so simple. Usually things are quite a bit more complex. But despite its (deceptive) simplicity it shows why forecasting is not an adequate basis even for purely adaptive behavior, let alone for the entrepreneurial decisions of long-range planning.

2. *Long-range planning does not deal with future decisions. It deals with the futurity of present decisions.*

Decisions exist only in the present. The question that faces the long-range planner is not what we should do tomorrow. It is: What do we have to do today to be ready for an uncertain tomorrow? The question is not what will happen in the future. It is: What futurity do we have to factor into our present thinking and doing, what time spans do we have to consider, and how do we converge them to a simultaneous decision in the present?

Decision-making is essentially a time machine which synchronizes into one present a great number of divergent time spans. This is, I think, something which we are only learning now. Our approach today still tends toward the making of plans for something we will decide to do in the future. This may be a very entertaining exercise, but it is a futile one.

Again, long-range planning is necessary because we can make decisions only *in* the present; the rest are pious intentions. And yet we cannot make decisions *for* the present alone; the most expedient, most opportunistic decision—let alone the decision not to decide—may commit us on a long-range basis, if not permanently and irrevocably.

3. *Finally, the most common misconception of all, long-range planning is not an attempt to eliminate risk.* It is not even an attempt to minimize risk. Indeed, any such attempt can only lead to irrational and unlimited risk and to certain disaster.

The central fact about economic activity is that, by definition, it commits present resources to future and therefore highly uncertain expectations. To take risk is therefore the essence of economic activity. Indeed, one of the most rigorous theorems of economics (Boehm-Bawerk's Law) proves that existing means of production will yield greater economic performance only through greater uncertainty, that is, through greater risk.

But while it is futile to try to eliminate risk, and questionable to try to minimize it, it is essential that the risks taken be the *right risks.* The end result of successful long-range planning must be a capacity to take a greater risk; for this is the only way to improve *entrepreneurial* performance. To do this, however, we must know and understand the risks we take. We must be able to choose rationally among risk-taking courses of action rather than plunge into uncertainty on the basis of hunch, hearsay, or experience (no matter how meticulously quantified).

Now I think we can attempt to define what long-range planning is.

It is the continuous process of making *present entrepreneurial* (*risk-taking*) *decisions* systematically and with the best possible knowledge of their futurity, organizing systematically *the efforts* needed to carry out these decisions, and measuring the results of these decisions against the expectations through *organized, systematic feedback.*

II

"This is all very well," many experienced businessmen might say (and do say). "But why make a production out of it? Isn't this what the entrepreneur has been doing all along, and doing quite successfully? Why then should it need all this elaborate mumbo jumbo? Why should it be an organized, perhaps even a separate, activity? Why, in other words, should we even talk about 'long-range planning,' let alone do it?"

It is perfectly true that there is nothing very new to entrepreneurial decisions. They have been made as long as we have had entrepreneurs. There is nothing new in here regarding the essentials of economic activity. It has always been the commitment of present resources to future expectations; and for the last three hundred years this has been done in contemplation of change. (This was not true earlier. Earlier economic activity was based on the assumption that there would be no change, an assumption which was institutionally guarded and defended. Altogether, up to the seventeenth century it was the purpose of all human institutions to prevent change. The business enterprise is a significant and rather amazing novelty in that it is the first human institution having the purpose of bringing about change.)

But there are several things which are new; and they have created the need for the organized, systematic, and, above all, specific process that we call long-range planning.

1. The time span of entrepreneurial and managerial decisions has been lengthening so fast and so much as to make necessary systematic exploration of the uncertainty and risk of decisions.

In 1888 or thereabouts, an old and perhaps apocryphical story goes, the great Thomas Edison, already a world figure, went to one of the big banks in New York for a loan on something he was working on. He had plenty of collateral and he was a great man; so the vice-presidents all bowed and said, "Certainly, Mr. Edison, how much do you need?" But one of them, out of idle curiosity, asked, "Tell me, Mr.

Edison, how long will it be before you have this new product?" Edison looked him in the eye and said, "Son, judging from past experience, it will be about eighteen months before I even know whether I'll have a product or not." Whereupon the vice-presidents collapsed in a body, and, despite the collateral, turned down the loan application. The man was obviously mad; eighteen months of uncertainty was surely not a risk a sane businessman would take!

Today practically every manager takes ten- or twenty-year risks without wincing. He takes them in product development, in research, in market development, in the development of a sales organization, in almost anything. This lengthening of the time span of commitment is one of the most significant features of our age. It underlies our economic advances. But while quantitative in itself, it has changed the qualitative character of entrepreneurial decisions. It has, so to speak, converted time from being a dimension in which business decisions are being made into an essential element of the decisions themselves.

2. Another new feature is the speed and risk of innovation. To define what we mean by this term would go far beyond the scope of this paper.

But we do not need to know more than that industrial research expenditures (that is, business expenditures aimed at innovating primarily peacetime products and processes) have increased in this country from less than $100 million in 1928 to $7 or $8 billion in 1958. Clearly, a technologically slow-moving, if not essentially stable, economy has become one of violent technological flux, rapid obsolescence, and great uncertainty.

3. Then there is the growing complexity both of the business enterprise itself, and of the economy and society in which it exists. There is the growing specialization of work which creates increasing need for common vision, common understanding, and common language, without which top-management decisions, however right, will never become effective action.

4. Finally—a subtle but perhaps the most important point—the typical businessman's concept of the basis of entreprenuerial decision is, after all, a misconception. Most businessmen still believe that these decisions are made by "top management." Indeed, practically all text books lay down the dictum that "basic policy decisions" are the "prerogative of top management." At most, top management "delegates" certain decisions.

But this reflects yesterday's rather than today's reality, let alone that of tomorrow. It is perfectly true that top management must have the final say, the final responsibility. But the business enterprise of today is no longer an organization in which there are a handful of "bosses" at the top who make all the decisions while the "workers" carry out orders. It is primarily an organization of professionals of highly specialized knowledge exercising autonomous, responsible judgment. And every one of them—whether manager or individual expert contributor—constantly makes truly entrepreneurial decisions, that is, decisions which affect the economic characteristics and risks of the entire enterprise. He makes them not by "delegation from above" but inevitably in the performance of his own job and work.

For this organization to be functioning, two things are needed: knowledge by the entire organization of what the direction, the goals, the expectations are; and knowledge by top management of what the decisions, commitments, and efforts of the people in the organization are. This needed focus—one might call it a *model of the relevants in internal and external environment*—only a long-range plan can provide.

One way to summarize what is new and different in the process of entrepreneurial decision-making is in terms of information. The amount, diversity, and ambiguity of the information that is beating in on the decision-maker have all been increasing so much that the built-in experience reaction that a good manager has cannot handle it. He breaks down; and his breakdown will take either of the two forms known to any experimental psychologist. One is withdrawal from reality, i.e., "I know what I know and I only go by it; the rest is quite irrelevant and I won't even look at it." The other is a feeling that the universe has become completely irrational so that one decision is as good as the other, resulting in paralysis. We see both in executives who have to make decisions today. Neither is likely to result in rational or in successful decisions.

There is something else managers and management scientists might learn from the psychologists. Organization of information is often more important to the ability to perceive and act than analysis and understanding of the information. I recall one experience with the organization of research-planning in a pharmaceutical company. The attempt to analyze the research decisions—even to define alternative decisions—was a dismal failure. In the attempt, however, the decisions were classified to the point where the research people could know what kind of decision was possible at what stage. They still did not know what factors should or should not be considered in a given decision, nor what its risks were. They could not explain why they made this decision rather than another one, nor spell out what they expected. But the mere organization of this information enabled them again to apply their experience and to "play hunches"—with measurable and very significant improvement in the performance of the entire research group.

Long-range planning is more than organization and analysis of information; it is a decision-making process. But even the information job cannot be done except as part of an organized planning effort—otherwise, there is no way of determining which information is relevant.

III

What, then, are the requirements of long-range planning? We cannot satisfy all of them as yet with any degree of competence; but we can specify them.

Indeed, we can—and should—give two sets of specifications, one in terms of the characteristics of the process itself, the other in terms of its major and specific new-knowledge content.

1. *Risk-taking entrepreneurial decisions, no matter whether made rationally or by tea-leaf reading, always embody the same eight elements:*

a. *Objectives.* This is, admittedly, an elusive term, perhaps even a metaphysical one. It may be as difficult for management science to define "objectives" as it is for biology to define "life." Yet, we will be as unable to do without objectives as the biologists are unable to do without life. Any entrepreneurial decision, let alone the integrated decision system we call a "long-range plan," has objectives, conscious or not.

b. *Assumptions.* These are what are believed by the people who make and carry out decisions to be "real" in the internal and external universe of the business.

c. *Expectations.* What future events or results are considered likely or attainable?

The three elements above can be said to *define the decision.*

d. *Alternative courses of action.* There never is—indeed, in a true uncertainty situation there never can be—"one right decision." There cannot even be "one best decision." There are always "wrong decisions," that is, decisions inadequate to the objectives, incompatible with the assumptions, or grossly improbable in the light of the expectations. But once these have been eliminated, there will still be alternatives left—each a different configuration of objectives, assumptions, and expectations, each with its own risks and its own ratio between risks and rewards, each with its own impact, its specific efforts, and its own results. Every decision is thus a value judgment—it is not the "facts that decide"; people have to choose between imperfect alternatives on the basis of their uncertain knowledge and only fragmentary understanding.

Two alternatives deserve special mention, if only because they have to be considered in almost every case. One is the alternative of no action (which is, of course, what postponing a decision often amounts to); the other is the very important choice between adaptive and innovating action—each having risks that differ greatly in character though not necessarily in magnitude.

e. The next element in the decision-making process is the *decision itself.*

f. But there is no such thing as one isolated decision; every decision is, of necessity, part of a *decision structure.* Every financial man knows, for instance, that the original capital appropriation on a new investment implies a commitment to future—and usually larger—capital appropriations which, however, are almost never as much as the amount mentioned in the proposal submitted. Few of them seem to realize, however, that this not only implies a positive commitment but also, by mortgaging future capital resources, limits future freedom of action. The structuring impact of a decision is even greater with respect to allocations of scarce manpower, such as research people.

g. A decision is only pious intention unless it leads to action. Every decision, therefore, has an *impact stage.* This impact always follows Newton's Second Law, so to speak. It consists of action and reaction. It requires effort. But it also dislocates. There is, therefore, always the question: What effort is required, by whom, and where? What must people know, what must they do, and what must they achieve? But there is also the question—generally neglected: What does this decision do to other areas? Where does it shift the burden, the weaknesses, and the stress points; and what impact does it have on the outside—in the market, in the supply structure, in the community, and so on?

h. And, finally, there are *results.*

Each of these elements of the process deserves an entire book by itself. But I think I have said enough to show that both the process itself and each element in it are *rational,* no matter how arbitrary they may appear. Both the process and all its elements can therefore be defined, can be studied, and can be analyzed. And both can be improved through systematic and organized work. In particular, as in all rational processes, the entire process is improved and strengthened as we define, clarify, and analyze each of its constituent elements.

2. *We can also describe long-range planning in terms of its specific new-knowledge content.* Here are the areas where such new knowledge is particularly cogent:

The Time Dimensions of Planning

To say "long-range" or "short-range" planning implies that a given time span defines the planning; and this is actually how businesses look at it when they speak of a "five-year plan" or a "ten-year plan." But the essence of planning is to make present decisions with knowledge of their futurity. It is the futurity that determines the time span, and not vice versa.

Strictly speaking, short-range and long-range do not describe time spans but stages in every decision. Short-range is the stage before the decision has become fully effective, the stage during which it is only "costs" and not yet "results." The short-range of a decision to build a steel mill is the five years or so until the mill is in production. And the long-range of any decision is the period of expected performance needed to make the decision a successful one—the twenty or more years above break-even-point operations in the case of the steel mill, for instance.

There are limitations on futurity. In business decisions the most precise mathematical statement is often that of my eighth-grade teacher: Parallels are two lines which do not meet this side of the school yard. Certainly, in the expectations and anticipations of a business the old rule of statistics usually applies that anything beyond twenty years equals infinity; and since expectations more than twenty years hence have normally a present value of zero, they should receive normally only a minimal allocation of present efforts and resources.

Yet it is also true that if future results require a long gestation period, they will be obtained only if initiated early enough. Hence, long-range planning requires knowledge of futurity: What do we have to do today if we want to be some place in the future? What will not get done at all if we do not commit resources to it today?

If we know that it takes ninety-nine years to grow Douglas firs in the Northwest to pulping size, planting seedlings today is the only way we can provide for pulp supply in ninety-nine years. Someone may well develop some speeding-up hormone; but we cannot bank on it if we are in the paper industry. It is quite conceivable, may indeed be highly probable, that we will use trees primarily as a source of chemicals long before these trees grow to maturity. We may even get the bulk of paper supply thirty years hence from less precious, less highly structured sources of cellulose than a tree, which is the most advanced chemical factory in the plant kingdom. This simply means, however, that our forests may put us into the chemical industry some time within the next thirty years; and we had better learn now something about chemistry. If our paper plants depend on Douglas fir, our planning cannot confine itself to twenty years, but must consider ninety-nine years. For we must be able to say whether we have to plant trees today, or whether we can postpone this expensive job.

But on other decisions even five years would be absurdly long. If our business is buying up distress merchandise and selling it at auction, then next week's clearance sale is "long-range future"; and anything beyond is largely irrelevant to us.

The nature of the business and the nature of the decision determine the time spans of planning.

Yet the time spans are not static or "given." The time decision itself is the first and a highly important risk-taking decision in the planning process. It largely determines the allocation of resources and efforts. It largely determines the risks taken (and one cannot repeat too often that to postpone a decision is in itself a risk-taking and often irrevocable decision). Indeed, the time decision largely determines the character and nature of the business.

Decision Structure and Configuration

The problem of the time dimension is closely tied in with that of decision structure.

Underlying the whole concept of long-range planning are two simple insights.

We need an integrated decision structure for the business as a whole. There are really no isolated decisions on a product, or on markets, or on people. Each major risk-taking decision has impact throughout the whole; and no decision is isolated in time. Every decision is a move in a chess game, except that the rules of enterprise are by no means as clearly defined. There is no finite board, and the pieces are neither as neatly distinguished nor as few in number. Every move opens some future opportunities for decision, and forecloses others. Every move, therefore, commits positively and negatively.

Let me illustrate these insights with a simple example, that of a major steel company today:

I posit that it is reasonably clear to any student of technology (not of steel technology but of technology in general) that steelmaking is on the threshold of major technological changes. *What* they are perhaps the steelmaker knows, but *that* they are I think any study of the pattern, rhythm, and I would say morphology of technological development, might indicate. A logical—rather than metallurgical—analysis of the process would even indicate *where* the changes are likely to occur. At the same time, the steel company faces the need of building new capacity if it wants to keep its share of the market, assuming that steel consumption will continue to increase. A decision to build a plant today, when there is nothing but the old technology available, means in effect that for fifteen to twenty years the company cannot go into the new technology except at prohibitive cost. It is very unlikely, looking at the technological pattern, that these changes will be satisfied by minor modifications in existing facilities; they are likely to require new facilities to a large extent. By building today the company closes certain opportunities to itself, or at least it very greatly raises the future entrance price. At the same time, by making the decision to postpone building, it may foreclose other opportunities such as market position, perhaps irrevocably. Management therefore has to understand—without perhaps too much detail—the location of this decision in the continuing process of entrepreneurial decision.

At the same time, entrepreneurial decisions must be fundamentally expedient decisions. It is not only impossible to know all the contingent effects of a decision, even for the shortest time period ahead. The very attempt to know them would lead to complete paralysis.

But the determination of what should be considered and what should be ignored is in itself a difficult and consequential decision. We need knowledge to make it—I might say that we need a theory of entrepreneurial inference.

The Characteristics of Risks

It is not only magnitude of risk that we need to be able to appraise in entrepreneurial decisions. It is, above all, the character of the risk. Is it, for instance, the kind of risk we can afford to take, or the kind of risk we cannot afford to take? Or is it that rare but singularly important risk, the risk we cannot afford *not* to take—sometimes regardless of the odds?

The best General Electric scientists, we are told, advised their management in 1945 that it would be at least forty years before nuclear energy could be used to produce electric power commercially. Yet General Electric—rightly—decided that it had to get into the atomic energy field. It could not afford not to take the risk as long as there was the remotest possibility that atomic energy would, after all, become a feasible source of electric power.

The Area of Measurements

I do not have to explain why measurements are needed in management, and especially for the organized entrepreneurial decisions we call "long-range planning."

In human institutions, such as a business enterprise, measurements, strictly speaking, do not and cannot exist. It is the definition of a measurement that it be impersonal and objective, that is, extraneous to the event measured. A child's growth is not dependent on the yardstick or influenced by being recorded. But any measurement in a business enterprise determines action—both on the part of the measurer and the measured—and thereby directs, limits, and causes behavior of the enterprise. Measurement in the enterprise is always motivation, that is, moral force, as much as it is *ratio cognoscendi.*

In addition, in long-range planning we do not deal with observable events. We deal with future events, that is, with expectations. And expectations, being incapable of being observed, are never "facts" and cannot be measured.

Measurements in long-range planning thus present very real problems, especially conceptual ones. Yet, precisely because what we measure and how we measure determines what will be considered relevant, and determines thereby not just what we see, but what we—and others—do, measurements are all-important in the planning process. Above all, unless we build expectations into the planning decision in such a way that we can very early realize whether they are actually fulfilled or not—including a fair understanding of what are significant deviations both in time and in scale—we cannot plan; and we have no feedback, no way of self-control in management.

We obviously also need for long-range planning *managerial knowledge*—i.e., knowledge with respect to the operations of a business. We need such knowledge as that of the resources available, especially the human resources; their capacities and their limitations. We need to know how to "translate" from business needs, business results, and business decisions into functional capacity and specialized effort. There is, after all, no functional decision; there is not even functional data, just as there is no functional profit, no functional loss, no functional investment, no functional risk, no functional customer, no functional product, and no functional image of a company. There is only a unified company product, risk, investment, and so on, hence only company performance and company results. Yet at the same time the work obviously has to be done by people each of whom has to be specialized. Consequently, for a decision to be possible, we must be able to integrate divergent individual knowledges and capacities into one organization potential; and for a decision to be effective, we must be able to translate it into a diversity of individual and expert, yet focused, efforts.

There are also big problems of knowledge in the entrepreneurial task that I have not mentioned—the problems of growth and change, for instance, or those of the moral values of a society and their meaning to business. But these are problems that exist for many areas and disciplines other than management.

In this chapter I have confined myself intentionally to knowledge that is specific to the process of long-range planning. Even so I have barely mentioned the main areas. But I think I have said enough to substantiate three conclusions:

First, here are areas of genuine knowledge, not just areas in which we need data. What we need above all are basic theory and conceptual thinking.

Second, the knowledge we need is new knowledge. It is not to be found in the traditional disciplines of business, such as accounting or economics. It is also not available, by and large, in the physical or life sciences. From the existing disciplines we can get a great deal of help, of course, especially in tools and techniques. And we need all we can get. But the knowledge we need is distinct and specific. It pertains not to the physical, the biological, or the psychological universe, though it partakes of them all. It pertains to the specific institution, the enterprise, which is a social institution existing in contemplation of human values. What is "knowledge" in respect to this institution, let alone what is "scientific," must therefore always be determined by reference to the nature, function, and purposes of this specific institution.

Third, the entrepreneur cannot decide whether he wants to make risk-taking decisions with long futurity; he makes them by definition. All that is within his power is to decide whether he wants to make them responsibly or irresponsibly, with a rational chance of effectiveness and success, or as a blind gamble against all odds. And both because the process is essentially a rational process and because the effectiveness of the entrepreneurial decisions depends on the understanding and voluntary efforts of others, the process will be the more responsible and the more likely to be effective, the more it is a rational, organized process based on knowledge.

IV

Long-range planning is risk-taking decision-making. As such it is the responsibility of the policy-maker, whether we call him entrepreneur or manager. To do the job rationally and systematically does not change this. Long-range planning does not "substitute facts for judgment," does not "substitute science for the manager." It does not even lessen the importance and role of managerial ability, courage, experience, intuition, or even hunch—just as scientific biology and systematic medicine have not lessened the importance of these qualities in the individual physician. On the contrary, the systematic organization of the planning job and the supply of knowledge to it should make more effective individual managerial qualities of personality and vision.

3

The Nature and Purpose of Planning[1]

Harold Koontz
and
Cyril O'Donnell

Planning is one of the functions of the manager and, as such, involves the selection, from among alternatives, of enterprise objectives, policies, procedures, and programs. It is thus decision-making affecting the future course of an enterprise.

It is sometimes said that planning is the primary managerial function which logically precedes all other functions, since, without planning, a manager would not have activities to organize, would not require a staff, would have no one to direct, and would have no need to control. However, the managerial job is actually one in which all the managerial functions take place simultaneously rather than serially.

While no manager can successfully accomplish his task unless he does all the functions well, it is nonetheless true that control is peculiarly dependent upon planning. Since control is the function of making sure that events conform to plans, no manager can control who has not planned. No one can ascertain whether he is on the correct path unless he has determined where he wishes to go. . . .

THE CONCEPT OF PLANNING

Planning is, as Billy E. Goetz has so effectively said, "fundamentally choosing," and "a planning problem arises when an alternative course

[1] By permission from *Principles of Management*, by Harold Koontz and Cyril O'Donnell. Copyright, 1955, McGraw-Hill Book Company, Inc.

of action is discovered."[2] If there were no alternatives in objective, policy, program, or procedure, planning would be so inflexible as hardly to exist. However, in practice there are probably few, if any, business problems for which some kind of alternative does not exist. Even in insolvent companies, which may seem to be doomed to bankruptcy, alternative courses of action are often still open. And should a company be forced into bankruptcy, there are usually legal alternatives available for accomplishing this unpleasant operation and, after bankruptcy, many alternatives for handling the bankrupt estate.

Planning is to a large extent the job of making things happen that would not otherwise occur. While seldom can the exact future of an enterprise be *made* to happen and while factors external to the firm or otherwise beyond its control may interfere with the actual operation of the best-laid plans, events, without planning, would be necessarily left to chance. Planning is thus an intellectual process, the conscious determination of courses of action, the basing of decision on purpose, facts, and considered estimates.

The pervasiveness of the planning function is not often fully appreciated. One often finds a tendency among middle and lower managers to regard planning as the exclusive activity of top managers. While it is true that more preoccupation with planning is found at higher levels, largely because the area of decision-making is larger, it is nonetheless a fact that any person who manages has a planning function. Even the foreman of a road gang or a factory crew, operating under fairly strict orders and procedures, plans. It is practically impossible so to encircle any delegation of authority that no area of choice remains. Within this area of choice of each manager lies *his* area of planning. As a matter of fact, it is interesting that in some of the studies of work satisfactions that have been made, one of the principal factors accounting for the success of foremen at the lowest level has been their ability to plan.[3]

THE NATURE AND VARIETY OF PLANS

In order to appreciate the nature of plans and understand their variety in typical enterprises, one should note the major kinds of plans.

[2] Billy E. Goetz, *Management Planning and Control* (New York, McGraw-Hill Book Company, Inc., 1949), p. 2.

[3] D. Katz *et al., Productivity, Supervision and Morale among Railroad Workers* (Ann Arbor, Mich., Survey Research Center, University of Michigan, 1951).

They may be classified as objectives, policies, procedures, budgets, and programs.

Objectives

The basic plan is the enterprise objective or objectives. This is the goal of the firm. While these are ordinarily subject to simple statement[4] and are essential to the proper planning, organization, staffing, directing, and controlling of any enterprise or any part of it, one often finds that a business or other enterprise has not considered what its basic objectives are.

A good argument can be made that in the United States all business enterprises have one and the same objective—to make a profit. This purpose is often covered under a series of platitudinous statements having to do with service to the public and opportunity for employees. Not that these objectives are improper: Certainly, the business enterprise that seeks to make a profit will tend to serve the public best by producing a good for which demand exists and at a price that will effectively meet the best efforts of others. A business that seeks to make a profit will likewise tend best to serve its employees. Good wages, security, and status for the employees are gained most effectively through a financially sound enterprise, efficiently operated and managed. The common element that identifies all business enterprise, from the newsboy and peanut vendor to the largest bank or insurance company, is thus the pursuit of profit.

And yet, it seems inadequate to speak of profit seeking as *the* objective of business. It is almost as though one said business is business. Furthermore, there have been too many cases of business owners with incentives other than profit. They may be interested in empire-building and power, social prestige, security of position, public acclaim, or any of the other strong motivations of human conduct. The business may be dominated by the desire to develop new things and try new ideas, as was the case of the owners of an engineering company with which one of the authors has worked. It may be to keep the business small, simple, and friendly, as a sort of fraternal group. Or it could be to beat their nearest, and larger, competitor, as was held to be

[4] For example, the *Announcement of the School of Business Administration* of the University of California at Los Angeles states that its central objective is "to provide a professional type of education for positions of administrative responsibility."

one of the principal objectives of the Ford Motor Company in 1952. But even though enterprise purposes are stated in these or similar terms, none of them is realizable unless the firm in question actually makes a profit.

Sometimes the motive of profit maximization takes the form of enterprise-value maximization. In other words, many businesses are operated not for the maximization of profits immediately or even for the short period, but for the purpose of increasing the value of the business in the long run. Many businesses have been known to pass by profits and pursue policies that will increase the capital value of the enterprise. Unquestionably, the principal motivation for this kind of maximization for the individual is the tax structure, which places lesser taxes on capital gains than on profits or normal income. But there are many entrepreneurs who receive satisfaction from seeing a business grow large, even though profits are passed by in the process. This motivation may maximize profits in the long run, although there have been many cases where even in the long run profits were not increased by so doing.

Another variant of the profit objective in business might be called maintenance of management security. Although evidence cannot easily be obtained on this point, since the controlling managers of a business would hesitate to admit that such is their objective, the fact is that managers sometimes follow a conservative path, which is not one that leads to maximum profits, in order to protect their position. This motive operates through an unwillingness to take even normal risks in order to gain a profit.

For example, the president of a large corporation told one of the authors that he would not approve embarking upon a certain expansion program, even though doing so promised great profits. He pointed out that if he did not approve this expansion and the company continued to make its moderate profits, the stockholders would not feel dissatisfied and would not press for his replacement. If his conservative path led to reduction in profits, the very fact that *he* had not done anything unusual made it reasonable to blame the turn of events on external business or political conditions. On the other hand, if he took a moderate degree of risk for the promise of high profits and succeeded, stockholders would merely think that he was doing a normal job and, while being happy and content that things had turned out so well, would not especially reward him. But should he assume

the risks of the expansion program and it did not turn out well, even through no fault of his own, stockholder reaction to losses might be quite adverse and he might lose his job. His reaction was, "Why take a chance? I like being president of this company!"

The motivation of management security is probably more widespread in business and more of an objective of planning than is generally realized. It is not surprising, either, when those responsible for the direction of an enterprise cannot often reap the advantages of profiting through the assumption of business risks. This motive, moreover, is not limited to persons at the top of businesses. Many department heads direct the energies of their departments toward the objective of maintaining their position as manager.

Policies

Policies are likewise plans. They are general statements, or understandings,[5] which guide or channel the thinking and action of subordinates in an enterprise or one of its departments. While a distinction has been drawn, largely for purposes of emphasis and clarification, between objectives and policies, it can be readily seen that enterprise objectives are policies, since they furnish the basic guide to thinking and action. Policies ordinarily have at least as many levels as organization, ranking from major policies applicable to the company as a whole, to major departmental policies, and to minor or derivative policies applicable to the smallest segment of the organization structure.

The varieties of policies in practice are legion. It may be a company policy to promote from within, to conform strictly to a high standard of business ethics, to compete on a price basis, to insist on pricing at fixed prices, to forsake civilian business for military, or to shun publicity. It may be a department policy to hire only persons with an engineering background, to require strict adherence to lunch-

[5] One can hardly refer to policies as simply "statements," since they are often implied from the actions of managers. While many policies are stated verbally, others grow like Topsy from one or more assorted decisions. The president of a company, for example, may strictly follow, perhaps for convenience rather than as policy, the practice of promoting from within: the practice may then be interpreted as policy and be rigorously followed by his subordinates. In fact, one of the problems of the manager is to make sure that subordinates will not interpret as policy a decision or a line of decisions made by him but which he does not intend to serve as a guide to their thinking.

hour schedules, or to encourage subordinates in the department freely to offer suggestions for improvement.

Policies, being guides to thinking and action, are seldom specific. It is the task of subordinates, therefore, to interpret policy though the exercise of initiative, discretion, and judgment. The amount of freedom will naturally depend upon the policy, which in turn tends to be a reflection of position in the organization structure. The president of a company with a policy of aggressive price competition has a broad area of discretion in which to interpret and apply this policy. The district sales manager of the company abides by the same basic policy, but the interpretations made by the president, the vice-president for sales, and the regional sales manager become derivative policies and tend thereby to narrow the scope of policy-making of the district manager.

Policies must, however, be consistent and must be integrated in such a way as to contribute to the realization of enterprise objectives. This goal is difficult to attain for many reasons. First, policies are too seldom written, and their exact interpretations too little known. Secondly, the very delegation of authority that policy-making is intended to implement leads through its decentralizing influence to widespread participation in policy-making, with almost certain variations among individuals. Thirdly, it is not always easy to control policy, in the sense of comparing actual policy against intended policy, largely because actual policy may be difficult to ascertain and intended policy not always clear.

Procedures

Procedures are also plans, for they involve the selection of a course of action and apply to future activities. They detail the exact manner in which a certain activity must be accomplished. Their essence is chronological sequence. Their pervasiveness in the organization is readily apparent. The board of directors may follow procedures quite different from those of the foreman. The expense account of the vice-president may go through quite different approval processes than that of the minor salesman. The vacation and sick-leave provisions and the procedures under which they are effected may vary considerably at various levels of organization. But the important fact is that procedures exist throughout an organization, even though, as one might expect, they become more exacting and numerous in the lower levels, largely because of the necessity for more careful control, the lesser need for discretion in action or decision-making, and the fact that the things done lend themselves to obtaining greater efficiency through prescription of the one best way.

Just as policies have a hierarchy of importance, so do procedures. Thus, in a typical large corporation, one may find a manual of corporation standard practice, outlining those procedures that apply to a corporation as a whole, and a manual of division standard practice, covering those procedures designed especially for division operations. There might also be special sets of procedures for a department, a branch, a section, or a unit of a business.

Procedures often cut across departmental lines. For example, the procedure for accomplishing the order-handling of a product in a large manufacturing company will almost certainly encompass the sales department (for the original order), the finance department (for proper acknowledgment of receipt of funds or for credit determination of the customer), the accounting department (for recording the transaction), the production department (for order to produce or authority to release from stock), and the traffic department (for proper determination of the shipping means and route).

In comparing procedures and policies, Billy E. Goetz has said:

> Policies are relatively general, reasonably permanent managerial plans. Procedures are less general but comparably permanent. A policy maps out a field of action. It determines objectives and limits the area of action. Procedures are stipulated sequences of definite acts. Procedures mark a path through the area of policy. They may fork, generally with adequate clues to determine clerical choice of the path; they may contain trivial gaps to be filled in at the discretion of a clerk; but there is little that resembles the extension of a policy. Procedures are not multidimensional; they do not cover areas of behavior; they have only chronological sequence. . . .
>
> Policy always sets an objective or delimits an area of action while procedures fix a path toward the objective or through the area. Sequence is the *sine qua non* of procedure.[6]

The relationship of procedures and policies may perhaps be indicated by a few examples. A company may have a policy of granting two weeks per year to each employee for a vacation. Procedures will

[6] *Op. cit.*, p. 84. For an excellent study of procedures, see Richard F. Neuschel, *Streamlining Business Procedures* (New York, McGraw-Hill Book Company, Inc., 1950).

be established to implement this policy, providing for scheduling of vacations to avoid disruption of work, methods and rates of pay, the maintenance of records to assure employees a vacation, and means by which an employee may apply for the vacation. Or a company may have a policy of shipping orders the day received; this policy will, of course, necessitate, particularly in a large company, careful procedures to assure that the order is handled expeditiously. A company may have a policy of requiring clearance by the public relations department of all public utterances by its employees. Naturally, to implement this policy, procedures must be established to make sure that clearance is obtained with a minimum of inconvenience and delay.

Budgets

A budget is essentially a plan, a statement of expected results expressed in numerical terms. It may be entirely expressed in financial terms, or it may be a statement of results anticipated in terms of man-hours, units of product, machine-hours, or any other measurement that can be reduced to numerical expression. A budget may be designed to deal with operations, such as the budget of expense and revenue; it may be designed to reflect expected capital outlays, such as the capital expenditures budget; or it may be formulated to show expected flow of cash, such as the cash budget.

Budgets are usually conceived as control devices, as indeed they are, and the principal discussion of them will be reserved for the chapters on control. However, the *making* of a budget is clearly planning. In fact, it is often the fundamental planning instrument in many companies. By being forced to establish for a period in advance a numerical compilation of expected cash receipts and expenditures, or anticipated expenses and revenues, or capital outlays, or man-hour and machine-hour utilization, whether the advance period is for one week or five years, a company is forced to plan. The budget cannot be used for control until it is in existence, and it cannot be in existence as a sensible standard of control unless it reflects plans.

Programs

Programs are a complex of policies and procedures, ordinarily supported by necessary capital and operating budgets and designed to put into effect a course of action. Programs may be as major as that decided upon in 1952 by the General Petroleum Company to put a $35-million refinery in the Pacific Northwest, or the five-year program embarked upon by the Ford Motor Company in 1946 to improve the status and quality of their thousands of foremen. Or they may be as minor as a program formulated by a single foreman in a parts manufacturing department of a farm machinery company to improve the morale of his workers.

While a budget of one kind or another is usually an instrument to implement a program, it may actually serve as a program. One of the authors recalls a company in difficult financial straits, which installed an elaborate budgetary-control program, designed not only to control expenditures but to instill a singular cost consciousness in the management of the firm. Furthermore, a budget may also encompass the entire program, with all other programs contained in it.

Programs may be basic, or they may be derivative, in the sense that they are required by the primary program. For example, in 1948, Trans World Airlines acquired twelve new Constellation aircraft along with necessary spare equipment, an order amounting to approximately $15 million, at a time when the company's entire assets were scarcely five times as much, its cash position extremely weak, and the company itself operating at a large loss, partly because of lack of equipment. This major program required many derivative programs. A program for provisioning the airline with adequate spare parts and equipment had to be developed. Pilots and flight engineers to man the new aircraft had to be hired and trained. It was necessary to prepare and expand maintenance facilities and hire and train new maintenance personnel. Ground personnel had to be hired and trained as the new kind of aircraft was scheduled to additional cities. A revised program of schedules was developed, along with an advertising campaign to notify prospective travelers of the new service. A program for financing the purchase of the aircraft and the spares was required. New insurance commitments were necessary. These and other programs had to be devised and effected before any of the new aircraft could be received and placed in revenue service. Furthermore, all these programs necessitated coordination and timing, so that all would be accomplished at the right time, since the failure of any part of the vast network of derivative programs would delay the major program with consequent unnecessary costs. It is also worth noting that some of the programs, such as the hiring and training of new personnel, could be accomplished *too soon* as well as too late, since needless expense would have been encountered if employees had been available and trained before their services were required.

Thus, one seldom finds that a program of any importance in business planning stands by itself. It is usually a part of a complex structure of programs, depending upon some programs and affecting others. Indeed, it is this interdependence of plans which causes so much difficulty and complexity in business planning. The results of poor or inadequate planning are seldom isolated, for planning is only as effective as its weakest link. Coordinated, and hence effective, planning requires extraordinarily exacting managerial skill.

THE IMPORTANCE OF PLANNING

The essential importance of planning has already been indicated. An enterprise, and every part of it, must plan if it would gain its objective or objectives. Without planning, business becomes random in nature; and decisions, meaningless *ad hoc* choices. It is as though an airplane pilot set out over the ocean blindfolded. Because business operates in an environment of uncertainty and change and requires the attainment of goals at the least possible costs, planning becomes a highly important function.

Planning may be likened to navigation. The navigator lays out a plan and sets a course toward an objective. But his job is not completed by so doing. Instead, he constantly rechecks his position as he proceeds toward his goal,[7] modifying his plan as errors or unforeseen circumstances prove that his course is leading to some point other than the goal sought.

Planning a Necessity Because of Uncertainty and Change

Since the future is characterized by uncertainty and change, planning is a necessity. Just as the navigator cannot set a course once and forget about it, so the business manager cannot establish his goal as profit and let the matter rest at that. It is true that certainty may lead to the elimination of all alternative courses of action but one and thus

[7] As the reader will readily understand, this constant rechecking is similar to the management function of control.

reduce planning to the minor function of confirming an obvious course of action. But future events are seldom very certain, and the farther in the future the results of a decision must be considered, the less the certainty. Thus, a business executive may feel quite certain that within the next month orders, costs, productive capacity, scheduled output, cash availability, and other factors of the business environment will be at a given level. Perhaps a fire, an unforeseen strike, or an order cancellation by a major customer may affect the actuality of these events, but in the short period this is unlikely. However, as the period for which this manager plans in advance becomes longer, the certainty of the internal and external business environment diminishes rapidly. With increased uncertainty, the possible alternatives of action become greater, and the rightness of any decision necessarily becomes less sure.

However, even where the future bears a high degree of certainty, some planning is necessary. In the first place, there are many ways to consider accomplishing an objective, and there is the necessity of selecting from among these the best way. With conditions of certainty, this kind of planning becomes primarily a mathematical problem, one of calculating which alternative course on the basis of the known facts will yield the desired results at the least costs. In the second place, when the decision as to a course of action is made, it is necessary to lay out plays or blueprints so that each segment of the business will contribute toward the job to be done.

Even though trends indicating change are easily discernible, difficult planning problems arise. The manufacture of stoves for family cooking purposes may be cited as a case in point. The change away from the use of coal and wood burners was distinct, but the change did not take place overnight. It was essential for the manufacturer of a half century ago to determine what percentage of his production should be assigned to the new burners and what to the old; it was also important to produce new burners in such a way as to retain efficient production of both lines. But there came a time when the small declining business of old burners became uneconomical. This was an obvious cutoff point. However, the manufacturer could have chosen an entirely different plan. Having satisfied himself with the certainty of change, he might have deliberately sacrificed some old-burner business in order to concentrate on the design and development of new burners, with the hope of becoming the leader among gas- and electric-stove manufacturers.

Where trends are not discernible, uncertainty is greatest. Many businessmen missed the significance of heavy government expenditures, pent-up demand, extensive savings, and rapid population growth, with their effect on the course of business following World War II. The recession expected by many did not occur, with the result that many firms missed opportunities for profit through under-expansion of capital facilities and lack of readiness for new markets.

It has sometimes been objected that planning in the face of great uncertainty is wasteful because plans must be changed continually and the margin of error is likely to be great. But, just as the navigator must premise some kind of winds in order to make a start toward his goal and must make corrections as necessary, the businessman must make his decisions against some kind of assumption as to the future. The existence of uncertainty implies not only that the manager must be alert to necessary changes in his plans as changes become discernible, but also that he would prefer to avoid making decisions that tie him irretrievably for a long period of time to a given course of action.

Planning Focuses Attention on the Enterprise Objective

Because the enterprise objectives serve as the goal of all activity and the end of all planning, the very act of planning tends to focus attention on these objectives. By continually measuring decisions against this kind of standard and acting in a manner to attain it, the various managers in an enterprise become consciously alert to the objectives of the firm.

This focus is especially important in that most policies, procedures, and programs are interdepartmental in scope. Without central goals, there is a very real danger that departmental goals will be established that may or may not be consistent with the objectives of the entire enterprise. Well-considered planning tends to direct the stream of interdepartmental activities toward one objective and consequently restricts the area of freedom in the development of purely departmental plans. It also has the collateral advantage of bringing attention to the need for possible revisions and extensions of plans. Managers, being typically inclined to concern themselves with immediate problems, tend to overlook the future and its effect. But if those who plan are forced to keep the attainment of purpose clearly in mind, they are far more likely to see the need for revisions.

Again, as Goetz has stated the problem, plans "focus action on purposes. They can forecast actions which tend toward the ultimate objective of economic efficiency, which tend away, which will likely offset one another, and which are merely irrelevant. Managerial planning attempts to achieve a consistent, coordinated structure of operations focused on desired ends. Without plans, action must become merely random activity producing nothing but chaos."[8]

Planning Is Economic

Because of the concentration on achieving the best way and because of the attempt to secure consistency, planning tends to minimize costs. It results in joint directed effort in the place of individual and piecemeal activity. It can replace uneven flow of work with even flow. It can result in studied decisiveness and designed action, as against recurring crises and snap judgments. In short, plans give rise to efficient and coordinated effort.

To guide subordinates requires careful planning at the top, as well as dissemination of adequate planning information to those who must exercise their authority to fill in the chinks of the major programs at the departmental level. It requires also an insistence that each manager recognize his duty to plan. Much of this endeavor can be accomplished through example, some through adequate clarity and information of top-management plans. Some can be effected through recognizing the ability to plan as a basic requirement for promotion or pay increases. And other results can be obtained by a thorough system of control to make sure that planning is done throughout the range of management.

Effective planning requires a careful understanding of plans and an agreement upon certain basic factors. If the production manager of a company is by nature a pessimist and figures that the company would not sell more than a certain volume of output, while the sales manager is an optimist and has hired salesmen to sell twice that volume, when, as a matter of fact, the market will most profitably absorb an intermediate amount, the loss in profits would be obvious. Individual managers are likely to differ in their outlook and appraisal of situations, and planning must be designed so as to channel their decision-making toward a unified objective if profits are to be maximized.

The economy of planning is easily understood at the production

[8] *Op. cit.*, p. 63.

level. No one who has watched the assembly of automobiles in one of the nation's large factories can fail to be impressed with the way that the parts and subassemblies come together. From one overhead conveyer system comes a yellow body, and from another the various appurtenances of the same color scheme. For another car, exactly the right engine or transmission or accessories fall into place at the exact appointed time. These events do not occur without extensive and detailed planning, and if such planning were not undertaken, the manufacture of automobiles would be chaotic and impossibly costly. While any manager sees the imperative necessity and economy of planning at the production level, it is surprising that other planning of equal and sometimes greater importance is occasionally left to chance and individual discretion.

Even where uncertainty causes plans to go awry, there is better chance for bringing about economy of effort by planning than by not doing so. Random, inconsistent, and uncoordinated activity is sure to give rise to unnecessary and high costs. With planning, these costs are avoided, even though the business may fail because of unforeseen changes. But to the extent that the unforeseen can be anticipated or circumvented and plans can be tolerably accurate, it is certain that the goals striven for will be attained at the least cost through adequate planning. Even a poor plan is better than no plan at all. As a successful business manager said to one of the authors, "To make poor decisions is understandable, but not to realize why a person made them or where he intended to go by making them is unforgivable."

Planning Essential to Control

The basic importance of planning for purposes of control has already been mentioned. A manager cannot determine whether his subordinates are accomplishing what he had hoped unless he has projected a future course of action. The navigator cannot check his route unless he has had a plan against which to measure it. As another top business executive told one of the authors, "After I leave my office at five o'clock this evening, I do not care what happened today, for I cannot do anything about it; I only care about what will happen tomorrow or the next day or next year, for they are the things I can do something about." Perhaps this is an extreme position, but it does serve to emphasize the point that the most effective control is one that looks to the future.

THE MULTIPLE HORIZON OF PLANNING

Shall plans be for a short period or a long one? How shall short-range plans be coordinated with long-range plans? These questions suggest that there exists a multiple horizon of planning, that, in some cases, planning a week in advance may be ample and that, in others, the desirable period may be that of years. Even within the same firm at the same time, various planning periods may exist for various matters.

The Planning Period

The National Industrial Conference Board, reporting on a survey of business planning in 1952,[9] disclosed, as might be expected, that businesses varied considerably in the period for which they planned. In some instances long-range plans were confined to two years in advance, while in others they were measured in terms of decades. But three to five years appeared to be the most common term for long-range planning, and few companies planned less than a year in advance. Moreover, the study disclosed a tendency toward lengthening the planning term, a tendency many companies attributed to tax policies and government actions.[10] On the other hand, certain business executives saw in the same factors influences limiting the length of their planning period.[11]

Observation of business planning leads to the belief that the long-run period tends to be picked on the basis of a period of years in which the management has some confidence that predictions bear a

[9] "Industry Plans for the Future," *Conference Board Business Record,* August 1952, pp. 324–328.

[10] As one company executive stated, "One reason why our long-range planning is getting to have a longer range is that, with taxes the way they are, we cannot afford to spend so much as we would like to in a year. Therefore, many things have to be held over." (*Ibid.,* p. 325.)

[11] For example, one manufacturer stated: "We are finding it more difficult to make long-range company plans because of the many uncertain factors which are ever-increasingly interrupting the normal thinking of today's businessman. I believe that every business should, as nearly as possible, be conducted on a long-range program, but find that it is necessary to inject so many 'ifs' into one's thinking that in the end what would normally be a long-range program has boiled down to six months or a year, on the average. We hope that before too long things will be established so that longer planning can be made a reality without too much interference from governmental activity." (*Ibid.*)

permissible degree of validity. The company that bases its long-run plans on a three- or five-year period may have picked this length arbitrarily or from the fact that other businesses do otherwise. But it is more likely that the period was selected because such a length of time was believed to be predictable.

Yet there must be some logic in selecting the right time-range for planning. In principle, this seems to lie in the nature of investment of resources of the enterprise. Capital is the lifeblood of enterprise. It is normally extremely limited in supply, relative to a firm's needs, and, when expended, there must be a reasonable possibility of recovering it through operations. When expended for various things, it represents a sunk cost that can only be recovered over time. For example, when Lever Brothers sank $25 million into a new soap factory on the West Coast, they were, in effect, making the decision based upon the belief that the soap business would justify the recovery of this investment over a period of time. If this period were twenty years, then logically the plan should have been based upon a projection of business for such a time. Of course, the company might reduce the risk (as the company did) by spending extra funds to give the plant possible usefulness for other production than soap manufacture.

Investments other than for plant and equipment should likewise be based upon a planning period that will anticipate the recovery of investment. If a company, for example, embarks upon a project that requires unusual training or if it spends funds to improve the quality of its management, these costs are in the nature of sunk costs.[12] In some cases they can be recovered in a short time; in others the recovery may require a fairly long period.

In fact this recovery-of-cost principle as one determining the planning period may be applied to short-range as well as long-range planning. Such planning is ordinarily for periods ranging from three months to one year. It usually emphasizes that portion of planning which has to do with revenues and expenses and, as such, tends to reflect the cycle of raw materials, production, inventorying, sales, and collection. The company offering a product with little raw material, no need for much equipment or a long labor commitment, and immediate collection of accounts can operate on a short-range planning period. For example, the gardener who tends lawns and collects his

[12] Even though these costs are expensed, they are nonetheless sunk in the enterprise at least to the extent that these are not tax offsets.

pay from his customers weekly has little need to plan further in advance than recovery of investment in his limited tools. On the other hand, a company manufacturing airplanes, which may require from four to six years from inception to final collection of funds, may literally be required to regard the short range as a four- to six-year period.

Despite the principle underlying determination of the proper planning period, there is a tendency for companies arbitrarily to limit the short range to six months or one year and the long range to three to five years. These periods are often compromises. The short range is selected to conform to fiscal quarters or years, because of the practical needs for conforming plans to accounting periods. And the somewhat arbitrary limitation of the long range to three to five years is usually based, as has been indicated, on the prevailing belief that the degree of uncertainty over longer periods makes planning of questionable value.

In any case, even with the application of the recovery-of-cost principle, it is abundantly clear that various appropriate periods will exist for various portions of the planning program. The planning period for the acquisition of a multipurpose machine will be shorter, because of its ready liquidity, than that required for a special-purpose machine. The planning period for almost any piece of machinery will tend to be shorter than that for a large capital investment with special applications, such as a new refinery.

Coordination of Short-Range Plans with Long-Range

Often short-range plans are made without reference to their relationship to long-range planning. This is plainly a serious error. The importance of attaining integration between the two can hardly be overemphasized, and no short-run plan should be made unless it contributes to the achievement of the relevant long-range plan. Many of the wastes of planning arise from decisions relating to immediate situations that fail to consider the effect of the action on more remote objectives.

The difficulty is that sometimes these short-run decisions not only fail to contribute to the long-range plan but may actually have effects which impede or require changes in the long-range plan. For example, if a small company accepts a large order for its goods without reckoning with the effect on productive capacity or cash position, it may so hamper its future ability to finance an orderly expansion as to require a complete reorientation of its long-range program. Or in another company, the urgency of obtaining needed small additions to plant may lead it to utilize vacant property, thus thwarting longer-range use of the land as the site for a large new plant. In other instances the decision of a plant superintendent to discharge workers without adequate cause may interfere with the company's longer-range objective of developing a fair and effective personnel program. The short-range decision of the late Sewell Avery, chairman of Montgomery Ward, to curtail expansion of the business after World War II, because of his belief that a serious recession was at hand, has probably interfered with what must have been his long-range program of enhancing the profitability of the company.

What is desired is that short-range planning contribute positively toward long-range plans or objectives. The company must, therefore, have long-range plans. Responsible managers, too, must understand them and provide continual scrutiny of the most immediate decisions to ascertain whether they contribute to the long-range programs. It is far easier to assure that short-range planning is consistent with long-range plans than it is to correct inconsistencies after they are made. Short-term commitments tend to set precedents for further commitments along the same line.

ECONOMIC THEORY AND PLANNING

It is in connection with the managerial function of planning that economic theory has much to offer. Holding that the profit motive is the mainspring of a capitalistic economy, economists have done much to develop principles applicable to decision-making. With the tool of marginal analysis, many of the aspects of choosing between alternatives yield to solution. This tool is simply one of finding the results of incremental changes. Thus, marginal cost refers to the *additional* cost incurred by producing an additional unit, and marginal revenue is the additional increment of revenue received by the sale of an additional unit. These increments are spoken of as the margins of the subject matter under consideration, and an entrepreneur producing and selling a good is thought of as operating at the margin when his additional costs are just compensated by the additional revenue received. As can be shown by analysis, this point is the one of most profitable output, for it is the point beyond which any additional costs incurred would not be recovered through additional revenues and below which the spread between marginal costs and marginal revenues would decrease profits.[13]

Planning and the Static Theory of the Firm

The static theory of the firm is postulated on the assumption that a kind of snapshot is taken of the firm at a given instant of time in order to rule out variations caused by uncertainty due to time. Under this kind of condition, that of "everything else being equal," planning becomes a matter of selecting from available alternatives based upon known market factors and input-output relationships. These variables are "timeless," and planning becomes a problem of finding the optimum plan, that which will maximize net receipts of the firm.[14]

In marginal terms, the optimum plan will be the one in which additional inputs (or costs) will just equal (but not exceed) *additional* receipts (revenues). Obviously, in a complex business plan, such as the location and construction of a new refinery, the number of factors bearing on costs and revenues are innumerable, and the determination of margins very complex. But the marginal analysis is a useful tool for the planner, for it highlights the importance of determining profit maximums by considering incremental costs and revenues.

Thus, a firm may already have a certain-sized plant and an overhead (service and supervisory) organization to operate it. If capacity for more production is available, the desirability of accepting a new contract should logically be decided upon the basis of the additional costs to be incurred and the additional revenue to be obtained. This kind of analysis implies that the customary system of using average costs, with a proration of all burden and overhead costs, may not al-

[13] A pioneer work in the application of economic theory to business planning is that published by Albert G. Hart in 1940. See his *Anticipations, Uncertainty, and Dynamic Planning* (New York, Augustus M. Kelley, Inc., 1951). This work, as well as that of other economists, is drawn upon here.

[14] *Ibid.*, p. 14. Hart refers to this as the maximization of "present discounted value of scheduled net receipts," in order to take into account the fact that future returns must be corrected for interest on a discounted basis. While this is indubitably an adjustment for the sake of strict accuracy, it is an adjustment that is seldom made in practice because of the margins of error unavoidably existing in planning. It is, in a sense, refining the unrefinable, and, in any case, the businessman enters interest as an offset against the revenues to be expected from a plan of action.

ways lead to the most profitable course of action, for it may lead the manager to turn down a contract that would more than pay for additional costs.

The marginal analysis also emphasizes the importance of fixed costs, whether these are in the nature of sunk capital investment or of an established minimum of service and supervisory personnel. Depending upon the range of output considered (obviously, if an increase in output would require a larger plant or a larger overhead organization, these new fixed costs become marginal to the problem under consideration), costs that are fixed in nature do not enter the planning problem, except in the sense of getting increased utilization of these facilities and personnel.

The fact that marginal analysis does not normally reflect all costs, but only additional ones, also serves to show the importance of flexibility in business planning. Flexibility is the quality of operations (facilities or personnel) that permits changes in kind and volume of output without undue costs. If machines or people can be utilized for different products or different volumes of production, without loss in investment already incurred, the firm may be regarded as having perfect flexibility, so far as production is concerned. But it may have other inflexibilities. If, for example, it could not obtain additional working capital for expansion of operations, the flexibility of production machinery and personnel would allow changes in output only at a level permitted by the working capital.

Problems of flexibility in business planning arise generally under conditions of dynamic planning, primarily because of the factor of uncertainty. However, even under static conditions, some question of flexibility exists. Where it is known that varying quantities of varying products will be produced, the manager plans for the flexibility needed for these changes, but he does so with complete certainty.

Planning Under Dynamic Conditions

The analysis of economic forces under static conditions is useful only to isolate the effects of uncertainty[15] and thereby develop tools

[15] *Ibid.*, pp. 25, 27. Hart adds capital-market imperfections and other market discontinuities to uncertainty as major factors that distinguish the dynamic from the static. These are important factors, since the firm cannot practically add or subtract extremely small quantities of capital and since orders are often for minimum quantities. It is a fact that in most real business situations the schedule of supply of capital or the schedule of demand for a product do not represent smooth connected

for analysis. Static conditions do not exist in practice, and business planning is, therefore, undertaken under conditions of change and uncertainty. It is this dynamic character of the business environment that makes planning difficult and the utilization of many economic principles of questionable value.

The central problem under dynamic conditions is the accuracy of a planner's estimate of the future. Obviously, the future is uncertain, although the degree of uncertainty may vary widely as between products, markets, geographical and political areas, and times. If a business manager makes an estimate of a future situation, he necessarily makes certain assumptions as to what will happen. As he weights his contingencies in one way or another, he obtains different results. Suppose, for example, that a manager were planning a new plant for the manufacture of a product and felt that he needed a ten-year span to be sure of recovering his costs. He might estimate the future with respect to markets, prices, labor costs, material costs, utilization of plant, labor efficiency, taxes, and other factors. Suppose further that he estimated six possible situations that he regarded as being most likely to occur, created out of different sets of assumptions as to what the future would bring. These might bring completely separate estimates of net profits to be obtained from the operation and could be charted, as in Figure 1.

As might be expected, all estimates for the first year or two are fairly close together, since the manager may feel more certain of near-term than of long-term results. But as the planning period is extended, the fact that this or that contingency may occur tends to make the estimate of accumulated profits vary from one of high profits, as in forecast A, to one of bare break-even (E), to one of projected loss (F).

Several observations may be made concerning this simplified model of planning under conditions of change and uncertainty. In the first place, the tools of marginal analysis are still useful in arriving at these various estimates of the expected situations. In each set of contingencies assumed, the planner would attempt to maximize profits by

---

lines. While these discontinuities have a significant bearing on planning and while other frictions exist (such as the desire of an owner of a small business not to use outside capital because of danger of loss of control), in this discussion simplification of the issues is obtained by dealing with the primary cause of dynamic conditions—uncertainty.

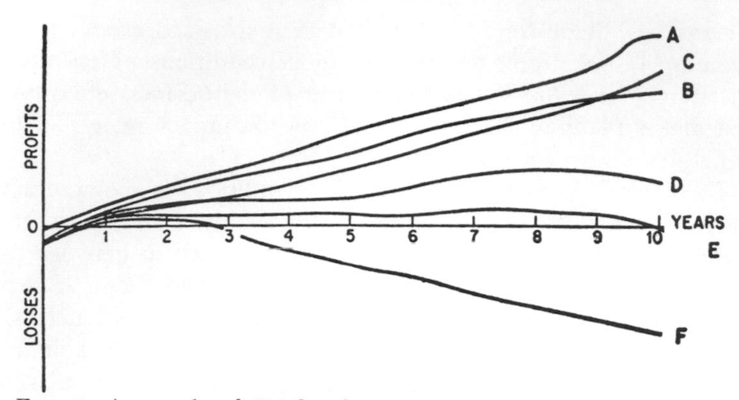

FIG. 1. Accumulated Profits from New Plant on Basis of Six Estimates of Future

assuring himself that additional costs are compensated by additional revenues and that, within the limits of divisibility of units of production, no opportunity exists for maximizing profits by increasing or reducing costs or revenues.

In the second place, this example may be ultilized to emphasize the fact that the uncertainties over time, plus the alternatives available to accomplish results under each set of uncertainties, give alternative possibilities astronomical in number. While only six possible forecasts are included here, the actual number may be infinite. In order for a manager to plan, therefore, especially where the subject is complex and the time period long, he must have some means of limiting his analysis to the most probable. In most cases, this is done by judgment and test. An experienced business analyst tends to have a feeling for problems, which grows out of his familiarity with the underlying factors. If he can consider the basic estimates from which his profit calculation is made and decide which are most likely to occur, he can soon limit the alternative projections to a few most probable ones. At this point, the adoption of a plan is likely to be based upon a weighing of the risks and benefits expected from these few probabilities in the light of the character of underlying uncertainties, the resources of the firm, and the ability and willingness to assume the risks involved.

As can be seen, the difficult problem in planning is the determination of underlying factors, such as future markets, prices, and costs. This is a matter of the forecasting and the calculation of probabilities.

For those companies that can afford the work of specialists in this field, with their utilization of mathematical, statistical, and market-research techniques, a fairly high degree of accuracy in forecasting can be attained. A forecaster may not be able to anticipate with any degree of accuracy such things as war, revolutionary invention, or cataclysmic economic changes, but within the framework of an assumption that one or the other major happenings will occur, forecasting can be undertaken with a workable degree of accuracy for periods of at least five years in advance.[16]

STEPS INVOLVED IN PLANNING

The nature and techniques of planning may be clarified by outlining the steps involved in major planning. Although they are presented here as dealing with a major program, such as the acquisition of a new plant or a new fleet of airplanes or the development of a new product, they are still steps that in their essential nature must be followed in any kind of thorough and logical planning. Minor plans may not be as complex, and certain of the steps may be more easily accomplished, but these differences should not obscure the fact that the planning process has a logical and practical set of techniques and principles of general application.

Establishment of Objectives

The first step in the planning process is the establishment of planning objectives. This must be first at the level of the entire enterprise, but the necessity for having an objective or objectives for each derivative or subordinate plan likewise becomes evident. Planning must be for or toward some goal to be meaningful, because the objective gives the key as to what basically to do, where to place the primary emphasis, and what to accomplish by the network of policies, procedures, budgets, and programs.

Regardless of the nature of objectives, they must be understood if plans of any meaning are to be pursued in the enterprise. Thus, the objective of the entire enterprise should control the direction of major

[16] In 1945 forecasters of three major airlines estimated that 1951 domestic airline traffic would reach approximately 10.5 billion passenger-miles. The actual figure for 1951 was 10.2 billion for the trunk lines and 10.5 billion for the combined trunk and feeder lines.

plans affecting the enterprise as a whole. These plans, then, in their reflection of this objective, define the objectives of the major departments. Major department objectives and plans give a key to the objectives of the derivative departments, and so down the line through the organization structure. Moreover, the lesser subdivisions will do their planning more effectively if they understand the over-all objectives of the enterprise.

But even this may not be enough. A group of research engineers in a military laboratory once remarked that, while they understood the objectives of the Defense Department and those of the military service for which they worked and while the detailed project plans of the laboratory were well understood, they did not always understand the objective of the project on which they worked. Their feeling was that, if they knew for what purpose their project was to be utilized, they might better be able to formulate plans for accomplishing more efficiently the principal objective. It is, therefore, of great importance that the entire hierarchy of objectives applicable to a department's planning be understood.

Establishment of Planning Premises

A second logical step in the planning process is the establishment of, agreement upon, and dissemination of, planning premises. These are forecast data of a factual nature and basic policies expected to be applicable for the future. Premises, then, are planning assumptions. They are the future setting against which all planning takes place.

The establishment of planning premises necessarily involves forecasts of the future. What kind of markets will there be? What quantity of sales? What prices? What products? What costs? What wage rates? What tax rates and policies? What new plants? What policies with respect to dividends? How will expansion be financed? It is important to realize that planning premises include far more than basic forecasts of population, prices, costs, production, markets, and similar matters.

Some premises are forecast policies that have not yet been made. If, for example, a company does not have a pension plan and if no policy with respect to having one has been made, those who would develop planning premises must forecast whether such a policy decision will be made and what it will contain. Other premises naturally grow out of policy decisions or plans already made. If, for example, a company has a policy of paying out 5 per cent of its profits before taxes for contributions and if there is no reason to believe that this policy will be changed, this policy becomes a planning premise for the future. Or, if a company has made large investments in special-purpose fixed plant and machinery, the very fact that this has been done becomes a planning premise of some importance for the future.

As one moves down the organizational hierarchy into divisional, departmental, branch, or section plans, the composition of planning premises tends to change somewhat. The basic outlook will be the same, but the existence of major plans and the development of new major plans will materially affect the future picture against which the managers of these lesser organizational units must plan. Plans affecting a manager's area of authority become premises for *his* planning.

Planning premises may be divided into three groups. There are those planning premises that are noncontrollable, in the sense that the individual firm doing the planning cannot do anything about them. These include such premises as population growth, future price levels, political environment, tax rates and policies, and business cycles. Then there are those planning premises that may be regarded as semicontrollable, in the sense that the individual firm cannot control them but can influence their happening to a greater or lesser degree. In this category may be assumptions as to the share of the market, the character of labor turnover, labor efficiency, company price policy, and even industry legislative policy. And finally, a group of typical planning premises may be characterized as controllable by the firm. Among these are those policy matters and programs that the company management can decide largely for itself. They may include such policies as expansion into new markets, the adoption of an aggressive development or research program, or the selection of a site for headquarters offices.

One of the difficulties with establishing a complete set of planning premises and keeping them up to date is the fact that every major plan, and many minor ones, tend to become planning premises for the future. The decision to establish a major factory in Kansas City, for example, will become an important premise for making other plans where this plant location will be important. Or a railroad, for instance, would find little sense in premising its future plans on reaching markets in Florida if its line were in the Pacific Northwest, and there could be no reasonable expectation of expanding to the Southeast. And when an airline equips its long-haul routes with one type of aircraft and builds maintenance and overhaul facilities for this purpose, this very act tends to become a premise for other plans.

It would be a matter of some surprise if all members of a company's management at all levels would agree independently as to the kind of future a company faces. One manager might expect world peace to last for ten years; another, world war for the same period. One manager might expect prices to go up 10 per cent in five years; another, 50 per cent; and another, that prices would drop.

The lack of planning coordination through use by managers of different sets of premises can be extremely costly to a company. Planning premises should, therefore, be agreed upon. A single standard for the future is a necessary step in good planning, even though this standard includes several sets of premises, with the instruction that different sets of plans be developed on each. In many companies, for example, it is customary to develop plans in prospects of both peace and war, so that, regardless of what occurs, the company will be ready. Obviously, however, a course of action taken for any future period can follow only one set of premises for that period.

Since agreement upon planning premises is important to coordinated planning, it becomes a major responsibility of managers, starting with those at the top of the company, to make sure that their subordinates understand the premises upon which they are expected to plan. In well-managed companies the top managers obtain unanimity with respect to premises for planning purposes, even if the chief executive must force a selection of the future outlook upon subordinates with differing views. In most cases, these major premises are the subject of careful study, including often extensive economic and other research, and of considered deliberation, so that the best thinking available in the company can be brought to bear upon them. It is not unusual for chief executives to force the top managers to come to some conclusion on the future that the company faces and, through group deliberation, arrive at a set of major premises that all can accept. But whether they are accepted by all or not, no chief executive can afford to chance a situation where his lieutenants are planning their portions of the company's future on substantially different sets of premises.

Established and accepted planning premises are only useful to those managers who are aware of them. As in other phases of the managerial job, it is important that planning premises be appropriately disseminated throughout the organization. This does not necessarily mean that all planning premises be communicated to all managers, but it does imply that each manager will have knowledge of those premises necessary for him to do an intelligent and coordinated job of planning.

Search and Examination of Alternative Courses of Action

A third step in the planning process is to search for and examine alternative courses of action. There is seldom a business plan for which reasonable alternatives do not exist. Moreover, before weighing alternatives and reaching a decision, one is wise to search for alternatives that may not be immediately apparent. Quite often an alternative not immediately seen proves to be the most profitable way of undertaking a plan.

Having searched for the alternative courses of action and having reduced the available alternatives to those few that seem to offer the best possibilities for fruitful action, the planner must next examine these alternatives. In the case of a major plan, this examination may be very complicated, leading to the preparation of detailed forecasts of costs and revenues, effects on cash position, and other considerations of a tangible nature, as well as to the consideration of many intangible factors. In deciding to build a new aluminum plant in 1950, the American Aluminum Company not only made a careful study of the costs of electricity at various locations in the country, the availability of suitable sites, the costs of transportation of raw and finished materials, costs of transmission of power, and other items that could be reduced to figures but also made a careful analysis of such intangible factors as the effect of the plant on local opinion and the question of taking the capital risk of building its own power-generating facilities.

Evaluation of Alternative Courses of Action

Having sought out the available alternatives and having made an examination of their strong and weak points, the planner must evaluate the alternatives. This evaluation involves the weighing of the various factors entailed. One alternative may appear to be the most profitable course of action but may require a large outlay of cash and a slow payback. Another course may be less profitable but involve less risk. Still another course of action may better suit the company's long-range objectives.

If objectives were simply to maximize profits immediately, if the future were not fraught with uncertainty, if a company did not have to worry about cash position and capital availability, and if there were not so many factors that could not be reduced to definite data, this evaluation would be easy. But the typical planning problem is so replete with uncertainties, problems of capital shortages, and intangible factors that the evaluation is usually very difficult. Even with relatively simply problems, the evaluation may not be easy. A company may wish to enter a new product line primarily for purposes of prestige. The forecast of expected results may show a clear loss. But the question is still open as to whether the loss, which is believed to be forecast within a narrow margin of error, is worth the gain in prestige.

Selection of a Course or Courses of Action

The fifth planning step is that of selecting the course or courses of action to be undertaken. This is the point at which the plan is adopted. Often an analysis and evaluation of available alternatives will disclose that two or more courses are advisable and the manager concerned may decide to do several things rather than the one best thing.

Formulation of Necessary Derivative Plans

But the planning process is not complete. Once a plan is adopted, there are almost invariably necessary derivative plans to be constructed to give effect to and support the basic plan. A derivative program may be necessary, as was the case mentioned above where the airline decided to acquire a new fleet of airplanes and, in turn, required plans for the hiring and training of ground and flying personnel, the acquisition and placing of spare parts, and other programs. In addition, it may be necessary to develop new policies and procedures for effecting the plan. And in most instances these plans will be accompanied by various cash, capital expenditure, and expense and revenue budgets to make sure that individual managers, in exercising their authority, will be contained within the framework of the plan contemplated.

In other words, plans do not accomplish themselves. They require a breakdown into further plans, with each segment of the company and each manager concerned executing the subsidiary plans necessary for making a basic plan a reality.

PLANNING WITHIN THE ORGANIZATION STRUCTURE

The type of planning in which a manager engages depends upon his position in the organization structure. Top-management planning has to do with broad over-all programs and policies important to the company as a whole. Planning within each department will, of course, be related to the departmental function and to the scope of authority delegation of the manager. In production or factory planning, for example, the programs devised and undertaken will be primarily concerned with scheduling machines, with utilization of manpower, and with procurement and use of materials.

The essential point is that the planning process is basically the same, wherever planning is undertaken. It may vary in complexity and breadth as the problem area and the kind of authority differ. As a matter of fact, planning at the lower levels of the organization structure, particularly in the production department, tends to be better and more thorough than that at upper levels. Among the more important reasons for this is that at the lower levels planning tends to be less a problem of dealing with the uncertainties of human reactions and more a problem of dealing with the definiteness of materials and machines. In addition, the emphasis on production management during more than four decades of scientific management development following the work of Frederick Taylor has resulted in more attention to planning at this level than any other. Another factor is that at this level mistakes in planning show up more quickly because the results of poor planning are soon disclosed by missed production schedules, confused operations, and high costs. While the quality of planning at top levels of an enterprise is of the greatest importance to management, sometimes the results of poor planning are not apparent until a company has lost an important market, has declined in financial strength or competitive position, or has become grossly inefficient.

What is often forgotten is that participation in planning is important at all levels in organization. It is even wise to have participation in *major* planning by all the managers in an enterprise. Every manager should be currently informed of all major plans affecting his area of authority. The informed manager is better able to develop suitable plans for his own department and to understand the part he is required to play. Furthermore, it is desirable for managers to be encouraged to contribute suggestions to top managers. Not only may these be of value to those making plans, but loyalty toward major plans can be nurtured from a feeling of participation. A third important element of participation is the desirability of managers being consulted in advance as to those plans they are expected to execute within their own department. Clearly, also, each manager must be required to make those plans necessary if his department is to carry out the objectives, policies, procedures, and programs of the enterprise, and he must be held responsible for checking continually upon the effectiveness with which his subordinates carry out the plans.

Participation in all planning affecting a manager's area of authority, through his being informed, contributing suggestions, and being consulted, contributes to good planning, loyalty, and managerial effectiveness. Yet one may ask how in a large plant the hundreds of foremen and superintendents, sales managers, and other managers *can* be consulted. One cannot imagine the top managerial team of the Ford Motor Company, for instance, consulting with their thousands of subordinate managers on the plans for a new line of cars.

Unfortunately, in large companies it is frequently not possible for this kind of planning communication to take place. Even so, there are devices available to management that can lead to wider participation of subordinate managers in the making of programs affecting their areas of operations. One is the use of a planning staff, which can spend time with key subordinate managers in developing plans and which will encourage these managers to discuss such matters with their subordinates. In some companies, this practice has produced valuable suggestions and greater understanding of what the top managers were trying to do.

Another valuable device is the establishment of suitable planning committees. While committees have limited administrative use, one of their most important values is improvement in communication. If appropriate committees are established at various levels and points of the organization structure, they can be effective in transmitting planning information, in eliciting suggestions, and in serving as a consultative device. They must be skillfully handled to avoid the expenditure of too much time, but, if properly used, they can pay handsome dividends in terms of helpful advice, understanding of objectives and programs, and in loyalty.

Still another helpful means employed successfully in some companies is the management club. This is an organization of all members of management, from the president to the foreman, and in a large company may be broken up into a number of divisional or territorial clubs. At a specified number of meetings during the year the president of the company or a team of top managers should conduct a meeting at which the planning and thinking of this top echelon are candidly reported to the management group and questions on these matters answered. The authors have noted that in several companies where this device has been tried the lower-management group has responded avidly and gained a strong feeling of unity of objective with the top management of the company. Even the dullest financial matters thus become vital, and the most complicated plan interesting. What many managers overlook is the simple fact that the rank and file of managers have a strong interest in these matters because, after their church and family, there is no more significant force in their lives than the enterprise for which they work.

But no device of encouraging participation in planning and the development of effective planning throughout an organization will replace managerial deficiencies in other directions. The strength of top leadership and the example given to lower managers, clear delegations of authority and careful descriptions of job duties, the development of managerial skills through proper training, and effective techniques of direction and control are among the priceless ingredients of good management that no system of communication and participation can replace.

4

General Features of a Good Plan of Action[1]

Henri Fayol

No one disputes the usefulness of a plan of action. Before taking action it is most necessary to know what is possible and what is wanted. It is known that absence of plan entails hesitation, false steps, untimely changes of direction, which are so many causes of weakness, if not of disaster, in business. The question of and necessity for a plan of action, then, does not arise; and I think that I am voicing the general opinion in saying that a plan of action is indispensable. But there are plans and plans; there are simple ones, complex ones, concise ones, detailed ones, long- or short-term ones; there are those studied with meticulous attention, those treated lightly; there are good, bad, and indifferent ones. How are the good ones to be singled out from among the others? Experience is the only thing that finally determines the true value of a plan, i.e., of the services it can render to the firm; and even then the manner of its application must be taken into account. There is both instrument and player. Nevertheless, there are certain broad characteristics on which general agreement may be reached beforehand without waiting for the verdict of experience.

Unity of plan is an instance. Only one plan can be put into operation at a time; two different plans would mean duality, confusion, disorder. But a plan may be divided into several parts. In large con-

[1] From Henri Fayol, *General and Industrial Management* (New York, Pitman Publishing Corporation, 1949), pp. 44–52. Used by permission.

cerns, there is found alongside the general plan a technical, commercial, and a financial one, or else an over-all one with a specific one for each department. But all these plans are linked, welded, so as to make up one only, and every modification brought to bear on any one of them is given expression in the whole plan. The guiding action of the plan must be continuous.

Now the limitations of human foresight necessarily set bounds to the duration of plans; so, in order to have no break in the guiding action, a second plan must follow immediately upon the first, a third upon the second, and so on. In large businesses the annual plan is more or less in current use. Other plans of shorter or longer term, always in close accord with the annual plan, operate simultaneously with this latter. The plan should be flexible enough to bend before such adjustments, as it is considered well to introduce [changes], whether from pressure of circumstances or from any other reason. First at last, it is the law to which one bows.

Another good point about a plan is to have as much accuracy as is compatible with the unknown factors bearing on the fate of the concern. Usually it is possible to mark out the line of proximate action fairly accurately, while a simple general indication does for remote activities, for before the moment for their execution has arrived sufficient enlightenment will have been forthcoming to settle the line of action more precisely. When the unknown factor occupies a relatively very large place there can be no preciseness in the plan, and then the concern takes on the name of venture.

Unity, continuity, flexibility, precision: such are the broad features of a good plan of action.

As for other specific points which it should have, and which turn on the nature, importance, and condition of the business for which the plan is drawn up, there could be no possibility of settling them beforehand save by comparison with other plans already recognized as effective in similar businesses. In each case, then, comparable elements and models must be sought in business practice, after the fashion of the architect with a building to construct. But the architect, better served than the manager, can call upon books, courses in architecture, whereas there are no books on plans of action, no lessons in foresight, for management theory has yet to be formulated.

There is no lack of good plans; they can be guessed at from the externals of a business but not seen at sufficiently close quarters to be known and judged. Nevertheless, it would be most useful for those whose concern is management to know how experienced managers go about drawing up their plans. By way of information or sample, I am going to set out the method which has long been followed in a great mining and metallurgical concern with which I am well acquainted.

METHOD OF DRAWING UP THE PLAN OF ACTION IN A LARGE MINING AND METALLURGICAL FIRM

This company includes several separate establishments and employs about ten thousand personnel. The entire plan is made up of a series of separate plans called forecasts; and there are yearly forecasts, ten-yearly forecasts, monthly, weekly, daily forecasts, long-term forecasts, special forecasts; and all merge into a single program which operates as a guide for the whole concern.

Yearly Forecasts

Each year, two months after the end of the budgetary period, a general report is drawn up of the work and results of this period. The report deals especially with production, sales, technical, commercial, financial position, personnel, economic consequences, etc. The report is accompanied by forecasts dealing with those same matters, the forecasts being a kind of anticipatory summary of the activities and results of the new budgetary period.

The two months of the new plan which have elapsed are not left without plan, because of provisional forecasts drawn up fifteen days before the end of the previous period. In a large mining and metallurgical firm not many activities are quite completed during the course of one year. Cooperative projects of a technical, commercial, and financial nature, which provide the business with its activities, need more time for their preparation and execution. From another aspect, account must be taken of the repercussions which proximate activities must have on ultimate ones and of the obligation to prepare far ahead sometimes for a requisite state of affairs.

Finally, thought must be given to constant modifications operating on the technical, commercial, financial, and social condition of the industrial world in general and of the business in particular, to avoid being overtaken by circumstances. These various considerations come outside the framework of yearly forecasts and lead on to longer-term ones.

Yearly and Ten-Yearly Forecasts

CONTENTS

Technical Section

Mining rights. Premises. Plant.
Extraction. Manufacture. Output.
New workings. Improvements.
Maintenance of plant and buildings.
Production costs.

Commercial Section

Sales outlets.
Marketable goods.
Agencies. Contracts.
Customers. Importance. Credit standing.
Selling price.

Financial Section

Capital. Loans. Deposits.

Circulating assets:
- Supplies in hand.
- Finished goods.
- Debtors.
- Liquid assets.

Available assets.
Reserves and sundry appropriations.

Creditors:
- Wages.
- Suppliers.
- Sundry.

Sinking funds. Dividends. Bankers.

Accounting

Balance sheet. Profit and loss account. Statistics.

Security

Accident precautions.
Works police. Claims. Health service.
Insurance.

Management

Plan of action.
Organization of personnel. Selection.
Command.
Coordination. Conferences.
Control.

Ten-Yearly Forecasts

Ten-yearly forecasts deal with the same matters as yearly ones. At the outset these two types of forecast are identical, the yearly forecast merging into the first year of the ten-yearly one; but from the second year onward notable divergences make their appearance. To maintain unity of plan each year the ten-yearly forecasts must be reconciled with annual ones so that at the end of some years the ten-yearly forecasts are generally so modified and transformed as to be no longer clear and [to] need redrafting. In effect the custom of redrafting every five years has become established. It is the rule that ten-yearly forecasts always embrace a decade, and that they are revised every five years. Thus there is always a line of action marked out in advance for five years at least.

Special Forecasts

There are some activities whose full cycle exceeds one or even several ten-yearly periods; there are others which, occurring suddenly, must sensibly affect the conditions of the business. Both the one and the other are the object of special forecasts whose findings necessarily have a place in the yearly and ten-yearly forecasts. But it must never be lost sight of that there is one plan only.

These three sorts of forecast, yearly, ten-yearly, and special, merged and harmonized, constitute the firm's general plan.

So, having been prepared with meticulous care by each regional management, with the help of departmental management, and then revised, modified, and completed by general management and then submitted for scrutiny and approval to the board of directors, these forecasts become the plan which, so long as no other has been put in its place, shall serve as guide, directive, and law for the whole staff.

Fifty years ago I began to use this system of forecasts, when I was engaged in managing a colliery, and it rendered me such good service that I had no hesitation in subsequently applying it to various industries whose running was entrusted to me. I look upon it as a precious managerial instrument and have no hesitation in recommending its use to those who have no better instrument available. It has necessarily some shortcomings, but its shortcomings are very slight compared with the advantages it offers. Let us glance at these advantages and shortcomings.

ADVANTAGES AND SHORTCOMINGS OF FORECASTS

The study of resources, future possibilities, and means to be used for attaining the objective call for contributions from all departmental heads within the framework of their mandate; each one brings to this study the contribution of his experience together with recognition of the responsibility which will fall upon him in executing the plan.

Those are excellent conditions for ensuring that no resource shall be neglected and that future possibilities shall be prudently and courageously assessed and that means shall be appropriate to ends. Knowing what are its capabilities and its intentions, the concern goes boldly on, confidently tackles current problems, and is prepared to align all its forces against accidents and surprises of all kinds which may occur.

Compiling the annual plan is always a delicate operation and especially lengthy and laborious when done for the first time, but each repetition brings some simplification, and when the plan has become a habit the toil and difficulties are largely reduced. Conversely, the interest it offers increases. The attention demanded for executing the plan, the indispensable comparison between predicted and actual facts, the recognition of mistakes made and successes attained, the search for means of repeating the one and avoiding the other—all go to make the new plan a work of increasing interest and increasing usefulness.

Also, by doing this work the personnel increases in usefulness from year to year, and at the end is considerably superior to what it was in the beginning. In truth, this result is not due solely to the use of planning; but everything goes together: A well-thought-out plan is rarely found apart from sound organizational, command, coordination, and control practices. This management element exerts an influence on all the rest.

Lack of sequence in activity and unwarranted changes of course are dangers constantly threatening businesses without a plan. The slightest contrary wind can turn from its course a boat which is unfitted to resist. When serious happenings occur, regrettable changes of course may be decided upon under the influence of profound but transitory disturbance. Only a program carefully pondered at an undisturbed time permits of maintaining a clear view of the future and of concentrating maximum possible intellectual ability and material resources upon the danger.

It is in difficult moments above all that a plan is necessary. The best of plans cannot anticipate all unexpected occurrences which may arise, but it does include a place for these events and prepare the weapons which may be needed at the moment of being surprised. The plan protects the business not only against undesirable changes of course which may bc produced by grave events, but also against those arising simply from changes on the part of higher authority. Also, it protects against deviations, imperceptible at first, which end by deflecting it from its objective.

CONDITIONS AND QUALITIES ESSENTIAL FOR DRAWING UP A GOOD PLAN OF ACTION

To sum up: The plan of action facilitates the utilization of the firm's resources and the choice of best methods to use for attaining the objective. It suppresses or reduces hesitancy, false steps, unwarranted changes of course, and helps to improve personnel. It is a precious managerial instrument.

The question may be asked as to why such an instrument is not in general use and everywhere developed to the farthest extent. The reason is that its compilation demands of managerial personnel a certain number of qualities and conditions rarely to be found in combination. The compilation of a good plan demands for the personnel in charge:

1. The art of handling men
2. Considerable energy
3. A measure of moral courage
4. Some continuity of tenure
5. A given degree of competence in the specialized requirement of the business
6. A certain general business experience

THE ART OF HANDLING MEN

In a large firm the majority of departmental managers take part in the compiling of the working arrangements. The execution of this task from time to time is in addition to ordinary everyday work and includes a certain responsibility and does not normally carry any special remuneration. So, to have in such conditions loyal and active cooperation from departmental heads, an able manager of men is needed who fears neither trouble nor responsibility. The art of handling men is apparent from keenness of subordinates and confidence of superiors.

Energy

Yearly and ten-yearly forecasts and special forecasts demand constant vigilance on the part of management.

Moral Courage

It is well known that the best-thought-out plan is never exactly carried out. Forecasts are not prophecies; their function is to minimize the unknown factor. Nevertheless, the public generally, and even shareholders best informed about the running of a business, are not kindly disposed toward a manager who has raised unfulfilled hopes, or allowed them to be raised. Whence the need for a certain prudence which has to be reconciled with the obligation of making every preparation and seeking out optimum possible results.

The timid are tempted to suppress the plan or else whittle it down to nothing in order not to expose themselves to criticism, but it is a bad policy even from the point of view of self-interest. Lack of plan, which compromises smooth running, also exposes the manager to infinitely graver charges than that of having to explain away imperfectly executed forecasts.

Continuity of Tenure

Some time goes by before a new manager is able to take sufficient cognizance of the course of affairs, the usefulness of employees, the resources of the business, its general setup and future possibilities, so as usefully to undertake the compiling of the plan. If, at such a moment, he feels that he will not have enough time to complete the work or only enough to start putting it into execution, or if, on the other hand, he is convinced that such work, condemned to bear no fruit, will only draw criticism upon him, is it to be thought that he will carry it out enthusiastically or even undertake it unless obliged? Human nature must be reckoned with. Without continuity of tenure on the part of management personnel there can be no good plan of action.

Professional Competence and General Business Knowledge

These are abilities just as necessary for drawing up a plan as for carrying it out.

Such are the conditions essential for compiling a good plan. They presuppose intelligent and experienced management. Lack of plan or a bad plan is a sign of managerial incompetence. To safeguard business against such incompetence:

1. A plan must be compulsory.
2. Good specimen plans must be made generally available. (Successful businesses could be asked to furnish such specimens. Experience and general discussion would single out the best.)
3. Planning (as a subject) must be introduced into education.

Thus could general opinion be better informed and react upon management personnel so that the latter's inefficiency would be less to be feared—a state of affairs which would in no wise detract from the importance of men of proven worth.

I shall not here go into detail about monthly, weekly, or daily forecasts which are in use in most businesses and which, like long-term forecasts, aim at marking out beforehand the line of action judged to be most conducive to success. All these forecasts must be made available early enough to allow time to prepare for their execution.

5

Does Planning Pay Off?[1]

George A. Steiner

Determining payoff is a matter of relating the value of planning results to the costs of planning. Every planning program should be examined to determine the margin between value and cost. On the whole, payoff calculations are probably more easily determined for short-range than for long-range plans.

Long-range planning may not pay off for five, ten or more years. It is because of the difficulties in making cost-value calculations, together with the length of time needed to draw conclusions, that questions often arise about payoff for long-range planning.

"EXTINCT BY INSTINCT"

Two extreme approaches seem to be taken by companies that either ignore or improperly face the question of payoff. One approach is to minimize costs by ignoring basic steps in planning. This method depends upon conclusions derived without encumbrances of carefully developed facts or lines of reasoning. For this approach the practitioner feels little need for a conscious and deliberate assessment of relevant considerations upon which judgments can be developed. In

[1] From *California Management Review,* Winter 1962, pp. 37–39. Used by permission.

common parlance this is called "flying by the seat of your pants." I prefer to call it the road to becoming "extinct by instinct."

"PARALYSIS BY ANALYSIS"

At the other extreme is overemphasis of value in relation to cost. With this approach there is recognition of the need for planning. An assignment is made to a dedicated, hard-working soul with a reputation for thoroughness. Work is begun without much reference to the complexities of the task, and before long a large number of people are involved at substantial cost.

Somewhere along the line, usually later than sooner, a voluminous report is prepared and promptly filed away "for future reference." Either the need for decision has long since passed or the report is too complex and bulky for busy people to read and digest. This I call the road to "paralysis by analysis."

COST-VALUE EQUATION

For planning to pay off, a happy balance between the two extremes must be struck. The precise payoff for any particular planning operation is difficult to determine. No one can do this without examining the cost-value equation for that program. But planning has paid off for companies that have considered this equation and achieved the balance required.

The Stanford Research Institute studied the question, "Why Companies Grow." One major conclusion of the study was that: "In the cases of both high-growth and low-growth companies, those that now support planning programs have shown a superior growth rate in recent years."

The Stanford study observed that most companies with formalized planning programs were enthusiastic about their value. Well might they be if, partly as a result of planning, their growth rates have been exceptional. For these companies planning has clearly paid off.

FORD'S EXPERIENCE

Ernest Breech, former chairman of the board of the Ford Motor Company, has observed: "We believe it is our business, and that of other large companies, to make trends, not to follow them. A confident aggressive spirit, backed up by intelligent planning and hard-hitting management, can be contagious." For Ford, planning has paid off handsomely, as the last ten years of that company's history will testify.

On the other hand the path to bankruptcy is strewn with corpses who failed to plan or planned poorly. A study by the Bureau of Business Research at the University of Pittsburgh concluded that among the ten companies chosen for intensive study every one was guilty of poor planning, and this shortcoming was the major cause of failure in the majority of cases.

It is probably true that the only certainty about long-range planning is that the conclusions will prove to be in error. There is no such thing as 20/20 foresight. But, one great advantage of forward planning is that coming to grips with uncertainty by analysis and study should result in a reduction of the margin of doubt about the future. Despite the fog enshrouding the future many companies have planned ahead and hit goals surprisingly accurately.

FORWARD PLANNING

Ralph Cordiner, commenting on this point in his book, *New Frontiers for Professional Managers,* has observed that one of the three principal new horizons ahead for managers lies in the area of long-range planning. As he put it, "In a time of radical world wide change, when every day introduces new elements of uncertainty, forward planning may seem to be nearly impossible—an exercise in futility. Yet there never was a more urgent need for long-range planning on the part of every business, and indeed every other important element of our national life."

The argument is often presented that for large companies the choices for investing funds are many and necessitate advance planning. But since a range of choice in investment of funds in a small single-product company does not exist, for it advance planning is a waste of time.

This idea is most erroneous. Small companies have just as great a need for long-range planning as large ones. They may not have the cash to support technical specialists, but there are other means to acquire the needed expertness. Many small companies, through long-range planning, have opened the door to successful expansion, new products, and new markets by multiplying ranges of desirable choices.

In considering payoff for long-range planning, value is generally considered to lie in the areas of improved profit stability, growth, more efficient sales, capital expenditure, inventory, research and development, or cost-reduction programs. Or long-range planning may prove its worth in better management-replacement and -improvement programs; or some other tangible and concrete activities of the enterprise.

II

STRATEGY

One must draw back to leap better.
—French proverb

But tasks in hours of insight will'd
Can be through hours of gloom ful-
fill'd.
—Matthew Arnold

6

Introduction

When we speak of the strategy of a corporation or other organization, we refer to the broad outline of future action contemplated by management. We refer to the set of goals and policies management has adopted. In the conceptual scheme of long-range planning, strategy comes before problems of organization and tactical programs. If it is not understood in proper perspective, long-range planning cannot be understood properly.

In this section we shall consider various aspects of strategy as it affects the planning effort. To begin, we take a discerning look at the problem of identifying goals. There are two parts to this problem, Tilles tells us in the next chapter: (1) what a company wants to *achieve,* and (2) what it wants to *become.* "For far too many companies," he asserts, "what little thinking goes on about the future is done primarily in money terms. . . . there is a basic fallacy in confusing a financial plan with thinking about the kind of company you want yours to become. It is like saying, 'When I'm forty I'm going to be *rich.*' It leaves too many basic questions unanswered. Rich in what way? Rich doing what?"

After Tilles' discussion we go to another excerpt—this one from a paper addressed to marketing people but, for all practical purposes here, pertinent for all policy-making managers. With a few simple changes in wording you can make McKitterick's thesis read for general management consumption. "The real challenge to marketing people," he argues, "is to get hold firmly of the idea that changing a business—finding it new roles, new customers, new markets—is even more important than operating it efficiently. . . . the profit rewards from endlessly doing old things more efficiently . . . are trivial." The author's challenge is not an easy one to forget.

The next chapter is one that appeared in the first edition (1958) of this volume. It is Weldon B. Gibson's "Guideposts for Forward Planning." Here we have a succinct statement of an idea that has been gaining increasing acceptance in this country—the role of images of the future in shaping behavior. "In one sense," the author states, "every long-range plan by an industrial organization is its image of the future."

In "The Company Creed" we undertake a more empirical examination of goals and aims. Specific company creeds are brought into view, and the purposes they serve are analyzed. Thompson is critical of certain types of creeds—"many such statements consist of grand phrases about nothing"—but he also reminds us that creeds serve varied purposes and work their benefits in more ways than one.

The Tilles, McKitterick, Gibson, and Thompson discussions just mentioned make an interesting first set in this series on strategy. They remind us of some fundamentals that have governed organizational success for many centuries. And they perhaps help us separate, define, and talk more productively about certain vital elements in managerial strategy.

Next we take a different kind of look at the strategy problem. Our concern from now on is more with the ways individual companies handle (or could handle) their strategic problems, more with the particular relationships in a company situation that may affect decisions, and more with the policy side of strategy than with the goals side.

For instance, Melvin E. Salveson gives us a highly original analysis of what makes for successful invention and innovation in a technical industry. Beginning with the available strategies and expected payoffs in two companies studied, he goes on to examine the "principles of design" of business enterprises, the development of entrepreneurial talent, the "criteria for business branching," and other provocative questions.

Percy and Roberts, in their chapter, reflect on the experience of Bell & Howell with profit-planning. In print for a number of years now, including in the first edition of this volume, their discussion contains a number of statements that have intrigued numerous businessmen readers. One such statement is that near the end: "Our theory used to be that when the [economic] indicators dropped down, then we buttoned down. Now we try to accelerate our new products ahead faster than originally scheduled and intensify our sales efforts. In other words, we, like other managements, will try to buck any adverse trend—that is our nature."

The last chapter in this section, also in the first edition, analyzes "Strategies for Diversification." It has been my impression over the years that this *Harvard Business Review* article has interested businessmen almost as much for its method of analysis—the emphasis is on the logical, analytical, and quantitative side—as for its conclusions. "While they are an integral part of the over-all growth pattern," Mr. Ansoff writes, "diversification decisions present certain unique problems. Much more than other growth alternatives, they require a break with past patterns and traditions of a company and an entry on new and uncharted paths."

CONTRIBUTORS TO THIS SECTION

Seymour Tilles was Lecturer on Business Administration and member of the faculty at the Harvard Business School when he wrote the article used in this section. He is now at the Pentagon working with the Assistant Secretary of the Navy for Financial Management.

John B. McKitterick is with General Electric Company as manager, Marketing and Public Relations Research Service.

Weldon B. Gibson is vice-president of Stanford Research Institute. He was formerly with Standard Oil Company of California, Burroughs Adding Machine Company, and other organizations.

Stewart Thompson is manager of research projects for the American Management Association, Incorporated. His writings include *Management Creeds and Philosophies,* a 127-page AMA Research Study (No. 32), which deals in considerable depth and detail with the topic of his chapter in this book.

Melvin E. Salveson is head of Management Sciences Corporation in Los Angeles, California. He was formerly with General Electric Company in its Management Consultation Services Division.

Charles H. Percy was president of Bell & Howell Company when he and William E. Roberts wrote their discussion of strategy. Since 1961 he has been chairman of the company.

William E. Roberts was executive vice-president of Bell & Howell when he coauthored the chapter with Percy. He was also executive vice-president and a director of Bell & Howell, Canada, Ltd.

H. Igor Ansoff is vice-president and general manager of the Industrial Technology Division of Lockheed Electronics Company, in New Jersey. At the time his article was written he was a development planning specialist with Lockheed Aircraft Corporation.

7

Identifying Goals[1]

Seymour Tilles

Corporate goals are an indication of what the company as a whole is trying to *achieve* and to *become*. Both parts—the achieving and the becoming—are important for a full understanding of what a company hopes to attain. For example:

• Under the leadership of Alfred Sloan, General Motors achieved a considerable degree of external success; this was accomplished because Sloan worked out a pattern for the kind of company he wanted it to be internally.

• Similarly, the remarkable record of Du Pont in the twentieth century and the growth of Sears, Roebuck under Julius Rosenwald were as much a tribute to their modified structure as to their external strategy.

ACHIEVING

In order to state what a company expects to achieve, it is important to state what it hopes to do with respect to its environment. For instance:

[1] From *Harvard Business Review*, July–August 1963, pp. 112–113. Used by permission.

Ernest Breech, chairman of the board of the Ford Motor Company, said that the strategy formulated by his company in 1946 was based on a desire "to hold our own in what we foresaw would be a rich but hotly competitive market."[2] The view of the environment implicit in this statement is unmistakable: an expanding over-all demand, increasing competition, and emphasis on market share as a measure of performance against competitors.

Clearly, a statement of what a company hopes to achieve may be much more varied and complex than can be contained in a single sentence. This will be especially true for those managers who are sophisticated enough to perceive that a company operates in more external "systems" than the market. The firm is part not only of a market but also of an industry, the community, the economy, and other systems. In each case there are unique relationships to observe (e.g., with competitors, municipal leaders, Congress, and so on). A more complete discussion of this point is contained in an earlier article of mine.[3]

BECOMING

If you ask young men what they want to accomplish by the time they are forty, the answers you get fall into two distinct categories. There are those—the great majority—who will respond in terms of what they want to *have.* This is especially true of graduate students of business administration. There are some men, however, who will answer in terms of the kind of men they hope to *be.* These are the only ones who have a clear idea of where they are going.

The same is true of companies. For far too many companies, what little thinking goes on about the future is done primarily in money terms. There is nothing wrong with financial planning. Most companies should do more of it. But there is a basic fallacy in confusing a financial plan with thinking about the kind of company you want yours to become. It is like saying, "When I'm forty I'm going to be *rich.*" It leaves too many basic questions unanswered. Rich in what way? Rich doing what?

The other major fallacy in stating what you want to become is to say it only in terms of a product. The number of companies who have gotten themselves into trouble by falling in love with a particular

[2] See Edward C. Bursk and Dan H. Fenn, Jr., *Planning the Future Strategy of Your Business* (New York: McGraw-Hill Book Company, Inc., 1956).

[3] Seymour Tilles, "The Manager's Job—a Systems Approach," *Harvard Business Review,* January–February 1963, p. 73.

product is distressingly great.[4] Perhaps the saddest examples are those giants of American industry who defined their future in terms of continuing to be the major suppliers of steam locomotives to the nation's railroads. In fact, these companies were so wedded to this concept of their future that they formed a cartel in order to keep General Motors out of the steam locomotive business. When the diesel locomotive proved its superiority to steam, these companies all but disappeared.

The lesson of these experiences is that a key element of setting goals is the ability to see them in terms of more than a single dimension. Both money and product policy are part of a statement of objectives; but it is essential that these be viewed as the concrete expressions of a more abstract set of goals—the satisfaction of the needs of significant groups which cooperate to ensure the company's continued existence.

Who are these groups? There are many—customers, managers, employees, stockholders, to mention just the major ones. The key to corporate success is the company's ability to identify the important needs of each of these groups, to establish some balance among them, and to work out a set of operating policies which permits their satisfaction. This set of policies, as a pattern, identifies what the company is trying to be.

THE GROWTH FAD

Many managers have a view of their company's future which is strikingly analogous to the child's view of himself. When asked what they want their companies to become over the next few years, they reply, "Bigger."

There are a great many rationalizations for this preoccupation with growth. Probably the one most frequently voiced is that which says, "You have to grow or die." What must be appreciated, however, is that "bigger" for a company has enormous implications for management. It involves a different way of life, and one which many managers may not be suited for—either in terms of temperament or skills. Moreover, whether for a large company or a small one, "bigger," by itself, may not make economic sense. Companies which are highly profitable at their present size may grow into bankruptcy very easily. Witness the case of Grayson-Robinson Stores, Incorporated, a chain

[4] See Theodore Levitt, "Marketing Myopia," *Harvard Business Review,* July–August 1960, p. 45.

of retail stores; starting out as a small but profitable chain, it grew rapidly into receivership. Conversely, a company which is not now profitable may more successfully seek its survival in cost reduction than in sales growth. Chrysler is a striking example of this approach.

There is, in the United States, a business philosophy which reflects the frontier heritage of the country. It is one which places a high value on growth in physical terms. The manager whose corporate sales are not increasing, the number of whose subordinates is not growing, whose plants are not expanding, feels that he is not successful. But there is a dangerous trap in this kind of thinking. More of the same is not necessarily progress. In addition, few managers are capable of running units several times larger than the ones they now head. The great danger of wholehearted consumer acceptance or an astute program of corporate acquisition is that it frequently propels managers into situations which are beyond their present competence. Such cases—and they are legion—emphasize that in stating corporate objectives, bigger is not always better. A dramatic example is that of Ampex Corporation:

From 1950 to 1960, Ampex's annual sales went from less than $1 million to more than $73 million. Its earnings went from $115,000 to nearly $4 million. The following year, the company reported a decline in sales to $70 million, and a net loss of $3.9 million. The *Wall Street Journal* reported: "As one source close to the company put it, Ampex's former management 'was intelligent and well-educated, but simply lacked the experience necessary to control' the company's rapid development."[5]

[5] "Rx for Ampex: Drastic Changes Help Solve Big Headache of Fast Corporate Growth," *Wall Street Journal* (New York), September 17, 1962, p. 1.

8

Focus on Profit Opportunities, Not Efficiency[1]

John B. McKitterick

Coming out of the Second World War, probably none of us would have conceived the miraculous transformation in our standard of living that was to occur in just fifteen years. However, in raising 50 million households from poverty to what by world standards can only be called opulence, we surely have changed our markets far more rapidly than we have been able to change our businesses in response. The most fundamental constraint on the growth of our economy, therefore, is the mobility of our corporations and the lethargy with which they react to new conditions. There is much more at stake here than merely the declining profits available in old markets that have become glutted with capacity, or the corresponding condition of chronic unemployment. Out of the pending trade negotiations with the Common Market looms the threat of serious import competition that will render obsolete entire industries that will fail to discover soon enough how to contribute to their market something of sufficient value to offset the inflated domestic wage scale. Even more fundamental, the American people, to whom we have taught great expectations of progress and impatience with delay, no longer will wait for business any more than they will wait for doctors or insurance companies or bankers. They will turn to government, and when they do, they will ir-

[1] From John B. McKitterick, "The Nature of the Involvement of Marketing Management and Profit Failure," in *Marketing Precision and Executive Action,* ed. Charles H. Hindersman (Chicago, American Marketing Association, 1962), pp. 84–88. Used by permission.

reversibly shrink the sector of economic activity in which the discipline of free choice among competing alternatives is permitted to operate.

Accordingly, the real challenge to marketing people is to get hold firmly of the idea that changing a business—finding it new roles, new customers, new markets—is even more important than operating it efficiently. If corporations aim to outlive the markets on which they are founded, then marketing must replace the lost function of the entrepreneur in the business planning process. Far too many of our companies today are filling their top management ranks with executives skilled in problem solving, when they should be seeking problem formulators—someone to specify tasks worthy of the organization's best efforts, someone who sees what the country really needs and is more dedicated to that vision than to forever attempting to repeat some past success.

By comparison, our planning has tended to become a mere administrative process of endless criteria, and the creative quality of the alternatives examined is scarcely worthy of the sterile perfection of the decision system applied. As a result, imaginative ideas entailing some real element of uncertainty tend to be cast aside in preference for safe trivia. Yet, as we have seen, the profit rewards from endlessly doing old things more efficiently also are trivial. Indeed, the obvious which is quickly imitated by competition may turn out to be a far more risky investment than some unique and original conception. It certainly is ironic that the very efficiency of the bureaucratic process within our businesses tends to create an atmosphere that is highly toxic to originality and risk-taking. But it should be a matter of particular concern when even the marketing ranks of a company become blockaded with individuals whose passion is conformity, because if marketing cannot furnish real empathy for change, then in the end the people cannot be served and profits will not be made.

On every side today we can find profit opportunities lost due to our fear of change. The increasing inversion of creative effort that shifts engineering attention from the customer's problem back into the factory production process, or diverts marketing research from the search for new opportunities to the evaluation of past results only mirrors the pronounced tendency of management to invest in old businesses at the expense of new undertakings. Our staggering outlay to improve our competitive position in static or even shrinking markets, backed by new facilities, product development programs, and costly sales promotions, is a chronic source of spiraling expense and sinking prices. It seems to me almost pathological that new growth businesses not infrequently are starved for similar support, and in fact are prematurely harvested in order to raise the very funds lavished on old markets. Obviously once a company rejects the future and loses confidence in its ability to replace present sources of sales revenue with new and better businesses, then existing market commitments tend to become a veritable obsession, because if these too are sacrificed, then the venture can have no future whatsoever. So it is not so hard to understand how a management can become frozen to its position in old markets. But the question we should ponder is: Why has marketing neither offered the business a worthwhile future nor shown it the harsh price of continuing to invest in its past?

Obviously, if marketing is to energize the mobility of the firm and make its planning responsive to new opportunities, it would do well to give a convincing demonstration of its entrepreneurial talents in these older product lines when the immediate profit leverage is always highest. One of the most urgent problems requiring market-oriented evaluation is connected with this whole matter of allocation of expense. When we see companies trying to contend with excess capacity by raising prices, or crying out that they cannot meet foreign competition—not because of direct labor but because of high overhead—it is high time for marketing people to take a look at the costs. What I am sure they will find is that a great deal of our total cost today is nothing more than the continuing expense of as yet unliquidated but nevertheless irremediable investment mistakes. The sooner these uneconomic plants and processes are declared obsolete and written off, the sooner costs and prices will become competitive, the sooner demand will revive, and the sooner profits will flow.

A further source of creative paralysis is to be found in our conception of the market itself. After spending a lifetime developing an efficient production base by skillfully blending conflicting customer requirements and straddling all possible issues, management often fails to understand that the cessation of further growth of demand essentially means that the market has become ripe for segmentation. In many mature businesses, rather than struggle to find ways to achieve a uniform penetration into every nook and cranny of the market, it would be far more profitable to attempt to capture all of one segment and ardently specialize the business in its service. Not only will prices tend to rise when suppliers thus become wedded to particular clienteles and insulated from each other, but volume also tends to expand in response to the new burst of creative products and marketing techniques brought forth. The real problem in segmenting a market is not so much the difficulty of finding a means to force realignment of suppliers and customers as the difficulty of persuading management to risk such an irreversible decision in the first place. Yet today in many companies we are face to face with the evidence that we have run out of profits because we have run out of courage to take the risk of being different.

A third opportunity for marketing to give old businesses a new lease on life will be found in Europe. The identical technology of production and distribution which brought many of our own markets to their present pinnacle of profitless maturity might prove just the right ticket if replayed overseas. Indeed, the very surplus plant equipment that we might do well to write off at home could be shipped abroad and set up to serve those markets with highly profitable results. Thereby the investments needed to protect our position in world trade could be acquired without grave injury to the prevailing balance-of-payments deficit, and produce a flow of income from resources that have no real profit potential as presently committed.

Some will remonstrate that the charming simplicity of this proposal is offensive because it exports potential jobs and capital rather than goods. However, as common sense suggests, mature industries vulnerable to foreign competition in the domestic market are rarely in a position to dream of exports to the very countries from which import competition is feared. Furthermore, the prospective growth and size of the Common Market are such that there is a far greater urgency for American businessmen to gain admission there than for European companies to win reciprocal accommodation here.

Indeed, if we now attempt to turn our back on these overseas opportunities, we will be in precisely the predicament of a Mom-and-Pop store when a new supermarket comes to town. The foreign manufacturer will be able to practice incremental pricing in our market without the slightest fear of any retaliation in kind. And as many of us have learned, foreign products need capture only a minor part of the demand in order to destroy the price level throughout an entire industry. If, on the other hand, we aggressively develop overseas manufacturing beachheads and build an efficient foreign distribution structure on those foundations, we undoubtedly will be able to export parts to these offshore facilities and even finished products to be moved through the served distribution outlets.

Summing up, the path to orderly and profitable growth for either a company or nation is largely a matter of common sense adherence to this objective on a day-to-day basis. Like good health, profits are rarely destroyed by an occasional lapse of judgment nor, once lost, easily regained by a brief episode of reform. Above all, our purpose must be firmly rooted in a commitment to the public interest and not easily distracted by the clamor of the bureaucratic struggle that rages within. To guide our decisions we have contrived no end of analysis of the internal state of our business and the flux of our economy. However, the most essential discipline for progress is not the numbers with which we score our results, but the vision of opportunity and resolve to realize its potential that comes from the passion to create. To achieve this is the real challenge to marketing management and the real answer to our nation's problem.

9

Guideposts for Forward Planning[1]

Weldon B. Gibson

Successful long-range business planning, and attainment of these plans, rests finally on business judgment, initiative, enthusiasm, and drive no matter what else is done or occurs. Naturally, a good product, process, or service must be offered. But the spirit of an organization springs from the very top; and the spirit must be right if an organization is to plan and grow successfully.

[1] From *Proceedings, Industrial Economics Conference* (Menlo Park, Cal., Stanford Research Institute, 1956). Used by permission of the author.

A prophecy of doom and gloom flowing down through a business soon stifles even the best of companies. On the other hand, an air of confidence in the future coming from the top soon infects an organization with drive and enthusiasm. The differences in spirit among companies often are subtle and hard to detect, but nevertheless they do exist. I am convinced that many companies have opportunities to succeed largely because they give the impression of being successful, on the move, dynamic, imaginative, and willing to invest patient money. Similarly, many companies in time decline because they somehow give an impression of being negative, self-satisfied, self-sufficient, hesitant, and seekers of the status quo. We might even say that a prerequisite for effective business planning in any company is an enthusiasm for growth and development.

We can take it as a heartening sign when leading businessmen of this country publicly express confidence in the future of their companies, their industry, and the country as a whole. Consider the impact of Robert E. Wood's faith in the country in 1945 and 1946 when Sears, Roebuck launched a growth plan just when many people expected a major business decline. The important point in all of this, as a guidepost for business planning, is that today, more than ever before, industry is making ambitious plans for the future. Optimism is the keynote even in spite of troublesome international problems.

This so-called spirit of the times is a significant economic reality. Many economists, Dr. Summer Slichter among them, maintain that the very fact of business planning on a grand scale works as a balance wheel on the business cycle and on long-term trends. In other words, planning for the future, and making business decisions on this basis, affects the economy of our nation in a profound way.

The entire idea of long-range planning is based in many ways upon concepts of the future as they arise in the collective minds of business leaders. There are indications that mere faith in the future is one force working to bring about conditions making up this future. Is it possible that this force may be stronger than it at first appears? At least one eminent social scientist believes this to be the case.

"IMAGES OF THE FUTURE"

In a book selected for the 1954 Council of Europe Award, Dr. Fred Polak, a Dutch economist, businessman, and social scientist, develops a theory that the future of a civilization, a country, or a people is determined in large measure by their "images of the future," their dreams, doubts, aspirations, and fears. He contends that it is possible to measure these images of the future, that it may be possible to alter or adjust them, and thus to guide a nation's or people's future. His two-volume work, *The Future Is Past Tense,* is now being translated for English publication.

According to Polak, if a society has optimistic ideas, dynamic aspirations, and cohesive ambitions, the civilization will grow and prosper. If it exhibits negative trends, uncertain ideals, and hesitant faith, then the society is in danger of disintegrating. The idea again is that by *thinking* about the future, man creates that same future according to his image.

It is easy to see that an image of the future has a bearing on long-range thinking in government, international affairs, and in broad social studies. But, does it have a place in business thinking? Polak thinks the answer is yes. All of our great industrial enterprises grow on the strength of a leading image of the future, whether these images be conscious or unconscious. Industrial expansion, consumer habits, and the world of advertising and public relations all depend upon an image created or stimulated both among producers and consumers.

In one sense, every long-range plan by an industrial organization is its image of the future. Certainly, the General Motors management in its billion-dollar expansion announcements is reflecting a collective image of the future. One of the surest ways to tear down some of the guideposts erected would be for American business in general to perceive gloomy and negative images of the future. One of the best ways to benefit from our guideposts is to see them as images of the future and to believe in their attainment.

But we know that mere believing, no matter how significant, is not enough in the business world. We must have action, we must have practical guidelines. There are problems, to be sure, though the general outlook may be good.

Business and industry must have money in great quantities if they are to plan and grow for the future. The final source of this money is business profits. Our thinking, our governing, our economic philosophy must recognize this fact. For if industry is unable to make the advances upon which our proposition is based—then we are in for trouble. It is encouraging that our country seems to be moving in the right direction on business policy. Wc must keep up the momentum. Our wealth is created in industry; it has a big job to do between now and 1975; industry must keep up with our expanding needs.

In keeping with the long view, we have given the spotlight to several guideposts for planning. Not the least of them is faith in the years to come, a faith bolstered by the onrush of applied science. One day in early 1945 Wood illustrated the point when he spoke to me along these lines: "My picture of the future is a country ten years hence with double our economic activity spurred on by an exploding technology. I lay my business plans on this picture."

Maybe we are too conservative. He missed the mark by only about 10 per cent.

10

The Company Creed[1]

Stewart Thompson

In order to resolve the orientation of a business with regard to its past experiences, its present competence, and its future objectives, managers of a number of firms have formulated company creeds. Other titles in wide use for statements of this nature are: "Basic Objectives," "Our Basic Policy," "Guiding Principles," "Our Aim," etc.

It may be useful to distinguish two broad purposes of the kinds of statements we are calling company creeds:

1 From Stewart Thompson, "New Dimensions in Creative Planning," *The Business Quarterly,* Summer 1959, pp. 86–90. Used by permission.

1. To formulate and state the present key assumptions and ideas basic to the operation of a particular enterprise, and which are the foundation of its relationships to customers, owners, workers, suppliers, the community, etc.

2. To formulate and state certain broad objectives which, although not sufficiently achieved at present (like teamwork, etc.), are to be achieved to an increasing degree in the future.

Here is an example of a company creed in use today in one Canadian firm:[2]

Primary Responsibilities
of
CANADIAN MARCONI COMPANY

1
TO THE SHAREHOLDERS,
for successful results

2
TO OUR CUSTOMERS
for price, quality and service

3
TO OUR EMPLOYEES
for fair dealing and continuing opportunity

4
TO OUR INDUSTRY AS A WHOLE
for constructive and ethical action

5
TO CANADA
for economic and social advancement

The statements developed by some companies are shorter than that of Canadian Marconi. Others are from twelve to twenty or more pages in length. That such a statement is brief, or that it is lengthy, is not significant outside the context of the particular company in which it is developed. Furthermore, the usefulness of such a statement to a par-

[2] See *Management Creeds and Philosophies,* American Management Association (Research Study No. 32), for a description of the development of this company creed, as well as that of four other corporations, and the related experiences of over fifty other companies.

ticular company cannot be discovered from either its length or its wording.

Two tables from the AMA Research Study are relevant to this article.

TABLE 1
PURPOSE OF THE COMPANY CREED

(Responses of 51 companies to the question: "What purpose was the creed intended to serve? Why was it prepared?" Some companies cited more than one reason for writing a company creed, thus accounting for the total of 73 responses.)

Response	Number	Per Cent
Formalization and clarification of basic philosophy and objectives of the company	26	36
Oriented to employee relations	12	16
Creed was intended to be a guide to basic operating procedure (emphasis on immediate operational procedure rather than long-term goals and principles)	11	15
Oriented to stockholders (often emphasizing profit as source of stockholder benefits)	6	8
Oriented to customer relations	4	5
Oriented to public relations	3	4
Unclassifiable	8	11
No answer	3	4
Total	73	99

Company creeds serve different kinds of purposes. In some companies the main purpose has been to produce a fine document which had created some enthusiasm at one time but which has little relevance to what actually are the ideas and objectives of the managers. In other companies the development of a company creed, that is, the process of thinking through, discussing, and making statements about those vital influences that are shaping the destiny of the enterprise, has provided an important medium for organizing and clarifying the otherwise random and perhaps unconscious purposes and ideas that are at work creating the future. In these companies the *process* of formulating and clarifying the ideas symbolized by the creed was of far greater importance and usefulness than any document which resulted.

TABLE 2
EFFECTIVENESS OF COMPANY CREEDS

(Responses of 51 companies to a question on the effectiveness of creeds. Some companies made more than one response, thus accounting for the total of 95.)

Response	Number	Per Cent
Made more effective development of managerial policy possible	35	37
Improved employee relations	25	26
Improved community and/or public relations	18	19
Helped in other ways	9	9
Benefit hard to measure or define	4	4
Creed is of no assistance or "don't know"	2	2
No answer	2	2
Total	95	99

A CASE IN POINT

The Objective of Ansul Chemical Company

The objective of our company and of everyone of us here at Ansul is to manufacture and sell products useful to our society and to receive an adequate return for them.

We do this while working together in an atmosphere of friendship and appreciation of each man's importance.

This statement of Ansul Chemical Company was written in 1948. It is displayed in the reception lobby of Ansul's offices. Its purpose, according to E. D. Schlutter, staff assistant to the president, was to emphasize the human values of the business, which, in Schlutter's words, "is something that Ansul has worked at diligently for the past eleven years to develop to even a higher degree in our present so-called participative management philosophy."

AID TO CREATIVE PLANNING

Every business has its own system of evaluation. By means of this system of evaluation the managers of a particular company determine that certain things are important, other things need emphasis, certain things are unimportant, etc. This system of evaluation establishes the over-all criteria by means of which the operation of the business is evaluated, changes made, risks taken, and so on. By means of its system of evaluation the limits and direction of company growth are established. The structuring of this system of evaluation, the formulation of the governing laws of the enterprise, is a unique function of top management. This function cannot be avoided, neither can it be delegated. The question is this: *Will the system of evaluation of a particular business be formulated thoughtfully and deliberately, periodically re-evaluated and restructured; or will it be formulated without clear convictions, without consistency and balance, without knowing what it really is?*

At one time the businessman "gathered all the facts" and made his plans. But now the function of management requires different skills and a different point of view. Now the businessman deals with *uncertainty.* He has few absolutes to guide him. But this increasing emphasis on the unknown, the increasing scope of our ignorance, highlights more and more the need for a thoughtfully formulated body of convictions, a system of evaluation, to aid the manager in determining those things—for the most part, those new kinds of things—that must be undertaken within his business in order for it to survive.

We are in an age of relativism. Through discussion programs, exchanges of opinions on various topics, etc., we are aware that our own points of view are not shared by others. Our points of view are "relative" to our particular culture, education, and so on. In some places and for some individuals this age of relativism has crippled initiative and has created persons who are indecisive and inconclusive on even the most urgent matters.

There is a time for gathering information and opinions, but there is also a time for making decisions and shaping convictions! Perhaps now more than ever before the businessman must be *convinced,* must have a body of organized ideas that give meaning and purpose to his decisions today and create the possibility of survival tomorrow.

CONCLUSION

This article has proposed that creative planning consists of reemphasizing the present and drawing dimensions on the future. It has been proposed that each business needs to have an organized system of evaluation by means of which it can sift out of the increasing range and complexity of alternatives those which are of particular relevance to the particular business at a particular time.

Some of the dangers and limitations of company creeds have been pointed out. To be sure, many such statements consist of grand phrases about nothing. As Kusik has pointed out, some company creeds are reproductions of ideas which have long since been reproduced by others. Nevertheless, this author proposes that there is an inherent potential for constructive contribution that can be generated by those who share in the examination of the basic purposes and the system of evaluation of their business. How can this inherent potential be brought out?

1. At the top-management level, recognize the importance of clarifying among the key decision-makers the convictions that should be common among these persons as they make their own unique contributions to the enterprise.

2. Identify and describe the real objectives the company is attempting to achieve. Develop from these objectives targets for corporate and individual improvement.

3. Relate the company to such influences as competitors, the government, labor unions, customers, shareholders, and suppliers, and to the public at large. What are the dynamic forces among these and other influences that the company should identify and exploit?

Of the many possible reasons why company creeds are not more common, perhaps these two broad and opposing differences in points of view typify the relative extremes in perspective on the subject:

1. Some managers already know all there is to be known about their business, its present competence and its future possibilities. Examination and reappraisal of the ideas of the business, of the sequence, logic, and relevance of its objectives, etc., is to these managers a waste of time.

2. Other managers regard the preparation of a company creed as a gross oversimplification of a critical and important process of management—the continuous reappraisal of the nature of the business and its governing laws.

Of course, some managers who would classify themselves under the second of these two categories might more factually be classified under the first. For other managers, the process of developing a company creed has provided an effective medium for clarifying their ideas and organizing for action.

Businesses are organized around ideas, not around people. Perhaps it is not so much the organization of people that causes some companies great difficulty as it is the kinds of ideas around which the people are organized. For example, there should be nothing to fear from the Atomic Age. The fear that confronts us is caused not so much by modern Atomic Age devices as it is caused by the grotesque combination of Atomic Age devices and Stone Age ideas.

And businesses *are* organized around ideas. The new dimensions in creative planning for each business can be discovered if its managers get together to organize their ideas, to test the relevance of these ideas, and to provide for their continuous redesign.

11

The Strategy of Innovation in Technical Industries[1]

Melvin E. Salveson

Long-range planning is becoming the *sine qua non* of every corporation which requires a continuing flow of profit for its survival and growth. The factors demanding increased LRP are many and impelling; the more important ones are summarized below. At the same time, the factors mitigating against effective LRP are many and impelling, and also are summarized below. Out of these countervailing forces, a broader view to LRP is suggested here. This view is concerned more with establishing the conditions for long-range "all-weather" *viability* and *profit;* less with attempting to pinpoint specific plans, steps, and events in an amorphous, opaque future. Thus, long-

[1] From Melvin E. Salveson, "Long-Range Planning in Technical Industries," *Journal of Industrial Engineering,* September–October 1959. Used by permission.

range planning as defined here is concerned with discovering and adapting business operations to the strong patterns and trends which underlie progress and change in an industry or in the economy.

The trends which create the heaviest need for LRP are found in the technical industries. Thus, this report is oriented to those industries. In large part, it is based on studies performed by the Center for Advanced Management for an electromechanical and electronics manufacturer in a highly technical industry.

A "technical" industry is defined broadly as one in which there is a high degree of scientific or technological knowledge required for performing its processes, for designing its product, or for manufacturing its equipment. Typical technical industries include the petrochemical, electronics, aircraft and missile, pharmaceutical, etc. An insistent problem in these industries requiring LRP is technological, or other, "change." However, the change is qualitatively different from that in "nontechnical" industries, and this difference creates the heightened need for LRP.

The women's garment industry illustrates the basic difference between change in the technical versus the nontechnical industries. In that industry, for example, there is change from season to season, year to year, and period to period. A recent scientific study by psychologists indicated these changes are motivated largely by the value of avoiding boredom in the wearer's appeal or attractiveness. Thus, different portions of the anatomy are emphasized under successive style changes; the style at one time emphasizing legs, at another the bust, at another some other portion of the anatomy. The important or significant factor here is, however, that there is no discernible change in the female anatomy. For our purposes it has always had these components, and happily, probably always will. The change is only in its covering apparel. Thus, new knowledge, new form, or new utility is neither created by the style change nor induces that change.

On the other hand, take the electronics industry as a counter example. Change has been frequent in that industry, perhaps up to the rate of change in the women's garment industry, but it has either been induced by or has resulted in new knowledge, new form, new utility. These, in turn, demand in that industry: new business enterprises, new equipment, new methods, differently trained personnel, etc. While some of the ideas and methods presented here may apply both to technical and nontechnical industries, the emphasis in this analysis is on the changes, the underlying patterns, and the trends in the technical industries as these relate to long-range planning.

The study which is reported here was cued by a large manufacturer's loss of market position and profit (call it Company A). The loss could have been expected three years before it was felt had top management been alert to the competitor's activities. But it would still have been too late to react and avoid the loss. Importantly, the whole mode of operation during these three years had been as good or better than before; so the loss was not due to any deficiency in Company A's current operations. Its difficulty arose because it was not concerned with those long-range activities necessary to keep its product and service competitive. The specific event which precipitated the problem for Company A was the introduction by a smaller competitor of a product based on far more advanced technology, thereby making virtually obsolete the company's leading line of products. But the lead had been lost several years before the competitor's product appeared on the market; indeed, it had been lost in the laboratory. Company A had to adopt an inordinately expensive crash program in order to regain its position.

It is in averting these kinds of reverses that long-range planning is concerned. Day-to-day operations also need to be efficient, of course, but unless they are carried out within the framework of broad, well-conceived LRP, they will lead only to the efficient collapse of profit, leadership, and market position. The following material resulted from analysis of the trends and patterns in the company's industry, and provided the basis for a course of action which would provide the foundation for long-range planning and action.

Analysis of the evolution of the industry concerned here revealed a significant fact: *It is impossible to predict.* That is, it was agreed, on presentation of the significant inventions and innovations in the industry in a chronology, that even the best-informed scientists would have been unable to predict these events, or even their incidence, plus or minus five years. The only predictable element was that there had been, and probably would continue to be, invention, innovation, and change, and that the relative frequency of these was roughly proportional to estimated research and development expenditures in the industry, lagged by some range of number of years.

The important Company A top-management conclusion and policy in response to this finding were that: (1) The company should plan systematically to spawn a continuing series of these inventions and innovations as the basis for a viable, growing enterprise. (2) It should establish the mechanism for this continuing flow of inventions, innovations, and developments. This flow and the mechanism for it henceforth would be considered as important as the flow of materials, goods, and services in producing its current products and the mechanism for that flow, the factory.

At this point, the results of a study made in one of my former employments (Company B) was introduced which reinforced the preceding decision. It also suggested a corroborative study of this company's different products. The purpose of the study was to determine the nature of the "game" which management plays in the long range: the strategies available, their expected payoffs, and the mixed or pure strategy which should be adopted in the long range.

Figure 1 presents the results of the first-mentioned study. This

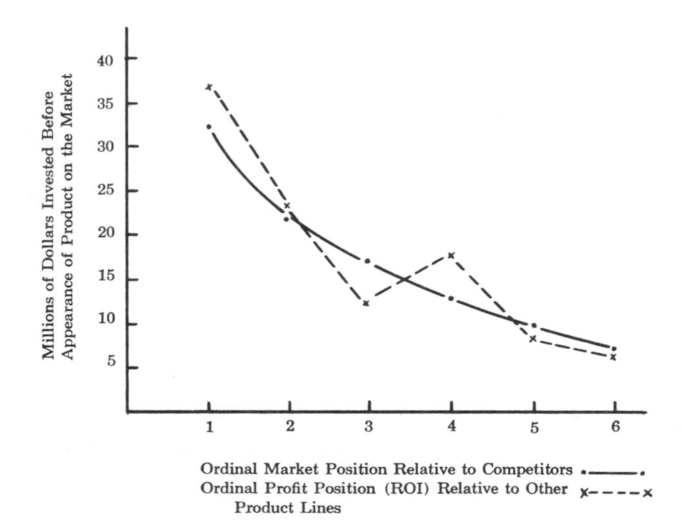

FIG. 1. Company B—48 Products
Average Return on Investment 23 Per Cent (*estimate*)

graph is interpreted as follows: Those products for which that former company was both in first position in its market and had highest return-on-(total product) investment also were the products in which it had invested the most money in the product development (on the average) prior to the original appearance of the product on the market. This is an exciting finding: To make more money, spend more on new-product research and development. However, before accepting the hypothesis unequivocally, the concept was tested by a similar analysis of Company A's products. The findings of this study are shown in Figure 2. The results are strikingly different. The meaning

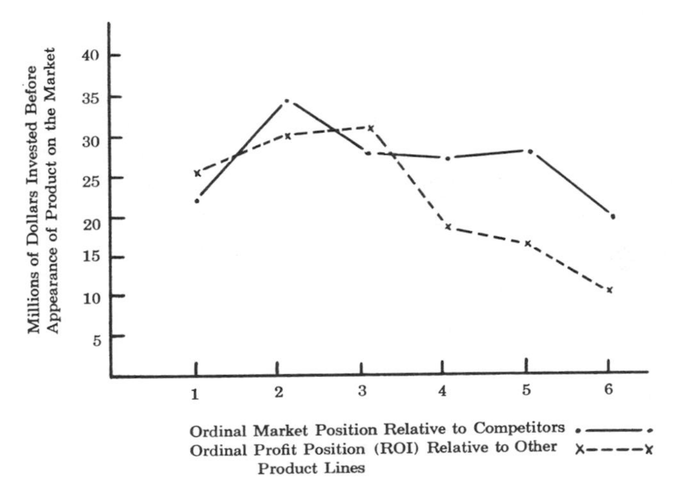

FIG. 2. Company A—26 Products
Average Return on Investment 17 Per Cent (*estimate*)

of the difference is clear. In Company A, large investment in advance of a product's first appearance did not tend to lead as strongly to first-market position. Indeed, relative to some of its second-place products, some of Company A's first-place products had achieved their position with less advance investment.

The study to determine the reasons for the different tendencies gave the following qualitative observations on each company. Company B maintained an aggressive research and development program, with expenditures for R&D very high as a percentage of sales—about 6 per cent. Company A was proportionately almost as aggressive as measured by R&D expenditures as a percentage of sales. The difference here did not seem significant.

Company B, through its advertising, company slogans, etc., presented a corporate image of "making progress," where progress included innovation and commercialization. However, it did so very conservatively. For example, one of its former chairmen of the board remarked, "Fifteen years is about the average period of probation, and during that time the inventor, the promoter, and the investor, who see a great future for an invention, generally lose their shirts. Public demand, even for a great invention, is always slow in developing. That is why the wise capitalist keeps out of exploiting new inventions."[2] While the policy at Company B subsequently has advanced, it did so only by developing systematic procedures for evaluating when and how, in detail, to develop and commercialize an invention.

On the other hand, Company A, through its corporate image, slogans, and policies, better represents the pioneering inventor. There is good, though nebular, evidence that this image represents the personality and policies of the principal executives. This is a significant difference, even though it is of a qualitative character.

If the preceding difference in fact did exist, it should manifest itself in other more measurable ways. The following are some of those ways:

	Company A	Company B
1. Percentage of R&D and engineering personnel in		
a. Central laboratory	54	38
b. Product-department laboratory	46	62
(Presumably reflects relative importance of product-oriented and "business-controlled" R&D personnel.)		
2. Average number of product lines per department or business profit center.	6.4	3.1
(Presumably reflects the relative importance of any single product line to a single profit-responsible management team.)		

[2] Rupert W. MacLaurin, *Invention and Innovation in the Radio Industry* (New York, The Macmillan Company, 1949).

3. Percentage of product lines directly traceable through evolution to original products without acquisition or merger (see Figure 3). (Presumably reflects purposiveness and ability to commercialize on inventions and innovations arising out of R&D related to its existing businesses.)	47	72
4. Percentage of products entering directly into the major over-all system produced by the company. (This factor presumably reflects singleness of management purpose in expanding its basic business.)	39	78
5. Percentage of engineering and R&D managers with training in management and business. (Presumably reflects commercial orientation in engineering and R&D.)	16	65 (estimated)
6. Percentage of R&D personnel's time which may be self-directed. (Presumably this reflects relative amount of direction toward company objectives.)	12.5	20

These differences cued further studies on the process of innovation, including invention, development, and commercialization. In order to disguise the companies, but yet to give concrete examples of this process, the early experience of the General Electric Company is given. Most examples and references here are from Passer,[3] but interestingly they form a striking parallel to the situations uncovered in this study.

The key person in the process of innovation and commercialization is the engineer-entrepreneur, the person with technical training who can see com-

[3] Harold C. Passer, *The Electrical Manufacturers* (Cambridge, Mass., Harvard University Press, 1953).

mercial possibilities in the application of scientific principles and who labors to perfect usable products and techniques. This kind of entrepreneurship has become increasingly important as the advance of science has made available new knowledge, new products, new production methods, and new resources. For in the long view the most significant manner in which to increase economic welfare (and company profit) is not through better administration of existing resources or (socialistic) change in the distribution of income, but through applications of science which increase national income.

Clearly, Company B is predominantly an "engineer-entrepreneur's" enterprise. It deliberately seeks opportunity to commercialize—mindful of the dictates of its chairman that without the test of marketability, any venture would be doomed to failure. It systematically extended its business through accretions always related to its product line and, hence, within the market and business which it knew well. Its engineering managers, as the above comparison indicates, have more training in and, presumably, understanding of the problems and methods of commercialization.

Another difference cited in the above comparison is the tendency to emphasize evolutionary entry into businesses. That is, Company B tends to enter companies through expansion into related products or through enlargements of the basic system which it produces and markets. For example:

> The economic orientation of Edison's inventive work in electric lighting defined his approach to the problem of subdividing the electric light [system]. His goal was to invent a system which could produce light at the lowest possible cost. And his inventions were inventions primarily because he was looking for a low-cost lighting system. . . . Edison was the first inventor to realize that an incandescent lamp which could operate in a constant-voltage parallel circuit would necessarily have to be of high resistance in order to keep the cost of the copper conductors from being prohibitive. . . . Edison's work on the dynamo was also directed toward reducing costs. . . . In each case, he perceived the function of the component in the system. He then determined the characteristic of that component which would result in a *system* with the lowest production cost of light . . . the lamp, the dynamo, and the distribution network were designed to form a lighting system using the minimum amount of resources, with a meter in the system to assure it.

Through the above, we can see the evolutionary chain via which the now General Electric Company entered into its various businesses and product lines, virtually all stemming directly from Edison's original lamp, the protozoa of that company. The General Electric chain of evolution is portrayed in miniature in Figure 3.

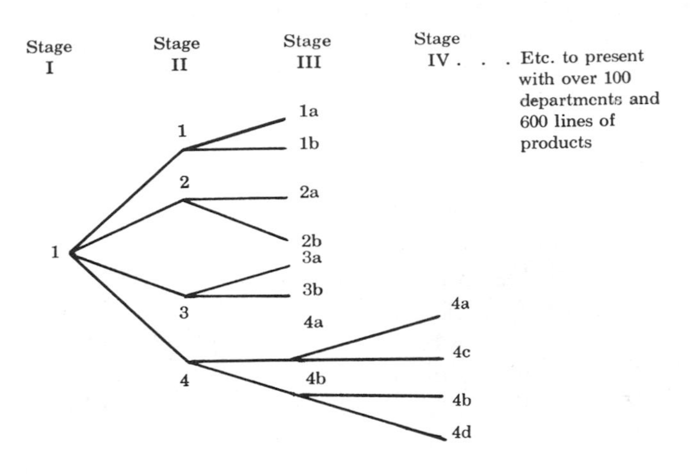

STAGE I

Edison developed the incandescent lamp, which he wished to commercialize. Alone it had no future; as part of a complete system he saw it had large potential. This prepared for the next stage.

STAGE II

1. The lamp business (*1*) required supporting businesses to make and sell a complete lighting system, including:

2. A meter business to supply meters (*2*) and measure energy consumed.

3. A distribution network business to provide the distribution equipment (*3*).

4. An energy conversion (thermal to electrical) business, to supply electrical generation apparatus (*4*).

STAGE III

1. The lamp business, through research on lamps, grew and spawned both indoor (*1a*) and outdoor lamps (*1b*).

2. The meter business involved measuring (*2a*) and instrumentation, thus leading via knowledge of instruments into the instrument business (*2b*).

3. Research and experience in distribution led to distribution hardware business (*3a*) through knowledge of electrical hardware and its properties and manufacture. It also led to transformers for conserving copper losses, and thus to the transformer business (*3b*).

4. The energy conversion business led naturally to knowledge and experience in both prime movers (steam engines and turbines) (*4a*) and to generators (*4b*).

STAGE IV

To abbreviate, only a small number of the evolutionary chains are shown, and the remainder of the narrative is reduced. Thus, at Stage IV, the prime-mover business led to building the engineering and marketing knowledge and skills on which to enter both the steam turbine and gas turbine businesses (the latter of which proliferated later into aircraft gas turbines and shipboard gas turbines). The knowledge and skills in the generator business led directly to the ability to enter also the electrical motor business. While neither aircraft gas turbines nor electric motors are required in the incandescent lamp business, pursuit of the latter business by competent engineer-entrepreneurs led to accumulating the knowledge, skill, and insight eventually necessary for entering those businesses.

The full evolution to date (1959) has led to the General Electric Company, with over one hundred separate departments producing six hundred lines of products in as many markets. Some evolutionary links have been terminal ventures, however. For example, governmental action restrained the company from operating electric utilities; and, the company found that, though it was helpful to finance these utilities, there was nothing in the skills of the engineer-entrepreneur which made him a good financier. Thus, General Electric withdrew early from the business of financing public utilities.

Return now to long-range planning, per se. Could Edison have visualized that his lamp business one day would have led directly to aircraft gas turbines and thence to rocket motors? Of course not; aircraft and rocket motors were unknown at that time. Even within much shorter periods, the links have led to unpredictable new businesses. If Edison, or any other scientist, could not forsee such basic events and turnings in his enterprise, how is it possible to plan for them in the long range?

The answer to the preceding question is in planning for the *flow of invention, innovation, and new businesses* which will evolve. This requires developing a deeper skill in and understanding of the processes of entrepreneurship. Planning for specific inventions and their commercialization is short-term, finite-period planning. This short-range planning requires knowledge and skill in the specific problems of the business to which the planning is directed. The longer-range planning for the continuing flow of corporate life blood requires a broader set of knowledge and skills—such as:

1. The general principles of how to design business enterprises, so that whatever evolves from invention and innovation can be profitably pursued or appropriately avoided.
2. How to recognize and develop not only required managerial talent, but more importantly, the entrepreneurial personnel to pursue new business.
3. How to set minimum, maximum, and expected rates of commercializable invention and innovation as the basis for growth and expansion.
4. How to determine criteria for branching at any node in the evolutionary chain, so as to enter only businesses which are compatible with acquired skills, knowledge and the collective self-image and corporate image.
5. How to determine the miscibility of different product lines and businesses into operating businesses.
6. How to establish the conditions and methods for effective entrepreneurship.
7. How to design the parent corporate structure and organization for the "flow of businesses" within that structure, from invention to innovation, to commercialization, and to replacement or abandonment, if appropriate.
8. How to perform the roles of chief executive and corporate staffs in a long-range plan embodying the "flow of businesses." That is, how to manage entrepreneurs, rather than how to manage other managers or individual contributors.

These areas of knowledge and skill would require many more pages to develop than are available here. However, a few paragraphs of explanation are in order.

1. *Principles of design of business enterprises.* This area is amply covered by the numerous texts and papers on business organization and management, together with the literature of managing the functional

components therein. However, one important lack is techniques for the integration of the various functional components into a single system, in the same manner that the engineer performs the system integration and synthesis function in designing a complex system. The newly developing techniques in operations research have important applications in the rational design and synthesis of business enterprises; as for example those being developed in the Operations Research and Synthesis Service at General Electric. Perhaps the existence of this service at General Electric reflects that company's unusual awareness of the need to bring to bear the most advanced and powerful techniques of science and engineering in designing the many evolving businesses within its corporate structure. Toward this objective, in a separate paper, I have attempted to describe methods and techniques for designing business organizations dynamically, in the same manner that engineers must design systems to both static and dynamic criteria.[4]

2. *Development of entrepreneurial talent.* The training and development programs for business are directed toward "managers"; the entrepreneur is hardly recognized. Yet, as Passer relates, "[he] is the key person in this process [of founding and growing new industries based on new technologies]." Unfortunately, the entrepreneur often may be greeted with untoward attitudes in established businesses, unless those businesses are organized to grow on the entrepreneur's labors. For example, MacLaurin writes: "Innovations, in fact, may be becoming inherently more difficult. The current trend toward emphasizing smooth human relationships as the principle qualification for administrative responsibility tends to militate against the rise of innovators [entrepreneurs] to top positions."[5]

To innovate and commercialize an invention or discovery, the entrepreneur necessarily must alter many facets of his environment: Change is his function; and new business, his output. But the capacity to change, or even to disagree—the first step in effectuating change—is a scarce commodity.

Torrance comments on the modern military entrepreneur, the Jet Ace:

[4] Melvin E. Salveson, *Dynamic Organization Planning* (New Canaan, Conn., CAM Press, 1959).

[5] Rupert W. MacLaurin, "The Sequence from Invention to Innovation and Its Relation to Economic Growth," *Quarterly Journal of Economics,* February 1953.

Research findings indicate that certain individuals show a generalized willingness to oppose others and disagree when the situation requires it. In our studies of Jet Aces in Korea, we found that this characteristic was typical of the Ace when compared to his less successful colleagues. Asch demonstrated a rather alarming similar picture. In "brainwashing" susceptibility experiments, Asch generated a disagreement between individuals and small groups on a clear and simple matter of fact in the environment. Only one-fourth of his subjects adhered to their own correct judgments, when confronted with the different and erroneous judgments of the (experimentally guided) groups.[6]

(The experiments involved deliberate expression of erroneous opinion by the group to determine whether the subjects would maintain their correct opinions. *Three-fourths did not.*)

To plan in the long range requires planned cultivation of entrepreneurs—those who can induce necessary change and who have the other moral and intellectual qualities for business leadership. Unless this key ingredient is provided, the best plan will remain dormant for want of the entrepreneurial spark.

3. *Rate of invention and innovation.* One of the principal findings from the study reported here is that there is a measurable rate of decay of the value of information as contained in products, processes, or methods. This is sometimes referred to as obsolescence. However, to recognize it as a problem in maintaining the continuous flow of new information gives the manager and the scientist (or engineer) a better basis for planning the R&D program, for planning the discovery and flow of new information, for anticipating the competitive decay of previously produced information, etc. The consequence of this insight in the study reported here was to study and project the trend in information decay rates, and to estimate the magnitude of the R&D staff and reinvestment required (1) to maintain fixed relative position; (2) to gain relative to competitors, assuming both their continuing at current rates and their accelerating their over-all reinvestment. The general nature of the findings on information decay rates is illustrated in Figure 4, and provides illuminating insight on the cost of remaining competitive and progressive.

To protect proprietary information, a weapons systems example is used, and the relative time span is expanded. However, the same trend

[6] Paul G. Torrance, *Function of Expressed Disagreement in Small Group Processes* (Reno, Nev., Stead Air Force Base, 1955).

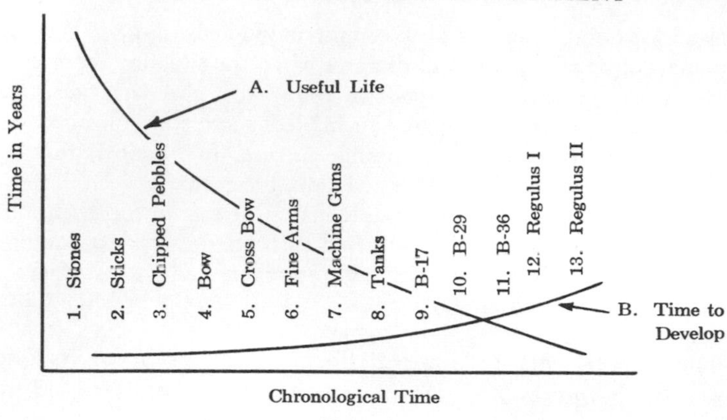

FIG. 4

was observed over short time spans and for a number of commercial products. To illustrate, curve *A* indicates the useful life of successive competitive weapons systems. Curve *B* indicates the time (or can be cost) to develop those systems. For example:

Nelson's tiny flagship was forty years old and still a first-rate ship-of-the-line at Trafalgar; Halsey's giant Enterprize at three years of age was obsolescent before World War II. The B-17 took about four years to develop and was operational for seven. The B-29 took about six years to develop and was operational for four. The B-36 was ten years in development and operational for only three. The Navaho was in development six years; it was abandoned before completion because of obsolescence. Regulus I and Regulus II had similar short lives.

Obviously, the increasing cost of R&D and the decreasing life spans of products counteract each other. The former tends to decrease a company's ability to do R&D; the latter increases the need for it. In between these, the rate of commercialization of inventions, then, needs to be controlled so as to insure an optimum program, balanced among the different phases, e.g., R&D, capital investment, advertising, market research, etc. Inasmuch as the problem of balancing and timing the various programs can be phrased in functional equations, it either becomes amenable to solution by calculus of variations, i.e., dynamic programming,[7] or these concepts greatly aid judgment solutions.

[7] Richard Bellman, *Dynamic Programming* (New York, McGraw-Hill Book Company, Inc., 1957).

The problem is somewhat complicated by the fact that the production or discovery of inventions has elements of uncertainty. This, however, is not difficult to handle if expected, minimum, and maximum rates are used and boundaries or tolerance limits are used in the computation. For example, an upper bound(s) may be used to help delimit the number and variety of programs which can be undertaken with available resources. The lower bound(s) determines minimum innovation necessary to maintain given levels of competitiveness. That is, the control of the flow of ideas is instrumental to corporate health; it must be neither too little nor too great.

4. *The criteria for business branching.* The General Electric Company's experience indicates that skills and knowledge are highly transferable, *vide* the branching and growth from lamps to such things as toasters, turbines, and transformers. However, some branches failed. The successes and failures together provide excellent guide lines. The following are key elements in predicting the success or failure of a branch.

Environmental or institutional knowledge. A working knowledge of trade practices, market characteristics, channels of distribution, contacts with key persons may provide at least part of the basis for a successful branching. For example, National Cash Register Company has had no prior background in large-scale computers. But its very close ties to an important market via a formidable marketing organization may well permit it successfully to enter the business computer field. It offers a point of entry into that business as the business data-processing technology expands and requires integration of the point of initial recording more intimately in the over-all data system.

Technical knowledge and skill. A prime example is General Electric's entry into the electric motor business. An electric motor is essentially a generator run in reverse. Thus, the technical knowledge and skills to design and manufacture generators provided a strong platform for entering the motor business. The basic data involved in the industrial analysis for this kind of branching are similar to those described by H. Igor Ansoff. The method described was used by Markowitz and Rowe as the basis for economic and military mobilization planning. The value of the analysis can be large: One company planned to branch into a business but found that the commonality of skills was only apparent, not real. It planned to operate a far-north aircraft engine repair station in the summer and a diesel repair station there during the winter while the diesel tractors were idle. Unfortunately, the skill carry-over from diesel to aircraft parts was too great; the mechanics repaired deisels to aircraft specifications, and vice versa. This was, of course, too costly and inefficient, and had to be abandoned.

Self-image and business flexibility. The self-image to which we refer here is a concept familiar only to those acquainted with psychoanalytic theory. Virtually only those individuals who have been successfully analysed will understand their self-images, and control the operation of them as the determinant of overt behavior. Others are conscious of their self-images only to the extent that they are or are not able to engage in one or another type of social, occupational, or other roles, but are not conscious of the reasons for their role inflexibility. An example is cited of a manufacturer of copper hardware that successfully competed in an industrial market where one pattern of occupational roles was required. The company was not successful in a commercial market, primarily because the executives' self-images unconsciously made them seek defensive refuge behind the mask of being "conservative engineers." While they consciously rationalized their preference for this role, to the trained observer it was obvious that it was a haven of defense against the incurrence of tensions and anxieties, induced by departing from their protective role. This unconsciously imposed inflexibility caused their commercial operation to be inefficient and unprofitable, even though the company already possessed a strong platform in manufacturing skills and facilities required for that commercial business.

Role-inflexibility problems often are resolved by "decentralization," so that each autonomous group, within the same company, can identify with that role(s) implicit in each of the several businesses which is compatible with the group's collective self-image. An alternative, which was used at least partially in this instance, is a psychoanalytically oriented training program to increase the personnel's flexibility to move between different roles. The organization, in this case, was not large enough to decentralize, hence required multiple role flexibility through personal flexibility.

The summation of the collection of self-images is the corporate self-image. This latter is one of the most powerful determinants of corporate flexibility—both because it reigns and operates through the unconscious and, hence, cannot be reasoned and reckoned with (except in analysis), and because it is self-reinforcing. No matter what course of action is followed, or attitude projected, it tends to be self-reinforcing: The negative attitudes, to be negatively reinforced; and the positive, positively reinforced—precisely because one or the other attitude already existed. Hence, the result of performing any business role is to enter that role with such unconscious predilections as create the responses from the environment which tend to confirm the predilection, in favor of or against the role.

Obviously, the greater the role flexibility of an individual, or of a business, the greater is its ability to capitalize on opportunities, regardless of the roles which they require. It is of little value to develop long-range plans and programs, only to find that a variety of apparently unrelated obstacles interpose themselves. These may take the form of "that is not our line of business," "the risk is too large," "the economy is uncertain," or other. Alternatively, they may appear as simple inaction, or delay. While it is possible to develop systematically the capacity for role flexibility, it is beyond the scope of this report to describe it.

Joint or by-products. A frequent basis for branching is when the production processes yield joint or by-products. This concept is obvious and needs no elaboration here.

The preceding are subject also to legal and moral limitations. For example, General Electric has been restrained by antitrust action from operating public utilities; the aircraft manufacturers, from operating airlines, etc. However, these concepts illustrate the evolutionary chain and branches in the growth and diversification of typical, successful, large companies. To reiterate, long-range planning for such growth requires as much the maintenance of the conditions for, and skills of, entrepreneurship as it does the development of specific action programs. Edison, in 1885, could hardly have planned for the evolution of the G.E. lamp business into the toaster and aircraft gas turbine businesses. But he and his successors, by maintaining the conditions for and skills of entrepreneurship, assured that evolution.

It was mentioned earlier that there is a minimum regeneration required for maintaining a viable business. Investment in innovation (as in R&D, new markets, new products, or other) must be at least at a certain minimum in order to sustain competitiveness and viability. In studying this phenomenon, the following observations were made.

There is a distinct, quantifiable, and measurable input-output relationship between successive stages in an innovation cycle. It was found that the "transfer function" can be used in long-range planning. Graphically, it is shown in Figure 5.

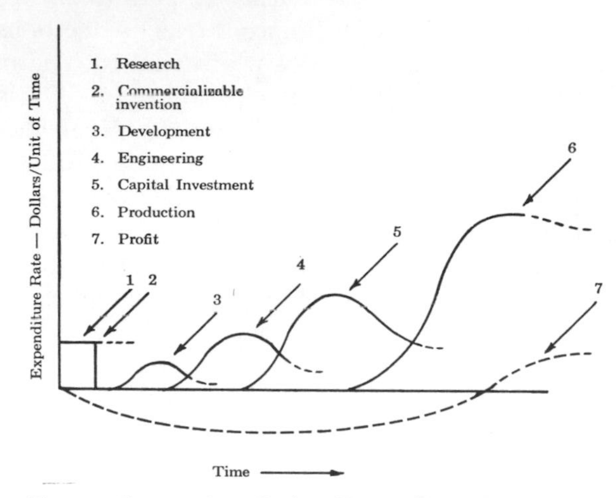

FIG. 5. Innovation Cycle—Expenditure Patterns

Several important relationships can then be sought for planning purposes. Some of these are:

1. What is the average, minimum, and maximum ratio of the area under each curve to the area under the preceding curve?
2. Is there a trend in these ratios over a period of time; are they increasing or decreasing?
3. What is the characteristic lead-lag relationship between the curves?
4. Do the ratios vary from product line to product line; and, if so, how?

This study was cued by an engineering occupations remuneration study. There, for example, it was found that the higher the rate of innovation in a branch of engineering, the higher the starting and top rates of pay. Similarly, it was found that the higher the rate of innovation in an industry—up to an upper bound—the higher the return on investment. It was found that the correlation between return on investment on a series of products, as a functional innovation investment, was not as high as it was on an industry basis. It appeared that there was random fluctuation on a product basis, which was averaged out on an industry basis. In particular, in a whole industry there is opportunity for the operation not only of primary breakthroughs, but also of supporting or facilitating discoveries.

Thus, it appears that whole industries tend to move together, while within these broad movements, the more aggressive innovators lead the way for the rest. But the leadership tends to be paced by the whole complex of limiting and facilitating innovations and advances.

In broader perspective, long-range planning must answer the question as to the division of innovational resources between:

1. Those programs which lead to lower cost (proportionately less employment)
2. Those which lead to more products

In the broad perspective, this is important: If the rate at which the work force is displaced through technological innovation is greater than the rate at which new employment is created on new products and services, unemployment is an inevitable consequence. In a political democracy with free enterprise, this balance can be maintained best through those free enterprises so planning their activities that the opposing tendencies are equilibrated. The alternative is social action, i.e., socialism.

In summary, long-range planning requires or achieves the following:

1. A business-wide perspective in innovation
2. A continuing flow of innovation for business viability and profits
3. A set of skills and conditions for successful entrepreneurship within the corporate framework
4. Organization components for pursuing the processes of entrepreneurship
5. Adaptation of the collective or business self-image to the roles implicit in foreseeable and evolving businesses, either through increasing personal flexibility or through organizational isolation of the roles (i.e., decentralization)

6. A balanced flow of resources to the phases in the innovation cycle

7. Recognition of and plans for the gradual reduction in the ratio of the direct labor force to the indirect labor force and overhead, as the result of technological progress.

12

Planning the Basic Strategy of a Medium-Sized Business[1]

Charles H. Percy
and
William E. Roberts

The foundation of "profit planning" at Bell & Howell is the company's sixty-month program. In setting our goals we take a retrospective look at where we have been, an objective look at where we are, and a hopeful look at where we want to go. We then chart a course which we believe will get us there. We keep an eye on economic forecasts, but we must admit that we do not let them influence our thinking too much. If the economic outlook is good, we are encouraged to go ahead with our plans. If it is foreboding, we try to determine how to buck the trend.

An important step is to analyze carefully our relative position in each field in which we compete. After a careful comparison of our past and present financial ratios—earnings to sales, return on investment, and inventory turnover—we establish goals to improve our position during each of the succeeding five years.

With the goals set, the detailed preparation of a sixty-month pro-

[1] By permission from *Planning the Future Strategy of Your Business,* ed. Edward C. Bursk and Dan H. Fenn, Jr. Copyright, 1956, McGraw-Hill Book Company, Inc.

gram begins. We analyze our existing product line and review our new-product development and research program. A sales forecast is made by months for the next fifteen-month period and on an annual basis for the following four years. Increases in hourly labor rates and salaries are projected, as is the lowering of unit costs through the anticipated effectiveness of cost-reduction programs. For expansion and capital equipment, future needs are analyzed, schedules are made, and financing is planned.

The sixty-month program is a living document which never becomes static. At no time has it ever been bound together between two covers as an "approved program" for the company. Most of the time it is in the form of rough layout sheets which are under constant revision.

The objective of the program is not only the program but also the thinking and planning that go into it. We are never satisfied with it, and we hope we never will be. Working constantly on a sixty-month program makes the preparation of our current year's profit and loss forecast a great deal easier, more accurate, and more satisfactory than it might otherwise be.

The merchandising division establishes a detailed sales forecast by months for all products and models, and submits it to manufacturing, financial, and administrative management for critical analysis. This same procedure is repeated frequently throughout the year. Desired inventory levels are established and manufacturing schedules drawn up. Cost of sales and divisional expense levels are established by the budget board in consultation with division managers. Programs and expenses are continually revised to maintain the current year's profit objective. The forecast profit-and-loss statement and the anticipated balance sheet position projected one year ahead are submitted to the board of directors at its December meeting.

ACTUAL VERSUS FORECAST PROGRAM

Flexibility is a must in a sixty-month program. Looking ahead five years from a constantly moving current date makes planning for the immediate twelve-month period easier. Both our long-range and short-range programs are constantly modified to meet new competitive products, the unforeseeable results of some of our own engineering and research efforts, the consolidation of newly acquired businesses, and other factors incalculable in advance.

Actually, our five-year planning is not directly measurable in terms of "batting averages." But in keeping us hitting in the right direction it has helped to achieve a good batting average in our short-term, twelve-month planning.

Over the past four years we have varied only slightly from our planned sales, expense, and profit budgets. Variation in expenses against budget, for example, ranged from 4.4 per cent in 1952 to 1 per cent in 1954. The variation from the preyear profit budget to the actual was only 3 per cent in 1954.

When deviations occur, as they frequently do during the year, we apply no magic formula for corrective action. Deviations are rapidly detected through weekly meetings of our sales analysis board. Then, pertinent division heads and executives are gathered to determine what action is necessary. The answer may be overtime, the addition of double or triple shifts, duplicate tooling, new capital equipment, or around-the-clock engineering effort; it may be a price change or the appointment of a special task force to nurse the situation back to normal.

We try to make our near-term budgets for profits, sales, and manufactured products realistic and attainable. They are rarely missed, although it sometimes requires ingenious and unusual effort to keep the program in balance.

Should some problem arise that cannot be remedied in time, we review earnings goals in the light of changed circumstances, and we immediately initiate steps to bring expense budgets into line.

Time will not permit a detailed review of our capital equipment planning. However, in brief, each division head develops and submits by November 1 a detailed list of his anticipated capital expenditures for the following year. The requested budgets are broken down in several ways. They are divided according to whether they are replacement, supplementary, or cost-reduction equipment. Each of these categories is, in turn, divided into two groups—"mandatory" and "desirable." The data are assembled by the controller, reviewed and balanced by the budget board, and then submitted to the president and the board of directors for approval.

Once approved, it becomes the total company dollar capital equipment budget for the ensuing year. However, each individual expenditure against the budget must be fully justified by the division head and approved by the controller before actual purchase. Cost-reduction equipment must presently meet a rigid rule of paying for itself within eighteen months. The measuring stick is almost always: What is the rate of return on investment?

COORDINATION OF MANAGEMENT EFFORT

At Bell & Howell we believe firmly that our business should be the expression of the ideas and objectives of our entire management group and, as far as humanly possible, of our employee group. We have experimented with many ways to encourage the free expression of opinion throughout the company, and have developed a pattern for coordinating our management effort and keeping us all running on the same track. The best way, we have found, is to have the top-management group help lay the track by participating in the development of the sixty-month and current-year forecasts.

But occasionally it helps to get far enough away from the program to take an objective look at it. To do this our officers and division managers literally move to the Fin 'n Feather Club in nearby Elgin, Illinois, once each quarter. Here we spend several days working together without the interruption of telephones or the pressure of supervisory responsibilities. The setting is beautiful, the atmosphere informal. Sports clothes are the order of the day, and, despite the customary skeet shoot, we have never lost an executive! In addition to crystallizing our thinking about our future program, this meeting helps to ease tensions that may have built up between purchasing and manufacturing, manufacturing and engineering, or engineering and sales.

For some time afterward the atmosphere is completely relaxed back in the organization—and then, suddenly, we know we have to go back to the Fin 'n Feather again.

Round-robin reports by division managers at our monthly staff luncheon keep each of us informed on all major developments within the company. Recent accomplishments can be reviewed and near-term forecasts analyzed.

We lean heavily on various management boards to coordinate the functional phases of our program. They are not committees. We feel about committees a little like the description by the chancellor of one of our large universities:

The first time he saw a camel, he got out of his jeep, stood right next to this ugly looking thing with its drooling jowls, baggy skin, and great humps, and he thought, "Good Lord, that looks like it was put together by a committee."

Although the responsibility of these boards is entirely advisory, they are effective in achieving a more closely knit operation and in tapping the specialized knowledge of top-management people.

The heart of our management program is the research board. All ideas for new products are first submitted to this board, which helps to guide new product ideas to fruition. The members of the board include the president, executive vice-president, and treasurer, the engineering, manufacturing, and merchandising vice-presidents, the head of our product-planning activity, and the assistant vice-president in charge of production engineering and tooling. Thus, all major operating divisions are able to contribute their viewpoints and participate in discussions and decisions on new-product development.

Market research and merchandising department ideas on product features, appearance, and price are usually obtained before the first line is made on a sheet of drafting paper.

Sales, engineering, manufacturing, and financing problems get a thorough going-over before—not after—new-product development work is begun.

RESPONSIBILITIES OF SPECIAL BOARDS

Our sales analysis board, which includes top merchandising, manufacturing, purchasing, and market research people and the executive vice-president, meets once a month. At these meetings individual product projections for the next fifteen-month period are studied month by month and compared with planned manufacturing and projected inventory schedules. The sales, manufacturing, and inventory programs are reviewed, and confirmed or modified in the light of changed conditions; weak areas are detected and corrective action planned. All statistical data are presented graphically.

Supplementing the sales analysis board, a smaller group meets each Monday and briefly reviews sales and manufacturing progress toward budget goals. Negative trends are thus detected in time to bend them back to meet or exceed budget.

The manufacturing board is composed of manufacturing, planning, tooling, production engineering, quality control, and methods engineering personnel. Acting as a two-way information channel and a sounding board for unusual problems or new manufacturing ideas or techniques, it coordinates the functions of the manufacturing division.

The budget board, which includes the president, executive vice-president, treasurer, controller, and vice-president of manufacturing, controls the purse strings of the company. It develops all budgets, in cooperation with the division heads, and recommends them for approval. Annual divisional expense budgets, manufacturing schedules, capital equipment budgets, inventory objectives, and the cash forecast are its responsibilities. It must operate within the current earnings target, with the sixty-month goals constantly in sight.

Our boards have become a device for overcoming the specialization that tends to divorce the outlook of operating experts in engineering from that of experts on sales or manufacturing. But they do not take major planning chores out of the operating people's hands; they do not take away from the division head the responsibility which is his for meeting company objectives; they do not become substitutes for the regular line and staff organization. The boards are merely superimposed on the operating organization as a device to make possible wider interdivisional participation by top executives.

EXECUTION OF PROGRAM

We would agree, I am sure, that the basic purpose of a free society is to develop the individual to the greatest possible extent. Should we not also conclude, then, that a company's chance for success is greatest when it encourages such growth and development on the part of each individual within the organization? We believe so, and therefore our objective is to try to create the proper working climate and sufficient incentive for every person to work as conscientiously and intelligently as if he were working for himself. This is the goal we keep constantly before us.

Once our target has been established, our job is to shoot for it—and to shoot with an expectancy of success. We are entirely dependent upon the people of our organization, to whom we delegate all necessary authority and responsibility. Decisions are made at the lowest possible level. We try, as much as possible, to manage through the rule of exception; that is, once a plan has been established and the authority delegated for its execution, no further authority is required from any higher source unless an exception must be made because of changing circumstances. This removes 90 per cent of the routine work from the manager's desk.

But top management would be remiss if it assumed that its job was now done. For in addition to the never-ending job of future planning, the president and the executive vice-president must go to work for the operating divisions of the company to help implement plans and programs already made. This job has many facets, but I will mention only two: the communications program and the continuing task of evaluating divisional and individual performance.

We have proved again and again Thomas J. Watson's words: "None of us is ever enthusiastic about anything until we understand it. Knowledge creates enthusiasm, and it is enthusiasm which inspires us to work and move foreward."

When the organization, from top to bottom, understands the overall aims, objectives, problems, hopes, and aspirations of the company, then it can do a better job of carrying out the company program. . . .

QUESTIONS AND ANSWERS[2]

From the floor: I am interested—and somewhat puzzled—by one aspect of Bell & Howell's "participation" management.

My organization has about five hundred people in it, and is pretty small in comparison with some of the large companies. We have a lot of talented young men, however, who are charged with ideas and raring to go, and we are anxious to hear their suggestions. And I couldn't help thinking, as Mr. Percy reported on the way his company operated, how bogged down we get when we try to get all these people into the act, how even our little organizational problems seem to get choked in committee sessions. Yet I understood from his presentation that Bell & Howell had around three hundred people getting together every month. How is it possible, as a practical matter, for a company to drag everyone into the act? And how can it control a management committee?

[2] The preceding sections are based on the authors' addresses at the Twenty-Fifth Annual National Business Conference at the Harvard Business School, 1949. In a later meeting, Mr. Percy answered questions pertaining to his formal presentation; this section is drawn, more or less verbatim, from the discussion that took place at this meeting. George P. Baker, James J. Hill Professor of Transportation, Harvard Business School, acted as moderator.

Mr. Percy: I became very enthusiastic about management participation—we had never had anything like it in the company before—but I must confess that at one point I made the unpardonable mistake of letting it go too far, and it was hard to pull it back on the track again. You just cannot let this type of thing get out of hand.

After we started having everyone at the meetings, these conferences had to be held after working hours. This made arrangements much more difficult, of course. When we found that meetings were unnecessarily long and that reasons for calling them were often invalid, we instituted a training program on conference leadership. We had agendas made out ahead of time, including the stated purpose of the meeting, the starting time, and the closing time. If the chairman conducted the meeting improperly, the committee members quickly criticized him for it and thus brought him back on the track. We no longer try to consider everything in these conferences. For instance, no one in the company is wise enough to judge how money taken in through sales should be prorated and expended; this is now a problem for the budget board.

I think we are no longer plagued by too much "meetingitis," as we called it, although we did have trouble for a while controlling our kind of participation management. We used to have dinner meetings once a month from 5:15 to 8:00, but we found we could save several thousand dollars a year by eliminating the dinners, and we now meet for only an hour and a quarter, from 5:00 to 6:15. This gives us plenty of time to present our monthly reports and to inform our executive staff and foreman about important company plans.

The smaller quarterly meetings of our top executives are another matter. They do need to be physically removed from the plant and free from all interference. These meetings, incidentally, provide a wonderful chance for our secondary line of management to run their divisions by themselves for a day or two every quarter. We think it is valuable experience for them to be completely on their own without any of the top-management staff about.

From the floor: Mr. Percy has stated that his long-range, five-year planning makes his short-range, one-year, and two-year planning a lot easier. How is this true?

Mr. Percy: By becoming familiar with what our cash position is likely to be several years in *advance* of any coming year—barring unforeseeable happenings such as the acquisition of a new business or our competition coming out with a revolutionary new line of product

—we find it much easier to estimate our position for any particular year. By the time 1955 came around, we had been planning and working on it for three or more years. Most of my personal time now is going into 1957 and later years—1957, incidentally, will be our fiftieth anniversary, and we have been thinking about it and working on it for many years. We think it will be a fine opportunity for a special drive in several directions. Detailed planning for 1957 should be much easier with all this general, long-range planning in back of us.

From the floor: In Mr. Percy's discussion of profit-planning, he has mentioned that he looks at the present objectively and the future hopefully. What is the point of this distinction between "objective" and "hopeful"?

Mr. Percy: "Hopeful" is one word that almost everyone associated with our company uses extensively. Businessmen have to be optimists; we would get nowhere if we looked with pessimism to the future. We have to figure ways for our company to keep going regardless of the way the economic indicators point and in spite of what our competitors may do. Our theory used to be that when the indicators dropped down, then we buttoned down. Now we try to accelerate our new products ahead faster than originally scheduled and intensify our sales efforts. In other words, we, like other managements, will try to buck any adverse trend—that is our nature. When I said that we look to the future hopefully, I meant we all believe that if any year doesn't turn out the way we thought, at least the approach we took made it better than it might have been.

13

Strategies for Diversification[1]

H. Igor Ansoff

The Red Queen said, "Now, *here,* it takes all the running *you* can do to keep in the same place. If you want to get somewhere else, you must run at least twice as fast as that!"[2]

So it is in the American economy. Just to retain its relative position, a business firm must go through continuous growth and change. To improve its position, it must grow and change at least "twice as fast as that."

According to a recent survey of the one hundred largest United States corporations from 1909 to 1948, few companies that have stuck to their traditional products and methods have grown in stature. The report concludes: "There is no reason to believe that those now at the top will stay there except as they keep abreast in the race of innovation and competition."[3]

There are four basic growth alternatives open to a business. It can grow through increased market penetration, through market development, through product development, or through diversification.

A company which accepts diversification as a part of its planned

[1] From H. Igor Ansoff, "Strategies for Diversification," *Harvard Business Review,* September–October 1957, pp. 113–124. Used by permission.

[2] Lewis J. Carroll, *Through the Looking-Glass* (New York, The Heritage Press, 1941), p. 41.

[3] A. D. H. Kaplan, *Big Enterprise in a Competitive System* (Washington, The Brookings Institution, 1954), p. 142.

approach to growth undertakes the task of continually weighing and comparing the advantages of these four alternatives, selecting first one combination and then another, depending on the particular circumstances in long-range development planning.

While they are an integral part of the over-all growth pattern, diversification decisions present certain unique problems. Much more than other growth alternatives, they require a break with past patterns and traditions of a company and an entry on new and uncharted paths.

Accordingly, one of the aims of this article is to relate diversification to the over-all growth perspectives of management, establish reasons which may lead a company to prefer diversification to other growth alternatives, and trace a relationship between over-all growth objectives and special diversification objectives. This will provide us with a partly qualitative, partly quantitative method for selecting diversification strategies which are best suited to long-term growth of a company. We can use qualitative criteria to reduce the total number of possible strategies to the most promising few, and then apply a return on investment measure to narrow the choice of plans still further.

PRODUCT-MARKET ALTERNATIVES

The term "diversification" is usually associated with a change in the characteristics of the company's product line and/or market, in contrast to market penetration, market development, and product development, which represent other types of change in product-market structure. Since these terms are frequently used interchangeably, we can avoid later confusion by defining each as a special kind of product-market strategy. To begin with the basic concepts:

The *product line* of a manufacturing company refers both to (1) the physical characteristics of the individual products (for example, size, weight, materials, tolerances) and (2) the performance characteristics of the products (for example, an airplane's speed, range, altitude, payload).

In thinking of the market for a product we can borrow a concept commonly used by the military—the concept of a mission. A *product mission* is a description of the job which the product is intended to perform. For instance, one of the missions of the Lockheed Aircraft

Corporation is commercial air transportation of passengers; another is provision of airborne early warning for the Air Defense Command; a third is performance of air-to-air combat.

For our purposes, the concept of a mission is more useful in describing market alternatives than would be the concept of a "customer," since a customer usually has many different missions, each requiring a different product. The Air Defense Command, for example, needs different kinds of warning systems. Also, the product mission concept helps management to set up the problems in such a way that it can better evaluate the performance of competing products.

A *product-market strategy,* therefore, is a joint statement of a product line and the corresponding set of missions which the products are designed to fulfill. In shorthand form (see Figure 1), if we let π represent the product line and μ the corresponding set of missions, then the pair of π and μ is a product-market strategy.

With these concepts in mind let us turn now to the four different types of product-market strategy shown in Figure 1:

Market penetration is an effort to increase company sales without departing from an original product-market strategy. The company seeks to improve business performance either by increasing the volume of sales to its present customers or by finding new customers for present products.

Market development is a strategy in which the company attempts to adapt its present product line (generally with some modification in the product characteristics) to new missions. An airplane company which adapts and sells its passenger transport for the mission of cargo transportation is an example of this strategy.

A *product development* strategy, on the other hand, retains the present mission and develops products with new and different characteristics that will improve the performance of the mission.

Diversification is the final alternative. It calls for a simultaneous departure from the present product line and the present market structure.

Each of the above strategies describes a distinct path which a business can take toward future growth. However, it must be emphasized that in most actual situations a business would follow several of these paths at the same time. As a matter of fact, a simultaneous pursuit of market penetration, market development, and product development

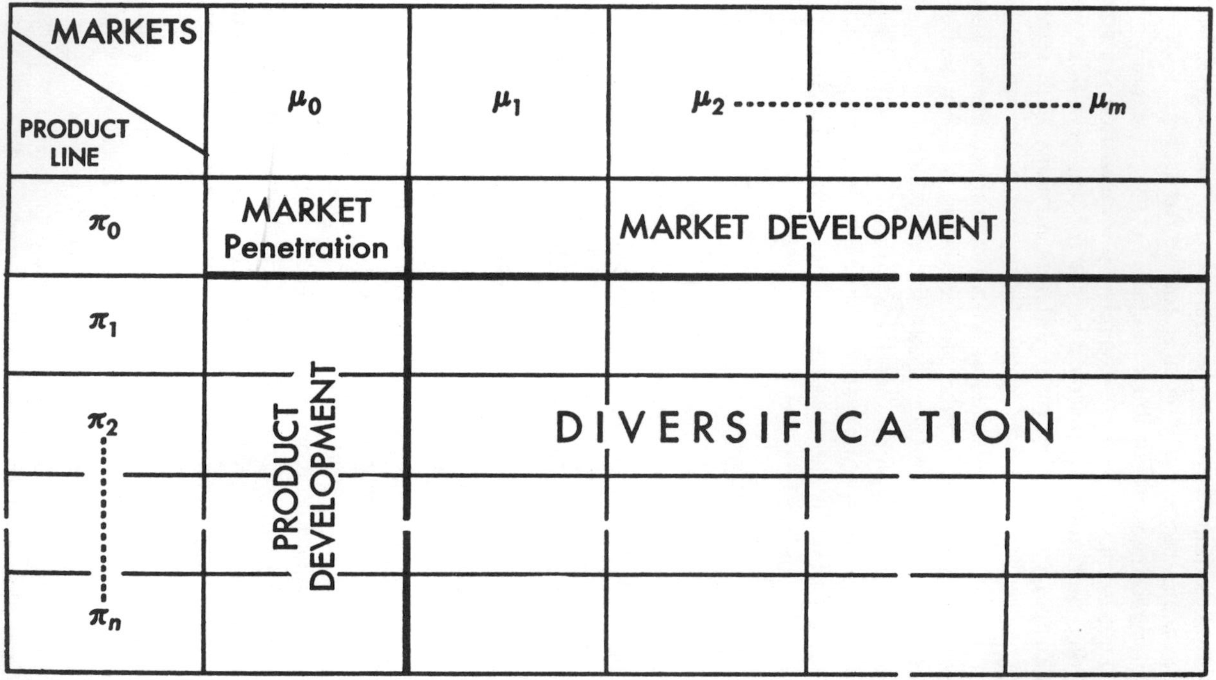

MARKETS / PRODUCT LINE	μ_0	μ_1	μ_2 .... μ_m
π_0	MARKET Penetration	MARKET DEVELOPMENT	
π_1	PRODUCT DEVELOPMENT	DIVERSIFICATION	
π_2 .... π_n			

FIG. 1. Product-Market Strategies for Business Growth Alternatives

is usually a sign of a progressive, well-run business and may be essential to survival in the face of economic competition.

The diversification strategy stands apart from the other three. While the latter are usually followed with the same technical, financial, and merchandising resources which are used for the original product line, diversification generally requires new skills, new techniques, and new facilities. As a result, it almost invariably leads to physical and organizational changes in the structure of the business which represents a distinct break with past business experience.

FORECASTING GROWTH

A study of business literature and of company histories reveals many different reasons for diversification. Companies diversify to compensate for technological obsolescence, to distribute risk, to utilize excess productive capacity, to reinvest earnings, to obtain top management, and so forth. In deciding whether to diversify, management should carefully analyze its future growth prospects. It should think of market penetration, market development, and product development as parts of its over-all product strategy and ask whether this strategy should be broadened to include diversification.

Long-Term Trends

A standard method of analyzing future company growth prospects is to use long-range sales forecasts. Preparing the forecasts involves simultaneous consideration of several major factors:

- General economic trends.
- Political and international trends.
- Trends peculiar to the industry. (For example, forecasts prepared in the airplane industry must take account of such possibilities as a change-over from manned aircraft to missiles, changes in the government "mobilization base" concept with all that would mean for the aircraft industry, and rising expenditures required for research and development.)
- Estimates of the company's competitive strength as compared to other members of the industry.
- Estimates of improvements in company performance which can be achieved through market penetration, market development, and product development.
- Trends in manufacturing costs.

Such forecasts usually assume that company management will be aggressive and that management policies will take full advantage of the opportunities offered by the different trends. They are, in other words, estimates of the best possible results the business can hope to achieve *short* of diversification.

Different patterns of forecasted growth are shown in Figure 2, with with hypothetical growth curves for the national economy (GNP) and the company's industry added for purposes of comparison. One of the curves illustrates a sales curve which declines with time. This may be the result of an expected contraction of demand, the obsolescence of manufacturing techniques, emergence of new products better suited to the mission to which the company caters, or other changes. Another typical pattern, frequently caused by seasonal variations in demand, is one of cyclic sales activity. Less apparent, but more important, are slower cyclic changes, such as trends in construction or the peace-war variation in demand in the aircraft industry.

If the most optimistic sales estimates which can be attained short of diversification fall in either of the preceding cases, diversification is strongly indicated. However, a company may choose to diversify even if its prospects may, on the whole, appear favorable. This is illustrated by the "slow growth curve." As drawn in Figure 2, the curve indicates rising sales which in fact grow faster than the economy as a whole. Nevertheless, the particular company may belong to one of the so-called "growth industries" which as a whole are surging ahead. Such a company may diversify because it feels that its prospective growth rate is unsatisfactory in comparison to the industry growth rate.

Making trend forecasts is far from a precise science. The characteristics of the basic environmental trends, as well as the effect of these trends on the industry, are always uncertain. Furthermore, the ability of a particular business organization to perform in the new environment is very difficult to assess. Consequently, any realistic company forecast should include several different trend forecasts, each with an explicitly or implicitly assigned probability. As an alternative, the company's growth trend forecast may be represented by a widening spread between two extremes, similar to that shown for GNP in Figure 2.

Contingencies

In addition to trends, another class of events may make diversification desirable. These are certain environmental conditions which, if

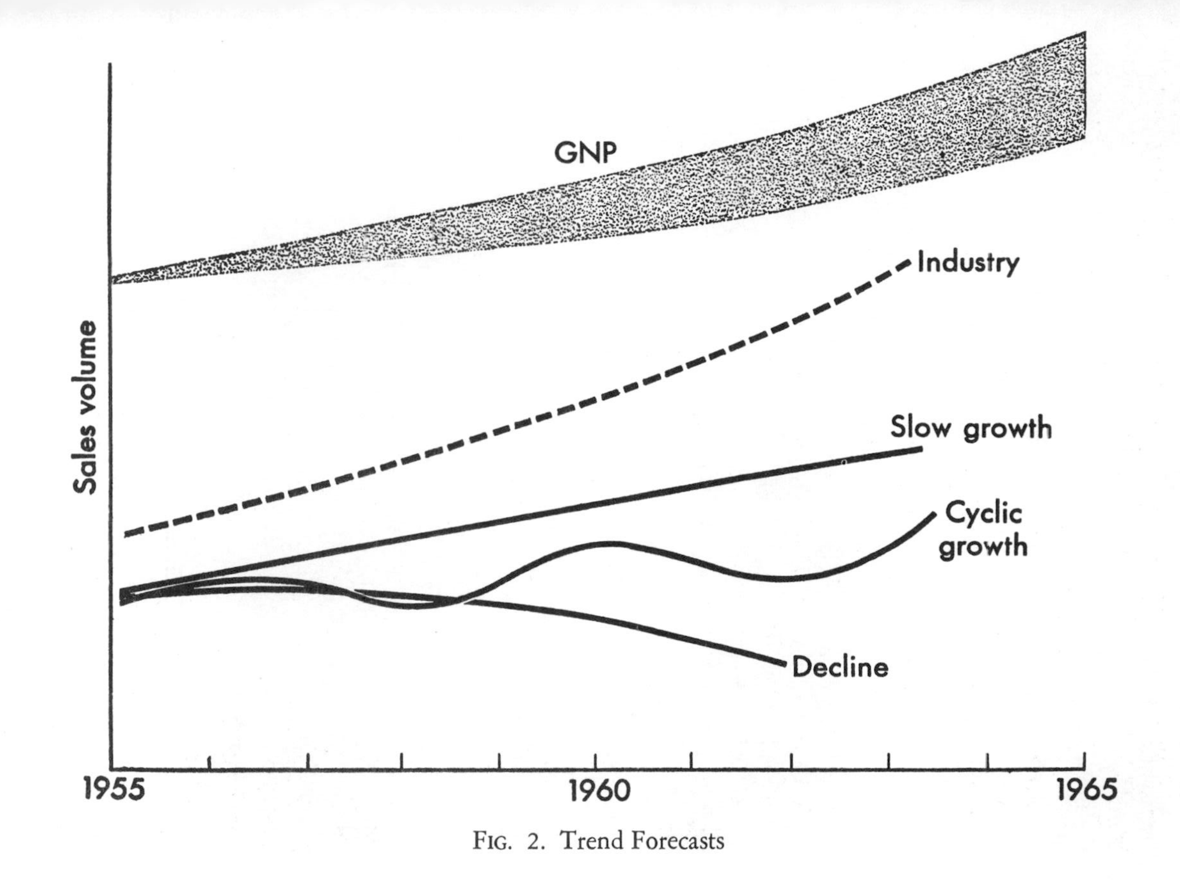

FIG. 2. Trend Forecasts

they occur, will have a great effect on sales; however, we cannot predict their occurrence with certainty. To illustrate such "contingent" events, an aircraft company might foresee these possibilities that would upset its trend forecasts:

- A major technological breakthrough whose characteristics the planners can foresee, but whose timing they cannot at present determine. (The discovery of a new manufacturing process for high-strength, thermally resistant aircraft bodies would be an example of this.)
- An economic recession which would lead to loss of orders for commercial aircraft and would change the pattern of spending for military aircraft.
- A major economic depression.
- A limited war which would sharply increase the demand for air industry products.
- A sudden cessation of cold war, a currently popular hope which has waxed and waned with changes in Soviet behavior.

The two types of sales forecast are illustrated in Figure 3 for a hypothetical company. Sales curves S_1 and S_2 represent a spread of trend forecasts; and S_3 and S_4, two contingent forecasts for the same event. The difference between the two types, both in starting time and effect on sales, lies in the degree of uncertainty associated with each.

In the case of trend forecasts we can trace a crude time history of sales based on events which we fully expect to happen. Any uncertainty arises from not knowing exactly when they will take place and how they will influence business. In the case of contingency forecasts, we can again trace a crude time history, but our uncertainty is greater. We lack precise knowledge of not only *when* the event will occur but also *whether* it will occur. In going from a trend to a contingency forecast, we advance, so to speak, one notch up the scale of ignorance.

In considering the relative weight we should give to contingent events in diversification planning, we must consider not only the magnitude of their effect on sales, but also the relative probability of their occurrence. For example, if a deep economic depression were to occur, its effect on many industries would be devastating. Many companies feel safe in neglecting it in their planning, however, because they feel that the likelihood of a deep depression is very small, at least for the near future.

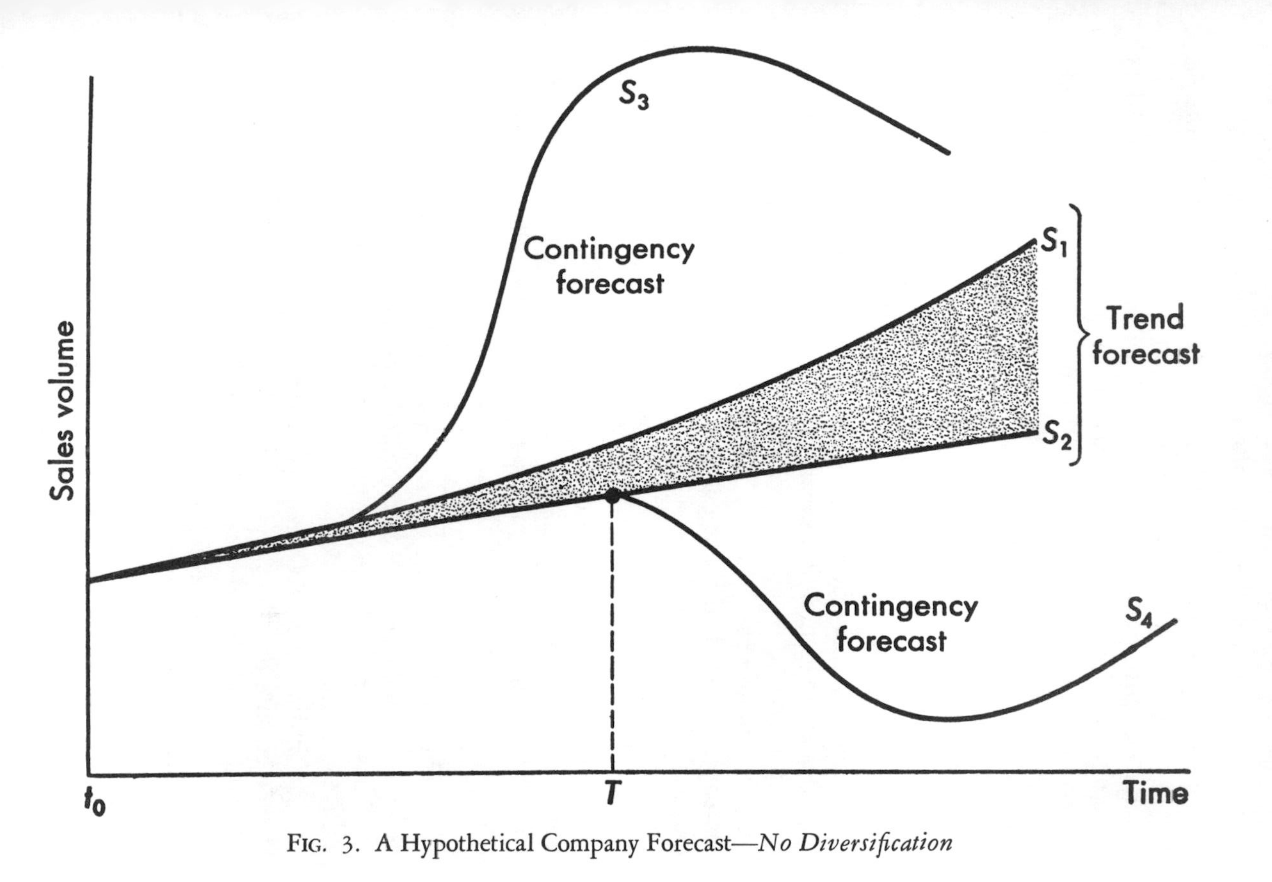

FIG. 3. A Hypothetical Company Forecast—*No Diversification*

It is a common business practice to put primary emphasis on trend forecasts; in fact, in many cases businessmen devote their long-range planning exclusively to these forecasts. They usually view a possible catastrophe as "something one cannot plan for" or as a second-order correction to be applied only after the trends have been taken into account. The emphasis is on planning for growth, and planning for contingencies is viewed as an "insurance policy" against reversals.

People familiar with planning problems in the military establishment will note here an interesting difference between military and business attitudes. While business planning emphasizes trends, military planning emphasizes contingencies. To use a crude analogy, a business planner is concerned with planning for continuous, successful, day-after-day operation of a supermarket. If he is progressive, he also buys an insurance policy against fire, but he spends relatively little time in planning for fires. The military is more like the fire engine company; the fire is the thing. Day-to-day operations are of interest only as they serve to improve readiness and fire-fighting techniques.

Unforeseeable Events

So far we have dealt with diversification forecasts based on what may be called *foreseeable* market conditions—conditions which we can interpret in terms of time-phased sales curves. Planners have a tendency to stop here, to disregard the fact that, in addition to the events for which we can draw time histories, there is a recognizable class of events to which we can assign a probability of occurrence but which we cannot otherwise describe in our present state of knowledge. One must move another notch up the scale of ignorance to consider these possibilities.

Many businessmen feel that the effort is not worthwhile. They argue that since no information is available about these unforeseeable circumstances, one might as well devote the available time and energy to planning for the foreseeable circumstances, or that, in a very general sense, planning for the foreseeable also prepares one for the unforeseeable contingencies.

In contrast, more experienced military and business people have a very different attitude. Well aware of the importance and relative probability of unforeseeable events, they ask why one should plan specific steps for the foreseeable events while neglecting the really important possibilities. They may substitute for such planning practical maxims for conducting one's business—"be solvent," "be light on your feet," "be flexible." Unfortunately, it is not always clear (even to the people who preach it) what this flexibility means.

An interesting study by The Brookings Institution[4] provides an example of the importance of the unforeseeable events to business. Figure 4 shows the changing makeup of the list of the one hundred largest corporations over the last fifty years. Of the one hundred largest on the 1909 list (represented by the heavy marble texture) only thirty-six were among the one hundred largest in 1948; only about half of the new entries to the list in 1919 (represented by white) were left in 1948; less than half of the new entries in 1929 (represented by the zigzag design) were left in 1948; and so on. Clearly, a majority of the giants of yesteryear have dropped behind in a relatively short span of time.

Many of the events that hurt these corporations could not be specifically foreseen in 1909. If the companies which dropped from the original list had made forecasts of the foreseeable kind at that time—and some of them must have—they would very likely have found the future growth prospects to be excellent. Since then, however, railroads, which loomed as the primary means of transportation, have given way to the automobile and the airplane; the textile industry, which appeared to have a built-in demand in an expanding world population, has been challenged and dominated by synthetics; radio, radar, and television have created means of communication unforeseeable in significance and scope; and many other sweeping changes have occurred.

Planning for the Unknown

The lessons of the past fifty years are fully applicable today. The pace of economic and technological change is so rapid that it is virtually certain that major breakthroughs comparable to those of the last fifty years, but not yet foreseeable in scope and character, will profoundly change the structure of the national economy. All of this has important implications for diversification, as suggested by the Brookings Study:

> The majority of the companies included among the one hundred largest of our day have attained their positions within the last two decades. They

[4] *Ibid.*

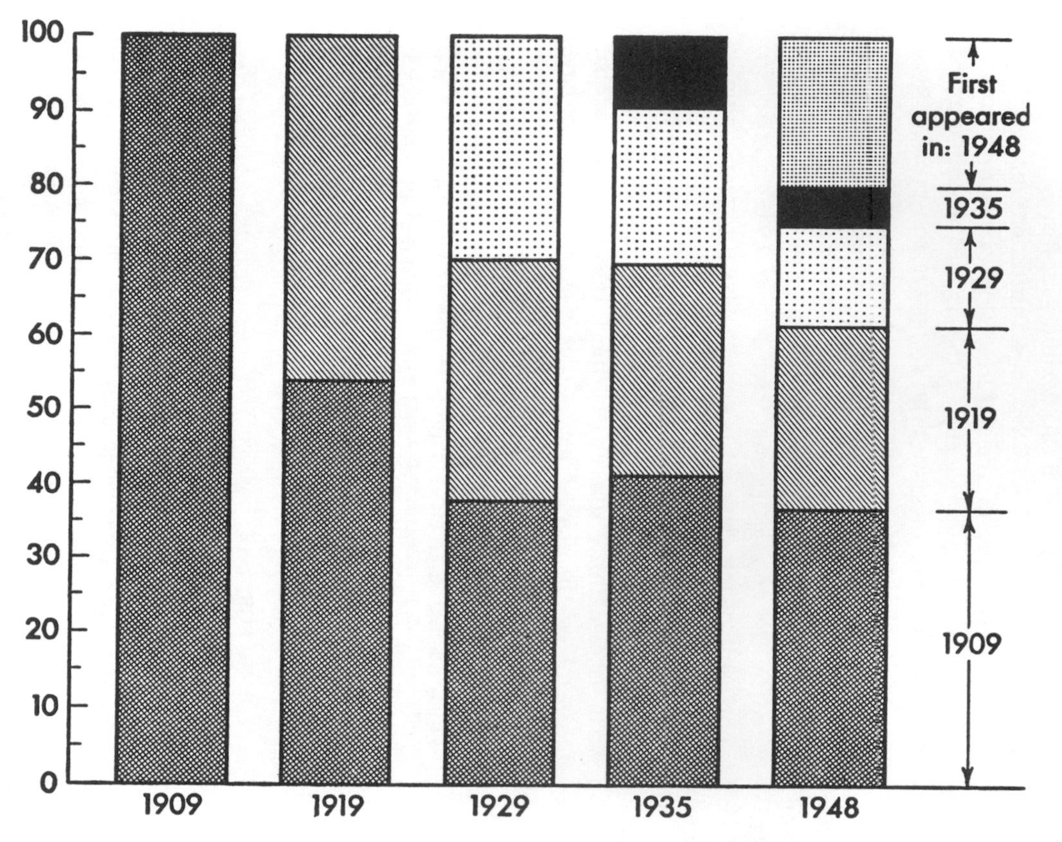

FIG. 4. Changes in List of the 100 Largest Industrial Corporations

are companies that have started new industries or have transformed old ones to create or meet consumer preferences. The companies that have not only grown in absolute terms but have gained an improved position in their own industry may be identified as companies that are notable for drastic changes made in their product mix and methods, generating or responding to new competition.

There are two outstanding cases in which the industry leader of 1909 had by 1948 risen in position relative to its own industry group and also in rank among the one hundred largest—one in chemicals and the other in electrical equipment. These two (General Electric and DuPont) are hardly recognizable as the same companies they were in 1909 except for retention of the name; for in each case the product mix of 1948 is vastly different from what it was in the earlier year, and the markets in which the companies meet competition are incomparably broader than those that accounted for their earlier place at the top of their industries. They exemplify the flux in the market positions of the most successful industrial giants during the past four decades and a general growth rather than a consolidation of supremacy in a circumscribed line.[5]

This suggests that the existence of specific undesirable trends is not the only reason for diversification. A broader product line may be called for even with optimistic forecasts for present products. An examination of the foreseeable alternatives should be accompanied by an analysis of how well the over-all company product-market strategy covers the so-called growth areas of technology—areas of many potential discoveries. If such analysis shows that, because of its product lines, a company's chances of taking advantage of important discoveries are limited, management should broaden its technological and economic base by entering a number of so-called growth industries. Even if the definable horizons look bright, a need for flexibility, in the widest sense of the word, may provide potent reasons for diversification.

DIVERSIFICATION OBJECTIVES

If an analysis of trends and contingencies indicates that a company should diversify, where should it look for diversification opportunities?

Generally speaking, there are three types of opportunities:

1. Each product manufactured by a company is made up of func-

[5] *Ibid.*, p. 142.

tional components, parts, and basic materials which go into the final assembly. A manufacturing concern usually buys a large fraction of these from outside suppliers. One way to diversify, commonly known as *vertical diversification,* is to branch out into production of components, parts, and materials. Perhaps the most outstanding example of vertical diversification is the Ford empire in the days of Henry Ford, Sr.

At first glance, vertical diversification seems inconsistent with our definition of a diversification strategy. However, the respective missions which components, parts, and materials are designed to perform are distinct from the mission of the over-all product. Furthermore, the technology in fabrication and manufacture of these parts and materials is likely to be very different from the technology of manufacturing the final product. Thus, vertical diversification does imply both catering to new missions and introduction of new products.

2. Another possible way to go is *horizontal diversification.* This can be described as the introduction of new products which, while they do not contribute to the present product line in any way, cater to missions which lie within the company's know-how and experience in technology, finance, and marketing.

3. It is also possible, by *lateral diversification,* to move beyond the confines of the industry to which a company belongs. This obviously opens a great many possibilities, from operating banana boats to building atomic reactors. While vertical and horizontal diversification are restrictive, in the sense that they delimit the field of interest, lateral diversification is wide open. It is an announcement of the company's intent to range far afield from its present market structure.

Choice of Direction

How does a company choose among these diversification directions? In part the answer depends on the reasons which prompt diversification. For example, in the light of the trends described for the aircraft industry, an aircraft company may make the following moves to meet long-range sales objectives through diversification:

1. A vertical diversification move to contribute to the technological progress of the present product line.

2. A horizontal move to improve the coverage of the military market.

3. A horizontal move to increase the percentage of commercial sales in the over-all sales program.
4. A lateral move to stabilize sales in case of a recession.
5. A lateral move to broaden the company's technological base.

Some of these diversification objectives apply to characteristics of the product; some, to those of the product missions. Each objective is designed to improve some aspect of the balance between the over-all product-market strategy and the expected environment. The specific objectives derived for any given case can be grouped into three general categories: *growth objectives,* such as objectives (1), (2), and (3) above, which are designed to improve the balance under favorable trend conditions; *stability objectives,* such as (3) and (4), designed as protection against unfavorable trends and foreseeable contingencies; and *flexibility objectives,* such as (5), to strengthen the company against unforeseeable contingencies.

A diversification direction which is highly desirable for one of the objectives is likely to be less desirable for others. For example:

If a company is diversifying because its sales trend shows a declining volume of demand, it would be unwise to consider vertical diversification, since this would be at best a temporary device to stave off an eventual decline of business.

If the company's industry shows every sign of healthy growth, then vertical and, in particular, horizontal diversification would be a desirable device for strengthening the position of the company in a field in which its knowledge and experience are concentrated.

If the major concern is stability under a contingent forecast, chances are that both horizontal and vertical diversification could provide a sufficient stabilizing influence and that lateral action is indicated.

If management's concern is with the narrowness of the technological base in the face of what we have called unforeseeable contingencies, then lateral diversification into new areas of technology would be clearly called for.

Measured Sales Goals

Management can and should state the objectives of growth and stability in quantitative terms as *long-range sales objectives.* This is illustrated in Figure 5. The solid lines describe a hypothetical company's forecasted performance without diversification under a general

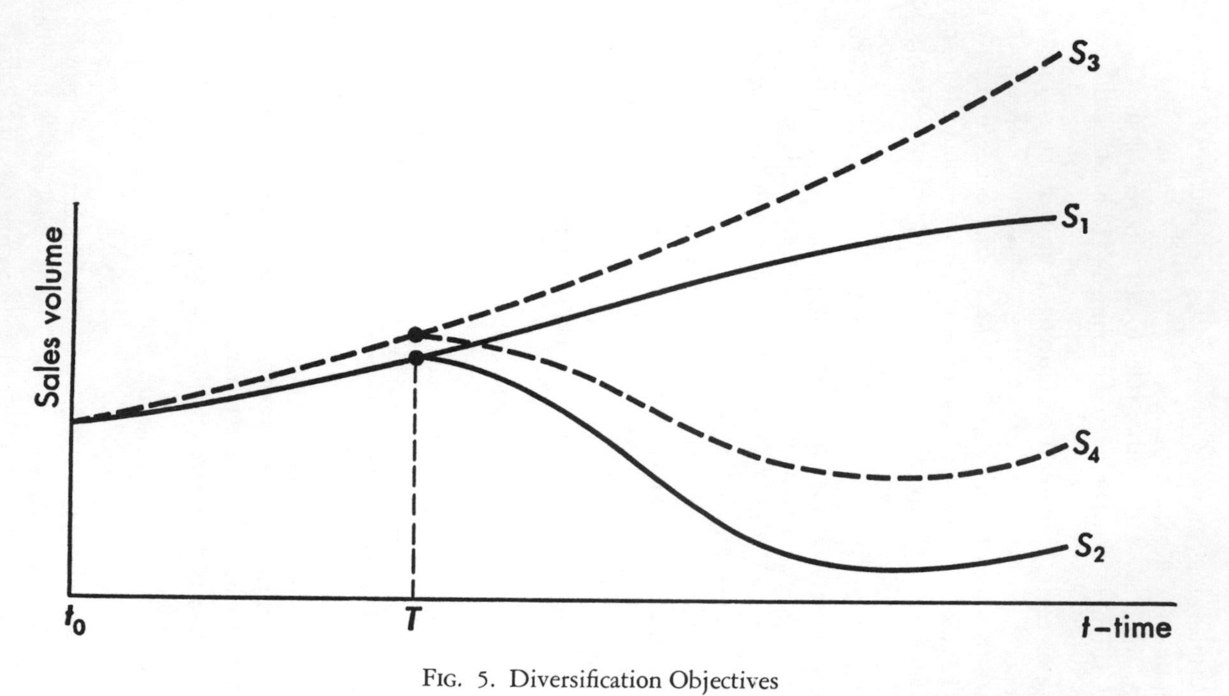

FIG. 5. Diversification Objectives

trend, represented by the sales curve marked S_1, and in a contingency, represented by S_2. The dashed lines show the improved performance as a result of diversification, with S_3 representing the curve with a continuation of normal trends and S_4 representing the curve in case of a major reverse.

Growth

Management's first aim in diversifying is to improve the growth pattern of the company. We can state the growth objective as follows:

Under trend conditions the growth rate of sales after diversification should exceed the growth rate of sales of the original product line by a minimum specified margin. Or to illustrate in shorthand, the objective for the company in Figure 5 would be:

$$S_3 - S_1 \geqslant \rho$$

where the value of the margin ρ is specified for each year after diversification.

Some companies (particularly in the growth industries) fix an annual rate of growth which they wish to attain. Every year this rate of growth is compared to the actual growth during the past year. A decision on diversification action for the coming year is then based on the disparity between the objective and the actual rate of growth.

Stability

The second effect desired of diversification is improvement in company stability under contingent conditions. Not only should diversification prevent sales from dropping as low as they might have before diversification, but the percentage drop should also be lower. The second sales objective is thus a stability objective. It can be stated as follows:

Under contingent conditions the percentage drop in sales which may occur without diversification should exceed the percentage drop in sales with diversification by an adequate margin, or algebraically:

$$\frac{S_1 - S_2}{S_1} - \frac{S_3 - S_4}{S_3} \geqslant \delta$$

Using this equation, it is possible to relate the sales volumes before and after diversification to a rough measure of the resulting stability. Let the ratio of the lowest sales during a slump to the sales which would have occurred in the same year under trend conditions be called the stability factor F. Thus, $F = 0.3$ would mean that company sales during a contingency amount to 30 per cent of what is expected under trend conditions. In Figure 6 the stability factor of the company before diversification is the value $F_1 = S_2/S_1$ and the stability factor after diversification is $F_3 = S_4/S_3$, both computed at the point on the curve where S_2 is minimum.

Now let us suppose that top management is considering the purchase of a subsidiary. How large does the subsidiary have to be if the parent is to improve the stability of the corporation as a whole by a certain amount? Figure 6 shows how the question can be answered:

On the horizontal axis we plot the different possible sales volumes of a smaller firm that might be secured as a proportion of the parent's volume. Obviously, the greater this proportion, the greater the impact of the purchase on the parent's stability.

On the vertical axis we plot different ratios of the parent's stability before and after diversification (F_3/F_1).

The assumed stability factor of the parent is 0.3. Let us say that four prospective subsidiaries have stability factors of 1.0, 0.9, 0.75, and 0.6. If they were not considerably higher than 0.3, there would, of course, be no point in acquiring them (at least for our purposes here).

On the graph we correlate these four stability factors of the subsidiary with (1) the ratio F_3/F_1 and (2) different sales volumes of the subsidiary. We find, for example, that if the parent is to double its stability (point 2.0 on the vertical axis), it must obtain a subsidiary with a stability of 1.0 and 75 per cent as much sales volume as the parent, or a subsidiary with a stability of 0.9 and 95 per cent of the sales volume. If the parent seeks an improvement in stability of, say, only 40 per cent, it could buy a company with a stability of 0.9 and 25 per cent as much sales volume as it has.

This particular way of expressing sales objectives has two important advantages: (1) By setting minimum, rather than maximum, limits on growth, it leaves room for the company to take advantage of unusual growth opportunities in order to exceed these goals, and thus provides definite goals without inhibiting initiative and incentive (2) It takes account of the time-phasing of diversification moves; and since these moves invariably require a transition period, the numerical values of growth objectives can be allowed to vary from year to year so as to allow for a gradual development of operations.

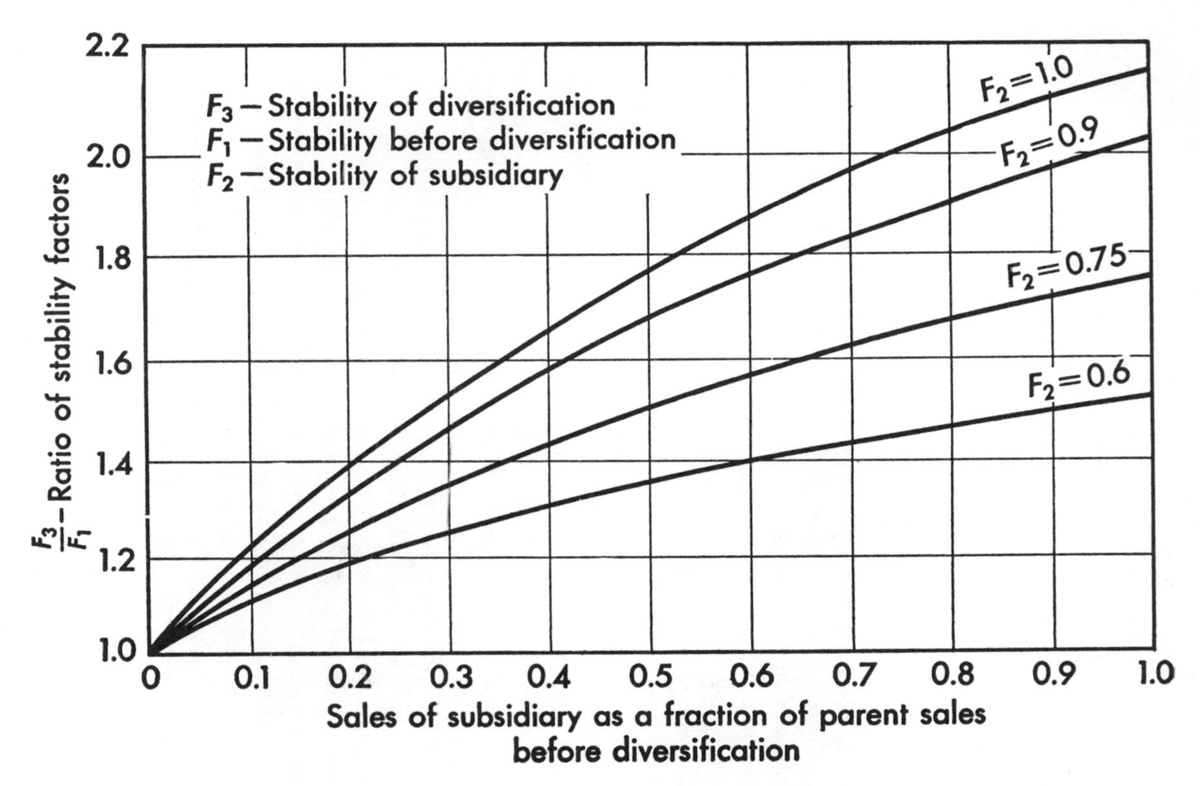

FIG. 6. Improvement in Stability Factor as a Result of Diversification for $F_1 = 0.3$

LONG-RANGE OBJECTIVES

Diversification objectives specify directions in which a company's product market should change. Usually there will be several objectives indicating different and sometimes conflicting directions. If a company attempts to follow all of them simultaneously, it is in danger of spreading itself too thin and of becoming a conglomeration of incompatible, although perhaps individually profitable enterprises.

There are cases of diversification which have followed this path. In a majority of cases, however, there are valid reasons why a company should seek to preserve certain basic unifying characteristics as it goes through a process of growth and change. Consequently, diversification objectives should be supplemented by a statement of long-range product-market objectives. For instance:

One consistent course of action is to adopt a product-market policy which will preserve a kind of technological coherence among the different manufactures with the focus on the products of the parent company. Thus, a company which is mainly distinguished for a type of engineering and production excellence would continue to select product-market entries which would strengthen and maintain this excellence. Perhaps the best-known example of such policy is exemplified by the Du Pont slogan, "Better things for better living through chemistry."

Another approach is to set long-term growth policy in terms of the breadth of market which the company intends to cover. It may choose to confine its diversifications to the vertical or horizontal direction, or it may select a type of lateral diversification controlled by the characteristics of the missions to which the company intends to cater. For example, a company in the field of air transportation may expand its interest to all forms of transportation of people and cargo. To paraphrase Du Pont, some slogan like "Better transportation for better living through advanced engineering," would be descriptive of such a long-range policy.

A greatly different policy is to emphasize primarily the financial characteristics of the corporation. This method of diversification generally places no limits on engineering and manufacturing characteristics of new products, although in practice the competence and interests of management will usually provide some orientation for diversification moves. The company makes the decisions regarding the distribution of new acquisitions exclusively on the basis of financial considerations. Rather than a manufacturing entity, the corporate character is now one of a "holding company." Top management delegates a large share of its product-planning and administrative functions to the divisions and concerns itself largely with coordination, financial problems, and building up a balanced "portfolio of products" within the corporate structure.

Successful Alternatives

These alternative long-range policies demonstrate the extremes. No one course is necessarily better than the others. Management's choice rests in large part on its preferences, objectives, skills, and training. The aircraft industry illustrates the fact that there is more than one successful path to diversification:

Among the major successful airframe manufacturers, Douglas Aircraft Company, Incorporated, and Boeing Airplane Company, have to date limited their growth to horizontal diversification into missiles and new markets for new types of aircraft. Lockheed has carried horizontal diversification further to include aircraft maintenance, aircraft service, and production of ground-handling equipment.

North American Aviation, Incorporated, on the other hand, appears to have chosen vertical diversification by establishing its subsidiaries in Atomics International, Autonetics, and Rocketdyne, thus providing a basis for manufacture of complete air vehicles of the future.

Bell Aircraft Corporation has adopted a policy of technological consistency among the members of its product line. It has diversified laterally but primarily into types of products for which it had previous know-how and experience.

General Dynamics Corporation provides a further interesting contrast. It has gone far into lateral diversification. Among major manufacturers of air vehicles, it comes closest to the "holding company" extreme. Its airplanes and missile-manufacturing operations in Convair are paralleled by production of submarines in the Electric Boat Division; military, industrial, and consumer electronic products in the Stromberg-Carlson Division; and electric motors in the Electro Dynamic Division.

SELECTING A STRATEGY

In the preceding sections qualitative criteria for diversification have been discussed. How should management apply these criteria to individual opportunities? Two steps should be taken: (1) Apply the qualitative standards in order to narrow the field of diversification opportunities; (2) apply the numerical criteria to select the preferred stratcgy or strategies.

QUALITATIVE EVALUATION

The long-range product-market policy is used as a criterion for the first rough cut in the qualitative evaluation. It can be used to divide a large field of opportunities into classes of diversification moves consistent with the company's basic character. For example, a company whose policy is to compete on the basis of the technical excellence of its products would eliminate as inconsistent classes of consumer products which are sold on the strength of advertising appeal rather than superior quality.

Next, the company can compare each individual diversification opportunity which is consistent with the long-range objectives with individual diversification objectives. This process tends to eliminate opportunities which, while consistent with the desired product-market make-up, are nevertheless likely to lead to an imbalance between the company product line and the probable environment. For example, a company which wishes to preserve and expand its technical excellence in design of large, highly stressed machines controlled by feedback techniques may find consistent product opportunities both inside and outside the industry to which it caters. If a major diversification objective of this company is to correct cyclic variations in demand that are characteristic of the industry, it would choose opportunities which lie outside.

Each diversification opportunity which has gone through the two screening steps satisfies at least one diversification objective, but probably it will not satisfy all of them. Therefore, before subjecting them to the quantitative evaluation, it is necessary to group them into several alternative over-all company product-market strategies, composed of the original strategy and one or more of the remaining diversification strategies. These alternative over-all strategies should be roughly equivalent in meeting all of the diversification objectives.

At this stage it is particularly important to allow for the unforeseeable contingencies. Since the techniques of numerical evaluation are applicable only to trends and foreseeable contingencies, it is important to make sure that the different alternatives chosen give the company a broad enough technological base. In practice this process is less formidable than it may appear. For example, a company in the aircraft industry has to consider the areas of technology in which major discoveries are likely to affect the future of the industry. This would include atomic propulsion, certain areas of electronics, automation of complex processes, and so forth. In designing alternative over-all strategies the company would then make sure that each contains product entries which will give the company a desirable and comparable degree of participation in these future growth areas.

Figure 7 summarizes the foregoing steps.

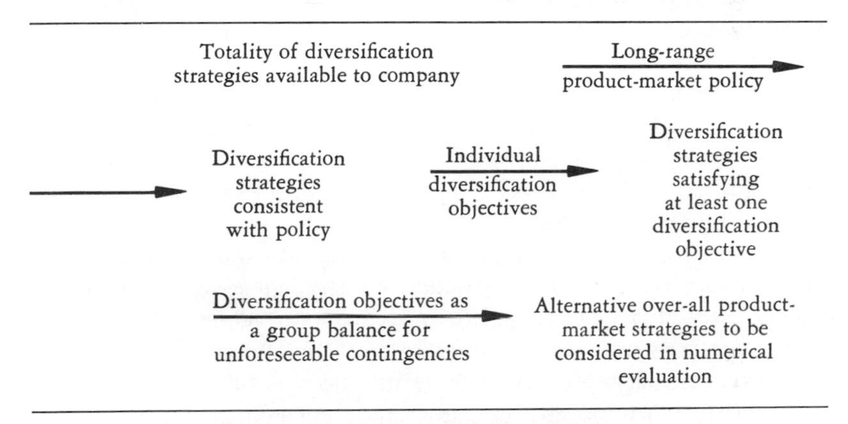

FIG. 7. Steps in Qualitative Evaluation

Quantitative Evaluation

Will the company's product-market strategies make money? Will the profit structure improve as a result of their adoption? The purpose of quantitative evaluation is to compare the profit potential of the alternatives.

Unfortunately, there is no single yardstick among those commonly used in business that gives an accurate measurement of performance. The techniques currently used for measurement of business performance constitute, at best, an imprecise art. It is common to measure different aspects of performance by applying different tests. Thus, tests of income adequacy measure the earning ability of the business; tests of debt coverage and liquidity measure preparedness for contingencies; the shareholders' position measures attractiveness to investors; tests of sales efficiency and personnel productivity measure efficiency in the use of money, physical assets, and personnel. These tests employ a variety of different performance ratios, such as return on sales, return on net worth, return on assets, turnover of net worth, and ratio of assets to liabilities. The total number of ratios may run as high as twenty in a single case.

In the final evaluation which immediately precedes a diversification decision management would normally apply all of these tests, tempered with business judgment. However, for the purpose of preliminary elimination of alternatives, a single test is frequently used—return on investment, a ratio between earnings and the capital invested in producing these earnings. While the usefulness of return on investment is commonly accepted, there is considerable room for argument regarding its limitations and its practical application.[6] Fundamentally, the difficulty with the concept is that it fails to provide an absolute measure of business performance applicable to a range of very different industries; also, the term "investment" is subject to a variety of interpretations.

But, since our aim is to use the concept as a measure of *relative* performance of different diversification strategies, we need not be concerned with its failure to measure absolute values. And as long as we are consistent in our definition of investment in alternative courses of action, the question of terminology is not so troublesome. We cannot define profit-producing capital in general terms, but we can define it in each case in the light of particular business characteristics and practices (such as the extent of government-owned assets, depreciation practices, inflationary trends).

For the numerator of our return on investment, we can use net earnings after taxes. A going business concern has standard techniques for estimating its future earnings. These depend on the pro-

[6] See Charles R. Schwarz, *The Return-on-Investment Concept as a Tool for Decision Making,* General Management Series No. 183 (New York, American Management Association, 1956), pp. 42–61; Peter F. Drucker, *The Practice of Management* (New York, Harper & Row, 1954); and Edward M. Barnet, "Showdown in the Market Place," *Harvard Business Review,* July–August 1956, p. 85.

jected sales volume, tax structure, trends in material and labor costs, productivity, and so forth. If the diversification opportunity being considered is itself a going concern, its profit projections can be used for estimates of combined future earnings. If the opportunity is a new venture, its profit estimates should be made on the basis of the average performance for the industry.

Changes in Investment Structure

A change in the investment structure of the diversifying company accompanies a diversification move. The source of investment for the new venture may be: (1) excess capital, (2) capital borrowed at an attractive rate, (3) an exchange of the company's equity for an equity in another company, or (4) capital withdrawn from present business operations.

If we let i_1, i_2, i_3, and i_4, respectively, represent investments made in the new product in the preceding four categories during the first year of diversified operations, we can derive a simple expression for the *improvement* in return on investment (ΔR) which will result from diversification:

$$\Delta R = \frac{(p_2 - p_1)(i_2 + i_3 + i_4) + (p_2 - r)\, i_1 - i_2 r + (p_1 - r)(i_2 + i_3)\, i_1/I,}{I + i_2 + i_3}$$

where p_1 and p_2 represent the average return on capital invested in the original product and in the new product, respectively, quantity I is the total capital in the business before diversification, and r is the interest rate.

We can easily check this expression by assuming that only one type of new investment will be made at a time. We can then use the formula to compute the conditions under which it pays to diversify (that is, conditions where ΔR is greater than zero):

1. If excess capital is the only source of new investment ($i_2 = i_3 = i_4 = 0$), this condition is $p_2 - r > 0$. This is, return on diversified operations should be more attractive than current rates for capital on the open market.

2. If only borrowed capital is used ($i_1 = i_3 = i_4 = 0$), it pays to diversify if $p_2 - p_1 > r$. That is, the difference between return from diversification and return from the original product should be greater than the interest rate on the money.

3. If the diversified operation is to be acquired through an exchange of equity or through internal reallocation of capital, then $p_2 - p_1 > 0$ is the condition under which diversification will pay off.

A Comprehensive Yardstick

The formula for ΔR just stated is not sufficiently general to serve as a measure of profit potential. It gives improvement in return for the first year only and for a particular sales trend. In order to provide a reasonably comprehensive comparison between alternative over-all company strategies, the yardstick for profit potential should possess the following properties:

1. Since changes in the investment structure of the business invariably accompany diversification, the yardstick should reflect these changes. It should also take explicit account of new capital brought into the business and changes in the rate of capital formation resulting from diversification, as well as costs of borrowed capital.
2. Usually the combined performance of the new and the old product-market lines is not a simple sum of their separate performances; it should be greater. The profit potential yardstick should take account of this nonlinear characteristic.
3. Each diversification move is characterized by a transition period during which readjustment of the company structure to new operating conditions takes place. The benefits of a diversification move may not be realized fully for some time; so the measurement of profit potential should span a sufficient length of time to allow for effects of the transition.
4. Since both profits and investments will be spread over time, the yardstick should use their present value.
5. Business performance will differ, depending on the particular economic-political environment. The profit potential yardstick must somehow average out the probable effect of alternative environments.
6. The statement of sales objectives, as pointed out previously, should specify the general characteristics of growth and stability which are desired. Profit potential functions should be compatible with these characteristics.

We can generalize our formula in a way which will meet most of the preceding requirements. The procedure is to write an expression for the present value of ΔR for an arbitrary year, t, allowing for possible yearly diversification investments up to the year t, interest rates, and the rate of capital formation. Then this present value is averaged over time as well as over the alternative sales forecasts. The procedure is straightforward (although the algebra involved is too cumbersome to be worth reproducing here[7]). The result, which is the "average expected present value of ΔR," takes account of conditions (1) through (5), above. Let us call it $(\Delta R)_e$. It can be computed using data normally found in business and financial forecasts.

Final Evaluation

This brings us to the final step in the evaluation. We have discussed a qualitative method for constructing several over-all product-market strategies which meet the diversification and the long-range objectives. We can now compute $(\Delta R)_e$ for each of the over-all strategies and, at the same time, make sure that the strategies satisfy the sales objectives previously stated, thus fulfilling condition (6), above.

If product-market characteristics, which we have used to narrow the field of choice and to compute $(\Delta R)_e$, were the sole criteria, then the strategy with the highest $(\Delta R)_e$ would be the "preferred" path to diversification. However, the advantages of a particular product-market opportunity must be balanced against the chances of business success.

CONCLUSION

A study of diversification histories shows that a company usually arrives at a decision to make a particular move through a multistep process. The planners' first step is to determine the preferred areas for search; the second is to select a number of diversification opportunities within these areas and to subject them to a preliminary evaluation. They then make a final evaluation, conducted by the top management, leading to selection of a specific step; finally, they work out details and complete the move.

Throughout this process, the company seeks to answer two basic questions: How well will a particular move, if it is successful, meet the company objectives? What are the company's chances of making it a success? In the early stages of the program, the major concern is

[7] See H. Igor Ansoff, *A Model for Diversification* (Burbank, Cal., Lockheed Aircraft Corporation, 1957); and John Burr Williams, *The Theory of Investment Value* (Amsterdam, The North-Holland Publishing Co., 1938).

with business strategy. Hence, the first question plays a dominant role. But as the choice narrows, considerations of business ability, of the particular strengths and weaknesses which a company brings to diversification, shift attention to the second question.

This discussion has been devoted primarily to selection of a diversification strategy. We have dealt with what may be called *external* aspects of diversification—the relation between a company and its environment. To put it another way, we have derived a method for measuring the profit potential of a diversification strategy, but we have not inquired into the *internal* factors which determine the ability of a diversifying company to make good this potential. A company planning diversification must consider such questions as how the company should organize to conduct the search for and evaluation of diversification opportunities; what method of business expansion it should employ; and how it should mesh its operations with those of a subsidiary. These considerations give rise to a new set of criteria for the *business fit* of the prospective venture. These must be used in conjunction with $(\Delta R)_e$ computed in the preceding section to determine which of the over-all product-market strategies should be chosen for implementation.

Thus, the steps outlined in this article are the first, though an important, preliminary to a diversification move. Only through further careful consideration of probable business success can a company develop a long-range strategy that will enable it to "run twice as fast as that" (using the Red Queen's words again) in the ever-changing world of today.

III

ORGANIZATION

No matter how much wisdom may go into planning, whether it be an insurance program, an armed invasion of a continent, or a campaign to reduce the inroads of disease, the measure of its success always will be the spirit and mettle of the individuals engaged in its execution. No matter how much treasure may support a project, or how elaborate its organization, or how detailed and farsighted its operational scheme, the human element is always the central one.

—Dwight D. Eisenhower

14

Introduction

To many people the most human, interesting aspect of long-range planning is how to organize for it. Here is where the personal element is high. There is nothing abstract or theoretical about this aspect. It is as real as the flesh and blood of managers.

For example, how do you get people to *do* planning? The results of effective planning often do not become visible for years, whereas time spent on everyday operating problems pays off quickly. Will the manager who invests time in planning be penalized in favor of the manager who is more "practical"? Will he be rewarded less, promoted more slowly? Hardly a symposium on long-range planning goes by in which these questions do not get asked in one way or another. No thoughtful executive can dismiss the problem. Our business corporations today tend to be hotbeds of management competition, much of it remarkably clean and hard but not all of it. (Sometimes the locale seems more analogous to a jungle full of guerrilla fighting!) The man who engages—or who *would* engage—in long-range planning cannot have both eyes on the corporation's need all of the time. He has himself and his family to worry about, too.

I wish I could say that the contributors to this section have sure answers for this kind of question, but I cannot. Perhaps no writer does. Indeed, perhaps no writer *can,* for it may be that only the chief executives who set the ground rules in a company have the power to provide such answers. But I do believe that the contributors to these pages are concerned about the problem and have done some thinking about it, and that their comments should prove helpful to many businessmen in companies large and small. If it is the wise, empirical, pragmatic view of the problem that you want most, see Wrapp's chapter; if you seek the revolutionary, novel, unusual proposal, see

Ross's chapter; and there are other pieces with shades of both chapters' qualities.

Then there is the matter of performance. Once you get executives committed to planning, how do you assure that they will do it *well?* What kinds of procedures and organizational relations will help keep them in the stream of things—active, influential, immersed in the give and take? This kind of question comes up most often in large and medium-sized companies, but variations of it arise in smaller organizations, too. Here we can develop answers that are less tentative. Business executives like Scheu and Tooker, for instance, can comment with much insight about the experience of their own companies, while Steiner and Drucker have sought out the lessons learned by a variety of firms.

In reading these chapters it is worth keeping in mind that knowledge can point the way to effective organization, but no more than that. *Doing* is the key. I believe it was the novelist James Cain who remarked that you cannot teach a writer to write by describing the process to him any more than you can teach a woman how to have a baby by having her watch somebody else have one; the only way he can really learn is by going through it himself. The same is true of organizing for long-range planning. The literature may be helpful. It may provide ideas. It may show how somebody else looks at the problem, which is always helpful. But its values will not materialize until the reader personally gets involved in the act, fitting planning into his own days, listening and persuading with his own facts, putting his own name on the line. It is at this point, and only this point, that one can say he knows how to organize for a planning job.

CONTRIBUTORS TO THIS SECTION

H. Edward Wrapp is Professor of Business Policy and director of The Executive Program at the Graduate School of Business, University of Chicago. He was recently associated with Automation Engineering Laboratory, Incorporated, and before that he was Professor of Business Administration at the Harvard Business School.

Sterling T. Tooker is executive vice-president, The Travelers Insurance Companies. His remarks were prepared for the Thirtieth Annual National Business Conference at the Harvard Business School, 1960.

Edward M. Scheu, Jr., is president of Good Humor Corporation and a board member of Thomas J. Lipton, Inc. and IBM Service Corporation. He also addressed the Thirtieth Annual National Business Conference.

Stewart Thompson, George A. Steiner, and *Peter F. Drucker* are all listed earlier in this volume. See the Introductions for Part I, page 6, and Part II, page 69.

Ronald J. Ross has managed research and development engineering programs in the instrumentation and inertial guidance fields for Sperry Gyroscope Company. When he wrote his article he was assistant to the engineering manager for a large instrumentation system program.

15

Organization for Long-Range Planning[1]

H. Edward Wrapp

Long-range planning has been high on the hit parade at management meetings and conferences in recent months, and as a technique it promises to be the next addition to the formula for "progressive" management. Moreover, the fact that consultants are much interested in it is a reliable harbinger that, ready or not, top executives are going to be hearing a lot about why they should embrace it. In fact the interest is so great—particularly as compared with accomplishment to date—that there is real danger of the whole thing rapidly becoming a fad.

But just because a fad sometimes turns into a fiasco when intro-

[1] From *Harvard Business Review,* January–February 1957, pp. 37–47. Used by permission.

duced in a company, it does not follow that management can ignore the long-range planning task. Fad or not, here is something management must look at seriously—cautiously, perhaps, but nonetheless purposefully—that is, unless the company wants to undergo deliberate or unconscious liquidation.

Unfortunately, as has been pointed out,[2] it is difficult to find plans to study and learn from. In the few companies where real projects of this kind have been undertaken there is reluctance to disclose the conclusions drawn by the planners, for fear that this might reveal to competitors the company's most closely guarded secrets on strategy and tactics. However, there is less hesitation to discuss *how* the planners went about getting the answers, and any executives who are considering the establishment of long-range planning in their firms can learn a great deal from a study of the ways in which other companies have approached the problem.

For this reason, and also because I think the administrative problem of introducing the planning activity and nursing it through the early stages is critical, I will concentrate on various organizational devices, on the approaches used to develop plans, and on some words of advice gathered from talking to executives who made a few mistakes along the way.

TRENDS AND COUNTERTRENDS

Long-range planning is that activity in a company which sets long-term goals for the firm and then proceeds to formulate specific plans for attaining these goals. There seems to be some indication that five years is the appropriate time span.[3] A shorter period hews too closely to operating problems and discourages the consideration of planning problems, whereas a longer period becomes too nebulous as a basis for developing "supporting" plans, i.e., detailed statements of what must be done in order to meet the long-term goals.

Up to now, not many companies other than the giants have done very much about such long-range planning on any formal basis. Typically, managements in small and medium-sized companies are too

[2] David W. Ewing, "Looking Around: Long-Range Business Planning," *Harvard Business Review,* July–August 1956, p. 135.

[3] See Mark W. Cresap, Jr., "Long-Term Planning," *Advanced Management,* January 1953, p. 34.

busy trying to make a profit for the current months to find time to think about what the company will be doing five years from now. Yet these same managements are making frequent decisions with long-term implications—decisions which, in many cases, are even more critical for them than for their bigger competitors—simply because they cannot as easily afford a costly error on a new product or a new plant.

Of course, no successful company is able to get along without some kind of forward planning. In the past, however, this has usually taken the form of one or two top executives setting the general direction of growth. It may have been no more explicit than a strong urge to expand sales. Even where companies have joined the rush to diversification, the purpose has often been expressed in terms of adding volume rather than in terms of making effective use of company resources or reinforcing particular weak spots. Only in isolated instances has a wide group of company executives been involved in laying out detailed plans for the growth of the enterprise which they manage.

What accounts, then, for the sudden flurry of attention to planning? In particular, why is so much interest being given to the committee type of organization for planning?

Certainly a part of the explanation lies in the fact that the financial analysts in search of growth companies have reacted favorably to those situations where management has attempted to forecast the specific shape and scope of potential growth and then taken positive action in anticipation of future demands. With this stimulus, a strong "follow-the-leader" influence has developed. More and more top managements, trying to get something started, have looked around at what others have done. And they have seized on the organizational devices used by the very big companies which, because of their size and complexity, have almost inevitably had to set up some kind of formal group effort.

Support and Opposition

However, the habits and traditions of the past are not easily overcome. Down the line, the feeling still persists that planning is the main function of the chairman and the president, and that vice-presidents and lower echelons should concentrate on running the company. So it is not enough for top management itself to *awaken* to the need for more formal planning. Someone very near the top must also take the initiative in *pushing* long-range planning of the company-wide kind; otherwise the chances are remote that it will ever be started.

Even in an organization conditioned to welcoming new developments and improvements in techniques, the long-range-planning function will probably not be self-generating. The trouble is that in most companies the rules of the game are such that the managers concentrate on short-term objectives. Budgets, performance ratings, and bonuses almost always are focused on the near term; accomplishments toward long-term objectives, by contrast, are more difficult to measure, and in most instances no attempt at measurement is even made. It is not surprising, therefore, that after years of conditioning under these circumstances managers are less than enthusiastic about the "obvious" advantages of long-range planning. For example:

The president of a company with five divisions, each of which was headed by a general manager who had complete responsibility for sales and production, was disappointed because his general managers were not taking a "long-term view." But as one of the general managers commented to an outsider: "I'm too damn busy with day-to-day problems to even think beyond the current year's operations. We have to submit budgets, and this takes us twelve months ahead, but that's as far as we go. I'm judged on profit performance year by year."

Another kind of resistance stems from the fact that, in order to be effective, long-range planning must be comprehensive and in the process "look under all corners of the rug." Often the initial reaction is to regard the development of a master plan as a meddlesome, unnecessary intrusion. Many vice-presidents and highly placed executives look upon it as a direct reflection on the caliber of the management in their respective departments; and, no matter how careful the precautions, the planners will find it difficult to avoid such an interpretation.

Indeed, I would venture the hypothesis that the most serious obstacle to long-range planning is not so much the drain on management time, the actual problems of doing good planning, or the danger of revealing company strategy, as it is the subtle, but occasionally open, opposition of some executives which appears in the early stages of the development.

Hence top-management support is absolutely essential. I am aware that if you add up all the speakers and writers who stipulate top-management support in the area of their particular interests, each and every activity in the company appears to need such backing—and that is a physical impossibility. But the argument in the case of long-range planning is overriding, if only because the activity has always been thought of as so distinctly top-level.

COMPANY APPROACH

Once the board of directors or the chief executive has committed the company to undertake long-range planning, the most critical decision to be made is how to approach the organizational problem—particularly the question of who is to be responsible for carrying the work through.

To get down to specifics, let me describe how one company approached this part of the long-range planning task, and then evaluate its efforts in comparison with those of several other companies.

OPERATING MANAGERS

The president of Company A appointed a senior vice-president with a background in sales as chairman of a planning committee. With the advice of the president, the chairman selected for the committee six managers from among the immediate subordinates of the vice-presidents: one each from product development, purchasing, staff engineering, research, production, and personnel. The chairman of the committee asked a junior executive from the market research department to serve as secretary of the committee, with the understanding that the task would require only about one-third of his time.

The chairman preferred not to assemble a special staff for the planning committee, and he suggested that the members of the committee draw upon existing staff personnel in their various departments for the studies required by the committee. An outside consultant was retained to meet with the committee, with the explicit understanding that he would act only as an adviser. Here is how the group functioned:

Sales Forecasts. The president had charged the planning committee with formulating a plan which would achieve a doubling of the company's sales within five years, without specifying how this goal was to be met. The committee decided to begin its work with an examination of the growth potential of the company's existing products. Considering such factors as population trends, a rising standard of living, and a high level of personal income, the planners estimated the total market for each of the products for the next five years.

They now attempted to estimate what share of the total market Company A could expect to get with each of its products. At this stage, the committee reckoned with expected improvements which the research group predicted for existing products, as well as with the best guess on the efforts of competitors in the various markets. The forecast assumed that expenditures for advertising, sales promotion, and sales salaries would rise proportionately with sales.

After surveying the domestic markets, the committee turned to the foreign markets and estimated the possible five-year growth in various countries over the world.

The total potential growth in existing products fell short of the total sales goal set by the president. To fill this gap the committee turned to new products. A detailed appraisal of the sales potential year by year was made for each of the four most promising new products then in various stages of development by the research department. Incidentally, the committee was the first to see that since one of the products had a large potential market yet was still in the early stages of research for large-scale production, there was both need and opportunity for making a closer study of possible acquisition of an existing company as an alternative to new plant.

At this point, the sales forecasts for existing products and new products were presented to the top executives. In their judgment, the estimates served as a reasonable basis for proceeding with more detailed studies of sales, production, manpower, and finances.

Subcommittees for Special Studies. With this general outline for company growth established, the members of the committee were able to break up into subcommittees to make more comprehensive studies in each area. For instance, the assumption previously made, that the dollars spent for advertising, sales promotion, and sales salaries would have to be increased proportionately as sales increased, had to be examined by a subcommittee of marketing specialists. The committee felt that as sales volume increased, perhaps a smaller percentage of the sales dollar would be needed for these purposes. On the other hand, as competitors intensified their efforts and as Company A sought an increasingly larger share of the total market, there was some reason to believe that a bigger share of the sales dollar would be needed to generate the expected volume of sales.

Before each subcommittee began any extensive studies, it was asked to prepare a description of how it proposed to collect the data needed for its final report. This proposed approach was presented to the entire committee for discussion, and many time-saving and money-saving suggestions were offered. For instance, the need for one expensive study was eliminated by the consolidation of two completed studies made by separate departments but not previously circulated outside the departments.

Concurrent with the sales study, a group of production representatives worked out a year-by-year schedule for existing production facilities. As shortages of facilities became apparent, they planned the type and location of new facilities needed over the five-year period. They also investigated the company's sources of raw materials and forecasted the pattern of price movements which might be expected. Finally, this group estimated the year-by-year capital requirements for the new facilities and predicted the manufacturing, freight, and warehousing costs for each product. A specialist on linear programming was called in to assist with this phase of the study.

A personnel group was also active. By keeping in touch with the deliberations in the sales and production subcommittees, it was able to draw plans for organizational changes, training needs, and recruitment requirements which would fulfill the expectations of the sales and production subcommittees.

Future Steps. The first five-year plan is not yet finished. The final stage is to compute the total capital requirements for new facilities and for working capital purposes. By projecting the budgeting procedure five years ahead, pro-forma profit-and-loss statements can be prepared for each of the years. Crude calculations of return on investment made at many stages to test the feasibility of certain individual projects will then be refined in the light of data available on all phases of the master plan.

Two years of the five-year planning period will have transpired before the committee is able to present a detailed master plan which the chairman believes is reliable as a basis for management action. The next task of the committee will be to project the plan for an additional two years. Each year thereafter the committee will review the four years of plans remaining and add a fifth year, so that a five-year plan will always be available for management guidance. The methods developed and the evidence gathered during the preparation of the first five-year plan will greatly simplify future projections, and the committee will concentrate on refining the projections and making detailed studies of proposals which have long-term implications for the company.

Solid Accomplishments

During the months of staff work and meetings, the committee members constantly found it difficult to avoid being sidetracked on studies of urgent operating problems; but under the subtle prodding of the chairman, who tolerated occasional detours, the group has made steady progress in assembling a mass of data, interpreting it, and drawing conclusions in terms of specific plans for future expansion. The president is enthusiastic about the committee's work; he sees a blueprint emerging that can serve as a general framework within which management can make specific decisions on sales, production facilities, new products, manpower needs, and capital requirements.

In addition, the planning committee has been a valuable training ground for developing future top executives. The members of the committee, who were already key operating managers, have been introduced to the difficult task of planning before being moved into positions where they have a major responsibility for thinking ahead. And having prepared and understood the plans, the members of the committee are ready to make the moves which will put those plans into effect when the go-ahead is given. In several instances, departmental projects have been initiated as a result of committee discussions without waiting for completion and approval of the over-all plans. The company enjoys the further advantage of having a real "team" of managers at the second level who have learned to work together.

Finally, the committee chairman has been able to sharpen his evaluation of each committee member's ability to put aside operating pressures and to devote a portion of his energies to the broader tasks of management. By combining executives who are especially imaginative and "creative" with men who tend to be more analytical and "scientific," and by mixing a great range of company experience, the chairman has been able to achieve a happy blend of bold, expansionist-oriented thinking and rigorously logical planning based on factual data.

Difficulties Experienced

Despite some solid accomplishments during its tenure, the planning committee's work has not always gone smoothly. The members of the committee, as well as the vice-presidents they report to, are extremely busy with operating problems; and while they recognize the value of the committee's work, both they and their bosses put top priority on immediate problems. In a way, this situation has been advantageous in that it has forced the committee member to delegate much of the spadework to subordinates, but without any question the committee's progress has been slowed by the continual preoccupation with immediate problems.

Also, the vice-presidents of the company are not charged directly with responsibility for planning, and this probably accounts for a certain amount of indifference toward the aims of the committee.

Another difficulty growing out of such an approach, which centers the planning function below the vice-presidential level, is that at certain stages the committee members may not be fully informed about proposals under consideration by the president and vice-presidents. Although most committee members have welcomed the opportunity to deal with broad company policies and problems, nevertheless they have experienced real frustration when, after weeks of study and discussion, a planning proposal has been rendered obsolete by top management's announcement of a move which the members of the committee did not know was under consideration.

Up to now, no workable line of communication has been set up for keeping the planning committee posted on the disposition of its proposals. As one committee member put it, following a two-hour presentation to the executive staff (composed of the president, executive vice-president, and vice-presidents): "There goes another four months' work down the well. We'll probably never hear from it again." Top-policy decisions are made by the executive staff; and since the committee members do not participate in these deliberations, they cannot appreciate the part that their studies may have played in the final decisions.

Another problem has been the sharing of information. As the subcommittees got set to work on various aspects of the master plan, some tended to hold off beginning their jobs until they had received the conclusions of other groups. Of course, it was to be expected that operating men would be inclined to plan within the specifications set by others; yet, to make the most effective progress, each group needed to be working with the others so that ideas could flow back and forth. For instance:

During the production subcommittee's study of the possibilities of expanding plant facilities, such factors as comparative costs, ease of distribution to markets, and availability of raw materials were considered. The group assumed that the management organization could adjust to whatever proposal it devised, and only after it had settled on a plan was a personnel subcommittee invited to prepare supporting programs for a management staff and a work force.

If, from the start, a personnel subcommittee had been studying the ideal expansion plan, considered from the standpoint of organization and personnel, it might have added an additional dimension to the production group's deliberations and thus have helped it to come up with a more practical proposal. As it was, the personnel subcommittee simply "planned" within the limits set down by the other subcommittee.

ALTERNATIVE APPROACHES

Top executives who anticipate or have experienced the shortcomings of Company A's approach may want to consider different systems. A company that began with a planning committee similar to Company A's, but was discouraged by the difficulty of combining planning and operating responsibilities in the same persons, abandoned this approach in favor of a group whose members were assigned full-time to the planning activity. As before, the members of the committee were selected from the various departments of the company, but under the new arrangement they were completely relieved of operating responsibilities.

There is a noteworthy advantage in such an approach in that a more detailed master plan could be developed sooner. But most chief executives would be horrified at the prospect of having a group of operating managers—at least, if they were good men—taken away from their jobs completely for a very long period of time. Almost immediately these operating managers would be tagged as *staff* men and, as a result, lose their preferred positions for influencing the line managers. This raises the question of what kinds of variations from Company A's approach are possible and practical.

Top-Level Vice-Presidents

Company B, which, like Company A, had a centralized management consisting of functional departments reporting to vice-presidents, decided in favor of the following kind of committee organization:

> The president of Company B gave his highest-ranking assistant additional duties as vice-president for planning and administration. This vice-president became chairman of a fifteen-man planning committee composed of all the other vice-presidents. A subcommittee was appointed for each project which the planning committee decided to investigate. (Note how much less comprehensive the aims of this group were than the aims of Company A's planning committee.) A vice-president was always selected as chairman of the subcommittee, which might include other vice-presidents

as well as company officials who were not members of the planning committee.

An assistant vice-president for planning was appointed. He became an ex-officio member of each subcommittee and coordinated their activities. The chairman of the subcommittee was responsible for the writing of the report to the planning committee, although he was free to call upon anyone to assist him in collecting and organizing data.

The planning committee did not attempt to formulate an over-all five-year plan, but studied a variety of individual projects, some of which were initiated by the president, some by members of the planning committee, and others by executives at various levels in the company. All of the projects had long-term implications.

Originally, a subcommittee was dissolved when its recommendations on a project had been accepted by the planning committee; but over a period of time, as the proposals began to fall into a definite pattern, the chairman of the planning committee decided to appoint standing subcommittees. For instance, the subcommittee on facilities came to be in continual operation and reviewed all projects which concerned the company's physical plant and equipment.

As the organization evolved, the top planning committee became a review committee, while the real spadework of collecting and interpreting facts and judgments went on in the subcommittees. The chairman convened the fifteen-man planning committee only to consider a report by one of its subcommittees. This happened on an average of four times per year.

The prompt and serious attention given to recommendations emanating from the planning activity created an extremely favorable atmosphere. There was never a delay in setting a meeting once the subcommittee was ready to report, and members gave top priority to attendance at these meetings. The president and board of directors responded similarly in taking up recommendations submitted to them. Because of this favorable top-management attitude, the subcommittees encountered little resistance in persuading various members of the company to undertake staff work, some of which was quite extensive.

At the same time, Company B's planning was not, obviously, as ambitious as Company A's. There was no master plan systematically accounting for the activities of all major company functions for a prescribed period of future years. It might be said, therefore, that in the short term Company B sacrificed the potentials of Company A's over-all planning for a thorough study of projects stemming from immediate problems. I do not mean to imply, however, that this is a case of "either-or," that there is no middle ground between the approaches of companies A and B. Indeed, as we shall see, other alternatives have already been proved practical—at least in the case of divisionalized companies.

Divisional Heads

Ordinarily, a company which is decentralized into divisions, each with a general manager responsible for sales, production, manpower, and profits, presents a simpler long-range-planning problem than that of either Company A or B. Within a division, the general manager and his staff are trained to work together on over-all divisional problems. Thus in effect each division becomes a separate planning center concentrating on a single product or line of related products. Such a setup can be advantageous in long-range planning, as the following example illustrates:

> The president of Company C asked each of his eight division managers to prepare a five-year plan for his division. Each plan was to be presented at an all-day meeting at the home office, attended by the president and all the vice-presidents. The home-office meetings were primarily intended to keep the top staff informed. The president and vice-presidents were free to comment on the plans, but any modifications had to be made by the general manager of the division.
>
> Members of the home-office staff were available to assist the general manager in preparing his plan, but for the most part the division personnel did the work. For instance, all the plant managers in a division were active in drawing up production plans. The division controller also played an important role in assembling quantitative data.
>
> The caliber of the initial presentations varied greatly. Moreover, they were so disparate as to organization, content, and criteria that comparisons among divisons were difficult. But by coordinating subsequent reports through a member of the home-office staff who was assigned the task, greater uniformity was attained.

At first there was resistance to Company C's planning attempt. Some managers argued that their divisions were doing very well in terms of profit and that they should not be dictated to on the question of whether or not to prepare a long-term plan. But since the first round of presentations, when several skeptics became convinced by what they saw come out of the other divisions, the opposition has dwindled, and almost without exception the managers have accepted the planning job with a high level of enthusiasm. They have discovered that a well-documented plan provides the best evidence they can muster to persuade the home office to allocate additional funds to their divisions.

At the same time, the presentation of long-range plans has put top executives at headquarters in a better position to judge the performance of the division managers. In a few instances the early presentations disclosed a lack of staff work even for day-to-day operations, much less for the more difficult task of forward planning. Those divisions with the most refined cost systems, budgets, and market research were able to produce more comprehensive plans from the outset. The emphasis on long-term planning in the meetings highlighted the efforts of those managers who were planning for long-term return on investment concomitantly with good profits from current operations.

It is interesting to note, in passing, that while top management effectively delegated the planning for the divisions to the general managers, it called on a consulting firm to help in drawing up an over-all plan for the company. The consulting firm was asked to study such problems as further diversification, the growth potential in existing divisions, and the prospects of competition from products and processes which might be introduced by other companies.

Specialists and Consultants

When the long-range-planning task is added to the already crowded schedules of a company's executives, progress on the plans may be painfully slow. To alleviate this problem, several companies have set up a special staff, usually reporting at a high level in the company, or have retained a management consulting firm to prepare the plans. For instance:

The chairman of the board of Company D hired an economist to develop a five-year plan. The economist brought three assistants with him. This group conducted extensive interviews and investigations in the company and drew upon sources close to the industry, such as the trade association, investment bankers, and government agencies. Within about eighteen months, the economist made a four-hour presentation outlining a master plan to the board of directors, which is composed mainly of the top officers in the company. The meeting broke up after a brief discussion, and the chairman asked that each member of the board study the 450-page report written by the economist and his staff. At the time this article was written, six months had elapsed since the initial presentation, but discussion of the report had not been resumed.

The lesson of this case is clear. The master plan was supported by a mass of evidence and had been carefully reasoned. As a starter, it was more complete and embodied a greater range of ramifications than most plans developed in companies that have relied on existing line and staff personnel. Yet I suspect that nothing will come of it. The understanding and confidence in a plan that can come only from months of painstaking development by the managers concerned are missing. Unless the chairman of the board presses hard, none of the major propositions in the plan will ever be acted upon. And the chairman probably has a bad case of indigestion as he looks at his untouched copy of the big report and thinks of the equally sizable bill.

I do not deny that at certain stages a special staff or a management consultant may be indispensable to a company planning group. Rather, someone with technical knowledge or broad experience in a market or industry quite often can assist tremendously by bringing a fresh and objective point of view to bear. But specialists lose their advantage when complete responsibility for the planning is turned over to them, and, unfortunately, many companies have foundered on this "easy" course of action. Part of the gain to be secured in long-range planning is the thinking through that the company itself must do, without regard for whether it ends up as pieces of paper with words and graphs on them.

THE STARTING POINT

The type of management organization, the diversity of products, and the extent of previous budget and research activity are probably the most important factors in deciding how to pick a starting point for the planners.

For instance, a company organized into divisions with a relatively autonomous general manager responsible for a single product or related group of products may be able to begin, as did Company C, by asking each division to prepare a five-year plan. Implicit in such a request is the assumption that the division will continue to expand so long as a satisfactory return on investment can be earned. Home-office management may even leave to the division manager the burden of presenting arguments as to what rate of return should be expected in his organization, although it will probably reserve the right of final decision.

Some home-office coordination may be required if comparisons are to be made of one division with another or if uniform yardsticks are to be applied. One company, for instance, developed a "standard" outline for each division's presentation:

The industry	Working capital
Our position	Return on investment
Competitors' activities	Location of new facilities
Sales forecasts	Manpower requirements
Present products	Management controls
New products	Pricing policies
Capital investment requirements	Appraisal of strengths and weaknesses

Special problem areas

If a company has had considerable experience with market research and budgeting procedures, the planning group may be able to start by setting five-year sales goals as did Company A. The point, however, is that sales and cost forecasting techniques are indispensable to this phase of planning. Unless the members of the planning group are familiar with such techniques—and certainly many operating managers are—they will probably be skeptical of the "crystal gazing" when first introduced to it. Because it is foreign to their own experience, the planning may seem to them like so much "guesswork."

Selection of Projects

For starting the work of the planning group, the most desirable kind of project is one which poses some operating questions, has long-term implications, and involves the operating experiences of several members of the committee. For instance:

If the committee sets out to formulate a plan for taking a new product from the research laboratory through the various stages of introducing it in a national market, the members can learn how to function effectively as a group; and at an early point they may derive a sense of accomplishment which will give them more "steam" for the forays ahead.

Also, since the time span for the introduction of a new product may be two or three years or even longer, the committee will get some practice in setting up timetables and in stating explicitly the action which needs to be taken at various stages. As an illustration, training assignments may be needed immediately if management personnel with proper qualifications are to be available three years hence, when the product reaches the market.

After working with one or two limited projects of this type, committee members should be more ready to tackle a more comprehensive planning assignment, if it happens to be called for. Interestingly enough, in this connection, one planning committee which has functioned successfully for several years has never in fact attempted to draw up a master long-term plan for the company's future. But look at some of the projects which have been undertaken:

Optimum size of main manufacturing facility (a major expansion is now under way as a result of the planning committee report).

Building versus renting home-office space (a large office building has now been started).

Employee housing adjacent to main plant (this was undertaken as a company project and subsequently developed into a major rehabilitation project by the community).

Scholarships (a policy on contributing to educational institutions was formulated).

Employee stock purchases (a plan for acquisition of company stock by employees at all levels evolved).

Reappraisal of an existing product (production and sale of this product were discontinued as a result of the planning committee's recommendation).

Note that the decisions reached in each of these projects represent *long-term* commitments. Moreover, the chairman's insistence that the committee produce definite recommendations and put them in writing has resulted in a series of carefully documented statements; and as these seemingly unrelated recommendations are accumulated, a very useful background of sales, production, and financial data is being built for a possible over-all company plan.

Perhaps more important, these studies have forced the planners to make more explicit the criteria which will guide the company's growth. For instance, in making a recommendation to expand its main plant, the committee found itself involved in long-term market forecasts for certain geographical areas. Once the commitment for expansion was made, the company was tied irrevocably to concentrating its marketing efforts in those areas.

The significant thing to keep in mind is that such "piecemeal" efforts would not be making a contribution to real planning if they focused on projects oriented toward operations. Unless such a focus is avoided, the committee may find itself falling into the role of supervising a sort of top-drawer suggestion box and never pushing on to the task of tackling long-range problems.

Within Real Limits

One good way to start, it seems to me, would be for the planners to make a study of the factors which will limit the company's growth in the future. This approach has the advantage of permitting a number of subgroups to begin simultaneous exploration of questions vital to the planning activity, and in addition it encourages realism.

Take the sales forecast, for instance. Management falls too frequently into the trap of planning how the company will increase its share of the market with only slight recognition of what its competitors are doing. It is certainly understandable that this happens when the sales outlook is worked out by a committee of enthusiastic marketing men. But a planning group composed only partly of salesmen is more likely to be realistic on this point.

Again, shortage of capital may put a limitation on a company's growth, and so it is a good question to study. Even when management can plan for a liberal return on additional capital, other conditions may prevent the attraction of funds to the company. Shortages of production facilities place still another limitation upon growth, albeit a short-term one; and also raw-materials supplies may present a problem.

An important limitation to examine is management personnel. Planners seem to have a tendency to assume that an existing management organization can undergo unlimited upgrading and that the lack of capable, trained managers need never hamper a company's growth. The almost universal experience of managers when they come face to face with expansion, however, is that this is not true.

GENERAL OBSERVATIONS

As I review the experience of several different companies that have organized for long-range planning, a number of general points and suggestions stand out in my mind. I shall set them forth briefly by way of conclusion.

By-Products

Several valuable by-products can be derived from a long-range planning effort:

"Crystallization" of executive thinking is more likely to take place if planners are expected to produce recommendations, and especially if these recommendations are to be put in writing.

Committee investigations and deliberations are an excellent means of keeping the top executives informed about different parts of the business. Such a channel may be particularly needed in a company which has been growing rapidly, for oftentimes there is no systematic means for top executives to learn of developments in a new division, especially if its managers come to the corporation as a part of a smaller company. (Incidentally, new executives in a company might be appointed to a planning group as a part of their indoctrination in over-all company problems.)

A planning group may find blind spots and potential problem areas which the regular management group might easily miss in a rapidly expanding firm. When given an over-all responsibility rather than a limited assignment, the planners should become skillful in catching up loose ends which are either being overlooked or perhaps even deliberately ignored.

The planning group may provide a company-wide sounding board for appraising the potential of new techniques. Linear programing, for example, may be introduced as a valuable planning tool for making decisions on plant location, production scheduling, and shipping patterns. However, the use of the technique requires the massing and interpretation of data from many parts of a company. A planning group composed of managers with diversified backgrounds is better equipped to judge the usefulness of such a complex device.

Common Blind Spots

The planners may find it difficult to persuade sales managers to disassociate sales estimates for planning purposes from the estimates they set as goals for the sales force. The practice of setting sales goals higher than those which are reasonably attainable is so habitual for the sales executive that he unconsciously carries over his heady optimism into planning work. Moreover, the objective of expanding sales volume can become such an obsession that the costs of expansion are ignored. For example:

In one company, the sales representative on a planning committee insisted that a certain volume of sales was attainable, in the face of opposition from every other committee member. Only when he was confronted with the costs of production facilities needed to back up his goal, and asked to vote on a recommendation that this expenditure be made, did he finally suggest that the sales estimates be scaled downward.

As previously noted, planners tend too easily to assume that enough management talent will be available no matter how ambitious the expansion plans may be. If their record is marred by one mistake, it is their failure to recognize that the "lead time" needed for building the management organization may be longer than that needed to adjust any other single factor to higher profit goals. Rather than the afterthought that it oftentimes is, manpower planning should figure prominently in the conception of a master plan.

Moreover, top management must not expect immediate results from long-range planning. It requires a type of thinking which is strange and difficult for most line executives, whose training and experience have prepared them to deal with operating problems but not to probe too far into the future. Unlike some new undertakings where the cream can be skimmed at the start, effective long-range planning will start slowly and gain momentum as more and more data are gathered to throw light on the future.

Any problem which is so complex as to require that it be analyzed piecemeal, and the analyses regrouped for an over-all appraisal, is particularly difficult in the early stages. The long-range planners usually have so few facts about other phases of the business that they must rely on wholesale assumptions in order to make progress; forward thinking based on such assumptions is alien to most practical operating men. However, once they can point to a tangible recommendation which sparked a line of action that otherwise would not have been taken, interest in long-range planning is sure to grow.

"Inside Job" Needed

If line officers are given the responsibility for developing the plans, they will be more ready to support them once they are translated into the action stage. The planning function strikes so close to the heart of the management task that line managers are almost certain to become defensive and resist intrusion if the board or the chief executive hires a consultant or an economist to master-mind the planning.

In working and talking with executives about long-range planning, I have been surprised, but agreeably so, that so many have resisted the temptation to begin by hiring a staff of specialists to do the job, and instead have taken the more difficult course of depending on the existing management staff to do the spadework.

If given the primary responsibility, specialists have a way of introducing new techniques and ways of thinking strange to a company, and such a start on long-range planning may saddle it with a handicap which can never be overcome. By dependence on the people already in the company, management gains another advantage in discovering the strengths and weaknesses of existing departments. As indicated earlier, however, the consultant can often serve usefully by giving *assistance* to the executives in charge of planning—for instance, by providing new leads or by making special studies.

Conditions of Success

Good long-range planning is expensive in more ways than one. The plans are inevitably complex, and many risks must be assessed. A comprehensive plan in which everyone can exhibit confidence will require hours of discussion even after the time-consuming collection of data has taken place. Management should not be led to believe that long-range planning can be added to the list of executives' tasks without making noticeable demands on their time. To have a set of plans based on less-than-thorough discussions and superficial investigations by the managers who design them is probably worse than to have none. Such plans are a dangerously shaky foundation for commitments of company capital.

At the start top management must give strong support to the planning activity. Not only is it time-consuming, but the kind of thinking needed is foreign to most executives, and the returns are difficult to predict. However, there is a brighter side of the picture. Unlike other activities calling for strong top-management support, the long-range-planning function need not be *perpetually* parasitic. If the top company officer and the board of directors show by their interest and action that they value planning, and if the planners can make one or two solid contributions, the activity should become self-sustaining.

The development of a master plan for growth probably must be entrusted to executives very near the top of the organization. In today's competitive scene, so many factors must be considered that only men with real management breadth are capable of assigning proper weights to the many different considerations involved in charting a future course of action. The specialist with a departmental point of view can make only limited contributions to an over-all plan for the company. Another argument in favor of placing the planning at the top level is the fact that the planners must have access to confidential information, and broad dissemination of such material in a company may provide dangerous leaks to competitors.

Finally, the planners should be near enough to the top to see their efforts as an influence on company policy. Planning has many frustrations, but the worst is to see top management making major commitments while failing to recognize or ignoring the long-term implications which the planning group could help to clarify.

These are some of the real difficulties involved in inaugurating a comprehensive and reliable long-range planning program. If management will face these difficulties, the rewards will be equally real.

16

The Attitude of the Line Executive[1]

Sterling T. Tooker

While the line officer's responsibilities may be limited as to time and scope, he is frequently concerned with the future of his operation based on estimates of his market, his production, his territory, his plant, or even his own career. Very often, his success as a line officer depends on his accuracy in making projections of this sort. It is when he is forced to participate in formulating the corporate big picture, in

[1] From *Managing America's Economic Explosion,* ed. Dan H. Fenn, Jr. Copyright, 1961, McGraw-Hill Book Company, Inc. Used by permission.

setting objectives and goals, that he most often feels unhappy and out of his element. This kind of long-range planning tends to demand a sacrifice of individual objectives and a diffusion of the line executive's sense of purpose and direction. Because of his intimate understanding of current operating problems, and his unique facilities for forecasting, he should be a valuable member of any long-range planning group. But how to engage him in this activity willingly without undermining his effectiveness as a line officer is a difficult and somewhat subtle process.

To put the problem in perspective, until the fairly recent past the concept of formalized long-range planning was relatively foreign to most business organizations. The typical executive was a line officer by training and temperament, even when he carried the title of president or chairman of the board. Very often he had built the organization from scratch, started it from his own idea and shaped it in his own image. His job as he saw it was to manufacture a product or produce a service at the lowest possible cost and sell it on the market place at the highest possible profit. If he was successful in this, he grew and prospered. If he was not, he turned his hand to something else; or he kept going at a slow but steady pace, and perhaps that suited him fine. The businessman generally viewed with suspicion and alarm the big thinker, the long-range planner, the starry-eyed dreamer. He flew his company by the seat of his pants, by hunch and intuition, and by that indefinable American something called "know-how." He prided himself that in *his* organization the impossible took only a little longer to accomplish than the difficult. For the most part, however, he solved his problems as they arose and did not spare the time or have the inclination to bother mapping the future.

In the years following World War II, long-range planning became legitimatized as a business function. The development of new techniques of economic forecasting, statistical analysis, and operations and market research made this transition possible. The business executive in our new economy cannot very well ignore these tools which science has placed in his hands. But it must be admitted that he is still uncomfortable using them and very often reluctant to admit they work.

As H. Edward Wrapp has pointed out, an increasing number of business organizations are presently restructuring themselves in an attempt to formalize long-range planning. They have been persuaded that the old organization chart, with its almost autonomous operating departments and separate financial, legal, and administrative staff functions, is not feasible for this purpose. The size and complexity of most modern corporations demands a greater degree of control and a far more effective use of the new business techniques.

So the line officer responsible for bringing home the bacon, turning a profit, developing a market, organizing a sales force, or manufacturing a competitive product has gradually found himself surrounded by an increasingly large number of staff officers. His traditional freedom to pilot his own ship is hampered, he often feels, by staff decisions in such areas as expense control, methods and planning, and research and development. No longer is he flying by the seat of his own pants. He is sitting instead before a complex instrument panel and often has the justifiable sensation that someone else is at the controls.

These are perhaps oversimplifications, but they provide a recognizable frame of reference for our problem. The line executive is convinced that *he* has a "responsibility" while the staff officer merely has a "function." One has to pay off directly and measurably. The other's impact may be felt only over the long pull. Thus, while it is apparently a staff function to develop company-wide plans for the future, the line officer must make the achievement of these plans possible every step of the way. And he believes he works best when he can keep his eye on the ball and not on the flag in the distant cup.

In the insurance business, we have traditionally been involved with long-range planning of a sort. Our product is a legal obligation to take effect at some definite future date, or upon the occurrence of a named contingency. In The Travelers, our price for the most long-range promises we make—our life-insurance contracts—is guaranteed over the lifetime of the policy, which may be generations. It must be based, therefore, on long-range projections of interest rates, mortality, and probable expense costs, all of which require planning of the highest order.

The line officer, however, who is responsible for the sale, service, or underwriting of these contracts, has traditionally divorced himself from this planning function. He has relied upon a staff of actuaries to develop his product and its price. This has, especially in a competitive marketing situation, made him impatient and at times dissatisfied. He, after all, knows *today's* market and *today's* competition and the kind of product that will be most attractive to his salesmen and their customers. He is frustrated by actuarial arguments as to why he cannot have precisely what he wants now. However, it often seems that he would rather use his creative skill in promoting the product as given than be involved with the long-range considerations so indispensable to the actuary. So strongly does he feel this way, and so uncertain is he of the "new techniques," that some firms purposely steer clear of the term "long-range planning."

The Travelers Insurance Companies have been pioneers in multiple line insurance, underwriting, and sales—and this has been our broad plan for thirty-five years. We produce all major forms of insurance: life, casualty, group, property, liability. We sell them through independent contractors. This multiple-line concept was conceived years ago as our unique long-range plan of operation. For decades, however, our line responsibilities were rigidly departmentalized. Strong operating executives developed independent organizations and methods. The life department and its agency force was almost as distinct an entity from the casualty operation as if it belonged to a separate company. And this was true right down the line from the department head to the new trainee. As long as the line officer was producing, he saw no need to alter his course. And no nonproductive staff executive had the right or the reason to tell him to do so.

Faced with a completely new marketing situation after World War II, with heightened public demand for all forms of insurance, some Travelers executives saw the need for a more cohesive view of our product and its sale. The burgeoning middle-income, surburban, family-centered, property-owning, and mortaged-to-the-hilt market needed our product by the package, not by the policy. It needed protection for family, home, car, life, and health *all at once* and needed some way of paying for it as it did for every other major purchase it made, by the month, in easy installments.

Needless to say, these were revolutionary concepts for a business which had never considered itself a factor in the rapidly changing mass market. To meet this situation, as we could project it into the future, line executives were asked to create new products and new marketing approaches. Committees were formed; surveys were made; interdepartmental groups held meetings. But for months nothing happened because each line executive was too much concerned with his present responsibility to take seriously a long-range activity which might change the whole method and philosophy of his operation. He was unwilling to jeopardize his ability to meet department goals by directing his energies and efforts toward an uncertain future.

What did we do about it? Essentially this: New staff positions were created to coordinate the sales and underwriting functions along the lines of our multiple-line, mass-marketing blueprint. These staff officers were charged with developing products and methods that would conform to this corporate thinking. Line officers were encouraged to contribute to broad planning either directly or through the services of selected junior staff members. Sales promotion, merchandising, advertising, and training were geared increasingly to this new marketing approach, and ultimately some line departments were actually merged.

Ours has not been a revolutionary approach. Line officers were not handed ultimatums to abandon their immediate responsibilities for the development of future programs. Instruments-in-being were created, both individuals and groups, to generate an atmosphere of change and to stimulate line officers to keep moving toward newly redefined corporate goals. The line executives, for their part, are not forced to dilute their energies or blunt their thrust. They can, however, feel the constant pressure of a prevailing wind and find it far easier to move with it than against it. The fact that our long-range, multiple-line plan is now proving its value for *other* insurance companies has given the entire concept a new respectability among formerly hostile or indifferent line officers.

We believe that merely to present the line executive with a fully developed program and say, "go to it," is to invite disaster because he will do just that and no more. He will go to it and not one step further. If it is a program that runs contrary to his training or his ingrained business experience, he may answer, "it is going to lose money," and lose money it will. If, however, he is permitted to operate in a total environment of directed change in which he is provided with constant opportunities for adaptation, he becomes a partner in planning, not an unwilling hostage to it. Most important, he perceives that all other operating departments are moving with him, in the same direction and at the same pace.

At The Travelers, it became increasingly apparent in the booming postwar years that we must make more efficient use of the masses of data being processed continuously—and that we must integrate the *methods* of processing as well. This could be accomplished only through increased mechanization and the centralization of procedures which were formally handled separately and departmentally.

The line executives involved were not prepared to give up their departmental prerogatives or to admit that present methods of operation could be improved in kind as well as degree. And so, after a period of trial and error, they simply were not forced to make this decision. Instead, key members of operating staffs were detached and placed on teams comprising an amalgamation of disciplines and skills. These teams were given the responsibility of redesigning the whole company's approach to data processing. Their work has not been joyfully accepted by all operating executives. However, as they resolve a problem, this solution becomes part of an integrated program. Their conviction that the ultimate goal *can* be reached pervades the atmosphere; and the line executive absorbs this change almost by osmosis.

In the area of new-product development, we soon found it impossible for line officers to agree on what they should develop and how best to accomplish radical changes in policies and programs. By creating a staff specifically charged with formulating plans for new products, we produced a brisk, energizing climate which the line officer soon found stimulating and challenging. Old prejudices and the natural desire to preserve a reasonably successful status quo are far more difficult to maintain in the presence of people actually working to alter this status quo. Rather than diverting the line executive from his primary responsibility, we have given him and his staff the opportunity to join in a general activity of product planning. As this work has gone on around him, his imagination has been stimulated and we have found him increasingly willing to devote part of his efforts to planning for markets beyond the present.

In our experience, then, the line executive is usually unwilling to change by directive an operation for which he is responsible, and in which he believes, simply because of someone else's long-range planning. Very often, abrupt shifts in method or direction can be destructive of his energy and his operational value. But as long as movement and direction are taking place around him, and as long as he is given a sense of participation, the line executive cannot help but make corporate planning a part of his own. Indeed, he will more willingly contribute to it when he sees it can enhance rather than undermine his basic responsibility. As each plan unfolds, as it is updated and altered to conform to changing events, his insights, data, and ability to forecast become an integral part of long-range planning. Of equal value, the planning itself gives an added significance to the objectives for which he is responsible.

Now we are undertaking a broad program to give *upcoming* management a larger perspective of the place of our company in the economy of our nation and of the world. Rather than remake the valued operating executive of today, we are enlarging the horizons of those to come. Ultimately, we hope, the distinction between planning and performance, function and responsibility, line and staff, will be less apparent. A new kind of executive, the corporate management man, will combine the skills of line operations with the techniques of long-range planning; he will be a participant in the future as well as a shaper of the present.

17

Getting Formal Planning Established[1]

Edward M. Scheu, Jr.

In pulling together my thinking about long-range planning I have come to two rather simple and very obvious conclusions:

1. Every businessman does long-range planning of sorts.
2. Long-range planning is not an easy task. There are no quick ways to establish it as an effective function.

[1] From *Managing America's Economic Explosion,* ed. Dan H. Fenn, Jr. Copyright, 1961, McGraw-Hill Book Company, Inc. Used by permission. (This discussion was originally under the title, "The Management of Planning," on pages 122–128.)

Though these two conclusions may look simple and obvious, I would like to elaborate on them briefly because they are so often overlooked.

In the first place, I say everyone is doing long-range planning. It is true, of course, that many of the good operators I know claim that long-range planning should be left to the so-called long-hairs on the corporate staff. These managers say that they cannot do their job of making daily profits if they have to be concerned with problems five years from now. Though these gentlemen are not being purposely facetious, they are in fact kidding themselves. Even if you are just operating a division, you have to be thinking five years in advance or you are going to find that the daily problems ultimately overwhelm you because you had not thought about them far enough ahead.

Why do these people feel as they do? First of all, most of these line operators are frankly a little hard-pressed to take the time to do the job of long-range planning. It is a hard job—no question about that; it calls for the burning of much midnight oil. It is no easy task to get a line sales manager who has been doing nothing but selling to sit down and formalize his thinking on product lines or future markets.

Secondly, I suppose the operator is a little worried, maybe subconsciously, that he will be putting something into the files which may finally prove that his thinking is somewhat erroneous. This familiar fear of error is a big stumbling block to planning. It should not be an obstacle, of course, because we should not be concerned if events do not work out completely according to plan. One of the great benefits of the process is that you get a good plan which allows you to make changes, even radical changes, as you go along instead of endlessly drifting with no chart at all.

Finally, the planning operator does not want to go ahead with serious formal planning, because he already has quite a bit of confidence in himself as an operator. He thinks he can and should keep himself flexible; he does not want a formal plan. He does not feel any necessity for setting his thinking or that of his top-management people down in writing. He will look back at the last five years and say: "Look, we have grown: our sales are up; our profits are up; what good would a five-year plan be?" More power to him; probably he has done a good job. But I am convinced that he would do a better job if he actually had a formal plan.

Secondly, this is no simple business. In itself, it must be planned, and not the least of the problems is the selection of the personnel to do the job.

My own first experience with formal planning was in a centralized organization. The company was a very fine one, one of the best on the industrial scene. Although we derived much good from the efforts of the so-called planning committee, of which I was a member, I feel that we failed to accomplish our mission—and for just one or two important reasons. One was the leadership of the actual planning function, which was assigned to a man who had been kicked upstairs from a top-line job. This executive was a very fine person, and top management hoped that this would be his opportunity to put himself back in as a strong member of the key group. But all they succeeded in doing was putting him in an almost impossible situation because when you do embark on planning it has to have the fullest support of the whole top-management team. They all have to be dedicated to the conviction that they are going to do this job. By appointing a man who has somewhat lost the respect of the management group, those responsible did a great deal to erode the effectiveness of the planning committee.

Then, instead of having the committee made up of top-management men, it was made up of the secondary people at the department-head or assistant-vice-president level rather than the vice-presidential. These men were really not in touch with all the information they needed to make up an intelligent plan; there was a good deal of material they simply did not have, or have ready access to. Furthermore, the top men—the vice-presidents—somewhat resented the fact that this planning function had been delegated to their subordinates. Although I do not think they openly sabotaged the efforts of this planning committee, they did not openly support it either. They rather looked down their noses at the whole operation. They seemed to say: "Well, you boys do all this fancy planning; then we will go out and buy another mill and that will destroy all your plans."

Some good did come out of these early efforts. We developed a great deal of interesting historical data, and I think we further stimulated an awareness of the importance of better planning.

Having chosen the right people, the first step in long-range planning is to develop an effective short-term plan. Too many companies launched into a long-term plan without a really effective blueprint for the immediate future. They are not really clear on where they have been or where they are going in the short run.

I do not mean simply looking at the last year's sales results or the sales results over the last five years or the production results. A company needs to study its last ten years of experience in terms of all the phases of its own operations and its competitors' as well. By putting all this down in readable and concise form, one places the past in better perspective so he can sail forth into the future.

To be a little more specific: When I moved into the job as manager of a medium-sized division of a large business, it was suffering as a result of a declining market. But it was suffering even more because of a complete lack of communication between the line organization at the division level and the corporate group. I am sure there was some planning going on, but it was of limited scope in the line organization; probably only a little more formal planning was being carried on in the corporate group. I soon found that once I had demonstrated to my staff that I was willing to revitalize the business, I was besieged with ideas of how to get this business off the ground.

I became convinced very soon that, rather than take the ideas and start to build, we should find out where we had been in the past. I asked all my department heads to give me a detailed analysis of where we had come from in the last five years. This was not only very interesting for me, being somewhat an outsider; it was twice as educational for my department heads. Most of them had been in the company for twenty years, and they learned much they had never known.

Once we had a reasonably clear picture of past performance, I asked each area to draw plans for the coming year. Generally speaking, this started off with a realistic appraisal of our financial budgets. Then we established production levels which were realistic with past sales patterns, not with the hopes and aspirations of the sales department. We also set up sales budgets that were consistent with production capacities. In looking at prior budgets, I found an amazing lack of coordination in this area. Also, there was very little knowledge of the price and cost trends which had put a lot of past planning out of whack. I found that many of the service groups were riding dead horses as far as their efforts went.

We had a mechanical development group working on a sizable project to automate a particular phase of our operation. But after a scanning of the sales projections, I was convinced we were going to be out of the business within about three years. It was just money going down the drain as far as our needs were concerned. All in all, from these studies we found we had a lot of problems. Unfortunately, many of them were too complex for an early solution. But the important point is that I felt that every person in my staff or in my organization, either line or staff or the top people, knew what our problems were; they knew the priority we had established for trying to solve them and to reach various goals that we had established over a short period.

I will be the first to agree that this is not really what I call long-range planning. But I was convinced that we were at a point where we were finally ready for long-range planning. First, we had collected a backlog of historical information, which I think is the foundation of any project. Then, I am convinced that we developed an attitude in our top-management group which was conducive to long-range planning. For example, when we developed a rather detailed marketing projection going off into two and three years, our sales manager, who was a hard-driving line man, saw the benefits that came from the struggle he had had for three months in trying to pull this thing together and put it down on paper.

This experience has convinced me of several points:

Do not leave the line people out of long-range planning. You can do a great deal to relieve them of the leg-work involved, but I am convinced that you cannot leave them out of the basic decisions.

Do not let yourself or your staff believe that your plan eliminates the need for future hunches or intuition or whatever you want to call it. I still feel this is what we all get paid for as managers; it is our ability to roll with the punches and not make a plan inflexible. For it is clear that long-range plans will fluctuate considerably.

When you do make hunches that go into long-range plans, do not let yourself or your organization be afraid to prove your hunches wrong. I found that a good and loyal organization will do some amazing things sometimes to prove that the boss—either the top boss or the boss down the line—is right.

I had a recent experience that illustrates my third "do not." We were forced to shut down a rather obsolete plant in one area of the country. It did not take any crystal ball to see that the plant would have to be shut down, but I was convinced that we were going to have to be back in that area with a new and modern plant within the next two years. I announced this not only internally, but externally to the general public in that area.

As a part of our two-year plan, I had a group specifically working on this problem and charged it with the responsibility of justifying my hunch. But for some reason I could not seem to get anything out of the group; it was dragging its feet terribly. I finally found out that my hunch was so completely erroneous that we had no business whatsoever building a plant in that area; and that the group was embarrassed to bring all this information to light because I had so foolishly announced publicly that we were going to be back in there soon.

When this group did present the report to me, albeit somewhat reluctantly, I think I surprised them a little by thanking them for saving me the future embarrassment of explaining the misappropriation of about $2 million.

In conclusion, planning is like any other area of the business which requires real management. I do not think you can put it up in some "ivory tower"; you have to bring it down to earth and make it a part of your daily operations. It has to stay flexible. Finally, a few top people have to be in the act.

18

Organization in a Steel Company[1]

Stewart Thompson

A sixty-year-old integrated steel company is the manufacturer of specialty steels in bar, billet, flat-rolled form, and sheet steel.[2] The firm has a subsidiary which makes welded tubing. Stainless steel and tool steel are major products. There are five plants, plus the tubing manufacturer and a Canadian company. There are approximately fourteen thousand persons on the company's U.S. payroll. Annual sales are approximately $250 million.

It was early in 1957 that steps were first taken to form what was to become the Corporate Development Department, "to assist in the planning and development of present and future business." Prior to that time the department was part of what is now the Technology Department. The Corporate Development Department has a staff of seven, plus its clerical and stenographic help.

The firm's manager of corporate development reports to the assistant to the president. Asked to outline the work of his department, he replied as follows:

"We make no decisions ourselves. We are purely a coordinating group. Our job is to coordinate the decisions of the president and

[1] From *How Companies Plan,* American Management Association Research Study 54 (1962), pp. 125–128. Used by permission.

[2] This company preferred not to be identified in the report.

his staff of vice-presidents, carrying these decisions into any ramification of the business and putting them all into a report with our recommendations.

"We have no authority to say, 'This is what we shall do.' We say, after investigating the subject, 'This is what we would recommend.' "

Question: "What kinds of circumstances bring you together with the president and the operating vice-presidents and other company executives?"

We might make a recommendation on a product, or perhaps on a cost-reduction project, or on a piece of new equipment, or on a plant that is being considered for acquisition. We would, in this latter case, recommend to the president whether, in the opinion of this department, our company should or should not acquire another firm, or another business.

Question: "What is the significance in the use of the term 'corporate development' instead of another label—'planning department,' for example?"

I believe our management feels that planning should not be assigned to any single department, because every department is expected to plan.

Question: "Can you give us some examples of the sort of work done in your department?"

When managers are setting company goals, I go back over reports of the different departments and may find—for example—that one department says, "Based on a certain goal, we plan to do thus and so." If the goal is incompatible with one established for another related activity, we call the managers' attention to the fact and persuade them to agree on compatible goals. We coordinate the planning of many groups.

We have pretty far-flung activities in the business. We have excellent people doing the planning in the various departments. But, as a hypothetical example, we might find that the Sales Department is deciding to get into a new market, selling something that we do not now make, but that the Operating Department is planning to do away with the equipment which might be used to make it. Our function is to uncover these inconsistencies. Periodically, we issue a planning document. We hope to make up a ten-year plan each year. So far, there have been two such documents.

I think the prime coordination of company plans comes from the planning document. Distribution of the manual is limited to our seven vice-presidents—and, of course, to the president. When they get the document (a mimeographed book of some fifty pages), they have an opportunity to comment on the various plans outlined in it.

The planning document states the nature of our business and gives general information about company products, our distribution system, and so forth. We describe the plans of the various individual departments; then we get into our product planning, where we set forth the goals in each major product category, such as stainless steel, tool steel, alloy steel, carbon steel, electrical and electronic equipment, titanium and refractory metals, and springs. These goals are set out in either tons or dollar sales.

First of all, our marketing research people set the over-all pattern of what they think the ten-year projection for each product should be. Then the top management people decide we should aim at so much for each of these markets. Then we have to make our plans, for the next ten years, to reach these goals.

Conferences between the president and the vice-presidents—I suppose you could call them the planning team—result in decisions as to what businesses we plan to stay in (or move out of). The assistant to the president, to whom I report, is a member of that group. They meet about every two weeks. Anything that comes out of that meeting which affects planning is passed along to me.

I think the benefit of maintaining my department (and it may have been the reason for initiating our work) is that we are not involved at all with the day-to-day operations of the business. I would say there is nothing we work on that is likely to happen within a year from the time we start on it.

Once the planning document is issued to the vice-presidents, it is reviewed by them and the president. After it is finally agreed upon, it becomes the plan for the company. At that point our work becomes that of monitoring the plan.

We follow along, as results are turned in by operating people. We point out instances where their work is not up to schedule.

As a result of information we receive from company executives and other sources, we may recommend that special studies be made.

We call these "projects." As these projects are undertaken, we review them periodically with our top executives. We are prepared to go into any amount of detail necessary in order to answer their questions.

Right now, there are about twenty-five projects under way. In addition, our department is presently involved in five other special projects. For example, when we set up our Canadian operation, some people worked on the planning project team for as long as two months, on a full-time basis.

Question: "How about the building of a new plant, for example? Would this constitute a project for the Corporate Development Department?"

Only so far as the *decision* to build the plant—not the actual building construction.

Question: "How are people selected to serve on the project teams?"

We suggest the kinds of people we need, and our recommendations are usually carried out. We may say we need an Accounting Department person, or an engineer. We usually have certain people in mind when we set up a project team. It is up to the department head of the individual concerned to decide whether he will be released from his regular work. Many parts of the work require, perhaps, two or three days' study, during which time the individuals are excused from their regular jobs. They may be called back to the project, from time to time, until it is finished. Two months is the longest I have known anyone to be away from his regular work.

Work on the projects is usually interesting. If someone performs well, he is noticed. Everyone who worked on the Canadian company project has had a number of promotions. That might be just by coincidence, I don't really know.

Question: "To what extent would compensation practices, or organization planning, for example, involve work for your department?"

With regard to compensation, we might be involved if plans were being considered to set up a whole new compensation structure, but we do not deal with the salaries of individuals.

The Employee Relations Department is responsible for organization planning. We would be expected to point out to the people there that some changes they propose making are in conflict with the basic plans that have been established, if we did uncover such a conflict.

Each individual department has to make its own plans. The departments tell us what they plan to do. If we don't think individual department plans fit in with company plans, we try to have the difference reconciled. For example: If it had been decided by top management that we were going to increase our share of a market by X per cent, it would be up to the Sales Department executives to determine what their marketing plans were going to be. They would have to decide whether they would need more salesmen, more product promotion, and so forth, to achieve the objective. We would match their own plans to the over-all plans. A top-management decision results in a mass of supplementary plans which we coordinate.

We are a staff, to the president and to the vice-presidents, for coordinating and seeing that planning is done. Like a labor relations department, for instance, we are set up to deal with one aspect of the work of the superintendent or the works manager. It isn't that the manager couldn't do adequate planning, but that he has too many other things to do. Our work is to coordinate plans for our managers.

Question: "Do you use economic consultants?"

Yes, we do. Our department schedules meetings with the consultants and our executives. We actually handle the physical arrangements for the meetings.

Question: "What improvements in the organization and work of the Corporate Development Department would you like to make?"

We are trying to set up to do a better job, I assure you. Our second planning document is vastly better than our first, and I hope that our third will be better still. But, as far as I know now, there is no likelihood that our approach to planning will be in any way different from what it is now.

One change that might come about in a few years is a formal method of cataloguing every company subject and project that deals with planning, a method similar to the one at Westinghouse Air Brake Company which was developed by Ed Green. Our coordination is no better than the means by which that coordination takes place. Those means involve personal contact, getting reports, and really understanding the reports. If we get a report and don't see how it relates to other departments, there is a flaw in our system. We may soon need a more thorough and elaborate filing system for keeping track of the development projects, as well as the departmental plans.

19

Stages in Development[1]

George A. Steiner

I have concluded on the basis of empirical study that companies with multiple divisions have gone through about five observable stages in the development of long-range planning programs. These steps were generally confirmed by the participants in, and papers prepared for, the University of California at Los Angeles research seminar on long-range planning (held in September 1962), and by a study of the Stanford Research Institute.[2] This evolution deserves more than passing mention in this paper.

Business firms generally get involved in formal long-range planning as a result of a major problem or the general feeling that since other companies are doing it perhaps they also should. In either event, an evolutionary process frequently sets in which typically goes through the following stages.

[1] From the Proceedings of the Academy of Management Annual Meeting, Pittsburgh, December 1962. Used by permission.

[2] R. Hal Mason, "Organizing for Corporate Planning," *Proceedings of the Long-Range Planning Service Client Conference* (Menlo Park, Cal., Stanford Research Institute, 1962).

Stage One is entered when an individual or a committee is assigned to look into the matter. If an individual is given the task he frequently is the controller, but he may be an assistant to the president, a vice-president, or a person interested in the job. If a group is assigned the task it is usually composed of the senior staff of the president. Staff specialists may be invited to advise the group on some problems. A good bit of information is collected and focused on special problems. Solutions are recommended and actions taken. Corporate objectives are developed and a more permanent and integrated planning program is discussed and recommended.

At the end of about one year a planning director is appointed and the next stage begins. He is given a small staff which includes economic, financial, engineering, and perhaps scientific talent. The mix depends, of course, much upon the company and industry. The work of this group does not follow a typical pattern but generally includes the development of corporate goals, examination in detail of the strengths and weaknesses of the company, analysis of the evolving environment in which the company will operate, surveys of where the company is heading, identification of new fields for corporate growth, and creation of a basis for the development of a comprehensive corporate planning effort. Division personnel participate in individual studies.

Around the beginning of the third year plans are laid for the first comprehensive plan, and the next stage begins. The central corporate planning group gives general guidance to the divisions for their development of a plan. Frequently, the plan covers the next five-year period. But parts of it may extend beyond five years. Once these plans are completed they are submitted to the central planning group for integration, aggregation, and assessment. The divisional plans are examined in the light of corporate goals, and often a gap appears between divisional projected developments and corporate goals. The problem then becomes one of how to fill this gap. Or, as often happens, divisional capital requirements are well beyond the financial capability of the corporation. This calls for drastic revisions of plans, tapping new sources of capital, or re-examining proposed courses of action. While the resulting plans are by no means considered by anybody as being perfect, they result in important decisions for action.

On the basis of the value to the corporation of this stage, the planning director is made a vice-president, and planning becomes formalized in the divisions. The central staff continues to give guidance to the divisions in the planning program but turns more to over-all corporate development problems. Presentation of division plans is made directly to top management. At the divisional levels, planning coordinators are appointed and report in a staff capacity to general managers.

Planning becomes firmly established in the company in the final stage, and the central planning staff begins to exercise a more critical evaluative review of divisional activities in relationship to company objectives. The work of the central planning staff expands in other directions to be noted shortly. At the divisional level the planning coordinators are given responsibility for both long-range and short-range planning, thereby assuring a close relationship between the two. In addition, they begin to take on control activities in conjunction with their current operating planning responsibilities. On behalf of the general manager these control activities concern evaluation of performance in relation to plans.

These stages seem to me to have been followed by so many companies and government agencies that they appear to be somewhat typical. Since we know so much more about planning today than we did ten years ago the sequence of stages of a company now entering the ranks of formalized long-range planners may be a little different; and the evolutionary process, considerably telescoped in time. For any individual company, of course, the sequence of stages and methods of operation may vary much from this presumably typical pattern.

20

The Divorce of Planning from Doing[1]

Peter F. Drucker

The second blind spot of scientific management is the "divorce of planning from doing"—one of its cardinal tenets. Again a sound analytical principle is being mistaken for a principle of action. But in addition the divorce of planning from doing reflects a dubious and dangerous philosophical concept of an elite which has a monopoly on esoteric knowledge, entitling it to manipulate the unwashed peasantry.

To have discovered that planning is different from doing was one of Frederick W. Taylor's most valuable insights. To emphasize that the work will become the easier, more effective, more productive, the more we plan before we do, was a greater contribution to America's industrial rise than stopwatch or time-and-motion study. On it rests the entire structure of modern management. That we are able today to speak seriously and with meaning of management by objectives is a direct result of Taylor's discovery of planning as a separate part of the job, and of his emphasis on its importance.

But it does not follow from the separation of planning and doing in the analysis of work that the planner and the doer should be two different people. It does not follow that the industrial world should be divided into two classes of people: a few who decide what is to be

[1] From Peter F. Drucker, *The Practice of Management* (New York, Harper & Row, 1954), pp. 284–285.

done, design the job, set the pace, rhythm and motions, and order others about; and the many who do what and as they are being told.

Planning and doing are separate parts of the same job; they are not separate jobs. There is no work that can be performed effectively unless it contains elements of both. One cannot plan exclusively all the time. There must be at least a trace of doing in one's job. Otherwise one dreams rather than performs. One cannot, above all, do only; without a trace of planning his job, the worker does not have the control he needs even for the most mechanical and repetitive routine chore. Advocating the divorce of the two is like demanding that swallowing food and digesting it be carried on in separate bodies. To be understood, the two processes have to be studied separately. They require different organs, are subject to different ailments, and are carried out in different parts of the body. But to be nourished at all, the same body needs both, just as a job must contain planning as well as doing.

Taylor's divorce of planning from doing was both specifically American and specifically late nineteenth century. It is a descendant of our eldest tradition: the New England theocracy of the early Puritans. It puts the priestly-elite concept of Increase and Cotton Mather into modern dress, but leaves it otherwise almost unchanged; and like the Puritan divines Taylor deduced a God-given right of the planning elite to rule. It is no accident that we hear this right to rule described today as the "prerogative of management"—the term has always been applied to right by divine or priestly anointment.

But the divorce of planning and doing was also part of the elite philosophy that swept the Western world in the generation between Nietzsche and World War I—the philosophy that has produced such monster offspring in our time. Taylor belongs with Sorel, Lenin, and Pareto. This movement is usually considered to have been antidemocratic. It was—in intent and direction—fully as much antiaristocratic. For the assertion that power is grounded in technical competence—be it for revolutionary conspiracy or for management—is as hostile to aristocracy as to democracy. Both oppose to it the same absolute principle: Power must be grounded in moral responsibility; anything else is tyranny and usurpation.

The divorce of planning from doing deprives us of the full benefit of the insights of Scientific Management. It sharply cuts down the yield to be obtained from the analysis of work, and especially the yield to be obtained from planning. [Tests at International Business Machines Corporation demonstrated] that productivity greatly increased when the workers were given responsibility for planning their work. The same increase in productivity (not to mention the improvement in worker attitude and pride) has been obtained wherever we have combined the divorce of planning from doing with the marriage of planner to doer.

21

For LRP—Rotating Planners and Doers[1]

Ronald J. Ross

In this article we shall examine a new approach to the problem of organizing for long-range planning. This approach is based on the concept of a rotating organization structure, with managers moving back and forth between operations and planning, first taking responsibility for the one, then the other. This rotation is done systematically. The aim is to integrate planning and operations and make *each* of them stronger through mutual reinforcement.

I do not propose this new organization scheme as a panacea for the problem of getting effective long-range planning started. It has limitations, as we shall see, and it will require careful administration. But it does represent an original approach at a time when fresh thinking and imagination are sorely needed. Some companies have made truly impressive progress in the organizational effort, but countless

[1] From *Harvard Business Review,* January–February 1962, p. 105–115. Used by permission.

others, with different problems and needs, seem to have got bogged down before really getting started.

The aim of the approach proposed here is to help some of the managements in the latter group to get going in earnest. It should help them to answer such questions as: Where should long-range planning be done? Should it be centralized in a formal group or carried out by other arrangements? To what extent should programing staffs get involved in follow-up and control? Where is the interface between long-range planning and operations?

I consider the new approach most practical for industries that have a ratio in the order of one professional (or person with equivalent experience) to eight, nine, or possibly as many as twelve lower-level skills. Many defense industries, as well as industries producing complex products for consumer or industrial markets, fit this category. The approach is probably less well suited to firms engaged in the kind of manufacturing that might be considered routine or highly repetitive in nature. The number of professional technical people in these companies is typically small in proportion to the predominant work force of lower skills. Eventually, however, the new organization structure may be more apropos to this industry group, especially as processes become more highly mechanized and the proportion of professional skills to lower labor skills reaches a narrower ratio.

MAJOR FAILINGS

Why is a new, nonconventional approach to the problem of organization needed? It is easier to understand the inadequacies of present systems if we remember that only in recent years have industrial managers begun to undertake serious study and application of long-range planning concepts. Merchants, politicians, spiritual leaders, and many more have, through the ages, studied and formulated the art of prognosis, but managers have not. If it seems odd that many responsible business executives are only now beginning to accept long-range planning as a significant development, bear in mind, too, that historical experience offers only limited guidance to the modern industrial planner. For instance, the aviation industry cannot turn back more than fifty years; the television industry, more than seventy; the nuclear reactor industry, more than twenty; and the space equipment industry, more than ten or twelve years.

While organizational frameworks for long-range planning vary widely in practice, even within a single industry, it is revealing that they are all based on rather conventional ideas. For some companies, long-range planning is accomplished by a committee comprised of a senior executive and immediate subordinate executives. Members of the committee are responsible for both day-to-day operations and long-range planning work. A committee of executives meets periodically on a formal basis to review progress. But the actual work of planning is an informal part of the day-to-day, week-to-week routine of individual executive officers.

In other companies one executive officer is appointed long-range planning director and reports directly to the senior officer. The planning director, in turn, appoints his own staff and is responsible only for conducting long-range planning; there is a minimum of interference from day-to-day operations.

In a few decentralized companies long-range planning is a responsibility of a central planning group which reports to the senior executive at headquarters. Managers of the decentralized organization submit either data or plans for their own operation to the central planning group, where the over-all long-term plan is interwoven into a master plan. In other decentralized organizations, managers of decentralized units make their own plans and receive approval from the central organization. And, of course, there are many variations of these schemes.

Now, in some of these firms a good deal of effort has gone into this planning, and in some of them it has even worked. Why, then, has progress been unsatisfactory in so many other cases? There are a series of reasons.

Dangers of Exclusiveness

In cases where the planning group is divorced from operations, it might seem desirable at first blush to keep members remote from day-to-day routine in order to retain long-term objectivity. On the other hand, planners lose contact with the immediate dynamics of firm operations, become narrow specialists, and lose much of the perspective and experience in current short-term management problems. It is doubtful that this loss can be recaptured through observation at the side lines, or by interviewing operating personnel.

Participation in planning is limited to a small specialized staff, either a group of senior officers or a small staff of planners gathered in a tight sphere around the senior executive. Personnel down the management ladder do not share in molding the future of their organization. Hence, middle and lower management people tend to regard planning as the exclusive responsibility of top managers; they acquire, at best, a hazy comprehension of long-term goals and objectives and of the reasoning behind actions to obtain these objectives. They are not able to apply their full capacities effectively to the long-term problems since they do not know exactly what the company is trying to do or what future problems to expect.

By neglecting lower management levels in long-range planning, a vast reservoir of knowledge and experience is left untapped. It is true that long-range planning specialists—especially those in engineering, finance, or marketing—are often a certain breed with insights and capabilities peculiar to their own field. But the critical analysis and constructive opinions of lower management groups can go far toward helping create a better working arrangement over the long term. In addition, there would be a better understanding and acceptance of problem solutions by the people most involved.

If subordinate executives or operating personnel help work out plans that are feasible from their point of view, they will not tend to regard necessary changes as mystifying, as arbitrary, or as based on unreasonable directives from above. They can see the purpose underlying new arrangements and the objectives being served. With understanding of the reasons for change, they can help lessen its impact on the various parts of the organization.

Preoccupation with Operations

Unfortunately, in many companies managers are entangled in day-to-day problems and concentrate on short-term objectives by dint of their immediacy. Typically, management is too busy trying to make profits for the current months to find time to project what the company will be doing five and more years hence. Yet the same management frequently makes decisions with long-term implications. Even among large organizations there is only a small group wherein executives are actually involved in laying detailed long-range plans, rather than expending most of their efforts on day-to-day and short-term problems.

Budgets, schedules, performances ratings, and the like are almost always focused on near-term objectives and accomplishments. By contrast, it is more difficult to measure long-term gains and accomplishments. Thus it is not surprising that after years of conditioning in short-range operations, managers are hesitant to broaden the time range of their attention, and find difficulty in making an effective move to start meaningful long-range planning activities.

Line-Staff Myopia

The businessman has two common business terms that apparently denote a sharp demarcation between organization functions. They are "line" and "staff." Although supposedly simple and precise definitions, they are in reality jargon. If taken too seriously, they may create roadblocks to the formation of new organization structures best suited to integrating long-range planning and company operations.[2]

It is distressing that many otherwise rational businessmen religiously adhere to the dogma that every function, position, job element, and whatever within their organization must be classifiable as either line or staff. This form of mental *rigor mortis* becomes evident in their disdain of exploring new principles of organization if the new propositions do not separate into neat line and staff functions. Since line and staff are not miscible, they argue that all functions must be readily defined; only then is it possible to proceed and evaluate the new ideas of organization.

But let five, ten, or more responsible and experienced businessmen review their own organization and they will certainly find, in practice, that there is a decided overlap in the so-called line and staff activities, probably in some cases a substantial overlap. For instance, the staff engineer often doubles as a line salesman; the line production manager can spend a significant part of his workweek assisting in staff planning activities; and the line sales manager participates in staff budgeting activities.

There are some companies that break down the functions of the manager into minute detail, employing charts, tables, and voluminous descriptive texts. Each aspect of a managerial job is sifted into functions and cross-functions and relationships and cross-relationships with respect to staff and line activities. This careful detailing probably has its place for studying and understanding the relationship of jobs and

[2] See Gerald G. Fisch, "Line-Staff Is Obsolete," *Harvard Business Review*, September–October 1961, p. 67.

job responsibilities in the firm. But its importance is overrated and can become, in fact, a guideline for stressing conformity to fixed patterns, ignoring realities of business change. Is it not more important that the manager be primarily concerned with the question of how to function and perform effectively in a dynamic business situation? He must, in essence, be aware that the work situation he oversees is not static, that preparations are continuously being made for change, and that he must act when change does *not* occur. Line-staff distinctions have little or no pertinence to this problem.

Inflexibility

Over the long run, the firm's organization structure needs to be flexible if management is to redirect its efforts effectively, utilize new methods and processes, and produce new products or new combinations of products. But few firms are in fact change-oriented. This is understandable because few organizations have the philosophy that change is fundamental; management has not imparted the logic that change is a condition of survival over the long run. Instead, the conventional organization structure is a foundation for an attitude of adherence to the status quo.

Of course, there are senior managers in the community of industrial firms who *believe* that they are change-oriented, but in reality they are likely to have little concept of action with true foresight. They dissipate substantial quantities of funds in advertising and in marketing new but improperly evaluated technological developments. Their actions are impulsive, haphazard, and unrelated to long-range business needs. This is not change orientation, but simple, short-sighted, organized chaos.

A NEW CONCEPT

How can the difficulties just enumerated be overcome? What kind of organization structure *will* help management to integrate long-range planning and operations so that each reinforces the other?

Rotational Scheme

Initially, consider a skeleton framework of an organization stripped of all duties except management tasks. Now, suppose that arrangements could be made to move managers from operations to planning, then back to operations, back to planning, and so forth in a cyclical rotation. Each executive would retain responsibility within his own field and commensurate with his management level in the firm.

Each man participates in planning a phase of the long-range program, then rotates into operations to execute that phase. The rotation period can be based on product cycles, cyclical changes in methods or processes, arbitrary calendar events, or any other periods significant to the conduct of the company's business. Rotation of managers can also be staggered to prevent transient changes in company operations.

This concept is called the *rotating organization structure,* or ROS for short. Fundamental to it are the assumptions that the company—

- Exists and operates under the enterprise system characterized by the American economy.
- Is motivated to earn profit.
- Desires to perpetuate itself and grow, and is nonspeculative in character.
- Has rational management.
- Utilizes long-range planning to attain broad business objectives.
- Applies long-range planning across the board—in marketing, engineering, manufacturing, and other major areas—for calendar periods compatible with the firm's long-range objectives (e.g., five, ten, or twenty years).

The operating principles of the ROS scheme are as follows:

1. Only managers above a specific level are included in the plan. The exact extent of participation varies from situation to situation since all companies do not have like characteristics, goals, or objectives. Participating managers are chosen to suit the needs of each individual firm. As an example, one firm might choose to have all managers above the level of department head, or the equivalent, participate in operations and long-range planning; another company with a different pattern of responsibility might include department heads and possibly certain of their subordinates.
2. No manager is responsible for long-range planning and operations concurrently. He is assigned to one *or* the other task.
3. Managers rotate within the same task responsibilities. For example, engineering managers will rotate between engineering operations and engineering long-range planning, manufacturing managers will rotate between manufacturing long-range planning and manufacturing operations, and marketing managers will rotate between marketing long-range planning and marketing operations.

4. Managers responsible for long-range planning and operations do not suffer reduction in rank, level of responsibility, or status in either operations or long-range planning assignments. Operations managers rotated to long-range planning activities, and long-range planning managers reassigned to operations, stay at the same levels and maintain the same status.

5. Managers performing long-range planning become responsible for controlling and executing the segments of the long-range plan they have developed, upon rotating back into operations.

6. Responsibilities are rotated on a systematic basis. The frequency and phasing of assignment changes must be compatible with the needs of the individual firm and the character of its business. For example, if the company changes its product or product mix frequently (e.g., every one or two years), rotation of managers might be advantageous on a product life-cycle basis. On the other hand, the company that experiences ten- and fifteen-year product life cycles might choose to rotate managers on a calendar basis.

7. As a general rule, rotation of managers is staggered to prevent a sudden break in organization relationships.

8. Both the long-range planning and operations managers should have supplementary staffs of specialists contributing to the tasks within their responsibility, but these specialists are not included in the scheme of rotating responsibilities.

Executive Relationships

Exhibit 1 portrays the ROS plan for a hypothetical company having a conventional pattern of authority (i.e., one man at the top, two men at the next highest level, and more men at succeedingly lower levels). For the sake of clarity, since the sole purpose of this illustration is guidance, I have focused here only on salient points and relationships, leaving out many details that would ordinarily be shown in a conventional organization chart. The notation M is the symbol for manager, subscript p denotes planning tasks, subscript o is for operations tasks, and superscripts 1, 2, 3, 4, and 5 denote the level of the managers, from 1 (the senior manager) down. The letter P denotes planning specialists, and the letter O is the symbol for operations specialists.

In a pyramidal form of authority such as this hypothetical company has, a planning manager ($M^2{}_p$) and an operations manager ($M^2{}_o$) report directly to the senior executive (M^1) under the ROS approach.

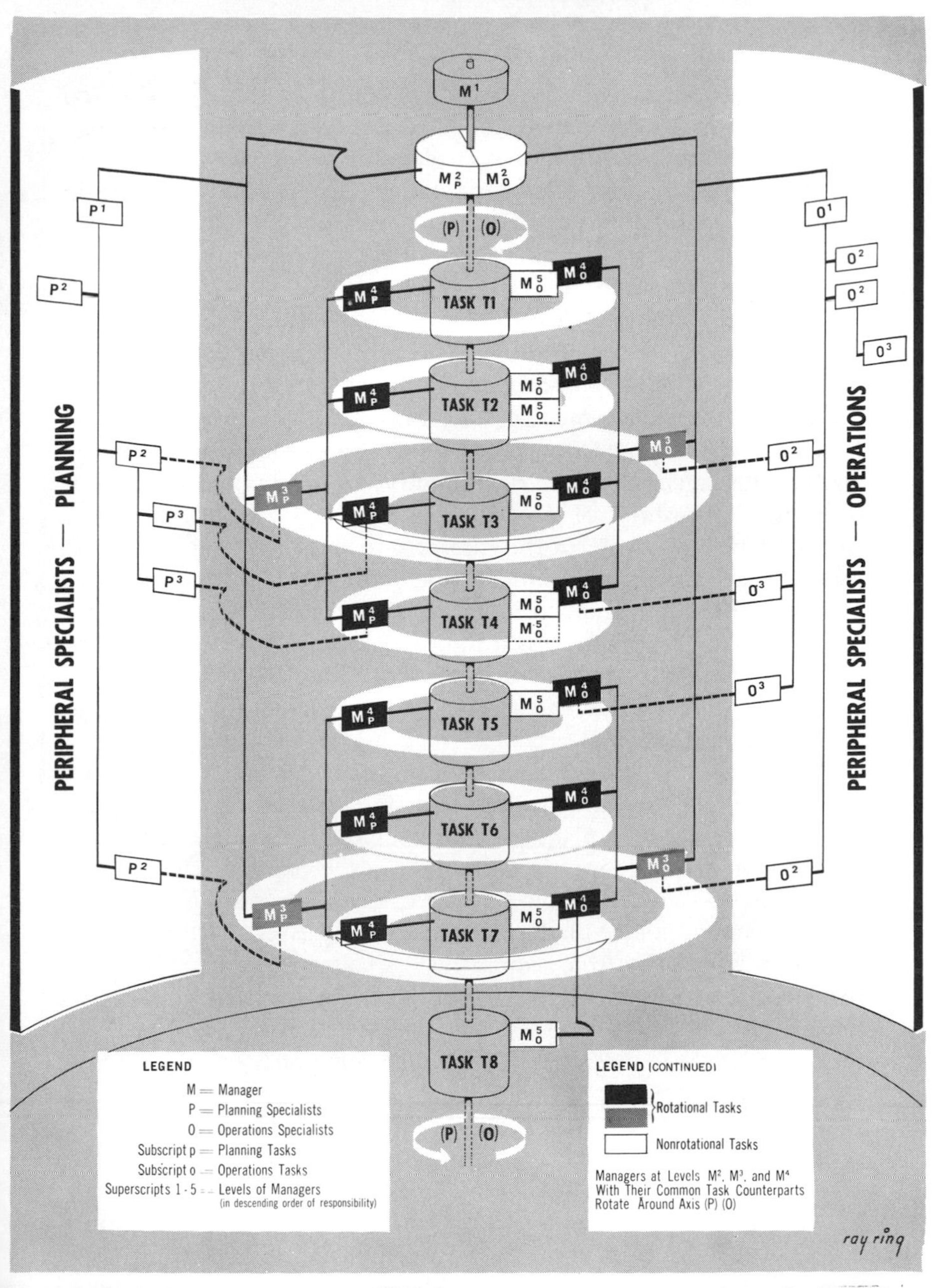

EXHIBIT 1. Rotating Organization Structure Arrangement for an Industrial Firm

Managers below the senior executive are rotated between planning and operations. All lower management people performing long-range planning report to the long-range planning manager through their levels of responsibility. Similarly, all lower management people in operations report to the operations manager in charge of their level. Managers performing planning are not responsible for operations, and the converse also is true.

Tasks are denoted *T1, T2, T3,* and so forth (only eight are listed for the sake of brevity). More than one meaning is associated with the word "task," and this choice is purposely made for flexibility of application. For the management of one firm, task may mean a specific function, such as production processes, cost accounting, or sales. For another management, task may signify all of the elements that comprise the business of producing a product or service from the initial to the final stage; in the case of our hypothetical firm, for instance, each task might include a wide variety of functions, such as sales, engineering, manufacturing, and all other activities which constitute the conduct of business through each stage. In brief, the word task does not imply specific functions, but rather those combinations of activities that best suit the specific requirements of the company to conduct its business.

An operations manager and planning manager are related to an activity and communication tie by a task. The task is the common bond and interface between planning and operations. Note that only the manager of task *T8* does not participate in the rotation scheme. It is a service task—let us say, raw stock maintenance—and this firm does not consider long-range planning essential in this area of work.

In our hypothetical company managers below Level 4 do not participate in the rotating scheme, nor do planning specialists and operational specialists. On the other hand, men at the second, third, and fourth levels rotate periodically, with the timing of their moves based on the product life cycle.

In the scheme of rotation, managers change between planning and operations on a staggered basis so that there will not be abrupt transitions in business activity. Long-range planning managers plan for the next cycle period and contribute to the modification of the firm's master long-range plan. It is also their responsibility to plan for their task activity, to keep close communication with the task operations manager, and to recognize and assist in solving the problems of integrating their task activities with the company's long-range business activities.

The operations manager, by contrast, is responsible for the day-to-day work that goes on in his task. He keeps a close communication tie with the task planning manager.

When the planning and operations managers rotate and interchange positions, the new operations manager becomes responsible for executing the plan he devised during his tour as planning manager, while the new planning manager begins the next segment of the long-range plan for his task.

The planning and operations specialists assist their respective managers in the more routine and detailed activities associated with the tasks.

Promotion is through the line of task managers. In moving to a higher level, the *manager* changes from operations at the lower level to planning at the next higher level, and begins his cyclic rotation at this point. Planning and operations *specialists* move vertically through the specialist ranks.

Distinctive Features

The idea of rotating managers through various organization positions has been used for years. But rotation as conventionally practiced is usually part of a management development plan, with personnel moving through various departments and across dissimilar fields to gain experience and background for promotion to higher levels. In this setup, the organization is essentially fixed; selected personnel are "spiraled" through the organization but do not return to the origin.

In the ROS system, by contrast, managers move through planning and operations *within a distinct project field,* and they move in a circle-like pattern back to the origin. What is more, the ROS system is not a training plan but an organization system for tying long-range planning into operations. Of especial importance, ROS is change-oriented. It leads personnel to expect changes in job assignments and exposes them regularly to the challenge of planning, where they make long-run projections and must maintain an attitude of change to fulfill their responsibilities. Moreover, having participated in the planning phase of a task, they are more likely to recognize and understand the time limitations of a program when they go back to the operations side.

INSTALLATION

At this point I should like to turn to some of the practical questions which the ROS plan raises.

I have discussed the plan with a number of businessmen—men in such industries as electronics, aircraft, steel, cosmetics, banking, insurance, and public service—and, as might be expected, they have asked about a wide variety of points. Of particular importance to them is the general problem of getting the ROS system started. Can it be installed without disrupting operations? How will the jobs be filled? Will top management end up losing control to managers down the line? Will staffing costs be increased?

To discuss these and other questions I shall use a hypothetical case:

> A company with a centralized management organization, a total complement of about forty-five hundred people, a varied product mix, and five distinct product lines wants to adopt the ROS plan. The current annual volume of business is about $125 million. The company has been an established firm for fifteen years, and its facilities are comprised of three plants geographically located within thirty miles of each other. One plant is the in this facility. The other two outlying plants are acquisitions purchased headquarters office, and three of the products are developed and processed seven and five years ago respectively. Each of the two outlying plants produces one product.
>
> There is no basic similarity among the five product lines; each has its own staff to generate new developments and processes and to manufacture and sell its product. The *average* of all product life cycles is about thirteen years, including development, transition to production, production, and final obsolescence in the market. The ratio of professional skills to labor skills is approximately one to ten.

How should the top management of this company be advised to make the transition to the new planning structure?

Initial Appointments

First, it must be emphasized that the senior executives making the change should not start out with the attitude that it is a trial marriage. The initial move to the new system will probably be the most difficult one to hurdle. Managers conditioned to solving current day-to-day business problems tend to procrastinate when faced with changes for the long range, and they must break with old practices and habits. The senior manager would be wise to prepare several alternatives of action to overcome bad starts or to revamp ideas that did not work as well as expected. If the only alternative is regression to the status quo before change, however, the senior executive is not really preparing for events ahead; he is, in fact, setting a subconscious attitude of retreat at the first sign of difficulty.

The senior manager's first step in effecting reorganization of the firm is to appoint and install his two top ROS managers (the second level in Exhibit 1). At the same time, he should move as quickly as possible to dissolve the functions and responsibilities of top-level managers under the old organization arrangement, and give these men responsibilities under the new framework. If the old organization managers do not have the abilities to fit into the ROS scheme, they can be shifted to the periphery of the planning or operations groups as specialists (denoted by *P* and *O* in Exhibit 1). The two top ROS managers should be selected for their ability to master a wide base of both planning and operations problems, rather than for experience or unusual capability in one or two fields of business.

The reason for installing the top men first is a very practical one. It means that each new group formed at a lower level will not buck resistance from the heads under the old organization structure. With a new arrangement of top managers under ROS, the attitude for change will be set, and new patterns will evolve more easily.

It would be preferable to launch ROS in a limited area only. In the case of our hypothetical company, the smaller outlying plant might well be selected as the first unit since the total staff, about eight hundred people, is smaller than any of the other product organizations and easier to handle in the first stage of gaining experience.

Third-level ROS managers should now be picked for the various jobs to be done. The needs might break down about as follows:

- Two sales (or marketing) managers for operations and planning.
- Two managers for finance, with responsibility for current operations as well as for new fundings for future operations (salary and wage administration will be under central control, within the responsibility of the second-level managers).
- Two manufacturing managers responsible for product fabrication processes and associated services.
- Two engineering managers responsible for both current product en-

gineering and development engineering (including product improvement and industrial research).

What if cost accounting, plant maintenance, raw stock control, and certain other specialized functions are organized separately? Management might consider two possibilities for fitting them in:

1. Since each product line is a complete task effort, special functions could be placed under the responsibility of the appropriate ROS managers as operations tasks, but not within the rotation scheme. In other words, they would be organized as task *T8* is in Exhibit 1.
2. The functions might be managed by ROS managers in the same way as are other tasks in the system. This alternative might be chosen if top management thinks it will be a problem to keep the special function moving apace with developments in other areas of the corporation.

Major Preparations

Now, the newly appointed ROS managers should spend about six months to a year working together as a group, preparing for the organization change-over. The group will spend most of its time with the senior manager, assisting in formulating a long-range master plan and also a long-range program (with alternatives) for the product line, preparing for operations in the first stage of the product plan, and preparing plans and operations procedures for all the business activities associated with the product including, for example, marketing, finance, product development and improvement, and manufacturing. The group should also devise a system to perpetuate performance measurements and performance goals that is continuously evaluated and revised. What is excellent, good, fair, and poor progress? What is failure? The parameters of this problem should include the timeliness and timing of the product and product improvements in the market.

These standards should then be related to alternative courses of action. Catastrophic failure of the business activity is least likely if, with the help of performance measurements, managers are continually prepared to change course in an orderly way when danger signs become evident. Such preparedness would be extremely important if our hypothetical company were, for example, a military aerospace or electronic equipment supplier and the demand for its products were highly dependent on national political and military uncertainties.

Once the new ROS group is confident that it is ready to move to the next phase of organization transition, the managers can be appointed at Levels 4 and 5. These men can be indoctrinated by assisting in the details of preparation for the change-over. In our hypothetical company, a total of twelve fourth-level and twenty fifth-level managers might be appointed to ROS positions.

Starting Rotation

When the ROS scheme goes into effect, the question of rotation arises. The frequency and timing of rotation can be tailored at will to company needs, as suggested earlier. In the case at hand let us suppose that the expected product life cycle is approximately fourteen years, including development time, transition to production, full production, and final obsolescence in the market, and that the expected life cycle is approximately one-half complete. It might then be reasonable, in the light of rapid technological changes, fluidity of the market, availability of funding, and changes in manufacturing processes, to start the first cycle of rotation ten months after ROS is completely installed, and to stagger rotation thereafter on an annual basis. Later on the cycle might be made longer, but for the time being ROS is a new experience in the firm, and a one-year cycle appears to be a better choice from the point of view of having managers gain a broad base of experience as rapidly as is practicable.

At the time fixed for change-over to ROS in the plant, one-half of the managers at all levels become responsible for planning, the other half for operations. The experience gained in the first year or two can be used by the next product group in the firm that adopts ROS. Succeeding groups should be able to change over at a more rapid pace, and possibly two or three organizations at a time might make the move.

MAKING ROS WORK

A case situation like the one just discussed has many limitations, of course, and I do not pretend to have communicated more than the rudiments of a picture. Accordingly, I should like now to cover a variety of questions that readers might raise about ROS, some of them related to what has gone before, and some of them not.

Transition and Change-over

How does a management operating under the ROS plan make the transition from an old to a new product?

Normally, each product area would be handled by a team of professional and technical people. Although the team builds its skills and background experiences around a specific product through its life cycle, its "tools of the trade" are common to many products and product areas.

If each product line has a complete staff to generate new developments, manufacture the product, and sell it, this group itself can be made responsible for developing new products or product lines to replace items completing a life cycle. In other words, ROS managers, when responsible for planning, would consider and prepare for the development of new products and product lines as a specific part of their tasks. The transition to a new product would not be spontaneous but well planned far in advance, and the transition phase would be a planned follow-through procedure.

In the event that a product line has a total demise in the market, or the company finds it is no longer profitable to continue the product line, then the ROS personnel, with their knowledge of the basic tools of the trade, can be shifted to other, fundamentally similar projects where their basic skills are needed.

If the corporation has a decentralized management pattern, is it equally practicable to install ROS?

Actually, in a decentralized company change-over to the ROS system can be accomplished with *greater* ease than change-over in the centralized company, particularly where the decentralized units have substantial autonomy. It would still be a good idea to make a pilot change-over first in one division, possibly a division initiating a new product or product line. And it would still be best to appoint and install the top ROS managers in the central organization first, to assure that the decentralized units will not buck the old top-level managers during the change-over period.

Personnel Problems

How does ROS affect the status of the company's senior planning executive?

Under ROS the senior manager of the firm does not relinquish his responsibility for formulating the master long-range plan. Participation in long-range planning by executives and supervisors down the line reinforces planning and provides better effectiveness in attaining the firm's long-term goals. By no means do the latter men usurp the prerogatives of the senior executive. He retains full responsibility for initiating master plans and strategy and for giving direction to the firm's business.

Can enough good men capable of "changing hats" be found to staff all the ROS positions in a company?

While operations or planning specialists can usually be acquired with a reasonable degree of ease, finding personnel equally competent in planning and operations might, at first, appear to be a nearly insurmountable problem. Not all organizations have many men who are potentially capable of taking on both planning and operations responsibilities, and the established firm steeped in traditional practices may indeed find it hard to identify the needed people. I do not think it is reasonable to conclude, however, that since managers do not conventionally rotate between planning and operations, personnel capable of doing this do not exist or else are too extraordinary for the average corporation to find.

Personnel for the management levels in ROS can be drawn from the immediate staff of many organizations. Qualified managers need to be trained, but building the skills of managers for ROS to broader-based capabilities is not impractical or impossible. In the ROS system, managers rotate between planning and operations within confined spheres of knowledge and experience. When the system is first installed, they do not cross automatically into unfamiliar fields. There is time for training and mental adjustment. The real roadblock, in my opinion, is less likely to be the potentials of management people than it is the attitude of senior managers and training specialists toward delegation and innovation.

Can a company really afford to pay two managers to do the same task?

The cost of two managers for each task has implications other than salary. These include greater flexibility and effectiveness in conducting the company's business over the long run, better communication ties, and more extensive utilization of managers on the job. By and large,

I think it would be reasonable for management to expect the cost of expanding the staff horizontally to be counterbalanced by economies in vertical compressions achieved through greater utilization of lower management capabilities.

What specific jobs would executives on ROS planning assignments have during the day?

To go back to the example of our hypothetical company, the executives would work full time on solutions to such problems as:

- Determining the direction of product-line development by (1) evaluating previous experiences to discover avoidable mistakes, and (2) exploring research work to learn of new technologies that can be utilized in short- and long-range product improvement.
- Evaluating automation techniques applicable to the company's production and making recommendations as to their usefulness (including plans for transition).
- Evaluating the capabilities of competitive companies, analyzing short-term and long-range trends and developments, and determining the corporation's anticipated position in the market.
- Examining facilities requirements for short- and long-range product lines and, when applicable, preparing for transition to the utilization of new facilities.
- Determining finance strategy, preparing anticipated long-range budgets for projected operations, and determining sources of funding for future operations and alternatives.
- Developing new administrative procedures and cost-control concepts that will be most effective for future operations.
- Exploring possible acquisitions which can strengthen or build the firm over the long run.
- Determining future personnel requirements and studying how, when, and where to acquire and train personnel.
- Evaluating more effective business housekeeping methods (e.g., electronic data processing) for new operations, and preparing for the transition to better methods as decisions are made for change.
- Evaluating and preparing changes in the firm's rotating organization structure.
- Studying and evaluating communication patterns in the company's entire organization and instituting changes for more effective communications in deficient areas.
- Evaluating labor relations trends and determining the firm's labor relations posture for the future.

• Modifying the existing system, or generating a new system, of performance measurements that will be more effective in evaluating operations.
• Modifying the master long-range plan to contain new decisions and strategies.

For other companies, the emphasis of such a list (which is by no means comprehensive) might be on different activities—i.e., selling and promotion, or financial management.

COMMUNICATIONS

How does the ROS scheme affect the possibilities of effectively communicating long-range goals to supervisors and to specialists on down the line?

In conventional organizations an outstanding cause for poor communication links between managers is the distances involved in managerial pyramids. Managers in these elaborate structures either filter information or create "noise" in the communication networks. By contrast, firms utilizing ROS will be able to avoid extensive pyramiding of managers. The information flow up and down through the managerial levels will therefore not be as susceptible to filtering, noise, and time delays. Lower-level managers will be better tuned to the senior executives' point of view, and vice versa. In addition, since ROS managers are responsible for broad aspects of business activity, they should be more prone to seek out information than is the manager responsible for a narrow field of activity who can get along satisfactorily with only limited information.

I feel reasonably certain that under the proposed system the most effective means for communicating objectives and plans down through the management levels is by informal, arm's-length verbal contact. Formal written statements and meetings will have value as supplemental communication media, but if vertical management pyramiding does not exceed a few levels, face-to-face communication should do the job. After all, the men reporting to the senior manager are busy people. Interferences with their work are aggravating and time consuming. Extensive meetings and formal discussions can become intolerable. As managers are frequently away from the plant on business trips, formal gatherings are often postponed to accommodate absent managers, and information disseminated loses its timeliness and impact. The formality of large and frequent meetings discourages discussion of important details of planning and operations. In addition, there are less personal ties between managers and the senior manager.

Accordingly, it seems to me that the senior manager might well decide that the most effective communication ties with his managers can be achieved if he—

- Directs that all ROS managers attend quarterly meetings.
- Makes the meeting time sacred.
- Uses the meetings for broad-brush treatment of objectives and plans, and gives managers the general direction for achievement of goals.
- Assigns the responsibility for communication transmission ties to ROS managers (the networks created should be tested through a trial period).
- Directs a small management group in ROS planning to take over the evaluation, modification, and installation of better communication networks as part of their responsibilities.
- Holds informal meetings with small groups of lower-level managers for the purpose of discussing objectives and problems on as extensive a "demand" basis as is practicable.

CONCLUSION

To recapitulate, ROS is an organizational scheme for integrating the company's long-range planning activities with operations so that each activity reinforces the other. Managers down through a certain level move back and fourth between operations and long-range planning in a cyclical rotation. Each manager continues with responsibilities commensurate with his position in the firm. Rotation is based on product cycles, changes in methods or processes, arbitrary calendar events, or any period significant to the conduct of company business.

Men at lower management levels who participate in long-range planning activities are responsible to the senior planning manager, while those responsible for operations are directed by a senior operations manager. Managers performing planning are not at the time responsible for operations, and managers in operations are not concurrently responsible for planning.

ROS is a means to use to the fullest advantage the capabilities and capacities of managers all down the line. They are accountable for contributing to the long-term master plan and for executing their segment of the plan. The ROS system is oriented to a philosophy of change. It provides a foundation for the development of dynamic attitudes that will contribute to the firm's survival over the long run.

The ROS system is also a means of tapping the large reservoir of experience of men at the lower management level to effect better working arrangements in the conduct of the firm's business. This in turn should help to provide top management with broader flexibility in its efforts to utilize new methods and processes and to introduce new products and services.

IV

STEPS IN MAKING A PLAN

If you have built castles in the air, your work need not be lost; that is where they should be. Now put the foundations under them.

—Henry David Thoreau

Be not the first by whom the new are tried, Nor yet the last to lay the old aside.

—Alexander Pope

22

Introduction

In this section we concern ourselves with steps, methods, techniques, and procedures for making effective plans. The section is divided into two parts: general guides and procedures; and quantitative techniques. The latter part reflects the influence of operations researchers, data processing experts, and management "scientists." The quantitative analyses included here are, of course, only a small sampling of the selections available, and only a suggestion of the possible uses of mathematical programing, probability, models, computers, and other methods.

It is sometimes said that executives rush too fast into the mechanics of plan-making without first creating the proper "climate" for it in the organization. ("Climate" usually refers to human relations, leadership quality, loyalty to the company, etc.) There is doubtless much truth in this observation. However, at the same time it should be remembered that a good plan, and hence any method that helps with formulating a good plan, contributes *itself* to the kind of climate in which it can survive and prosper. This is because such a plan provides an organized body of knowledge about where a company is going, how, and when. Unless the administrative situation is quite poor, and there is no support at all from chief executives, the plan will be talked about. When managers admit its existence, and especially when they begin to depend on it in any way, its goals and steps become one of the many influences on executive behavior. In time, they may well assume a priority over personal power and advantage.

Such an event has important implications. It means that the power of an executive does not depend alone on his ability to sell himself, to manipulate others to his point of view, to see a temporary advantage. He and all other managers are committed to a plan of action or criteria for action. His ability to understand, interpret, and act within this framework becomes an important factor in his influence.

No longer, then, must men at the middle and lower management levels feel that direction from the top is subject to the momentary tides and currents of "politics." Politics there will be as always, but the plan exerts a powerful force in favor of *predictability*. With supervisors down the line having the feeling that "we know where we're going" (as opposed to just "we're going somewhere"), attempts to persuade necessarily are made more in the context of established long-term thinking.

If, for instance, a good deal of research, development, and planning has gone into Product X, the chances are better that an impulsive switch in marketing emphasis will not undermine the chances for Product X to succeed when the time comes for advertising, promotion, and distribution. If a new head takes over in the marketing department, or a new supersalesman becomes a power in shaping policy, he may personally have many reservations about Product X, but the plan has him committed to it. He *may* succeed in switching the strategy around, but it will be harder to do than if there were no formal set of aims and assumptions to work around.

To take another example, one large oil company I know of has very carefully spelled out criteria for corporate activities. Program managers have great leeway in the choice of new investments *providing* that the outlays can earn a certain return on investment. There is little chance in this company that top-management "politics," a sudden shift in key personnel, or some other such factor can suddenly change the ground rules and start the pouring of company funds into a project that does not meet the minimum return standards that others have had to meet. Research men, accountants, salesmen, staff specialists, and others down the line can pretty well count on this. On this score, at least, there is comparatively little room for cynicism and disillusion.

Such an atmosphere is the very one that long-range planning needs most for survival. Once company personnel can be made to feel that there will be consistency and continuity in the firm's programs—and the long-range program itself, as indicated, is an instrument for accomplishing this—then the way is made easier for those who *would* invest time and money in planning. Hence, efforts to improve the mechanics of planning are not entirely separate from efforts to create the right climate for planning. There is a circularity of effect rather than progress in independent stages.

CONTRIBUTORS TO THIS SECTION

Bruce Payne is president of Bruce Payne & Associates, Incorporated. He is a former president of the Society for Advancement of Management, and also a former president of the Harvard Business School Association.

L. Eugene Root is group vice-president of Lockheed Aircraft Corporation and president of Lockheed's Missiles and Space Company.

George A. Steiner is listed in the Introduction to Part I.

Clarence A. Danielson is with Archer-Daniels-Midland Company as controller. He has been with the company since 1948. He was formerly controller at Bell Oil and Refinery Company.

Stewart Thompson is listed in the Introduction to Part II.

Mark W. Cresap, Jr., was chairman of the Executive Committee and president of Westinghouse Electric Corporation at the time of his death in 1963. He was formerly with the consulting firm of Cresap, McCormick and Paget, of which he was cofounder.

Maurice E. Waring is division accountant with Independent Metal Products, a division of Fruehauf Trailer Company in Omaha.

Paul W. Demarest is with Independent Metal Products as divisional controller.

James Dowd is a principal associate with Cresap, McCormick and Paget. From 1945 to 1949 he served with Air Reduction Company, Incorporated in various staff capacities.

Leo A. Rapoport is with Esso Research & Engineering Company as a research associate.

William P. Drews is also a research associate at Esso. He and Rapoport have been active for a number of years in developing mathematical programing and operations research studies for Jersey Standard's operations.

E. Leonard Arnoff wrote his article as associate professor and assistant director of the Operations Research Group at Case Institute of Technology.

William J. Platt is director of the Economic Development Division of Stanford Research Institute.

N. Robert Maines was formerly also at Stanford Research Institute. He is now manager of long-range planning for J. C. Penney Company, Incorporated.

23

Steps in Long-Range Planning[1]

Bruce Payne

Long-range planning is the one really new technique left to management that can give a company a major competitive advantage. Looking back, we have seen how industrial engineering, market research, control, and other techniques have given progressive companies an important edge over competitors. Looking ahead, I see long-range planning as another concept that will spell the difference between success and mediocrity in business.

One of the advantages of the new technique is that it enables a company to go farther than it would otherwise dare to in taking advantage of its strengths. Management can safely extend itself more, get more mileage out of its assets, flex its muscles more. There is less holding back because of needless fears about how far and how fast the firm can go. We live in an expanding economy. Some companies need to expand at unprecedented rates just to stay in competition. Long-term planning, properly conceived, answers the question, "How fast should we grow?" It points up the obstacles to growth and prepares management to overcome them.

Among successful companies such planning is often supervised only in a broad, general way by the chief executive, even though it is one of his main responsibilities. This is natural, for many presidents are

[1] From *Harvard Business Review,* March–April 1957, pp. 95–106. Used by permission.

temperamentally unsuited to the kind of work that is involved. They are too impatient to guide the plodding, thorough fact-finding which is necessary. But they do, of course, make the key decisions affecting the organization, scope, methods, and aims of planning. Here are some of the questions and propositions facing these chief executives which I shall discuss in the pages to follow:

What is a true long-term plan? Here we will need to look at some concrete examples of the work of successful companies.

How should the work be set up? The essential proposition here is that the development of a five- or ten-year plan is not an "ivory tower" job for one or two gifted individualists to do, but a very practical, factual, down-to-earth assignment which makes a team approach absolutely necessary.

How should the planning team go about setting objectives? A new method, *marketing variables analysis,* has proved extremely valuable in making projections. However, the really basic problems are to decide what kinds of products, selling, expansion, and organization the firm should have, and to keep company activities in balance during a period of expansion.

What about the timing of a company's future moves? Several lessons from experience will be discussed in regard to the scheduling of early and later steps in the plan of action.

How should modifications in the plan be handled? One of the most important concepts is that the planning team should *expect* gyrations in the market. The possibility of future reverses makes a long-term program more important, not less important.

How can top executives tell whether or not a plan submitted for their approval is a good one? I shall outline six criteria which have been found especially helpful.

TRUE PLANNING

Much of the work that goes on under the name of "long-range planning" today does not deserve the title at all. True long-range planning is still rare, and it involves a unique set of activities. Let us look at the kinds of things executives do when they work out a really effective program.

Activities Involved

Such executives are likely to begin with present products, appraising future sales potentials and the hurdles to be taken. Next they may look at possible future products and ideas for service; in so doing, they consider the direction of future growth. Then they analyze company strengths and weaknesses—manpower, finance, production know-how, marketing organization, and the rest. They go on to ask: What are our potentials? What is the best we can do?

Next—and this should be done only at the top-management level—they try to pull together all the information developed in the foregoing inquiries and look at it as a whole. They try to summarize the different possibilities for growth by merger, research, better marketing, and so forth, with special attention to *return on investment.* They decide to promote one line harder, cut down on another; to consolidate the company's position or push hard to expand; to turn to the merger route or grow from within. They look at every facet of the business for five, ten, or fifteen years ahead—whatever length of time is necessary.

Two Models

What they end up with is a plan that tells management (1) *what* it is going to do, (2) *how* it is going to proceed, and (3) *when* it will take action—developed in broad terms first, then in specific steps to be accomplished during each month of each year. As illustrations of what such a plan looks like on paper, I have taken the summary overall plan of Company A and a portion of one year's detailed program of Company B. (Other disguises have also been used to protect the identity of the concerns involved.) Each case represents an actual, successful experience with long-term planning:

Company A. This company is a fairly autonomous subsidiary of a large eastern manufacturer. Its product is hardware, some lines being marketed to retailers and others to industrial buyers. Prior to 1951, the company had been losing ground steadily to competitors and was showing a poor return on investment.

Exhibit 1 sets forth the plan. Drawn up for the president in 1951, it incorporated a series of decisions reached after analyzing the company's problems and potentials. One of the most important conclusions was that the retail and industrial businesses of the company had become so different that they could not now be run efficiently by one management group. This conclusion was the basis of many of the moves planned for 1952, 1953, and 1954.

The exhibit shows the steadily rising sales goals for each of the two

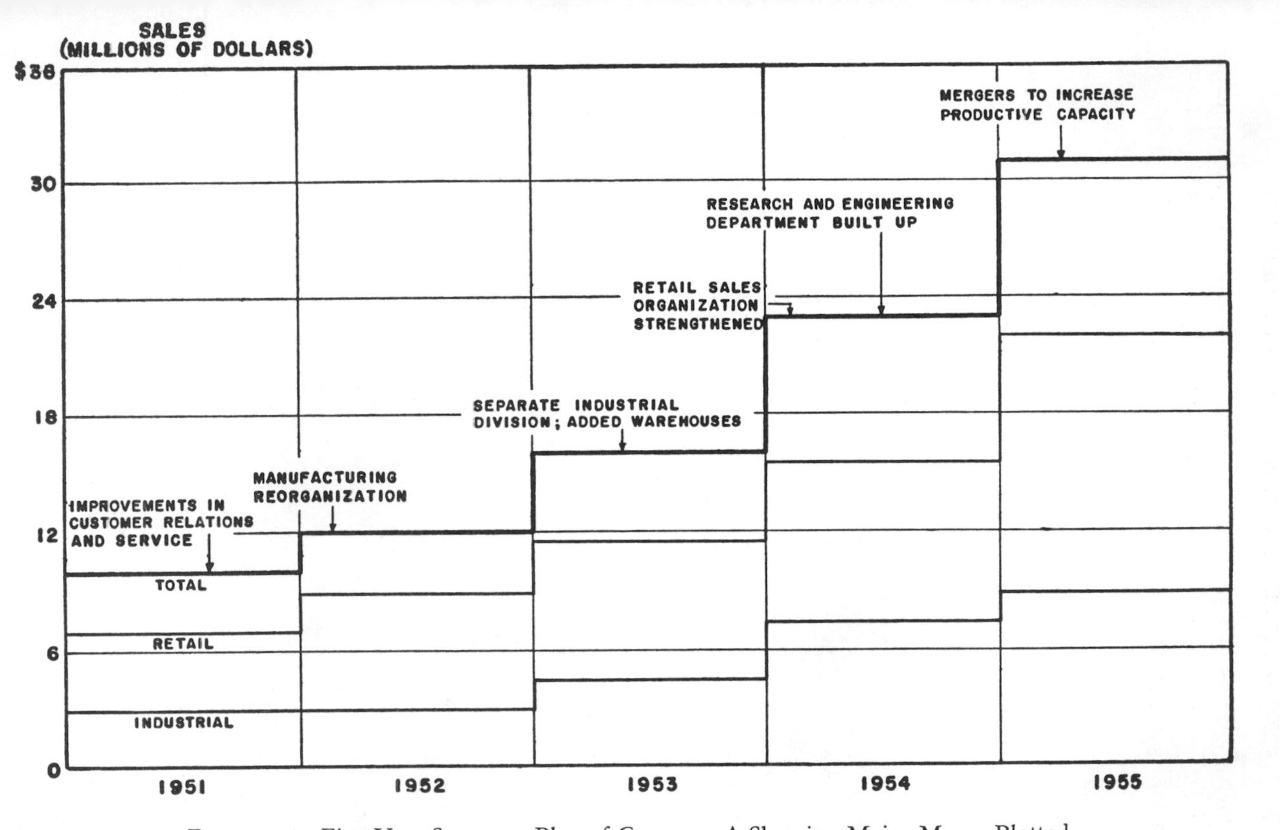

EXHIBIT 1. Five-Year Summary Plan of Company A Showing Major Moves Plotted Against Sales

product lines, the major steps to be taken, and the timing of these steps. Each part of the plan was laid out in detail in separate programs not shown.

Here I should emphasize that no five- or ten-year plan runs as such for more than a year. With the passage of each year, another year must be added to the plan, with all recent changes taken into account. In other words, in 1952, the Company A management would have extended its plan to cover 1957, and the continuing impact of the Korean War might very well have changed its thinking about the immediate future.

Company B. This company manufactures home appliances in the Midwest. Several different lines are produced, each priced for a different consumer market. Long-range planning was started in 1952 as a result of a disagreement among senior executives over policy and of growing concern about the firm's falling profit margins.

Exhibit 2 reproduces part of the detailed program for the first of several years covered by the over-all plan (not shown), which called for a large increase in volume and profits. The executives agreed that this growth was possible if certain steps were taken to reduce costs, merchandise more aggressively, and meet other needs. The exhibit reproduces the program for only five management functions, which are enough for illustration; but similar plans were made for other company areas. The three major product lines are designated as X, Y, and Z; the latter two came in for the most attention since they were believed to have the largest unrealized sales potentials.

Just because a plan is on paper does not mean, of course, that it is a good one, although a written statement gives the program definiteness and makes it harder for management to ignore. Rather, the crucial questions are whether the goals are sound; whether the moves and timing are realistic; and, perhaps of first importance, whether management is ready to implement the plan. Let us examine these questions carefully.

TEAM APPROACH

A concept of planning such as the one described means that the program cannot be the brain child of any one man, even a genius. In the first place, he cannot possibly know enough or be objective enough. In the second place, other executives will inevitably react with some such comment as, "What ax is he grinding now?"

EXHIBIT 2

PORTIONS OF DETAILED FIRST-YEAR PLAN OF COMPANY B

Time	Marketing Organization	Sales Effort	Advertising	New Products and Styles	Production Control
November 1952	Formulate sales organization plan, sales policies, pricing plan, forecasting program.		Plan catalogues, national advertising, and cooperative advertising.		Construct factory-fixed budget for 1953; make sure historical cost system is accurate and accepted by all personnel.
December 1952	Complete new sales plans.		Consult with advertising agency.	Select industrial designers.	Determine IBM requirements; manually schedule production of products X, Y, and Z.
January 1953		Outline new policies and programs to personnel.	Analyze media for X, Y, and Z product lines.		Begin work on over-all production control plan; as departments go on new standards, construct variable budgets for each department.
February 1953	Select assistant sales manager; select Southern, Southwestern, and Canadian sales directors.		Select media; complete cooperative program.	Consult with designers on Y and Z product lines.	Complete production control plan; begin experimental run of plan.
March 1953	Begin recruiting new salesmen.	Introduce new selling procedures; lay out routes.		Mock-up construction Z product line.	Hire production control and scheduling supervisor.
April 1953		Continue sales training with films, role-playing, etc.	Begin planning outdoor advertising campaign; announce cooperative advertising program; distribute catalogues and dealer aids.	Mock-up construction Y product line.	
May 1953		Start new salesmen.	Begin national advertising program.		
June 1953			Begin regional advertising Y and Z product lines.	Market tests for all new Z product line styles.	Review all production schedules; prepare progress reports and continue expediting.
July 1953	Recruit new salesmen for South and Southwest.	Assess new sales plan at sales meeting; hold meetings with new dealers.		Market tests for all new Y product line styles.	Hire industrial engineering assistant.
August 1953					Meetings on quality control and inspection standards.
September 1953			Outdoor advertising campaign Chicago, Detroit, Milwaukee, and other cities.	Show selected new Z product line styles at fall trade shows.	Inventory modernization program to reduce inprocess inventories.
October 1953	Appoint new Medwest district managers.	Special consultations and meetings with managers of Y and Z product lines.		Show selected new Y product line styles at trade shows and conventions.	Fixed and variable budgets for 1954 with tighter operating budgets.

Often the burden of long-range planning has been carried by a controller or some financial executive. But neither officer has the expert knowledge of marketing or production required to develop a plan in which marketing or production executives will have real confidence. This was the case not too long ago in one of the country's larger corporations:

The president gave the job to an extremely able executive in the financial department. Although the executive went to the production and sales managers for his facts, the plan was primarily an individualistic one. He did not work with those men every day; and after his fact-finding interviews he did not keep in touch with them out of habit. Also, as frequently happens, the long-range planning job was just a springboard for him—a temporary proposition. Nobody was surprised when he was promoted to a higher management position. Nobody should have been overly surprised, either, when his work was quietly filed away.

The trouble with handing the task of planning to such a man is not just that he is likely to have difficulty gaining the confidence of his associates. More important, he cannot "crank into" the plan he draws up any real depth of experience and know-how. The ideas will seem biased or impractical to others, even if they like him. A frequent comment is: "The facts are hazy." When this is the situation, the management team as a whole tends to be skeptical of the program.

Here, in a nutshell, is one of the main causes of failure in long-range planning today. Controller, sales executive, economist, production manager—it makes no difference. No one man can carry the burden alone of getting the broad factual background "in depth" (particularly the company's competitive strengths and weaknesses) which will make other managers willing to *commit themselves* to what is written out on paper.

Specifications

Reviewing successes and failures in setting up the job of long-term planning, it appears to me that three important lessons have been learned:

1. The work should be directed by someone who is in more or less *continuous* contact with the different managers concerned, so that the results reflect a team approach. (And if a consulting firm is called in, it should be one which can make available a parallel *team* of specialists as needed.) In

this sense, the planning head must have the same continuing relationship with all top executives as the president has.

Incidentally, there seems to be an illusion that planning can be done by getting a bunch of executives together and "going off into the hills" for a couple of days, away from telephones and other interruptions. This is useful for "brain-storming" purposes, but it is no way to get the factual work done—the groundwork which is the basis of a good plan.

2. A long-range plan is so confidential—its contents may be worth many hundreds of thousands of dollars to competitors, and this is only a partial measure of the cost—that it is risky to bring anybody into the final stages of it who might resign and join a competitor. The man in charge should therefore be a trusted officer of the firm. Equally important, he should be a man who has *shown ability to take normal calculated business risks.* Often the "elder statesman" does not qualify, therefore, although he may be ideal in other respects.

3. The planning head needs a particular kind of temperament. He should be one who is not afraid to say that this is right and that is wrong. Something of a "let the chips fall where they may" attitude is ideal—an indifference to the personal implications of fact-finding and analyzing in the most objective way possible.

If the planner tackles his work in the way described, he may run into resistance from other executives when he is drawing up the plan; but, once it is down on paper, much of this resistance usually disappears. And he has one real advantage. There is a kind of impersonalness about long-range planning which, when combined with objective, realistic preparation of a program, makes it less controversial. It does not center around individuals as much as short-range planning does, simply because it is hard to say who will be sales manager or manufacturing vice-president four or five years hence.

These comments on the question of organization are far from comprehensive and have dealt primarily with the problem of getting facts. For other aspects of this question readers should refer to H. Edward Wrapp's article, "Organization for Long-Range Planning."[2]

SETTING GOALS

The problem of setting goals is one of the most fascinating and fundamental ones in long-range planning. And it is not easy. Goals should be not hopes but realistic, attainable objectives. Moreover, set-

[2] Chap. 15, above.

ting goals is far more complex than forecasting. You can get a pretty good forecast, if you manufacture for a few large customers, by asking them what their needs will be; or if you sell color television, by doing a good market research study; or if you make building supplies, by having a good economic analysis made. But much more than this is involved in setting targets in forward planning.

What Should We Be?

Management's first step in setting goals is to answer the question: What kind of business should we be in? (By "kind of business" I mean type of product sold, type of selling, kind of expansion needed, and so forth.) Getting executives to think inquiringly about this question is probably as challenging a job as any the president and planning heads have. To illustrate the possibilities:

A midwestern firm has always specialized in the manufacture of the founder's basic invention. It has always conceived of its business as doing the best it could with that one product. Changing conditions now force it to consider merging with another company making a related but quite different product. By merging it can make more money—but management will have to divide its attention among several different lines of manufacture. Does its strength lie in manufacturing one kind of product—or what? Will its business security be enhanced by merger? Is a larger return on its investment a true measure of its business success?

A large eastern manufacturer of a staple product finds that it cannot expand and keep its share of the fast-growing national market with the simple management organization it has traditionally had. To keep its market share, it must completely reorganize its sales organization, production system, and management assignments. Does management conceive of the company as a well-known national producer, or is its business to operate its present plan as profitably as possible?

The management of a prosperous lumberyard business in the West anticipates that in a couple of years the demand for housing, the main prop in its market, will fall off for a period. Should it sell its lumberyards and go into the booming prefabrication business, or should it get into commercial construction?

A materials producer, undertaking for the first time to make an end product, begins to worry about the implications of moving into a market where the company will be competing with some of its present customers. Will they look at the firm as a less desirable source of supply and turn to some other supplier? Should the company back out of the retail market as soon as possible?

How can questions such as the foregoing be answered by anyone except top management itself? No one else can tell management what kind of business it should be in because so much depends on what management *wants* to achieve. At the same time, it is important to realize that the question cannot be answered realistically and constructively just by sitting back and reflecting, at however high a level in the organization. Down-to-earth analysis is called for; and the most important things to study, as I shall indicate later, are: (1) the key influences in the growth of the industry and (2) the strengths and weaknesses of the company as compared to those of its present or potential competitors.

What Rate of Growth?

One of the most decisive factors to consider in making goals realistic is the desirable rate of expansion. As every executive knows, all companies have their limitations. In the early stages of a new industry, these limiting factors are most likely to be internal. But as competitors come into the market and the company loses its quasimonopolistic position, the major limiting factors become external. Often the external limitations become so severe after a time that the firm must get a new product or process.

Of the different factors to watch in planning the growth rate, personnel is certainly as important as any. For instance, one nationally famous concern purposely holds back the rate of launching new products so that volume will increase no more than a certain percentage every year, because the board feels that the executive organization simply cannot take a faster rate of expansion.

Finance as a growth factor is probably overemphasized by businessmen. The tendency in long-range planning has been to focus attention on capital expenditures, other cash requirements, profits, working capital, and similar considerations.[3] Once a comprehensive plan is completed, however, finance is likely to appear as a relatively small and obvious part of the program.

If anything, marketing is the key to a long-term plan. But even this statement must be qualified. The program of Company A, a good case in point, took into account marketing, manufacturing, organization, and finance. Although marketing underlay and formed the basis

[3] See, for example, "Industry Plans for the Future," *Conference Board Business Record,* August 1952, p. 324; and Wrapp, *op. cit.*

for the other three, each was planned for and integrated into a course of action that would provide a step-by-step attainment of objectives. The planners realized that it was of the greatest importance to keep each basic activity in phase with all the others, and to guard against opportunistic moves which might endanger other parts of the organization.

What I am arguing for, in other words, is a concept of *balanced* expansion. It is tempting to consider one problem or area the "key" to the speed of growth. Such a temptation should be guarded against. It may be harder and more painstaking to plan the rate of growth so that the different company activities are continually reinforcing each other, but it is certainly the most successful approach.

Making Projections

Now I wish to outline a method of projecting growth and volume which has proved helpful in a number of situations where long-range planning has been done. This method should *not* be confused with forecasting. Forecasting is a part of it, but only a small part.

The unique value of this method, which I call *marketing variables analysis,* is that it begins with the market and ties sales objectives to the steps in finance, production, and so forth that are necessary to accomplish them. In other words, planners using the approach come up not only with sound, realistic targets but also with the elements of a plan of action. (Incidentally, the basic procedures can be used in setting production goals too, if desired.)

In principle this method is similar to an approach used by chemical engineers to analyze the effect of change on a system. When a system has a series of known inputs, the engineer can postulate on paper what will happen if one input is changed and the others are held constant; with this data he can design changes in the system or diagnose trouble where it has occurred if the output or performance varies by a certain amount from standard.

Similarly, in setting marketing objectives, the planners agree that sales volume is a function, let us say, of brand management, territorial sales, dealer effectiveness, advertising, promotion, and sales effort. Next they ask how much the management of these functions could improve in, say, two years if certain changes in staff, policy, and budget are made. Then they ask what will happen to sales in two years if performance is improved in *one* of these functions (e.g., a 30 per cent increase in advertising effectiveness) but not in any of the others. They record this change, ask the same question about each of the other functions, and on the basis of all of the changes estimate a realistic over-all goal in sales volume.

Each projection should be made by two or three men, not one, in order to reduce the margin of error. Also, the projections should be made first for the functions which can be analyzed in the most factual way, and last for the functions where the most assumptions and guesswork are involved.

In making these last estimates, the planning team should adjust the *assumptions* used in the light of the first few estimates. For example, it might be tempting to assume a highly elastic demand for a product and estimate that a very great increase in volume would result from heavier promotion and advertising. This temptation might be resisted if it had earlier been predicted that great improvements in brand management and sales territorial work would produce only moderate sales increases. Taking the earlier, more factual estimates into account means that errors in them may be compounded, of course; but this risk is more than offset by the value of these estimates in "anchoring" the assumptions used in the later, more speculative predictions.

Example of Analysis

Let us take a hypothetical example which, although oversimplified, is in principle similar to other cases where marketing variables analysis has been applied:

Projections made. Let us suppose that Company C manufactures small boats in twelve branded models priced from $350 to $1,000. The main plants are located in Wisconsin, and the sales territories include the Great Lakes and the inland lake areas of Wisconsin; Minnesota; Michigan; Illinois; Ohio; and Ontario.

Beginning with a sales territory analysis (fairly good factual estimates can be made here), the planning team figures for each territory the percentage of actual sales to potential sales (computed on the basis of population, income, competitors' sales, etc.) of the lower-priced models. They find that the highest percentage is in the northwest Michigan territory—65 per cent of the total potential.

Some unusually favorable circumstances are at work here, however, and so 65 per cent is not considered a good target for other territories. The planners agree that a more realistic target would be the 50 per cent figure for the Green Bay territory. If all territories could reach or surpass this target, the planners estimate, actual sales of the lower-priced models would increase 35 per cent. A similar analysis for the higher-priced models indicates that their sales can increase 45 per cent and that *total sales volume of all models could reasonably be expected to increase 40 per cent with improved territorial management alone.*

Next, the planners predict how much sales can be increased with better brand management, if no changes in other phases of the marketing effort are made. They choose this function because here again a good deal of reliable factual evidence is available. They examine the total sales of each of the leading brands as a percentage of total potential sales. They ask: Do these sales figures look right? What should they be? Are we doing a good enough job on the best-selling brand to use it as a goal for the others? They conclude that *with better brand management total dollar sales volume could be increased 35 per cent.*

The planners go on to make similar analyses for all other functions, estimating what would happen if the number of dealers in the different territories were increased, advertising stepped up, the selling effort improved, and so forth. Estimates for these latter functions vary from 10 per cent to 80 per cent, with greater margins of error being allowed for because more unknowns and intangibles are involved.

Plan of action. Many of these projections assume that certain steps are taken in other areas of the company as well as in marketing. For instance, an increase in the number of dealers and better average sales performance from them may require establishment of a more efficient inventory system to cut down backlogs; improved brand management may call for better quality control, because customer dissatisfaction with quality has been a factor in the lagging sales of certain brands; and an increase in total units sold may mean that funds must be raised for new plant and equipment.

In addition, the projections help in scheduling activities because the different sales-increase estimates are made for specific units of time, i.e., two-year periods.

Growth line. Theoretically, management could concentrate on improving one function at a time, in which case estimating total sales goals in the future would be easy. Actually, of course, this will not be the case; progress in all the areas will be going on concurrently, and management will be dividing its attention and resources among all of them. A judgment will have to be made, therefore, as to what is a reasonable five-year sales goal. When this is done, the results of the analysis can be summarized in some such form as Exhibit 3.

On the vertical line above 1959 (two years hence) the planning team plots the five independent estimates of the increases in sales volume pos-

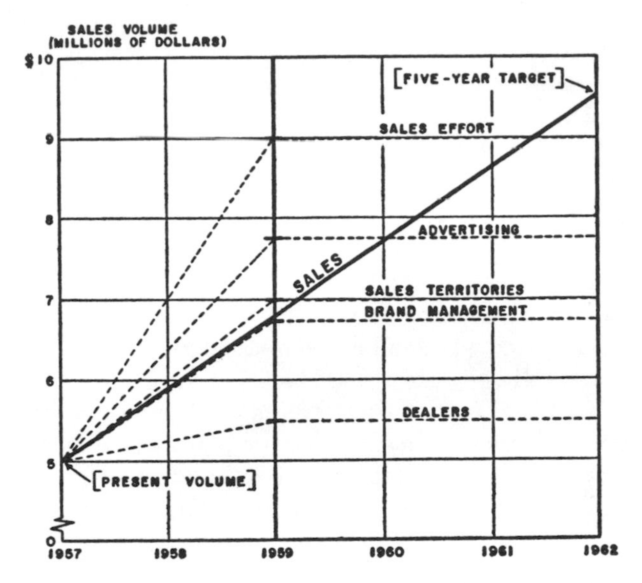

EXHIBIT 3. Five-Year Sales Growth of Company C

sible. Horizontal lines are drawn through these points to indicate the continuing benefit of improvement in the function.

The diagonal line begins with current sales and represents a conservative estimate of the growth of volume over the five-year period. Actually, of course, the growth will probably not be linear, but the line serves as a rough estimate. In drawing it, the targets for territorial sales and for brand management, which were computed with a minimum of guesswork and checked out closely, are especially important. However, the line is based mainly on management judgment, using the five estimates only as bench marks. Usually, management will be inclined to make its five-year goal conservative. The goal of $9 million in Exhibit 3 is a very conservative one in the light of the two-year estimates.

NOTES ON APPLICATION

The sales goal obtained by the method described is not necessarily the sales goal which will appear in the master plan for the company as a whole. For instance, it may develop that too much expenditure on new plant and equipment is called for in view of the company's limited financial resources, with the result that the sales goal will have to be lowered. (Such revisions would necessarily have to be downward, because the sales goals represent the *maximum* possible growth of the company.)

The number and kinds of projections made will, of course, vary from company to company; it is up to the planners to pick out the pertinent factors in the market. For instance, public relations would be a major factor in some companies' sales, although not for Company C. Also, the facts and forecasts used in making the projections will vary. In Company C's situation, obsolescence (of small boats in use) would be an unimportant factor; but in the machine tool industry it would be a very important one indeed, and the annual obsolescence data collected and published by the industry each year would be studied carefully.

Finally, it should be noted that the projections for each function depend not only on its present efficiency but also on the company's position in the market. To illustrate, a greater effort in advertising and promotion ought to result in a fairly substantial increase in sales in the case of Company C if it has only 15 per cent or so of the total market; but a similar increase in the advertising effort of a competitor with a larger share of the market would be expected to produce a smaller increase in volume because sales resistance would develop more sharply. In this respect a company like E. I. du Pont de Nemours & Company, for example, which is often selling in new markets, enjoys an advantage over companies like Ford Motor Company and General Motors Corporation, which have large shares of long-established markets.

PROBLEM OF TIMING

The problem of timing a company's major moves is especially intriguing to the top two or three executives working on a long-range plan. Certainly no other aspect of the work calls more for native good judgment, experience, intuition, and imagination.

If any one lesson stands out in practical experience with forward planning, it is that the senior planners must *set a date* for the completion of projects scheduled or else they will not get done. A case in point is that of a Midwestern manufacturer of industrial equipment:

The executives visualized a $36 million operation for their company some day, and they had a pretty good idea of where the added volume would come from and of some of the steps that would be necessary to attain it. But whether that volume should be attained in five years, seven years, or ten years was a question they had not decided. Their sales objective was, therefore, meaningless. Until they put that $36 million down with a date on it, they could not think of it in terms of the organizational, production, financial, promotional, and other steps that were essential if their planning was to become *real.*

In other words, it is not enough to set objectives, however carefully thought out, and say, "That's our goal." There must be a timetable.

Flexible Timetable

It is a good idea to keep the timetable flexible, especially where financing is an important factor. Planners must often make a very careful forecast of the funds that will be required to support the major moves, and estimate the extent to which retained profits and depreciation reserves can provide these funds. In such cases flexibility becomes a much-needed safeguard against the forecasted results being obtained either ahead of or behind schedule. The fewer the commitments to a precise timetable in production, marketing, and organization, therefore, the better.

How much flexibility is needed? This can be judged in the light of the alternative courses of action planned to meet possible company reverses or dips in sales (to be discussed in a later section). But the planning group may find it more practical to switch to substitute plans (in case of certain contingencies, such as war, for example) than to try to build a great deal of flexibility into the basic plan itself.

Sometimes it is wise to make timing conditional upon certain other things happening, with a clear understanding that any dates put down are tentative only. For example, management may have, as at least one large corporation has, a concept of what is an ideal economic unit—a figure of so many thousand people per plant, arrived at on the basis of such factors as management effectiveness, recreational facilities needed, schools, and past operating experience. It will not commit itself to building a new plant until it has to, but it will state in the plan that the company *will* build when sales volume gets to a certain point, and estimate as well as possible when that time will be.

Quick Versus Slow Start

The timing of the first major moves is strictly dependent on the degree to which the company house is in order. To put long-range planning in high gear on top of unsolved current problems is obviously foolish. In Company A's case, for instance (Exhibit 1), major moves to increase sales were postponed because the company was saddled with a bad delivery problem; until that was straightened out and better customer liaison established, it would have been premature to launch into large-scale promotion, salesmen recruitment, and so forth.

Another factor that may make a slow start advisable is overhead; it may need to be either cut or *increased* before the organization is ready to take on new responsibilities.

The time needed to prepare the organization for increases in volume or for a change-over to a different type of production can be used often to very great advantage, particularly in this day of increasingly complex marketing strategy. For example, take the problem of a materials producer who wants to promote a product utilizing a new material he has developed:

> If he begins by trying to sell to the manufacturers who would normally manufacture and sell the new product to retailers (or use it in other products they sell), he may run into considerable resistance. These manufacturers tend to favor the products they are already set up to produce, and if they hesitate to adopt the new idea, reports discrediting it have an opportunity to circulate. But if the product can first be publicized quickly and effectively to the ultimate consumer, the materials producer can go on and in a short time build up pressure on manufacturers to buy his idea. The consumer is *their* market.[4]

In cases of this kind where an indirect approach, while taking more time at the start, succeeds in creating sales faster in the end, the strategy can be doubly helpful by allowing the manufacturing organization extra time to straighten out any problems it has. The possible value of delaying the sales "burst" is therefore well worth looking into.

In terms of the *number* of steps planned in the annual schedules, the foregoing may mean considerably more activity in the fourth or

[4] For a fuller discussion of this problem, see E. Raymond Corey, *The Development of Markets for New Products* (Boston, Harvard Business School, 1956), p. 81.

fifth years of a five-year plan than in the early years. To refer to Company A again:

> During the first three years a lot of hard work was planned in developing present customers of the firm. On paper this groundwork would not have looked particularly impressive. But a detailed plan for the fourth year, when the new business was to start coming in, would have shown new salesmen and supervisors going out on new routes, catalogues being issued to acquaint new customers with the business, preparations for mergers being made, plant space added, research additions, and many other activities coinciding with a marked rise in volume. It took several years, in other words, before forward planning could really "look good" on paper.

MAKING A PLAN WORK

The biggest danger of long-range planning, according to many men who have had experience with it, is atrophy. Company managers must understand the *why* of the steps and timing planned, or they will give up the plan when they are under pressure. Earlier in this article I outlined a special method of setting objectives. It is a good case in point. It works beautifully *if* executives keep in mind how the objectives were set. And that means some pretty strong leadership at the top. One of the best planners I know put it this way:

> Modifications will be necessary even in the best plan. But from time to time managers down the line will *think* that more changes should be made than really are needed. The chief executive needs to be the kind who can say, "Al, that's a good idea, but it isn't our policy."

Usually there are five or ten key decisions that lead to the final conclusions in a plan about market share, volume, and so forth. In one company these conclusions may be drawn from such things as projections of population increase and trends in consumer use; in another, from such things as the probability of new technological applications of a product and projections of the needs of a few large industrial buyers. Whatever these conclusions are, the top planners must "watch them like a hawk," reviewing them carefully from year to year and keeping them before the men who run the company.

I think that one of the most important concepts of forward planning is that it does *not* assume there will be ideal business conditions or smooth sailing. Unexpected things will happen—gyrations in the market or the loss of a key man—but they in no way affect the practicality of planning. As a matter of fact, one of the values of a good long-term program is that it helps to keep executives from panicking when reverses happen or dips occur. Let me illustrate the kind of top-management perspective that often spells the difference between success and failure:

A Southwestern manufacturer of plumbing equipment had a plan predicated on a series of rising sales levels. One year house construction slowed unexpectedly, and naturally the company's sales fell off. The pressure was on to abandon the plan. But the planners checked their original assumptions and projections and found that the same number of homes still had to be built as first thought. So top management stuck with the plan—and before too long a 22 per cent spurt in sales occurred which the company was ready to take advantage of, thanks to its having gone on with the steps in the program. But competitors, plugging along on a day-to-day basis, were caught unprepared by the rise in demand.

The same sort of crisis confronted a large firm manufacturing appliances when sales took a serious slump. Reviewing the economics of demand, it decided not to cut back, although one of its leading competitors did. Some months later sales shot up again. The company was ready for the increase while its competitor was not, and as a result it got back its No. 1 sales position.

Modifications

As a rough guess, I think that management more often finds it necessary to revise *timing,* when modification is necessary, than to change the steps or actions that were planned.

What often happens is something like this. The planners find that there is a lot of room for expansion, and in their five-year plan they map out steps to increase production, suppliers, dealers, and so forth. But the sales manager who was supposed to turn the reins over to a younger man delays doing so, with the result that nothing happens to sales despite the fast-rising levels drawn on paper. Obviously, in such a case, management needs to suspend (but not shelve) the plan. Once it can find a way to take care of that sales management problem, however, it can go back and use much of the thinking that went into the original plan, including not only the actions recommended but also some of the time relationships.

As those who have had experience with modifications realize, although the different steps in a plan are dependent upon each other in a great many ways, there are also many divisible parts. When a plan is laid out, one can usually predict right at the outset which parts, if any, will not have to be changed and which ones will most likely have to be revised because they are contingent on forecasts of supply or sales. For instance, product development and engineering schedules can be followed even though it is still far from certain when and in what plants the products should be produced. Again, the product restyling program of Company B (Exhibit 1) might have been followed with only minor changes even if major revisions had become necessary in other parts of the plan.

SIX CRITERIA

By way of conclusion, let us suppose that a true long-range plan is submitted to the president or board of directors. How can they tell whether or not the program—one along the lines of those shown in Exhibits 1 and 2, for instance—is a good one? In short, what are the earmarks of a good plan?

It seems to me that top management ought to keep in mind six criteria, which can best be stated in the form of questions:

1. *Has the planning team determined the key influences in the growth of the industry and evaluated the influence of each?* These influences vary from industry to industry. In the case of a hosiery or sugar company, sales potentials are obviously tied to per capita consumption, and management can project the market fairly accurately, barring any revolutionary changes. By contrast, in the case of the atomic energy industry, the key influences are likely to be research and technological developments. Most companies, however, have to take both types of influences into account. To illustrate:

> A manufacturer of an improved, more heat-resistant bearing may find that the key influences are not only the rising number of bearing users and projected expenditures on heavy machinery using bearings, but also developments in the use of faster machinery which would increase the incidence of bearings freezing.

2. *Have the strengths and weaknesses of the company been accurately evaluated?* This is without doubt one of the most important

questions in forward planning; an incorrect answer here has probably caused more failures than inadequate research on any other topic.

To add dimension to their appraisal, the planner should look at the strengths and weaknesses of *competitors* as well as of their own firm. Why has one rival been able to get a larger share of the market than others? Maybe its costs are not the lowest in the industry by a long shot, but that does not matter if selling effort is the key. The implications of this question for planning are tremendous:

A holding company's strengths may be money and large tax carrybacks; its weakness may be that most of its subsidiaries are in a declining industry. The question arises, then, whether it should not plan to buy and sell its way out of the industry.

A company with an excellent distributor organization might well plan to move into other industries where jobbers are important; but a firm with a weak distributor organization would not be in a position to make such a move.

In his article on "Conditions of Marketing Leadership,"[5] Arthur Felton cited the case of a large eastern manufacturer of a staple product considering the building of a large new plant fifteen hundred miles away, where the greatest *future* sales potentials were believed to exist. Here one of the company's strengths was an almost certain boom in national consumption of its product, while one of its weaknesses was that the center of the market was gradually moving westward, with all that meant for higher warehousing and freight costs if production continued to be centered in the East.

3. *Have the capacities of different company functions to support the plan been projected far enough ahead?* This is not a hard question in the case of, say, industrial relations, personnel, or advertising; if the main plan covers four or five years, that is as far ahead as these functions need to be carried. But the question can be a subtle one where financing and research are important factors. For instance:

I know of one company considering a large plant expansion program which wisely carried its *pro forma* balance sheets ahead fifteen years. If it had not, the planners would never have recommended the program which they did, because nine years were needed to reach the break-even point on the planned investment. The prospect of a very high return on investment after nine years was so good that the long look ahead was completely justified.

[5] *Harvard Business Review,* March–April 1956, p. 117.

4. *Is there a practical timetable?* It needs to be detailed for the forthcoming year (as in Exhibit 2) but progressively less detailed for later years. The timetable should not be rigid. Thus, if mergers are planned, it does not conflict with the principles of good long-range planning to make an opportune purchase a few years in advance of the time scheduled. It *is* inconsistent, however, to make such a move without considering the effects it may have on the rest of the plan by diverting limited financial or executive resources.

5. *Have alternatives been considered?* To put this in terms of a specific situation, did the planners of Company A decide to increase productive capacity after first looking at the make-or-buy question? Did they consider the possibilities of cooperative research with one of the institutes organized for that purpose before deciding to expand the company's research and development program as much as they did? And perhaps most important of all, how seriously did they explore, with top management, the question of what kind of business the company should be in?

6. *What provisions have been made for future reverses?* A number of companies have found it possible to include safeguards in their plans in case future expectations do not materialize. For example:

> One company's policy is to manufacture not more than 50 per cent of its requirements, so that if sales fall off unexpectedly, it can cut back purchases from suppliers rather than its own production.
>
> A large company has a reserve of products that have gone through the research-and-development stage but have not yet been put on the market. If sales fail to meet expectations, new products can be put on the market faster than planned.

The best built-in form of protection that a plan can have, however, is good planning—not only good execution of the program but also steps to keep the company effort in *balance.* In Company A's case, management could expect a measure of protection to come after the fourth year from the increasing research and development effort. Again, for a company dominated by engineering thinking, the best long-run protection may be to strengthen the marketing effort.

To the extent that the planners can anticipate future reverses against which there is no protection, management should have a pretty good idea of what it is going to do if these reverses occur. With such steps spelled out, operating managers will be in a better position to foresee in what direction the company will move when and if the reverses come. Also, they will tend to "think together" better when crises approach.

Profit Insurance

So much for the criteria of a good plan. In addition to any practical value they may have, I hope they serve to indicate the dynamic nature of long-range planning. Here is where it differs from certain other management functions which also deal with the future and are therefore sometimes confused with planning. While the aim of forecasting is to show what future trends will be, forward planning aims to *take advantage of them.* And while budgeting involves forecasts, coordination, and control of future management actions, planning goes into the what, how, and when of these actions—and for a longer period of time.

Long-range planning is certainly one of the most creative aspects of management, and it is easy to see why it gives management such a tremendous advantage in competition. No wonder many executives are so excited about it that they are referring to long-range planning as their "profit insurance."

24

The Lockheed Aircraft Corporation Master Plan[1]

L. Eugene Root
and
George A. Steiner

This analysis is divided into three parts. The first concerns the origins and basic objectives of the Lockheed Master Plan. The second treats the principal methods used in constructing the plan. The third deals with the underlying philosophy and uses of master planning.

ORIGIN AND OBJECTIVES OF THE LOCKHEED MASTER PLAN

In speaking of the beginning of a program as broad and complex as the master plan it is well to get behind the surface record of who asked who to do what and when. Basically, the plan developed because management recognized the need for an organized, cohesive, and balanced evaluation of future growth patterns and alternative profitable courses of action upon which current decisions could be made. Many problems in and characteristics of the airframe industry explain why management felt the need for such a tool. We would like to highlight just a few of these.

[1] From a presentation given by George A. Steiner to the Controllers Institute of America, Los Angeles, September 20, 1956. Used by permission of the authors. The first half of this article is based on L. Eugene Root and George A. Steiner, "Development Planning for Management Decision," in *Organizing for Executive Systems Planning and Control,* American Management Association Special Report No. 12 (1956).

Two important characteristics of the airframe industry necessitate not only long-range planning, but long-range planning in considerable detail. They are the extended production lead-time (up to ten years from concept to flight for complicated airborne weapons) and an extremely dynamic technological rate of advance (one which has been greater in the past few years than in the entire history of man's efforts to conquer the air).

The development of a turbine transport illustrates the type of long-range planning problems these considerations create. Actual production of such planes is some time ahead in the future. In the meantime, Lockheed, or any company interested in such airplanes, must answer such questions as these: What specific research and production facilities will be needed? What type of people will be required for research? For production? Where should the facilities be located? How much will they cost? These matters, it will be recognized, must be resolved at least tentatively and some decisions made a long time before the production of one single airplane.

This states a problem, but it fails to portray the magnitude and complexity of such questions. The scope of these problems when coupled with the nature of the business is such that a very large part of the company's resources—engineering, scientific, and management brains, as well as money—could easily and inevitably become firmly committed long before income was generated from the venture, assuming the outcome was successful. Add to such problems the fact that a large part of the demand for the company's products depends upon a cloudy foreign political situation, or that the product mix can easily change rapidly with substantial leverage on profits, and the urgency to get an informed look at the future becomes even more understandable. In this light, there is not much margin left for off-the-cuff vague decisions, or for decision-making on the principle of Donnybrook Fair—"Hit a head when you see it."

Like all major planning efforts the Lockheed Master Plan (LMP) has multiple objectives. Courtlandt Gross, Lockheed's President, established the superior objectives for the plan when he launched LMP (II) in December of 1955. He said: "Our primary objective is to develop solid bases for important management decisions at all levels in the corporation. These decisions, of course, are those necessary to insure that Lockheed will meet major technological challenges which lie ahead, maintain and improve its market position, and make an ever effective contribution to the national security posture of the United States.

These broad corporate goals were reduced to more concrete objectives for Lockheed's master planning work, as follows:

To indicate:	Future product characteristics and demand, both military and commercial.
To analyze:	Development and manufacturing needs to meet new product requirements, including investigations into facilities, organization, financing, and manpower needs.
To present:	Desirable growth patterns for a long period of time, at least one decade, for each division and subsidiary and for the entire corporation.
To recommend:	Preferred policies over a broad range of specific management actions to guide the corporation toward preferred patterns.

Although these objectives suggest a pattern of approach, many different methods could be used to meet them. We think that Lockheed's methodology is uniquely suited for achievement of these objectives. In this light, a summary account of the basic methods used by Lockheed in preparing its master plans may be of general interest. Although the basic patterns have been established, future plans will certainly modify methods used in the past. What we are about to describe relates to the plan prepared in the summer of 1956.

THE BASIC METHODS USED IN PREPARING LMP (II)

By way of introduction to this section the four main structural members of the plan are given in capsule form.

First is a detailed forecast of probable sales. By "detailed" we mean projections of specific models of airplanes, missiles, and other products in units, time, and dollars. Injected into these data are the manifold considerations which are associated not only with the levels of output but with the technical characteristics of production.

Second is a detailed projection of the fixed capital investment required to meet the probable sales level, as well as research and development facilities necessary to maintain a desired technical competence. Individual buildings and major pieces of equipment are specified.

Dates for their construction or acquisition, as well as dollar costs, are determined.

Third is a detailed projection of balance sheets and profit-and-loss statements.

Fourth is an analysis of emerging problems and suggestions for solving them. Ample opportunity is provided for setting forth and examining alternatives. Different patterns and projections are developed, based upon selected possibilities in such areas as sales, new models, financial capability, organization, plant location, technical and executive manpower availability, general industry competitive conditions, and product diversification.

The nature of the problems considered in the plan dictates coverage of a long span of years in the analysis. Sales, capital investment, financial, and most other areas of analysis are made for a ten-year period. It is recognized, however, that some feel for the decade succeeding the one analyzed is essential for long-range planning. For example, it is clear that any effort to determine the nature of research and development needs, or of production facilities, required in the years 1960–65 will depend much upon products to be made and the demands for them in the decade 1965–75. Hence, some parts of the plan cover two decades.

Organization for LMP (II)

Something should be said about the organization for completing LMP (II). LMP (I) taught Lockheed that organization into a team effort is required for such a large undertaking. A great many people have been and will continue to be involved in master planning. The successful completion of a task of such magnitude and importance requires sound organization.

Courtlandt Gross's letter of December 8, 1955, to top corporation officials not only launched LMP (II) but set the basic patterns for organization and methodology. At the very beginning of his letter, Gross observed: "We all realize that preparing a revised Master Plan is a formidable undertaking. It is one that will require the energies of our best talent over an extended period of time. . . . As we proceed in our periodic revisions of the Master Plan we must develop as effective a team operation as possible."

In conformance with this team spirit, and with the need for central guidance, an *ad hoc* organization was erected to complete the plan.

Exhibit 1 shows the basic outlines of this organization. At the very top stands the Administrative Committee (now called the Policy Committee). Directly underneath are the director of development planning and the controller. These executives work as a team in guiding the effort. They head a Steering Committee, the general functions of which are, as noted to the left of the chart, providing guidance and planning assumptions; coordination; evaluation; and recommendations.

Executives throughout the corporation, of course, help the committee in discharging its functions. One type of help is made available by working groups. Three were established. They are indicated to the right of the chart. The corporate sales directors spearheaded the work of the Working Group for Sales Assumptions. It was the function of this group to develop the basic guidelines and assumptions upon which the divisions prepared detailed sales estimates, and to make appropriate evaluations of the work done by the divisions.

The next committee, called Working Group for Investment and Finance, was headed by the corporate manager of budget and financial forecasts. This group had the job of preparing the instructions for division reporting of fixed capital investment programs and the financial forecast. In addition, the committee set forth some broad guides to be used in evaluating submitted data.

The next group, called the Technical Group for Research and Development Investment Program, was headed by the assistant director of the development planning department. This group was responsible for guiding and evaluating the research and development programs submitted by the divisions.

The work of all these groups was reviewed and approved by the Steering Committee before being sent to the divisions. The divisions had an opportunity to see and criticize instructions prepared for their guidance before these were officially sent.

In the middle of the chart are shown various central corporate offices. These are permanent offices which, in their fields of responsibility, act on behalf of the Steering Committee. As noted to the left of the chart, they supervise the work of the divisions, serve as channels of communication between the Steering Committee and the divisions, and make preliminary analyses of work done by the divisions in their respective areas of responsibility.

Finally, of course, one always finds on a chart—usually at the bot-

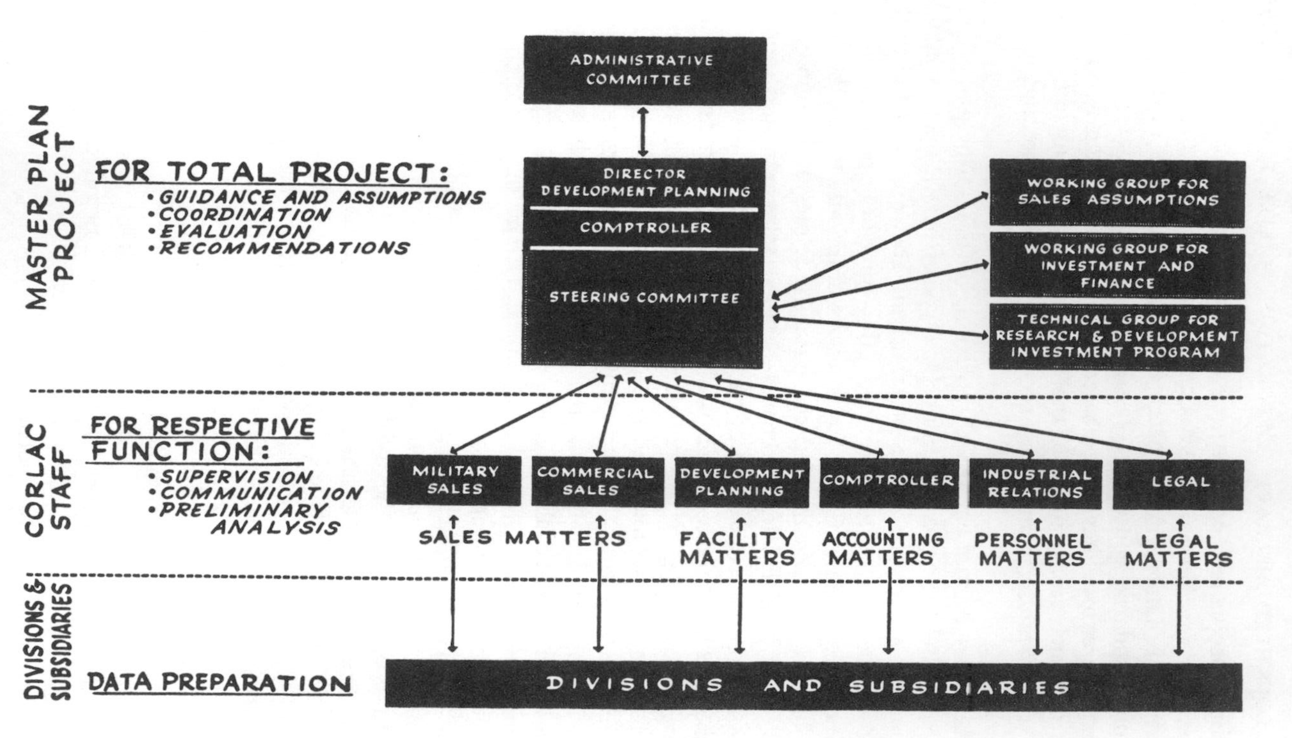

EXHIBIT 1. Organization for Lockheed Master Planning

tom—the people who do most of the work. In this case it is the operating divisions and subsidiaries of the corporation. In our arrangement of things, to maul Tennyson somewhat, "theirs is not to do or die without reasoning why." They are partners in the enterprise. They do in fact prepare detailed working data under broad top-management guidance. But they have a chance—which they take—to review any work touching upon their interests done by the Steering Committee.

Major Steps in Completing the Master Plan

With this backdrop, what was the work flow pattern in completing LMP (II)?

The first step obviously had to be the establishment of basic objectives. The next step was to fix guidelines and assumptions. Needless to say, these should be formulated with great care if the basic factual detail is to be prepared in the most useful and accurate manner. Of major significance are assumptions concerning sales projections, fixed asset requirements, and balance sheet and profit-and-loss statements. The treatment of sales assumptions illustrates the thoroughness with which such assumptions were prepared.

Three sales projections were prepared for LMP (II). The first and most important was the "probable" sales level. The other two were the high and low possible sales levels.

The Steering Committee prepared detailed assumptions to guide the work of the divisions in forecasting probable sales. Many of the assumptions were the subject of detailed and scholarly analyses. They covered only one ten-year period of the plan. They were (1) continued cold war, which was derived from a thorough analysis of the international political situation; (2) increasing emphasis on air power; (3) increasing total defense expenditures; (4) guided missiles will cut into aircraft procurement in the future; (5) general business conditions will be prosperous; (6) present military airframe manufacturers will continue to compete; (7) missiles systems responsibilities will go increasingly to nonairframe manufacturers; (8) government influences and attitudes will remain about as they now are; (9) there will be no major technological break-throughs in the planning period; (10) divisions will generally stick to types of products they are now producing; (11) Lockheed will constantly endeavor to expand when sales and profit expectations warrant the risk; and (12) personnel availability will be similar to that in the 1952–55 period.

In addition to these assumptions there were a number of others associated with the commercial market, such as airline availability of funds, competition, and market potentials. Wherever appropriate, assumptions (e.g., gross national product and defense expenditure forecasts) were quantified.

The high and low possible sales calculations were made by the corporate staff with some division help. A great deal of work went into the examination of various possible events which could lead to sales much higher or substantially lower than the probable levels. Care had to be exercised in appraising the probability of many assumptions and possible events.

On the *low* side, possible events such as the following had to be appraised in terms of their likelihood and the resulting impact on Lockheed: disarmament and the level of military spending in general and for airborne weapons in particular, economic depression, competitive conditions in the arcraft industry, and possible technological advances. On the *high* side, the following types of possibilities had to be judged: small wars, technological developments among major competitors, and unusual Lockheed sales successes. Once the assumptions were laid down, detailed dollar and unit sales projections were made.

Division Investment Programs

There is no need to get into deep detail about the instructions to the divisions for calculating the fixed capital investment program associated with the probable sales level. But to understand how the divisions prepared and reported their fixed investment programs some of the pages from principal facility reporting forms are given in accompanying exhibits.

As Exhibit 2 shows, the first page provided space for the usual type of facility information. There were blanks for the name of the reporting division, name of the facility, its function, and physical description, including land, installations, and machinery.

The next page (Exhibit 3) provided for cost data relating to land, land improvements, buildings, building installations, and machinery and equipment. Two basic estimates were required. The upper group of boxes were for desired specifications and the desired time schedule of construction. The lower boxes provided space for yearly costs for minimum specifications and maximum deferral. Also note the provision for estimating the extent to which the federal government might be expected to help finance facilities.

The next page (Exhibit 4) provided space for division responses to specific questions about their facility program. Brief answers were requested to questions concerning the difference between cost and

I. FACILITY TITLE ______ II. ORIGINATING DIVISION (CHECK ONE) CALAC ___ GELAC ___ MSD ___ LAS ___ LAT ___ CORLAC ___ III. FACILITY NUMBER ______

IV. FACILITY FUNCTION ______ RESEARCH ___ DEVEL. ___ MFG. ___ ADMIN. ___ SERV. ___ OTHER ______

V. PHYSICAL DESCRIPTION

A. LAND AREA IN ACRES ______ NOW LAC-OWNED? YES ___ NO ___	B. LAND IMPROVEMENTS	
C. BUILDINGS BUILDING NO. (1) (PRIMARY)	BUILDING NO. (2)	BUILDING NO. (3)
FLOOR AREA ______ AVERAGE NO. OF EMPL. ______		
D. BUILDING INSTALLATIONS		
E. MACHINERY & EQUIPMENT		

EXHIBIT 2. Individual Facility Report—Lockheed Master Plan II Fixed Asset Requirements 1956–65

FACILITY NO. ________

VI. DESIRED SPECIFICATIONS DESIRED SCHEDULE (A)	(B) COMPLETION DATE DESIRED	(C) TOTAL FACILITY COST (OMIT 000)	(D) AMOUNT GOV'T. FINANCED (OMIT 000)	(E) LAC SCHEDULE OF EXPENDITURES (OMIT LAST THREE 000) 1956	1957	1958	1959	1960	1961	1962	1963	1964	1965	TOTAL
(A) LAND:														
(B) LAND IMPROVEMENTS:														
(C) BUILDINGS:														
1.														
2.														
3.														
(D) BUILDING INSTALLATIONS:														
1.														
2.														
3.														
(E) MACHINERY & EQUIPMENT:														
1.														
2.														
3.														
	TOTALS													

VII. MINIMUM SPECIFICATIONS MAXIMUM DEFERRAL (A)	(B) COMPLETION DATE DESIRED	(C) TOTAL FACILITY COST (OMIT 000)	(D) AMOUNT GOV'T. FINANCED (OMIT 000)	(E) LAC SCHEDULE OF EXPENDITURES (OMIT LAST THREE 000) 1956	1957	1958	1959	1960	1961	1962	1963	1964	1965	TOTAL
(A) LAND:														
(B) LAND IMPROVEMENTS:														
(C) BUILDINGS:														
1.														
2.														
3.														
(D) BUILDING INSTALLATIONS:														
1.														
2.														
3.														
(E) MACHINERY & EQUIPMENT:														
1.														
2.														
3.														
	TOTALS													

EXHIBIT 3. Individual Facility Report—Lockheed Master Plan II
Fixed Asset Requirements 1956–65

(PLEASE ANSWER THE FOLLOWING QUESTIONS IN THE SPACE PROVIDED)

APPENDIX A – FACILITY QUESTIONNAIRE – GENERAL EXPLANATION AND REMARKS

FACILITY NO. ________

I. PLEASE EXPLAIN PRINCIPAL CONSTRUCTION VARIATIONS THAT ACCOUNT FOR THE COST DIFFERENCES IN SCHEDULES VI AND VII.

II. DOES THE DIVISION CONSIDER THE STATED AMOUNT OF GOVERNMENT FINANCING TO BE:

1. IN SCHEDULE VI OPTIMISTIC ☐ PESSIMISTIC ☐
2. IN SCHEDULE VII OPTIMISTIC ☐ PESSIMISTIC ☐

III. A. IS THE REQUESTED FACILITY REQUIRED BY AND TIED DIRECTLY TO A SPECIFIC ANTICIPATED CONTRACT(S)? MILITARY OR COMMERCIAL?

YES ☐ NO ☐

B. WHICH CONTRACT(S)?

IV. A. DOES AN AVAILABLE FACILITY SIMILAR TO THE ONE REQUESTED EXIST NEAR THE DESIRED FACILITY LOCATION? YES ☐ NO ☐

B. IF "YES", PLEASE EXPLAIN WHY THE EXISTING FACILITY CAN NOT FILL THE DIVISION'S NEEDS:

V. A. IF THIS REQUESTED FACILITY IS PROVIDED, WILL EXISTING FLOOR SPACE BE VACATED? YES ☐ NO ☐

B. IF "YES", PLEASE ESTIMATE

(A) VACATED SPACE ______ SQ. FT. (TOTAL)

(B) VACATED HIGH BAY SPACE ______ SQ. FT.

C. WHAT DOES DIVISION SUGGEST BE DONE WITH VACATED SPACE?

VI. IF THE FACILITY BEING REQUESTED CANNOT BE PROVIDED, WHAT WILL THE DIVISION DO?

VII. REMARKS. (ENTER ANY COMMENTS THE DIVISION FEELS SHOULD BE A PART OF THIS REPORT.)

EXHIBIT 4. Individual Facility Report—Lockheed Master Plan II Fixed Asset Requirements 1956–65

timing variations in the two programs presented, the existence and location of available facilities similar to those requested, the floor space to be vacated if the facility were built, what the division would do if the facility were not built, and so on.

Exhibit 5 shows the type of questions asked about research and development facilities. Divisions were requested to report for all such facilities technical data on dimensions or capacity, quantities and characteristics of elements to be controlled, special technical features, abnormal hazards, the exact nature of work to be done in the facility, what the company would do if the facility were not constructed, and whether experienced people would be available to operate the facility.

Detailed instructions for the reporting forms were prepared. These, of course, provided liberal illustrations of the precise type of information to be given.

Another set of complementary assumptions was prepared for the financial forecasts.

This by no means completes the guidelines for or the information requested on facilities. It merely illustrates the degree of detail, the general scope of requested response, and the methodology for reporting fixed capital requirements.

Future Projections

With the basic guidelines earlier discussed, the operating divisions, along with the central corporate offices, were in a position to begin the third step in the planning process. This was to produce the detailed analyses, data, and related information concerning future projections and growth patterns. The divisions prepared basic information in three main areas: (1) probable sales, (2) plant and equipment requirements, and (3) balance sheet and profit-and-loss statements. While this work was moving along the corporate staff studied, from an over-all corporate point of view, various problems and policies associated with these growth patterns.

The process of evaluation then followed. It is not hard to list the major steps in evaluation. They were validation of data inputs, aggregation of all relevant factors bearing upon a problem, application of judgments to facts, and examination of and choice among alternatives.

The final step was that of preparing results for presentation, first to the Administrative Committee and then to others in the corporation.

No fixed patterns have been established for either the drafting or

FACILITY NO. ________
LAB/UNIT NO. ________

ORIGINATING DIVISION:
___ CALAC ___ GELAC ___ MSD
___ LAS ___ LAT ___ CORLAC

APPENDIX B - TECHNICAL EXPLANATION AND REMARKS
(SPECIAL FORM FOR EXPERIMENTAL RESEARCH & DEVELOPMENT UNITS ONLY)

INDIVIDUAL LABORATORY OR TEST UNIT TITLE: ________

REMARKS BELOW APPLICABLE TO DESIRED ☐ OR MINIMUM ☐ SPECIFICATIONS

I. FACILITY PURPOSE

II. MAJOR ITEMS OF EQUIPMENT

III. PERTINENT DIMENSIONS AND/OR CAPACITY

IV. QUANTITIES TO BE CONTROLLED

V. SUPPLY REQUIREMENTS

VI. SPECIAL FEATURES

VII. GROWTH POTENTIAL

VIII. ABNORMAL HAZARDS

IX. NOISE AND/OR VIBRATION PROBLEMS

X. UTILIZATION ANTICIPATED

XI. BY WHAT MEANS COULD THE NECESSARY DATA BE OBTAINED IF LOCKHEED DID NOT HAVE SUCH A FACILITY?

XII. AVAILABILITY OF EXPERIENCED PEOPLE

DESIGN:
CONSTRUCTION:
OPERATION:

XIII. REMARKS

EXHIBIT 5. Individual Facility Report—Lockheed Master Plan II Fixed Asset Requirements 1956–65

the presentation of the results of the planning process. In the case of LMP (II) a short-range problem triggered the official presentation to the Administrative Committee. As a result the presentation took place in steps. The initial report, tailored to fit the immediate problem, summarized basic results about future sales, capital investment, and the financial result of operations. In each of these areas such matters as the following were treated: major trends and growth patterns, major current and future problems, and suggested corporate actions to correct some problems. Analyses of the master plan not given to the Administrative Committee in the initial presentation were presented later.

In the meantime, of course, the divisions utilized their part of the master plan as guides to operations. Their decision-making process reflected the larger patterns for the entire corporation set by the Administrative Committee following the initial presentation of the plan.

So long as the data of LMP (II) can serve management in the decision-making process it is a living program modified, of course, by decisions made upon the basis of it and other information at the disposal of management. When major decisions are made which affect importantly the future, or when external factors alter enough to make the existing plan relatively obsolete, a new plan is formulated.

PHILOSOPHY AND USES OF THE LOCKHEED MASTER PLAN

This concluding section treats some of the ideas with which master planning is approached at Lockheed and some of the many uses this work has in the development of the corporation. These two matters can appropriately be considered together.

Concepts underlying the methodology of the master plan have much to do with approaches to the work, the value of the information contained in any plan, and how the corporation may and will use the information to maximum advantage. To speak of the master plan without dealing with philosophies and concepts associated with it would be like describing a man in terms of his flesh and bones and omitting his personality characteristics.

There are eight major uses of the master planning process at Lockheed. They follow:

First, the master plan is a basis for management decision at all levels in the corporation and over a broad range of policy and operations. The use of the materials in the plan for this purpose covers a rather wide field of activity. Hence, we shall touch upon only a few major points.

To begin with, the plan identifies major problems ahead before they arise or become acute. It seeks to find out the *right questions* to which management must give attention. The toughest problem in management is not to find the answer to a problem. It is rather to find the right question to be answered at the right time. LMP (II) seeks to place the right question before management for solution.

The company has benefited considerably by the fact that the master plan has clearly delineated some important future problems. Being forewarned is to be forearmed. Because of action today, many of the problems detected will not assume the proportions they otherwise might have, or will not arise at all. Master-planning therefore *highlights important future problems and gives the corporation time to solve them.*

The planning operation also provides a *long-range perspective,* as well as a basic policy frame of reference, for all sorts of current decisions. Many decisions made at lower echelons in the corporation reflect the guidelines which the decision-maker found in the master plan as well as top policy formulated by the Administrative Committee. The proclivity of the human animal to seek support for his actions in some ground, as well as a genuine need for the larger perspective in arriving at decisions, makes this understandable.

The plan and subsequent revisions of it provide not only a base for current decisions but also a model by means of which the impact of current decisions on future operations can be measured. Robert E. Gross (now chairman of the board and chief executive officer of the company) pointed out in a management memorandum on the subject of the master plan: "Our plan suggests appropriate management policies and decisions to be taken to achieve desirable growth patterns for at least the next ten years. . . . The plan influences decisions that we must make today for the course of our production operations through the next five to ten years. It does not commit us, however, to irrevocable courses of action beyond the implication of immediate and near-term decisions."

The corporation recognizes that data collected today about the long-range future cannot be considered to have unchanging validity.

There are many events that will alter "the best-laid plans of mice and men," to take plenty of license with Robert Burns. It is also recognized that the further out in time the planning, the less certain one can be about the precision of numbers. As a basic principle in planning it is understood that in the longer range, details merge into trends and patterns. For these and other reasons, the master plan drafted today cannot stand like the Tablet of Moses for years to come as the one and only oracle for a dynamic corporation like Lockheed.

The master plan is considered to be very flexible. Everyone recognizes the need for continuous adjustment and improvement in it. There is an understanding of the need for periodic review of the entire plan, re-examination of basic assumptions, restudy of market estimates and trends, and a fresh appraisal of strategic judgments and alternative choices.

One other important aspect of the plan and the decision-making process is that the plan does not present alternative courses of action or suggested solutions for *all* major problems. This is done only for some questions. Nor does the plan presume to make top policy decisions. The master plan is a basis for decision. It incorporates past decisions. But it does not make new decisions to meet new major problems. That is the prerogative of top management.

The master plan is not, therefore, a blueprint of fixed action steps over time which the Administrative Committee can pull out of a bottom desk drawer in the coming years to find the answers to a particular problem. Rather, the plan periodically seeks to lay out feasible, rational, and desirable patterns of future growth. It is a basis for clarifying fundamental objectives of the corporation and the divisions. It is a basis for determining the major problems which must be met and faced in achieving objectives. It also provides a framework for working out the best alternative courses of action by means of which corporate and divisional objectives can be met and problems in their achievement solved in an acceptable way.

You will recognize these things as ingredients needed by top management before it makes an important decision. Good decision-making is not simple. Elementally the process requires finding the right problem, defining the problem, analyzing the problem, developing alternative solutions, and choosing the best solution. Our master plan is an organized effort to do these things.

Rather than a blueprint, the plan is a malleable model which alters and changes over time. Clarification of objectives, problems, and policies in any master plan will constitute important guides in the development of the next one. New environmental forces operating on the corporation must also be reflected in ensuing plans. Thus, each plan is a link in a chain of analyses supporting management decisions over the broad range of actions importantly affecting the company's future.

This point deserves elaboration. The materials in each master plan are organized facts and judgments based upon past decisions, future desires, and rational expectations inside and outside the corporation. Matters in the plan concerned with new policy decision problems and alternative solutions are proposals. They are not prophecies of new decisions to be made. It is the Administrative Committee that solely is the maker of major decisions for the corporation. To a lesser degree—within their areas of responsibility and in light of Administrative Committee decisions or knowledge of top-management attitudes—the divisions also make decisions during and after the compilation of the plan.

When the Administrative Committee receives the plan, in whole or in part, it does not bless the plan in its entirety. Rather it deals with problems presented in the plan. It weighs the risks of different solutions to problems and determines the solution that achieves the maximum result with the minimum effort, establishes right timing, and relates the decision to the organizational structure. These are tasks of the highest difficulty and responsibility. When a decision is made it is transmitted to the appropriate divisions in the corporation through regular line organizations. It is not transmitted as a part of the master plan.

Such a plan supports major decision. It reflects past decision. It is not the vehicle or instrument for either transmission or control of decision and resulting actions.

In a sense, most of the other uses which are here ascribed to the master plan can be subsumed under this one subject of aid to management decision-making. There is, however, a case for segregating them.

Second, the plan establishes a basis for getting at the major determinants of Lockheed's future. Not everything that goes on in the corporation or outside it carries equal weight as a determinant of Lockheed's future. Hence, some trends and forces will have more importance than others. The master-planning technique provides a mechanism for segregating such strategic forces and giving them the analysis and weight they deserve within a unified and understood framework.

Third, the plan establishes a framework for organizing value judgments. No one should suppose that a master plan such as described here is completely unbiased, purely scientific, and always probable. The data in the plan are derived from or importantly reflect personal value judgments. But the methodology of the plan provides a focal point for measuring one judgment against another. It provides a central frame of reference for testing individual judgments, weighing them, and getting a reading. It does not, of course, force conformance to one collective judgment. By this process, however, not only does there tend to be registered consensus of judgment about important matters by people most competent to judge, but the possibility that an extreme position held by a forceful individual may get too much attention is reduced.

Fourth, this type of plan opens up new horizons for further profitable exploration. The mere fact that it brings to light important problems which otherwise would be dim or not perceived means that analysis is merited if the solution is not readily discernible. Master plans have launched a number of important study programs which ultimately will result in major policy decisions. Some of these undoubtedly would have been undertaken without the master plan. One wonders, however, whether they would have been made at the same time, in the same general context of corporate expectations, and with the same strength of support for top policy decision.

Fifth, the master plan stimulates thought about and information concerning basic company policy, strategy, and future developments to all who should be aware of such matters.

New ideas, suggestions, self-appraisal, and criticisms are more freely generated when they have a chance of being heard and properly evaluated at appropriate management levels. One good way to choke initiative, silence self-criticisms, and formalize the outdated, the outworn, the outmoded, the wrong, and the costly is to insist on formal conventional channels of communication or to have no such community of thought between the top management and lower line and staff personnel.

We do not mean to imply that the company has now or had prior to the master plan a poor method of communication. We wish merely to point out that in our judgment, the plan, for matters within its purview, provides a new, fresh, and adaptable channel of communication to the highest management level in the corporation. Because the plan is reviewed at the top-management level, because everyone knows this, and because everyone knows that the Administrative Committee considers the plan and its associated analyses highly important, it becomes a fresh channel of communications. It broadens the opportunity for more and more people at all levels of line management and staff to contribute information and suggestions that ultimately promote soundness in final decisions.

The plan also has served a useful function in disseminating important information downward. The mere organization in the plan of basic corporate objectives, premises, policies, reflections of top-management points of view, and evolving problems gives the corporate organization the same unified body of facts and operating plans at the disposal of top management.

One other aspect of this subject of communications deserves mention here. All groups have semantic problems in communication. Words mean different things to different people. Confucius said that the first thing he would do if he were to become Emperor of China would be to fix the meaning of words, for actions follow words. Lack of understanding of the meaning of words is a serious baffle in any system of communications. The master plan has served to fix the meaning of many words. There is more agreement than before in the company about such words as corporate objectives, planning, forecast, major problems, probable sales, corporate technical competence, research and development, rate of return on investment, and master planning. The substantive elements of such words have also been more clearly delineated. In addition, the meaning of words and concepts important to Lockheed has become, as a result of master planning, part of the mental equipment of more and more people. In mind are such terms as gross national product, alternative costs, acid-test ratio, elasticity of demand, constant versus price-inflated forecasts, net worth, and return on investment.

Sixth, the master plan is an important integrating force. To begin with, it has served as a catalytic agent in fusing line and staff, in both the corporate offices and the divisions, in a team effort to tackle important problems affecting each other and the entire corporation.

The mere fact that the plan provides a common meeting ground for exchanging ideas and testing them against the judgment of others is healthy. Beyond this, however, the plan serves as a framework within which the many areas of knowledge and expert talents in the corporation can be welded together to support management decision. We refer to areas of importance in management decision such as the technical, military, personnel, production, organizational, financial, administrative, accounting, and economic. Top corporate policy reflects elements of all these disciplines. To ignore any one or give any one too much weight can be costly. Hence, any means to integrate and balance them has great value.

It is not suggested that the master plan forces unanimity of opinion in all these areas on a given problem. No comprehensive plan can do that. It has served, however, to produce a surprising degree of concurrence on matters which, without it, would probably stimulate strong, entrenched, diverse points of view. When there are diverse points of view, the plan serves as a mechanism for organizing the differences and insuring that they receive an appropriate hearing and weight.

Seventh, the master plan helps to prevent piecemeal solutions to problems. There is a natural tendency in most operating organizations to concentrate on immediate problems. In the absence of long-range planning, current decisions often are made within the context of short-range considerations. In addition, each problem tends to become isolated from other problems. The result may well be that operating decisions not only conflict in the short term, but run quite contrary to the long-range interests of the enterprise. The existence of such a management tool as the master plan not only reduces the number of piecemeal *ad hoc* solutions, particularly in the capital investment and financial areas, but helps to insure that decisions made currently do not jeopardize the desirable long-range growth patterns of the corporation.

Eighth, and closely associated with the foregoing point, the master plan brings a comprehensive, coordinated, and uniform picture of the present and future business of the corporation as a whole to those who must operate the business. Without this sort of framework, pieces of strategic information—on sales, capital investment, profits, and so on—would come before top management individually and would not be so well related with other important elements in the operation of the business.

In sum, the master plan has multiple objectives and uses. Topping all is its use as a tool for management decision. Abraham Lincoln once observed that "if we could first know where we are, and whither we are tending, we could then better judge what to do, and how to do it." The master plan translates this keen observation into action at Lockheed.

25

How We Took Hold of Long-Range Planning at A-D-M[1]

Clarence A. Danielson

To identify promising areas of expansion, investigations were made [at Archer-Daniels-Midland Company] of our research, marketing and production activities. The leading consideration here is marketing, i.e., what we can expect to sell. Under the heading of marketing falls the identification of the major external factors that affect the company's sales volume and profits. Important external variables we looked for were:

1. Trend of national business conditions.
2. Trend of business conditions in the company's industry.
3. Relative strength, technically and economically, of competitive companies.

Few companies are fortunate enough to have well-defined arithmetical relationships of sales and major external factors. Overattention to national trends holds a danger in that it injects a note of

[1] From *NAA Bulletin,* March 1962, pp. 7–12. Used by permission. Portions at the beginning and end of the original text are omitted.

hopelessness if businessmen feel subject to the indications. But businessmen should be setting trends, not following them. It would be better to ignore economic trends than to be enslaved to them, but they can be useful if an objective effort is made to determine the extent of their influence on the company's business and to design methods of countering adverse trends, rather than submitting to them as inevitable. Selection of indexes is a factor. Gross national product, total industrial production, and population trends are complex indexes and not specific enough to be useful for our product lines. Our method of handling the economic trend problem was to identify a reasonably logical index with which sales of each major product line might vary. The index chosen closely relates the product and the service it performs.

Competitive factors were counted among the external influences involved in making sales projections. The written plan ultimately contained a paragraph discussing the abilities of leading competitors in each field, including a brief identification and appraisal of foreign influences. A summary of the best information available quickly brought out some of the important items that were pertinent in correctly gauging the strengths and weaknesses of competition.

Sales projections were made for each product line by volume and estimated per cent of market. These were supported with substantiating data or reasons why the projections were realistic. Proposed marketing programs, business indexes, new products, etc., were used to show how the forecasts were determined. Whenever possible, our sales forecasts were based on at least two independent sources of information. Usually, field reports from salesmen were compared with statistical predictions, providing the opportunity for one source to serve as a cross-check on the other. How these sales forecasts shaped up is diagrammed in Exhibit 1 against five years of experience and five of projection. Even with luck and a lot of refinement of technique a sizable error can occur in the sales forecasting, especially for a five-year period.

This can be disconcerting but, in our estimation, does not necessarily render the plan useless for, with the possible exception of the first year, accuracy is not the most important feature of long-range plans. Planning is not budgeting. Budgeting requires greater accuracy. Long-range planning, by its very nature, must cover a span of years. The kind of thinking required for this is frustrated by a demand for pin-

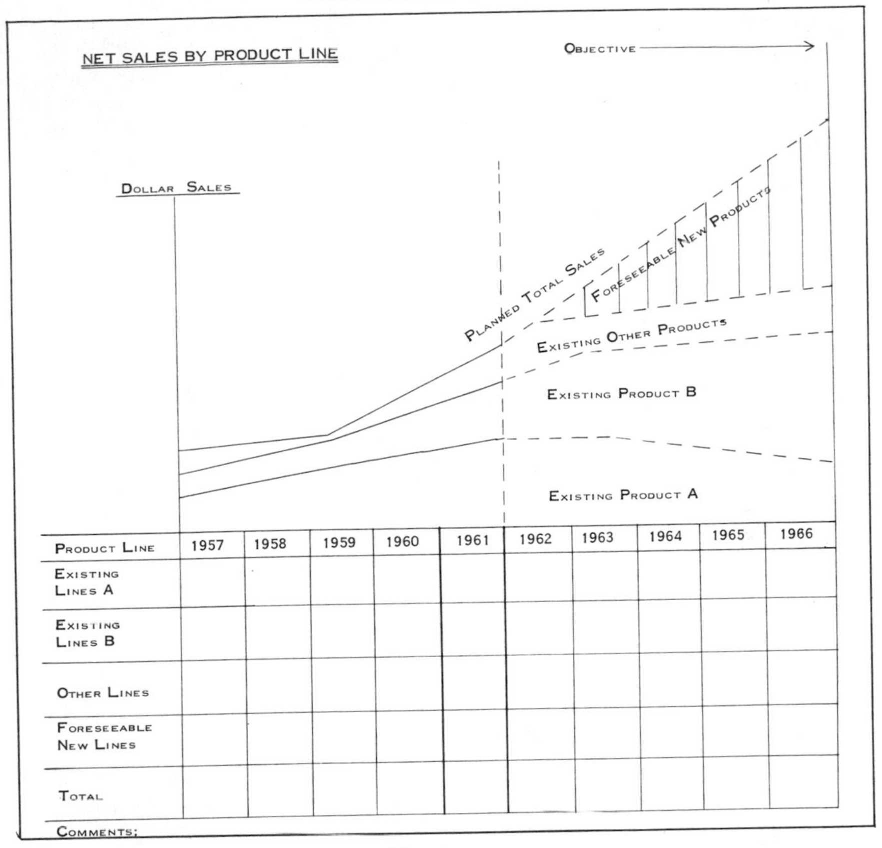

EXHIBIT 1

point accuracy. Our sales forecasts are the honest anticipation of sales and costs, without demanding provable accuracy. They represent the best estimates at the time. The first year, which is described in some detail, is actually a budget; the next few years are more loosely forecast.

NEW VENTURES—WHAT AND HOW?

In order to classify and categorize new ventures for growth through research or possible acquisition, a general survey was made in those areas that appeared to be the most promising. This program was segregated into two phases. The first consisted of the development of criteria for judging areas of growth, collection of growth ideas, study and evaluation of the more promising areas for growth, and development of recommended areas of expansion. A review was made of all previous studies and recommendations the firm has had over the past years. It required contact with all people who might contribute ideas for growth, such as research, marketing, production, development, and outside research groups. Ideas were screened and classified by general industry categories. The more promising areas were then studied in depth against the criteria available for all facts pertinent to those products and/or industries that survived the original judgment evaluation. The second phase involved the development of recommendations for new products to be acquired through research or through other companies considered prime candidates for acquisition.

In evaluating research objectives, certain key ideas and motivations apply. These are as follows:

1. Capture of certain segments of the market which have previously been inaccessible.
2. Diversification of uses for present products or present types, i.e., application of present technology and research to new industry.
3. Improvement in quality, production, engineering, cost-reduction techniques, plant modernization, etc.
4. Development of completely new products, product types, industries, new technology in manufacturing, and other ideas for further evaluation.

Research ideas once conceived must be evaluated and approved. This is no easy matter because sometimes a good deal of time elapses before the original idea can be brought to a point of fruition. Therefore, research ideas must be constantly re-evaluated as progress implementing these ideas and expanding them continues. The point at which research ideas are actually formalized and incorporated into definite future fields will vary according to the complexities of the program. However, when such new ideas have been fully developed and evaluated, they will become a firm part of our long-range planning.

Growth through acquisition sometimes is more rapid than growth through research; however, there is a tremendous element of risk in the latter. [Efforts to assess and evaluate strengths and weakness and to identify promising areas of expansion] evolved directions of thought and pointed to those industries and areas where acquisition opportunities might be possible. Industries approved for expansion will be checked to determine which firms in that industry might be the most desirable for acquisition. Much information about good and poor companies in each industry is already available within the present company structure. Individual companies will be checked against criteria hitherto developed, on the basis of all available information. For the purpose of developing the plan, it will not be necessary initially to contact any outside firm which might be a candidate for acquisition. However, enough information must be developed so that, at the proper time, negotiations can be started in a promising manner.

LONG-TERM GOALS AND PROJECTION OF PRESENT OPERATIONS

From the criteria developed in the activities described in the foregoing sections of this paper, it was possible to set tentative long-range goals five years ahead. Projections were then made to determine the results of present operations and the outlook for the period of the long-range plan. It was felt that these studies might reflect that a certain segment of our industry is in a declining position, while others are in a growth position. Such projections of present operations were then added to the plan forecast at the proper point in time. This was also done for forecast results of operations from new developments through research or acquisition. The projection of present operations, as a whole, made it possible to undertake a study and review of the long-range goals.

The narrative portion of the plan was reviewed to determine whether the goals were attainable within the scope of the firm's capabilities. A realistic and factual appraisal was made of each segment of the plan. If the goals were too high and the proper management, manpower and technical skills were not available, such requirements were to be added or, if impossible to add, the goals were reduced to come within the scope of the firm's capabilities. Conversely, it could have revealed that a potential exists within the firm capable of goals much higher than those originally set. In this case, revision should be made fully to utilize the firm's capabilities to the maximum.

THE PLAN IN WRITING

After thorough review of the tentative plans and establishment of long-range goals, the entire program was formalized and reduced to writing to permit continuing review and revision. It was also necessary to reduce the plan to figures for proper financial planning. The written plan consists of an introduction followed by detailed reports. The introduction is a concise narrative summary of the firm's present position in industry, briefly highlighting the present operations. The objectives of the long-range plan and ultimate goals which are to be achieved are stated. A brief review of the firm's marketing position, production facilities, research capabilities, and management skills was also included. Contemplated major changes were highlighted, as well as summaries of necessary capital requirements. In addition, we indicated the projected effects of the plan on the financial position of the company.

The detailed reports were subdivided into five sections as follows:

1. Marketing
2. Manufacturing or production
3. Research and development
4. Management
5. Financial analysis

Marketing

This section contained a detailed appraisal of the strengths and weaknesses of the present marketing organization and a forecast of sales. Charts relating the progress of the firm to projections and to applicable economic indexes were submitted. A review of the major customers and names of competitors and types of competition which exist and can be expected were included. Some attention was given to the necessity of advertising expenditures and their relationship to increased business. This section also included a review of the present and projected marketing personnel. Possible acquisitions of other companies, with a narrative disclosure of the likely magnitude, type of acquisition, and contribution of these acquisitions to the firm, were summarized in some detail in this section.

Manufacturing or Production

A detailed review of the firm's manufacturing facilities, stating their present condition together with modernization or expansion programs was included in detail for each facility. Present and projected capacity for each facility was scheduled. Distribution and warehouse requirements, present and projected, were fully covered. In this section, a projection of inventories, as well as details of total manufacturing costs, was made. Charts were prepared projecting production capacities against projected sales. Charts were also prepared showing projected savings from plant modernization and expansion programs. Also prepared was a review of the company's labor relations, union contracts, and status of negotiations, with projections into future labor relations.

Research and Development

This section dealt with present technical manpower capabilities of research and development staffs. Projects which were in progress, as well as those contemplated, were shown in detail. Charts were presented by year, showing the estimated expenditures for research and development in relationship to projected sales. The expenditures were further subdivided to include classifications such as basic and pioneering research, product and process improvement, assistance to sales, investigation of new ventures, etc. We assigned an estimated dollar cost to each of these classifications. Available historical evaluation of completed research products was included as an indication of the magnitude of this expense as compared with revenue over a period of time. We anticipated and stated general trends of the research and development plan, and the direction which it will take.

Management

In order to record management strengths, complete analyses of top and middle management were made. Description of the organizational responsibilities, as well as an organization chart, was prepared and included as part of this section. If long-range planning goals necessitated increased management personnel or a change in organization, such items were spelled out; a projected organizational chart was included as part of the formalized plan. Necessities for recruitment, on-the-job training, and outside training programs were set forth and evaluated.

Financial Analysis

A summary was made, covering the analysis of capital expenditures necessary for the implementation of the plan. This capital expenditure analysis was for each year of the plan. It was given in five sections as indicated below:

1. Basis for cash flow—years in which capital expenditures will be made.
2. Basis for return on investment—year in which project will be completed and capitalized.
3. New depreciation as a result of capital expenditures.
4. The effect of capital expenditures on level of inventories.
5. The effect of capital expenditures on level of accounts receivable.

A profit-and-loss projection was made for each year of the long-range plan. With this and the foregoing schedules, it was possible to project complete cash flow schedules, balance sheets, and return-on-investment schedules. Numerical reduction of the long-range plan is merely one of the evaluating procedures which management must use in appraising the soundness and tentative results of the plan.

26

Planning at American Machine & Foundry Company[1]

Stewart Thompson

Through its nineteen divisions and subsidiaries, AMF manufactures a wide range of products: bowling equipment and supplies, sporting goods, bicycles, electrical relays and timers, equipment for the gas and oil industry, missile ground-support equipment, and weapons systems

[1] From *How Companies Plan,* American Management Association Research Study No. 54 (1962), pp. 128–132. Used by permission.

and components, as well as automated machinery for the bakery, tobacco, and other manufacturing industries. Annual sales approximate $293 million, and $69 million is received in rentals.

Planning is headed by J. P. D'Arezzo, vice-president of planning and marketing, who is also a corporate officer. The Planning and Marketing Division consists of four major departments: Planning, Acquisitions, Products and Market Analysis, and Advertising Services. The planning staff consists of a supervisor, two staff analysts, and two trainee analysts who also serve the Acquisitions Department.

The history of planning as it is presently conceived at AMF began in February 1958 with the appointment of Carter L. Burgess as president of the corporation. Although the company has experienced its rapid growth largely by acquiring other businesses, it was Mr. Burgess's belief that more planning should be undertaken before future assignments. Accordingly, soon after his appointment to the presidency, he directed that two steps be taken to aid him in formulating plans for the company: (1) A small Planning Department was established, with a director of planning as its head; (2) a planning committee of top corporate officers was formed.

The initial assignment of the newly created planning department included these four directives:

1. Develop an approach to planning.
2. Formulate a plan for the corporation.
3. Consider the over-all corporate organization structure (whether divisions should be formed by marketing areas, product groupings, or geographical areas).
4. Investigate and negotiate acquisitions of companies.

Largely because of Mr. D'Arezzo's interest and previous experience in AMF's Commercial Research Department, he was appointed director of planning and marketing, in March 1959. (It was believed that planning at AMF should be oriented to marketing. Consequently, the people selected for the planning staff were selected from the Commercial Research Department.)

During April–September 1958, the planning staff undertook a historical review of the corporation and its divisions. Managers of each of the twenty-five profit centers were asked to submit information on their departments, under such classifications as "five-year projections of sales," "profits," "new products," "sales territories," "market penetration," "changes in sales approaches," "profit prospects," and "profit characteristics of industries served" (by each center). This information was compiled in a planning data book dealing with over-all company performance in the past and expected performance under future economic conditions. The historical study included conversations with executives who had participated in the early decisions that had led to the growth of the business. Among these executives was Morehead Patterson, chairman of the board. The growth of the business since the early 1900's, when AMF was a division of American Tobacco Company, was carefully studied.

By late 1958 the first basic corporate plan was prepared, covering the period 1959–62. Since that time a new five-year planning document has been drawn up each year for approval by the "executive office." Mr. Patterson, the corporate chairman, participates actively in the formulation and approval of the corporate plan.

Besides encompassing statements of specific profit and sales objectives for each profit center, the corporate plan incorporates a marketing review of all products of the business in order to assess the outlook for each. Decisions are made as to whether certain elements of the business ought to be expanded, or disposed of, or whether additional studies should be undertaken. It may be decided, for example, that expenditures for product development in a certain area ought to be increased, or, if they are unjustified, that they should be discontinued. The planning staff makes recommendations on the addition or expansion of product lines and production facilities, and reviews all budgets.

Reporting to Mr. D'Arezzo is the planning staff, headed by Harry G. Jones, supervisor of planning, and two trainee analysts. In the acquisitions analysis group are three persons, while the product-and-market analysis group and the Advertising Services Department are staffed by a total of thirty-three people. Chart 1 shows the organization of the entire division.

There is also a planning committee which meets each month, usually after the meeting of the board of directors. The chairman of the planning committee is an economist employed on a consulting basis. (This, it will be noted, is an unusual arrangement.) Company managers on the committee are the president, executive vice-president, vice-president of the bowling products group, vice-president of planning and marketing, vice-president of the international group, vice-president in charge of bakery products, the treasurer, the controller,

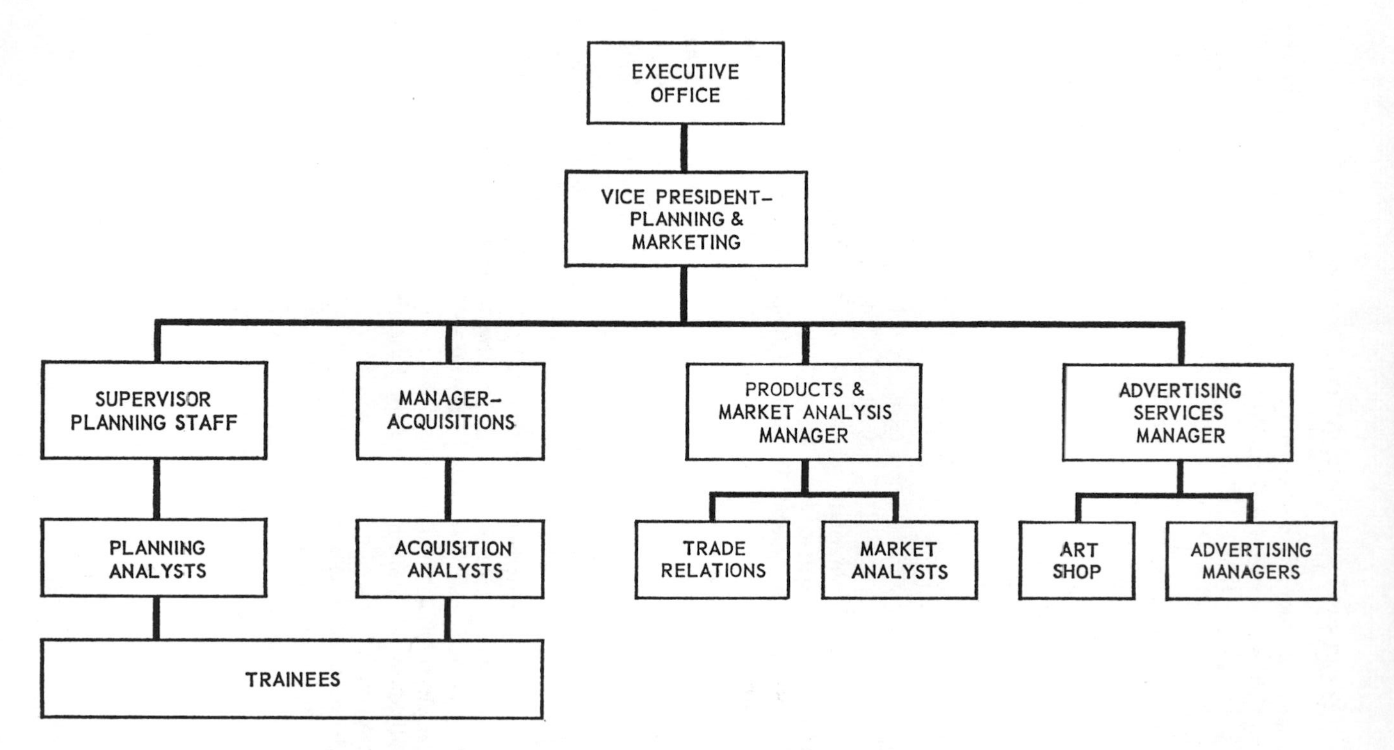

CHART 1. Planning and Marketing Division of the American Machine & Foundry Company

and an aide to the board chairman. Not currently serving on the planning committee are the corporate secretary, the vice-president of personnel and industrial relations, and the vice-president for research and development.

Mr. Jones was asked to describe his company's approach from his viewpoint as supervisor of planning. He replied as follows:

We look on planning as a line responsibility. However, we do not assign this responsibility to line people without providing specialized staff assistance. Planning in AMF is the collection of data in an organized manner and the use of this data to prepare a planning document.

A previous effort to draw up plans by operating managers without assistance resulted in a weighty collection of documents reflecting various degrees of market research, the use of excessive detail, and occasionally an inflexible or a somewhat unrealistic course of action. We collected too much information, with the inevitable result that an impressive file of material which could not be understood was assembled.

To ease the implementation of planning within each of AMF's business units or profit centers, we have found, uniformity and simplicity are vitally important. Formal written plans appear to be the only effective ones. Therefore, to simplify each unit's task and achieve a uniform format for ease of analysis, we have developed a series of planning forms. The sequence of facts to be presented follows a logical, step-by-step development of a plan for each business or division.

Our plans are primarily marketing-oriented, with secondary emphasis upon R&D, manpower, facilities, and capital requirements. Each five-year plan sets forth, by year, the goals of that particular unit with the major actions proposed to achieve its goals. To provide continuity, the results of the previous five years' performance are also submitted. In developing the American Machine & Foundry Company's five-year plan, each division is requested to prepare information on the following seven major categories of the program:

1. The market.
   a. Present major product lines and proposed new major product lines.
   b. Total industry volume and unit sales volume in each.
2. The competition.
   a. Present major product lines and proposed new major product lines.
   b. Total industry volume and unit sales volume in each.
3. Factors affecting unit performance.
   a. Future price structure for products.
   b. Direct and indirect labor costs.
   c. Market strategy.

   d. Trends within the industry.
   e. Technological changes affecting product cost and use.
   f. Market penetration (per cent and dollar volume).
4. Unit requirements.
   a. Spending for research and development.
   b. Spending for machinery and equipment.
   c. Spending for buildings.
   d. Market research program.
   e. Advertising program.
   f. Personnel and training.
5. Operations summary.
   a. Net revenues.
   b. Pre-tax profits.
   c. Assets employed.
   d. Profit margins.
   e. Asset turnover rates.
   f. Return on assets employed.
6. Cash flow.
7. Acquisition opportunities.

Individual business units' reports of projected performance and plans are received by the Planning Division late in the year. This is, however, prior to the time when unit managers submit, to the executive office and controller, the detailed operating budget for the unit for the next year. Before they are submitted for top management review, these unit plans have been evaluated, screened, and modified by the group executive—if any—who oversees the unit. Individual unit plans are then carefully analyzed and consolidated into an over-all company projection and plan of action. The separation of unit plans from budgets is important, because each differs in purpose.

In general the corporate plan consists not only of the individual unit plans, modified as necessary by the introduction of corporate priorities and goals, but also of the introduction of those programs conceived at the corporate level. Corporate programs usually deal with such matters as the development of major new products, and acquisitions.

The plan resulting from the critical analysis of the unit plans and their consolidation with corporate priorities is presented to the company's planning committee. It is important that the plan be presented in a form that enables the committee to make its decisions promptly. Broad strategic and economic considerations encompassing the over-all corporate picture are stressed, with supporting detail kept to an absolute minimum. The plan submitted to the planning committee should enable those on the committee to discuss such questions as these: "Where do we go now?" "How did we get here?" "Where will we go, without policy changes?" "Is this where we would like to be?" "How can we modify where we are going?" "With this change, will we be close to our objectives?"

A formal checklist used in planning at the American Machine and Foundry Company is reproduced below.

CHECKLIST OF QUESTIONS FOR PLANNING
AMERICAN MACHINE & FOUNDRY COMPANY

1. *Where are we now?*
   a. What businesses are we really in?
   b. Who is our competition?
   c. How big is our market, and what share do we have?
   d. What are our present strengths (and weaknesses)?
      (1) People.
      (2) Money.
      (3) Product.
      (4) Facilities.
2. *How did we get here?*
   a. What is past and present market position?
   b. How important were former technical developments in our growth?
   c. Did our past success rest with a few key people?
   d. Does our past financial policy help us today?
3. *Where will we go, without policy change?*
   a. What will be our future markets?
   b. How strong will our competitive position be?
      (1) (Future price structure.)
      (2) Reputation.
   c. Will we have adequate resources (men, money, and plant)?
   d. Will present levels of R&D result in enough new products?
   e. What sales and profits are expected from various profit centers, in contrast to the resources allocated?
4. *Is this where we would like to be?*
   a. What criteria can we use to measure satisfaction?
      (1) What theory of business operations do we want to hold?
      (2) What objectives can we set for this theory of operation?
      (3) What specific goals must be reached?
   b. How does the present operation and its projection into the future stand against these criteria?
5. *How can we modify where we are going?*
   a. What new products should be sought?
   b. Can new markets be opened up for present products?

c. Will shifts in marketing strategy benefit us?
d. Should major expansion of facilities be considered, or should they be reduced?
e. What new people are needed?
f. Will organizational changes be in order?
g. How can we strengthen our financial structure to meet future needs?
h. Will we grow "internally" (i.e., R&D and new products) or "externally" (i.e., acquisitions and licenses)?

6. *With this change, will we be close to our objective?*
a. What is the net effect of all these changes?
b. What priority should be given to each of these changes?
(1) What is the timing of an action program?
c. Who is responsible for each of these programs?

27

Determining and Reporting Division Objectives at American Brake Shoe Company[1]

The purpose of objectives or targets is to set a level of performance toward which divisional plans of action will be directed. Objectives are redetermined each year for each of the next succeeding three years. They are determined for each product line or plant and for the division as a whole. Once formulated together with their supporting programs, they become an integrated plan for the control of operations.

[1] From the company's *Guide to Profit Improvement Program,* August 1, 1959. Used by permission.

Objectives are determined for each product line or plant and for the division as a whole for:

1. Share of the market
2. Sales volume
3. Earnings
4. Necessary investment
5. Return on investment

What constitutes a product line is largely for division determination. However, . . . the important thing is that all concerned know what is included or excluded in the product line and the industry or market. . . . The objectives to be reported should be determined within the framework of the following:

1. In August each division will be furnished a forecast of the outlook for general business which to the extent possible will encompass the industry groups which comprise Brake Shoe's principal customers. The forecast will be revised quarterly to reflect changes in the general economic climate. The principal value of the forecast will be that of a guide to the general level of business during the period for which objectives are to be determined.

2. Objectives are to be determined for each of the next succeeding three years. Data with respect to the current year should be actual up to the time of determining objectives plus forecasted results for the balance of the year.

3. Known or reasonably anticipated changes in costs and selling prices for 1960 should be targeted. Objectives for 1961 and 1962 should be on the same basis of costs and prices (both purchased materials, wages, and services and products sold) as were used for 1960.

No attempt should be made to predict inflationary or deflationary movements in general wage levels and prices. Thus objectives set in 1959 for 1960, 1961, and 1962 should be in terms of the material prices, wages, and selling prices used for 1960 objectives. Changes in salary rates for 1960 can be anticipated and reflected in accordance with the Salary Planning Program submitted by the director of personnel services.

4. The amount to be included in division objectives for each of the next succeeding three years for the services of the Research Center should be determined by mutual agreement between the division president and the company vice-president for research and development

after agreement has been reached as to the research projects to be sponsored by the division.

5. The amount to be included in division objectives for each of the next succeeding three years for the services of the construction and maintenance and the industrial engineering departments should be determined by mutual agreement between the division president and the respective department heads after a joint review of division plans for the use of such activities determined on the basis of the standard rate per hour for each department.

6. Divisions will be advised by September 10 of the cost to include in determining objectives for each of the next succeeding three years for the services of Headquarters. In the absence of unusual circumstances, the amount given for the next year ahead will not be changed.

7. Objectives for cost, earnings, and investment should be established on the basis of sales volume objectives. They should reflect not only the improvement in the rate of earnings to sales and investment turnover which can be expected from higher volume, but the other operating improvements, which flow from better control of variable costs, burden, and investment.

In order to assure reasonable consistency in reporting practices the following forms (distributed each year by the comptroller's department) are to be used:

Form CO-164 Product Line or Plant Objectives
CO-166 Division Earnings Objectives
CO-168 Division Operating Investment Objective
CO-169 Summary of Division Objectives[2]

Instructions as to the use of each form are given on an explanation sheet accompanying a sample of the form.

On all forms, data shown on the line styled "target" or "present estimate" for years prior to the current year should be actual figures.

[2] This form, which is similar in format to the others, is reproduced, with the accompanying instructions for its use, on pages 276–277 following—ED.

FORM CO-169
SUMMARY OF DIVISION OBJECTIVES

This form is used for reporting objectives for the division as a whole. It provides, on one piece of paper, in summary form a picture of division objectives expressed in dollar amounts.

The explanations which follow are numbered to correspond with the arrow overlays on each of the areas of the accompanying sample of the form.

1. *Sales Value of Normal Operation*
   The sales value of normal operations is reported here. The amount so reported should be equal to the sum of that shown on line 1 of individual Forms CO-164. Provision is also made for recording previously reported normal operation targets.
2. *Markets*
   Entries for the dollar volume of market or industry should only be made here if the division is in only one market or industry. If such is the case then the amount entered should be equal to the total reported on line 3 of Form CO-164 for each plant. Comparisons where applicable should be made with previous market determinations.
3. *Shipments*
   The shipments objective for the division is entered here. This amount should agree with line 2 of Form CO-166. Comparisons with previous targets should be made where applicable.
4. *Earnings Before Taxes*
   The earnings objective is shown here as well as its percentage relation to shipments. The amount entered for each year should agree with line 19 of Form CO-166. Comparisons with previous targets, where applicable, should be made.
5. *Average Operating Investment*
   The division investment objective as well as investment turnover and return on investment are reported here. The amounts shown for average operating investment for each year are found by reference to line 16 of Form CO-168.
6. *Number of Employees End of Year*
   Provision is here made for reporting the number of employees at the end of each year.

SUMMARY OF DIVISION OBJECTIVES
(Thousands of dollars)

DIVISION: ______________________

		1	2	3	4	5	6	7
		1956	1957	1958	1959	1960	1961	1962
	SALES VALUE OF NORMAL OPERATION [1]							
1	Target							
2	Previous target	-	-	-				-
	MARKET [2]							
3	Present estimate							
4	Previous estimate	-	-	-				-
	SHIPMENTS [3]							
5	TARGET							
6	% of normal operation							
7	% of market							
8	PREVIOUS TARGET	-	-	-				-
9	% of normal operation	-	-	-				-
10	% of market	-	-	-				-
	EARNINGS BEFORE TAXES [4]							
11	TARGET							
12	% of shipments							
13	PREVIOUS TARGET	-	-	-				-
14	% of shipments	-	-	-				-
	AVERAGE OPERATING INVESTMENT [5]							
15	TARGET							
16	Turnover							
17	% return before taxes							
	NUMBER OF EMPLOYEES - END OF YEAR [6]							
18	Wage earners							
19	Salaried employees							
20	Total							

CO-169

FORM CO-169

28

Some Guides and Standards[1]

Mark W. Cresap, Jr.

Another technical question is whether to project goals and other elements of plans on a trend or a cyclical basis. I favor the former, i.e., projections following normal trends without regard to cyclical fluctuations. In the first place, the prognostication of yearly economic fluctuations is a function of the most hazardous species. Trend forecasting is difficult but I am convinced that trend projections, on the whole, have been vastly more accurate than guesses as to cyclical swings. *Fortune* magazine recently displayed a mortality table of the cyclical predictions of professional economists. It revealed a high correlation between forecast and prediction—but in reverse. And yet, if you examine the more soundly based long-term forecasts in recent years, taking for examples national product, electrical energy, and steel production, the correlation, while by no means perfect, is not of the reciprocal type.

My second reason for favoring the trend basis of planning is that the long-term development of a business should be geared to long-term movements and should not be governed by guesses as to short-term swings. Employment of the latter procedure involves a company in the risk of being strategically whipsawed and of losing its position

[1] From "Some Guides to Long-Term Planning," *N.A.C.A. Bulletin,* January 1953 (published by the National Association of Cost Accountants). Portions at the beginning and end of the original text have been omitted. Used by permission.

in growing markets. The trend approach to planning accepts the fact that there will be periods (of a reasonably short duration, it is hoped) when some plant capacity will be temporarily idle. But such an approach recognizes that, if the alternative is to delay action in the face of reliable indicators of future market growth—to delay for "more favorable circumstances"—action should be taken.

In fact, it is more speculative to attempt to time long-term strategical development by cyclical guesswork as to the "right moment" than to move ahead sure-footedly when the distant signal is clearly "green," at the same time assessing the extent of the risks involved and reflecting this assessment in the long-term plan by appropriate provisions for periods of retrenchment. Reasonable periods of idle plant capacity are far less costly than the loss of basic competitive and market status, the recapture of which may prove a crippling effort.

THE USE OF RATIOS IN BUSINESS PLANNING

A great deal of attention has been devoted to the question of what the most pertinent bases are for expressing objectives and measuring performance as regards the profitability of a company's operation. While the choice of such a basis is again dependent, to a large extent, upon the nature of an individual business, the most accepted and appropriate performance ratios for most manufacturing companies appear to be these:

1. Net income to net sales billed.
2. Return on gross fixed assets.
3. Return on current assets.
4. Return on total assets, representing the sum of gross fixed assets and current assets.

Some explanation of these ratios is relevant, since the manner of computing each is highly important, particularly if comparisons are to be made of operations within a company, and between a company and others in the same line of business. In computing these ratios, net income after taxes is employed instead of a before-tax figure, for two reasons: (1) The only effective result of a company's operations is the net amount remaining for reinvestment and dividends; and (2) it is past experience and the future expectation that, on a long-term basis, the effect of changing tax rates on net income margins is not permanent. This statement would not apply to short-term projections or annual budgets, in which cases sudden changes in tax rates have a direct and substantial effect on profits, as in 1951 and 1952. But a fifteen-year comparison of tax rate trends and after-tax corporation income ratios will quickly and convincingly confirm the fact that taxes do not necessarily affect net income margins over the long pull.

The ratio of net income to plant investment is based on the gross fixed assets figure, instead of the net amount remaining after depreciation, as a means of injecting a rough adjustment factor to provide some equalization of facility values of various divisions of a company or of comparable companies—between those with old plants built at relatively low cost and those with new plants built at high cost. By dealing with all plant values at their gross book value, the distortion of respective ratios of return on plan investment is minimized and it is felt that the relative inefficiency of the older plants is compensated adequately by their relatively lower gross value, without deduction of accrued depreciation. The use of gross plant figures does not result in truly reliable comparisons, but, unless a realistic basis for evaluation of plants on an appraisal basis is feasible, it is the most practical approach available.

The key performance standard and measure is the ratio of return on total assets. Some argue that return on net worth is preferable. The total asset basis is preferred because it measures management in terms of profits returned on total capital employed, without injecting consideration as to the sources of capital. A net worth basis of measuring profit return is pertinent to a financial evaluation, but the total asset basis is the best for appraising management's basic responsibility for earnings. I was interested to note that, in a recent survey of practices in this regard among a representative group of large companies, the measurement of return against total assets, with the fixed assets included at gross value, was the predominant approach.

The four profit performance ratios which have been mentioned serve not only to establish objectives and to measure performance but also to provide standards for evaluating the desirability and value of a new or existing product line.

Application of these standards must reflect the fact that, because of inherent characteristics, product lines will vary in their profitability ratios as between (1) "margin" of profit and (2) return on investment. Some lines with high margins produce a low return on investment because "turnover" is low—that is, the volume of sales in relation to capital employed. Other lines with moderate margins are able to produce a good return on investment because of high turnover. Often heavy special-purpose machinery is in the first classification and standardized mass production items (automobiles, refrigerators) in the second. Nevertheless, the more significant of the two measures of profitability is return on investment (rather than per cent profit to sales), since it evaluates a proposition in terms of the earnings generated by stockholders' investment, which in turn influences the rate of dividends and the market price of the company's shares.

The key criterion as to a product line, therefore, should usually be the return which it produces on its investment, expressed in terms of the ratio of profit on total assets. The component ratios of return on fixed assets and on current assets, while helpful in analysis, are useful only in an auxiliary manner. Some situations involve high fixed investments and low current assets, while others are of the reverse type. The real measure is the return on total assets. From the standpoint of risk, of course, situations requiring relatively greater current investment than fixed investments are more attractive, but only from the standpoint of risks. Funds permanently required for working capital represent the employment of capital as truly as investment in plant and equipment, and a true gauge of management's ability to return profits on investment must reflect all capital employed, both fixed and current.

The use of existing price levels as a basis for projections is advocated because of the difficulty of forecasting movements in the price level and because of the complications and dangers inherent in attempting to make all of the various adjustments required in the relationships between price realization and costs incident to fluctuations in the value of the dollar. The use of current price levels provides a stable basis for making projections. The goals can be understood and interpreted more readily by hinging them to current price levels than otherwise. Furthermore, with regular and frequent revisions of objectives, projections can be adjusted to new price levels when these revisions are made. Then, too, if major emphasis is placed on performance objectives in terms of ratios (per cent market, per cent margin to sales, per cent return on investment), the problem of varying price levels is not as acute as would be the case if the dollar objectives were stressed.

29

The Follow-Through—Necessity in Planning[1]

Maurice E. Waring
and
Paul W. Demarest

One phase of long-term planning ignored by most of its proponents is that it is a costly activity, especially so if such forecasts are carefully developed but never checked to see that planned results are attained. Each year numerous firms put together carefully thought out budgets, and we venture to say that actual results in many cases do not come too close to the predetermined objectives. A recent remark of a leading company executive emphasizes this point: "We spend a lot of time and money every year setting up fancy budgets, and everything is fine until business drops, and then my budget goes to pieces."

A budget or forecast over one year or longer is usually based on results anticipated by management. If the enthusiasm that created the original and usually ambitious goals becomes dulled by complacency, results are bound to be less than desired. Another factor contributing to the failure of forecasts is that expenses get out of hand. It is here that the accountant can step in and show management where the company is straying from the long-run objective. In the day-to-day decisions required of management, the cost of actions taken must be evaluated by the accountant within the framework of the budget or forecast.

There is still a psychological barrier between the accountant and the executive. It used to be that accountants were criticized as simply being

[1] From *NAA Bulletin,* August 1962, pp. 83–84. Used by permission. Portions at the beginning and end of the original text have been omitted.

after-the-fact reporters. Of late, accountants have become in effect . . . a society of sophisticated fortune-tellers, provided a highly complex series of conditions are furnished to them. Many executives are inclined to ridicule such predictions in the light of daily demands by this or that department. If the accountant fails to keep track of actual versus anticipated actions, the forccast becomes a thing of the past.

In reaching pre-established goals, many company departments become enmeshed in internecine warfare. This type of situation is typified by remarks like, "My department is doing its part. We'd be all right if Charley over there would get his group going." Long-range effort gets lost in this type of nonsense. The fine programs developed by the economic expert will be meaningless if one department falls behind and blames its failure on another. It is a teamwork operation that is needed to implement the accountant's carefully devised prognostications, and for this the accountant must spell out these goals in terms of each department's operations.

30 The Board of Directors Looks at Long-Range Planning[1]

James Dowd

The directors are properly concerned not only with *who* has had a hand in long-range planning, but with *how*. They would begin to get a sinking feeling if a company officer said, "Some of us did it in our spare time." But again the board needs to probe deeper:

[1] From *The Controller,* November 1962, pp. 538–540. Used by permission. Some introductory material in the original text has been omitted.

How many executive man-days does this nicely bound document on long-range planning represent?

Were there frequent conferences between the planning committee and top management, or just a few?

And now that this document has been produced, has the planning committee disbanded?

Attitudes are all-important: Directors know that planning is a difficult and often thankless task. And so they pay attention to the president and listen between the lines.

Has he properly emphasized from the start, and on suitable occasions thereafter, the importance of long-range planning to his entire executive staff?

Was there a formal announcement, or merely a few lines in the employee newsletter?

Were any of the committeemen relieved of their regular assignments, or any of their duties transferred to others?

In particular, alert directors are aware of any connotation that a nicely bound document "constitutes our long-range planning." The document is a *plan,* but planning is not a document. It is an activity; it is a continuing affair and not an event. Therefore, directors will listen for possible hints that the company's executives think the job is done, that the plan has been completed, or that "Next time, I hope they get someone else to work on that project." The word "project" is quite a clue. It suggests that one does the planning and gets it over with. It is like lashing down the helm, abandoning the bridge, and expecting the ship to cross the ocean and make port.

If the board finds no evidence that periodic reviews of the long-range plan are contemplated, it would have grounds to suspect the quality of the work and the caliber of management as well.

THE PLAN ITSELF

And now, the directors look at the document itself:

Did it have to be 100 pages thick?

It is not that directors are lazy, but how can one say so much about the future?

How reliable, or even worth reading, is this document?

How many executives in the company are going to wade through this and refer to it as a guide in their regular work?

Let us suppose the vice-president for finance has issued this document. His staff economist has picked up a couple of long-range forecasts of gross naitonal product (GNP) made by well-known authorities; company sales are related to GNP and *viola!* here is the long-range sales forecast.

That may seem just a little too pat, so the board asks the vice-president for marketing if the sales in each of his product lines are growing at the GNP rate or at different rates. The answers here may be revealing:

Different rates, are they?

Some declining?

Some industries using less of certain product lines?

The export market is more and more of a problem?

A major competitor has just come out with a new line which appears to have wide customer acceptance?

Does this company have a new line coming out?

When?

Indefinite?

The directors may also pursue some related points:

How is the industry as a whole going to fare while the company's sales are growing à la GNP?

The major competitors—will they get bigger?

Are mergers likely?

How about price-cutting?

In other words, what is the probable competitive environment five or ten years from now?

You will recognize that this is a far different and far more qualitative approach than the usual quantitative statement of a long-range sales forecast. It is more enlightening because it poses a question: *What is this long-range plan disclosing or intimating regarding the future problems likely to be in store for the company?*

Leafing further through the planning document, the directors see that the sales forecast has been used as the basis for projecting detailed statements of profit and loss, source and application of funds, balance sheet, earned surplus, and financial ratios—for each year covered by the long-range plan. All these statements are supplemented by comparative historical data exhumed from the company's past.

The directors examine the direct-cost-of-sales figure and discover that it bears an unvarying relationship to sales. They inquire about the variation in cost of sales by product line and about assumptions regarding future product mix. They look at the factory burden figure and see that it is inching ahead in the future as in the past. They ask the vice-president for production about possibilities for automation, about his need for new machinery, his opportunities for changes in production lines and quality control techniques and inventory methods. They inquire about labor relations and product development work.

The directors learn quite a bit, but they have difficulty relating what they have learned to that sterile cost-of-sales projection. The directors are told that there are too many imponderables, no exact schedule for modification of production facilities, no advance information on forthcoming union demands—in fact, they are given every good reason why those cost-of-sales figures are what they are—and incidentally, why they should distrust them. The clincher comes when the directors are told, "After all, these are only projections." *Only?* That old question of attitude comes back to haunt the board.

WHAT ARE THE FLAWS IN THE PLAN?

This is the crux of FALLACY NUMBER ONE:

Is management giving only lip service to long-range planning?

Is it going through the motions of what it feels is proper corporate ritual for "progressive, modern management"?

Is it mistaking the form for the substance?

Is this physical, tangible, nicely bound document its idea of what long-range planning is?

Then, as the directors scan the pages of supporting schedules, the further thought occurs that this is primarily a *financial* document—an attempt to portray as faithfully as possible what the company's future profit-and-loss statements and balance sheets may look like. A planning document which is devoted to this approach may possess a certain kind of usefulness—like the Coast and Geodetic Survey's publication of tide tables for various points along the seacoast. But tide tables do not shed much light on the problems of navigating past hidden shoals or weathering a hurricane.

What the company's executives need is something less figure-happy in the way of a long-range plan, with much more emphasis on contingencies and alternatives—with the spotlight on potential opportunities as seen today, and on possible catastrophes or handicaps to the business. *What is the imminence of these opportunities and handicaps, and what is their significance to the executives in purchasing and production and research and sales?*

This brings us to FALLACY NUMBER TWO:

Is the company's long-range planning a practical road map?

Is the planning document useful as a regular guide to middle as well as to top management?

It is the *pertinence* of the document to the present activities of the company that gives it value in helping to shape these activities toward the future. But if the long-range plan is disconnected from the present—if it merely portrays a bright future, without any hint of how to get there—sooner or later the directors are likely to hear some harried middle-management executive complain: *"If things are going to be so good, why don't I feel better? Why have I got all these problems?"*

Of course, too often planners dwell in ivory towers. This brings us to a consideration of FALLACY NUMBER THREE:

Just how "real" is this long-range planning document?

Is it something more than an automatic extrapolation of trend lines or the pet theories of engineering or sales?

All of us remember the advertisements appearing during World War II, promising utopia once the shooting was done. Good for morale, good publicity for companies temporarily without consumer products to sell—but very optimistic, very unreal. Never a hint of postwar problems for the producer or the consumer. Directors will very likely be wary of long-range planning which does not identify basic problems for their industry and for their company.

Let us now look at FALLACY NUMBER FOUR. If the directors read in the long-range plan about problems and prospects, and if they substitute for 1965 or 1970 the dates 1955 or 1960, and if the statements they read still seem appropriate, then the directors will quickly sense a fallacy: the projection of the present business climate into the future.

All the directors have to do to spot this particular error is merely to review in their own minds how many changes have taken place in the past five or ten years in the company, in the industry, in the customers, in business generally. Long-range planning requires the contribution of an informed imagination, grounded in historical perspective—or the plans will simply lag. The company will not be able to anticipate; it will be continually taken by surprise; and its executive decisions will be reactions to competition and circumstance, rather than a display of initiative and foresight.

WHAT'S AHEAD?

The essence of long-range planning lies in devising a strategy for the business over the coming years—not in prescribing yesterday's tactics for tomorrow. Without the new and the different, there is no possibility for adaptation to economic change.

But the directors will also be quick to catch an excess of enthusiastic expansionism—a vision of practically unlimited possibilities for business growth:

Is it sensible to grow that much?

Is there an optimum size, before the company becomes unwieldy?

What is the practical share of the market it can secure?

What about these diversification plans?

Is there talent in the company to manage something so different?

In trying to cash in on the new opportunity, will the company spread itself too thin?

Is the profit opportunity really there?

These are questions which will occur to the board as it looks at FALLACY NUMBER FIVE: escapism.

The board might well reflect that this kind of long-range planning suggests an immaturity in management—a preoccupation with the dreams for a gilt-edged tomorrow rather than with the unpleasant necessity for better management of today's lower-margin business.

To sum up, there are at least five fallacies the directors may find in the company's long-range planning:

1. *Are executives giving lip service to the need for long-range planning but acting on the basis of business as usual? Is long-range planning a fad?*

2. *Do the long-range plans have practical significance for influencing the thinking and the current decision-making of middle as well as top management?*

3. *Are the plans realistic? Are problems as well as opportunities identified? Or have the plans been put together in a vacuum?*

4. *Are there any valid projections of the business environment? Or are these projections just rehashes of the present and the past?*

5. *Is the long-range planning a blue-sky alibi for today's indifferent performance?*

As a matter of fact, the directors may begin to ask corporation management just how good its *short*-range planning is:

How well is it managing its annual budgets and operating programs?

Is its market research really good?

How about management development?

Are enough good people coming along in the junior management ranks?

The best of plans still need good people to translate them into reality.

And this reminds the directors:

How about the statement of company objectives?

Does the company have any?

Are these objectives more explicit than merely "to make money"?

Do they make good sense, in terms of profit, return on investment, industry position, product emphasis, R&D goals?

All these things—annual budgets and programs, market research, management development, company objectives—are essential foundations for good long-range planning.

Planning takes thought, rather than paper. Planning takes daring, rather than ritual.

"Often, unfortunately," says Beveridge in his remarkable book, *The Art of Scientific Investigation,* "committees are too inclined to play safe and support only projects which are planned in detail and follow conventional lines of work. Worthwhile advances are seldom made without taking risks."[2]

He was writing, of course, about laboratory research, from which new products spring, but his words apply equally to the deliberations of long-range planning committees.

Big volumes and major projects are not the answer to long-range planning. I have seen one sheet of 8½" x 11" paper express a valid and illuminating long-range plan, because there had been previous

[2] William I. B. Beveridge, *The Art of Scientific Investigation* (Melbourne, Australia, William Heinemann, Ltd., 1950).

broad-gauge thinking about the future, and because there was initiative and appetite for opportunity.

Whatever some executives may think, a board of directors *is* capable of taking a hard-boiled look at the top-management group. And when it does:

What will it see? Intelligent drive? Or just energetic treadmilling?

Does the board see evidence of entrepreneurial instinct, of an appetite for the calculated risk?

Or are these executives in love with their traditions, with pictures of "our founder" all over the place, and a good retirement plan?

Private enterprise is a wonderful thing, but when the emphasis gets put on the *private* instead of the *enterprise,* the board has a real problem on its hands.

No effective long-range planning is possible in an atmosphere like that, because, fundamentally, long-range planning is an attitude—a state of mind.

Under these circumstances, a board of directors might well issue a deadline ultimatum to company management to shape up—or resign.

31

Mathematical Approach to Long-Range Planning[1]

Leo A. Rapoport
and
William P. Drews

• How can mathematical programing help management decision-makers shift their attention from the technicalities of planning to long-range goals and risks?

[1] From *Harvard Business Review,* May–June 1962, pp. 75–87. Used by permission.

• What unique features distinguish linear programing from conventional approaches to planning problems and make it more useful for executives?

• How specifically can programing studies help management to evaluate the effect of various events on costs and profits and then make the best possible revisions in policies and programs?

The growing application of advanced mathematical techniques to the fields of business and economics may very well be one of the most far-reaching developments of the last decade. Whether we are actually on the verge of a revolution in the technology of business administration, as suggested by some forecasters, is still difficult to confirm. But it is a fact that mathematical methods of programing and optimization are increasingly used for the study of industrial and business operations.

Like most new "techniques," mathematical programing has gradually gained acceptance on the basis of a number of special applications. Thus, it is used today as a routine tool for such problems as products blending, setting up refinery running plans, scheduling machine utilization, allocating supplies to plants and warehouses, and designing and controlling transportation systems. Unquestionably, there is still room for many more worthwhile applications of mathematical programing to other specific, technical facets of industry. At this stage, however, the most significant gains can probably be achieved by focusing attention on the over-all treatment of business systems, viewed as a composite of marketing, manufacturing, procurement, finance, and such other interdependent functions.

In this article, then, we will discuss the use of a mathematical programing approach to long-range investment planning and to operations scheduling for integrated corporations. The particular approach to be considered is *linear programing.* Inasmuch as the theory of this approach is well established and has been widely discussed, we need not concern ourselves with the underlying mathematics and computational procedures.[2] Instead, we shall—

• Briefly examine the conceptual *implications* of integrated planning from the viewpoint of how to allocate funds and resources in the most effective way for the whole corporation.

[2] Alexander Henderson and Robert Schlaifer, "Mathematical Programing: Better Information for Better Decision Making," *Harvard Business Review,* May–June 1954, p. 73.

- Illustrate the *content and general structure of a mathematical "model"* describing a system of interdependent activities as it evolves through time.
- Outline the *various uses* to which such a mathematical planning model can be put.

In the course of these discussions we hope to make it apparent that mathematical programing is not a "black box" substitute for decision-making. Rather, it should be viewed as a discipline aimed at developing a vast, organized body of information. Utilization of this discipline could permit management to shift much of its decision-making activity from the technicalities of planning to the area of goals, policies, and risks.

ALLOCATION AND OPTIMIZATION

For purposes of illustration, it is convenient to begin with a "bird's eye view" of an integrated business like the one shown in Exhibit 1. Thus:

The basic function of this oil company would consist of extracting and processing crudes and of ensuring the movement of all products to the sales terminals so as to meet a certain demand through time. For the sake of simplicity we consider that this oil business deals only with two types of crudes—heavy and light—and with three classes of products—gasoline, kerosene, and industrial fuel. It thus reflects the general characteristics of most integrated industrial enterprises. The crude oil reservoirs may be considered equivalent to sources of raw materials; and the refineries, equivalent to manufacturing or assembly plants producing the finished products. Note that the marketing activity as such is not included in our example. Only the results of marketing, in the form of providing a certain demand on the system, are considered.

The structure of the business is divided into three major technical functions: production, transportation, and refining. These functions work "in series" along the flow path of the crudes. Such an arrangement in series necessarily entails strong interdependence of the different technical functions, since the output of one function serves as an input to the next. At the same time, however, each major function or activity is composed of parallel elements—for instance, two refineries and a number of oil fields or crude oil supply areas operating "side by side." Such a parallelism, in turn, suggests that the operation of the integrated system offers a wide choice of alternatives. These two combined aspects, functional interdepend-

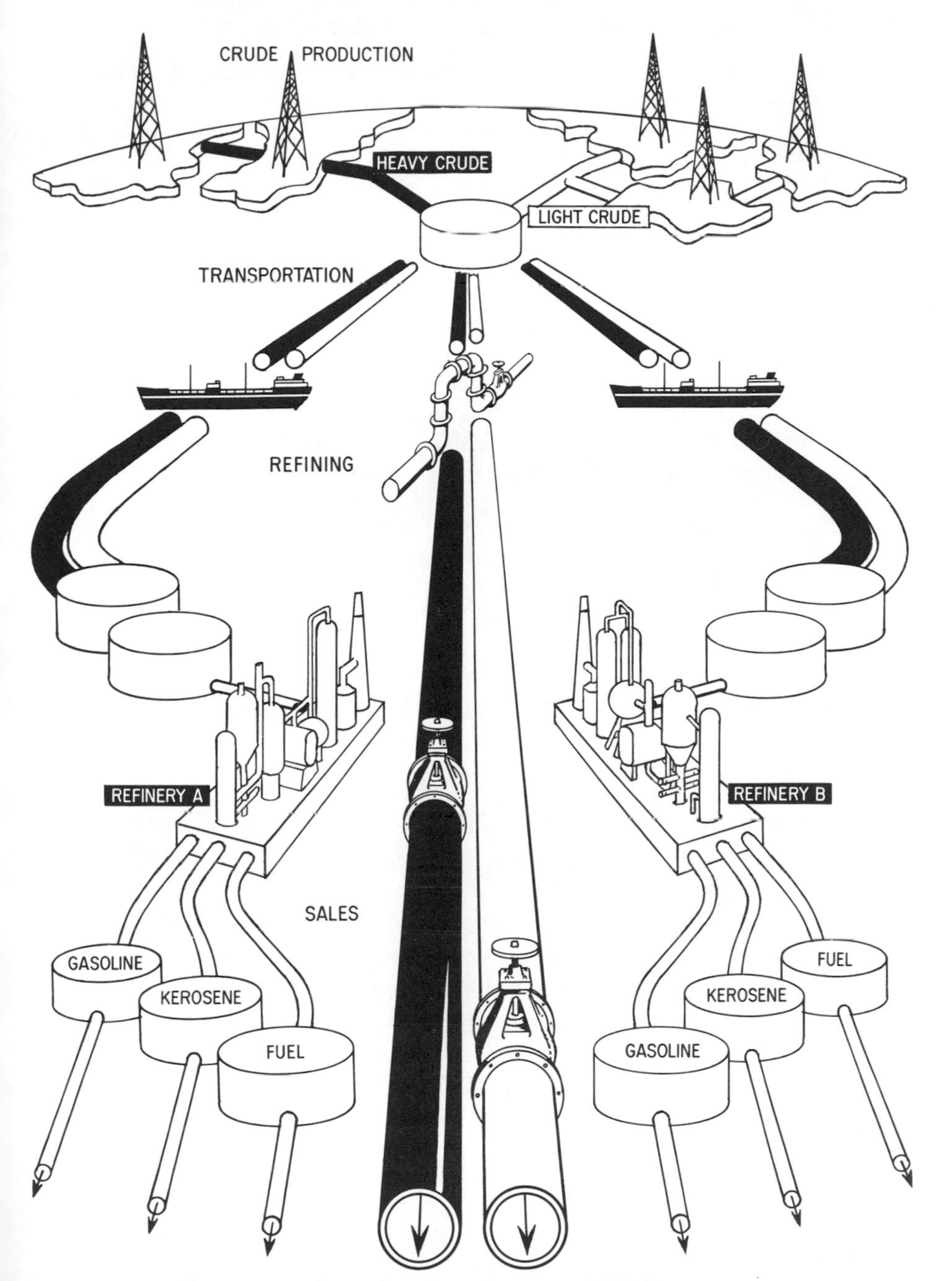

EXHIBIT 1. Operations in an Integrated Oil Company

ence and choice of alternatives, lead naturally to the notions of "allocation" and "optimization":

¶ To clarify the notion of *allocation,* note that one oil field can be produced or developed in preference to another; different kinds or different amounts of crude can be channeled to the various refineries; and the refinery yields, along with the expansions of refinery installations, can be selected with a certain degree of freedom. However, all these different possible alternatives must be coordinated and scheduled so as to ensure smooth intermeshing of operations. This, in turn, implies appropriate allocation of funds and/or resources to the component parts of the integrated enterprise.

¶ The notion of *optimization* arises from the fact that the different operational and investment alternatives entail costs which are usually different. It is not sufficient to assign activity levels or allocate funds merely to ensure a feasible plan. Rather, the ultimate objective is to allocate funds or resources to *maximize the over-all profitability of the integrated business.* In short, it is the effectiveness of the corporation as a whole in which top management is interested. (This "effectiveness" is commonly defined in terms of corporate profits. However, other definitions of a broader nature might often be preferable.)

These concepts of allocation and optimization are useful in discussing long-range planning, and the terms will appear frequently in the remainder of this article.

The Whole Versus the Parts

Almost everybody will agree that over-all optimization is desirable. At the same time, however, there still is a widespread belief that the best plan for an integrated business will be obtained by letting each of the component activities improve its own efficiency as much as possible. Another common view is that for purposes of optimal planning it suffices to evaluate and screen projects or budget proposals on the basis of their individual profitability. These are serious misconceptions.

Mathematically it can be demonstrated that the maximum of a composite function generally does not correspond to the values of variables which maximize the individual components of that function. A simple graphical illustration of this situation in the context of economics appeared in a recent article by Edward G. Bennion.[3]

[3] "Econometrics for Management," *Harvard Business Review,* March–April 1961, p. 100.

The optimization principle has also been stated in clear terms by Peter F. Drucker:

> . . . If there is one fundamental insight underlying all management science, it is that the business enterprise is a *system* of the highest order. . . .
>
> The whole of [such] a system is not necessarily improved if one particular function or part is improved or made more efficient. In fact, the system may well be damaged thereby, or even destroyed. In some cases the best way to strengthen the system may be to *weaken* a part—to make it *less* precise or *less* efficient. For what matters in any system is the performance of the whole. . . .
>
> Primary emphasis on the efficiency of parts in management science is therefore bound to do damage. It is bound to optimize precision of the tool at the expense of the health and performance of the whole.
>
> This is hardly a hypothetical danger. The literature abounds in actual examples—inventory controls that improve production runs and cut down working capital but fail to consider the delivery expectations of the customer and the market risks of the business; machine-loading schedules that overlook the impact of the operations of one department on the rest of the plant; forecasts that assume the company's competitors will just stand still; and so on.[4]

Admittedly, the above statements are somewhat general and, therefore, might appear as unfounded abstractions to the hardened skeptic. A simple example, however, might help to illustrate their practical importance:

> In the case of our hypothetical oil company in Exhibit 1, suppose that one of the refineries should find it most profitable to install a particular processing unit of Type T in order to utilize a certain low-price crude, C_t. The installation of this unit would be justified *from the refiner's viewpoint* by showing an attractive return on incremental investment. This "conventional" approach, however, may overlook the aspects of functional interdependence.
>
> Bear in mind that the installation and efficient utilization of a processing unit of Type T would commit the producing function to a continued supply of crude, C_t. This crude, although low priced (on the outside market), may not, in fact, be the least costly to produce, nor would it necessarily remain the least costly as greater amounts of it become required in the future. Accordingly, from an over-all viewpoint, it could prove more desir-

[4] "Thinking Ahead: Potentials of Management Science," *Harvard Business Review*, January–February 1959, p. 26.

able to install a different processing unit of Type S. This other unit might be more expensive to install or to operate than Type T. In compensation, however, it would permit utilization of some other crude, C_t, which in the long run might be less costly to produce than crude, C_t.

Under such conditions, it is apparent that over-all company economics could actually be improved by *weakening* the economics of one of the refineries.

Danger of Suboptimization

The preceding example, oversimplified as it is, highlights one of the basic shortcomings of the conventional methods of economic analysis. This shortcoming amounts to excessive "suboptimization" from the viewpoint of investment planning. In many instances, investment planning is based on a simple ranking of projects in terms of their return on investment, credit status, or present-value profile. Such a direct ranking procedure permits comparison of different proposed projects under the assumption that the projects stand independently on their own merits. However, this ranking approach usually does not evaluate how much each of the projects under consideration affects the profitability of existing operations. Moreover, it basically ignores how much the profitability of each of the currently considered projects may be affected by other projects and operations in the future, and vice versa.

To overcome these shortcomings of suboptimization, it is clearly necessary to look simultaneously at all pertinent projects and operations of the integrated system as they evolve through time and impinge on each other. This actually implies keeping track of and evaluating all the repercussions caused by a modification or adjustment in any one of the individual operations within the system. Such a task naturally brings to mind the desirability of resorting to a formal, systematic approach—that is, mathematical programing.

Aid to Judgment

The basic implication of a formal programing approach to planning is to describe the economic or business processes under consideration in mathematical language—much hte same as the physicist employs mathematical expressions to describe natural phenomena. In turn, when this is done, we can take advantage of the analytical power of mathematical techniques combined with the capabilities of modern, high-speed computing equipment.

From a procedural viewpoint, the first step in a mathematical-programing approach to planning is to define the quantifiable factors which are pertinent to the functioning of the business system under consideration. This definition implies, in particular, specification of those factors which are, or might be, considered controllable and those factors which are not. The former we will call the *variables,* while the latter may be designated *parameters* or *coefficients.*

The next basic step consists of formulating appropriate mathematical expressions which describe the interrelations of all of the pertinent variables and parameters. Such formulations, reflecting the interdependence of the actual operations as well as the various limitations imposed on the activities of the business, represent, in effect, a *mathematical model* of the business system. Such a model—describing the technology and economics of a business—consists essentially of a set of simultaneous equations and inequalities.

The most significant aspect of mathematical programing, then, consists of determining what is called an *optimum solution* to the set of model equations and inequalities. This implies finding numerical values for all the controllable variables in such a manner as to satisfy the interrelations and limitations characterizing the business system, while at the same time maximizing profits, or minimizing costs, or coming as close as possible to some other goal or criterion. Inasmuch as each of the variables employed in the model formulation serves to designate a specific operation or level of activity, the mathematical solution provides a direct description of an optimum operating and investment plan.

From the foregoing it should now be apparent that mathematical programing is incomparably broader in scope than, and in fact quite different from, what is often implied by using the term "programing" to designate adaptation of a technical problem to machine computation. (For example, there is no similarity between the programing we are concerned with and the kind of programing pertaining to data processing or clerical operations.) However, the broad scope of mathematical programing does not mean that it is equivalent to an automatic decision-making device. In particular, *the establishment of criteria as to what is actually best for a business enterprise is altogether beyond the realm of mathematics.* The charting of a course for a business requires consideration and weighing of a number of intangible factors (long-range technical trends, evolution of markets, political pressure, and so on) which have to be evaluated on the basis of intuition, judgment, and experience.

Thus, mathematical programing should be viewed essentially as a helpful supplement to judgment and intuition. The help that it can provide stems from its ability to deal efficiently with large amounts of information and to explore systematically a great number of alternatives and restrictions characterizing the functioning of a complex business system.

MODEL FORMULATION

Let us now turn to a concrete illustration of mathematical programing (and of linear programing in particular) as applied to integrated planning. We shall try to show how a mathematical model is actually formulated by:

1. Introducing and defining the pertinent variables
2. Reviewing the relationships employed to describe the activities and the constraints of the business system
3. Examining how these relations are expanded to reflect the changes in operating conditions and facilities as the system evolves through time
4. Discussing how the economic aspects or objectives of the business can be expressed in mathematical form

With these points in mind we will later consider the basic methodology and conceptual innovations contributed by the mathematical-programing approach.

USE OF VARIABLES

In setting up a mathematical model for purposes of planning, it is convenient to distinguish between *operational variables* and *investment variables*. The operational variables serve to specify the levels at which the different activities within the business system are carried on. From a financial viewpoint, these variables are essentially associated with operating costs. The investment variables, on the other hand, pertain to the installation of industrial facilities, i.e., they specify the expansions of the various plant or operating capacities. Accordingly, the investment variables are associated with capital expenditures.

If we were to take our hypothetical oil company and list the operational and investment variables that are basic to planning, we might come up with a set such as the one shown in Exhibit 2. More specifically:

EXHIBIT 2

BASIC VARIABLES FOR PLANNING

OPERATIONAL VARIABLES		
Amounts of crude production from various oil fields	Heavy crudes	X_1, X_2, X_3
	Light crudes	X_4, X_5
Heavy crudes transported to gathering station		X_6
Light crudes transported to gathering station		X_7
Heavy crudes allocated to Refineries A and B		X_8, X_9
Light crudes allocated to Refineries A and B		X_{10}, X_{11}
Heavy crudes allocated to outside sales		X_{12}
Light crudes allocated to outside sales		X_{13}
Amounts of gasoline produced at Refineries A and B		X_{14}, X_{15}
Amounts of kerosene produced at Refineries A and B		X_{16}, X_{17}
Amounts of industrial fuel produced at Refineries A and B		X_{18}, X_{19}
INVESTMENT VARIABLES		
Expansion of production facilities	Heavy crudes	Y_1, Y_2, Y_3
	Light crudes	Y_4, Y_5
Expansion of pipeline capacity		Y_6
Expansion of processing installations	Refinery A	Y_7
	Refinery B	Y_8

The *operational* variables are defined as the amounts of crudes or products processed by each activity over a given time period, say per year. Thus, X_1 would represent the yearly production of heavy crude from Oil Field No. 1; X_8, the yearly amount of heavy crude processed by Refinery A; and so on.

The *investment* variables are defined as the increments in yearly production and/or throughput capacities. Thus, Y_1 would represent the increase in heavy crude production capacity resulting from the installation of additional wells in Oil Field No. 1; Y_7 would represent the increase in refining capacity resulting from the expansion of processing facilities at Refinery A; and so on.

These variables define the operational and investment activities for a given time period, say, the year 1962. A similar set of variables would be

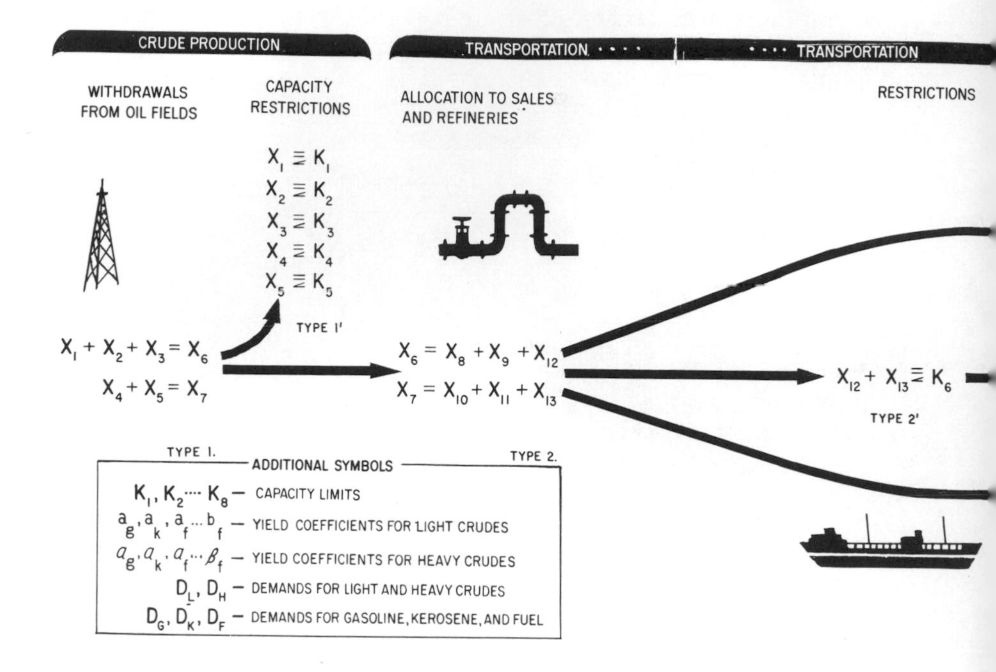

employed to define the activities of 1963, still another set for 1964, and so on. (Usually, the variables defining a given activity for successive time periods are designated by the same symbol but associated with different superscripts. For the sake of simplicity, these superscripts have been deleted from Exhibits 2 and 3.)

As we will see, the operational variables are used in describing the interdependence of the various activities of the business system within any given time period. The investment variables then serve to link activities through time—within a given period as well as between periods—by specifying the effect of new installations on current and future operations.

Description of Operations

The manner in which the operational variables can be employed to obtain a basic description of the business system in a given time period is illustrated in Exhibit 3. This description consists primarily of a sequence of balance equations, which link one activity of the system to

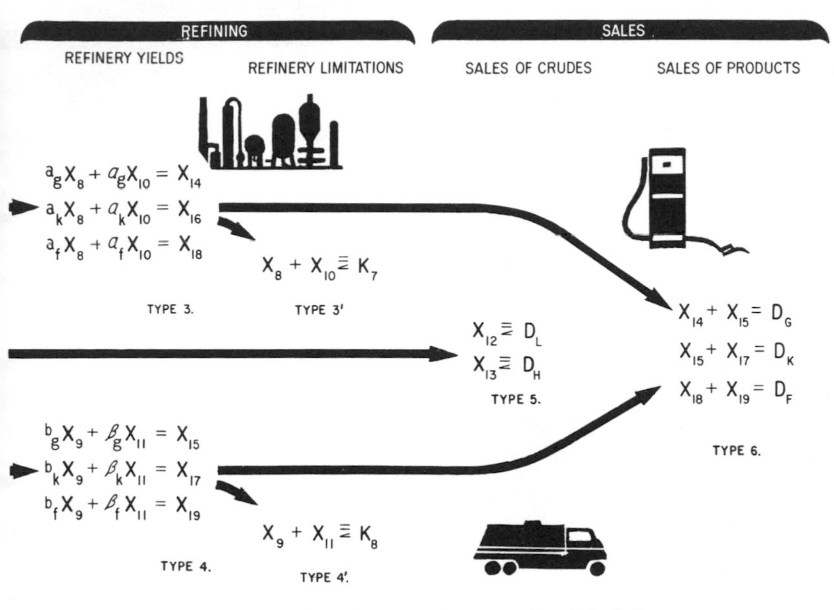

EXHIBIT 3. Programing Model

the next. (These balance equations are shown inside the white circles.) For instance:

Equations of Type 2 list the yearly crude productions from the various oil fields and state that these amounts of crude are transferred to the transportation activity. (The transportation variables are identified in Exhibit 2 as X_6 and X_7.) Equations of Type 2 describe the distribution of crudes between direct sales and refinery allocations. Equations of Types 3 and 4 then define the relationships between crude allocations to the refineries and the resulting slates of manufactured products, i.e., gasoline, kerosene, and fuel. These relations, greatly simplified for purposes of this example, correspond to a description of refinery yields, based on the consideration of certain yield coefficients, a_g, a_k, a_f, α_g, and so on.

The final set of relations required to complete the description of the flow of crudes and products throughout the system is illustrated by expressions 5 and 6, which represent the demand stipulations. These stipulations, relating the amounts of crudes and products generated by the system to the external demands, are particularly significant, since they actually trigger the behavior of the entire system.

Aside from the statements of balance or equality, the description of the business system also requires a representation of the various *limitations* imposed upon or existing within the system. These limitations, pertaining to the many practical considerations which can only be stated in a somewhat indefinite form, are mathematically expressed by means of inequalities (shown inside the white boxes in Exhibit 3). Thus:

- The relations of Type 1′ serve to state that the amount of crude taken from each oil field cannot exceed the existing yearly production capacity, K, of that field.
- Relation 2′ expresses the fact that the total amount of crude sent through the pipeline to the sales terminals cannot exceed the pipeline capacity, K_6.
- Expressions 3′ and 4′ serve to state that the yearly refinery runs cannot exceed certain limits, K_7 and K_8 at Refineries A and B, respectively.

It is important to realize that many of the administrative, political, or contractual restrictions of a business system can also be expressed, like the technical limitations, in the form of inequalities. This is illustrated in Exhibit 3 by one of the demand stipulations, the relations of Type 5. These relations could, for instance, reflect an agreement with a purchaser of crude who would be willing to accept any amount of heavy crude up to D_H barrels per year and up to D_L barrels per year of light crude. On the other hand, the general company policy, "at least 60 per cent of our total crude production should be processed in our own refineries," would be expressed just as simply by the inequality:

$$X_8 + X_9 + X_{10} + X_{11} \geqq 0.6\ (X_1 + X_2 + X_3 + X_4 + X_5)$$

Evolution Through Time

The relations just described provide only an instantaneous picture of the business system. A whole sequence of such snapshots is required to describe the evolution of the system through time. This is accomplished by repeating essentially the same type of formulation for each of the time intervals under consideration. Thus, a description of the system over five successive years would involve five sequences of equations and inequalities similar to the one illustrated in Exhibit 3. Of course, the coefficients figuring in the various relations should be modified from one time period to the next so as to reflect the variations in demand and modifications of technological characteristics. In addition, the changes or expansions of facilities carried out in each time period must be explicitly stated by means of separate "capacity expansion equations." To illustrate:

The variations in demand would be represented by assigning, in accordance with the demand forecast, different values (for successive time intervals) to the requirement factors D_H, D_L, D_F, D_G, and D_K, which figure in relations of Types 5 and 6. On the other hand, as previously indicated, changes in facilities will generally be expressed by means of the investment variables. Then this leads to additional equations (not shown in Exhibit 3). For example:

$$K_7^2 = K_7^1 + Y_7^1$$

This relation simply states that in the second time period under consideration the processing capacity K_7^2 available at Refinery A is equal to the previously existing capacity, K_7^1, plus the incremental capacity, Y_7^1 installed during the first time period. Similar equations describing the various expansion or investment alternatives apply, of course, to all other types of facilities.

These expansion equations, then, provide the logical and necessary linkage between the sets of relations describing the activities of the system in each particular time period.

In summary, to describe an integrated system of activities evolving through time we use a sequence of similar sets of structural relations, e.g., those illustrated in Exhibit 3. Each of these sets is linked to the next one on the basis of the investment variables and certain capacity-expansion equations which define the changes in operating conditions. In turn, because of this linkage through time, the sets of structural relations corresponding to the different time periods must all be considered together in order to view the business evolution in proper perspective.

Economic Objectives

The foregoing sections have dealt with physical operations and the flow of materials. To provide a complete view of the business system, we must describe the flow of cash associated with the movement and processing of materials and products. This can be accomplished by considering appropriate unit-cost and unit-revenue coefficients which enable us to express the expenditures or revenues of each activity in terms of the corresponding operational and investment variables. For instance:

¶ In the case of our oil company, it may cost c_1 dollars to produce one barrel of heavy crude from Oil Field No. 1. Accordingly, the expenditure associated with the production of X_1 barrels from this oil field will be c_1X_1, while the expenditure corresponding to the production of heavy crude from Oil Field No. 2 will be c_2X_2. Similarly, the expenditures associated with the transportation of crudes to the central gathering station will be c_6X_6 (for the heavy crudes), c_7X_7 (for the light crudes), and so on.

¶ On the other hand, the capital expenditure associated with the installation of Y_7 barrels per year of incremental processing capacity at Refinery A may be expressed as i_7Y_7; and similar expressions will apply to the investments pertaining to the expansions of pipeline and producing facilities.

¶ The revenue corresponding to the sale of X_{12} barrels of heavy crude will be $r_{12}X_{12}$, that corresponding to the sale of X_{14} barrels of gasoline will be $r_{14}X_{14}$, and so forth.

In general, we can see that when the cost and revenue coefficients are known, the cash flow picture of the business system is readily obtained by simple algebraic summation of the successive yearly expenditures and revenues associated with each activity. (It is, of course, understood that the cost and/or revenue coefficients associated with a given activity may be different for the different time periods encompassed by the planning formulation, in accordance with anticipated changes in technology, escalation of wages, market prices, and the like.)

Thus, the total outgoing cash flow for the system would be described by the following expression, summed over all time periods under consideration:

$$Z_c = c_1X_1 + c_2X_2 + \cdots c_{19}X_{19} + i_1Y_1 + i_2Y_2 \cdots + i_8Y_8$$

where the symbols X and Y represent the different operational and investment variables (see Exhibit 2), while the coefficients c and i are the corresponding unit operating and investment costs. The expression Z_c is usually referred to as the "cost functional" or, more generally, the "objective function." It describes the particular economic objective—in the above case, the total costs—in terms of which the operation of the system is to be studied.

Of course, various other economic criteria or objectives for the business system can be studied and formulated. For instance, if we desired to consider gross profits rather than costs, we would define a profit functional as follows (with the expression again summed over all time periods under consideration):

$$Z_p = r_{12}X_{12} + r_{13}X_{13} + \cdots r_{19}X_{19} - Z_c$$

This profit functional is obtained simply by multiplying all the volumes of crudes and products sold by the corresponding unit revenues, r, and then subtracting the previously defined cost functional, Z_c.

Proceeding in a somewhat similar manner, we could also define an objective function in terms of net profits after taxes or in terms of dividends over a succession of years.

Note, too, that we can formulate the objective function so as to describe the present worth of the anticipated costs and/or profits. To do this we only need to multiply the cost of revenue coefficients corresponding to the successive years by appropriate discount factors. In turn, different objective functions can be formulated for different interest rates, i.e., different values of the discount factors.

From the preceding discussion we see that the value taken by the objective functions, Z_c or Z_p, depends on the values assigned to all of the operational and investment variables. With this in mind we can now summarize the planning problem in concise mathematical form. Determining the best plan of action or the "optimum solution" for an integrated business system consists of finding a set of values for all the variables so as to maximize—or minimize—the objective function while at the same time satisfying all the structural relations which describe the physical operation of the system.

FEATURES OF PROGRAMING

When a problem such as the one just described is solved mathematically, how is the job done? It is not necessary to describe a solution in detail here, but it is worthwhile to review the basic features of the method.

To begin, the particular formulation we have discussed is that of a linear programing model. The model is so called because the equations and inequalities employed to describe the business system, as well as the objective function, Z, are in the form of linear relations between the variables. (If the original relations in the problem are not linear, often they can be replaced by suitable linear approximations.)

Speed in Computations

Since the algebraic relations employed in the model formulation are clearly quite elementary, why is a special mathematical technique required? The need arises from the fact that while each of the relationships is very simple, there are many such relationships to be solved simultaneously. To illustrate:

> The greatly simplified problem in Exhibit 3 involves 19 variables which must be selected so as to maximize the profit functional while satisfying 13 equations and 10 inequalities. Extension of this schematic example over five successive time periods would lead to 95 operational variables and 115 equations and inequalities. In addition, we would consider at least 32 investment variables and 32 expansion-type equations (eight per time period) linking the successive time periods to one another.
>
> Moreover, each of the basic operational and/or investment variables considered in our oversimplified formulation must in reality be expressed in terms of specific technological factors. For instance, in order to obtain a meaningful representation of the system, the yearly production from each oil field should be explicitly related to the number of wells, to the underground pressure decline characteristics, to workover and development drilling activities, and so on. Thus, realistic representation and planning over five successive periods of our hypothetical company would actually involve the manipulation of perhaps 500 variables and about 400 equations and inequalities.

While the conventional algebraic paper-and-pencil methods are in principle applicable to these problems, the actual size of the equation systems involved would make the use of such methods so time consuming as to be entirely impractical. In contrast, the linear programing approach includes basically more efficient equation-solving procedures, coupled with specially designed techniques for high-speed machine computation. These specialized computational techniques represent a significant advance in the handling of voluminous information and, in turn, contribute greatly to the solution of practical planning problems. At present, for example, linear programing optimization problems of about five hundred equations and a thousand to fifteen hundred variables can conveniently be solved on the IBM 7090 computer in a matter of a few hours.

Greater Reach

Is linear programing simply a means of carrying out conventional problem-solving procedures more rapidly and conveniently? It is true that the technique deals with a problem that is very familiar to economists, businessmen, and engineers; namely, determining how to use or allocate limited amounts of resources and/or facilities to best advantage. However, the methodology introduced by linear programing to help solve this type of problem draws on mathematical concepts that are relatively novel and unconventional. The example in Exhibit 3 illustrates this aspect:

> The salient feature of the formulation is that it contains more variables than equations. Besides, we have a number of relationships which are not neat, exact equations, but inequalities. Under such conditions, classical theory indicates that there may be not one but an infinite number of solutions to the problem. This indefiniteness is characteristic of most practical planning problems and moves them out of the realm of conventional algebra. No longer is it enough to find a solution to a large set of equations; it is important to find among all the possible solutions the one that is best in accordance with a given objective.

The conventional approach to the kind of planning problem shown in Exhibit 3 consists essentially of carrying out a series of case studies. Often, without even taking advantage of a basic formulation, considerable effort is devoted to arriving first at a feasible solution. Then, the whole effort is resumed and another feasible solution or case is worked out and compared to the previous one; and so on. In spite of the guidance provided by judgment and experience, this testing of solutions—in effect, by trial and error—can readily become a very tedious and confusing affair for any business system of respectable size. Moreover, it is clear that only a limited number of solutions can be tested. Thus, management has little assurance that the best solution has been attained—or perhaps even envisioned—when the studies are made.

Linear programing, in contrast, deals basically not just with the mechanics of producing a solution to a set of equations but also with the automatic ordering of multiple solutions for problems that are characterized by a certain degree of indefiniteness (provided, of course, that the relations in the problems are, or can be made, linear). The process works as follows:

1. The simplest possible solution to the problem is determined. This first solution or planning program is often deliberately trivial.
2. Any calculated solution or program, including the first one, is subjected to a testing routine to determine whether it can be improved, i.e., to find out whether any of the values assigned to the different variables can be changed so as to decrease the cost functional or increase the profit functional, whatever the case may be.
3. If the test indicates that a solution can be improved, a revision is carried out in accordance with a procedure which automatically ensures that the new solution will be at least as good as or better than the preceding one.
4. Succeeding revisions are made until the testing routine indicates that no further improvement is possible. At that stage an optimum or best solution has been attained.

(High-speed computing codes are available to carry out all the above operations in minimum time and without introduction of human errors.)

Thus, we see that the linear-programing approach permits exhaustive exploration of many alternative solutions and systematized search for an optimum solution. A most significant by-product is that the opportunities for improving the planning solution are evaluated on the basis of every variable and in regard to each of the restrictions contained in the problem. Thus, linear programing provides numerical information of an analytical nature and concepts of problem exploration not encompassed by conventional planning methods.

USES OF MODEL

What different types of studies are possible with the help of linear programing? What kinds of information pertinent to long-range planning decisions can be developed?

From the foregoing analysis it will be apparent that the direct, basic function of a mathematical planning model is to determine the best possible schedule of operations and program of investments over a period of time. The simplest use of the model would be to evaluate such a plan for a fixed set of conditions, i.e., for a certain demand forecast and a given economic objective, with a given set of costs and technological parameters (e.g., shipping capacity, yield factors, and production limits).

However, with the gradual accumulation of practical experience and continuing theoretical advances, the scope of programing model applications has been greatly extended. Therefore, we can now consider three broad areas of application:

1. Exploration of planning programs over a range of conditions.
2. Economic interpretation of restrictions and policies.
3. Sensitivity analyses.

Whereas studies of the first type are mainly concerned with maximizing profits, minimizing costs, and other aspects of optimization, studies of the second and third types are essentially of an analytical nature. In their case the model formulation is used, in effect, as a mathematical framework to investigate how the integrated business system would react to variations of its component elements and/or external factors.

Exploration of Plans

Planning decisions are, of course, largely governed by the picture of anticipated demands. It is therefore interesting to investigate the implications of meeting different patterns of demands through time, and to study systematically how the potential long-range profits of the business may vary in accordance with different possible demand patterns. Such broad exploratory studies can also serve to develop a better basis for coping with the uncertainties of future demands.

In developing planning information relative to a spectrum of possible demands, the first step is to submit different sets of demand stipulations to the programing model. The model formulation is then solved, or optimized, using each of the demand stipulations in turn. The determination of an entire set of optimum solutions can be obtained rapidly and at low cost by virtue of the computational efficiency of linear programing. This is especially true if a special feature referred to as "parametric programing" is used. This procedure consists essentially of submitting to the model a range of possible demand patterns and of gradually shifting from one limit of this range to the other. As a result, an entire array of optimum planning solutions is created automatically.

Note that a linear-programing formulation permits extremely rapid development of plans for a multitude of demand cases and that each of the developed plans is an optimum. Accordingly, the effects of different demand patterns can be compared on a well-defined, consistent basis—under conditions of optimum utilization of existing facilities and investment opportunities. Such studies, in turn, can provide a measurement of the incentives for modifying demands, e.g., an evaluation of the justifiable increments in marketing expenditures for purposes of developing additional outlets and/or intensifying sales efforts.

In dealing with the problem of uncertainty over future sales and demands, the ability of linear programing to evaluate entire arrays of solutions can be used to generate a least-risk plan. In this application, the mathematical model would be instructed to: (1) develop the entire sequence of feasible solutions, and (2) seek a program which may not be optimum relative to any one of the possible demand patterns, but which is acceptable for and the least removed from optimality in regard to the whole set of demand patterns that are foreseeable.

A serious difficulty which often arises at the very outset of corporate planning studies is to find an acceptable definition of long-range company objectives. This is a very basic problem which stems in many instances from the desire to pursue or simultaneously consider different objectives. Thus, management may be confronted with different viewpoints, some of which will stress the desirability of maximizing gross revenue or long-range volume of business, while others might emphasize maximization of net profits, and still others may focus primarily on the minimization of costs.

Mathematical programing can help to resolve such a difficulty by permitting systematic evaluation of the best strategies for attaining different objectives. This can be done conveniently by writing out in mathematical form each of the contemplated possible objectives. The model formulation would then be solved for optimal programs, using each of the objectives in turn. In this manner it is possible to develop a comprehensive, quantitative picture of the operational and economic implications associated with the pursuit of the different goals. This, in turn, will clarify the extent to which different objectives may be compatible with one another, and it can provide valuable background information for decisions pertaining to basic long-range policies.

Guidelines and Evaluations

A mathematical model is entirely objective but not creative. It can process and optimize a large number of alternatives, but it cannot originate any innovations. More concretely, the model cannot think up new ways of running the business, nor consider alternatives not previously submitted to it.

However, while the solution to a programing formulation will always be within the bounds of its own framework, each solution contains explicit information as to how much its profitability could be increased by changing or shifting any one of the bounding restrictions. By analyzing the "potential profit increment numbers" that are contained in the programing solution, management can use the model to:

1. Detect which changes in existing or contemplated facilities or policies are most desirable.
2. Determine explicitly and quantitatively the economic significance of technological, administrative, and political restrictions and/or interrelations.

Thus, a programing model can actually assume a somewhat creative role by providing analytical information and guidelines extending beyond the specific boundaries of model formulation. A case in point is the detection of potential bottlenecks in an integrated system and the evaluation of incentives for removing them:

In the case of our hypothetical oil company, for example, the optimum planning solution generated by the programing model may call for the fullest utilization of the catalytic cracking unit (which serves to increase the gasoline yield) at one of the refineries. Under such conditions the solution will contain a number which can be interpreted as the number of additional dollars per year that could be earned by additional "catcracker" capacity. If this number is sufficiently large, compared to the investment for catcracking capacity, it can be interpreted as a sign that a new catcracker may be profitable. Similar profit increment numbers or "opportunity costs" will of course be obtained in regard to any other technical bottlenecks. This information can be used in a systematic search for investment opportunities.

Going one step further, a programing model might be used for estimating the worth of technical innovations. This would be done by incorporating into the model formulation an entirely new element, such as a hypothetical refining process or perhaps a new secondary recovery scheme. Programing would then supply a number representing the potential increment in corporate profits that could be realized if the hypothetical process were actually available. This would provide a measure of the cost at which a new process would become attractive.

Finally, a programing solution will often contain information that can be used for evaluating the worth or potential profits associated with possible changes in rules and policies. An operating policy usually appears in the model formulation as an inequality (or sometimes as an equation) in form similar to the physical restrictions on production capacities or other technical limitations. Should a given policy be found to be actually binding in the context of an optimum operating plan, a corresponding number will appear in the programing solution. This number is a measure of the increased profits which might be attained by setting that policy aside. In effect, the number represents the "shadow price" associated with a given policy. Such shadow prices are helpful to management in deciding whether it is desirable to relax or modify certain policies.

Sensitivity Analysis

How much change can there be in the data on which a planning formulation is based without undermining the soundness of the plan itself? How accurately must management know cost coefficients, production performance figures, and other factors before it can make planning decisions with confidence? These questions are of real practical importance. Many of the basic data (in particular, the cost figures) required for the development of long-range plans are uncertain. While these uncertainties cannot be avoided, management can employ programing to study how critical they are. And that in itself can often help planners through a large part of their problem.

The procedure for doing this job, which we call "sensitivity analysis," is essentially this:

1. An optimum planning solution is calculated for a given set of conditions or estimated costs.
2. The computed optimum solution contains numerical elements which by appropriate grouping will automatically define the total change in profitability of that solution for a 1 per cent (or for a $1) change in any of the basic cost figures.
3. Each cost figure which is fed into the problem can also be tested to see how far it can be changed without actually calling for a different strategy or planning basis.

The important point here is that within certain limits of cost variation the basic strategy indicated by an optimum planning solution might still remain desirable, even though the profit picture varies in accordance with the cost changes. But when or if some of the changes in cost figures exceed certain limits, the programing formulation indicates that a new basis or strategy should be considered.

In the course of a sensitivity analysis it is generally found that some of the cost data are more critical than others; these could be the data which, if subjected to only a slight numerical change, would call for a different over-all course of action. Detection of such factors enables management to channel more attention to the truly sensitive areas in the cost picture.

Sensitivity analysis can be used as well for evaluating the significance of purely technical factors. When thus applied, it may have a bearing on the allocation and orientation of research and engineering efforts. A considerable amount of development work and engineering is continuously applied to refine or improve the prediction of technical performance characteristics. However, in many instances there is a question as to how much engineering detail and sophistication is really needed in order to provide management with an adequate basis for planning. The most objective way to answer this question, we believe, is to find out how critical the data are by using the procedures just outlined.

In a general sense, sensitivity analysis is actually the key to the development of practical mathematical models of manageable size. Planners may readily start out with the simplest and smallest possible planning formulation, rather than try at the outset to describe all operations in fullest detail and with greatest accuracy. They can put down approximate numbers in the formulation and then come back to sharpen them up later, if sensitivity analysis should prove that these are critical. This approach can be extended beyond specific data to include also successive improvements regarding the form of the interrelations used in the program. Thus, a mathematical-programing model is not a static device but a flexible tool which should be continually revised and refurbished as additional studies are made.

CONCLUSION

To sum up, we have tried to show that the true function of mathematical programing is:

1. To evaluate planning factors and alternatives as they arise, rather than to prescribe courses of action.

2. To provide the planner with systematic, more powerful means of analysis, rather than to reduce his responsibility by the use of automation.

3. To help management explore policies and objectives in greater depth, but not to introduce a substitute for decision-making.

32

Operations Research and Long-Range Company Planning[1]

E. Leonard Arnoff*

Operations research may be defined as the application of scientific methods to problems of the executive, that is, problems of the manager responsible for integrating the operations of functionally distinct organizational components.[2] Teams of scientists and engineers of diverse backgrounds examine all aspects of a problem and draw from a wide range of scientific concepts, methods, techniques, and tools those which are most applicable to the problem at hand. Out of this integrated and synthesizing research procedure, the executive is provided with an objective basis for making decisions and establishing

* The author wishes to express his indebtedness to Walter R. Van Voorhis for his valuable comments and constructive criticism contributing to the preparation of this chapter—D.W.E.

1 From *Implementing Long-Range Company Planning* (Menlo Park, Cal., Stanford Research Institute, 1957). Used by permission of the author.

2 A complete and detailed discussion of operations research and its definition; history and development; methods, techniques and tools; areas of application; and of the administration, selection, and training of personnel for operations research can be found in Reference 7 (see References at end of chapter).

policies which best serve the organization as a whole, rather than any one—or combination of less than all—of its individual parts.

The method of operations research may be described in the following terms: By analysis of the objectives and operations of the organization, a particular problem is formulated in its broadest possible terms. Then, a scheme is developed to express the "effectiveness" of the organization. The manner in which the organization's effectiveness is dependent on the constant and variable aspects of the system is then usually described in a mathematical way. This functional relationship is called a "model," and is essentially an expression of the assumptions upon which analysis is based. Values of those variables which are subject to control are then determined so as to yield maximum effectiveness. These results are then tested, both for validity and practicability. Once validated and shown feasible, these results are applied in plans and procedures in a form which provides for their continual re-evaluation as conditions change.

Most of the applications of operations research reported on to date have occurred in areas which might be classified as short-range planning, both strategic and tactical. There are relatively few published operations research studies primarily concerned with long-range planning. This lack, however, is readily explained. In the first place, operations research is a new science, and management has not as yet had sufficient opportunity to develop confidence in the merit of utilizing an operations research approach. Consequently, operations research teams are often initially obliged to consider problem areas where the results of their efforts can be evaluated in a rather short time. . . .

In the second place, even when management confidence is present and when the operations research team is permitted to consider long-range planning problems, short-range planning is still a necessary prelude. . . .

DEVELOPMENT OF CRITERIA FOR LONG-RANGE PLANNING

In business and industry, long-range planning manifests itself in one or more of several ways. These include new product development, market development, expansion and acquisition, and other areas. . . . Fundamental to each of these major paths of company growth is the development of criteria, measures, and standards for accurately and realistically guiding the research and, in turn, gauging the effectiveness of the team's efforts and plans. The importance and value of establishing such criteria can be illustrated by referring briefly to a particular company of which the executive committee wished to evaluate certain plans of action that pertained to the company's operations over a forthcoming five-year period.

Management agreed upon a list of five-year objectives. These objectives were:

1. Continuation of existing management
2. Guaranteed 6 per cent return to the owners on their original investment
3. Ability of the company to make up to 15 per cent return on investment if market for the product stayed in the range of 100 per cent or 200 per cent of current demand
4. No layoffs, and reasonable promotion of key company personnel
5. Stable labor relations (as evidenced, for example, by the absence of strike threats and a minimum of hiring and layoffs)
6. Technological leadership
7. Community service over and above legal requirements

The objectives were then weighed by management to determine their relative importance.[3] The final distribution of relative weights was as follows:

Objective	*Relative Weight*
1. Security of existing management	0.25
2. Financial security	0.30
3. Financial opportunity	0.10
4. Key personnel	0.15
5. Labor stability	0.05
6. Technological leadership	0.05
7. Community service	0.10

These weights were then accepted by the team as basic data.

The company executive committee was considering three possible board policies which, in abbreviated form, were:

A. Projected 200 per cent expansion of the company's operations in two years, including new products and markets.

B. Maintenance of the present size of the company, with emphasis on improvements in models of existing products.

[3] For a description of the weighting procedure used, see Reference 7, Chapter 6.

C. Maintenance of the present size of the company, with emphasis on the replacement of less profitable products by new products.

A company committee, composed of representatives of all of the major functions of the company, then evaluated each policy on a numerical scale with respect to each objective. More specifically, evaluations were assigned which were assumed to measure the probability that a specific objective would be attained under a given policy. The resulting evaluations were then appropriately combined (as with weighted probabilities) and the relative weight (*utility*) of each policy was determined, yielding:

Utility of policy A	0.28
Utility of policy B	0.38
Utility of policy C	0.34

In other words, Policy B was judged to be of greatest expected value in terms of achieving the specific objectives of the company. By this means, the company was able to establish an "optimal" policy for its future planning. Note particularly that this policy, i.e., maintenance of the present size of the company with emphasis on improvements in models of existing products, is not the kind of policy usually associated with long-range planning. If the various policies had not been evaluated in terms of objectives, the company would probably have planned by means of Policy A, i.e., in terms of a projected 200 per cent expansion of the company's operations in two years, including new products and markets. Such a planning policy would have been expected to yield results which would not necessarily have been compatible with the stated objectives of the particular company.

The appropriate standards and measures for long-range planning, once established, guide the next phase of the research along the proper path of company growth. Thus, in the preceding example, the selection of Policy A would have required that a planning program include consideration of new products and also new markets. Policy C would have required emphasis only on consideration of new products, whereas Policy B required only a concentration on improving the existing products.

In order to illustrate in specific terms the application of operations research to long-range planning involving some of the major paths of company growth, I shall summarize briefly several company case histories which reflect the use of the operations research approach.

OPERATIONS RESEARCH IN PRODUCT SEARCH AND EVALUATION[4]

One of the most common paths of company growth is that involving new products—whether required for the sake of keeping up with a rapidly changing technology, for expansion, or for diversification.

The well-known investment firm, J. H. Whitney and Company, reported that, of twenty-one hundred new product propositions, only seventeen were considered by them to be of merit. Of these seventeen, only two proved to be conspicuously successful on the competitive market; five were moderately successful; six were considered to be of a borderline nature; three were still too young to appraise; and one was a distinct failure, even though its production was recommended. In this vital area of product expansion, product improvement, and product diversification, this is indeed a very dismal record. It would appear evident, therefore, that there is a great need for improved methods of product search and product evaluation.

The search process in obtaining new products for expansion or diversification is principally one of selection, in that many ideas and suggestions must be examined and those meriting further investigation must be evaluated. The final objective of the researcher is to obtain a group of alternate possibilities, each of which has been subjected to intensive research and deliberation, and has also passed various criteria of acceptance. A product evaluation procedure is then carried out for each of these remaining possibilities to determine the final choice.

Recently, the Oster Manufacturing Company, well known for its line of pipe- and bolt-threading machines, announced its entrance into the billion-dollar materials-handling field through a line of multipurpose, hand-propelled, hand- and battery-operated portable lifts. This move by Oster culminated a three-year study into new products and their market potential which had been conducted in cooperation with the Operations Research Group at Case Institute of Technology.

The first stage of the Oster new-product study consisted of establishing suitable criteria, standards, and measures. These items reflected

[4] This section is a brief summary of an article on this subject written jointly by the author and Dr. Paul Stillson, director of operations research, Shell Chemical Corporation (see "Product Search and Evaluation," *Journal of Marketing*, July 1957, pp. 33–39).

the current status, facilities, capacities, and objectives of the particular company. Some of the initial criteria of acceptance were:

1. Can use be made of the existing distribution facilities?
2. Can use be made of the existing production facilities?
3. Can use be made of the present raw materials?
4. Can use be made of the present technical knowledge?
5. Can patents and copyrights be obtained for the product?
6. Has the new product been tested adequately—marketwise?
7. Has the new product been tested adequately—engineeringwise?

These criteria were ranked according to their relative importance by one of several procedures that have been developed and successfully applied.[5] Then, products obtained from such publications as *The Thomas Register of American Manufacturers* or from consideration of new materials and new manufacturing techniques were studied with respect to these criteria of acceptance.[6] This yielded a greatly reduced list of products which were initially acceptable and ready for further sifting.

Consideration was then given to the relationship of each proposed product with the existing company product line. Specifically, the following basic questions were answered:

1. Why is a new product being searched for at this time?
2. Will the inclusion of this new product affect the operational stability of the company?

A new product is usually considered for one of the following reasons:

1. Promotional: to extend the product line and increase the over-all sales volume for all products.
2. Aggressive: to extend the company's products into new areas and to diversify the product line.
3. Defensive: to provide an additional outlet for the company's facilities in the event of a market decline in the current product line.[7]

[5] There are, of course, serious limitations on the use of such ranking devices as well as on the validity of the results obtained therefrom. These are considered in Chapter 6 of Reference 7. See also Reference 17.

[6] For a discussion of methods of evaluating such products with respect to criteria of acceptance, see Reference 7, Chapter 6, and Reference 17.

[7] This might also be phrased as seeking a product line which will compensate for the economic peaks and valleys of the demand for the current product line and which will provide a means of maintaining a certain degree of labor stability under all business conditions.

Only those products which conformed to that objective selected from the three were retained for further consideration in a second-stage sifting process.

To answer the second question, it was necessary to consider the basic nature of the company's operations with respect to such items as:

1. Its ability to process certain raw materials
2. Its ability in tooling
3. Its ability in the finishing of products
4. Its ability in packaging
5. Its current marketing and distribution channels

Consideration of items of this kind entailed considerable analysis. However, the successful determination of the company's objectives and its philosophy of operation are essential ingredients of any scientific product search.

The selection criteria will vary with each company and with each product classification. However, the final result in each case is a much narrowed-down list of truly "acceptable" products, each of which must then be evaluated.

Product Evaluation

The method of product evaluation can be stated in terms of three tasks:

1. Determine the minimum market requirements for each product.
2. Analyze these market requirements with respect to production planning, manufacturing facilities, and manpower, and supervision.
3. Determine whether these market and production requirements can be met.

Task 1. Minimum Market Requirements

In order to stipulate a minimum acceptance level for gross sales, it was necessary to make certain assumptions or estimates concerning manufacturing costs, sales mixture, administrative expenses, overhead, and the like. These costs, either historical or estimated, must reflect the adaptation of the present system to incorporate the new product. Factors such as dealer's discount, acceptable net rate of return, product mix, and others, may be unknown but can be expressed in terms of parameters. For example, there was some doubt as to the sales commission that should be allowed on a given new product as well as to the minimum acceptable net rate of return. The evaluation, then, was carried out for low, medium, and high values of each of these factors. The resulting evaluation was then a function of both parameters. Thus, a table of the following form (data fictitious) was prepared to exhibit the minimum market requirements as a function of the sales commission and the net rate of return:

Rate of Return	*Sales Commission*		
	0.02	0.05	0.08
0.10	386,000[a]	455,000	555,000
0.15	516,000	650,000	873,000
0.20	783,000	1,132,000	2,055,000

[a] All values within the table are based on gross sales per year.

Task 2. Production Requirements

The minimum market requirements thus established must then be translated in terms of specific production requirements. Here, one must consider problems of inventory, time, and manpower requirements, capacity allocations, planning and scheduling, and other elements. These problems can be solved by means of the many operations research techniques of production and inventory control, linear programing, queueing theory, and the like.

Task 3. Market Analysis

The third and last task in this evaluation procedure is to determine whether the market and production requirements indicated by Tasks 1 and 2 can be met. Here, one must consider the feasibility of capital investment, facility expansion, and material procurement, as well as the determination of the potential market for the new product through the use of sales forecasting, market research, and market testing.

Observations on New Product Search and Evaluation

Once these tasks had been completed, management was provided with information and facts with which it could make an effective decision. In general, the method for searching for new products as outlined above subjects management to critical self-analysis concerning long-range objectives and goals and incorporates these policy decisions into future expansion plans. It defines an acceptance standard for present as well as future company operations, and it suggests other profitable areas for further research in the fields of product improvement, product expansion, and product diversification.

Operations Research in the Long-Range Planned Expansion of an Electric Utility System[8]

Any electric utility company expands its system in order to be able to fulfill its customer demands for power with some prescribed measure of reliability. Since future customer demands can only be estimated and since generators and auxiliary equipment (boilers, turbines, and the like) are subject to forced outages (e.g., breakdowns), a utility system is required to maintain a reserve of installed generating capacity in the form of "extra" turbogenerator units. Therefore, the problem of system expansion is essentially equivalent to the problem of determining and maintaining a proper (or optimum) installed, reserve generating capacity. Failure to have a sufficient reserve (sufficient as measured by some criterion) leads to customer shortages with resulting customer dissatisfaction and loss of revenue, both direct and indirect. On the other hand, a surplus of generating capacity means additional inventory costs—costs associated with direct charges on idle or unnecessary capital equipment.

The "reserve" problem, then, is to ascertain the best balance between these two costs—the cost of a shortage and the cost of excess inventory. The determination of this optimum balance point then indicates when a new unit should be added to the system, thus giving the best reserve policy for the particular system and, hence, determining the optimum expansion program for the company.

In the electrical utility industry, the reserve question is usually phrased in terms of "What is the optimum reserve generating capacity?" wherein the existence of one single reserve percentage is implied. For example, a rule of thumb in the industry is that the reserve capacity should generally be no less than 15 per cent of the system capacity. However, as will be seen later in this paper, there is no *one* optimum percentage, since the optimum varies with the size of the generators in operation. Furthermore, since hte reason one seeks to ascertain the optimum reserve is to know when additional capacity is required, it seemed much more reasonable to rephrase the research question in

[8] This section is, with only minor modifications, the paper described in Reference 3. It appears here with the kind permission of the editor of *Operations Research.*

terms of "When should generating capacity be added to the system?" Then, having answered this question, one can readily determine the optimum reserve capacity for any given generating system.

An associated problem, and one for which the answer is, in a sense, already implied in the determination of the optimum reserve policy, is that of determining the optimum size of unit to be added to the system. Varying the size of the unit affects coal costs, maintenance costs, labor costs, holding costs, and other factors. Here, in considering large as opposed to small units, one seeks a "best" balance between installation cost savings, coal savings, and labor and maintenance savings, on the one hand, and increased costs of investment, on the other.

A method for answering the first question—that of determining the optimum time to add generating capacity to a system—will be discussed first. Then, the second problem, that of determining the most economical size of unit, will be considered, subject to restrictions stated later. The methods described here were developed in a study recently completed for an electric utility company.

Determination of Optimum Reserve Generating Capacity

Analysis of the company system showed that the following factors affect the determination of the optimum time for acquiring generating capacity and, hence, must be taken into account:

1. *Available Capacity:*
   a. The number and sizes of the generating units now in the system
   b. The size of new generating units to be added to the system
   c. The amount of additional power available from (1) interconnections and, to a much lesser extent, from (2) voltage drops, (3) dropoff of customers whose contracts permit reductions in power, and (4) large industries within the system area that have their own generating units
2. *Requirements* (consumption of power or of power-generating capacity):
   a. Customer demand (since this is not known, it must be forecast, and errors due to forecasting must also be taken into account)
   b. Scheduled, or preventive, maintenance
   c. Unscheduled, or emergency, outages due to breakdowns
3. *Costs:*
   a. Purchase price of the generating equipment

b. Installation cost of the generating equipment
c. Operating cost of the generating equipment: (1) coal, (2) labor, and (3) maintenance
d. Fixed charges on capital equipment: (1) cost of money, (2) income tax, (3) real estate and personal property taxes, (4) depreciation, and (5) miscellaneous
e. Costs due to shortages[9] (or maximum allowable risk of shortage)

Certain of these factors had fixed values and could be determined immediately: for example, the number and sizes of the existing units in the generating system. Additionally, the scheduled maintenance program is an established one and, thus, it is safe to assume, at least for the moment, that it will be continued in its present form during the period of time under study. (A variation of the scheduled maintenance program is also evaluated in a later section of this paper.) Finally, the costs associated with installation and operation of the generators are also known.[10]

Certain other factors could be assigned values, but these values were not unique. Such factors are:

1. *The probability of forced outage* (i.e., the probability that a generating unit would not be available owing to a breakdown). Studies conducted on a national scale by the Edison Electric Institute showed that the national average for forced outages, for weekdays only, for all types of generating equipment is approximately 2 per cent. Roughly, this indicates that one can expect generating equipment to be out of commission approximately 2 per cent of the time because of an emergency, or forced, outage, either because of turbogenerator or boiler trouble.

Analysis of the company system showed that forced outages were being experienced only 1 per cent of the time. Accordingly, both figures were used in the study. Using both the 1 and 2 per cent figures also enables management to measure the value of its excellent preventive maintenance program, because forced outages are affected by the rigidity (i.e., frequency and nature) of the preventive maintenance program.

[9] A shortage occurs whenever the sum of customer demand, forced outages, and scheduled outages (due to maintenance) exceeds the total system capabilities.

[10] Since the purchase price of any generating unit will vary with time, this factor was treated essentially as a variable, and results were obtained for various price levels.

2. *The amount of additional power available* to an electric utility company is largely dependent upon contractual arrangements with interconnecting companies. Inasmuch as this amount can vary with respect to the future, several varying amounts of additional power were assumed, namely, 100, 200, and 400 megawatts (MW). Not only does this enable us to provide answers to the reserve question, but it also serves to measure the value of the interconnection and the amount of power for which one should contract from the interconnection.

3. Since a system would require an *infinitely large amount of generating capacity* in order to provide for no shortages whatsoever, management must decide upon a certain risk of shortage which is "acceptable" from a practical, operating point of view.

In the electric utility industry, a rule of thumb exists as to a *maximum acceptable risk of shortage*. This, of course, assumes much as to the homogeneity, from one system to another, of the type of customer, sizes of units in the system, costs of shortage, cost of holding excess inventory, and so forth. Within the industry, however, this shortage policy is not too well defined. Accordingly, several shortage policies were assumed and evaluated with respect to total expected cost. In particular, three policies were considered and evaluated. These assumed the maximum allowable risk of shortage to be (1) one day in two years, (2) one day in five years, and (3) one day in ten years.

4. Inasmuch as the research study also included the determination of the optimum size of new units to be added to the system, the alternatives of adding distinct *sizes of generating units* were studied. In particular, two systems were studied, involving the addition of units of 240-MW and 340-MW size.

5. Since the purchase price of new generators will vary with time, study was also made of the effect of various levels of incremental *cost of purchase*. Thus, for a comparison of the addition of 340-MW units with the addition of 240-MW generators, cost differentials of 0, 1, 2, 4, and 8 millions of dollars were considered.[11]

Finally, there were the following factors whose values had to be established: (1) the probabilities of forced outages of varying amounts for the system as a whole, and (2) the determination of ex-

[11] These cost differentials include incremental installation costs.

pected customer demand. From these two factors and the known scheduled maintenance requirements (as well as the system capacity and other factors) one must then determine (3) the probability of a shortage. Finally, since there will be errors due to forecasts of customer demand, one must determine (4) the amount of reserve capacity required to provide for various levels of protection against forecasting errors.

Determination of Customer Demand

In the determination of expected customer demand, it is normally of interest to ascertain only expected daily peak demands, since the ability to satisfy customer requirements at peak loads implies the ability to satisfy off-peak demands as well. Furthermore, since weekend and holiday peak loads are only 50 to 75 per cent of the normal weekday peak load, it is assumed that, for all practical purposes, shortages will not occur on week ends and holidays. Hence, in the analyses to follow, only peak loads occurring during weekdays are considered.

To determine the distribution of peak loads, a method was developed that is based upon the company's forecast of annual kilowatt-hour (kwh) consumption. A study of this annual kwh-consumption, by months, revealed a consistent variation in monthly demands. Furthermore, study also revealed that the distribution of daily peak loads within any given month was also predictable.

Therefore, by means of statistical analyses, the distribution of daily peak loads within each month can be obtained and, hence, the nature of customer demand for each month. Following is an example of such a distribution of daily peak loads for a sample month.

Determination of Probabilities of System Outages

Methods of calculating probabilities of outages for a given system range from the rigorous method of Calabrese to the approximation method of Lyman.[12] For a system such as that discussed here, where unit sizes vary over a very large range, a rigorous computation of system probabilities of outages would require the use of a large electronic computer. Accordingly, the device below was employed.

[12] See References 4, 5, 6, 13, and 15.

SAMPLE MONTH

Peaks (MW)	*Expected Number of Days*
1230	0.32
1240	0.57
1250	0.84
1260	1.28
1270	1.68
1280	2.00
1290	2.31
1300	2.35
1310	2.31
1320	2.00
1330	1.68
1340	1.28
1350	0.84
1360	0.57
1370	0.32

The actual system under study was represented by a system of generating units whose sizes (i.e., capacities) are multiples of 25 MW. This yields a model of the system whose joint probabilities are then easily calculated. Care was taken so that any errors due to this simplification would be in the direction of increasing reserve requirements.[13]

DETERMINATION OF WHEN UNITS ARE TO BE ADDED TO THE SYSTEM

Once having determined (1) expected customer demand, (2) expected frequency and amount of forced outages, and (3) scheduled maintenance requirements, these three factors can then be combined to yield the total expected demand on the system for each month.[14] Such a combination led to the type of total expected monthly demand tabulation shown in Table 1. Then, with the total expected

[13] Since the results obtained from the model of the system are assumed to represent the actual system, several models were tried and the results compared with observed (historical) values, from which the "multiple of 25 MW" system was selected.

[14] Treating the expected forced outages as a demand on the system is a very useful device which enables one to consider the capacity of the system as fixed.

TABLE 1
TOTAL EXPECTED DEMANDS FOR "TYPICAL" MONTH

Total Demand, Including Forced Outages (1)	Expected No. of Days for Month (2)	Expected No. of Days for Month, Indicated Demand or Greater (3)	Indicated Demand Expected No. of Days for Year, or Greater (12 × Col. 3) (4)
1400	1.282	21.000	252.0
1425	1.361	19.718	236.616
1450	3.521	18.357	220.284
1475	4.400	14.836	178.032
1500	2.949	10.436	125.232
1525	2.511	7.487	89.844
1550	1.746	4.976	59.712
1575	0.854	3.230	38.760
1600	0.688	2.376	28.512
1625	0.508	1.688	20.256
1650	0.319	1.180	14.160
1675	0.228	0.861	10.332
1700	0.197	0.633	7.596
1725	0.147	0.436	5.232
1750	0.097	0.289	3.468
1775	0.073	0.192	2.304
1800	0.047	0.119	1.428
1825	0.024	0.072	0.864
1850	0.018	0.048	0.576
1875	0.012	0.030	0.360
1900	0.007	0.018	0.216
1925	0.005	0.011	0.132
1950	0.003	0.006	0.072
1975	0.001	0.003	0.036

monthly demand on the system determined, this demand is associated with total system capabilities and maximum allowable risks of shortage so that, finally, it is possible to determine when new generating units should be added to the system. The procedure for doing so may best be explained by means of the following example.

EXAMPLE

Assume the following conditions to be true:

1. Maximum allowable risk of shortage: 1 day in 5 years. (I.e., the system is permitted to have a shortage no more frequently than 0.2 days per year.)

2. Internal system capacity: 1,725 MW.

3. Additional capacity (e.g., from interconnection): 100 MW. (It is assumed, therefore, that the total system capacity is 1,825 MW.)

Assume that we are considering the month depicted in Table 1. By referring to Table 1, we see that, for this month, a demand of 1,850 MW or more to occur at the rate of 0.576 days per year can be expected (Column 4). Since the total system capacity is only 1,825 MW, 0.576 represents the expected number of days per year that the system will be short. Since 0.576 exceeds the maximum allowable shortage of 0.2 days per year, more generating capacity must be added during this illustrative month.[15]

Thus for each month a table of total expected demand on the system is determined by combining (1) expected customer demand, (2) expected frequency and amount of forced outages, and (3) scheduled maintenance requirements. By comparing the expected number of days per year that the system will be short with the maximum allowable risk of shortage, it can then be determined when (i.e., in which month) additional generating capacity will be required.

Such an analysis was conducted for combinations of the following values of the factors:

1. Probability of a unit outage: 1 and 2 per cent.

2. Additional power available from the interconnection, etc.: 0, 100, 200, and 400 MW.

3. Maximum allowable risk of shortage: 1 day in 2 years, 1 day in 5 years, and 1 day in 10 years.

The results are summarized in Table 2, which shows not only when the next unit should be added to the system for various assumptions, but also the corresponding percentage of reserve available in the system at that time.

The method just presented assumes, essentially, that there are no errors in the forecasting of customer demands. In practice, however, if adjustments are not made for errors in forecasting, shortages will occur with less frequency (in comparison to the forecast just developed) 50 per cent of the time (since the forecast will be high 50 per cent of the time), and shortages will occur with more frequency 50 per cent of the time (since the forecast will be low 50 per cent of the

[15] Were the expected number of days short less than 0.2, the system would be deemed sufficient, and the next month's demand would then be analyzed.

TABLE 2
INSTALLATION DATE FOR NEXT UNIT

Probability of Outage (per cent)	*Additional Power (MW)*	*Risk of Shortage*					
		1 day/ 10 Yrs.	Per Cent Reserve	1 day/ 5 Yrs.	Per Cent Reserve	1 day/ 2 Yrs.	Per Cent Reserve
1	0	Dec. 57	22.0	Apr. 58	18.6	June 58	18.6
	100	July 58	18.6	Apr. 59	11.7	July 59	11.7
	200	May 60	6.2	Dec. 60	4.6	Mar. 61	1.8
	400	Mar. 62	− 5.0	July 62	− 5.0	July 62	− 5.0
2	0	Dec. 56	31.3	Apr. 57	27.4	Dec. 57	22.0
	100	Dec. 57	22.0	June 58	18.6	July 58	18.6
	200	Dec. 58	13.9	May 59	11.7	May 60	6.2
	400	Apr. 61	1.5	Nov. 61	0.0	Mar. 62	− 5.0

time). Accordingly, an additional amount of reserve capacity is required to provide a margin of safety against such errors, that is, in order to reduce the percentage of time with which more frequent shortages will occur or, equivalently, in order to increase the percentage of time during which fewer shortages will occur.

Calculations were made, based on a four-year forecast, showing the additional reserve capacity required for various percentage levels. Results are shown in Table 3.

TABLE 3
ADDITIONAL RESERVES REQUIRED BECAUSE OF FORECASTING ERRORS

Per Cent of Time Fewer Than Max. Allowable No. of Shortages	Per Cent Additional Reserves Required
60	2.1
70	4.3
75	5.6
80	7.0
85	8.7
90	10.7
95	13.7
97.5	16.3
99	19.4
99.5	21.5

Analyses were also made of the economics associated with various values for:

1. Probability of unit forced outage: 1 and 2 per cent.
2. Maximum allowable risk of shortage for 1 day in 2 years, 1 day in 5 years, and 1 day in 10 years.
3. Additional power available from the interconnection: 0 MW, 100 MW, 200 MW, and 400 MW.
4. Incremental cost of purchasing new 340-MW generating units as compared with 240-MW generating units: $0 million, $1 million, $2 million, $4 million, and $8 million. (I.e., a system which involved the addition of new 340-MW units was compared with one adding 240-MW units for various cost differentials.)

These analyses were based on the method discussed earlier and yielded the results to be discussed subsequently.

Effect of a Rigid Preventive Maintenance Program

As mentioned earlier, the company system experienced forced outages only 1 per cent of the time, rather than the national average of 2 per cent, because of an excellent preventive maintenance policy. This has resulted in a reduction of forced outages that has reduced the capacity requirements and, hence, resulted in substantial gross cost savings. These savings must then be compared with the increased costs of maintenance required to obtain the 1 per cent forced outage rate in order to determine whether or not the rigid maintenance program is economically justified. The gross savings due to this more rigid maintenance program are given in Table 4. (The numbers in

TABLE 4
Additional Costs, 2 Per Cent Outage Rate vs. 1 Per Cent Outage Rate
(millions of dollars per year)

Size of Units Subsequently Added	*Maximum Allowable Risk of Shortage*								
	1 day/2 Yrs.			1 day/5 Yrs.			1 day/10 Yrs.		
240 MW	1.3	1.1	0.4	1.8	1.3	0.5	1.9	1.7	1.0
340 MW	1.2	1.0	0.6	2.2	1.7	1.2	2.4	1.9	1.2
Additional power available (MW)	100	200	400	100	200	400	100	200	400

Table 4 represent the annual savings obtained by comparing the costs for a 1 per cent unit forced outage rate with those for a 2 per cent unit forced outage rate.)

Maximum Allowable Risk of Shortage

In this study, the "cost of shortage" and "maximum allowable risk of shortage" have been used rather interchangeably. Ideally, one would like to be able to determine the costs caused by shortage (including the impact on customer good will, loss of future sales, and the like) and thereby arrive at a definite answer to the reserve question. However, the costs caused by shortage are not known, nor are they easily determined. Hence, the alternate approach of analyzing several maximum allowable risks of shortage was used. Thus, although management is obliged to decide upon a suitable shortage policy, it is nevertheless supplied with a firm quantitative basis for establishing this policy.

Table 5 shows the cost reductions associated with shortage policies

TABLE 5
Reduction in Costs for Risk of Shortage Greater Than 1 Day in 10 Years
(millions of dollars per year)

Risk of Shortage	*Size of New Units*	*Probability of Forced Outage* 1%				2%			
1 day/5 yrs.	240 MW	1.0	0.8	0.3	0.2	1.0	0.9	0.7	0.6
	340 MW	1.0	0.9	0.6	0.3	1.0	1.2	0.8	0.3
1 day/2 yrs.	240 MW	1.9	1.5	1.0	0.3	2.0	2.0	1.7	0.9
	340 MW	2.4	1.7	1.1	0.4	2.3	3.0	2.0	0.9
Additional power available (MW)		0	100	200	400	0	100	200	400

of one day in two years and one day in 5 years as compared with a policy of maximum acceptable risk of shortage of one day in ten years.

Additional Power Available from the Interconnection

Throughout this discussion, it has been apparent that a very important factor is the amount of power available from the interconnection. Thus, in applying Table 1, varying the level of the amount of power available from the interconnection would affect the decision to add or not to add additional capacity. Also, as the other tables show, the costs and savings vary quite markedly with the amount of such additional power. Accordingly, analyses were made of the differences in costs associated with power available from the interconnection in amounts of 0 MW, 100 MW, 200 MW, and 400 MW. The amount of 100 MW was used as a base, and all costs were compared accordingly. The results are given in Table 6.

TABLE 6
EVALUATION OF INTERCONNECTION (BASE: 100 MW)
(millions of dollars per year)

Additional Power Available	*Size of New Units*	*Probability of Forced Outage* 1%			2%		
0 MW	240 MW	−2.0	−1.9	−1.6	−2.0	−1.9	−2.0
	340 MW	−2.5	−2.4	−1.8	−2.0	−2.2	−2.8
200 MW	240 MW	1.8	1.3	1.5	2.0	1.9	1.7
	340 MW	2.0	1.7	1.3	2.5	2.2	1.5
400 MW	240 MW	3.8	3.1	2.6	4.7	4.4	3.5
	340 MW	4.2	3.6	2.8	5.5	4.6	3.4
Maximum allowable risk of shortage		1 day/ 10 yrs.	1 day/ 5 yrs.	1 day/ 2 yrs.	1 day/ 10 yrs.	1 day/ 5 yrs.	1 day/ 2 yrs.

As mentioned earlier, a tabulation such as Table 6 thus furnishes management with a sound basis for determining the amount of power for which it should contract from the interconnection.

DETERMINATION OF SIZE OF NEW UNITS TO BE ADDED TO THE SYSTEM

A highly essential question which must be answered in planning for the expansion of a utility system is that of determining the most economical size of unit to be added to the system.[16] Two basic plans of expansion were considered: (1) Each new unit is of size 240 MW, or (2) each new unit is of size 340 MW. Since actual purchase costs were not known and would vary with time, computations were made for various incremental cost levels, thus permitting determination of those purchase cost levels for which one unit is more economical than the other. These comparisons, using the 240-MW unit as a base, are given in Table 7, and are obtained by taking into account (1) fixed

[16] See Reference 2.

TABLE 7

COMPARISON OF 240 MW AND 340 MW UNITS[a]

Probability of Outage (Per Cent)	*Additional Purchase Cost of 340 MW vs. 240 MW*	*Maximum Acceptable Risk of Shortage* 1 Day/10 Yrs.				1 Day/5 Yrs.				1 Day/2 Yrs.			
1	0	3.7	7.7	7.6	8.1	3.9	7.8	9.9	9.4	8.8	9.0	5.5	8.3
	1.0	2.3	6.3	6.5	7.3	2.5	6.6	8.9	8.6	7.5	7.8	4.6	7.5
	2.0	0.9	5.0	5.4	6.5	1.1	5.4	7.9	7.8	6.1	6.6	3.6	6.7
	4.0	—1.9	2.4	3.3	4.8	—1.6	2.9	5.9	6.3	3.5	4.2	1.7	5.2
	8.0	—7.1	—2.7	—0.8	—1.7	—6.7	—1.7	2.2	3.3	—1.6	—0.2	—1.9	2.3
2	0	2.1	2.2	7.1	6.9	1.3	5.1	7.3	3.0	4.8	11.4	8.4	6.2
	1.0	0.7	0.8	5.8	6.0	—0.1	3.7	6.0	2.2	3.4	10.4	7.3	5.4
	2.0	—0.7	—0.6	4.5	5.0	—1.5	2.4	4.8	1.3	2.0	9.0	6.2	4.6
	4.0	—3.5	—3.4	2.0	3.2	—4.3	—0.3	2.0	—0.4	—0.8	6.4	4.1	2.9
	8.0	—8.8	—8.6	—2.8	—0.4	—9.5	—5.3	—2.2	—3.7	—6.1	1.4	0	—0.2
Additional power available (MW)		0	100	200	400	0	100	200	400	0	100	200	400

[a] Figures are in millions of dollars for period 1958–67. The negative values indicate the conditions under which the 240-MW generator is preferable to the 340-MW generator.

charges on capital equipment and (2) differential costs in (a) coal, (b) labor, and (c) maintenance.

Observations on Planned Expansion

The utility system case study illustrates a method for solving the problem of long-range planned expansion of a company. Specifically, the method enables a company to determine when additional generating capacity should be added to the system and, also, to ascertain the optimum size of these new generating units. These conclusions, however, presuppose that management has already made certain decisions as to:

1. The probability of unit forced outage to be used, that is, establishing the preventive maintenance policy.
2. The maximum allowable risk of shortage.
3. The amount of power to be made available through the interconnection.
4. The safety level deemed essential for protection against forecasting errors.

Once having answered these questions (with the assistance of the cost comparisons previously described), it can then be readily determined when new units should be added to the system, what the size of these units should be, and, hence, the best long-range expansion program for the company.

THE APPLICATION OF OPERATIONS RESEARCH TO OTHER LONG-RANGE PLANNING PROBLEMS

The following case history summaries reflect in further degree the broad applicability of the operations research approach to the problem area of long-range planning.

Allocation of Sales Effort

In 1955, Russell L. Ackoff reported on a study conducted jointly by the Lamp Division of the General Electric Company and the Case Institute Operations Research Group.[17] This study was concerned with the allocation of sales effort and recognized that, before a salesman can operate most efficiently, three questions must be answered:

[17] See Reference 1.

1. How frequently should a salesman call on a specific account?
2. How many accounts should be assigned to a salesman?
3. What kind of man makes the best salesman for what type of account?

The study concentrated on providing answers to the first question. . . . The study also provided data from which conclusions and suggestions were derived affecting the use of sales time. These are:

1. The breakdown of how a salesman spends his time
2. The allocation of sales calls to prospects
3. The breakdown of salesman time into sales and service activity

Specifically, the study showed that a considerable average reduction in the number of sales calls could be made without affecting the sales volume; that is, the existing number of salesmen in the Lamp Division could carry considerably more accounts without affecting their return per account.

At the time of the study, the Lamp Division was preparing for a reorganization which indicated the need for a greater number of salesmen than that currently employed. The study showed that, contrary to this belief, additional salesmen were not required. The operating cost implications of this result were considerable.

Planning for an Integrated Operation

The reorganization of the Lamp Division of the General Electric Company was reported by Walter Glover and Russell L. Ackoff early in 1956,[18] and is another illustration of the application of operations research to the problems of long-range planning. Glover and Ackoff discussed "Five-Year Planning for an Integrated Operation" and told how objectives were established, how policies were set, and how resources and organizational operations were coordinated for the entire Lamp Division.

The resulting five-year plan covered the following major areas:

1. Specification of objectives for the next five years
2. Specification of operating policies by which the objectives could best be attained
3. Specification of the resources required to carry out the policies
4. Specification of the resources required to carry out the policies within the framework of existing resources

[18] See Reference 14.

The new organizational structure and the corresponding objectives were announced by the General Electric Company in January 1955. Although it is obviously too early to completely evaluate this study at this time, it has been stated that the objectives set for the first of the five years were met and, in some cases, surpassed.

Long-Range Planning by Means of Operations Research on the Consumer

There is a most important class of operations research studies on long-range planning in which the research is conducted on (and for) one's customers. An example of an extensive use of this type of approach to the problem of long-range planning is that reported by Roger Crane.[19] He describes how the Westinghouse Air Brake Company conducted research on consumers in order to help establish an effective company-wide research and development program.

Since most of the company's business was with the railroads, the initial objective of the research project was to carry out research on railroad operations in order to obtain a thorough and comprehensive knowledge of railroad operations. As time progressed, the scope of this activity broadened to include the study of all present and potential customers of the company.

Among the problems considered by the Operations Research Group at Westinghouse Air Brake Company were the following:[20]

1. Analysis of the operations of a railroad classification yard
2. Determination of the optimum length (number of cars) of a train
3. Study of the distribution of freight cars in a large terminal area
4. Purchasing of new rail and its allocation on a railroad
5. The flow and utilization of information on a railroad

LONG-RANGE PLANNING AND MANAGEMENT DEVELOPMENT

In this final section, I should like to call attention to the fact that long-range planning must also include some program for the development of management personnel within the company. It does not suffice to consider expansion and growth only in terms of plant, land, and/or machinery, or solely in terms of balance sheets, working capital, and the like. Without trained, intelligent, and competent manage-

[19] See Reference 8.
[20] See References 9, 10, 11, and 12.

ment, "the best laid schemes o' mice and men gang aft a-gley." Toward this end, many companies have recognized in operations research a valuable training ground for tomorrow's managers and have either selected men skilled in operations research for managerial positions or have assigned prospective managers to their operations research teams as part of a management development program. In either case, they are providing for a corps of inspired and trained managers—scientifically trained managers—who will be in a much better position to accept and use effectively the greater amount of information and answers about their present and future operations which is being provided for them through operations research.

The importance of having managers who are conversant with operations research and scientific methods is pointed out very well by the chairman of the board of the Cummins Engine Company, J. Irwin Miller, who writes:

> If the head of a business indulges in research, as many do, just to solace his own fears of the future, and plays no personal part in this agonizing function, then he will only come to the end of his cycle all the sooner. If research is to be fruitful, it must be a daily concern of top management, and if it is to succeed, those who conduct the research must have a solid understanding of the true needs of their company, of its industry, and of its customers.[21]

REFERENCES

1. Russell L. Ackoff, "Allocation of Sales Effort," *Proceedings of the Conference on "What Is Operations Research Accomplishing in Industry?"* (Cleveland, Ohio, Case Institute of Technology, April 5–7, 1956).
2. "An Investigation of the Economic Size of Steam-Electric Generating Units," *Combustion,* February, 1955, pp. 57–64.
3. E. Leonard Arnoff and John C. Chambers, "On the Determination of Optimum Reserve Generating Capacity in an Electric Utility System," *Operations Research,* August 1956.
4. G. Calabrese, "Determination of Reserve Capacity by the Probability Method—Effect on Interconnections," AIEE *Transactions,* 69 (1950), Part II, pp. 1018–1020.
5. ———, "Determination of Reserve Capacity by the Probability

[21] See Reference 16.

Method," AIEE *Transactions,* 68 (1949), Part II, pp. 16[illegible]–1688.
6. ———, *System Generation Reserve Requirements,* monograph submitted to the Subcommittee on the Application of Probability Methods to Power System Problems, July 9, 1953.
7. C. West Churchman, Russell L. Ackoff, and E. Leonard Arnoff, *Introduction to Operations Research* (New York, John Wiley and Sons, Inc., 1957).
8. Roger R. Crane, "Operations Research on Industrial Consumers, *Proceedings of the Conference on "What Is Operations Research Accomplishing in Industry?"* (Cleveland, Ohio, Case Institute of Technology, April 5–7, 1955).
9. Roger R. Crane, Frank B. Brown, and Robert O. Blanchard, "An Analysis of a Railroad Classification Yard," *Operations Research,* August 1955, pp. 262–271.
10. Roger R. Crane and Frank B. Brown, "Theory of Maintenance of Rolling Stock," *Mechanical Engineering,* December 1954.
11. Roger R. Crane, "Some Examples of Operations Research Work," *Proceedings of the Railway Systems and Procedures Association Winter Meeting,* 1953.
12. Roger R. Crane, "A Discussion of Certain Maintenance of Way Problems," Seminar on Operations Research, Railway Systems and Procedures Association, February 1954.
13. "Forced Outage Rates of High Pressure Steam Turbines and Boilers," *Combustion,* October, 1954, pp. 57–61.
14. Walter S. Glover and Russell L. Ackoff, "Five-Year Planning for an Integrated Operation," *Proceedings of the Conference on Case Studies in Operations Research* (Cleveland, Ohio, Case Institute of Technology, February 1–3, 1956).
15. W. J. Lyman, "Calculating Probability of Generating Capacity Outages," AIEE *Transactions,* 65 (1945), pp. 1471–1477.
16. J. Irwin Miller, "Executive Planning for 1970," *Indiana Business Review,* May 1956.
17. Paul Stillson, "A Method for Defect Evaluation," *Industrial Quality Control,* July 1954.

33

Pretest Your Long-Range Plans[1]

William J. Platt
and
N. Robert Maines

¶ How can management evaluate the quality of its long-range plans?

¶ Must management wait for history to be written to see whether today's planning decisions will pay off?

¶ Although sales and earnings statements are the final test, are there any ways by which long-range plans can be pretested in some sort of "decision laboratory"?

¶ Since operations researchers claim to be developing the science of decision, can they help in evaluating or even in formulating long-range plans?

The purpose of this article is to consider the importance of planning, then to take a glimpse into the decision laboratory to see what kinds of plans are being or could be pretested and what research techniques are applicable.

NEED FOR PRETESTS

The dynamic character of our economy has made continuous business planning an essential for the successful company. This is a conclusion which is widely accepted, and it is supported by a study that

[1] From *Harvard Business Review,* January–February 1959, pp. 119–127. Used by permission.

followed the fortunes of about four hundred companies from 1939 to 1957.[2]

An objective of that study was to find what characteristics, if any, distinguish companies of high growth from those of low growth. A number of characteristics were identified, including the presence in high-growth companies of organized programs to seek and promote new business opportunities. This was measured by such quantifiable indicators as whether or not the company had a formal planning organization for long-range planning, whether or not the company had a product research laboratory, and whether or not the company moved by plan into new major product fields or markets.

The study revealed that more high-growth companies support long-range planning functions than do low-growth companies. But the existence of a formal long-range planning function in a company does not, of course, guarantee successful plans. The value of the activity can be curiously elusive, because a period of years must elapse before a set of long-range plans can be evaluated on the basis of results and performance. Thus there is inherent in any long-range planning activity the possibility that ineffective or unprofitable plans will go undetected for months or years.

To prevent being misled by glib staff planners, management is therefore interested in subjecting the planning activity to whatever objective tests can be found. How can it tell *in advance* whether or not a program is sound?

Pretests of plans not only reveal flaws but encourage bolder approaches to future planning. If a company has no experimental means by which to make its planning mistakes inexpensively, it tends to adopt plans that have proved themselves in the past—and avoid those which, although promising, do depart sufficiently from experience to pose severe risks. Conservative behavior is a natural consequence of the lack of valid experimental techniques.

It is for this reason that a decision laboratory is attractive. If management can pretest at least parts of its planning in a decision laboratory, then costly full-scale or "real world" tests can be eliminated and, possibly, better plans developed. Pretesting may be new to business strategists, but it is not new to scientists. Indeed, without laboratory experimentation, progress in physical and biological science would

[2] "Why Companies Grow," *Nation's Business,* November 1957, p. 80.

have been drastically impeded. In business and industry, on the other hand, until now there has been no corresponding laboratory. The world of experience has been the only way to test policies, decisions, and planning.

THE DECISION LABORATORY

The efforts of management scientists and operations analysts to pretest new plans and decisions by analytic and experimental techniques are still far from maturity. Enough progress has been made, however, to justify management scrutiny of these approaches in its planning and decision-making.

Certain planning topics receive, and deserve, more emphasis than others in top management's long-range planning:

1. Changes in production equipment and distribution facilities
2. Changes in allocation of company resources
3. Changes in products by development and diversification
4. Changes in markets, both geographical and with respect to type of customer

We shall confine our examination of planning to the foregoing topics, recognizing nonetheless that many worthy subjects of management planning lie outside these areas—subjects such as labor relations, executive development, and capital sources, to name only a few. It should be remembered that the changes mentioned can include both additions and eliminations in products, markets, and facilities.

It is our intention to describe the relationship between business planning, as just outlined, and certain operations research approaches that may help management to evaluate the quality of planning. This description can best start by terming operations research *the science of decision* and the professional man who practices operations research *the management scientist*. Further, *decision laboratory* will be used to identify the group consisting of the company planner, the management scientist, and the latter's electronic assistant, the computer.

Operations research utilizes the techniques of mathematics, statistics, economics, and other disciplines to help solve operating problems and determine business policy. It seeks to improve decision-making by setting forth the implications of alternative decisions, by eliminating the less desirable ones, and by predicting the consequences of the remaining alternatives. It provides quantitative information for the exercise of enlightened management judgment.

The impact of operations research is spreading rapidly in industry. In an American Management Association survey, 51 per cent of 631 companies replying to a questionnaire reported that they were using operations research in 1957. But virtually none of them used it in 1951, and only 13 per cent of them used it in 1953.

Versatile Models

A principal tool of operations research is the mathematical model, which describes in a quantitative sense the operation of a real process or system. Basically, a model can be thought of as a computing procedure. It is used to determine the consequences—usually measured in numerical terms—of particular decisions if carried out in a particular environment. Thus:

¶ An inventory model will compute inventory level, number of stock-outs (or delays), and number of orders placed. It will make these computations for any set of given assumptions about the external environment, such as delivery or lead times and the daily demand for materials.

¶ A transportation model is now being used by a major oil company to plan optimum means for serving its widely dispersed terminals. Probable future costs by use of pipelines, barges, tank cars, and so on are being related to projected changes in volumes and product mix at each terminal.

The beauty of all models, whether it be a physical model of an airplane in a wind tunnel or a decision model in operations research, is that the scientist can pretest solutions without hazardous, expensive, and time-consuming tampering with real-world operations. If the model bears a sufficient resemblance to appropriate aspects of reality, the scientist can predict with some confidence the outcome of actual operations. Models can also accept specified degrees of uncertainty or randomness about environmental conditions.

An excellent example of a dynamic model relating to business decisions is suggested by Jay W. Forrester.[3] This is an inventory model which starts in simple form but to which additional complexities of the real world are added. By using this model in an experimental way, management can anticipate the consequences of shifts in product de-

[3] "Industrial Dynamics: A Major Breakthrough for Decision Makers," *Harvard Business Review,* July–August 1958, p. 37.

mand and can design ordering and scheduling response systems to accommodate such shifts.

The Company Planner

In the functioning of the decision laboratory, the company planner performs the vital role of identifying the planning questions most important to management and of setting forth hypothetical plans in each area of future operations in such a manner that tests for these plans can be devised. The company planner must also provide a statement of constraints imposed by company policy which must be taken into account in future operations—for example, restrictions on the geographical location of plants, degree of product diversification, rate of expansion, and level of customer service.

While he himself may not be an economic forecaster, the planner is responsible for securing the market, price, cost, and other projections that are needed. Of course, forecast data do not translate automatically into figures or values that can be used in the mathematical formulas, and so the planner will need to apply his judgment here—sometimes a good deal of it. This he, and only he in the decision laboratory, should be well prepared to do. As a regular part of the planning function, he is studying trends and developments, assessing their significance to his company, and estimating the probability, timing, and magnitude of change. Against this background he can select likely alternative values, estimate reasonable probability factors, and indicate values in which randomness should be expected.

The Management Scientist

To provide the means for testing plans and for supplying other needed information to management, the management scientist devises the required model. An important ingredient in this model construction is the description of the environment in which the system operates. By environment we mean the set of factors which affect—but are unaffected by—the operation of the system. For purposes of company planning, a description of future environments is essential. It is here that collaboration with the company planner may be most fruitful in model construction.

One example of a future environment for which many companies must plan is that developing in the European Common Market:

Under the terms now established, there is to be a twelve- to fifteen-year period during which tariffs within the six signatory nations are gradually removed and external tariffs are made uniform. These transitional tariff adjustments are part of the environment which the management scientist must accommodate in his model.

The management scientist conducts the experiments in the decision laboratory. In establishing his model and in probing for solutions he must balance carefully the wants of management against the capability and validity of his methods—particularly the degree of significance in forecasts and the limits on computational complexity such as exist even in large computers.

THE COMPUTER

Although the electronic computer has quantitative limits and can make no computations that cannot be made with pencil and paper, its data processing and calculating capability will allow the management scientist to conduct analyses and experimentation which would be entirely impractical with manual methods. The enormous advantage a computer confers is speed. With this advantage, more complicated models of real problems can be analyzed for purposes of finding the best decision policy with respect to a given statement about the environment.

Even more important, with high-speed computers a policy that seems best given to one environment can be evaluated for many different environments. To put it in other words, almost any given statement about the environment that may exist in a future period is tinged with uncertainty (for example, estimates of future demand in the inventory control problem mentioned earlier).

Thus, if rational decisions are to be made, it appears essential to test out a policy under conditions which depart from those underlying its specification. For example, what if an automobile manufacturer's program for new warehouses and factory capacity is *not* supported by the market-share projections that management is so confident of?

Because of the remarkable capability of the computer, the company planner and management scientist are not confined to analysis of the most *probable* environment but are encouraged to explore the many *possible* environments which may exist. Thus, they may become aware of special opportunities or difficulties which will confront their company if a certain environment prevails; preparations for these eventualities can be made accordingly.

Testing Methods

We are now ready to go into the decision laboratory to see if the management scientist has useful techniques which can pretest company plans.

Three approaches will be described here, but the reader should realize that there are many others suitable for the decision laboratory. None is all-embracing in the sense of being a unified scientific theory of over-all company operations now and in the future. While each depends on the use of models and, in most cases, electronic computers, each works in a different way. The three types of "laboratory equipment" used are these:

1. *Current operational models* of production and distribution systems, useful in experimenting with the effects of particular decision rules under a wide variety of assumptions as to the business environment, and yielding conclusions which are applicable to long-range plans.
2. *The business game,* for testing useful strategies in allocation of resources under competitive conditions.
3. *Ecological models* of the sales of a company's future products (or services), appropriate to the planning of market strategy and product development strategy.

OPERATIONAL MODELS

Through manipulation of the models of current company operations which they construct, management scientists attempt to simulate the behavior of the real system whose salient features they have translated into mathematical terms. Use of the electronic computer makes it possible to incorporate in these models a great deal of the complexity which exists in the real system.

The solution of current problems by the use of computer experimentation obviously is not a means of testing long-range plans. Nevertheless, important guides to the future development of the company may be derived from these experiments.

Two over-all problems that lend themselves to computer experimentation are the following:

1. How can existing production and distribution facilities be used in such a way as to yield minimum total cost for given levels of customer service?

2. What configuration of production and distribution facilities in the future will make for minimum cost for given levels of customer service?

In studying problems of the first type the analyst can program a computer to test rules and policies for a future period for which specific assumptions have been made. For example, values for annual sales at distribution facilities may be generated by the computer on a basis which includes any specified degree of chance (i.e., the less likely the possibility that such-and-such a sales volume will be generated, the less the value attributed).

In the second type of problem the planner is not restricted to existing facilities and capabilities but is seeking to find the number, locations, and throughputs of production and distribution facilities for the most profitable operation. Well-developed techniques exist for some of the problems which may arise—for example, the linear-programing method for determining activity within a specified distribution network. It is possible to supplement these proven analytic techniques and attack broader problems using extensive computer experimentation.

While no complete mathematical "solution" exists for the more complex problems, the computer gives the scientist the opportunity to explore for solutions in a systematic way. Thus:

> In reviewing additions to production or distribution capacity, the analyst can start the process by selecting, from a list of feasible site locations, a series of reasonable combinations that can be examined under different assumptions about future conditions.[4] The effects of uncertainties in such future conditions can also be explored for purposes of selecting that combination of capacities, uses, costs, and levels of customer service which is most consistent with the over-all objectives of management planning.

A multitude of other suppositions as to future developments can be tested equally as well. By judicious manipulation of his model, the management scientist can answer the planner's questions: "What would happen if . . . ?"

[4] Robert E. Johnson, "The Use of Operations Research in Plant Location Problems," *Operations Research Reconsidered,* New York, American Management Association Report No. 10 (1958), pp. 120–127.

THE BUSINESS GAME

Another approach to pretesting plans, particularly with respect to allocation of company resources, is through use of business games (similar in general concept to the parlor game "Monopoly," but in many ways quite different). G. R. Andlinger has defined the business game as "a set of rules that corresponds to the economics of a business as realistically as possible within the limitations of a game structure."[5] By selecting various aspects of business economics, an infinite number of business games can be designed.

Business games are being constructed primarily to improve executive training. The management planner should watch closely the developments that are occurring in games, however, for they offer some promise of becoming an important means of pretesting company plans.

The fact that computers can be applied to the play provides fresh stimulus to develop new business games. Computers make it possible simultaneously (1) to reproduce with increasing realism a complex business environment, and (2) to calculate rapidly the consequences of decisions when affected by random fluctuations in (and changed relationships among) inventories, measures of customer service, and supply of working capital.

Games go operational models one better. In the experimentation with models, fixed decision rules are established and the computer then tests them against changing situations. In the business game, however, changing situations—including those brought about by intelligent competition—are described to the player, and the umpire or computer asks, "What decision rules do you want to apply? What do I do next?"

MECHANICS OF PLAY

Business games have received considerable management attention. One developed for the American Management Association[6] and one by McKinsey and Company, Incorporated,[7] are the best known, but

[5] "Business Games—Play One!" *Harvard Business Review,* March–April 1958, p. 115.

[6] See Richard Bellman, C. E. Clark, D. G. Malcolm, C. J. Craft, and F. M. Ricciardi, "On the Construction of a Multi-State, Multi-Person Business Game," *Operations Research,* August 1957, p. 469; and Lawrence A. Appley, "Executive Decision Making: A New Strategy," *Think,* December 1957, p. 2.

[7] See Andlinger, *op. cit.*

others have been designed which emphasize financial planning, production planning, and general business principles.[8] These games have been played by representatives of middle and top management in many companies, with generally favorable reactions as to the value of the game for training purposes. As for the general procedures used:

¶ In the usual business game, each competing team makes a play by deciding how to allocate its resources to production, marketing, research, and plant investment for the ensuing period. Referees then take the decisions of all teams and calculate, according to the design of the game, the effect of the decisions on the share of the market that each team obtains, the unit cost of production of each, and other consequences. The calculation may be performed manually or on an electronic computer. If the game is designed for electronic computation, it can be more complex and therefore a more complete representation of reality.

¶ After reviewing results obtained from the referees, each team makes new decisions for the next period. The process is repeated to simulate as many years of operations as is desired, and the relative performance in share of market, growth of assets, net profit, and other indicators is recorded by the referees.

¶ The effects of decisions are calculated by the referees according to the rules and the relationships designed into the game. These relationships can reflect the sensitivity of one aspect of a business to another, such as the lower product costs obtainable by investing in advanced plant equipment; they can also allow for realistic time lags in system response to certain decisions, such as the cumulative effect of advertising or its decays (or "half life") when terminated, and the lags associated with implementing the results of research and development.

¶ When the game is over, the teams and the referees critically review the results and the decisions that generated them.

Values for Planning

In a sense, the business game can be viewed as a means of compressing time in a way that will simulate the essentials of several years of business experience in the period of a few hours or days. Thus the players have an opportunity to experiment with alternative management policies and to observe the outcome of their planning in a competitive, dynamic environment.

The business game is also attractive in its ability to incorporate key

[8] See G. R. Andlinger, "Looking Around: What Can Business Games Do?" *Harvard Business Review,* July–August 1958, p. 147.

aspects of a changing external economic environment—such as the market—which is uninfluenced by decisions of the competitors. A simple form of such external change might be the secular growth in a market brought about by increases in population and in per capita income. A more complex form of external change is that mentioned earlier with respect to the European Common Market. In a game where the players represent competitors for shares of a European market, they would have to make decisions appropriate to the simulated "years" in which they were competing.

A valuable feature of these games is the way in which random factors can be programed into play when this helps to achieve a more faithful representation of reality. For certain factors and relationships which may be difficult to estimate, random numbers can determine results (within a range of probability), thereby permitting the game to reflect the effect on plans of some of the uncertainties experienced in real life—the successes and failures of salesmen, for example, or the unpredictability of investments in new equipment.

There is no intent in a game to arrive at the one best strategic solution. What the game can provide is a dynamic tool for working through the various consequences of competitive actions. By keeping records of the outcome of many "plays" and the strategies that dictated the moves within the game, one may be able to get some insight through statistical inference into the sets of strategies which appear more effective over the long run than other sets of strategies.

Possible Variations

It is entirely possible to design a game expressly for the planning problems confronting a given industry. Some of the decision areas that might be allowed for in such a game include:

1. *Outside acquisition of capital*—The American Management Association and McKinsey games allow only for self-generation of capital, a restriction which reduces the game's realism for many planning activities that are dependent upon heavy investment. If outside money were brought in as a factor, then dividend policy could also be introduced as a subject for decision, since a company's performance in this respect influences the ease with which it can obtain financing.

2. *Innovation and technology*—In the American Management Association game structure, expenditures for research are reflected only in improvements in the unit cost of the product, and not in the ability to intro-

duce new products. The McKinsey game makes provision for increased sales due to product improvements resulting from research and development expenditures.

There is much to be learned before we can describe in quantitative terms the cycle from research through engineering to marketing of new or improved products. Nonetheless, we could perhaps make some reasonable assumptions about the probable fraction of research and development efforts which will succeed, the investments in testing and other preproduction costs required for successful research projects, and the lags required to pass through these phases. These assumptions, some of which are probabilistic, would permit design of a game that gives competitors a chance to try alternative innovation strategies in the larger context of business competition.

3. *Merger and company acquisition*—Many of the important pros and cons of expansion through merger or acquisition can be reduced to formulas and included in a business game. The alternative opportunities would be presented to the player for evaluation and action.

In sum, the major contribution that the business game approach makes to long-range company planning lies in its ability to combine the strengths of man and of computer in experimenting with alternative strategies. The human players can test their plans and their judgment in an environment of conflict, while the computer can quickly assess the effects of decisions in terms of known relationships among the components of a business and of the market. The computer can even introduce random elements into calculating these effects, thus adding to the uncertainty, or luck, already present by reason of human competition.

ECOLOGICAL MODEL

The dictionary defines ecology as "the branch of biology which treats of the relations between organisms and their environment." The term is a useful one in economics because products or services in a product-market environment have some of the characteristics of biological organisms in their environment.

In an age of technological advance, a product or service can be created, mature, have its day in the economic sun, and then perish through obsolescence and competition. And while accelerating technology is tending to make the sales life of a product or service shorter, the very complexity of this same technology is tending to make the research and development, or gestation, period longer—often up to five or ten years in the case of advanced electronic, chemical, or pharmaceutical products.

Practical Benefits

"Ecological model" may sound strange and occult, but the concept is practical. To illustrate:

An ecological model from the military—e.g., the projected long-term air defense of the United States—must consider, among other factors, weapons systems already under development by our military, the probability of successful production, the timing of initial production, costs, and the effectiveness of defense against enemy weapons (which are expected to increase progressively in capability for destruction). Each new weapons system in turn will be expected to attain predominance in our air defense system, then be supplanted by another more advanced and more effective weapon.

In military planning there has long been some tendency to evaluate a weapons system outside its true time environment. An illustration of this error would be a study showing that an air defense weapon available in quantity in 1960 appears to be very effective against a bomber that has been available since 1954. The same weapon may appear superior to another air defense weapon available in 1958. The realities of the situation, however, require that *contemporary* defense weapons be compared in effectiveness and cost against a *contemporary* threat.

If the time dimension is treated explicitly and carefully, significantly more realistic results are obtained than if it is treated casually. The pace of military technology is now so rapid that availability of weapons is being measured with some of the same care that is given to measuring performance.

The translation of the foregoing ecological approach in weapons planning and succession to the commercial product-planning scene is quite apparent. Whereas in the military problem accelerating technology dictates an explicit treatment of the time dimension and the changing military environment, so in commercial product planning do changing technology and changing market conditions dictate explicit treatment of the phasing of product development, production, and marketing against the competitive conditions expected to be contemporary with merchandising of the product. To illustrate:

¶ A radically new type of wooden box for packing fresh produce at first appeared very attractive in comparison with existing packaging. When it was placed in the future environment of competition with certain known paper and plastic developments, however, it did not appear to be competitive. It was therefore dropped, and an investment of very high risk was avoided.

¶ Similarly, a pharmaceutical manufacturer has to keep his development program for relief-giving drugs in balance with his and other firms' progress toward cures for the same diseases.

The ecological model differs from what we have previously described as the current operational model in that it focuses on the long-range plans for changes in *markets* and in *products* rather than on changes in production and distribution facilities. Products and their supporting technologies must be considered in a time dimension.

The aim is to help management foresee what succession of decisions will best assure the company's success at any given time in the future, taking into account that each of the firm's products is in a continually varying stage of its life cycle, that the expected capability of competitors is always changing, that consumer demand is fluctuating, and so on. This means the market environment must be projected into the future at least as far as is necessary to span the cycle time for the product from conception to merchandising.

Data Analysis

Now let us be a little more specific. What types of information does an ecological model require to produce useful results? What demands does it place on the planner?

1. The first need is for data about the market environment. Here one should include all secular influences, together with special trends that can be anticipated, such as the wave of household formation that will occur in the 1960's as a result of the wartime and postwar baby crop. Other environmental data that need to be related to time are the foreseeable changes that will affect the business of one's customers and of one's suppliers—back through all tiers of suppliers to extracted raw materials and forward through all tiers of customers to the ultimate consumer. For example, in Lockheed Aircraft Corporation's development planning for the airline market, the needs of passengers and air cargo shippers were fully explored.

2. The extension of forecasting far into the future demands an immense breadth of knowledge on the part of the company planner. His concern with both economic and technical changes must spread into industries

peripheral to his own, where competitive threats of many kinds can develop and where, conversely, opportunities for his own company may be revealed. Little wonder that planners express a growing need for information on and analysis of significant changes in industries other than their own.

3. Against the backdrop of the market environment, the next step is to plot the company's sales capabilities by product or product line. Nearly all companies make master sales and workload forecasts for one or two years in the future. What is proposed here is that forward planning of sales and workload be greatly expanded in time to ten or fifteen years and in scope to the research and technology which underlie products or product lines.

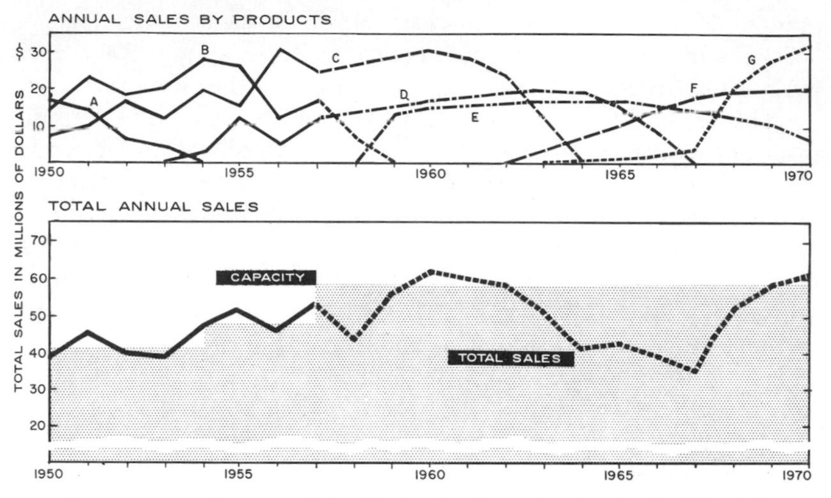

EXHIBIT 1. Company Sales Projection Based on Ecological Model

Exhibit 1 summarizes hypothetical results drawn from one type of ecological model. The upper part indicates annual sales by product for seven products, and the lower part shows the sum of the upper curves. The lessons to be learned from this case are that there will be declines in the company's market in 1958 and in 1964–67. It may be that some rephasing of research and development effort can help fill the latter gap. If not, other corrective action, such as product or company acquisition, might be undertaken.

MAKING PROJECTIONS

The forecast of product development and of sales must be based on a profound comprehension of the technological environment and its possible effects (in terms of probabilities for success) on the outcome of research and development projects. Here the call may not be so much for an "economic superman" as for the kind of thorough, systematic, plodding spadework that has been outlined in *Harvard Business Review* articles discussing the organizational aspects of planning.[9] Projections of sales by product depend on market environment, of course, and must lie below the umbrella of maximum planned capacity.

The model of the management scientist has great value in analyzing the many combinations of circumstances that may prevail in both the market and in product development. If many alternative values and probabilities are incorporated in the computation, the electronic computer can be used to advantage.

Algebraic expressions of product-market relationships have been developed by many management scientists, but usually for the solution of near-term problems. Many of the considerations involved in long-term product and market planning and several of the mathematical approaches have been discussed by H. Igor Ansoff in terms of their applicability to evaluation of products for diversification.[10]

The exercise of plotting product or service life cycles in a time frame has the effect of revealing gaps in a company's future capability, due either to attrition of products or to expected inability to compete. Given appropriate lead time, these gaps can be filled by setting up new research and development projects or else by acquiring outside the company a development, or product, or even another company whose outlook will be helpful at the time the gap is anticipated.

The ecological approach is certainly not one that can be done once, and then frozen. Instead, it is effective only if it is a continuing dynamic plan that adjusts previous programs in the light of external and internal developments.

It can be seen that the ecological approach does not try to optimize future operations in the sense used by the management scientists. Its principal usefulness is to the company planner in reducing to a mathematical or graphical expression his conclusions as to likely alternatives

[9] See H. Edward Wrapp, "Organization for Long-Range Planning," Chapter 15, pp. 147–167; and Bruce Payne, "Steps in Long-Range Planning," Chapter 23, pp. 216–238.

[10] "Strategies for Diversification," Chapter 13, pp. 115–142; and "A Model for Diversification," *Management Science,* July 1958, p. 392.

facing his company. Thus it offers an orderly way of assessing the dynamics of a company's product-market future.

CONCLUSION

Since today's actions inevitably foreshadow tomorrow's operations, there is always a planning job to be done. It is our belief that management should do this job aggressively, not allowing external factors, by default, to determine a company's destiny.

There are not now, and may never be, any all-embracing models in operations research that can be relied on to evaluate over-all long-range company planning. However, if management chooses, it can now begin to pretest its planning in the decision laboratory. The use of computer experimentation, business games, and ecological models should yield valuable test reports that can direct management toward better long-range plans.

SPECIAL FUNCTIONS AND AREAS

Nae man can tether time or tide.
—Robert Burns

Planning isn't really a prediction of the future. You can't predict the future. What I think you can plan for is change itself. This, I think, is quite important. If you think of planning in terms of an organization's flexibility in preparing for the unknown and of anticipating possible crises and system changes, this really seems to be the essence of it.
—Kenneth Boulding

34

Introduction

In this section we turn to some specific functions and areas of organized activity in which long-range planning has significant possibilities. It should be obvious that the areas listed are not the only ones where planning is useful. My selection reflects partly the gaps in the preceding material and partly what is available at this time in the literature. As we shall see in the Conclusion, the literature of long-range planning is far from complete despite great strides in the past six years.

As might be expected, the chapters in this series draw rather heavily on concrete cases and situations. In considering research and development, for instance, we catch glimpses of planning activities at Bell Laboratories and a series of manufacturing firms. When we come to new products we take a case history from Aluminum Company of America—not written as an analysis of planning but with obvious implications for students of the subject. In the article on production and control we examine some problems of instrumentation. In the series of studies of forecasting we look at situations experienced at Lockheed Aircraft Corporation and other organizations. In the study of fiscal planning we have a singular case study from education as well as analyses of corporate problems. In the part on personnel we have (among others) a study made at Minnesota Mining and Manufacturing. And the chapter on overseas operations shows what Standard-Vacuum has done.

I think that case studies of this depth and variety reveal a significant truth about long-range planning. Planning makes no sense unless related to specific organizational situations. As an abstract exercise it is futile. Planning methods and approaches should be induced, not deduced. It is the particular problem that should justify the plan, not someone's "book" of principles. The function of the literature and classroom teaching is to provide resources and guides.

If you want a rationalization for this conclusion, you might proceed as follows: (1) Managers in nearly all organizations make decisions with long-term implications. For example, a simple decision to build or not build a warehouse, or to increase or not increase salaries, makes assumptions—often very important assumptions—about future needs and resources. (2) These decisions are necessarily pragmatic. They rest on particular sets of facts, feelings, and interpretations of facts and feelings. (3) Long-range planning makes sense only as the framework for these decisions. Planning adds the time dimension, the strategy dimension, the resources dimension to a stream of decisions that would, in part, run on in some way whether planning existed or not. (4) Therefore, planning, too, must be pragmatic. You can judge the usefulness of a plan or program only if you know what and whose decisions it is supposed to guide.

People ask, "Should a long-range plan be in writing?" or "Should planning begin with marketing and then work around to the other functions?" or "Should planning go at least five years ahead for all major activities?" I do not think you can answer these questions correctly without reference to particular situations. Written profitability targets may be very well for a Westinghouse or a General Mills—but what about for the firm where there is no agreed-on understanding among managers as to what return on investment really is or should be? Ten-year programs may be very appropriate for a timber company—but what about for a toy manufacturer? Detailed cost-reduction programs showing sequences of activities and goals may be fine for some corporations—but what about for the company where a top-management cost-reduction drive has come to mean, to lower management, pressure and meanness and insecurity?

These are the kinds of questions we begin to ask when we get down to cases!

CONTRIBUTORS TO THIS SECTION

James Brian Quinn is Associate Professor of Business Administration at the Amos Tuck School at Dartmouth College. His two-year study of research management in business covered a wide variety of companies and industries.

Morton Hunt did his interesting piece on Bell Laboratories as a

free-lance writer. He was president of the Society of Magazine Wr
in 1956.

Harry L. Hansen is Professor of Business Administration at the Harvard Business School. He is also director of the School's new Division of International Activities.

E. Raymond Corey is also Professor of Business Administration at the Harvard Business School. His books include *Industrial Marketing,* published in 1962 by Prentice-Hall.

George M. Muschamp is vice-president—engineering for the Industrial Products Group of Minneapolis-Honeywell Regulator Company. He is responsible for integrating product programs and the technical evaluation and planning of long-range needs in several systems.

Burnard H. Sord, at the time he helped write *Business Budgeting,* was Assistant Professor of Management at the College of Business Administration, The University of Texas.

Glenn A. Welsch, the coauthor, was Professor of Accounting at The University of Texas.

William H. Newman is Samuel Bronfman Professor of Democratic Business Enterprise at Columbia University's Graduate School of Business.

Gerald A. Busch is director of planning—eastern region for Lockheed Aircraft Corporation. He was formerly associated with Douglas Aircraft Company, Incorporated.

Ernest W. Walker is Professor and Chairman of the Department of Finance at the College of Business Administration, The University of Texas.

William H. Baughn is also at Texas University's College of Business Administration. He is Associate Dean and Professor of Finance.

Manley Howe Jones, when he wrote the book from which his chapter here is drawn, was Associate Professor of Business Management at Illinois Institute of Technology.

Sidney G. Tickton writes his paper as consultant to The Fund for the Advancement of Education. The paper originally appeared as a chapter in a pioneering book edited for McGraw-Hill by Dexter M. Keezer, *Financing Higher Education, 1960–70.*

James W. Oram is vice-president of public and employee relations for The Pennsylvania Railroad Company.

Wendel W. Burton made his contribution as employment manager of Minnesota Mining and Manufacturing Company.

at the time of his address to the Harvard Business sixth Annual National Business Conference in 1956, ırd-Vacuum Oil Company as manager, economic co-

361

35

Top-Management Guides for Research Planning[1]

James Brian Quinn

What kind of guidance can and should top-level management provide in the planning of its research operations? Its most essential activities in this sphere are:

1. Establishing meaningful objectives for research
2. Seeing that the organization is attuned to the company's major long-term technological threats and opportunities
3. Developing an over-all business strategy into which research is integrated
4. Developing a procedure which evaluates research projects in light of company goals and capacities

[1] From *Technological Planning on the Corporate Level,* Proceedings of a Conference Sponsored by The Associates of the Harvard Business School, ed. James R. Bright (Boston, Harvard Business School, 1962), pp. 169–205. Used by permission.

AUTHOR'S NOTE: This paper is based on a two-year study which included interviews with over 120 top research, operating, and planning executives in 35 major companies in the chemical, electrical, electronics, basic metals, and pharmaceutical industries. The author gratefully acknowledges a research grant from the Alfred P. Sloan Foundation.

5. Organizing research and operations for a maximum transfer of technology from research to operations

This paper will analyze why each of these activities is critical, what problems each involves, and how these problems can best be overcome.

OBJECTIVE SETTING

As with any other aspect of industrial planning, research planning should begin with the establishment of the targets the activity is to shoot toward—over-all organizational objectives. But in most organizations there is great confusion over the nature and use of objectives in planning. What are objectives? Why are they needed? How do they come into being? Where and why do failures occur in establishing objectives for research? These are common questions. If we can dispel some of the major misunderstandings about these issues, perhaps management can avoid one of the most common pitfalls in research planning—inadequate objective formulation.

What Are Objectives?

Objectives are targets or goals. They state the results that the organization or any of its components should accomplish. Objectives do not take just one form. They should exist at all levels in the organization in a definite hierarchy.

At the top of the pile are the relatively permanent "value objectives" of the total organization. These link together the value premises which should guide the organization's actions. They state the firm's desire for employee happiness, value of products, honesty to all, profits to stockholders, etc. These are selected by the owners or general management for the whole organization and generally express some distillation of the moral values of the times (although you can always have value objectives like those of the Al Capone organization which are rather individualistic). While value objectives may well serve as guides for potentially errant managers, they are of relatively little use in planning.

But in business enterprises—immediately subordinate to the value objectives—there is a group of "over-all business objectives" which are critical to the planning process. These establish the intended nature of the specific business enterprise and the directions in which it should move. These over-all business objectives are somewhat less permanent than value objectives, but nevertheless usually stand for years. General management should, of course, establish these objectives, because they are targets for all elements of the organization.

Below this level are a series of less permanent goals which define targets for each organizational unit, its subunits, and finally each activity within the subunit. The critical objectives here are those at the over-all business objective and the "organizational objective" levels. Formulation of both is a top-management responsibility. Below this level top management's concern is just to see that those who establish goals keep them consistent with higher-level objectives.

Why Define Objectives for Research?

There are three overwhelming reasons for setting clear objectives for research:

1. Objectives provide the only usable criteria for judging the adequacy of research plans. If present (or proposed) programs will not propel the company to its goals, they must be replanned. For example:

One large company set as its goal a 10 per cent annual sales growth rate. Because of the company's size and the nature of its markets, antitrust laws foreclosed the possibility of acquisitions. Growth therefore had to be internally generated. Market planners thought that if present products were given adequate technological defense and were skillfully marketed, the company would achieve a 2 per cent to 3 per cent growth rate because of population factors. But research planners evaluated 85 per cent of current research and development programs as essentially defensive. By a simple ratio analysis it became obvious that the company was in effect expecting each dollar of offensive R&D —i.e., the other 15 per cent of its program—to yield approximately $25 per year of new-product sales. To expect such a high impact ratio was entirely unrealistic. Consequently the company had thoroughly to reassess its offensive programs and its total program balance.

2. Objectives allow self-planning in creative organizations. They do not *constrain* action like other plans, i.e., policies, procedures, or methods. Properly established, objectives tell the organization *what* it is to accomplish, not *how* to do it. Creative persons are thus left free to select their own approaches to needed solutions.

3. Objectives provide the only criteria by which actual research performance can be judged. On a national level we have an outstanding

example of the confusion that is caused when this maxim is not followed.

The U.S. missile program was conceived primarily to support goals of national defense and scientific investigation. Whether or not the decision was a good one, the program initially was not intended particularly to enhance the national image in the eyes of the world. The R&D program as drawn up and executed appears to be successfully meeting the goals originally set for it. Hence, it should be considered a success. But suddenly the goal of national publicity has been retroactively applied. The result is disillusionment and confusion.[2]

How Do Objectives Come into Being?

Granted the need for objectives, how do they come into being in an organization? They can originate in three different ways: (1) by "enunciation," i.e., by management's carefully assessing the organization's future purposes and communicating these in an organized system; (2) by "appeal," i.e., by subordinate groups' submitting proposals to management until its pattern of decisions indicates that an organizational objective exists (even though not formally enunciated); (3) by "external imposition," i.e., by outside pressures such as those of the government, labor unions, or the international situation, forcing the company in certain directions. In most complex organizations objectives originate by all three methods.

But consistent management decisions are the only way to keep an established objective in existence. Once decisions begin to contradict understood objectives, the organization cannot direct itself toward the goal with confidence. At this point the utility of the objective—no matter how clearly and how often enunciated—has ceased. Enough decisions consistently contradicting a given goal will eventually create a new goal. Until then confusion reigns. Consequently, all key decision-makers must have a clear idea of the firm's objectives and back these with consistent decisions throughout the organization.

Key Problems in Establishing Objectives

Let us look at some of the major causes of failure in establishing objectives for research and some of the approaches specific companies

[2] This argument is developed in depth in R. E. Lapp, *Man and Space—The Next Decade* (New York, Harper and Row, 1961).

have found useful in dealing with these problems. The most common failures can perhaps be classified as follows:

1. *Objectives change too often.* Managements allow "urgent competitive pressures" to dominate decisions. Hence the whole organization becomes oriented to the "profit now" objective and overdiscounts —or ignores—future needs until they become crying present realities. Thus longer-term fundamental and applied research either lack guidance altogether or are essentially converted into short-term service activities supporting current marketing or production goals.

2. *Objectives are distorted by the organization.* This problem can never be completely overcome. For each time an objective is transmitted from one person to another, the person receiving the transmission reinterprets the objective within his own framework. Thus small distortions introduced by somewhat inconsistent top-level viewpoints are likely to be amplified by each link in the chain of authorities transmitting the objective down into the organization. Researchers can only self-direct themselves meaningfully if these distortions are minimized by careful management action.

3. *Objectives are too general.* A most common problem where objectives are enunciated formally is to express them too vaguely for use as planning guides or criteria for judging action. Such overgeneralized goals usually take the form of value objectives. But too frequently even over-all business objectives are thought out in such vague terms as "growing as rapidly as possible," diversification in any profitable direction," etc. While not imposing constraints on research, such objectives do not help stimulate research in desired directions.

4. *Objectives can be too specific.* Some organizationally immature operations overplan research by setting goals in too great detail. Such goals take either of two forms: (a) specific materials, pieces of hardware, test measurements, components, etc., demanded by operating groups, or (b) step-by-step experimental goals. Such goals occur when operating or staff groups dominate the research function. The obvious result is that research is constrained in its approaches to problems since it is told *how* to do the job, not *what* is to be done.

The experience of several companies may demonstrate some interesting ways of attacking these problems.

On the issue of the short-term orientation of decisions, the chairman of the board of one large concern said: "Any damn fool can make a profit for a month—or even a year—by gutting the organization's future. Top management's job is to keep the company 'future-oriented.' We try to do this by using a complex of *long-term* management controls. We play down the use of current profit and return standards in any rigid sense. And we purposely use intuitive judgments concerning how well each operating unit is building its organization and technology to meet future demands. So far we have resisted taking on board members from banks and financial houses because we think such people overemphasize current profits at the expense of future strength."

A pharmaceutical company reports that its president and chief technical executives visit the central laboratory once a month and talk with individual researchers about their work and evolving company goals and needs. The executives get to talk to each researcher about once a quarter. The company reports that the activity is a real stimulus to researchers because they feel management has a positive interest in their work and they genuinely understand company objectives.

A large company has both a centralized planning group and divisional planning groups. The central group reports to an Executive Committee, consisting of general corporate managers. Each year, to initiate the company's planning process, the Executive Committee—with the help of Central Planning—draws up and circulates a statement of general corporate goals for the next five years. Targets for each division are included as a part of the statement. Before formal division planning begins, appropriate representatives of the Executive Committee personally discuss these targets with each division manager and his planning manager. Each division then draws up a set of plans—supported by budgets—to meet agreed upon goals. All plans are screened by the Central Planning group and then sent to a Long-Range Planning Committee (of the Executive Committee) for final coordination into the corporate plan. The corporate plan then becomes the basis for appraisal of budgets, and the division goals expressed within it become standards against which division performance is evaluated.

Types of Objectives Needed

Fortunately the kinds of objectives which are most vital to research planning can be established—with proper care—to avoid the pitfalls noted above. A later section on "The Research Mission" will describe the kinds of organizational objectives which should be considered for research. Formulation of these logically follows the forecasting of technological threats and opportunities and the establishment of a research strategy. The following examples will illustrate what over-all business objectives[3] are most critical to research planning and what issues these should resolve for maximum effectiveness:

The kinds of businesses the company wants to be in. These can be best expressed in terms of the kinds of markets the company will sell in and the functions its products must perform for customers. Thus an "electronics" company should consider whether it will be in the "communications" business, the "industrial controls" business, the "consumer appliance" business, the "quality laboratory measurements" business, etc. Each of these businesses requires a different kind of research backup in terms of program scope and balance. Obviously, a broad-based company will seek a position in several such businesses simultaneously. This simply means that it should be careful to back each with the research needed to accomplish its goals.

Method of growth intended. Is growth to be achieved by acquisition, merger, internal development, or a combination of approaches? Each approach carries different financial and organizational commitments and affects research program size and balance.

Direction of growth. Is the company to grow vertically toward markets or raw materials or horizontally into new areas at the same level of distribution? Should it find new fields or further penetrate present markets? Should the company be a broad-line producer or specialize in limited fields? Should it hedge cyclical products with countercyclical products, etc.? Such considerations obviously affect the internal balance of the research program tremendously.

Rate of growth. Recognizing the limits of its personnel, resources, and markets, how fast should the company reasonably hope to grow? What should the timing and pattern of such growth be in each market area and over-all? This requires careful thought because too rapid growth can be as dangerous as too little growth. Unless all resources including technology are carefully built up to support a new market

[3] I have amplified some of these in "Long-Range Planning of Industrial Research," *Harvard Business Review*, July–August 1961, pp. 88–102.

position, the company will be easy prey to a slower-moving competitor with better-developed backing for his product or service.

Allowable dependence on suppliers. Are the company's raw material markets stable or should alternative materials be sought? Is competition among vendors sufficient to insure technical progressiveness and low cost? Are individual vendors strong enough to support technical programs of their own or should these be supplemented? Management must decide how much of a risk it is willing to take on supplier relationships. A company can often gain some degree of control over its supply markets and individual suppliers by obtaining superior knowledge of the properties of purchased materials, processes for manufacturing purchased items, or possible substitute items. Again, the company's goal of "independence of supply" affects research program scope and emphasis.

The kind of capital structure desired. Particularly in smaller companies the desired capital structure affects the length of time the company can wait for research payoffs, the amount of technology the company can exploit without damaging ownership goals, the degree of risk the company can assume on projects, etc. These, in turn, influence total program size and balance on long-term versus short-term projects.

The degree of stability desired. Because of stock price considerations, ownership needs, banking relationships, etc., a given company may desire earning and sales stability as opposed to more rapid but risky growth. The degree of stability needed will affect the emphasis placed on more "sure fire" applied projects and smaller-impact technology which may sacrifice potentially greater gains for lower risk.

Other business objectives. Other objectives commonly stimulate or restrict certain research programs. These include: the desired company image, its intended size, the allowable degree of government control, the percentage of market to be held in total and by geographical areas, the degree of technical flexibility desired, the price-volume and profit-volume markets the company wants to be in, the degree of decentralization intended, the company's desired size, and rate of return on investment.

Obviously initial decisions concerning objectives will be modified as information from later planning stages becomes available. But orderly research planning must begin with a clear understanding of the directions the company wants to go and the confidence that these directions will not be constantly changing. Without such guidance the program will inevitably drift toward studies that fascinate individual scientists, toward pet projects of key executives, or toward sales service—or similar short-term activities—which bear little relationship to long-term company needs.

DETERMINING TECHNOLOGICAL THREATS AND OPPORTUNITIES

Research must be responsive to technological flows from three sources: the *scientific community* generally, the company's present and potential *customers,* and the company's *competitors.*

Let us see what is involved in assessing the threats and opportunities offered by each of these three flows. Since other papers at this conference discuss elements of how such technological forecasts are made, I shall concentrate on the top-management questions they raise: What kinds of organizations have been found useful for forecasting technology? What kinds of information should management expect forecasters to consider and to provide for the planning process? And what kinds of problems are encountered in forecasting technological threats and opportunities?

CONCEPTS OF TECHNOLOGICAL FORECASTING

The first thing to emphasize is that forecasting is *not* planning. Forecasts assess future environments and the mutual impact of these environments on the company and the company on the environments. Planning occurs later when management takes forecast information and converts it into goals, policies, programs, and procedures which guide action. Forecasting can be delegated to staff groups. Planning from the forecasts should always be a line of activity. Planning requires that action decisions be made and followed up with authority delegations, assignments of responsibilities, and controls to see that these assignments are carried out. This is where many "planning programs" fail. Staff planning groups anticipate problems or foresee opportunities. They evaluate alternatives and even recommend action in reports which are carefully "accepted" by management. But then nothing happens. Line managers continue to make decisions as if the staff group's analysis—and the problems and opportunities themselves—never existed. Top management thus should see that technological forecasts are used for decision-making or else not waste money on them.

Another important point. Management is interested in forecast accuracy, not precision. No one can forecast the precise technologies which will be needed and available three to seven years ahead. Yet management decisions on staffing new knowledge areas, planning exploitation of present research results, making major organizational changes, and so on, demand such lead times. Fortunately, what such decisions require is information about the *direction* future technology is likely to take and the *probable ranges* of technologies which might be faced. As the future unfolds, early long-range decisions can be modified, nullified, or reinforced—provided sufficient flexibility has been built into initial plans. Forecasters can be expected to provide accurate enough range forecast information for these early plans to propel the company in proper directions.

Finally, unlike other areas of forecasting, mathematical formulations are almost worthless in technological forecasting. The requisites are human judgment, a knowledge of the scientific field under study, a real sense of the economic implications of science, and imagination without stargazing. To be effective, each phase of such forecasting must be the specific responsibility of some competent individual or organization. Let us see what kinds of approaches have been used in evaluating each of the three technological flows affecting research.

The General Scientific Environment and Competitive Technology

Forecasts of the general scientific environment—and the impact of competitive science in particular—may take several possible forms. The following examples offer an excellent overview of major approaches:

Some companies have developed grids[4] of all the basic sciences which might potentially impinge on their operations. On a preset schedule they review each scientific field on two bases. First they investigate whether the science: (1) is beginning to show promise of breakthroughs, (2) is highly active, with major contributions being made rapidly, (3) is slowly approaching saturation, or (4) is scientifically dormant. Second, they evaluate whether the science is developing

[4] One such check list is provided by the Specialties List of the National Register of Scientific and Technical Personnel.

in directions which appear to be more (or less) closely associated with the company's long-term goals. These two parameters help determine whether a given field needs increased or decreased emphasis in the company's fundamental program. Such reviews are made by the company's most competent available scientist(s) in each field with such outside support as the company may feel is warranted.

Other companies select for study specific knowledge areas which researchers or executives think might eventually impinge on their company's operations. Staff groups then assess the scientific potential of these individual fields and their potential economic implications if certain solutions are found. An individual study could take several man-months and usually involves an investigation of the "state of the art," important knowledge gaps, the current work being done, the magnitude of the field's potential economic impact, and the availability of qualified personnel to man the field.

Many studies—both within and without industry—have projected the future state of the art in various technological fields. These have attempted to estimate what technology will be needed and available in such end-use fields as computers, automatic production devices, transportation, space, communications, energy, etc.[5] The technique most commonly used in such studies is to forecast critical sociological factors whose change will create certain demands for technology.

Present technology is compared against these needs and gaps are noted. The forecaster then identifies the missing key facts which compose these gaps. Present fundamental and applied programs indicate which of these problems are being worked on and with what seeming progress. Past experience with similar problems provides a basis for determining probability of success and the potential timing of solutions. Then, by cataloging significant breakthroughs and trends, the forecaster can extrapolate developing knowledge into the future and estimate the future technical configuration of the field under study.

Many companies evaluate competitive technology both formally and informally. In fundamental research liberal publication policies and free informal exchanges make it relatively easy to evaluate the scope of competitors' programs. Many research directors say they know to a man who is working on what in competitors' fundamental re-

[5] Published examples include: Lapp. *op cit.*, note 2; Harrison Brown, *Challenge of Man's Future* (New York, Viking Press, 1954); Hans Thirring, *Energy for Man* (Bloomington, Indiana University Press, 1958).

search. Several companies keep accurate tabulations of publications and patents by competitors and break them down into knowledge areas to assess competitive progress in critical spheres. Many companies make annual product comparisons to identify where their products are superior or need defensive support.[6]

Forecasts of the scientific environment are typically provided by one of three organizational devices: (1) a staff analysis group, (2) a research committee, or (3) an *ad hoc* special study group. Each approach presents its special advantages and problems. Two interesting combination approaches illustrate solutions some companies have found useful.

Several research directors indicated success in having research scientists assist a respected staff group in preparing forecasts. They say this approach both utilizes the special skills and information sources the staff group has and forces the researchers involved to think rigorously about the potential of their scientific fields and their contributions to it.

The vice-president of research in one electronics company annually assigns a team of newly hired Ph.D.'s to study the potential impact of their own scientific specialties. As new personnel they are not influenced by past company biases. Their report goes directly to the research committee.

Customer Needs

Of all possible technology flows, the company is most interested in those which impinge on the needs of its present and potential customers. Projecting technology to support present lines is not uncommon. As a matter of routine some market research groups look ahead to customer needs three to five years in the future. But too often market research groups get bogged down in problems of the present. Some of the more sophisticated *organizational devices* to insure a longer-term orientation to the needs of present and potential customers include the following:

A chemical company invites its customers' technical and management personnel to seminars at which they discuss their developing scientific problems and learn about the sponsor's own current research

[6] Several systems for doing this are found in J. B. Quinn, *Yardsticks for Industrial Research* (New York, Ronald Press, 1959).

programs. The company then tries to meet defined needs through its own R&D program and through cooperative research with customers.

AT&T has long supported a sizable systems engineering group which (on the basis of demographic data, call information, system problems, anticipated new means of communication, and so on) expresses needed future technology in terms of "black boxes" (of known performance characteristics) to be developed by R&D. The group must constantly look far enough into the future to keep adopted technology from creating system-wide bottlenecks ten to twenty years ahead.

One company has a long-range marketing research group of technical people whose sole responsibility is to contact those charged with long-range thinking in customer and potential customer companies. On the basis of this information they try to meet future technical needs —three to ten years ahead. The group claims to be able to spot needs and opportunities that customers themselves cannot see because of operating biases and the fact that they are constantly putting out technological "brush fires."

Some specific *techniques* used in identifying areas where longer-term research could propel the company into new or expanded markets are also interesting:

A glass company considers those properties of its product (glass) which are unique unto it, i.e., exceptional tensile strength, chemical resistance, translucency, ductility, etc. It then seeks to identify present and potential markets in which consideration of one or more such properties is a dominant factor. Its applied research program then seeks glasses with intensified properties needed to meet recognized market needs. Its fundamental program seeks primarily to further isolate and understand the properties of various glasses.

A basic metals company by extensive field research seeks to identify those applications where its products can most nearly be substituted for the dominant competing product. It then identifies the performance limits which preclude its present product's entry into the desired market. Where economically feasible, applied research works on the improvement of these performances limits. Fundamental research investigates the phenomena limiting the performance of the metal's compounds and alloys.

A chemical company seeks what it calls "the critical operating characteristic" of each of its major products. This is the characteristic which—if improved slightly—will most dramatically influence product sales. This becomes the focal point for applied research. For most products the nature of this critical characteristic is said to remain stable over a moderate—two-to-five-year—period.

Such market research guidance helps stimulate long-range research in useful directions but does not constrain scientific approaches by overdetailing the specifications of needed products.

Top-Management Considerations

Obviously, top management does not need to be involved in the details of technological forecasting. But it should expect research planning to be based upon adequate forecast data and to see that proper organizational devices exist to provide it. These organizations must look far enough ahead to allow research planning adequate lead time and not be overly biased by short-term considerations or by traditional ways of attacking problems. The effects of the latter kind of bias can be tragic. For example:

In a large chemical company a product area had been disregarded as "too small relative to our operation" to be worth the company's while. A brief discussion established the fact that if certain solutions could be found, the product had an annual potential of $10 billion. This sounds fantastic, but the company had only considered the traditional way of doing things in the market under consideration. It had not thought about what chemistry could do to change the field totally.

Significantly, the *most profitable opportunities* and the *most serious threats* offered by technology frequently come from looking at old problems in entirely new ways—not from traditional approaches gently mutating accepted technology. As examples:

The indigo industry was subverted not by traditional dye sources, but by the development of synthetic dyes through chemistry. Polymer research—not agricultural research—recently transformed the textile field and the rubber business. Solid state physics is revolutionizing electronics. Plastics are on their way toward transforming the housing, packaging, and metals fields. The accidental discovery of penicillin brought about a whole new approach to the attack on certain medical problems. Psychology has recently made dramatic advances—not because of traditional therapeutic techniques but because of chemistry.

Finally, technological forecasting must take a broad enough viewpoint to insure that research planners recognize the opportunities and threats posed by change in the general economic and sociological environment. This means that they must consider trends in economic conditions, the demographic structure, shifting expenditure priorities, the role of government in the economy, public and legal attitudes toward business, international affairs, future labor conditions, and so on. Analyses of such factors have led particular companies to research policies which more limited commercial considerations would not have dictated. For example:

Some companies are beginning to orient some of their technological thinking toward arms control. This move is based on a changing U.S. and international attitude toward such activities, as well as the growing potential of a multibillion dollar business in arms control devices.

Demographic analyses have shown the need for research into many fields: geriatrics, nonfossil energy sources, synthetic foods, recovery of water and chemicals from the sea and air, water purification, sewage disposal, traffic control, exotic sources of food and raw materials, and chemical means for contraception—to name only a few.

Recognizing potential public and legal pressures, some companies have established broad fundamental research programs and even entire laboratories for the primary purpose of producing technology for the public good. Others take on certain defense or health contracts—outside their normal spheres of interest—on a nominal (or non-) profit basis and contribute resulting knowledge to the public domain. Some companies restrict research and growth which would apply to areas that might create cries of "giantism" or "stifling competition." Many freely exchange basic technology with competitors although this induces a higher degree of competition in markets they could otherwise dominate.

STRATEGY FOR RESEARCH

The next major top-management consideration in research planning is to develop the over-all business strategy which research is to help support. An initial problem here is that the concept of strategy itself is so often misunderstood.

A strategy is a plan so complete that it takes into account possible countermoves of opposition groups. A strategy is an *implementing* plan. It supports an objective—or set of objectives—by determining *how* the organization can best achieve its desired ends in light of competitive (or other) opposing pressures and its own limited resources. Every competitive organization which survives in the long run must be stronger in some respects than its competitors. Conversely, its competitors must exceed its strength in certain areas or else they would not survive.[7] The essence of strategic planning then is to marshal the organization's resources so that its comparative strengths are emphasized and the opposition's comparative strengths have the least negative effect on the organization.

This means, in research, that no company can be pre-eminent in all technological fields. Because of limited resources, each company must expose itself to some risks and pass up some opportunities. The research strategy problem is to establish—in light of expected competitive action—where the company should: (1) concentrate its research efforts, (2) remain "on the grapevine" in touch with the scientific community, or (3) virtually ignore developing technology. Each company's peculiar strengths, weaknesses, and objectives will determine its optimum strategy. Let us look at the typical considerations in research strategy.

Major Research Programs

First, the company must minimize serious technological threats to its existence. As a starting point, it looks at positions which must be defended at all costs. Then it saturates these areas with research. Almost every company has a few lines or processes which are its "bread and butter." These must be defended with strong research commitments until design maturity eliminates returns from research or the company decides to phase out the products or processes themselves. Carefully forecasting customers' technological needs and watching competitive programs will indicate areas which need heavy developmental and applied research support. Cataloguing the limits of knowledge supporting these areas helps to delineate fields for strong *longer-range* research efforts.

For example, one large, limited-line electronics equipment manufacturer said:

> Our company got into fundamental research because things were becoming too complicated to continue without it. We needed to know

[7] Of course, if either party is nurtured by a benevolent third party—such as the government or Fate—it can have no comparative strengths and nevertheless survive.

the physical limits of certain kinds of matter in order to develop machinery which could operate at increasingly high speeds and with increasing complexity. Purchase of our kind of equipment is a straight technical decision. The fastest, most reliable equipment for a job will sell. No other will. Consequently, whoever first obtains the basic knowledge in our field will dominate it. And we cannot afford to lose our present number one position. As a result, 80% of our fundamental program is now on composition of matter problems which we think pertain to our one primary equipment line. We try to exceed competitors' talent commitments in all these problem areas.

Next, the strategic plan outlines areas where optimum technological opportunities exist. Top management must determine these by a critical analysis of the company's particular strengths and weaknesses. Examples from the chemical industry illustrate three completely different strategies in actual companies:

Company A tries to make itself indispensable to its customers by high performance of its chemicals and special services. The company refuses to make chemicals which may face fierce price competition. The company makes only high-margin specialties whose volume is too small to interest the industry's giants. It sells mostly to small companies who tend to regard Company A as their own research department. To do this Company A must keep intimately in touch with its customers' needs and be a research leader in a few scientific fields tailored specifically to these needs. The company backs up its carefully restricted research program with a team of engineers highly specialized in flexible small-plant operations.

Company B only enters fields requiring the complex technical skills it already has and/or raw materials to which it has special access. Its real strength lies in exploiting highly competitive situations by applying offbeat process technology. Consequently, the company plans to grow only in fields with large, long-run volume potentials, not in those having short-term, high-margin potential and high technological obsolescence. The company backs up its strategy with a strong raw materials and process-oriented research commitment. It attempts to expand its range of technical skills slowly, but develops great depth in each skill it takes on.

Company C combines research with an acquisition strategy. After World War II, the parent company found itself with large amounts of cash, but with heavy investments in overseas resources and low-margin cyclical products and services. The company decided to diversify into the chemical field by acquisition. After several successful acquisitions made on a somewhat random basis, the company found itself with successful operations at both ends of the chemical spectrum—chemical specialties and heavy chemicals. But to fill out its line and provide profit stability, it needed intermediate-range—medium volume and margin—chemicals. With this as a target Company C started a long-range research program to provide: (1) the know-how to back up acquisitions of desirable small companies in these fields and (2) new intermediate-range chemicals on which to build a new division of its own.

Such considerations determine where a company's program should be strongest. Here the company must exceed competitors' talent commitments—not necessarily their dollar commitments—area by area.

Grapevine Programs

The strategic plan must also ensure: (1) that sudden advances in certain areas of science will not catch the company unaware and completely demolish a major segment of its business, and (2) that the company does not overlook exceptional exploitation opportunities offered by rapid developments in new scientific areas. Such is the function of "on the grapevine" or "connecting" programs. These programs keep the company aware of impinging technology so that, as major advances occur, it can move rapidly to (1) force competitors to cross-license otherwise damaging technology, or (2) develop market positions for itself while avoiding pre-emption by competitors.

Research groups in each connecting area tend to be small. But they must be staffed with first-rate men who can be on the informal grapevine that exchanges scientific information freely. These men must make contributions themselves, and the company must allow them maximum freedom to publish and to participate in scientific meetings. Two examples will show how this element of strategy is implemented in practice:

One large company considers its laboratory a "window on the world." The laboratory's primary function is "to be in the main stream of pertinent science in order to be able to appreciate the implications of new science as it becomes available."

This means that the company can initiate crash programs in time to avert developing technological threats and can move rapidly to use new technology which is relevant to its operation. To be in the main stream of science, the company feels its laboratory must contribute "a fair share" to fundamental knowledge in all areas which might impinge on its operations. It therefore makes sure its program scope includes all active related sciences. And the company liberally encourages its researchers to publish their own scientific contributions.

A large chemical company uses a planning technique it calls the "limit forecast." In effect, it annually surveys all pertinent scientific fields and plans its program so that it can never take more than five years to catch up with major new technology hitting its field from any unconventional source. Such planning is possible because of (1) the company's own substantial financial capacities, (2) inertia in its markets and (3) long lead times in the industry caused by sizable investment requirements. The company feels that a five-year crash development program could put it into a good position to deal with any major threat either through cross-licensing or direct competition.

Problems in Strategic Planning

While the above concepts are straightforward, strategic planning is fraught with hazards. Let us look at the more common and significant problems in strategic planning for research.

The first big problem is determining objectively the critical strengths or weaknesses of the company. Two approaches are provocative:

A medium-sized electronics company made a study of the relative *market penetration* of its various products. The products with high penetration and profit return were considered successful. Those with low penetration *or* low profit return were considered unsuccessful. Top management tried to assess what factors had contributed most to the success of "successful lines." It also analyzed what factors had caused the failure of "unsuccessful" lines. It then tried to assess why the leading competitor was most successful in each area where the company had failed. The study indicated that the company's strengths lay in designing special components for precision jobs and selling such items directly. Its weaknesses were in competing in mass markets where low cost and advertising "pull" techniques were important. It then started a program to "spin off" the latter activities and to retrench into specialized markets backed by a fast-moving engineering group and pilot scale plants.

A coal company used an *investment analysis* approach. It found that its investments were almost exclusively underground. Because of the technological maturity of the field, management felt further investments in the highly competitive underground operations would offer limited returns. It decided to do research which would yield aboveground investment opportunities leading to special market positions. With this broad goal its research was most successful.

Unless a company adequately assesses its particular strengths and weaknesses and develops its resources properly around these, it will eventually be a "me too" operation, unsatisfactorily trying simply to meet competition on all fronts.

A second major problem: Many managements do not recognize that in organizing the company's resources a "growth-through-research" strategy must be backed by kinds of financial and organizational commitments entirely different from more conventional market development or acquisition strategies. The research approach requires: (1) that management think in terms of a five- to seven-year payback period instead of the two- to four-year period common to other investments, (2) that management be willing to make research investments with less certain information and a potentially higher risk than normal operating investments, (3) that a flexible long-term capital plan be developed to meet the unpredictable investment spurts and long investment cycles characteristic of research, (4) that operating departments be more technically oriented and highly coordinated to achieve maximum benefit from research technology, and (5) that the over-all organization be planned to grow flexibly from within rather than through acquisition of entire experienced operating units from outside. Lack of such long-term thinking has often caused research failure in companies dominated by "merchant" or "financial" management whose approach is geared to near-term profit considerations.

Finally, strategic thinking is frequently biased by "the way things have always been done." This leads to problems like the following:

1. Many companies tend to balance their R&D programs to match present product lines' sales or investment patterns rather than building programs to meet maximum technological threats and to take advantage of greatest technological opportunities.

2. Few companies tend to balance their investment risks by purposely taking on extremely high-risk projects a certain percentage of the time. Instead, they tend to research traditional products on tradi-

tional sets of components and fail to look for really offbeat approaches which could upset the whole field. Although scientists themselves frequently would like to take a broader range of risks, they are often constrained by management's attempt to hold research to too detailed a profit contribution standard over too short a time base. Conversely, by limiting the scope of their research, these companies are simultaneously (and often unwittingly) exposing themselves to the threat that an entirely new technological approach taken by an outsider could completely upset their traditional market positions.

3. Few companies have defined their research strategies broadly enough to defend themselves adequately against the eventual costs of "gadget changing and molecule manipulation" short-term technical orientations. Business is the institution our society has established to take its risks. In fact, the only logical justification for "big business" besides economies of scale—and these are surpassed as soon as a company decentralizes—is to take risks other economic units cannot. Perhaps the paramount element of risk-taking today is in scientific and technological spheres. Yet—despite a significant change in attitude in recent years—too few companies have really faced up to supporting the truly long-term research which is needed to kep U.S. industry in the technological forefront. Instead much of such research is still forced onto institutes, the federal government, and educational institutions. In the long run, this exposes business to several extremely unpleasant possibilities:

a. Specific industries can be more easily attacked by public groups with the eventual goal of greater public control over the businesses' operations. For example: The pharmaceutical industry today would undoubtedly be less prone to attack and eventual regulation if it could point to significant fundamental research contributions as justifying high margins and returns. Despite truly impressive developmental accomplishments, the industry does not enjoy as favorable a scientific image as it easily could in the eyes of the public or the medical profession.

b. The groups supporting longer-term research will eventually control large areas of basic knowledge and can make business subject to royalty payments and/or specific controls if it uses such knowledge. Atomic energy is a case in point.

c. The government itself has another wedge to use in entering open productive competition with private enterprise. It has already entered the power-producing field (not by this route however) and now has powerful technological entrees into the air transportation and satellite communications fields should it choose to use them.

d. The total long-term research done in the United States may not be adequate. The result can only be that eventually certain foreign countries will usurp desirable markets which would otherwise belong to U.S. businesses.

e. Even in considering U.S. markets many companies tend to overlook or discount rapidly developing *institutional* markets and the potential of new *public* consumption areas.

Such threats may in the long run be among the most serious of all strategic considerations for business.

Top management must overcome these serious difficulties and develop a broad research strategy which minimizes technological threats from present and potential competitors yet maximizes the company's own potential gains from the use of technology.

The Research Mission

The research organization can support any given strategy in a variety of ways. And it is up to top management to specify which types of support it expects from research. Is research to be the dominant source of new product and process ideas, or is this the function of sales or operating managers? To what extent should research simply service present products and processes? Is research to be the technological arm of management consulting on all aspects of the company's technological situation? Or should research be just a highly skilled pool of technical specialists available to answer problems beyond the talents of divisional personnel? To what extent is research to support itself through patent income? Is research to provide a scientific "intelligence service" to keep the company aware of impinging technological threats or opportunities outside the sphere of traditional operations? To what extent is research technology to be the basis of new-product growth, new processes, or a general technological reputation for the company? Answers to such questions are crucial in designing a research program which best fits the company's needs.

By not defining the research mission carefully, many managements, in effect, set research adrift without specific responsibilities in the over-all organization. Like any other organization, research can and must be held accountable (over a suitable period of time) for accomplishment of a particular portion of the company's goals.[8] *Proper definition of corporate goals, strategies, and the research mission provides a firm basis by which management can hold the research organization responsible for specific accomplishments. Yet, if properly developed, these plans do not constrain the scientific approaches research uses in carrying out its mission.*

PROJECT SELECTION

Next top management must be sure that it has a project selection procedure which fits research into company goals. The process, of course, is exceedingly complex and requires much intuitive judgment, but project selection for an integrated research program essentially follows a three-step sequence: planning technology (1) for present products, (2) for foreseeable new products, and (3) for entirely new applications.

Present Products

The process begins by assessing the technology needed to support present lines two to ten years in the future. The first step is prediction of the company's potential market for each product class. Partly, this involves assessing what technology will keep the products attractive to customers despite inroads of substitute items, competitive technology, and changing customer needs. Customers' technical needs and potential competitive technology are defined by the technological forecasting techniques already noted.

Planners then compare present technology with needed technology, and identify gaps. If enough key facts are available to fill these gaps, defensive development or applied programs can be introduced (or continued) to fulfill established needs in the shortest possible time (usually within two to five years) and with a high probability of success. But if key facts are missing, the company will have to undertake "support" studies in the specific disciplines underlying needed technology.

Because scientific areas within which these studies are needed can often be rather clearly defined, their probability of technical success is usually reasonably high. Average lead times often lengthen to three to seven years if support studies are introduced. But past experience in

[8] See Quinn, *Yardsticks for Industrial Research.*

the specific scientific areas supporting the product should be used as the guide to expected lead times and the number of people needed to staff each area. Regardless of whether the developmental or the combined developmental-support-fundamental approach is used, planned technology for existing lines proceeds from recognized needs to specific programs.

NEW PRODUCTS

In a dynamic technological environment, however, present products —plus planned acquisitions—are unlikely to fulfill all company goals (see Figure 1). The next step is to find new market applications for present or new technology and then (through the forecasts noted) identify the specific technology needed to fulfill these applications.

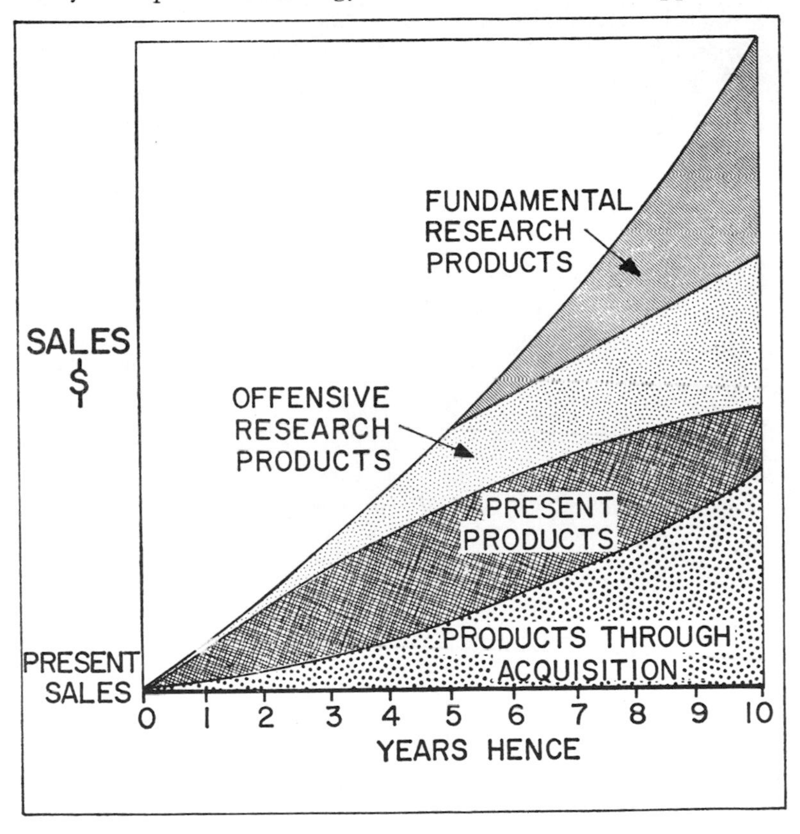

FIG. 1

The needed technology is again matched against present technology and gaps noted. As before, the gaps can be attacked by either of two methods—support research or development. Before making substantial commitments to either approach the company should make exploratory investigations to determine the technical feasibilities of the various possible courses that are open to it.

As in the case of present products, if exploratory work indicates that enough key facts are known, development and applied programs can be undertaken with a high probability of success and a probable impact within two to five years. If key facts are missing, support programs in defined areas can be initiated. Again, experience indicates the general probability of success and lead-time pattern in any given area, and specific project sizes are based on this estimate. These factors are typically determined by intuitive judgments. Only when research has reached quite applied stages are mathematical projections at all useful. But even in applied work, experience indicates that, while time schedules can be met by massing personnel on projects, budget estimates are only accurate within broad ranges.

Again, note that planning new lines first identifies market needs and then works back to sequential programs to meet these needs. Thus, optimum levels for both present and new-product support are best developed by aggressively (1) seeking specific market needs, and (2) analyzing past experience in technological support areas to obtain the best possible estimates of success probabilities and project cost.

Fundamental Research

Addition of the offensive program still may not enable the company to meet its goals (see Figure 1 again). The company may need technology which develops entirely new applications beyond the scope of those presently foreseen. The company then needs a "fountainhead" fundamental research program. Here the planning process is reversed. First, technical planners must identify scientific areas which may provide the foundations for commercial end products compatible with company goals. Within these fields management should support specific project inquiries based on:

1. The rapidity with which technical advances are occurring.
2. The competence and enthusiasm of company personnel in the particular field.

3. The availability of qualified persons to staff scientific areas new to the company.

4. The anticipated amount of information yet to be discovered in an area.

5. The relative pertinence of the area's knowledge to company goals.

There is no alternative to an element of faith in planning fundamental research. Here the probability of a given project's leading to a commercial end product is low or unknown. Either it will yield "commercializable" technology or it will not. However, a rather stable percentage of the projects undertaken in a given field will frequently have commercial implications. Several companies with mature fundamental programs made statements like the following:

> We can predict with some accuracy that we will have one major new capital-absorbing development as a result of fundamental research in that area next year. We don't know what the development will be; we do know we can expect it.

Despite the fact that many companies have analyzed their experiences over a long period of time and have come up with ratios showing so many dollars of sales (fixed investment or profits) per dollar of research, I know of no company which has found enough reliability in such ratios to use them rigorously for planning specific fundamental programs. Nevertheless, intuitive, "order-of-magnitude" judgments of these relationships, *scientific field by scientific field,* must—and do—underlie all determinations of whether the company has enough fundamental research to meet its goals. Management should, of course, bring to bear any data which may help reveal possible trouble spots in the fundamental program. But it should avoid using any figures rigidly. Ultimate decisions on this element of program balance must be left to trained scientists in whom management has confidence.

Detailed fundamental research planning indeed occurs from the "bottom up." Each researcher should be encouraged to select his own specific inquiries within his scientific specialty. Since these researchers should know more about their specialties than anyone else in the company, management's primary control is to make sure that their judgments are tempered by those of competent scientific executives who understand company goals and needs.

A large chemical company stated how its management gives the researcher maximum scope in selecting inquiries, yet does not lose control of this critical planning process:

> We expect the individual researcher to come up with project proposals within the area of his specialty. He discusses any new idea with his director. If the director is enthusiastic, he suggests that the researcher make a literature search, perform exploratory investigations, and report back in one month. If at the end of the month the area looks promising to the researcher and a small committee of research directors, the researcher is allowed to go ahead for another three months. His progress—and the promise of the field—is then checked again. If things are encouraging, he is given a commitment for six more months' work. The six-month review is the last informal review. If the project continues, it is thereafter reviewed annually by the Research Committee in the appropriate budget review cycle.

Other Technology

Although fitting projects into goals has been described in terms of sales and/or profit goals and present or new product lines, similar approaches are used to fit other technology into company goals. If specific needed technology can be defined, the program develops from the desired result back to the specific research project. If specific technology cannot be defined, the company plays the probabilities that fundamental research in broad scientific areas will produce applicable technology. These concepts apply whether the technology is for new processes, new raw material sources, greater human safety, improved product quality, information for the public good, or any other of research's many possible outgrowths. The important factor is to work *from* company goals *to* a balanced research program that will meet these goals.

Program Balance

The final stage of project selection is balancing the final package of projects to meet company goals and strategies. So many detailed decisions are involved in the planning process that intended final program balance may be lost if management does not step back and take a careful overview of its final program. It must see that emphasis is balanced among:

Phases of effort—By seeing that long- and short-term goals are supported by adequate fundamental versus applied versus developmental research. More fundamental stages must feed new scientific possibilities to later stages and must find principles which are bottlenecking more applied programs. Applied and developmental programs should provide concrete evidence of research payoff in the near future.

Offensive versus defensive research—By making sure that the company is giving adequate attention to growth goals versus maintaining present businesses. This breakdown applies only to applied and developmental phases because earlier phases cannot be identified as to results sought.

Product lines supported—By subdividing applied and developmental programs to see whether each present and potential product line is getting sufficient offensive and defensive support to fulfill its particular subgoals.

Operating divisions supported—By seeing that each division's needs receive adequate attention when divisions and product lines do not coincide (as in the refining, distributing, transporting, and producing of oil).

Scientific areas—By ensuring, particularly in fundamental phases, that program scope includes all scientific fields presenting major long-range scientific threats or opportunities within the company's sphere of activity.

Types of results sought—By supporting goals with the proper levels of product technology, process technology, raw materials technology, public-good technology, pursuit of general scientific understanding, and so forth.

No mathematical techniques can tell managers what the "right" balance is for their program. What is right for one company is wrong for another. The proper balance for any particular company depends solely on its goals, capacities, and strategies. These must be determined by seasoned management judgments. But this balance must not be regarded as a rigid cast. As certain project areas begin to produce results, they should receive added emphasis. Others become less attractive and must be de-emphasized. The result is a constant dynamic rebalancing as the program progresses. In fact, one sure sign of program weakness is a static balance of emphasis over a long period.

RESEARCH TO OPERATIONS

One more crucial area for top-management advanced planning is in facilitating the transfer of technology from research to operations. Two sets of biases tend to restrict this transfer. On one hand is the researcher, who often either does not recognize the commercial implications of his work or will not release his work until he has covered all of its possible scientific ramifications. On the other hand, operating groups often term research technology "impractical" because it was "invented by people who don't understand operating problems."

Perhaps the most insidious restriction appears when operating managers—many of whom are held to profit or return-on-investment standards—resist taking on research ideas which will add marketing or engineering development costs to their operations in the short run—despite the long-run desirability of such ideas. Involving operating personnel in program planning and reviews tends to enhance their understanding of research progress and prepares the way for transfer of research technology to operations. Beyond this approach and the usual exchange of reports, individual companies have found the following organizational devices useful:

A large chemical company has formed a development division which it refers to as a "large flexible plumbing and cooking establishment." The development director is held to a profit responsibility. He makes his profit by pilot-plant production and sale of new products conceived in research. As soon as a product or process is successful in development, the appropriate operating division can request that the product be transferred to it. The development director has to try to pull other research ideas up to commercialization as soon as possible to continue making a profit. Consequently, there is a positive impetus to get ideas out of research, and operating managers do not resist taking on proven profitable ideas.

A pharmaceutical company pays the researcher a percentage of profits on any idea commercialized and encourages him to follow the product or process through to commercialization, if he has the talent and interest. In effect, the company sets up a small new profit center and operating division for each new product. The researcher thus has an interest in pushing his ideas, and there are no operating managers to resist taking on new products or processes.

By simple accounting entries a steel company segregates the "debugging" or "market introduction" costs of a new operation and puts them into a separate pool which is not charged directly to any operating division. These costs are only amortized to the specific operation after it has had sufficient time to get established.

A large electronics company emphasizes that the managers of its decentralized operating divisions are not held to a short-term profit standard, but are held to a complex of standards, an important one of which is "technical progressiveness." Management judges technical progressiveness by comparing each division's actual use of research technology against an estimate of how much research-produced technology *could have been* used by the division—the standards beings, of course, subjective.

Such devices assist the transfer of technology from research to operations. But they are not total solutions in themselves. Optimum transfer of research technology to operations will occur only when research is properly integrated into the company's over-all plans by the kind of top-management coordination outlined above.

SUMMARY

Top management's function in research planning thus is:

1. To provide research with a clear understanding of company goals and strategies and to define a specific mission for research within the context of these plans
2. To see that appropriate organizational arrangements are made:
   a. To assess carefully the major technological threats and opportunities the company faces
   b. To facilitate transfer of research technology into operations
3. To develop a project evaluation procedure which results in a balanced package of projects to meet company objectives

From this point on management must continuously evaluate its program to see that both research and operating units carry out their intended functions in developing and utilizing technology to support company goals.

Q. You described one firm's procedure of having the researcher present his proposals to the director of research, of making the researcher do exploratory work and report in a month; then sending this to a screening committee; and so on through to an annual budget. Surely this procedure kills exploratory research?

A. No! This is a very successful research operation. The secret is that the entire company is highly science- and technical-oriented. The research directors are themselves former major contributors to science and are very liberal in approving projects. The screens they place over projects are primarily their applicability to company goals. The committees are all research committees. In this screening process (until budget reviews) they do not bring in outside operating people, although in something like 80 per cent of their operating units the manager is a former research man.

Q. I think a research man has to be given a little freedom. Keep the committee out of it until the man has time to do things for himself.

A. I agree. The great problem is where to begin screening for feasibility to make sure that the man is not just tearing off in a fruitless direction.

Q. Do you have any recommendations on how to organize to clarify business objectives? How do you get research objectives to be laid down by corporate management?

A. An elaborate procedure used by a large company is described in the paper. The essence of this problem comes down to two processes—either "enunciation" or "appeal." If the managements do not perceive the needs for objectives, the enunciation process is likely to be out of the question. Lower-level managers can try to encourage their bosses to get together and come up with goals, but this probably isn't going to get too far unless the top men think in such terms themselves.

I know of one situation where the research operation was literally at loose ends and couldn't get a feeling of where it was supposed to go and what its purpose was. So this particular group undertook the appeal route on purpose. It just kept putting proposals up to management: "We'd like to do this and can't do that. Why not?" Over a period of time research developed for itself a pattern of objectives which all could understand. This is one way of solving your problem.

If you cannot convince the management that clear objectives are needed —if they have not already recognized this themselves—there are other ways of getting research goals. The usual way is to sit down in some rather quiet place (like Buck Hill Falls) and try to work out a consistent pattern of some sort. I can think of one company that has taken this particular approach. Its top managers spent a whole week in this manner, then came back and put the defined objectives aside for a period of a month. Then they went back and spent another week on it, and so forth. Finally they came up with a package they thought was pretty good. Then they did a most extraordinary thing. They took the package of over-all company objectives and split it like this: They kept the total objectives to themselves —top management—and only handed out pieces of the objectives to one person in the operating organization, one piece to another man, and so on. How they expected to maintain coordination I'll never know, but at least the formulation stage of the objectives was rather well done.

Q. Isn't there a danger that top management is eager to do a big "objective-setting job" but doesn't know what its objectives should be; so they get pushed into it and may set the wrong objectives?

A. It can certainly happen. However, you can always change the objective once it comes into being. You can do this by probing, by means of the proposal (or appeal) route. Although over-all objectives must be fairly permanent, you can always review these objectives if the company genuinely needs to be headed in a new direction.

Q. You formerly stressed the importance of stable objectives.

A. Objectives have to be changed over a period of time, but the time span is a several-year time span, and not a short-term, one-year, six-month, or three-month time span which is too common.

Q. You've emphasized "top management" all the way through here. You said nothing about operating divisions, divisional managers, and their responsibility for long-range planning.

A. My paper was purposely cut off at the level right above operating divisions. It seems fairly clear to me that if planning is to be done in a realistic sense, there has to be interplay. One company illustrates how this can be done. Its management first comes up with a set of objectives at the corporate level. These objectives then become the beginning point for the long-range planning process down in the operating division. They go out to each operating division manager. The operating division managers then draw up long-term plans whch will meet these goals. As they draw up their long-term plans, if for any reason they feel that the goal itself may not be appropriate, the managers have the right to appeal the goal. They have, in effect, a contact man on the corporate level with whom they work in this connection. Final goals are worked out early in the planning process. Then the individual plans to meet these goals are fed up from the operating groups to a long-range planning committee at the corporate level.

The long-range planning committee's function is to take the plans which have come up from the operating divisions, work these together, and make sure that they mesh over the long period. They then convert, by means of staff units reporting to them, these long-range plans into a long-term capital plan. This is eventually approved at corporate level. The company maintains a decentralized operation despite this by not allowing *operating* budgets to be involved. It only allows capital budgets to come through this process, and the operating budgets are handled in an entirely separate fashion. Again, this exceedingly complex thing comes down to communications: One individual with a group; a group with one individual. It is a constant interplay situation and very difficult to sort out in a solid sense. There are a variety of ways it can be done, and it depends on the individuals involved.

Q. You have a very fine structure to your paper, and I have no criticism, but it seems to be organized around the consumer nondurable industry.

A. Would you like to develop this a little bit further? I had not particularly intended that this be the case. The examples I have chosen, I must confess, for probing out customer desires and things of this sort were chosen because it is easier to find good solid examples in certain fields.

Q. You've covered those industries and firms serving the consumer rather than those having a tradition of doing the research and producing new products before the customer can tell or is aware of what he needs or wants. Many firms are working in larger and larger systems and in different patterns of research.

(Comment) What you're saying is, I think, something along these lines: That the consumer doesn't really know what he wants in a finite sense. Consequently the company has to propose to the consumer that they have a product he might like before the consumer is aware of his own innate desires.

A. But, again, I think you could identify the parameters that are present. The consumer has certain desires—for example, entertainment, and for certain types of entertainment. These basic parameters are present. Certainly there was disagreement on whether television would be a wonderful thing or not all the way through, but basically there was a feeling that the consumer would some day like home video entertainment. Isn't that right?

Seriously, I do think that you have to approach any field with basically the same viewpoint: try to identify needs, desires, or wants where you can and work back into the development and applied research process. Obviously, you will come up with ideas occasionally that are unique. Then you have to screen these ideas at various stages as they move forward from research into the expensive stages of development, scaleup, and market introduction.

Q. In our industry we've had two examples involving new physical phenomena. Nobody knew what they were going to do with that. No market research would tell. If you started with market research, you'd be excluded from the business of the relatively new technical material from which you eventually develop products.

A. No, I'm not excluding this by any means. I'm saying that there are two routes by which technology comes to the market. One route is to identify a technological desire, want, or need. This is step one—trying to find out about as many such things as you can; then trying to work programs to fit them. Clearly, an applied research program or fundamental research program that's really successful is going to come up with technologies that you cannot plan in advance. This is where the "bottom-up" planning process occurs, when you first plan to get the technology. Then, when you get the technology, you begin to screen it for its commercial implications. I hope that you would agree with me that you don't move these items into costly development stages until you have made some market assessment, even though these may be very crude at first.

Q. One of the most important considerations when you plan the program is to first decide the actual amount of dollars that you can afford to spend on it. What's the criterion or procedure to go about arriving at this answer?

A. I wish that I had a handy-dandy, home-cooked solution for you here. I do not know of any way except to go through [them all,] project by project, proposal by proposal, and analyze each in light of its potential contributions to company goals and strategies. As the project progresses it must be assessed against a range of criteria which vary from very intuitive criteria (in the early stages) to relatively precise mathematical criteria as you get way out to the end of the development spectrum. Assess each one of these proposals. If the item looks as though it's going to be useful and have a value sufficiently greater than the cost of attaining it—in an intuitive sense or however you have to measure this—you should try to support the project. Again, you have to pass the project through a set of screens established by company goals—and the limits of the company's capacity. You obviously can't support all interesting projects and be predominant in all fields. You simply have to expose yourself to some risks and pass up some opportunities.

Q. But if you go through this synthesis and come out with a number, then don't you have to compare it with, say, the company's capabilities for generating capital? . . . If you tried to apply such a criterion, it might turn out to be a pitifully small number.

A. Yes, this is certainly true.

Q. You've got to have a feedback whereby, having synthesized total program cost, you compare it against a framework of limitations.

A. Certainly. There are a number of checks. Essentially the process is to come up with a program package and compare it with your capacity limits.

Q. From your experience, Professor Quinn, how often do research planners get together with corporate management officers in order to determine the capital requirements with respect to technological research and long-range planning?

A. It can be simply at the time the research budgets come up for review. The financial officer may be involved only at this stage. In some cases, an over-all commitment as to general funds level is established before the research planning process begins. Then the package of programs is built up, and compared against the general funds limitation. The funds limitation may be changed or the package of products may be modified at the end of this cycle. There are many ways of doing these things. Financial considerations must get involved in any company [if it is] to have integrated planning.

36

Bell Labs' 230 Long-Range Planners[1]

Morton M. Hunt

The contemplation of the future has long been a favorite pastime of poets and dreamers. For industrialists, however, it is a serious and workmanlike business. One of the most remarkable organized efforts to foresee the future is being made, day in and day out, by the long-range planners and the "systems planners" of the Bell Telephone System—a thousand or more specially oriented scientists and executives scattered strategically throughout its huge laboratories and affiliated companies.

These down-to-earth seers grapple with the future from nine to five daily, trying to outguess the vagaries of unwritten history. For

[1] From *Fortune,* May 1954. © 1954, Time Inc. Reprinted by special permission.

obvious reasons, successful prophecy is far more important in the communications business than in the diaper, auto, paint, or paper businesses. The telephone first made possible easy contact between separated people—and the sweeping impact of that commonplace facility is almost impossible to gauge. Hardly anyone realizes, for instance, that the telephone on his desk is but one set of controls in a single electric machine that lies spread across the three million square miles of the United States; his phone is physically linked with over 50 million other telephones by 185 million miles of wire and 200 million complex electric relays. An individual conversation by telephone is an act one takes for granted; but last year Americans made 56 billion phone calls, and quite obviously a major part of the affairs of the nation could not have been conducted without the transmission of this ocean of talk.

The United States, with only 6 per cent of the world's people, owns 59 per cent of the world's phones. Britain has only one-third as many phones per million, West Germany one-sixth as many, and Russia one-sixtieth as many. To what extent this is responsible for the United States being the world's richest and most productive nation, one can only speculate; yet since man is distinguished from the beasts principally by the facility with which he communicates, it must be that the telephone network has been vastly influential in making American civilization what it now is.

For such reasons, officials of the Bell System feel the weight of destiny on their shoulders, and pay well for the services of expert planners. The Bell System consists of the American Telephone & Telegraph Company, the headquarters organization; Western Electric, which makes and installs the equipment; Bell Telephone Laboratories, the research-and-development outfit; and twenty-one "operating companies," which actually provide the telephone service. In each of these parts of the Bell System there are specialists in planning, from the businessmen of AT&T to the scientific directors of Bell Labs, to the managers of the local companies, who try to keep up with the growth of their cities but not outrun them.

In addition to all this, Bell Labs has in recent years set up an entire department whose sole function is to assess the probable needs of the future, and to make judicious speculations as to how those needs can best be met. Systems Engineering, as the department is called, consists of over 230 thoughtful, inquisitive engineers, physicists, and mathematicians who are occupied full time with the express duty of acting as scientific seers and architects-of-the-future.

The boss of these engineer-dreamers is a short, amiable, balding man named George Gilman. His planners are an assortment of scientists of all ages, shapes, and backgrounds, from old experienced telephone engineers to shiny-faced lads with fresh Ph.D.'s. All of them are clean of hand and shirt; they sit in offices, reading, arguing, doodling endless diagrams, and collecting masses of data, but seldom doing physical work. "We avoid inventing things," Gilman says. "It prejudices our neutral position."

"Anyhow," he adds with an Olympian wave of his hand, "we don't have to actually *build* a new mechanism to know that it is possible. When we need a new thing, we think out what it should do, talk over its hypothetical characteristics with the development engineers, and they build it for us."

Gilman's systems planners are scattered about the upper floors of the Bell Labs building on West Street, overlooking the New York waterfront. A future-predicter at work is nothing exciting to watch. He sits at a desk, reading technical reports and memoranda; he scratches his chin thoughtfully, tilts back in his chair, lights and relights a pipe monotonously, scribbles a few equations, and doodles a few diagrams. Sometimes he shuffles in and out of the great laboratory at Murray Hill, New Jersey, looking for new theories and inventions to help him, asking innumerable questions, and nodding in unconvinced affability. He cannot talk without a pencil or a piece of chalk; he spoils hundreds of sheets of notepaper, tablecloths, menus, and napkins with scribbled diagrams. He may perform a study known as "systems evaluation" to see how well some part of the Bell System is currently functioning, and he may go on to use the mathematical tools of operations analysis to disclose which factors can best be altered in the interests of greater efficiency; but systems planning—the architectural designing of the future—goes far beyond both of these.

AUTOMATIZATION, VINTAGE 1910

Long-range planning is an old and honored policy in the Bell System, going back long before there was any special department entitled Systems Engineering. Originally the key planners were simply high-level engineers scattered about the Bell System in various jobs. Just about the shrewdest, yet simplest, piece of forecasting in telephone history was made some . . . [fifty] years ago. The subject in question was the use of operators versus some new and seemingly visionary devices for automatic (dialed) telephoning.

A few of the more farsighted telephone engineers began to wonder about the far future. (This was about 1910.) They looked at the curves of telephone growth; they dared to wonder if someday every family might have a phone; they pored over charts and worked on equations of probability. After a while, a few of these genteel radicals put down their pencils and agreed on one thing. "Unless we put in dialing by the customers themselves," they told the vice-presidents, "the telephone system will someday collapse of its own growth. Within a generation you won't be able to hire enough girls to run the phone system even if you could get every eligible girl of the right age and education in the whole country." Within ten years automatic exchange equipment and dial phones were perfected and being installed throughout the country.

Since that time the number of phones in the United States has grown sixfold; if no automatic switching equipment had been developed, the phone company today would need 1,500,000 full-time operators—and it currently has a hard time finding and keeping a mere 250,000 of them.

Equally remarkable foresight was displayed in a few small laboratory rooms at Bell Labs thirty-eight years ago, when inventor Herbert Ives and several associates began to tinker around with whirling disks, spirals made of little lenses, and other improbable-looking mechanisms in a system called "television." In 1927 they invited a delegation of newsmen into the offices of Bell Labs and let them goggle at a flickery picture of Commerce Secertary [Herbert] Hoover, speaking from a brightly lit telephone booth down in Washington, his face and voice being sent to New York over telephone wires. Within the next three years they had also transmitted two-way telephone television, color television, and had even foreseen the future to the extent of transmitting a movie over a TV circuit from Philadelphia to New York.

None of this was for the purpose of getting the telephone company into the TV-producing business. (For that matter, nobody in Bell knew whether there would ever be a TV business, or how it could compete with movies and radio.) But the planning specialists of the Bell System had figured out that this thing logically had to become big in the future; when it did, the images and sound would have to be carried around the country via the telephone network, and it behooved them to find out how it would work, and what kinds of long-distance wires, amplifiers, filters, and the like would have to be built into future telephone installations to make that possible.

THE TV SYSTEM NOBODY KNOWS

It is likely that many people believe (if they think about it at all) that the TV networks themselves developed, installed, and operate the coaxial cables and radio-relay towers that carry TV across the country. The actual facts are quite different. Broadcasters have rented the long-distance facilities of the Bell System since the early days of radio, and TV has followed the same pattern. In almost all cases, when the picture and sound leave the control room of a TV studio, they travel downstairs in telephone-company wires, under city streets to a "TV operating center" run by telephone engineers, and are transmitted cross-country by Bell System radio relay or coaxial cable—both of which the Bell System owns, and which its own engineers designed over twenty-five years ago, in response to the earnest pleading of the planners to make radio relay and coaxial cable capable of carrying not only great new loads of phone conversations, but television as well. At the far end, other telephone engineers receive and reroute the impulses via underground lines into the local TV station's own control room, where the studio engineers finally take charge of shunting it into the local transmitter.

Neither radio relay nor coaxial cable, excellent as they are for carrying TV signals cross-country, is economically feasible for this local distribution of the signals within a city from the TV operating center to control room, or vice versa. The fine-gauge paper-covered wires that carry ordinary telephone conversations around a city could be pressed into service only by using expensive special repeaters (amplifiers), and even then two miles would be the practical limit because of introduced distortions. So back in the early 1940's the design engineers developed for this special purpose a husky shielded wire called a "video pair." Video pairs, far cheaper than coaxial, were still expensive; moreover, they would take up valuable space in telephone conduits that might be better used for ordinary telephone wires. Yet at a time when no huckster, producer, or business analyst was willing to bet his reputation on the future of TV, the systems planners of Bell Labs advised the directors of the telephone companies to start putting video pairs into the ground as part of every new telephone-cable installation when those cables ran past stadiums, theaters, or radio-studio buildings. Long before TV was a paying proposition the telephone companies had stuffed into the ground millions of dollars' worth of video pairs—useless for anything but TV—in the firm belief that the special wires would be needed mighty soon.

All this sounds simpler than it really is. The systems engineers of A.T.&T.'s Operation and Engineering Department and systems engineers of Bell Labs had to do more than merely conclude TV was a coming thing. They had to estimate what demands it would make on a national communications system, and put together a theoretical system—based on equipment that would become available in time—that could handle these demands, be compatible with the rest of the Bell System's business (which is, after all, basically one of handling telephone conversations), *and,* beyond that, be economically justifiable.

The biggest trouble with TV, from the engineer's point of view, is that it takes up too much space. Each channel occupies as much room on a radio-relay or coaxial-cable circuit as would serve 600 to 1,000 simultaneous long-distance telephone conversations. And *that* is a serious matter; for frequency space is a valuable and hard-won commodity.

"Television," the planners warned the management of A.T.&T. in the mid-thirties, "now looks as though it would use up anywhere from two to four million cycles of bandwidth—the equivalent of 600 conversations. That much bandwidth can't be crammed onto ordinary wires." Management wanted to know what to do about it. The planners said that several researchers in the laboratories had an idea that although wide bands of frequencies would leak off a regular wire, they would stay on the inside surface of a tube with a wire down the middle of it. Other researchers, they added, had some notion that high-frequency radio waves, carrying a wide band of frequencies, could be focused like light and beamed from tower to tower. Either method would solve the problem of future telephone traffic—and of TV at the same time. After listening to these alternatives the A.T.&T.

management boldly spent an additional $10 million to perfect coaxial cable (the hollow tube) and nearly as much on radio relay, though neither of these systems would be needed for nearly ten years.

A special feature of systems planning known to most canny businessmen is the strategy of hedging one's bets. Lesser men than systems planners might, fifteen years ago, have occupied themselves with the question of *which* system—radio relay or coaxial cable—was the better one, and which should therefore receive the full force of future development. In the truly long-range view, however, both seemed excellent, lacking only the perfection of special unknown devices to make either one a whole workable system. So both were pursued; both were perfected; and today both operate together—compatibly—serving the same functions within the transcontinental telephone network. In soft, level soils, where a plow can speed along easily, cable goes in cheaper; in mountainous regions, radio-relay towers perched on ridge crests are a better solution. As for the future, the best minds at Bell Labs will venture no guess as to which system will eventually win out. Right now, 11,000 route miles of radio relay are strung across the country, and 9,500 miles of coaxial cable are buried beneath its soil.

BEFORE COLOR, A SCRUBBING JOB

Color TV raised a whole new complex of problems. The big trick in color is to crowd much more information into no more frequency space than that allotted to black-and-white TV. Ideally, black-and-white TV is allotted a bandwidth of about four megacycles; but in actual practice, especially when coaxial cable is used, it gets somewhat less. That does not matter much, since the upper third of the bandwidth carries information which does not affect the picture perceptibly. Even when the upper 1.3 megacycles are chopped off, the televiewer can barely perceive any difference in picture quality.

Color TV, however, has to be sent on four full megacycles, and even so, the only place where TV engineers can squeeze in additional signals to signify hue and intensity is in the upper part of the band, just where loss and distortion are most pronounced.

For this reason, a group of systems engineers have been working out plans for new terminal equipment, repeaters, equalizers, and methods of maintenance to make the present coaxial-cable and radio-relay circuits capable of passing the color TV signal without distortion or loss. "We're doing what you might call 'scrubbing up the circuits,' " says one of the group. To date, the Bell System has "scrubbed up" circuits for color TV between New York and California; other circuits will be improved as the broadcasters need them—but plans are so far advanced that upgrading any particular circuit would take only a month or two.

FREQUENCY SPACE: A LIMITED RESOURCE

Such matters are the legitimate province of systems planners; but actually the finest grist for their intellectual mill consists of far larger issues, problems that exist over periods of decades. One of the largest is the matter of a vanishing natural resource—frequency space. Every message sent over radio occupies a certain range of frequencies, and the more traffic there is, the more difficult it is to fit everything in.

By modern techniques, it is possible to send and receive radio signals covering a range from about 100,000 cycles per second (the 3,000-meter wave length) clear up to 30 billion cycles per second (the one-centimeter wave length). That seems like room enough for all, especially in view of the fact that Morse code needs only about 100 cycles, and a phone conversation needs only about 4,000 cycles. Radio, however, needs up to 15,000, and TV about 4 million per station. As a result, the FCC has already divided up and parceled out the entire useful range of radio frequencies. There is practically no empty space left, except at extremely high frequencies that the engineers do not yet know how to use.

If the radio waves are so crowded, perhaps the better answer for the phone company is to expand along the lines of improved coaxial cables and wires. But this is no easy answer either; the wider the band of frequencies put on wire or cable, the more amplifiers the engineers have to insert into the circuit, or the bigger they have to make the cable. That soon becomes cripplingly expensive.

In another generation, from past indications, the volume of telephone talk may easily double or triple, the number of mobile radiotelephones increase tenfold, the volume of transatlantic telephone business grow a dozenfold, and TV expand into fields only dimly foreseen. Such facts might give any systems planner pause. But having so paused and reflected, several of Gilman's men and others from AT&T recently worked out plans in which it appears possible that the enormous potential load (even including theater network television) could nevertheless be shunted around the country by Bell System facilities, by modifying present cable, radio-relay, and switching systems. "We expect to be able to meet whatever load may arise," one of Gilman's assistants says, "and without lousing up the whole radio spectrum, either."

WAVES BEAMED THROUGH PIPES

One of the inventions that figure heavily in their long-range thinking about the frequency-space problem is called a "waveguide." Above 30 billion cycles per second, there is a great area of radio frequencies that are not used. Unfortunately, these frequencies begin to act a little like light—they are stopped not just by solid objects, but by clouds, smog, or even rain. Bell inventors started over twenty years ago designing hollow pipes in which the radio impulses could travel in their own atmosphere. Confined within their waveguide—which will be only a couple of inches in diameter—these waves will neither be affected by outside radio waves, nor affect any outside receivers. In contrast to older systems, which carry several dozen to several hundred phone conversations at one time, a single waveguide pipe could easily carry many thousands. One hitch, unfortunately, is that the copper pipe must be microscopically precise, both in manufacture and in installation; also, each will require a fortune in terminal facilities to stack up and later unscramble the thousands of simultaneous messages. (Waveguides a few hundred feet long are actually in use nowadays on radio-relay towers, and cost about $12.50 per foot. No Bell System engineer will even hazard a guess as to the cost of a transcontinental waveguide.)

Other frequency-saving mechanisms are now in the experimental stage. These handle human voices and TV pictures the way the Army handled milk and eggs in the last war—powdering them, shipping them, and reconstituting them later on. How this could be done was explained in "The Information Theory," *Fortune,* December 1953.

Another major concern of the systems planners is the customer—a cantankerous, ornery, and noncontrollable piece of the system. A small group of Gilman's men is continuously trying to analyze the ways in which customer habits affect the telephone network.

PHONES IN A JAM

One of the things they worry about is the possibility that too many customers will choose the same moment to pick up their phones to place calls. Ordinarily, the telephone system is geared to handle about one phone in twenty, at any given instant. If one phone in every ten were to be picked up at once, a serious jam could ensue. If one exchange were to be so jammed, the automatic equipment in other exchanges would hold its calls, waiting to get through, and so the jam might fan out from one exchange to another throughout parts of a city, or even a whole city.

This is no theoretical nightmare. During World War II a Washington, D.C., radio station announced free nylons to the first few callers; the resultant eruption of calls swamped one central exchange, backspread to others, and seriously snarled phone connections in the nation's capital and some adjoining points for more than two hours.

The job of the planners, of course, is to specify systems large enough, and with safeguards enough, to prevent this kind of thing in everyday use; on the other hand, for good economic reasons, they dare not overdesign the capacity of the system by any huge factor. In general, their planning is sufficiently adroit so that attacks of paralysis in the phone system have been extremely rare and short-lived.

But the big question is: What would happen if a major disaster or surprise bombing attack were to cause millions of people to make a frantic dash for the phone? The resulting snarl might temporarily immobilize all defense and rescue efforts. After considerable study, the planners suggested and the operating companies have adopted a safeguard to be used only in the gravest emergencies. In each major telephone exchange of the nation, an attendant by merely flipping several switches can temporarily cut off outgoing calls from some or all of the nonessential phones, allowing the civil defense setup, the military, the Red Cross, and other critical agencies to go about their business unhampered by fears of an overload. This emergency system has been tested in a few local situations, such as storm and flood, and has worked beautifully.

Officials of the operating telephone companies do the same kind of planning on their own, often without the assistance of Gilman's group. They have been planning the routes of new cables and radio towers so as to avoid paralysis if any one city were wiped out. For instance, all national TV programs, all overseas telephone calls, and until recently all long-distance calls in and out of New York passed through one switching center in a building on lower Sixth Avenue. One good blast over that part of the city would have cut North and South apart, and isolated us from Europe. Today a series of alternate exchanges in Newark and other points are handling about one-third of New York's long-distance business. Similar plans are being carried out in a dozen major cities.

AN ASH CAN FULL OF PLANS

Among the sundry uncertainties with which Gilman's department has to contend, perhaps the greatest of all is the unpredictability of new discoveries and inventions. A few years ago, for example, several physicists at Murray Hill got interested in the odd properties of the metallic element germanium. When they got through investigating it, they had invented the transistor—a pea-sized object that will do most of the things vacuum tubes do, last perhaps twenty times as long, use almost no power, and take up almost no space. As a result, several hundred pounds of plans, which had been worked out with excruciating care, and which dealt with such matters as the amplifiers, modulators, varistors, and such that boost your voice in loudness $10^{1,500}$ times (i.e., 1 followed by 1,500 zeros) as it crosses the country, may soon be ready for the ash can.

The transistor did little, however, to alter the larger outlines of the biggest and finest scheme ever concocted by the prophets of the telephone company. That scheme is called FACD ("foreign-area customer dialing"), which means long-distance dialing by the customer. In the full-fledged FACD system, a subscriber will pick up the phone, dial three digits plus the local number of any other subscriber in the country, and that's all. No fuss, no operators, no waiting; all America in his own backyard.

That idea, so simple and appealing, is actually the longest-range piece of planning ever undertaken by the Bell System. It dates back to 1933, when Dr. Frank B. Jewett, then president of Bell Laboratories, invited his associates to consider the problem of long-distance automatic dialing.

The heart of the problem was the nature of central-office switching equipment. The early automatic machinery for handling dial calls consisted of banks of fast-moving rotary switches and relays called "step-by-step" equipment. This equipment is logical, but unimaginative; it has to be told everything, including not only the destination but the best route. If it were to be used for long-distance dialing, a subscriber might have to dial a number like this: 057 076 097 157 2345. Even so, the machine could not automatically take any bypaths or alternates.

The planners concluded that a completely different type of central-office equipment was needed. They told the development engineers in broad terms what they wanted to do. "Make a system," they said, in effect, "that can accept the dialed numbers from the customer; hold them in an electrical memory while it figures out the ultimate destination; look over all the routes from its own position to the destination; pick out and test the shortest or best one; if that one is busy, pick out the next shortest one or the next until it finds a free circuit; operate all the necessary switches; make sure it has the right number; and then disengage itself and get busy with someone else." As though that were not enough, they also wanted it to be able to call a human operator when the customer dialed an impossible number, wait for him if he forgot the last couple of digits and had to look them up, pull the plug on him if he took too long about it, and in general do everything in a judicious, intelligent manner.

The machinery that was finally perfected to fit this prescription is called the "crossbar system." The first toll crossbar installation went into operation in Philadelphia ten years after the engineers started trying to make it. A more recent version of crossbar required a patent application as big and heavy as a copy of *Gone With the Wind.*

NOTHING HAPPENS OVERNIGHT

Although FACD has been in the works for nearly a generation, it is emerging slowly because such a vast amount of expensive equipment in the United States was made and installed to do the local switching job before the planners had begun concocting their great plan. The cost of the change-over will run into many hundreds of millions of dollars. As a result, FACD is going to have to be born a finger at a time.

To some extent, it's born already. Formerly, anywhere from two to eight operators had to talk to each other to put through a long-distance call. Today, because of the installation of many crossbar exchanges and toll offices, 44 per cent of all long-distance calls are being dialed directly by the first operator the customer talks to. The next step will simply let the customers in those same areas (where the operators now dial long-distance calls) do the dialing themselves. This ultimate achievement is no longer just a paper dream: It went into effect in the suburban community of Englewood, New Jersey, in November 1951.

Since that time, the 10,000 telephone customers of Englewood have been able to dial directly any one of some 13 million telephone numbers in the United States, covering large areas of the East, Midwest, and West. They dial the ten digits and wait about fifteen seconds[2] while the incredible nationwide machine makes its thousands of split-second decisions, tests its routes, double checks its own handiwork, and then rings the other phone, anywhere up to 3,000 miles away. Another 10,000 customers just outside Detroit and 10,000 more outside Pittsburgh got FACD during 1953, and more communities will get it each year from now on. The job should be completed within fifteen or twenty years.

WHO MAKES OUT THE BILLS?

The FACD plan solved many problems, but raised new ones. Who, for instance, would record and charge the customer for the long-distance call, if no operator were involved? The planners foresaw this need and predicted long ago that an automatic billing mechanism would have to be developed. Ten years of work in Bell Labs have since resulted in AMA (automatic message accounting). On a wide tape, AMA machinery records your phone number, the number you dialed, and the beginning and ending time of your conversation. Later other machines rerun the tape, pick out your call from all the other calls recorded on it, figure out how much to charge you, and write out a charge slip.

And how, the planners wondered, could a wholly automatic long-distance system be guarded from mechanical failure, with no operators checking on each call? (Actually, there will be even more em-

[2] In 1920 the average long-distance call was put through in fourteen minutes; in 1953 it went through in ninety seconds.

ployees than there are today, because business will be so much greater.) The solution lay in giving the crossbar machine and the big automatic toll centers the ability to recognize when something goes wrong in their intricate mechanisms. When any part of their many circuits goes wrong, certain automatic checking devices fail to get the right response to coded testing signals they continually send out. The faulty part causes the automatic testing brain to punch a mark on the appropriate part of a long ticket, which graphically portrays in terms of preprinted code symbols thousands of possible trouble conditions.

ROBOT REPAIRMEN?

The obvious next step—and one that would surprise no one in the planning department—would be the development of servomechanisms that will analyze the printed trouble report and make simple repairs automatically, plugging in spare relays and tubes, pending the semiannual visit of the repairman.

All this sounds like plenty to work on for years to come. But in their more expansive moments around the conference table, the planners talk about even bigger things. Their FACD plans already make room for Canada and Mexico in the ten-digit dialing setup. But that's not all. "You may think world-wide dialing sounds silly," says one switching expert, "but we've thought about it a good bit, and aside from the backward state of telephone systems in some countries, it's well within the framework of our present plans."

Another remote subject of planning efforts involves a system that might, for the lack of any other name, be called "televisiphone"—the sending of TV images along with the voice signal. Bell engineers first hooked up a two-way telephone-and-television combination in 1930. The picture was miserable, and the cost would have been staggering to any customer. But it was a fascinating idea.

Today, twenty-four years later and with TV a nearly perfected art, the Bell planners are still thinking hard about televisiphone. It would put a terrific new demand for frequency bandwidth on the telephone wires and undoubtedly cost a good deal. One idea that planners have recently been considering involves sending not a moving image but a series of stills at five-second intervals; this would use up only a narrow band of frequencies and be much cheaper.

Dr. Ralph Bown, vice-president of Bell Labs, feels that the use of vision on the phone is as little appreciated today as the use of speech was when Bell invented the thing three-quarters of a century ago. "People used to ask who'd want to talk into a tin box," he says. "Today they can hardly get along without it, but they ask who needs TV with his telephone. But in today's world, sight and sound go together. Some form of vision with the phone is inevitable."

Other new devices that already exist, or should exist in the future, and for which the planners have great hopes, include an automatic telephone-answering machine to take your calls for you when you are out; a machine that understands the numbers zero to nine, and can ring a phone number upon spoken command; an electronic calculator that will design and draw plans for new pieces of technical equipment when told what that equipment has to do; and another calculator that will be able to translate from one language to another.

"However all that may be," Gilman said recently, staring at the ceiling with his hands clasped behind his head, "we can't afford to deal in idle dreams. We're simply trying to use every reasonable idea and prospective invention that may fit into the broad picture, so as to help solve the problems that will be arising in the future.

"The main thing is not to get too smug."

37

Timing of New-Product Introduction[1]

Harry L. Hansen

A difficult problem in timing . . . is whether or not a company should be the first one to offer a new type of product on the market. What are the advantages and disadvantages of being the first or being the follower?

Undoubtedly a great deal depends upon the nature of the product, its uniqueness, and the question of whether or not the company has any long-run advantage, as for example through the control of patents. In thinking about a problem like this, take for example the question of frozen orange juice. Supposing Minute Maid Corporation, a newly formed company and one of the first (as Florida Foods, Incorporated) on the market with frozen juices, was attempting today to break into the field. In all likelihood the company would have a difficult time competing against today's well-established sellers, such as General Foods, Incorporated, and Libby, McNeill, and Libby. In contrast, the California Fruit Growers Exchange, which came late into the frozen orange juice field, encountered only normal difficulty in getting retail stores to handle its frozen orange juice, because its brand, Sunkist, was well known on fresh oranges.

Take another illustration. Suppose the executives of a large paper

[1] From Harry L. Hansen, *Marketing: Text, Cases, and Readings* (Homewood, Ill., Richard D. Irwin, Inc., 1956), pp. 115–119. Used by permission.

company, such as West Virginia Pulp & Paper Company, well established in selling printing and industrial papers, might think that it would be desirable for the company to enter the consumer facial tissue field. Here we have a field dominated by several strong brands of which one of the strongest is Kleenex, made by the International Cellucotton Products Company. In some markets Kleenex is very substantially ahead of all other brands in consumer acceptance, probably outselling all others combined. In such a situation, West Virginia, despite its large size, would have an extremely difficult time in offsetting consumer preference for Kleenex.

Take as another example the marketing of electric blankets. General Electric was the first seller in this field, entering it in an attempt to try to expand the sale of its electric wiring. What difference does it make to a company like the Chatham Manufacturing Company, a blanket manufacturer, if Chatham enters the field later? Can General Electric establish so strong a brand preference that it would be difficult for Chatham to break into the market? Probably not, since presumably market acceptance of this product would be so slow that a seller entering the market late could expect consumers to shop and compare electric blankets.

Take, for example, a record which, it is claimed, will induce sleep through hypnotic suggestion. Does it make any difference here whether or not the seller is the first one to make available such a record, or is this fact immaterial?

Large sellers may be able to afford to delay in introducing new products. An illustration of this is Dictaphone's entrance into the field of electronic dictating machines. For several years this company, with an older type of dictating machine, lagged behind the smaller companies in their development of such machines; but when it finally developed a machine, it had overcome certain of the disadvantages or difficulties that were evident in earlier competitive makes. With its well-known name it had little difficulty in regaining its market position. Another illustration might be taken from the field of the electric razor. The first electric razors to be popularized were sold by Schick; but when a large company, Remington Rand, followed, it rapidly assumed a position of leadership. These illustrations suggest that the small seller does not have an easy time merely because it is first in the field. Typically it escapes only temporarily the job of combating large competitors, and it has the difficult job of developing demand by itself. Some small companies will attempt therefore "to ride on the coattails" of larger sellers. For instance, many small frozen food packers have capitalized on the acceptance for frozen foods created by the pioneer frozen food seller, Birds Eye Division of General Foods, Incorporated.

Since new products are often a gamble, a company can lessen its risk by avoiding radically new products or by following the moves of competitors and letting these sellers make the mistakes of market appraisal. A frequently quoted example of the risk in the introduction of new products that require buyers to think in radically different ways was Chrysler's move in the 1930's in introducing a streamlined line of cars. The design turned out to be too radical for consumers to accept. On the other hand, it is sometimes a greater risk not to be the first company in the field with a new product. For example the financial rewards were high for those who pioneered chlorophyll toothpaste and antihistamine cold remedies, even though the continuing markets for these products turned out to be far smaller than originally they were heralded to be.

Thus, it is difficult to generalize whether the risk is greater to be first or later in the field. To find the answer one must estimate total market size (a difficult job for a new product), and predict the speed at which buyers will accept the product (no less difficult a job).

One general observation can be made even though there will be exceptions to it, namely, that generally buyers, both consumer and industrial, are usually slower to accept new products or services than the seller expects, even though in the seller's eyes these new ideas are obviously desirable. This buyer hesitation or skepticism is often minimized by the seller in his enthusiastic belief in his product or service. Naturally, there are all degrees of buyer skepticism. Buyer reaction to an electric rattrap is likely to be more cautious than toward more conventional rodent killers. Paper bathing suits for women are viewed with some misgivings, whereas a new synthetic fiber woven into men's suits may cause only momentary doubts.

The seller therefore often has the difficult appraisal to make: How far ahead of buyer product experience can he afford to get? A minor product improvement, like a wrap-around windshield, may be accepted by buyers quickly; a major change or an entirely new product, like a garbage-disposal unit, may require years of selling effort before it is widely accepted.

NEW-PRODUCT GROWTH CURVES

How long should it take to establish a product on the market? The answer depends upon the strength of the underlying demand for the product, the financial resources of the seller, and the skill which he brings to bear upon the problem. Despite the probable overriding control of the individual . . . situation, there always is an interest in the possibility of approximating a normal new-product growth curve. There is not much known about such curves. This general lack of information is probably traceable to a series of considerations. Basically, sellers usually regard individual product sales figures as confidential. If the product has been evaluated as unsuccessful, the seller does not normally want to reveal data that may properly or improperly be taken to be a reflection on his business judgment and performance. Apart from these considerations, many sellers look upon the study of past experience as of only limited value for future experience in a world where there have been so many dynamic changes in the last quarter century. World depressions, wars, booms, strikes, and major technological bursts tend to discourage reliance on statistical curves. Despite these difficulties the basic idea in theory is an intriguing one.

Butler, moreover, writing in 1946 on this subject, indicated that in his company, a cotton textile manufacturing company, normal growth patterns could be defined. The technique was relatively simple. In order to compare products selling in different volumes and with different potentials, sales were converted to "per cent of objective" calculated by years. The objective might be set at three, five, or ten years, depending upon the situation. When the data were plotted on a grid with the per cent of objective on the vertical scale and years on the horizontal scale, a normal growth pattern was observed. Actual per cent of objective for new products was then compared with the normal curve. If a product appeared to be growing more slowly or rapidly than normal, study was then made to determine the reasons. Experience indicated that there were different normal growth patterns, depending upon the merchandising effort used. Exhibit 1 illustrates the technique employed by Butler. In order to smooth the actual growth curve, he has used a three-year moving average.[2]

[2] Ralph Butler, "Growth Patterns for New Specialty Products: A Case Study," *Journal of Marketing,* July 1946, p. 27.

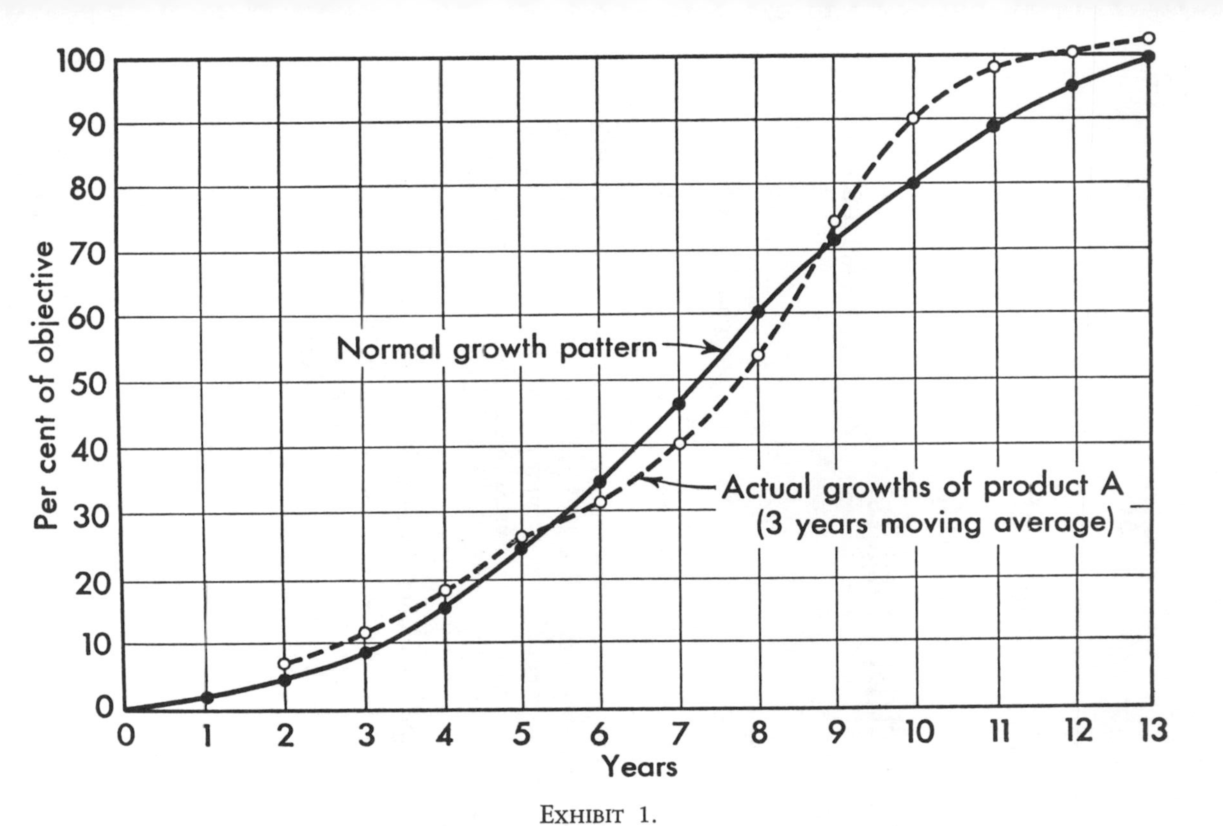

EXHIBIT 1.

SOURCE: Ralph Butler, "Growth Patterns for New Specialty Products: A Case Study," *Journal of Marketing*, July 1946, p. 29.

38

The Strategy of Market Introduction for Industrial Products[1]

E. Raymond Corey

In planning the introductory marketing program, it may be difficult to anticipate the reactions which various market groups may have toward the appearance of the new product in the market and, hence, to determine where to concentrate sales effort. In addition, the appearance of the new product in the market may generate unanticipated forces of resistance which obstruct the creation of initial demand and delay the integration of the new product into established channels of manufacture and distribution. Such complexities were present in the history of Alcoa's development of a market for aluminum sleeve bearings.

In 1936 the Aluminum Company of America had initiated laboratory work on the development of an alloy suitable for use in aluminum sleeve bearings. This work was undertaken after Alcoa personnel had learned that both the British and the Germans were successfully using such bearings in aircraft engines. Within a year Alcoa laboratory technicians had developed Alcoa alloy 750 as the material most suited for use in bearings. This alloy contained 6.5 per cent tin, 1 per cent copper, 1 per cent nickel, and 91.5 per cent commercially pure aluminum by weight.

Experimental bearings made of alloy 750 were made available in

[1] From E. Raymond Corey, *The Development of Markets for New Materials* (Boston, Harvard Business School, 1956), pp. 82–98. Used by permission.

1937 to a large diesel engine builder to be installed for testing on a few diesel engines. Alcoa's management believed that the testing should be restricted because of the functional importance of engine bearings and because of the damage that faulty bearings could do to large engines. Sufficient test data, it was believed, would take two to six years to accumulate.

The shortages of tin during World War II precluded the possibility of further development work, although the diesel engine builder's test installations were still operating. By 1944, however, when limited amounts of tin again became available, the performance characteristics of aluminum bearings had been thoroughly studied, and test data had proved the suitability of aluminum in this application. In 1945, therefore, the diesel engine builder ordered solid aluminum bearings from a bearing manufacturer for all its diesel engines.

The logical market for aluminum bearings, the Alcoa management had concluded, was the large diesel field, i.e., all diesel engines over truck-size. There were approximately ten large manufacturers of diesels for large tractors, locomotives, and power plants. The reason for ruling out smaller type diesel and gasoline engines was that their design called for a thin-walled bearing, and aluminum had to be used in a bearing that had a ratio of wall thickness to diameter that was greater than could be accommodated in smaller engines. It was possible, however, that either through further alloying development or through changes in engine design, a solid aluminum bearing might at some future date be developed for small diesels as well as automotive engines.

In large diesels, however, pronounced advantages were claimed for aluminum. Solid aluminum bearings resisted corrosion by chemicals much better than conventional bearing materials. Corrosion was a matter of increasing concern with the greater usage of engine lubricating oil additives. Second, aluminum dissipated heat rapidly so that when any possible high spots on the inside bearing surface and on the shaft rubbed against each other, the frictional heat was dispersed before the two metals could expand and the bearing freeze on the shaft. Third, solid aluminum bearings, it was claimed, would outwear other bearings many times over, and there had been no instances in any tests of "fatigue failure."[2] The chances of fatigue

[2] Fatigue failure was a fracturing of the inside bearing surface, which spreads, causing pieces of the inside bearing surface to break off.

failure occurring had increased as engines were designed for greater power output. A fourth, and particularly important, advantage claimed for aluminum was that in case of failure for such reasons as inadequate oil supply or insufficient clearance between the bearing and the crankshaft, the bearing would not damage the shaft. In large diesel engines, an engine shaft might cost as much as $4,500 to replace.

Aluminum bearings, furthermore, would cost less to make than the types of bearings they were designed to replace. An aluminum bearing was made from a cylindrical casting, machined on an automatic lathe, and finished to close tolerances in a boring machine.

Two processes, each requiring more skill and more tooling than the above process, were used in making conventional bearings. In the one process, flat sheet steel (to serve as the backing or outside surface of the bearing) was bonded to a thinner sheet of inside bearing surface material, such as Babbitt metal. Pieces of the bonded metal were sheared off, and these flat blanks were formed into bearing halves in a punch press. The inside dimensions of each half were machined to close tolerances, and then the entire piece was plated with an alloy of copper, lead, and tin.

A second process for making bearings used seamless steel tubing. Such a bearing was made by coating the inside of the tubing with a molten copper and lead alloy, machining this inside surface, and then coating all bearing surfaces. The application of the inside bearing surface material required a great deal of skill. Consequently, this type of bearing was the most expensive to make.

Although no adequate estimate of the cost of making an aluminum bearing was available in 1944, one aluminum bearing manufacturer subsequently reported that his cost for making such bearings was 25 per cent to 50 per cent less than what he would have had to pay to purchase a Babbitt metal steel-backed bearing and between 35 per cent and 60 per cent less than the price of a copper-lead bearing.

INITIAL MARKET DEVELOPMENT

Satisfied, then, on the basis of both its own laboratory tests and the early diesel engine builder's experience that alloy 750 aluminum bearings was a sound application, the Alcoa management made plans in 1945 to market bearing castings. The decision to market castings rather than alloyed metal in ingot form was based primarily on the desirability of doing as much as possible to maintain bearing quality. Alloy 750 required special foundry techniques, and it was likely that even if Alcoa was not to make castings, most cases of bearing failure would reflect ultimately on the company. In addition, foundries that might make such castings would almost invariably have no technical service facilities to help customers with application problems; consequently, this function would be likely to fall on Alcoa's staff. Another reason for the decision to make castings was the hope that as volume of business increased, prices could be reduced. This possibility was all the stronger if all casting was done by one organization rather than scattered among a number of foundries. Finally, by making bearing castings rather than supplying ingot to foundries for this purpose, Alcoa would realize a higher dollar volume of sales and accordingly would increase its opportunities for profit.

In 1945 Alcoa undertook a national advertising campaign on aluminum bearings. The advertisements were designed to generate customer inquiries. These requests for further information were answered with letters listing the largest bearing manufacturers in alphabetical order and suggesting to the sender that an order for a trial set of bearings be placed with one of these companies or with his present supplier. Alcoa Development Division personnel also called on large diesel engine builders and, after creating some interest, suggested that these companies contact their normal bearing suppliers. When Alcoa could learn who the bearing supplier was, a salesman was detailed to call on this supplier and advise him of his customer's interest in aluminum. Bearing manufacturers indicated a great interest in the new development and asked about the introductory work that was being done with bearing purchasers. Shortly thereafter it was learned that salesmen for some bearing manufacturers were following up Alcoa calls and were frequently recommending their own bearings rather than aluminum bearings.

In the meantime, many smaller bearing manufacturers indicated a great deal of interest in aluminum bearings. Alcoa representatives tried to work with these concerns, but it soon became evident that their customers did not include the manufacturers of large diesel engines.

Alcoa then shifted the direction of its promotional work. On calls to bearing users, Alcoa offered to make a test set of bearings in its laboratory machine shop for trial purposes. When the bearings had been tested, Alcoa designers made up sets of blueprints which the engine builder could use to order bearings from his normal supplier. Instances in which this approach was successful included those cases where the user made his own bearings and did not buy from a bearing manufacturer. Three diesel engine manufacturers had made their own Babbitt metal bearings and were well equipped to take on aluminum. A fourth diesel engine builder had machine capacity which he could use for this purpose, and when he became convinced of the desirability of using aluminum he decided to make his own bearings. These four companies then used aluminum bearings exclusively.

This last company of the four had previously been the customer of Tyler Bearing Corporation,[3] a large supplier of bearings for diesels. When the decision to convert to aluminum was made, therefore, orders placed by this company with Tyler were canceled. In the meantime (early 1946) Sawyer Diesel,[4] another Tyler customer, had given Alcoa an order for a test set of alloy 750 bearings. Tyler's president therefore requested the Alcoa management to let him take over the order for this test set. Alcoa readily consented to this arrangement.

In the next year, Tyler submitted many sketches of different types of bearings to Alcoa and requested bearing prices on each. In the meantime, Sawyer Diesel did not receive the set of aluminum bearings it had ordered. In early 1947 a letter was received from Tyler saying that the company had had great difficulty in taking test measurements on some aluminum bearings it had tried to make, and its readings were completely inconsistent with each other.

An Alcoa representative working with the Tyler plant manager, however, straightened out the machining difficulties. Sometime thereafter, Tyler informed Alcoa that the company still found aluminum impossible to machine accurately. This concluded any activity on the part of Tyler with aluminum bearings as far as Alcoa was concerned.

With these delays, interest at Sawyer Diesel in aluminum bearings had waned considerably. Alcoa representatives in their contacts with the Sawyer Purchasing Department were not able at that time to revive interest in solid aluminum bearings.

Several years later, however, it developed that some users of Sawyer diesels were having bearing trouble. The problems had arisen in part from the fact that Sawyer was designing new engines with

[3] Fictitious name.
[4] Fictitious name.

increased power output, and that standard bearings could not always standup under the greater loads.

In the late summer of 1952 the Alcoa Development Division received word from one Sawyer customer that the company was purchasing a new diesel engine and would like to have a set of aluminum bearings installed. The bearings were machined in the Alcoa laboratory shop and then installed at a cost of approximately $1,000. Shortly thereafter another bearing company reported a bearing failure on a Sawyer diesel. The faulty bearing had badly scored a $4,500 crankshaft, and this engine user, too, wanted to get a set of aluminum bearings from Alcoa. Subsequently, operating people from two other companies using diesel engines made similar inquiries at Alcoa after learning of these instances in which aluminum bearings had been successfully installed.

Another attempt to get aluminum bearings adopted at Sawyer seemed timely, therefore, and a meeting was then arranged with Sawyer executives. In this meeting the company's general manager stated that Sawyer was not using aluminum bearings because the engineers had not recommended it. The chief production engineer then said that there was a belief that aluminum bearings would damage a crankshaft in the event of seizure.

The Alcoa representatives indicated that this was a misconception, and that laboratory tests would prove the opposite to be true. It was then arranged to run such tests, and it was agreed that if the results were satisfactory, Sawyer would order trial sets of aluminum bearings for further testing. Accordingly, bearings were placed on a crankshaft set up for test purposes in the Sawyer shop, and the oil supply was cut off. The bearings seized but in failing did not damage the shaft.

In a short time, Alcoa received an order from Sawyer's purchasing department for ten sets of aluminum bearings to be tested in actual use. This order was subsequently canceled because of some differences of opinion among Sawyer executives with regard to the test program. At a later meeting between Alcoa and Sawyer representatives, however, the order was reinstated.

In the meantime, Alcoa had learned of numerous other companies which were interested in solid aluminum bearings. The Alcoa Development Division management believed, therefore, that such an important testing program ought to be broadened in scope to include more concerns than those Sawyer had planned to select. This matter was taken up with the Sawyer management, and it was agreed then that an Alcoa representative should visit various additional companies using diesel engines. It was also agreed that Sawyer would give Alcoa a list of the power companies at which it planned to install trial bearings, and in all cases both Alcoa and Sawyer engineers would be on hand to watch the installation of trial sets.

The first company which an Alcoa representative visited was interested in the possibility of testing a set of aluminum bearings but did not want to take action until the district sales manager for Sawyer could be consulted. The Alcoa representative then called on the Sawyer district manager, who expressed a desire to cooperate as fully as possible in this program. At his suggestion a Sawyer salesman was assigned to make calls with the Alcoa representative on Sawyer customers. This salesman, however, sometimes told customers on these calls that Sawyer was recommending one of its regular bearings; that solid aluminum bearings were being tested, and if they proved to be satisfactory Sawyer would so inform its customers. In another of Sawyer's sales areas, the Alcoa representative was asked not to visit Sawyer customers since one set of aluminum bearings had already been allotted to this area for trial purposes, a fact of which Alcoa had not been apprised.

As time went on, interest in aluminum bearings seemed to be increasing as certain diesel engine users, having encountered difficulties in some instances with conventional bearings, successfully replaced them with aluminum bearings. Nevertheless, certain diesel engine builders exhibited a great reluctance to add aluminum bearings to their present lines.

In spite of these difficulties, Alcoa's sales of aluminum bearing castings had been rising steadily since 1947. Annual sales as of 1954, however, were only a small fraction of the annual sales potential this application was estimated to hold for aluminum. The great bulk of sales was being made to diesel engine builders who made their own bearings. One large bearing manufacturer was accounting for some of the volume because he had had firm specifications calling for aluminum bearings from one of his customers. Under these circumstances, the Alcoa management was considering four alternative courses of action: (1) continue the present work with engine builders and other bearing users; (2) try to persuade as many engine builders and other bearing users as possible to undertake the manufacture of their own bearings; (3) build a machine shop that could handle production orders for finished bearings; (4) acquire an interest in an established bearing manufacturing firm.

The history of Alcoa's efforts to build the market for aluminum bearings illustrates the difficulty of appraising at the outset all the factors and conditions which may affect the success of a marketing program. While Alcoa originally planned to function as a supplier of bearing castings, lack of success with this approach required the company to try other approaches, sometimes singly and sometimes in combination, over a period of time from 1945 to 1954. As in this case, inability to predict market reception of the product may leave a company no other alternative but to try a variety of approaches until one is successful.

The philosophy has been expressed that when a new application is basically a good one, the product will eventually find its place in the market. That aluminum bearings represented a "good application" is supported by the facts that several diesel engine manufacturers have been using aluminum bearings for large diesels, that aluminum bearings have been succesfully installed in numerous instances where conventional bearings failed, and that sales of bearing castings have continued to grow after the war until the present time. Nevertheless, with benefit of hindsight, it may be pertinent to speculate as to why Alcoa's introductory marketing program did not succeed, quickly and easily, in creating as great a measure of demand for aluminum bearings as Alcoa's management had hoped might be developed.

In this instance, four market groups may be identified as having a potential interest in aluminum bearings. These groups are large bearing manufacturers, small bearing manufacturing concerns, diesel engine builders, and diesel engine users. In commenting further on Alcoa's experience in this case it may be useful to consider each of these groups in turn—its reactions to the idea of aluminum bearings and possible reasons for these reactions.[5]

RESISTANCE OF THE BEARING MANUFACTURERS

Alcoa's introductory marketing program for solid aluminum bearings had encountered resistance from bearing manufacturers shortly

[5] The analysis which follows is an effort to interpret, from the point of view of the materials producer, the significance of the reported facts. This interpretation is the author's own analysis, based on the information provided by one company. It was not practical, within the scope of this study, to obtain facts and opinions from all groups and companies concerned in this case history.

after its inception. Through its advertising program, Alcoa had generated inquires from engine builders, which were referred to large bearing manufacturers for action. Certain bearing manufacturers had then responded to Alcoa's efforts by attempting to divert the expressed interest in aluminum bearings to an interest in the types of bearings which they regularly made and sold.

While this response may have seemed to be aimed at undermining the Alcoa program, it may more usefully be interpreted as an effort on the part of bearing manufacturers to pursue a program in accord with their own interests. Large bearing manufacturers would probably have no strong incentives to promote the use of aluminum. Any sales volume that could be built up in the new line might simply replace sales of the other types of bearings they regularly sold. In addition, since the manufacturing process for aluminum bearings differed from processes by which conventional types were made, any shift in emphasis away from conventional types to aluminum bearings might require important changes in the production program.

In addition, the introduction of an aluminum bearing more simple to make than other bearing types possibly presented somewhat of a challenge to an important element in the bearing manufacturer's competitive strength, his technical know-how, and his production skills. The fact that it required less machinery and less processing skill to make aluminum bearings from castings than to make conventional bearings created the possibility that bearing customers might adopt aluminum bearings and then choose to make their own instead of purchasing them from bearing suppliers. One engine builder's decision to make his own aluminum bearings from Alcoa castings might easily have sufficed to turn disinterest in the new product on the part of bearing suppliers into active resistance to it.

It is likely, too, that the bearing manufacturer would not be completely in favor of a market approach by Alcoa which involved the latter in the bearing manufacturer's relations with his customers. It would probably be a matter of some concern to him that, if an improved product was available, he should be the one to introduce it to his customer. The bearing manufacturer's technical reputation is likely to be based in part on his ability to keep abreast of new product developments and, when these developments have been evaluated, to make them available to his customer. It is logical therefore that when the initial introduction of the new product does not come through the framework of this supplier-customer relationship, the first reaction on the part of the supplier might be to discredit it.

Another reason for resistance on the part of large bearing manufacturers might possibly have been some uncertainty with regard to the future role of the aluminum producing companies in the bearing market. The development of demand for aluminum bearings might possibly attract the aluminum companies to compete for a share of the market for bearings, particularly if a satisfactory aluminum bearing should be developed for use in automotive engines.

The growth of active resistance to a new product on the part of established manufacturers, once started, may tend to be self-perpetuating and may be difficult to overcome. Once the established manufacturer has taken the position with his customers that he does not recommend a new product, it may be psychologically difficult for him to reverse his stand.

MARKET POSITION OF THE SMALL BEARING MANUFACTURER

Failing at the outset to enlist the active support of large bearing manufacturers, Alcoa had the possible alternative of approaching market development through the smaller concerns. Smaller bearing manufacturers might have utilized the new product to increase their market shares and hence would have reason to work aggressively on establishing aluminum bearings in the market. This approach has been successful in other cases. Why might it not have been effective in this instance?

Alcoa's experience indicated that small bearing manufacturers did not typically sell to large diesel engine builders. There were also indications that relationships between the large bearing manufacturers and their customers were exceptionally strong and, hence, that it might be difficult for outside suppliers to sell to these customers. In many instances diesel engine builders probably relied greatly on the technical assistance of bearing manufacturers both to design their bearings and to recommend specific types for their use. Furthermore, the supplier-customer relationship in many instances was probably one of long duration and may have been one around which strong personal ties had developed.

Unless there were compelling reasons for making changes, the engine builder could be expected to rely, then, on his regular bearing suppliers for bearings and for technical service and technical advice. As long as a diesel engine, and the bearings in it, performed satisfactorily for the user, there would be no impetus for change even though aluminum bearings had superior performance characteristics. Under these circumstances smaller bearing manufacturing concerns may have found the development job a somewhat difficult undertaking.

REACTIONS OF DIESEL ENGINE BUILDERS

When Alcoa first began to offer to supply trial sets of finished bearings to diesel engine builders, the company enjoyed some initial successes with four engine building concerns which were interested in making their own bearings rather than purchasing them from established bearing manufacturers. The comparative simplicity of finish-machining aluminum bearings was a consideration strongly favoring their adoption. In these cases, evidently, the only finished bearings which Alcoa sold were trial sets, and thereafter it supplied bearing castings to this group of engine builders.

Efforts to interest some other diesel engine makers in converting to the use of aluminum bearings were notably unsuccessful. It seemed difficult for Alcoa salesmen to interest these concerns in taking bearings for trial use. When engine builders could be persuaded to conduct either field tests or shop tests, these trials were sometimes carried out under something short of favorable conditions. Why was it that, with the exception of those firms interested in making their own bearings, diesel engine builders as a group did not exhibit greater interest in adopting aluminum bearings?

To understand the engine builder's position, it might be useful first to define the product as it relates to *his* selling program. Understandably, the type of bearing in a diesel engine might not be an important sales point for the engine builder to stress in sales to customers, since it would normally be assumed by his customer that the engine builder would use bearings which, with proper care, would last the life of the engine. Cost of the bearing would probably have a relatively insignificant effect on the cost of the engine itself and consequently would not be translated into a lower price to the engine user.

Type of bearing used in an engine may become important only when users experience particular difficulties with this engine part.

Under such circumstances, the bearing would then achieve an importance that goes beyond the part itself. Bearing failure might do damage to an engine that would be considerably more costly than the bearing. Additionally, excessive difficulties encountered with this one part can reflect unfavorably in the user's mind on the over-all quality and design of the engine.

Hence, it might be said that bearings may be important in somewhat of a *negative* sense to the engine builder. The *positive* appeal of the product for *some* engine builders was the fact that it was relatively simple to machine finished bearings from castings. Hence, engine builders for whom this consideration was important would have a strong reason, in addition to the advantages of the product itself, for adopting aluminum bearings.

For other diesel engine manufacturers, there might be a natural reluctance to make a change. In the absence of particular problems with conventional bearing types, engine builders have no compelling incentive to adopt aluminum bearings. If, on the other hand, customer difficulties with bearings bring up the question of whether a new type of bearing might be used, engine builders might tend to rely for technical advice on bearing suppliers—both because of the highly technical nature of the par and because of the close relationships that may have developed between engine builder and bearing supplier. It might be unlikely under the circumstances that bearing manufacturers would recommend the use of aluminum bearings.

In addition, engine builders might be inclined, of their own accord, to develop some resistance to aluminum bearings when this product appears in the market as a remedy for the difficulties customers have experienced with engines they have made. The failure of one engine builder to develop strong enthusiasm for a field-testing program which involved his customers and to work harmoniously with the Alcoa representative in this undertaking may easily have been due to a sensitiveness about such difficulties.

INCENTIVES OF ENGINE USERS

Engine users seemed to exhibit real interest in adopting aluminum bearings. With the development of diesel engines with high power output and with the increased use of engine lubricating oil additives, engine users began to encounter difficulties with the use of conventional bearings. Their interest in aluminum bearings therefore sprang from a recognized need to find a type of bearing that would require less frequent replacement and would not cause engine maintenance problems.

It is significant that engine users came initially to Alcoa and that orders received from this group were evidently unsolicited. Had these purchasers not recognized a strong need to find a better product than the bearings then in use, it might have been difficult to focus sales effort at this level in an attempt to create demand for aluminum bearings. Engine users might tend to follow the technical advice of engine builders on matters such as bearings. Hence, it is of particular interest that some engine users were willing to try aluminum bearings although it was necessary to obtain these sets from a source other than their regular sources of supply.

If engine users could be identified as that group of customers having both the greatest incentive to adopt the new product and the least resistance to it, initial efforts to introduce aluminum bearings might logically have been expected to be most successful in this segment of the market. If it is likely then that the engine user's existing supply sources would tend to be an influence opposing adoption of the new product, the approach to end users might have been more effective than it was if it had been a direct approach—one not taken through, or in the name of, the end user's regular supply service.

When an Alcoa representative visited the customers of one diesel engine building concern to solicit their participation in a bearing test program, his efforts in creating demand for the new product were possibly less effective than they might have been in the absence of this tie-in with the engine builder. Had the field salesman simply been selling finished bearings and representing Alcoa alone, he might have been in a position to emphasize to a greater extent than he may have done both the cost and the functional advantages of aluminum bearings. As it was, he may have hesitated to draw critical comparisons between aluminum bearings and the conventional bearings which the engine builder was then using.

Hesitancy to approach end users directly may arise from an unwillingness to jeopardize relations with the end user's regular suppliers if it is anticipated that at some future time this group will be the one through which the product will be regularly sold. Thus Alcoa representatives may have been hesitant at the outset to approach engine builders out of consideration for the maintenance of good relations with bearing manufacturers. Later on, hesitancy to approach engine users directly and aggressively might have been based in part on a desire on Alcoa's part to maintain good relations with diesel engine builders.

Such hesitancy, however, may possibly prolong the achieving of initial acceptance of the product in the market if it means minimizing the aggressiveness of the selling program. Approaching the market as they did, first through bearing manufacturers and then through engine builders, Alcoa representatives were not enabled to sell "against" conventional bearings and to take full sales advantage of the difficulties which were being encountered with conventional bearings in certain makes of diesel engines. Prolonging the initial stages might have had the effect then of permitting the development of increased resistance at all levels of the market to the new product.

When the new product can be introduced quickly and effectively at an end-user level, it may be psychologically easier for other groups in the market to concede its advantages and to incorporate the new product advantageously in their own operations. Once groups in the market have time to generate resistance to the product and have an opportunity to sell against it, ultimate adoption tends to become a concession and may therefore be long in coming. Reports discrediting the new product have an opportunity to circulate. Such reports become the basis for explanations as to why manufacturers and end users are *not* selling or using the new product, as the case may be.

Successful sales efforts with end users, however, may be expected to create pressure on their chain of supply (in this case the engine builder and the bearing manufacturer) to have the new product available. Whereas these suppliers may have hesitated originally to sponsor an unproven product, they would now be motivated by the desire to preserve market share by keeping abreast of technical developments.

When it seemed apparent that demand had been created at the end-user level and that adoption by the chain of supply was in process, it might be appropriate at that point to shift the focus of sales effort away from end users. Serving the end-use market directly may not in the long run be either satisfactory or economical for the materials producer. If not, then distribution through the established chain of supply may provide broad coverage of the market and may put the new product in channels where a sales and a servicing program can be carried out effectively.

SUMMARY

In the initial stages of market development the materials producer's efforts to create demand for the new product may be focused either on potential manufacturers of the new product or on potential end users. Some conscious choice needs to be made, therefore, with regard to which of these groups can most effectively be approached on a direct basis.

The choice ought probably to be based, first, on a definitive analysis of the product, the process by which it is manufactured, and its end-use applications. Second, the choice should be based on a judgment as to whether potential manufacturers or potential end users of the new product will have the greatest incentives to adopt it initially and which groups in the market can be expected to register the greatest resistance to its adoption. Finally, some appraisal should certainly be made of the character and the strength of the relationships between potential end users and their suppliers. When incentives to adopt the new product at the end-use level conflict with the influences of a strong end-user–supplier relationship, the incentives may not be strong enough to assert themselves in the face of these contrary pressures.

On the basis of such an appraisal a decision may then be made as to whether the creation of demand for the new product can best be achieved by focusing sales effort at an end-use market level in an attempt to *draw* the new product into, and through, the chain of supply. Alternatively, the materials supplier may choose to *push* the product through this chain by seeking to interest manufacturers in assuming major responsibility for developing demand at the end-user level.

When there is potential resistance in the market to the new product, the introductory marketing program may lose effectiveness if it is complicated by efforts to reach more than one group of customers at the same time. In attempting to preserve his relations with both potential end users and their suppliers, the materials producer may find that he has modified the aggressiveness of his marketing program.

The result may be to reduce the competitive impact of the new product on products which it seeks to displace.

If the materials producer chooses to focus initial sales effort at the end-user level, the success of this program may be signaled in time both by increasing sales to end users and by the growing interest of other concerns in making and selling the new product. At this point a second stage in the marketing program might evolve out of the first phase. In the second stage the materials producer may change his focus of sales effort from end users and may concentrate his sales program on the end user's regular sources of supply.

At what point in time the transition should be made between the first and second phases is a matter of judgment. On the one hand, the materials producer may not long wish to jeopardize relationships with his eventual customers by competing with them in the end-product market. On the other hand, he will want to be assured that growth of the market will not be deterred by the discontinuance of his own direct sales efforts to generate demand at the end-user level. The over-all selling effort may conceivably lose some of its aggressive flavor when the product becomes integrated in the established chain of supply. Continued market growth may then depend upon whether the level of end-user demand is self-sustaining and upon whether some suppliers will want to sell the new product aggressively in order to increase market share against their competitors.

39

Tomorrow's Integrated Offices and Plants[1]

George M. Muschamp

Automatic controls are experiencing an explosive growth. Industrial processes and their control systems are becoming larger and more complex. And this growth of automaticity is being paralleled in the office.

As exasperating as the area of automatic control is in its complexity—and it promises to become even more so—the challenges it offers provide it with a fascination for all who work in it. Every industry and most professions have a big stake in it.

I want to discuss here a subject that, in my opinion, is the most important single issue confronting not only those in automatic control but every industrial enterprise of any consequence. That is the eventual "marriage" of two massive developments—the automatic operation of the plant and the automatic operation of the office.

I firmly believe that the bringing together of these developments will constitute the greatest industrial event of this decade. As they now stand, the automatic controls in the plant and the automatic operations in the office are linked mainly through people. These arrangements are often loose and inefficient, but elusive as they are, they are a wide open target for automatic controls' big guns.

Each of these areas of automaticity—the office and the plant—has evolved over a long period. Each has had a complex and varied

[1] From *Automation,* May 1961. Copyright, 1961, Penton Publishing Company, Cleveland 13, Ohio. Used by permission.

career of its own. And each has incorporated the latest scientific and engineering techniques that now provide the means for bringing them together. Automatic control people are the ushers of this colossal wedding.

PLANT AUTOMATION

Let us look first at the plant. The staggering variety of manufacturing processes in all industries defies any simple classification. Automatic control people often divide all manufacturing into the continuous processes and the batch processes, but I have found considerable disagreement as to what degree of continuity is necessary in a process for it to be called continuous. Strictly speaking, there are few, if any, truly continuous processes.

It is also a gross oversimplification, of course, to think of all manufacturing as divided into the "wet" or liquid manufacturing processes and the "dry" or hardware manufacturing processes. However, there are distinctions between the two. In the so-called wet processes, such as those which are predominant in the oil and chemical industries, automatic control in the thirty years that I have known it has grown from relatively simple and often independently operating control systems to huge and complex systems measuring and controlling many variables. In these processes data are acquired on temperatures, pressures, flows, and the like in various parts of the process and quality or characteristics of a product both in the course of its production and at the conclusion of the manufacturing cycle.

Some of this data is transient. It is fed into control instruments, which do their work; and the data may then be forgotten. Other data, however, are recorded for use in accounting, inventory control, nonautomatic quality control, or engineering and management analysis. Although derived from the plant, they definitely are office data.

"Dry" processes, such as those which are predominant in the metals, food, textile, and paper industries, among others, share many of the characteristics of the wet processes. For example, they also use feedback control loops. Here again, the measurements are of two kinds: Those which can be used within closed automatic control loops and have no further utility; and those which are used for further nonautomatic control purposes, that is, for office or management purposes.

Dry processes such as are found in the metal cutting and forming industries, the electronic industries, and other so-called discrete parts industries, often depart rather widely from the wet processes even though many have a high degree of production continuity. However, such operations as numerical machine controls, which embody automatic feedback principles, have much in common with the automatic control systems of the wet processes. One does encounter, though, in many metal-cutting processes, discontinuities which characterize the process wherein many people are involved with taking and using data.

For example, the manual inspection of a batch of machined parts has two purposes. One is to provide data from which we can control the operation of the machine to produce acceptable parts. The other is to provide accounting or inventory data. The first purpose is served by a man-machine data or control loop including the machine, the operator, the inspector, the foreman, and sometimes many others. In the assembly of the parts even more communication or data-passing among people may take place. Between these manufacturing operations and the business operations such as accounting, production control, and sales forecasting, data-passing becomes a career for many people.

It appears then that throughout industry we are acquiring two categories of data or information about the production processes. One is the information that is automatically taken and automatically fed into control systems which automatically control specific processes in the plant. This information, for the most part, has little use beyond the requirements of the automatic control system. Therefore, people have little to do with this kind of information. Then there is the information about the plant that is automatically or manually taken and which goes to people for making decisions and taking actions. Often the actions are only to pass the information on to other people. It is perfectly plain that the more we enlarge the first category by creating more automatic data or control loops, the less data need be given to people and the fewer decisions they must make.

OFFICE AUTOMATION

Let us look at the office, where much of this information finally goes. It is not necessary for me to elaborate upon the degree to which electronic data processing has invaded office operation and the impact it has had upon the clerical and technical operations of business. It has been the means of extending the available work force to meet a workload that simply could not have been met manually. There are few large manufacturing plants that do not enjoy it in some degree for office work.

The tremendous technological changes that have taken place, and are continuing to take place in electronic data processing, are exemplified by the experience of Minneapolis-Honeywell. In the space of five years our company has developed two generations of computers of radically different design, each of million-dollar size. The development of such equipment represents enormous capital outlays and expenditures of scientific and engineering talent.

To simplify our discussion, let us consider office processes as falling into two large classes. One class of office process is that whose final product is primarily information. The other class of office process is that in which the information is incidental to the manufacture of some real product.

In the first category—the information office—fall all of the record-keeping operations of insurance companies, banks, and nonmanufacturing enterprises of all kinds, as well as research testing of industrial laboratories, engine test laboratories, and missile ranges. This category is not of immediate concern in the coming wedding of plant and office because no physical product is involved.

What does concern us is the second category—the real-product office—which embraces all office operations of all the manufacturing plants referred to in connection with automatic control in the plant. To some degree, testing operations can be included.

Our concern is with the *whole* manufacturing process for products. This includes the manufacturing equipment, its immediate automatic controls, *and* the data acquisition, processing, and computing equipment in whatever departments of the organization it may be lodged. Less and less, it seems to me, will there be a clean line of separation between what is automatic control equipment in the plant and what is automatic data processing equipment in the office. The immense challenge before us is the minimization of the intolerable and costly overlapping which surely will occur if we continue the separate pursuit of plant and office automatization.

EVOLUTION OF INTEGRATED CONTROL

What is now possible, if we face up to it, is the merging of plant and office functions. We can reorganize the paper work, which is the present end product of most automatic office equipment, so that the information, in addition to serving as a record, can be fed automatically into the plant control systems as required. We can automatically acquire, from the process, the information needed for automatic control of the process together with the information needed for accounting. We can automatically feed the necessary information back to the process for automatic control. We will then have more automatic parallel operations in place of the present man-machine serial operations.

This has been characteristic of the evolution of control systems. First you measure. Next you record, usually collecting more records than are needed—records that are used by people who adjust the process and so make man-machine control loops. Then you automatically control, with parallel recording, gradually eliminating all but the records required for monitoring or for the future. The process goes on in ever-widening loops.

This same kind of evolution will occur in the joining of office and plant operations. Presently, the targets for manufacturing operations are set through office operations with respect to the factors of profit, cost, quality, delivery, and production control. However highly mechanized these office operations have become, their output is now primarily designed for the use of people, not for directly feeding into plant automatic control systems. The intervening people now adjust the plant automatic controls.

Bit by bit and with increasing acceleration, ways will be found to join automatic office equipment to automatic plant controls. The development will be impeded by the fact that there is relatively little standardization among companies as to how things are done in this area. However, we will learn how to make these connections on an experimental basis. First we will simply record and observe their effects. Then we will allow them automatically to control with parallel recording of monitoring information, and finally we will minimize the information-gathering step, as the automatic control proves itself.

BUILT-IN FINANCIAL CONTROLS

Few companies today attempt to operate without some means of market forecasting. These predictions are the inputs to the production control mechanism. The production control mechanism goes on to provide parts breakdowns which form the demands on the manufacturing departments. Cost information is generated and related to prices —an operation that can be mechanized in varying degree. Compilation of salary, wage, and other information may be done automatically, including various "control" reports.

Anything which purports to be a control is of consuming interest to us. It must, however, contain performance versus a criterion or it is not a control at all. If it has these, then it has the elements necessary for *automatic* control. For example, if a product is to yield X per cent gross profit and the automatic data processing equipment determines that a given product line is not meeting that target, presto, a switch can shut down that line. Ridiculous? It would be surprising how many corporate directors would rush to buy such a device if they could be sure the figures were reliable. Sales contentions that an unprofitable product helps sell products that are profitable would be more objectively examined.

Or instead of shutting down the line, perhaps the switch could electrify into action the department foreman, an industrial engineer, or the design engineer. Think of all the many things that could be done with just this profit-by-product-lines criterion.

Suppose, for example, that a continuous refinery under full automatic control is capable of turning out, dependent upon the respective adjustments of the control instruments, two different products from the same crude input. Suppose, also, that these adjustments are controlled automatically from a computer which, in effect, possesses a "profit switch." Suppose, further, that the market situation is such as to make the two products equally acceptable. Then, obviously, the profit switch could be actuated to set the control system in the refinery so as to make the profitable as opposed to the unprofitable product. This can be paraphrased for several industries in which the attempt is now being made to incorporate over-all economic factors in automatic plant operation.

What is significant about such operations in terms of the wedding of plant and office is that market and economic information processed in computers is directly applied to the automatic control system of the plant.

This business will not be as simple as the profit switch, but in the entire interaction of the elements of an enterprise, the operation will consist of a multiplicity of such operations automatically programmed and monitored by people as they properly should be. While control systems for a whole enterprise can become quite complex, they nevertheless can be built step by step. A case in point is that of a large metropolitan electric company which serves several million users with a system of great complexity. It soon will have an on-line digital computer to help it solve the problem of producing electricity at minimum cost.

Each generator in each generating station has a machine control system for keeping constant the characteristics of its output despite variations in load to meet changing power demands. This is done by varying the supply of steam or hydraulic power to the turbine from a source which has its own control system. Also, generators in a station usually have different efficiencies requiring that, for optimum economy, the load should be apportioned among them according to their relative efficiencies at different levels of load. This is the station control system. Furthermore, the stations also will vary in over-all efficiency and be miles apart, introducing line loss factors. The relationship of all the factors involved in such a system is so complex that the solution to the economic dispatch formulas and the automatic adjustment of the network, station, and machine control systems to maintain over-all system efficiency at an optimum lies in a general purpose digital on-line computer.

There is another complication which enters the picture. Power networks are interconnected so that one company may buy or sell power from another as demand dictates. Thus, a half-dozen or more other networks may be supplying power to a network or receiving power from it. Whenever this happens, further variables are introduced into the system control, involving, in addition, intercompany economics, since obviously there must be an accounting of the power produced by one company and used by another.

The on-line digital computer, whose primary job is automatically to direct the control system, performs a secondary function. That is the obtaining of basic data for intercompany billing of the delivered power. The significance of these economic and business operations in the automatic control system is the bringing together in a fully automatic way the things which have in the past been regarded as separate plant and office operations.

It is impossible at this stage to specify the exact degree to which the automatic operations of office and plant will merge. I do not contend that there will not also be separate and independent office or plant systems. So long as they are dealing respectively with information or data that in amount and kind has little in common, there is not much point in merging them except for machine economy.

LINKING REMOTE LOCATIONS

It is typical of the enlarging loops of automatic control and data processing alike that the communication function is becoming increasingly important. In the power control system just cited, the generating stations and the tie points with adjoining networks are many miles apart. This requires communication between the various measuring and control points and the central control locations—in this instance, telemetering over telephone lines. In the operation of pipelines, the state of development of telemetering and remote supervisory control systems is so high that many large stations are completely unattended.

Thus, in practically every field telemetry is rapidly making possible the joining of operations formerly linked by people or not linked at all. Where wire connections are not possible, in cases such as airborne and other vehicular systems, radio will have an important place. The frequency spectrum is being exploited from one end to the other for industrial communication purposes—from d.c. control systems to microwaves and above. The opening by the Federal Communications Commission of frequency bands above 10,000 megacycles for private communication systems now makes it possible for industrial firms to have their own networks for data links, automatic control, and voice. All of this communication activity will accelerate the joining of office and plant systems.

ROLE OF TOP MANAGEMENT

No matter how passive a role top management plays in these two evolutions of automaticity, that in the office and that in the plant, each will evolve as economics dictate. As they meet, however—and they are now starting to do so in a significant way—they will not necessarily mesh in a logical pattern. It is already apparent that, in the absence of a deliberately planned program, the chance is rather remote that the automatic plant controls and plant information gathering equipment will be compatible with the office data processing equipment. This is not surprising when one recognizes the wide gamut of systems and designs of equipment now available in both areas.

But management can not afford to do nothing. It will be faced with some costly improvisations if it does not have an over-all plan to insure compatibility. How does management get this insurance? There are two efforts looming up in answer to this. First, some managements are recognizing the wide scope of these movements by establishing upper-echelon committees or task forces under a corporate officer to study and plan the acquisition of automatic equipment. Secondly, equipment manufacturers are supplying more and more systems engineering and are recognizing the need for compatibility by providing "common language" input and output signals for the various pieces of equipment and by supplying single-source responsibility for systems. It was in recognition of this trend that our company set up a division devoted exclusively to advanced systems engineering.

Management and engineering consultants will become involved in this evolution to a greater or lesser extent, depending upon the degree to which an enterprise can provide these services from within. This has been the traditional role of the consultant where plant design, construction, finance, and organization have been concerned. There appears to be no reason to expect this relationship to change. But where these consultants in the past have been specialists in one area or the other, they, too, will need to provide several services collectively. I know of several formerly pure accounting firms now employing operations research departments.

ENGINEERING THE SYSTEMS

The many problems of joining the plant and office are large. Ironically enough, they do not arise from a basic lack of machine techniques, but from a lack of process knowledge which, in the office, means procedure knowledge. It involves also a vast lack of procedure standardization in both the plant and the office, calling for special solutions that are often uneconomic. That is to say, the differences in the ways that different companies do things prevent use in a second plant of the system and application engineering carried out at a first plant.

It is upon this problem area that operations research has made an assault with varying degrees of success. Those who have tried operations research and found it wanting would, I feel, do well to ask whether it was this approach which failed or whether they were not asking operations research to do some things which should have been done by other means. Common-sense systems or application engineering in some cases might have been the answer.

One can not perform either the user's role or the equipment manufacturer's role in this evolution without the most advanced systems engineering which applies to the problem. This means using mathematical models where they are applicable. It means using dynamic analysis and servomechanism theories where they are justified. It means using common sense when none of the sophisticated techniques applies.

In my opinion, there have been two erroneous impressions created in the art. One is that complete mathematical models are widely applicable at present and widely used. It is true that a great amount of study and theorizing and some experimentation are taking place. Yet we are not often able to provide accurate mathematical models for real processes nor able to provide quantitative data for such models. This is not to disparage the effort which I sincerely hope and expect will continue, will accelerate, and will succeed.

The second is the impression that one can not advantageously use data processing equipment or computers without complete mathematical models. There are many functions of processes that have been well known that required too much time and manpower to be handled manually but which can now be advantageously handled by computers. There are many functions not known to us, as specifically as the mathematician might like, that can be handled by computers.

A good example is the three-mode controller. Either in its pneumatic or electrical form, it is an analog computer. It has been in wide industrial use for twenty-five years and can be tuned or adjusted to the process whose specific quantitative characteristics are not known. I happen to know that these were originally developed without the benefit of servomechanism theory or much mathematical knowledge of the process. Their basic contribution to the development of industrial processes is history. Many processes could not operate without them. I see no reason why large digital machines can not be used in the same general way by recognizing the greatly increased complexity of the larger system.

What I want to emphasize strongly is that we should not be frightened because there is so much that we do not know. We should realize we know enough to effect vast changes if we do so studiously.

Study does not mean mathematics alone. I believe that any presently successful enterprise can find enough qualified personnel within its organization to make an impressive start in this field, relying, if necessary, on outside assistance for help in specialized areas. If we did nothing more than broaden the horizons of our industrial engineering departments, we could make tremendous strides. Too many of these departments have been limited to the role of tool design or specific process or method formulation and have not been given enough breadth of scope in their activities. It is management's job to correct this.

APPROPRIATE INFORMATION USE

Since we are dealing with the production of real products and the use of information in the production process, let us orient our information to manufacturing. We have four sets of information:

1. That which is now directly incorporated in manufacturing automatic control loops and has no other use
2. That about the manufacturing process which is either automatically or manually taken and which has further use by the plant operators and others
3. Business and technical information generated within the enterprise
4. Business and technical information generated [outside] . . . the enterprise

The first and second categories of information relate in a way that is obvious but terribly important. If information has no use beyond its function in an automatic control system, then we should stop collecting it, once the automatic control system is installed. Obvious as this is, it is surprising how often we fail to recognize that the man-machine loop has been replaced by the automatic feedback loop and the man no longer needs nor can use certain information.

We do need the second category of information about a process even when it is under automatic control. An operator needs certain performance information for monitoring the whole effort. Quality control, engineering, accounting, and various levels of management need information. A transitional step in bringing plant information into the office system is automatic data collection.

Business and technical information peculiar to the individual manufacturing operations is a mixed bag. Part of this data may be automatically read *out* of the plant, processed with other data and then be automatically read *into* the plant. If we want automatic control, it is this part that has to be carved out of a mass of other data which may exist for other purposes.

The fourth, the external category of information, is usually not susceptible to inclusion in the automatic control system unless we happen to be considering one plant of a multiplant enterprise. In that case, our system may be extended to the whole enterprise.

In summary, plant automaticity has reached a high state of development. Office automaticity is rapidly approaching the same point. We are on the threshold of a colossal wedding of these two dynamic movements in company-wide automatic operations. New developments in communications will accelerate the movement, and systems engineering will play a leading role. The effect of this wedding will be to produce more goods, to provide more jobs better suited for people, to require more education to fit people for these jobs; and for the present it will mean more work for management to bring this off economically as a union and not a collision.

40

How Economic and Sales Forecasts Are Made[1]

Burnard H. Sord
and
Glenn A. Welsch

A forecast represents an attempt to predict what probably will happen under certain assumptions concerning the future. We believe that sound management planning necessarily must be based to a large

1 From *Business Budgeting* (New York, Controllership Foundation, Inc., 1958), pp. 132–144 (from Chapter 5, "Long-Range Planning and Forecasting"). Used by permission.

degree on forecasts of both internal and external economic forces. Current economic trends should be analyzed, and the effect of these trends on future operations should be considered. Economic and competitive conditions change from year to year. Industry positions in the economy may be altered by changing technology and other developments. When management attempts to formulate definite profit objectives, the level of general business activity should be appraised and the probable effect of this level on revenues and expenses should be determined.

The vital importance of the sales budget, coupled with the necessity for reasonable accuracy in sales forecasting, has caused many companies to develop both economic and industry forecasts at regular intervals. Where economic and industry forecasts are developed they serve as invaluable aids in developing a realistic sales budget for the firm. The importance attached to forecasting was clearly evident throughout the study[2] as is indicated in Figure 1.

Many of the companies interviewed develop forecasts of (1) general economic conditions, (2) economic conditions of the particular industry, (3) share of market, (4) prices for products, and (5) sales volume. Table 1 presents the interview results.

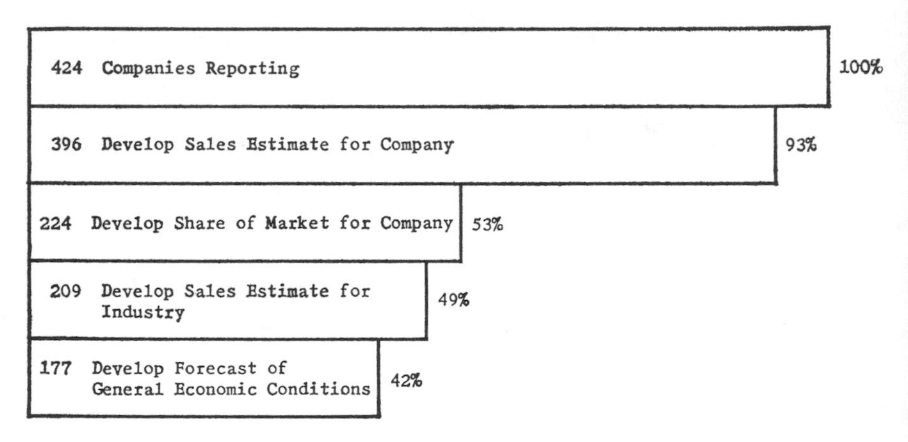

FIG. 1. Per Cent of 424 Companies Developing Economic and Sales Forecasts Within Their Firms

SOURCE: Tables 1 and 2.

[2] [The study covered 424 companies in the United States and Canada—Ed.]

TABLE 1
Number and Per Cent of the 35 Companies Interviewed
Developing Economic and Sales Forecasts

Type of Forecast	Number of Companies Developing Forecast	Per Cent
General economic conditions	18	51
Sales estimate for industry	19	54
Share of market for company	24	69
Sales estimates for company	35	100
Sales prices for product	25	71

It is highly significant that more than 50 per cent of the companies participating in the interviews employ all of the more common types of forecasts generally used for business planning.

The sales budget is generally considered to be of prime importance to the individual firm, since other company planning is predicated to a large extent on sales plans. All thirty-five of the companies interviewed use the sales budget as a primary basis for other plans in the business. Thirty-four of the companies use the sales budget as the basis for production (or equivalent) planning.

The importance of a general economic forecast should not be minimized, but at any one time the growth patterns of a specific industry might or might not be following the growth patterns of the economy as a whole. The growth of an industry might be stabilized or declining, or it might be following the general economic growth, but at a faster or slower rate. This is one of the primary reasons that so many companies consider industry forecasts to be valuable tools in developing a realistic sales budget. Industry forecasts also provide a basis for determining per cent of market that should be obtained by a particular company. In this connection the competitive position of a firm in its own industry is of primary importance.

Table 2 presents a tabulation of the types of forecasts employed by the companies replying to the mail questionnaire. Comparison of these results with those developed during the interviews (Table 1) reveals somewhat lower percentages in general for the mail questionnaire group. Despite these differences it is significant that so many companies develop economic, industry, and share-of-market forecasts in particular.

TABLE 2

PER CENT OF COMPANIES DEVELOPING ECONOMIC AND SALES FORECASTS WITHIN THEIR FIRMS AS REPORTED BY 389 COMPANIES BY INDUSTRY AND SIZE[a]

TYPE OF FORECAST	INDUSTRY CLASSIFICATION									
	Manufacturing		*Public Utilities, Transportation*	*Wholesale and Retail*	*Finance and Insurance*	*Miscellaneous*	*Total by Size*			
	Durable	Nondurable					S	M	L	Total
Total Replies	186	131	40	16	10	6	118	150	121	389
				PERCENTAGE DISTRIBUTION						
General economic conditions	35	40	55	69	60	33	29	33	62	41
Sales estimate for industry	51	53	25	63	30	33	40	46	61	49
Share of market for company	56	54	23	63	40	33	49	49	56	51
Sales estimate for company	94	94	90	100	60	83	92	94	93	93

[a] Percentage analysis will not add to 100 per cent because more than one answer could be checked.

Analysis of Table 2 reveals the influence of size on the types of forecasts developed. Only 29 per cent of the small companies develop general economic forecasts, while 62 per cent of the large companies develop such forecasts. Sixty-one per cent of the large companies forecast sales for a particular industry compared with 40 per cent of the small companies. Forty-nine per cent of both small and medium companies forecast share of market as contrasted to 56 per cent of the large companies.

In comparing the types of forecasts developed by various industries, the low percentage of public utilities and transportation companies preparing sales forecasts for the industry (only 25 per cent) and share of market (only 23 per cent) stands out. Public utility companies normally do not prepare such forecasts. Such companies generally are the sole operators in a particular area; therefore, industry forecasts or share-of-market forecasts are thought to be relatively unimportant.

The high per cent of wholesale and retail companies preparing the various types of forecasts attests the importance which these companies place on forecasting. Forecasting is highly developed in this industry for several reasons. Traditionally, the wholesale and retail companies operate on very close profit margins and must carefully plan the purchase of merchandise. Many such concerns must also deal with style and all the inherent problems connected with style changes.

The data in Table 2 indicate that there is very little difference in the percentage of durable manufacturing companies and the percentage of nondurable manufacturing companies developing economic, industry, share-of-market, and sales forecasts.

DEVELOPING SALES FORECASTS

Among the executives interviewed, it was generally agreed that sales budgeting is the most difficult task in profit planning. Many company executives readily admitted that they are not always able to estimate total sales volume with sufficient confidence. However, the most difficult sales-budgeting problem generally does not concern *total* sales volume, but rather the inability accurately to estimate the sales of specific products or specific sales areas. Many executives stated that actual total sales are often within 5 per cent of the total sales originally budgeted, whereas actual sales of specific products or areas often deviate by as much as 25 per cent from budgeted sales. This condition does not appear to be peculiar to a specific type or size of business.

Historical sales data are extensively used as a basis for sales budgeting; and a variety of sales-forecasting techniques are employed, some of which do not utilize historical data extensively. The procedures used in developing sales forecasts as reported by the companies participating in the study are shown in Figure 2. The procedures of the companies interviewed are shown in Table 3.

TABLE 3
PRINCIPAL PROCEDURES USED IN DEVELOPING SALES BUDGET IN 35 COMPANIES INTERVIEWED

Procedure	Number of Companies Using Procedure	Per Cent
Past sales trends of company	29	83
Sales department estimates	29	83
Survey of company executives' opinions	18	51
Correlation of company sales with general economic indicator	15	43

The following description by one controller illustrates the technique of use of company executives' opinions:

The controller, treasurer, economist, production planner, and purchasing manager are all members of the forecasting committee. In October the forecasting committee meets to formulate the basic assumptions to be considered in the sales forecast. These basic assumptions are presented to the president for review and approval. After the president's approval the various divisional managers are notified of the basic assumptions to be considered in determining the divisional sales forecast for the coming year.

With the basic assumptions in mind, each division develops its own sales forecast by product lines for the coming year. These forecasts from the divisions are reviewed by the forecast committee. If the forecast committee disagrees with the forecast of a division, the committee will submit its observations and disagreement in writing along wth the sales forecast to the president. The president will then approve or disapprove the sales forecast.

A budget director described their procedure as follows:

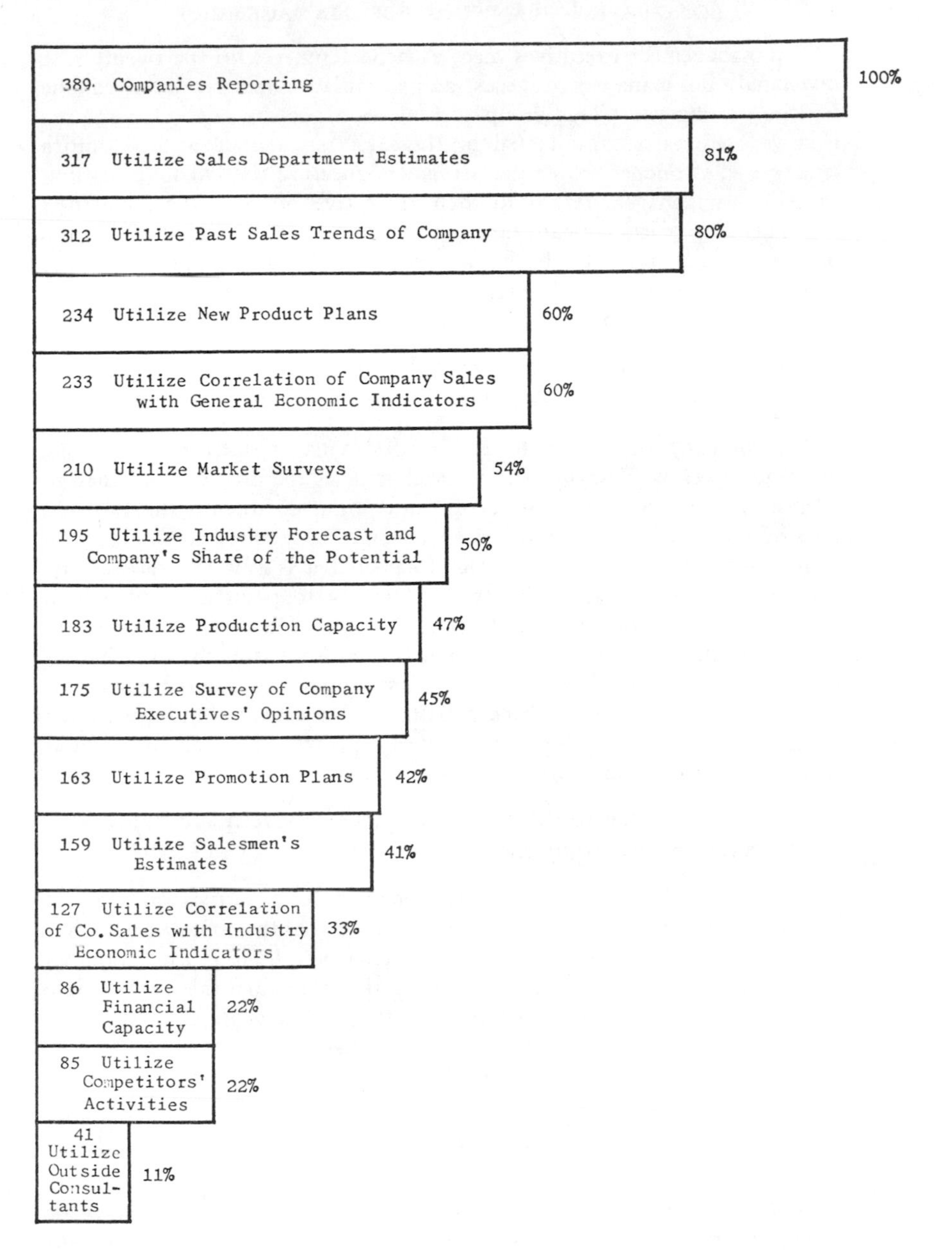

FIG. 2. Procedures Used in Developing Sales Forecasts
SOURCE: Table 4.

Top-management executives meet each September with the twenty-four divisional sales managers to discuss and formulate a tentative sales volume for the coming year. This group formulates a general sales plan for the next year which is consolidated by the sales research department into a tentative sales budget. After the September meeting the twenty-four divisional sales managers return to their respective districts and have their regional sales offices prepare detailed sales budgets. These detailed sales budgets are submitted to the home office for review and approval. Once these sales budgets have been approved by top management, these are considered the sales goals for the year.

The use of estimates from the field force in developing the sales budget is described by an assistant to the president as follows:

The company sends to each branch sales manager questionnaires to be filled out by each salesman. These questionnaires require each salesman to estimate by six-month periods for the next eighteen months the expected sales of each model. The branch sales manager is required to consult with each salesman and to develop a sales forecast that is mutually satisfactory. The branch sales manager utilizes this meeting to point out both strong areas and weaknesses for the individual salesman. He uses the occasion to guide the salesman toward more productive efforts. After the branch sales managers have finished talking with all salesmen, the economist and the marketing director meet with each branch sales manager and review the sales forecast. Once the forecast has been approved by these three, it is submitted to the president for review and final approval.

The same assistant to the president quoted above made the following observation concerning the accuracy of salesmen's estimates:

It is almost impossible to get salesmen to make a satisfactory forecast beyond a six-month period. We use eighteen months, but the last two six-month periods are not very significant. However, there is a real value in having these two periods included. It gives the individual salesman a place to put prospects. If you do not provide them with a place to put these different prospects, there is a tendency for them to put them in the immediate six-month period. We repeat our forecast every six months.

SALES-FORECASTING PROCEDURES

One of the questions on the mail questionnaire asked for the principal procedures used in developing the sales forecast[3] . . . The re-

[3] [In Sord and Welsch, *op. cit.*, Appendix A, Question 17—Ed.]

plies are tabulated in Table 4. Study of the figures in this table reveals considerable variation in industry practices. Of 389 companies, 80 per cent use past sales trends and 81 per cent use sales department estimates. Analysis of Table 4 also reveals that companies of all sizes rely heavily on these techniques. In contrast, only 60 per cent of finance and insurance companies use past sales trends, and only 30 per cent of these companies use sales department estimates.

Forty-one per cent of the companies use salesmen's estimates in making sales forecasts; the percentage variation between the small, medium, and large companies using this technique is only 4 per cent. However, only 6 per cent of the wholesale and retail companies use this procedure. This is probably due to the caliber of sales personnel used at lower levels in retail companies.

Sixty per cent of the respondents to the mail questionnaire use correlation of company sales with general economic indicators. This reflects the importance of the general economic forecast discussed earlier. Analysis of these figures reveals that 50 per cent or more of all industries, except finance and insurance, use this procedure. The influence of size is reflected by the fact that 75 per cent of the large companies use correlation of company sales with general economic indicators in making the sales forecasts, as contrasted with 51 per cent of the small companies and 55 per cent of the medium-sized companies.

In analyzing the industries using new-product plans in making sales forecasts, the pattern of replies reflects industry differences. Seventy-three per cent of the durable manufacturing and 66 per cent of non-durable manufacturing employ this procedure, contrasted with only 18, 19, and 20 per cent of the other industries.

Relative to the use of market surveys, the influence of size is indicated in Table 4. Sixty-seven per cent of large companies use market surveys, while only 47 per cent of small and 49 per cent of medium-sized companies use this device. The large companies use production capacity, share-of-market, correlation of company sales with some industry economic indicator, competitors' activities, promotion plans, financial capacity, and outside consultants more than medium-sized companies. The medium-sized companies use these latter techniques more than small companies. This observation is true generally of every technique included in Table 4 except past sales trends of company, salesmen's estimates, new-product plans, and sales department estimates. These data are indicative of the importance that larger

TABLE 4

PER CENT OF COMPANIES UTILIZING VARIOUS PROCEDURES IN DEVELOPING SALES FORECASTS AS REPORTED BY 389 COMPANIES BY INDUSTRY AND SIZE[a]

Procedures Utilized in Developing Sales Forecasts	Industry Classification						Total by Size			
	Manufacturing		*Public Utilities, Transportation*	*Wholesale and Retail*	*Finance and Insurance*	*Miscellaneous*				
	Durable	Nondurable					S	M	L	Total
Total Replies	186	131	40	16	10	6	118	150	121	389
	Percentage Distribution									
Past sales trends of company	78	82	93	94	60	17	80	81	79	80
Salesmen's estimates	52	37	25	6	20	17	39	43	40	41
Correlation of company sales with general economic indicators	61	56	70	69	40	50	51	55	75	60
New-product plans	73	66	18	19	20	–	60	54	68	60
Market surveys	55	62	48	31	20	17	47	49	67	54
Production capacity	54	51	33	–	–	50	28	51	60	47
Industry forecast and company's share of the potential	56	52	28	38	20	67	38	51	61	50
Sales department estimates	85	82	75	94	30	50	81	79	84	81
Survey of companies' executives opinions	45	42	53	56	40	33	44	43	48	45
Correlation of company sales with some industry economic indicator	34	30	43	38	10	17	20	33	44	33
Competitors' activities	22	28	5	19	20	17	19	17	30	22
Promotion plans	33	52	50	63	40	–	38	40	48	42
Financial capacity	30	15	15	25	10	–	16	19	31	22
Outside consultants	11	12	10	–	–	17	5	9	15	11

[a] Percentage analysis will not add to 100 per cent because more than one answer could be checked.

companies place on the use of forecasting. It probably also reflects the ability of the larger companies to develop and use a greater variety of forecasting procedures.

The low per cent of public utilities and transportation companies (5 per cent) using competitor's activities reflects the character of the industry. Public utilities usually do not have competition within a specified area.

Perhaps the most significant aspect of the data given in Table 4 is the high per cent of companies using the various forecasting techniques. This table clearly reflects the serious concern of management in developing reliable sales forecasts.

One of the primary purposes of the interviews and the mail questionnaires was to identify the principal planning practices employed. Both the long-range and short-range planning practices employed by the companies participating in the study have been presented. Survey findings[4] . . . reveal extensive use of short-range profit objectives and of an integrated plan of operation. The study bears out the generally accepted belief that the plan of operations is supported by detailed objectives in all areas of activity.

The data presented thus far clearly indicate that top management actively participates in and finally approves the plan of operations. The importance of the staff role of the controller and budget director in the coordination and scrutiny of plans is clear. The importance attached to participation by all levels of management in the planning process is also revealed in the development of objectives. The phase of the study devoted to planning clearly shows budgeting to be one of the principal tools used in developing and in communicating operational plans. The value of planning lies in the use made of plans. The degree of coordination actually achieved depends upon the ability of management to guide the activities toward the objectives included in the plans.

4 [Given in *ibid.*, Chap. 2–5—Ed.]

41

Dealing with Unreliable Forecasts[1]

William H. Newman

Administrators who wish to enjoy the benefits of planning can at least partially overcome the limits imposed by unreliable forecasting in two ways. First, they may make studied attempts to *improve* their *forecasts*. Thousands of companies subscribe to one or more forecasting services or employ some economic consultant to advise them. Many companies have made great strides in the compilation of data upon which to base predictions; for example, the automobile companies receive from week to week the sales, automobiles on hand, used car prices, and other market information from all of their dealers throughout the country. Several of the larger companies have a separate division whose sole mission is to prepare business forecasts. Of course, if the uncertainty relates to internal conditions, forecasting can often be improved by exercising closer control—as will be discussed in later paragraphs.

A second way to deal with unreliable predictions is to *detour* around the areas of greatest uncertainty. For instance, if securing an objective within a definite time is of sufficient importance, as it often is in military operations, alternative programs may be developed and started in operation; then, when it becomes apparent what the operating conditions actually will be, the most effective alternative is

[1] From William H. Newman, *Administrative Action* (Englewood Cliffs, N.J., Prentice-Hall, Inc., 1951). © 1951. Used by permission of the publishers.

followed to its conclusion. Obviously it would be more economical to follow only the one alternative finally used, and in most business enterprises the pressure for economy dictates that a single course be followed even though it is admittedly more risky.[2]

In a few situations unreliable forecasting may be counteracted by hedging; that is, by arranging operations so that losses in one area will be offset by gains in another, or vice versa. In a narrow sense, hedging is applicable only to protection against price changes for a limited number of commodities; the general principle, however, is sometimes applicable in other situations, such as offering two or more styles of products with the expectation that if one does not appeal to customers the other will, or locating plants both in the United States and abroad so as to be able to serve the foreign market regardless of the changes in foreign exchange rates.

The most common way to detour around unreliable forecasts is to separate those parts of the operation that will not be affected by the uncertain factor—volume, style, weather, or whatever it may be—and then make a tentative plan for the remaining segment in considerable detail. When the uncertain factor is finally settled, it is, relatively, a simple job to pull the various parts of the program together. It is quite possible, for example, to do the design work and develop engineering specifications for a product before it is practical to decide when, and perhaps in what plant, it will be produced. Many an advertising campaign has been mapped out, copy prepared, media selected, and all completed except for the timing, which depended upon factors difficult to appraise when the planning was initiated.

These means of overcoming unreliable forecasts are at best only partial remedies. Improved forecasting technique may push forward the time span of confidence, but the practical limits are soon reached for most enterprises. The detours around unpredictable elements are only applicable in certain circumstances, and even then apply only to part of the operations of the enterprise. Consequently, the inability to forecast accurately remains one of the factors that limit the period and the detail in which planning is practical.

[2] The danger of following a single though risky course may sometimes be partly offset by insurance. As a rule, however, insurance is practical only for catastrophes that are quite unlikely to occur, and hence are not covered in the regular planning.

42

Prudent-Manager Forecasting[1]

Gerald A. Busch

The practicality of long-range planning is a controversial question in industry today, and in the planning area itself one of the most disputed topics is long-range sales forecasting.

How, businessmen may argue, can a firm foretell the future with certainty? The answer, in the opinion of a growing number of executives, is that forecasts do not *need* to be certain. Then how, ask the critics, can long-range forecasting be of much help in planning? The answer is that long-range planning can be effective *without* dealing in certainties.

According to this thinking, it is enough if management can work with probabilities—with the likelihood of certain potential markets and certain market penetrations occurring under certain conditions, the chances of other conditions developing which will affect the forecasts, the probabilities of various alternative developments. In other words, management's aim should be to gain not a hard and fast outline of the future but an evaluation of probabilities on which it can make informed decisions.

This is the thinking that has animated an approach developed at Lockheed Aircraft Corporation. We have used the method, dubbed "prudent-manager forecasting," with some success for a number of years. We believe that many other companies could also use it with

[1] From *Harvard Business Review,* May–June 1961, pp. 57–64. Used by permission.

profit, especially firms selling products and services to markets characterized by relatively small numbers of large buyers and sellers.

To apply this technique, management (1) brings together a small group of seasoned specialists representing such functions as marketing research, marketing, finance, engineering, and administration, and (2) asks them to assume the role of decision-making managers in a customer firm that is evaluating one of the firm's products for purchase. In effect, this group of specialists assumes the position of the customer's management. In so doing, it attempts to evaluate prudently the facts available and to arrive at the preferred procurement decisions —preferred from the *customer's* point of view.

In a way, this is very much like the "role playing" used in management training, in that company people put on the hat of somebody else and assume that "somebody else's" point of view. The origin of the idea probably lies in the sociodrama that has been used with some success by clinical and group psychologists in ironing out family problems.

PREPARATORY STEPS

But prudent-manager forecasting cannot take place in a vacuum. It will not work unless it is preceded by a great deal of staff work. To be successful, those who are asked to serve as prudent managers must be provided with adequate, carefully organized information to draw on in the decision-making process. They should not be expected to make decisions without having the facts necessary for rational judgment. This is where the work of the market-research staff comes in.

Since the preliminary, analytical work is so vital to the successful application of the prudent-manager technique, I shall begin with a brief discussion of some of the major stages of preparation. Note that the steps described are actually those involved in the classic analytical approach to forecasting, and in themselves will provide a forecast that may be sufficient for certain purposes. However, when top management requires a longer-term sales forecast, the addition of the prudent-manager technique is far more than frosting on the cake. As we shall see, it adds substance, acumen, and depth of viewpoint to management's expectations.

The main steps in forecasting can be illustrated from Lockheed's experience. Executives of other companies should not find it difficult to visualize data from their own studies in place of the specifics shown here.

Ground Rules

It is typically necessary to narrow the scope of a study so that it will be compatible with the elapsed time, manpower, and other resource constraints surrounding the study. Accordingly, we start with certain ground rules which are tailored to the specific forecasting problem at hand. For example, in a study in 1959 having to do with our electronics sales outlook, we set forth three categories of ground rules and assumptions—economic, political, and technological (see Exhibit 1).

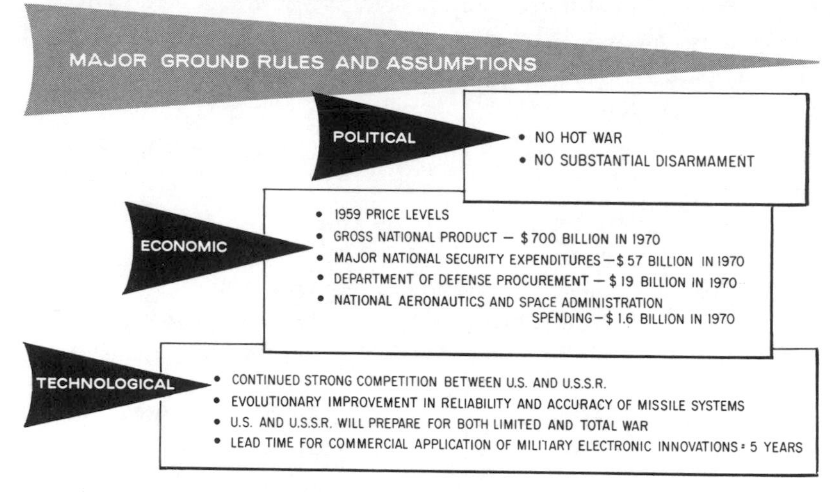

Exhibit 1. Major Ground Rules and Assumptions

In each case we drew on the best thinking of both line and staff executives. To illustrate from Exhibit 1:

1. *Some of the points were derived from previous studies focusing on the subject at hand.* The last four items in the "economic" group are a case in point. Here we dealt with projections of the gross national product, total major national security expenditures, and certain components of the latter—for instance, Department of Defense procurement and procurement by the National Aeronautics and Space Administration. These were all areas in our business warranting continued investigation. (In the case

of a company selling, let us say, bearings to large manufacturers of diesel engines, a similar statement might be made about projections of the number of end users, transportation trends, gross national product, and related factors.)

2. *Some assumptions were simply based on informed judgment.* For instance, our "political" assumptions were that there would be no hot war and no substantial disarmament. These appraisals may, of course, turn out to be completely wrong. And yet, we had to make assumptions to begin with, and these seemed like the most reasonable ones.

3. *Some assumptions were based on specialized technical knowledge.* Examples here are the "technological" estimates that the improvement in missiles would be evolutionary rather than revolutionary, and that a five-year lead time would be needed for commercial application. (In the case of the bearings manufacturer, comparable projections might concern the development of new materials affecting the use of bearings.)

You may quarrel with individual items in this list of ground rules; and, of course, we do not recommend them for other companies' programs. The point is that in long-term sales forecasting you generally cannot afford the luxury of a "womb to tomb" approach; so limiting ground rules are necessary. Management should make a practice of stating these *explicitly.*

Characteristics of Demand

The next stage requires a look at the historical characteristics of supply and demand in the markets that management is concerned with. Ordinarily this means studies not only of demand for different products but also of the buying behavior of different customers. At Lockheed, for example, we are deeply interested in such customers as the military services, other government agencies, and certain commercial buyers; and in the demand characteristics for aircraft, missiles, space vehicles, electronics, ground-handling equipment, and a host of other products.

Exhibit 2 shows a study we made last year in one area of importance to us—Air Force spending of its aircraft procurement budget. This analysis gives us a picture of how these funds were expended during the decade of the 1950's—for bombers, fighters, transports, trainers, and other types of aircraft, as well as for spare parts, ground-handling equipment, and modification. From this type of study we can make comparisons and correlations with concurrent operational, technological, political, and economic events, and then develop appropriate fore-

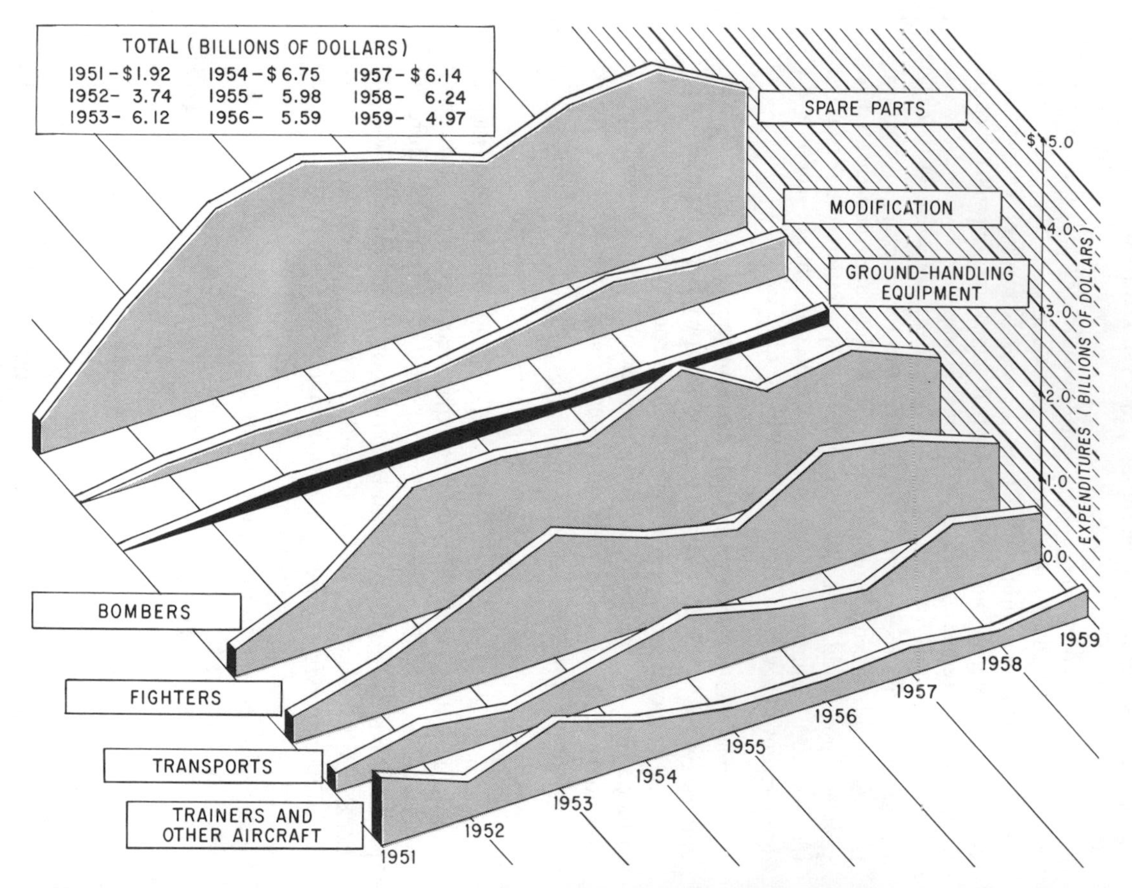

EXHIBIT 2. Historical Characteristics of Demand for Manned Aircraft by the U.S. Air Force

cast indicators. Personally, I am a great believer in the value to the forecaster of a good hard look at history.

Economic Indicators

Next comes the development of economic indicators. Correlation analysis may be very helpful here. A case in point is a Lockheed study of the relation between cargo transportation and gross national product. Exhibit 3 . . . portrays (1) the effective demand for cargo transportation service in the U.S. domestic market since 1929 as compared to (2) the gross national product in terms of constant dollars.

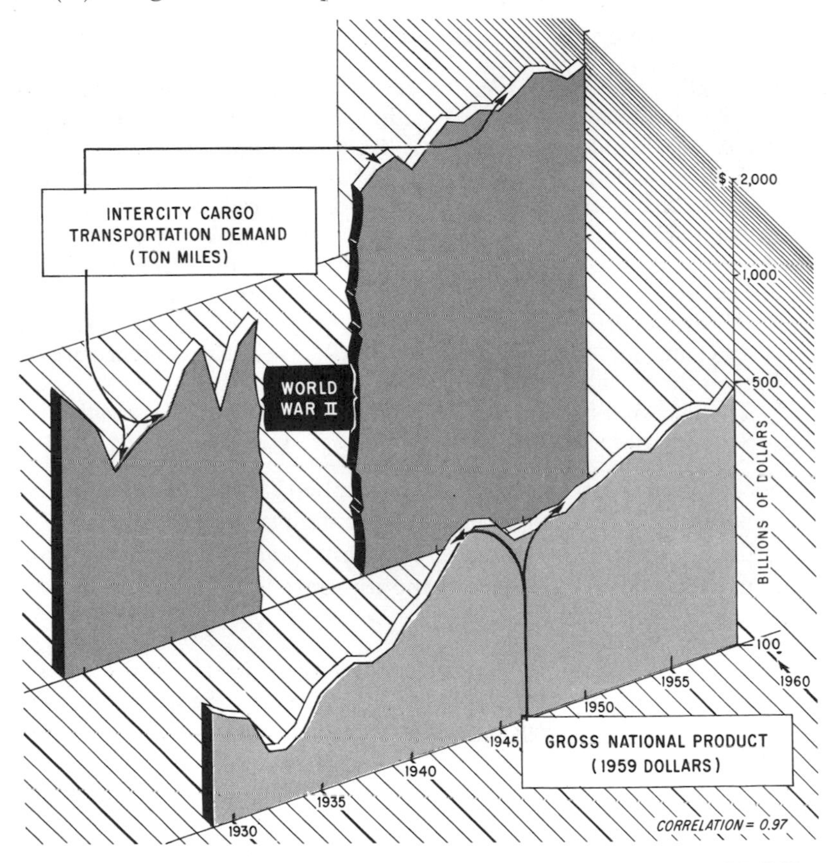

Exhibit 3. Correlation Between U.S. Domestic Cargo Transportation Demand and GNP

The correlation between these two series is 0.97—high enough to permit us to project the demand for cargo transportation on the basis of our forecasts of gross national product. We at Lockheed are interested in the total cargo picture, of course, because the total demand is relevant to the demand for air cargo, in which we are more directly concerned.

I should add that it is seldom that we get such a high correlation as in Exhibit 3. As forecasters know, the closer to the actual product an analysis gets, the lower is the correlation usually obtained.

The next step is to derive a parameterized market projection. In such an analysis the aim is to look at the effect on the market of changes of the key variables. Briefly, the procedure is as follows:

1. For the problem at hand, the forecasters select the significant variables (like consumer income, price and availability of service, system performance) and decide what the "most likely" future levels will be.
2. Then, assuming that these "most likely" levels will turn out to be correct, they make an estimate of demand for the product or service.
3. But they must make allowances for other possibilities; the "most likely" levels may not in fact be realized. Therefore, they make projections of demand based on other levels that may reasonably occur.
4. When they have a range of demand or "output" figures correlated with different "input" levels for one variable, they take another variable and repeat the process.
5. The final result is a matrix of projections showing how sensitive the forecast is to various changes in each of the input variables.

Such a "sensitivity analysis," as it is called, is valuable to the prudent managers when, subsequently, they deliberate over the forecast. It is likely to show, for instance, that certain variables are more important to watch than others. Let me illustrate again from the experience of Lockheed:

Exhibit 4 . . . shows a "parameterized" forecast made a few years ago. At the left is the historical trend in the distribution of the demand for air, rail, and bus transportation in the United States. At the right are shown five alternative projections:

• In Projection A all of the inputs are at their "most likely" projected levels.

• Projection B shows what demand would look like if we held all other inputs constant, but restricted the availability of air coach service to no more than what it was in 1953.

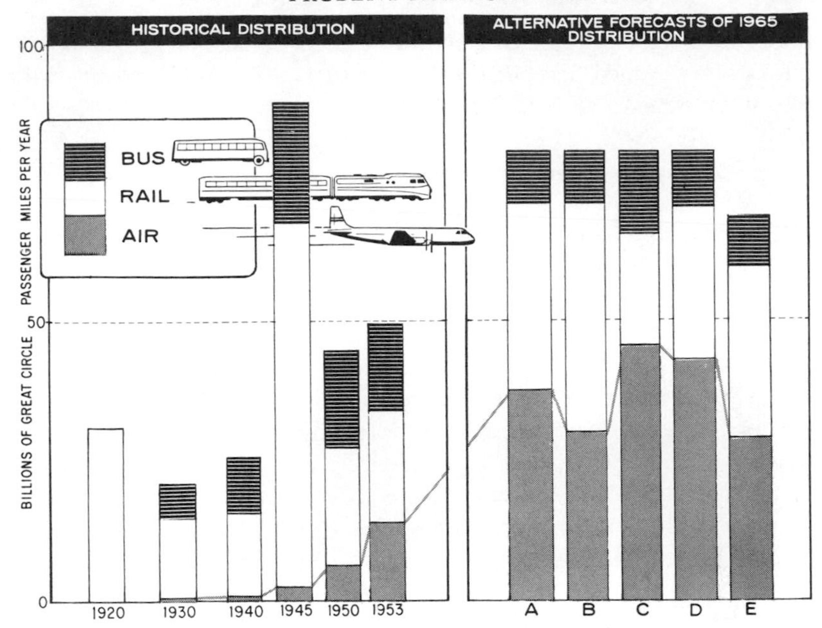

EXHIBIT 4. Distribution of Demand for Bus, Rail, and Air Transportation

- In Projection C we have restricted the performance of the surface systems—bus and rail—to their 1953 levels.
- In Projection D we have increased the unit valuations on the time of the traveler by 50 per cent over the projected levels.
- And in Projection E we show what the effect on the picture is in the event that the rate of expansion of the economy of the United States should turn out to be somewhat less than our other studies suggest.

Thus we see at a glance how variations in the input variables will affect the total demand for air passenger transportation in 1965. Incidentally, the staff did not make firm conclusions or choices among the several situations. We concluded that the demand for airline transportation would increase between threefold and fivefold from 1953 to the early 1970's and that, *assuming all inputs were at their "most likely" projected levels,* the potential air transportation demand would be about 57 billion great-circle passenger miles per year at that latter time. But we pointed out that this conclusion was highly sensitive to two of the inputs—(1) the projected expansion of the U.S. economy, and (2) the projected performance of the surface transportation systems. (Note that air transport is highest in Projection C, where it is assumed that performance of surface transport systems will stay at the same level as in 1953.)

COMPARISONS WITH COMPETITORS

The next step is to take an objective look at the company's product or service in comparison with its competition. It is important to select those characteristics for comparison which are of particular concern to the *potential buyer.* To illustrate, Exhibit 5 shows a few of the characteristics of competing transport-type aircraft of concern to Lockheed's customers. Here we see comparative data on speed performance, pay-load range performance, unit operating cost performance, and return on investment. With comparative data such as these, the prudent managers can subsequently make judgments as to the relative importance in the eyes of the customer of, say, differences in block speed and return on invested capital.

ROUNDING OUT THE FORECAST

Now, with all this work done, the market research staff is able to make a forecast of sales of the Lockheed product—again preferably in parameterized form. This it does on a customer-by-customer basis, if feasible. The procedure is as follows:

1. The major customer categories are separately analyzed. For instance, in making a study of the sales outlook for a certain type of electronic end equipment, the Lockheed staff looked at prospective sales to the government, including the Air Force, Navy, Army, and NASA, and to the nongovernment agencies.
2. Within each customer category, the sales in each application are separately forecast, as in Exhibit 6. (To simplify this chart, I have shown the data in nonparameterized form.)
3. The staff puts all of the individual forecasts together and comes up with an aggregate sales forecast.
4. The aggregate figure is subjected to a test of reasonableness. After adding up all the individual forecasts, the staff asks itself, "Does the resulting total appear reasonable? Is it in consonance with our traditional percentage of the market? Does it appear too pessimistic or too optimistic? Is too much weight given to some factors and too little to others?" Only after the forecast has been subjected to questions like these and, if necessary, revised, is the stage set for the prudent managers.

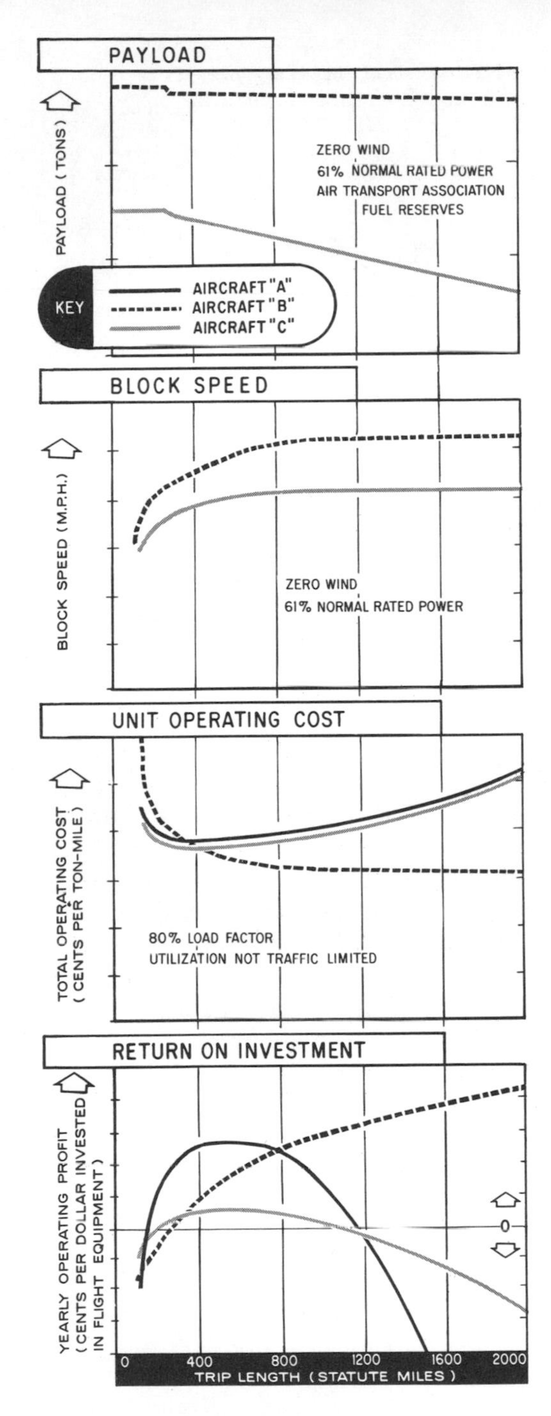

EXHIBIT 5. Comparative Performance Characteristics of Cargo Transport Aircraft

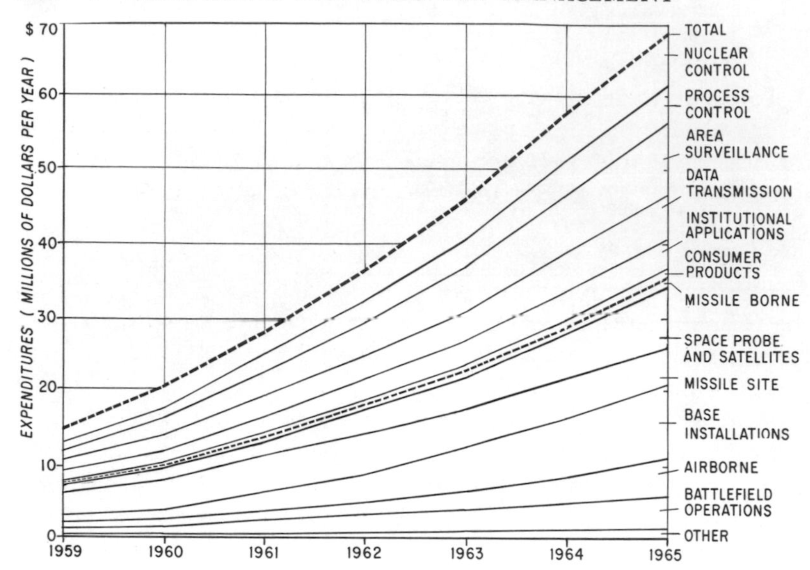

EXHIBIT 6. Estimated Procurement of an Item of Electronic End Equipment for Different Applications

MORE REALISTIC JUDGMENTS

All of the steps and techniques I have described up to now are part of the staff work of forecasting in many companies. At Lockheed, some details may be changed or emphasized more in anticipation of what comes later, but in the main the type of work just outlined is essential to any intelligent type of forecasting, and even by itself would lay the groundwork for informed managerial decisions.

But it does have the disadvantage of inbreeding. It is done by staff people like myself who sometimes may become bemused with figures and, in their concentration on the tools and techniques of their craft, lose contact with the reality with which they should be dealing and which, in effect, they are trying to forecast.

Therefore, to reintroduce this factor of outside reality and to help assure that our sales forecast will give service to the commanding importance of the customer's point of view, we like to expose the staff analysis to a balanced group made up predominantly of non-market-research people, and get their evaluation. This brings us to the essence of the prudent-manager approach.

ORGANIZING THE CONFERENCE

To begin, there is the question of how these non-market-research people should be organized. Our experience at Lockheed indicates that it is a good idea to try to make up a conference from a representative group, but we have found it essential to keep the number of participants small.

So far as it is practical to do so, we use Lockheed people. We will usually include a representative from finance who knows firsthand the financial situation of our customers, one or two representatives from marketing who are very knowledgeable of the market and the customers in question, and one or two managers from the technical side of the house who have a detailed knowledge of the product's performance. Occasionally, we include an outside consultant—an economist from a university, perhaps, or a business consultant. And we always include a senior market research staff member who is familiar with all of the preparatory work done by the staff.

In general, the participants should be mature, seasoned in their areas of specialization, objective in their approach to problems, and able to both give and take in the negotiating process.

We have found that it is desirable, prior to the first get-together of the prudent managers, to provide each man with copies of the preliminary staff reports in order that he may do some "homework" on the subject beforehand.

At the first formal meeting, the prudent managers are briefed in detail on the staff work. Sometimes we devote as much as one day to this briefing, so that the participants will know in detail how each input was developed, how the variables were integrated, and so forth. From there on, the group is on its own. I stress the importance of adequately briefing the prudent managers—for if this is not done well, there is the distinct danger that the group will resort to that insidious technique which I call "feet-on-the-deskmanship."

REACHING CONCLUSIONS

Now let us turn to the deliberative process itself. For the sake of being specific, let us suppose that the managers are considering the problem of arriving at a long-term sales forecast for a proposed new passenger transport airplane. How do they go about making their judgments?

To begin with, they put themselves in the place of each major potential customer in turn, starting with the larger airlines and later dealing with relatively homogeneous groups of small airlines. In this position, and generally accepting the analytical work done by the staff as "gospel," they carefully review the judgments made by the staff—and typically interject others which the staff may have overlooked.

To be more specific still, let us suppose that the customer under consideration is Air France, a major foreign airline. Each participant figuratively stands in the shoes of the manager of Air France and attempts to answer questions such as these:

- What new aircraft procurement policy must I pursue in order that my airline will remain competitive and retain or improve its standing in the market over the next decade?
- How does the proposed new Lockheed plane stack up aganst competitive offerings?
- Will I be able to finance my new aircraft?
- How many planes should I buy, say, in 1965?
- What will be my needs over short-haul routes, long-haul routes, and so on?
- How much money can I make with the Lockheed aircraft as compared to what I can make with competitive planes?
- What about return on investment?
- What about operations into marginal airports?

In pursuing this approach, each participant tries to appraise dispassionately the Lockheed product vis-à-vis competing products in each customer's application. The prudent managers must be hardheaded about this—just as hardheaded, we hope, as they would be if they were charged with the responsibility of actually running the company they are considering. Very often they know something about the personal failings and strengths, the preferences and prejudices, of the men whose positions they are assuming. For example, Mr. A likes pod-mounted engines, while Mr. B has been publicly thumping the drums for high-density coach configurations. All these items are taken into account as they argue out and discuss the probable buy the customer will make.

Next, the prudent managers work out a forecast of that customer's likely purchases of the Lockheed airplane. Then, having settled on what they think is the most probable purchase of one customer, they pass on to another and start the whole process over again.

When they have covered the whole field of potential customers, they total the probable purchases and come up with an aggregate forecast. This result is then compared with the staff results and, as in the staff procedure, is subjected to the general test of reasonableness.

The result, we think, gives a closer approximation to what may in fact actually happen than can mere staff work alone.

TESTS OF EFFECTIVENESS

How effective prudent-manager sessions are depends in part, of course, on the thoroughness of the staff work done in preparation for them, for a lot of the managers' thinking is based on this work. But effectiveness also depends on how well the talents and viewpoints represented mix together.

Generally speaking, the level of competence increases as the organizational level of the members of the team increases, because the men higher in the organization are generally those with the greatest knowledge and acumen, and the broadest point of view. But there are drawbacks to inviting men who sit too high in the organization. For one thing, they may not find it possible to stay with the group because of other demands on their time. For another, a vice-president sitting with men two levels below may unknowingly tend to constrain valuable give-and-take discussion.

Beyond this, we have found that there are some people who have a natural talent for this sort of discussion. They have the imagination to put themselves in someone else's place, the ability to judge dispassionately and realistically, and the breadth to consider all phases of the problem. Generally speaking, we have found that people in senior staff jobs in the company measure up best in this respect.

CONCLUSION

To sum up, certain lessons based on experience in using the prudent-manager techniques should be emphasized.

In organizing a conference, these are the most important points for management to remember:

1. Keep the number of participants small.
2. Include a balanced representation of technical specialities. Bring in:

- Selected "in-house" specialists.
- A senior market research staff analyst.
- An occasional outside consultant, as needed.

3. Give the participants a detailed briefing on the background and results of the staff study.

To make the deliberative process a success, each prudent manager should:

1. Assume the position of decision-making executives in the customer firm
2. Dispassionately appraise the performance of competing products that the customer firm might consider buying
3. Make a forecast of the purchasers that he thinks the customer will make
4. When the individual forecasts are pulled together into an aggregate forecast, join with the other participants in testing its reasonableness

Keep in mind throughout all this that prudent-manager sessions are not a substitute for sound staff forecasting; they are merely a refinement on it. Certainly they should never be used instead of such staff work. Management should also be forewarned that the technique is relatively costly—particularly in the early years of its application. As a rule, at Lockheed, we "roll over" our important long-term forecasts every year or two. The time and effort required in the second and subsequent passes is significantly less than in the original forecast.

I do not suggest that prudent-manager sessions are the answer to all forecasting problems or, indeed, that they should even be applied to all such problems. But I do suggest that, where the sales forecast is of particular importance to top management in its long-range planning, and where objectivity and realism are primary goals, this technique may be a useful addition to present forecasting methods. There is every reason to believe that the benefits gained at Lockheed can be duplicated at many other companies.

43

Planning for Total Financial Requirements[1]

Ernest H. Walker
and
William H. Baughn

There are four key questions that underlie the over-all financial plan:

1. What is the total amount of assets to be employed?
2. When will various financial requirements materialize?
3. How long will the requirements continue?
4. What will be the sources for funds to acquire assets?

The total volume of resources committed to a given business enterprise is the result of judgment, chance, and availability of funds. Business expansions and contractions involving changes in the level of assets employed may come from carefully conceived plans of management or from external forces that bring about changes not contemplated by management. In other cases, management may wish to expand but may be limited by lack of available capital.

Insofar as the decisions to employ additional resources in the business are made by plan and not by chance, it is recognized that such plans are the responsibility of top management. Even though the success of a financial plan depends upon basic decisions on the use of funds, the finance officer may have little to say in these basic decisions. Under such circumstances he is expected to provide the necessary funds to cover needs controlled by others. Yet the earning power of total

[1] From *Financial Planning and Policy* (New York, Harper & Row, 1961), pp. 88–113. Used by permission.

resources employed will determine the finance officer's success in securing funds. No financial plan is a good one unless it is built upon a solid foundation of carefully planned use of funds. Business firms today realize that the net productivity of assets acquired must be matched against total costs of funds used to secure the assets. In this matching process the finance officer should play a major role.

Securing the proper amount of funds at exactly the time given assets are to be acquired is not easy. It may be desirable to anticipate needs and hold excess funds in liquid form even for relatively long periods. There are several factors which might explain the holding of idle (from the standpoint of the business) funds. If expansion occurs in large units and is financed from internal sources, excess funds must be held for long periods. Second, anticipation of changes in the availability and costs of funds from outside sources may result in a firm's securing funds prior to the time they are to be used. Third, economies from the use of large security issues rather than numerous smaller ones will result in excess funds until the resources can be properly employed. Fourth, delays in carrying out expansion plans often result in unanticipated excesses. Although it will not be possible to time sources and uses of funds precisely, a good financial plan calls for an evaluation of the costs of holding funds idle as compared to the advantages gained. Proper timing is an important element in the financial plan.

Illustrations[2] of the recognition of the costs of idle funds are found in the extensive use of short- and intermediate-term credit to carry expansion plans up to a certain point before securing longer-term funds. Since long-term funds may be secured in large blocks, the firm finds it advantageous to have its planned expansion well under way before going to the market.

Essential also to financial management is a careful matching of source of funds with the length of time the funds will be needed.

[2] When long-term issues are announced in the financial press, it is very common for the purpose of the issue to be explained in terms of replenishing working capital that has been reduced by capital expenditure programs in progress. Two such cases are described in the news story "Continental Can in a Big Offering," *New York Times*, September 28, 1960, p. 51C. In reference to the $30 million Continental Can offering, the article said: "Proceeds from the debentures . . . will be used to replenish working capital, which has been reduced by the company's capital expenditure program. These outlays amounted to $89,000,000 last year and $49,000,000 in the first six months of this year." In regard to a $12 million issues by Indianapolis Power, it stated: "Proceeds will be used to repay bank loans and for construction."

Payout periods vary with the type of asset acquired. Financing should be commensurate with that period. Permanent capital needs should be financed in appropriate ways, but generally not on a short-term basis. Conversely, temporary financial requirements should not be met with long-term inflexible contracts. The estimate of the length of time for which given funds will be needed will influence the conditions under which the funds are acquired.

The exact type of financing to be used will be governed by a large number of factors, to be discussed below. The number of variables that enter the decision will be determined by a combination of internal and external factors. In the final analysis, the choice will be based upon conflicting evidence. Constantly changing techniques of finance and varying business practices mean that the right answer today may not apply tomorrow.

OBJECTIVES OF THE FINANCIAL PLAN

In a private enterprise all decisions are weighed in terms of their effect upon the net return to the owners of the business. Financial decisions are no different in this respect. The over-all criterion for judging the soundness of a financial plan is its effect upon net profit. However, adequate consideration must be given to future as well as current profits. For this reason, the expected return from the increased resources must be balanced against all foreseeable costs—direct and indirect. The general objectives of the over-all financial plan are:

1. To provide adequate funds to enable the firm to employ resources up to the point where expected returns cover costs of funds, plus a profit necessary to justify the assumption of increased risks
2. To minimize the cost of funds by securing funds under the most advantageous circumstances commensurate with the risks owners are willing to assume
3. To balance costs with risks, in order to protect owners from the hazards of loss of control or loss of the business
4. To provide a flexible financial plan which will enable the firm to adapt its financial structure to changing conditions
5. To keep the financial plan as simple as is consistent with the other objectives

These general objectives provide the criteria upon which financial decisions must be weighed. Each of the objectives is important in its own way. Yet in the decision-making process equal weight cannot be given to all criteria. Under some circumstances certain of these criteria will be much more important than others and will govern. But experience has shown that none of these general considerations must be ignored. Continuous evaluation of the financial plan is necessary to insure a proper balance among these major objectives.

VARIABLE DETERMINANTS OF THE FINANCIAL PLAN

A financial plan is good or bad depending upon how it fits specific circumstances. No plan is perfect, and few can be considered to have been built upon an accurate evaluation of all variables involved. Many variables affect the applicability of a given financial solution to a given problem. These factors influence both the firm's ability to employ resources profitably and its ability to secure funds under various arrangements.

It is the number of variables, their subjective nature, and the changing functional relationship among them that present the challenges in financial management. No finance officer is ever certain that he has given proper weight to each of these determinants. Only with a grasp of the problem that comes from experience and a command of available analytical tools can these variables be assessed adequately.

Industry Characteristics

Both the need for funds and the logic with which resources can be committed to the enterprise will be affected by certain basic industrial characteristics. In addition, the terms under which investors will furnish capital will be influenced by the same industry characteristics. The degree of risk associated with financial decisions is related to the nature of the industry.

Among the characteristics of the industry most influential in financial matters are: (1) stability of both business volume and earnings rates, (2) the earnings rate in relationship to assets employed and sales, (3) growth factors, including degree of maturity of the industry, (4) business practices within the industry, including the nature of competition, (5) seasonality, and (6) structure of assets.

Variations in the stability of business volume (as measured by both physical output and sales), as compared to earnings, are shown in Figure 1 for three broad industry groups. Industry A (electric utilities), as might be expected, exhibits a remarkable degree of stability around a smooth upward trend. Physical output, sales, and earnings follow almost exactly the same upward trend. Under such conditions, financial planning can be more definite than in other cases.

Both Industry B (chemicals) and Industry C (paper) show considerable more stability in business volume than in earnings. Thus, their need for financial resources does not vary so much as the profit base upon which funds must be secured. In the chemical industry there has been a tendency in the last thirteen years for average prices to decline, as evidenced by the fact that the sales line falls below the index of physical output. The reverse is true for the paper industry—sales revenue has risen faster than production. The three industries in Figure 1 were selected at random to illustrate these basic industry characteristics. Each industry group has its own peculiar pattern which varies itself with time.

Three widely varying growth patterns are shown in Figure 2 for three separate industries. One industry (airlines) has enjoyed almost uninterrupted growth, with a sharp upward trend since 1936. A second industry (wheat flour) expanded slowly from 1936 to 1947, but has declined since that time from its peak output. Because of the demand characteristics of flour, it is not expected that the industry will show any significant growth. A majority of the expansion in output during the period 1945 to 1948 was due to foreign aid programs. Industry C (cement) has enjoyed a substantial growth since the end of World War II, and a pattern of growth that is unusually stable for such a product.

Financial planning for Industry A would be very different from that for Industries B and C. Firms in industries with sustained rapid growth have to use every available financial tool to provide enough capital to cover this rapid expansion. In Industry C the slower expansion rate does not create the same pressure for new funds, and in Industry B financial planning centers around maintenance of capacity and the securing of equipment to increase efficiency.

An industry composed of aggressive competitors will cause the firms to face continual financial problems associated with modernization, research costs, and new marketing methods. Less aggressive competition

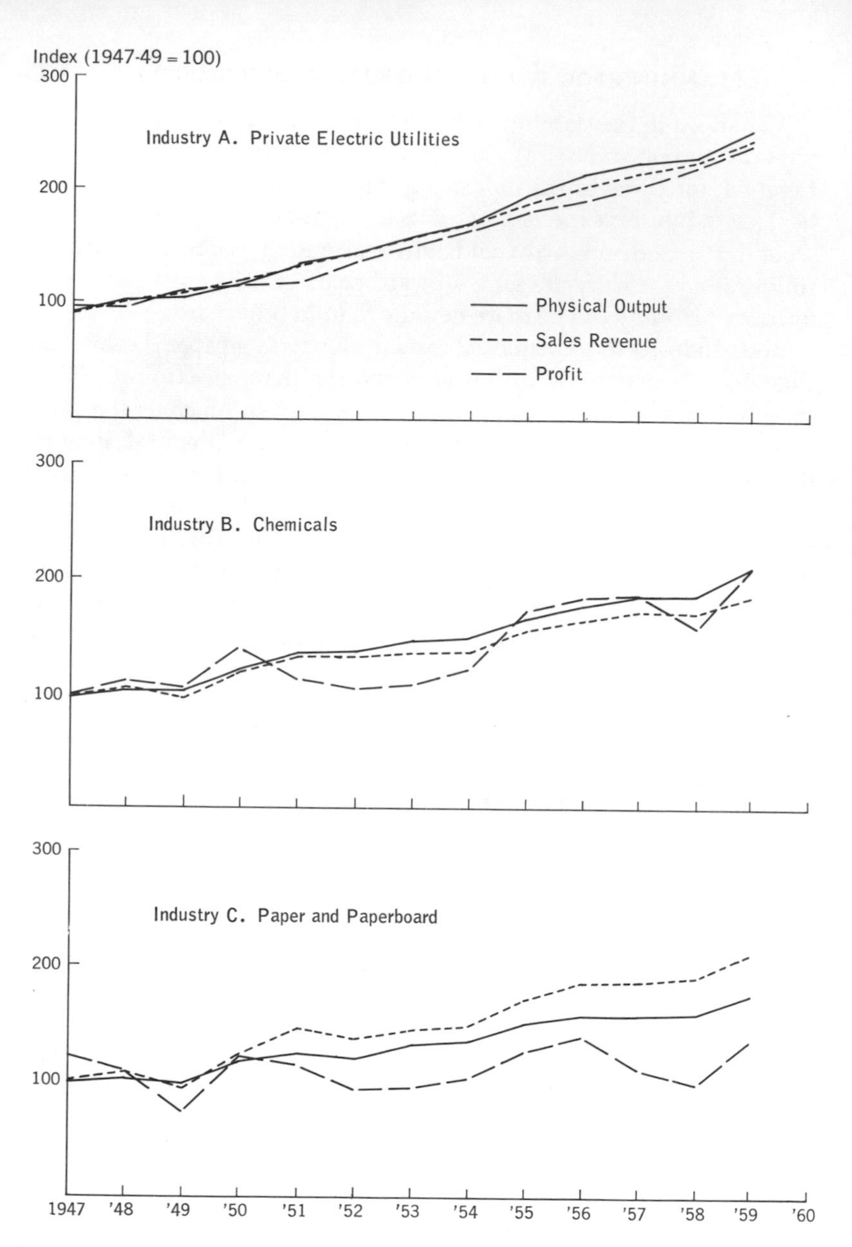

FIG. 1. A Comparison of Stability of Physical Output, Sales Revenue, and Profit for Three Broad Industry Groups

SOURCE: 1957 biennial edition of *Business Statistics* and subsequent issues of *Survey of Current Business,* both published by the U.S. Department of Commerce.

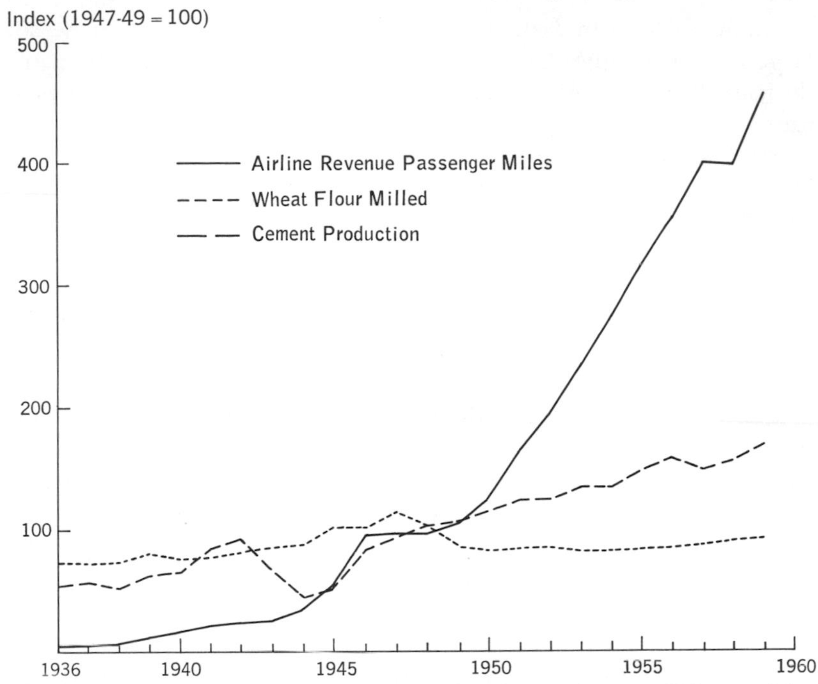

FIG. 2. Growth Patterns of Three Broad Industry Groups (Measured by Physical Output)

SOURCE: 1957 biennial edition of *Business Statistics* and subsequent issues of *Survey of Current Business,* both published by the U.S. Department of Commerce.

will allow the firms to follow established products and methods and worry less about obsolescence. Seasonality is a basic determinant of working capital management. The structure of assets will affect terms under which funds can be secured and the length of time that funds must be committed to various uses.

STATUS OF THE FIRM

Although the industry pattern will influence the financial plans of firms within the industry, it is the status of the specific firm that will determine both what is a desirable financial plan and also whether it is possible to carry out the plan. Since industry characteristics are averages of firm characteristics, it is obvious that an individual firm may fall above or below the industry average in terms of either plus or minus factors. In fact, dispersion within an industry may be so large as to make the use of industry data meaningless. In other industries, firm data may deviate only slightly from the industry picture.

Most of the factors enumerated above that affect financing for the industry hold true for the firm. Stability of sales and earnings, growth patterns, and seasonality become more meaningful when applied to the firm. These are basic determinants of the needs for funds and the willingness of investors to supply those funds. But before a finance officer assumes that his firm is capable of carrying the same debt structure as the industry average, he should analyze his firm in relationship to his industry. . . . Since many modern firms cut across industry lines and market a variety of products, the firm's stability may be different from that of the industry.

Other firm characteristics are also important to its financial management. Age, size, and geographical coverage are very influential. It is recognized that new businesses encounter special financial problems during the period when the success of the venture is not sufficiently apparent to attract investors. Size alone, not related to age, will be a major factor in the firm's ability to tap certain sources of funds. Even a new business that starts with large-scale operations will have financial advantages over a smaller firm of the same age. Geographical coverage, in terms of market area or ownership of physical assets, may determine the number of financial institutions available to the firm. It is well known that banks and other financial institutions prefer to deal with businesses in their geographical area.

Less objective considerations will also influence the ability of a firm to solve its financial problems advantageously. These include:

1. *The past record of the firm, including its reputation within the industry and its credit standing.* Blotches on a firm's credit record or a reputation for taking advantages of contractual loopholes will give the finance officer substantial trouble when he seeks funds.

2. *Management's reputation as to experience, training, and aggressiveness.* A firm may have a good credit rating, but if it has not provided for proper management succession, it may experience difficulty in securing long-term funds.

3. *Management's attitudes toward various financial matters.* Prejudice and ignorance on the part of top management often eliminate desirable alternatives to the finance officer. A board of directors or

president who refuse to understand and accept desirable changes in financial practice can reduce earnings just as if they had refused to market new products.

Risks to Be Assumed

Inherent in any financial plan other than one based entirely upon owners' funds is some degree of risk of losing the business to creditors or being forced into liquidation. Yet practically every business in operation today owes money. The commonly accepted practice of financing a part of current requirements through debt does not carry over as extensively into long-term requirements. There are considerable differences among industries and firms within an industry in risk assumption by the use of debt capital. Later in this chapter the question of equity versus debt financing is discussed in detail. It is sufficient to say here that there is no precise answer to what is the proper ratio. In the final analysis, it will be the attitude with respect to risk of the top decision-making authority in the business. Inevitably, the actual decision is a compromise between cost considerations and the degree of risk.

Also basic to financial management is another aspect of risk. Liquidity is expensive from the standpoint of use of funds. Insufficient liquidity may be more expensive if it results in financial embarrassment. Some firms, because of their internal controls, careful planning, and efficiency, can operate at a lower liquidity level than others and with no greater risk. However, for any firm the reduction of liquidity increases financial risks. This again is a decision of the firm, either by plan or by indifference, and reflects the attitude of management toward risk assumption.

Future Growth Plans of the Firm

Most business firms expect to grow larger than they are. It is easy to say that a firm should know the direction in which it would like to develop and plan for it. Similarly, one often hears the statement that a firm should know when to stop expanding. But from a practical point of view neither matter is easy to resolve. There is no simple answer to the question of how far a firm should plan its total commitments.

At any one time a business does have some concept of both its ability to expand and its plans to do so. Even if the plans are mere hopes which have taken no definite form, the current financial plan should take those ideas into account. If no discussions have been held by management concerning long-run plans, the finance officer often can ascertain future patterns from past developments. Making current financial decisions with the view of being able to provide for tomorrow's growth is fundamental to effective financial management.

Regularity and Magnitude of External Capital Requirements

Adjustments to various size levels of operation may be made in small segments or in large blocks. If expansion is continual and divisible into relatively small units, and if this expansion is to be financed predominantly from external sources, proper financial management will require considerable interim financing. Short-term funds will be used for long-term needs and be funded in lumps into more permanent capital in order to reduce the number of times the firm goes to the financial market. On the other hand, if expansion is in big units with long periods in between, it will be easier to match the securing of funds with use of funds. A workable capital structure is the responsibility of the finance officer. Demands for expansion funds are generated elsewhere in the business. The ease with which needs can be met without the sacrifice of logic in the capital structure will be affected by the timing of expansion requirements.

Privacy of Company Data

The attitude of management toward making public company operational and financial data will help determine sources of funds. Securing short-term credit usually requires the submission of some financial data, and the private placement of longer-term securities is accompanied by statements. However, in these cases only those granting the credit are informed of the firm's status. Until a company is ready to make its statements available to the public, it is denied access to public sources of funds.

Availability of Alternative Sources of Funds

A very practical determinant of a financial plan is the number and type of potential supplies of funds. The market structure for funds, immobility of capital, imperfect knowledge on the part of finance officers, and other factors may prevent a firm from obtaining capital under the most preferred arrangements. Many financial institutions are regional or local in character and do not enter other markets. The larger the firm and the sounder its financial record, the greater will be the number of alternative sources, and the easier the finance officer will be able to secure his desired financial structure.

Government Regulations Affecting Finance

Government regulations may affect financial policy both directly and indirectly. Monetary and fiscal policy influence both availability and costs of funds, and will be a major factor in the relative costs of debt and equity capital. In addition, sharp shifts in monetary policy result in equally sudden changes in interest rates. Since the finance officer cannot forecast these changes accurately over long periods, the probability of rate-level fluctuations means that flexibility must be a major objective of financial policy.

Direct government regulation in business finance is limited in its influence upon financial management. Except for the public utility field and in the areas of corporate reorganization, these regulations pertain to protecting the investor against false and misleading information. These regulations do not appear to interfere with sound financing policy or handicap legitimate enterprises. On the contrary, a good case can be made that regulations have actually facilitated corporation finance by instilling confidence in the investing public concerning securities.

Since 1935 public utility financing has been specifically under the control of the Securities and Exchange Commission. Objectionable practices associated with the use of multiple holding companies led to this control. The extent to which the restriction of the financial policies of utilities is detrimental to stockholders in the long run is a matter of personal judgment. Similarly, certain abuses which benefited insiders at the expense of legitimate investors and practices in the reorganization of distressed corporations have resulted in specific regulations with better protection for the public.

TOTAL CAPITAL REQUIREMENTS

No precise objective standards can be used to measure capital adequacy. In specific cases one can conclude that a firm has surplus funds committed to the business, and in other cases it is obvious that, for the given level of business, the firm needs additional capital. Between the two extremes, conclusions as to the adequacy of firm capital will depend upon assumptions made. There is no way to remove subjective considerations from this aspect of financial policy.

The terms *capital, capital structure,* and *capitalization* are used differently by various writers on business finance. In order not to add further confusion to the usage, the definitions which appear to be the most logical and most common will be accepted in this text.

The *capital* of a business firm refer to total funds committed to the business, that is, total assets. Residual claims to business assets will be referred to as *ownership capital* or *common stock equity. Capital structure* is synonymous with total capital, except that this term refers to the make-up of the credit side of the balance sheet, or the division of claims among trade creditors, bank creditors, bondholders, stockholders, etc. The counterpart of capital structure for the debit side of the balance sheet is the *asset structure.* Specific segments of the assets and liabilities will be referred to by name, such as *current assets, long-term debt,* or *capital stock.* These latter two items when used together will be called *long-term capital,* and not capitalization. The use of *capitalization* to refer only to long-term debt and capital stock is erroneous and infers that short-term creditors do not constitute suppliers of capital. In reality, total capital is furnished by short-term creditors, long-term creditors, and owners.

Undercapitalization versus Overcapitalization

The question of whether a business is over- or undercapitalized has been discussed from many angles. Some of the confusion has been due to use of conflicting terminology, and some to divergent approaches to the question. A firm is said to be overcapitalized when it has trouble earning enough to pay an adequate return on capital stock, and undercapitalized when the rate of profit is too high.

To correct overcapitalization in this instance presumably would involve a mere reduction in the stated amount of capital stock, so that owners would receive a higher return upon the reduced value. (It is difficult to see how the owners benefit from this action.) Certainly, the correcting of such an "over-capitalization" would *not* involve taking assets out of the business; conversely, undercapitalization would be corrected by a write-up of equity capital, so that the return, expressed as a percentage, would be more modest. (Still nothing has been accomplished!) Proper corrective action would *not* be to have additional assets acquired, whether needed or not, to reduce the average return on assets employed to a lower level.

The above use of over- and undercapitalization relates to the relationships between earnings and stated capital, and not to whether the firm has adequate capital. The return on stock is not only related to adequacy of capital, but also to (1) the profitability of the business venture (as a result of luck, good management, or other factors), and (2) the conditions under which the stock is acquired. If the stock has been "watered" so that some owners contributed assets and others did not, the average return per share will be less than if all had contributed assets that were profitably employed. However, this question has little to do with whether or not the firm needs more capital. This use of overcapitalization really refers to an improper valuation of assets offset with enough net worth to equate the two sides of the balance sheet.

The real value of net worth is the earning power of the business. Total earnings divided by the number of shares of stock is a much more important determinant of the value per share of stock than is stated net worth divided by the number of shares. A firm with total common stock equity of $250,000 divided among 25,000 shares earning only 10¢ per share might explain its situation in one of several ways. (1) The stock may have been issued 10,000 shares to promoters, with an inflated asset structure to compensate, and 15,000 shares sold for $150,000. (2) All 25,000 shares may have been sold at $10 per share, but in spite of the fact that the stock was not "watered," the business is still not profitable. (3) All 25,000 shares may have been sold for $1 per share, and subsequent profitable operations have resulted in retained earnings which increased the equity to $250,000, but in recent years operations have not been profitable. The stock of the company is selling for $1 per share.

From the standpoint of the owners, does it make any real difference which of the above explanations is true? Under the general definition the company is "overcapitalized." Yet with an additional $100,000 of capital the firm might take advantage of new opportunities that would expand earnings and stock value. In such a case an "overcapitalized" company's major trouble is that it is short of capital.

Because of this confusion, perhaps the term *overcapitalization* should be dropped completely and more clear-cut terms used. When assets are overvalued according to reasonable standards, the situation should be called *inflated asset structure;* if a firm needs additional funds, it can be said to be *short of capital;* and if it has excess funds not needed for the business, it can be said to have *surplus capital.*

Since funds employed cannot be adjusted constantly to the need of the business, total firm capital (or assets) will be based upon average needs for a given period. Total requirements of the business, as measured by the volume of assets that can be employed at a profit, then become a composite management decision based upon expectations. As business opportunity changes, the finance officer should adjust capital to needs, with the shorter-term adjustments being made by variations in debt, rather than ownership, capital. Assets should be acquired when expected return exceeds costs of funds by a margin to compensate for the degree of risk involved.

Proper financial management begins with the basic business decisions as to what assets will be acquired and when. The control of use of funds falls to all decision-making units in the firm. Common policies in all segments of the business as to the expected rate of return on acquired assets is fundamental to good financial planning. Total financial requirements, then, are the sum of each type of need, properly considered and based upon the most accurate estimate of productivity that can be made.

A firm has the "right" amount of capital when all of its assets are effectively employed and, under given conditions and expectations, no additional assets could be used in the operation that could be expected to increase profit sufficiently to compensate for added risk. Assets employed, in this sense, include necessary liquidity in cash and other forms to carry out transactions and act as a shock absorber for unanticipated variations in revenue and costs. Too little capital exists when the firm is unable, by manipulation of its assets, to secure the necessary funds to function most profitably. Excess capital is committed to the business when unnecessary liquidity exists, or when the firm has excess investments in assets not needed in the business now or in the future.

Thus the determinants of capital requirements are the same factors which determine business size and nature of operations. These factors may be divided into two broad groups, one group of factors being those related to the nature of the enterprise, and the other group those related to the particular firm's management.

1. Factors related to the nature of the enterprise
   a. Industry stability
   b. Operating characteristics of the industry
      (1) Rapidity of assets turnover

        (2) Size of physical plant requirements
        (3) Length of production period
        (4) Distribution methods
        (5) General level of profits
        (6) Sales terms
        (7) Growth patterns
2. Factors related to firm management
    a. Efficiency of management as measured by its ability to modify industry ratios in favor of the firm
    b. Management's decisions as to degree of risk to be assumed
        (1) Extent to which certain risks are covered by insurance
        (2) Decisions as to necessary liquidity
        (3) Decisions as to other risks to be assumed
    c. Management's decisions as to the extent property will be purchased rather than leased or rented
    d. Management's decisions as to both scale of operations and capacity that are justified by the future outlook for the firm

It is easier to decide whether a firm has too much or too little capital committed for a given level of business than it is to determine whether the level or scale of operations is proper. When to stop investing in additional assets is a major question that must be resolved by top management. The finance officer should exercise a major influence in that complex decision. He has primary responsibility for the determination of whether the firm is too "lean" or too "fat" for a given scale of activity.

Problems that can result from inadequate capital include:

1. Inability to carry an inventory commensurate with optimum operating level
2. Restriction of buying policies and inability to take advantage of quantity or cash discounts
3. Chronic pressure on cash position, which will impair credit standing
4. Inability to make necessary outlays for machinery and equipment to improve efficiency
5. Inability to take advantage of sudden changes in business opportunity

6. Required retention of earnings at the expense of proper dividend policy
7. Inability to weather minor reversals in business conditions and the resulting threat of insolvency

On the other hand, excessive capital employed in the business can have certain undesirable results:

1. Contributes to loose financial policies such as excessive inventories and poor credit policies
2. Encourages unnecessary expenditures for unproductive assets and services
3. Contributes to inefficiency of operations
4. Reduces earnings in ratio to equity capital
5. May encourage unwise expansion plans simply because funds are available to carry them out

Observation indicates that by a considerable margin business difficulties stem more from inadequate capital than from surplus funds. In too many instances the shortage results from inadequate consideration of needs or overly optimistic estimates of revenue. Both underestimating expenses and overestimating revenue by a single firm quickly result in "running out of money" even before the production plans receive a fair test.

Shortages of capital can also develop from underestimating business volume. Unexpected increases in sales generate additional capital requirements to (1) carry a higher level of inventory, (2) finance increased receivables, and (3) enlarge the physical plant in line with the expanded volume. It is likely under such circumstances that the volume of forward commitments will increase, requiring added financial resources. Expenditures for research can easily squeeze financial resources by opening up opportunities for profitable expansion before the firm is in a position to secure additional permanent capital to carry them out.

In recent years there appears to have been chronic pressure on business as a result of capital shortages. Inflation has pushed wages up (or perhaps wage increases have caused inflation), inventory and receivables investments have been constantly expanded, and any machinery or equipment acquired has had to be financed at much higher costs.

Depreciation charges based upon original cost, with the resulting tax effects, have not furnished a proportionate share of funds. Firms have had to use more and more capital, even for a given level of operations. When capital was not available it was necessary to curtail operations; many did not do this and faced financial difficulties from which some did not survive.

Certain financial arrangements are used to "stretch" equity capital as far as possible. In addition to the usual methods available to the firm to improve specific turnover ratios and thus conserve capital, practices commonly used include:

1. Lease or rental rather than purchase of equipment
2. Special arrangements by officers, directors, or principal stockholders of small corporations to provide collateral for loans or to guarantee loans, or to make subordinated loans themselves to the business.
3. Securing advances on sales, factoring receivables, or securing longer credit terms from suppliers

Each firm must determine whether or not its capital is adequate for its current needs; concurrently it must plan for its future requirements. Finding the proper balance will be a compromise based upon risks and costs as compared to prospective advantages. In the solution to this continuing question there can be a conflict between what is desirable to management (if management does not own a large amount of stock) as compared to stockholders. Management's tasks are made easier if funds are not too scarce. The pressure on management might even be reduced further by its having available surplus funds. Since excess funds are a luxury and are held at the expense of stockholders, this easy situation might not be to the best interest of the owners of the business.

TYPE OF CAPITAL

Permanent versus Temporary Capital

The proportion of total capital funds coming from short-term sources as compared to more permanent sources should be based upon the asset structure and the nature of firm operations. Although there are some general principles which will aid in this decision, the actual solution to the problem will be influenced by the willingness of owners to assume risks.

Only that proportion of ownership funds not available for dividends can be considered "permanent" capital in the strictest sense. Since all bonds issued by American business firms have maturity dates, many with provisions for retirement prior to maturity, no debt capital is permanent. However, for purposes of this discussion, permanent capital will include all ownership funds and debt capital furnished for more than ten years. Short-term capital will include debts due in less than a year, and intermediate-term capital falls between those two extremes. Both short- and intermediate-term capital are considered here to be temporary capital.

Two general rules usually applied to the division of capital between temporary and permanent sources are: (1) Permanent capital should be sufficient to finance all fixed assets, plus minimum working capital. In this case *minimum* usually refers to working capital at its lowest point during the year. (2) The payout period for the asset acquired should be matched with the debt contract under which the necessary funds are secured.

Let us consider the first of these principles. Its origin can be linked to the familiar commercial banking theory that all firms should be out of debt to their bank at least once during the year. It supposedly followed that, if good banking practice required that a firm pay off its debts in full once each year, then it must be necessary for the firm to have enough permanent capital to tide it over during that period. With the increased use of term lending, banking practice has been modified in this respect. In addition, the availability of funds specifically designed for working capital needs from specialized finance agencies may mean that a firm does not need to have enough permanent capital for even minimum working capital requirements. The rule usually should apply, and exceptions from it should be made only when the firm is certain that it will benefit from the exception. Again, costs of alternative sources and risks involved will govern.

The data in Table 1 show how this principle might work out for an individual firm. The ABC Company enjoyed continued growth from 1955 through 1960. To keep abreast of this growth it invested additional funds in fixed assets each year, financed by added sales of common stock to old stockholders. Maximum and minimum working capital needs, not financed by the firm's own trade creditors, are shown

TABLE 1

SUMMARY OF FINANCIAL DATA: ABC COMPANY

(thousands of dollars)

	1955		1956		1957		1958		1959		1960	
	Max.	Min.	Max.	Min.	Max.	Min.	Max.	Min.	Max.	Min.	Max.	Min.
Current assets (less trade creditors)	420	160	480	240	500	270	600	400	600	420	660	450
Fixed assets	400	400	500	500	600	600	700	700	720	720	750	750
CASE I												
Short-term borrowing	260	0	240	0	230	0	200	0	180	0	210	0
Long-term debt	40	40	36	36	32	32	28	28	24	24	20	20
Common stock	500	500	600	600	700	700	800	800	850	850	850	850
Surplus	20	20	104	104	138	138	272	272	266	266	330	330
CASE II												
Short-term borrowing	260	0	240	0	230	0	200	0	180	0	210	0
Long-term debt	40	40	116	116	142	142	268	268	250	250	310	310
Common stock	500	500	600	600	700	700	800	800	850	850	850	850
Surplus	20	20	24	24	28	28	32	32	36	36	40	40
CASE III												
Short-term borrowing	260	0	320	80	340	110	440	240	410	230	500	280
Long-term debt	40	40	36	36	32	32	28	28	24	24	20	20
Common stock	500	500	600	600	700	700	800	800	850	850	850	850
Surplus	20	20	24	24	28	28	32	32	36	36	40	40

for each year. It will be noted that as business expanded, the proportionate gap between the peak and lowest working-capital requirements tended to narrow. The firm's profit ratio is very favorable and it enjoys an excellent credit position. The long-term debt shown in Cases I and III is being paid off in ten equal annual installments.

If the firm follows the principle that its permanent capital must equal fixed assets plus minimum working capital, it might follow either Case I or III. In Case I, dividend policy is carefully controlled so that retained earnings are sufficient to increase surplus (and capital stock by stock dividends) each year in the amount necessary to hold short-term borrowing to the difference between maximum and minimum requirements. This enables the firm to show a zero amount in short-term borrowing once per year, but at the expense of reduced dividends.

In Case II dividends are at a higher level, and the firm increases its long-term debt each year by an amount sufficient to enable it to pay off its short-term borrowings once each year. It thus follows the rule regarding permanent capital.

Suppose the firm chooses not to pay off its short-term borrowings completely each year. In Case III, it follows the same dividend policy as in Case II but does not increase its long-term debt. As a result, with expanding working capital requirements, the short-term borrowings not paid each year increase. Up to 1960 the suppliers of these funds are willing (and even anxious) to renew the notes. If that rate of growth continued and similar policies were followed, the questions of ownership capital in relation to debt and business volume would no doubt be raised by lenders at a later date.

Up to 1960, which of the three policies is most beneficial to the firm? Obviously, Case I gives it a more conservative financial structure and a better credit rating. But owners may wish to draw high dividends in order to make other profitable investments. In Cases II and III, total debt is the same, but in Case II the rule is followed and longer-term debt is increased. Case III violates the rule and uses short-term borrowing for "permanent" needs. Which is better? The long-term debt supposedly would avoid the hazard of being hurt by sudden reversals which might cause the short-term lender to refuse to renew the debt. In addition, the firm might secure long-term funds cheaper than short-term money; but the reverse can be true also. The long-term debt contract might require annual payments, and a default on one of these could be as serious as difficulty in meeting a short-term note. Another problem to be considered is the fact that business volume *might* decline and working capital needs would contract. It would be easier (unless unusual flexibility existed in the long-term debt contract) to adjust to lower levels under Case III than under Case II.

The above illustration also raises the question as to when "permanent" capital should be adjusted upward with growth. One authority says that if growth is permanent, working capital should be financed from permanent sources.[3] Many business firms are not in a position to know when or if growth is permanent. Table 2 contains the variations in current asset requirements based upon given sales levels for eight companies (selected at random) for the nine-year period ending in 1959. This was a period of relatively stable business conditions, characterized by general economic expansion. Yet none of the firms showed an uninterrupted increase in current assets on the same statement date each year. At what point should each of these companies consider the increase in its working capital requirements to be permanent? Based upon the data for these years, it appears that Quaker Oats Company would be safer than the other firms in concluding that each successive increase in working capital requirements was permanent. The record for Liggett & Myers Tobacco Company would not support definite conclusions as to whether or not changes in current asset requirements were permanent.

The decision as to when working capital requirements have "risen to a new plateau" can be based only upon individual company experience. If requirements expand each year and suffer no decline in the business adjustments (such as those of 1953–54 and 1957–58), a firm would be relatively safe in increasing its permanent capital accordingly. On the other hand, cycle-oriented firms should be careful in concluding that gains, even those sustained for three or four years, are permanent. Two conclusions seem justified:

1. The provision for expanded working capital needs may be met either by temporary or permanent capital, depending upon (a) the relative costs involved, and (b) the probable ease with which sudden changes in requirements (either up or down) can be met.

2. When it appears that expanded working capital requirements are permanent and long-term capital is acquired to meet these needs,

[3] J. F. Weston, "Financial Implications of Growth," *Controller,* March 1958, p. 118.

TABLE 2

TOTAL SALES AND TOTAL CURRENT ASSETS OF SELECTED COMPANIES, 1951–59[a]

(millions of dollars)

		1951	1952	1953	1954	1955	1956	1957	1958	1959
Virginia Carolina Chemical Company	Current assets	32	35	36	34	32	32	33	35	40
	Sales	71	78	82	85	77	70	71	68	81
Quaker Oats Company	Current assets	52	76	75	76	79	92	93	98	99
	Sales	229	264	265	266	276	277	303	315	322
Bond Stores, Inc.	Current assets	39	41	44	40	42	46	46	47	50
	Sales	79	83	86	—[b]	85	87	90	84	85
Kelsey-Hayes Company	Current assets	30	34	42	32	39	53	60	51	58
	Sales	104	103	138	124	141	155	202	170	202
Spencer Kellog & Sons	Current assets	28	27	21	26	25	25	25	26	28
	Sales	128	108	111	106	90	93	135	128	131
Borg-Warner Corporation	Current assets	169	194	190	184	245	273	275	260	297
	Sales	369	354	407	380	552	599	609	533	650
Cluett, Peabody & Company	Current assets	44	44	42	44	52	55	54	54	57
	Sales	80	76	84	83	87	110	106	99	114
Liggett & Myers Tobacco Company	Current assets	452	461	468	459	425	445	417	370	365
	Sales	540	603	587	549	547	565	570	556	555

[a] For accounting periods ended during these years and according to company statement dates.

[b] Change in accounting period, data not available.

SOURCE: *Moody's Industrial Manuals*, 1951–60.

the new capital should be secured under contracts which allow expansion or contraction in amount without injury to the firm.

A survey of actual practices among listed firms with respect to the amount of temporary capital reveals a whole range of practices. A great many firms[4] show short-term notes on the balance sheet very infrequently. Either these firms close their accounts and issue statements uniformly at the time of year when all bank debt has been paid, or they are providing for all capital requirements, other than trade credit, from permanent sources.

There are very sound reasons why a firm might not resort to short-term borrowing. Many of today's business enterprises are so diversified and geographically dispersed that the "peak" period has disappeared from the sales pattern. Even where there is still some fluctuation in sales, careful financial planning can match expected outlays against expected income so that no short-term credit is required. In fact, a major objective of planning is to eliminate seasonality. The joint consideration of fixed and working capital needs can result in proper timing and reduce pressure on financial resources.

In cases where permanent capital is the only source of outside funds except trade credit, the firm that is not able to smooth out its outlays to match revenue exactly will have surplus funds at certain periods. The difference between the cost of the permanent capital and available short-term capital, the length of time the surplus exists and the extent of the surplus, and the possible earnings on the surplus funds when invested in the market must be weighed together to determine if the exclusive use of permanent capital is desirable. Of course, if the arithmetic comes out in the marginal zone, the permanent capital should be given serious consideration. That alternative eliminates the time and trouble involved in negotiating varying levels of short-term credit, and the risk of not being able to arrange for it at exactly the right time and on desirable terms.

The use of permanent capital to finance working capital needs (less trade credit) and equipment as well as long-life assets makes meaningless the second principle quoted at the beginning of this section. No effort is made to match the payout period of the asset acquired with the debt contract. Funds are not secured for specific purposes

[4] Examples: S. S. Kresge Co., W. T. Grant Co., Winn-Dixie, Pepperell Manufacturing Co., Sunbeam Corporation, and Hershey Chocolate Corporation showed no short-term borrowing on their annual statements between 1951 and 1959.

(increases in capital are usually explained in terms of "added working capital needs," "modernization," "to acquire new assets," or "expansion"), but for general business use. Machinery and equipment wear out and become obsolete at a fairly uniform rate. The finance officer is concerned with his total level of funds and cash availability, not the financing of specific projects and assets.

For a smaller firm with a definite seasonal pattern and one that acquires major fixed assets only every few years, financial planning becomes an entirely different problem. Of major concern is the question of how the peak inventory or receivables will be financed, or how the new machinery will be acquired. Short- and intermediate-term credit in such cases must be a part of the financial structure. Permanent financing would be ruled out on a cost basis.

It is possible for a firm to have such a pronounced seasonal pattern that more permanent capital must be held in the business than is really desirable. The firm must have "excess" equity capital in order to be "credit worthy" for its peak borrowing. In Table 3 is shown an example where this might apply. Peak needs during the period May–

TABLE 3
MONTHLY BALANCE SHEET DATA: ABC CANNING COMPANY
(month-end amounts in thousands of dollars)

	Jan.	Feb.	Mar.	Apr.	May	June	July	Aug.	Sept.	Oct.	Nov.	Dec.
Cash	4	4	3	3	3	2	2	3	4	4	4	4
Inventory	20	25	30	50	70	50	40	30	25	20	20	20
Receivables	5	5	10	20	40	60	40	40	30	20	15	15
Total current assets	29	34	43	73	113	112	82	73	59	44	39	29
Fixed assets	10	10	10	10	10	10	10	10	10	10	10	10
Total assets	39	44	53	83	123	122	92	83	69	54	49	39
Accounts payable	5	7	10	17	20	17	13	10	8	5	5	5
Bank loans	0	3	9	22	69	71	45	39	27	15	10	0
Capital stock	30	30	30	30	30	30	30	30	30	30	30	30
Surplus	4	4	4	4	4	4	4	4	4	4	4	4
Total	39	44	53	83	123	122	92	83	69	54	49	39

June might require a restricted dividend policy so as to increase equity capital, although during a large part of the year capital funds are adequate. If the inventory was suitable for collateral loans, the firm might be able to meet its seasonal requirements without increasing equity capital. Or capital might be stretched by personal endorsements on the notes covering the excess amounts of loans.

Ratio of Debt to Equity Capital

One of the most difficult components of financial planning is the choice between debt and equity capital. Since both forms of capital have obvious advantages to the firm, the decision is often the result of conflicting opinions and evidence. In some instances the question is easy to resolve, but in the many marginal cases the choice will be affected by management's willingness to assume risks.

The use of debt capital in proper proportion to equity has specific advantages:

1. In terms of financial charges, interest on debt capital is normally less than the dividend rate necessary to attract equity funds.
2. The use of debt capital avoids the sharing of the voting control of the company.
3. Present tax laws reduce effective interest charges to 48 per cent of the coupon rate and thus widen the cost gap mentioned in 1.
4. The use of debt capital increases net return to equity shareholders through the principle of financial leverage.

To counterbalance the above advantages, a high equity capital proportion has certain advantages:

1. It does not risk loss of the business to creditors as a result of economic reversals.
2. The use of equity capital to a maximum extent results in the most conservative capital structure and enhances the credit standing of the firm.
3. Since the use of financial leverage results in more widely fluctuating earnings to stockholders, the higher the proportion of equity capital, the more stable will be net profit.

Actually, a combination of equity and debt is the proper answer for the majority of firms, not a choice between the two. One is not a substitute for the other. The problem is, then, not which to use in the capital structure but rather what proportion of debt and equity is the optimum under given circumstances. The three influencing factors in that decision are (1) relative costs, (2) relative risks, and (3) availability of funds as affected by the investor criteria normally used in the debt-equity ratio.

The actual cost of debt capital (if no financial difficulties are encountered) is relatively easy to measure. This cost includes (1) the cost of getting the funds or underwriting fees and legal expenses, (2) interest expense, and (3) redemption cost, especially if retired prior to maturity. But the cost of equity capital to a corporation cannot be measured precisely. If the firm is a proprietorship or partnership the cost of equity funds would simply be the expected average earnings accruing to the new capital divided by the amount of new capital. However, this is *expected* cost, not *actual* cost. Actual cost can be determined only after a lapse of time.

The cost of equity capital to the corporation cannot be measured; the cost criterion must be applied to what the cost is to present stockholders. Even if we assume that the expected profit rate actually materializes, there would be a difference of opinion as to the extent of the cost. Suppose that a corporation is earning (after taxes) $100,000 each year, that there are 100,000 shares of stock outstanding, and that dividends amount to 60 per cent of earnings.

1. If we assume that by the sale of an additional 50,000 shares of stock earnings would increase $50,000, what is the cost of the new equity capital? If dividends continue at 60¢ per share, then the added payout is $30,000 per year. But is there any cost to the old stockholders? The new capital expands earnings proportionally to new ownership, and the old stockholders are exactly where they were.

2. If we assume that the additional capital expands earnings by only $40,000, the costs to old shareholders partly depend upon whether the dividend rate is maintained or reduced. If the 60¢ dividend is maintained, have the old shareholders lost ground? Their current dividend has not been reduced, but their claims to earned surplus are diluted. If the dividend is reduced to 50¢, the added capital inflicts injury on the old stockholders, unless long-run prospects offset the decline.

3. If earnings expand as a result of the new capital by 60,000, the old shareholders benefit either by an increased dividend or a proportionate claim to larger earned surplus.

In none of the above cases are costs related to the amount of funds secured, since no mention was made of the contribution to the company of each new share of stock. Now assume that the new stock was sold for $10 per share; can the cost of funds be figured? If we decide that the 60¢ dividend alone attracted the capital, the evident cost of funds was 6 per cent. But the new stockholders have an equal claim to the other 40¢ earnings per share. Then was the cost of funds 10 per cent? In the second case when earnings per share dropped as a result of the new capital, if dividend rate was maintained, the costs of funds was again 6 per cent in dividends; but earnings per share dropped to 93⅓¢. If the cost of funds in the first case totaled 10 per cent, in this instance the total was 9⅓ per cent. If the earnings rate was reduced, was there a lower cost of funds? In the third case earnings per share increased. Again, if the dividend rate was maintained at 60¢, the paid-out cost of funds remained 6 per cent, and the total cost jumped to 10⅔ per cent as a result of increased earnings. If the earnings rate is increased, does this mean that the capital was more expensive simply because it was more productive?

From the above it becomes clear that there is only *one* logical method for computing the cost of new equity funds, and that is alternative cost to the old shareholders. The hypothetical case in Table 4 illustrates the computation of the alternative costs.

Since debt capital is generally considered to be cheaper than equity capital, the choice between the two broad sources of funds would be an easy one if it were not for the risk factor. The risk rests upon the possibility that earnings may not be sufficient to cover debt service, which is a contractual obligation, thus resulting in default. The extent of the risk assumed, therefore, can be related to (1) the level of earnings in relation to debt service and (2) the degree of fluctuations in earnings. An adverse situation in one of these relationships may be partially compensated for by the other factor. A relatively high coverage of financial costs will tend to reduce the risks of fluctuations in earnings. Stability of earnings reduces the risks of lower coverage of financial charges. For example, it is difficult to say which of the two illustrations in Table 5 represents the higher degree of risk. Example A has the advantage of a higher debt-service coverage during the seven years shown, but considerably more variation in operating income; Example B has lower average coverage, but with more stability in income.

The question of the "safe" debt limit for a firm is often discussed but with little meaning. Most of the rules of thumb that are used by

TABLE 4
COST COMPARISON OF DEBT AND EQUITY CAPITAL

Before new financing:

Total assets	$150,000
Liabilities	50,000
Common stock	100,000
Earnings before taxes	10,000
Earnings after taxes	7,500
Earnings on common (as a per cent of book value)	7.5%
Dividends (payout rate 66⅔%)	$ 5,000
Dividend rate	5% on book value

It is estimated that $50,000 in additional capital will double present profits (before taxes or financial costs). The tax rate is 25 per cent.

If new financing is by common stock:

Total assets	$200,000
Liabilities	50,000
Common stock	150,000
Earnings before taxes	20,000
Earnings after taxes	15,000
Earnings on common (as a per cent of book value)	10%
Dividends (payout rate 66⅔%)	$ 10,000
Dividend rate	6⅔% on book value

If new financing is with borrowed capital at 6% per year:

Total assets	$200,000
Liabilities	50,000
Common stock	100,000
Long-term debt	50,000
Earnings before taxes and interest	20,000
Interest cost	3,000
Earnings after taxes	12,750
Earnings on common (as a per cent of book value)	12¾%
Dividends (same payout percentage)	$ 8,500
Dividend rate	8½%

(Plus the fact that old common shareholders have a claim to a larger earned surplus per share.)

The cost of the equity capital as compared to the debt capital is:
In terms of earnings rate: 12.75% − 10% = 2.75%
In terms of dividend rate: 8.5% − 6.67% = 1.83%

finance officers to decide whether further debt financing is too risky are based upon a ratio that someone (economist, accountant, or otherwise) was brave enough to set up as a rule. If such ratios are to be

TABLE 5

COMPARISON OF DEGREE OF RISK FROM DEBT FINANCING

	1953	1954	1955	1956	1957	1958	1959
			EXAMPLE A				
Operating income	$100,000	$60,000	$120,000	$140,000	$80,000	$40,000	$100,000
Debt service	20,000	20,000	20,000	20,000	20,000	20,000	20,000
Debt coverage (ratio)	5	3	6	7	4	2	5
Average debt coverage = $4\frac{4}{7}$							
Average fluctuation in income from average of previous and succeeding year = 36%							
			EXAMPLE B				
Operating income	$80,000	$70,000	$90,000	$100,000	$90,000	$80,000	$100,000
Debt service	30,000	30,000	30,000	30,000	30,000	30,000	30,000
Debt coverage (ratio)	$2\frac{2}{3}$	$2\frac{1}{3}$	3	$3\frac{1}{3}$	3	$2\frac{2}{3}$	$3\frac{1}{3}$
Average debt coverage = $2\frac{9}{10}$							
Average fluctuation in income from average of previous and succeeding year = 11%							

used, they should be determined from firm-industry experience, and not be just averages of what all corporations have done in the past. Setting a safety limit must be based upon a prior decision as to what magnitude of busines fluctuations is likely to occur in the future. This is usually done by assuming that future cycles will be no greater or less than past ones. If financial plans are made within that framework, safety is not guaranteed. Our conclusion is, therefore, that the choice between debt and equity capital must be based upon individual firm considerations—stability, earnings levels, general outlook, and management's attitude toward risks. The choice should not be made upon the basis of ratios found in some "authoritative" source.

A survey of actual debt-equity ratios of corporations will show that no patterns are followed. In given industries firms with about the same stability in earnings and approximately the same earnings rate on assets will differ widely in their debt-equity balance. In rare instances there is a pattern for the industry. As an example, among several large cement companies there had been little long-term debt in the few years prior to 1956. By 1957, three companies had outstanding long-term debt in roughly the same proportion to equity capital (25 per cent). There appears to have been a sudden change of attitude toward debt capital in that industry. Each of the three companies, even with 25 per cent debt, had at least a twelve-times coverage of debt service (before taxes) in 1957.

There is good evidence that the financial policy covering the use of debt capital may in many cases be too conservative rather than too risky. American industrial companies may not be borrowing enough, if we consider only the magnitude of the business cycle since World War II. Debt service coverage for many industrial corporations (from among those with long-term debt) runs unusually high.

A comparison of two similar industrial companies in Table 6 illus-

TABLE 6
ILLUSTRATION OF THE EFFECTS AND RISKS OF DEBT-FINANCING: TWO BUILDING PRODUCTS COMPANIES

Year	*Per Cent of Total Long-Term Capital* Debt	Preferred	Common Equity	*Times Debt Service Earned*[a]	*Per Cent Earnings to:* Net Worth	Assets	*Net Income Before Taxes and Debt Service* (ratio to 9-year average)
				COMPANY A			
1951	3.6		96.4	Over 100	18.2	13.9	1.09
1952	3.2		96.8	Over 100	15.7	12.3	1.00
1953	2.8		97.1	Over 100	13.1	10.3	0.87
1954	2.6		97.4	Over 100	10.8	8.4	0.72
1955	2.3		97.7	Over 100	14.1	10.8	1.05
1956	1.8		98.2	Over 100	12.1	9.6	1.16
1957	1.7		98.3	Over 100	8.5	6.9	0.74
1958	1.2		98.7	Over 100	9.9	7.7	1.01
1959	0.9		99.1	Over 100	12.3	9.7	1.35
Average	2.2		97.8	Over 100	12.7	10.0	1.00
				COMPANY B			
1951	22.5	12.9	64.6	38.6	12.3	8.4	0.69
1952	27.5	11.0	61.5	27.4	11.0	7.2	0.75
1953	28.0	9.0	62.2	20.0	10.7	7.0	0.74
1954	25.9	9.1	65.0	25.1	16.1	11.7	0.90
1955	20.7	7.3	72.0	30.5	14.5	10.7	1.12
1956	17.4	6.1	76.5	28.3	10.6	8.3	1.03
1957	16.9	5.9	77.1	24.6	9.2	7.3	0.91
1958	15.8	5.2	79.0	29.7	10.2	8.1	1.15
1959	14.6	4.4	81.0	36.4	12.6	10.2	1.73
Average	21.4	7.9	70.2	29.0	11.9	8.8	1.00

[a] Before taxes and financial charges.
SOURCE: *Moody's Industrial Manuals*, 1951–60.

trates how consideration of nothing more than the debt-equity ratio for long-term capital may be misleading in determining earnings on net worth. Company A had very little long-term capital during the period, whole B averaged 21.4 per cent debt funds and 7.9 per cent preferred stock. A earned an average of 10 per cent on assets employed, and B earned 8.8 per cent. B's use of approximately a fourth long-term debt in financing raised its earnings on net worth to 11.9 per cent as compared to 12.7 per cent for A. B financed a larger proportion of assets by long-term capital, including debt. A, with the more conservative debt-equity ratio in its long-term capital, tended to have a higher proportion of its assets financed by current liabilities, especially trade credit. In total, there was little difference in debt-equity ratio between the two firms, and thus they had about the same spread between the earnings-assets ratios as between the earnings–net worth ratios. A look at the stability of net income (before taxes and financial costs) shows that there is little difference in the two firms' ability to carry extensive debt when measured by these criteria. However, the profitability of both the firms during these nine years would warrant further long-term debt financing, if only debt service coverage is considered. The minimum debt service coverage was 20 times in 1953 for Company B.

The individual firm's decision as to the extent of debt financing will also be influenced by investor attitudes on what the acceptable debt-equity ratio should be. The rules of thumb used by investors do affect the ratings on securities and therefore the costs of funds. Of course, the norms established vary with type of business and generally consider the ratio of total debt to equity capital as well as the ratio of long-term debt.

The actual ratios will vary with the business cycle, and whether the rules are applied to the ratios at the time the debt is incurred or to averages for a period of time is a matter of choice. The total debt (current and noncurrent) for all manufacturing corporations at the end of June 1957 was 53 per cent of equity capital; at the same time in 1953, the proportion was 58 per cent.[5]

Whether the rules followed by investors are reasonable or are just the perpetuation of ratios that looked logical at one time does not seem to matter. These rules affect security ratings and costs of funds; the firm must comply or pay the penalty. State laws limiting certain types of investments to securities with specific ratings narrow the market for issues not meeting those minimums.

[5] See H. C. Sauvain, "Has Business Borrowed Too Much?" *Business Horizons*, Winter 1958, p. 53.

The timing of borrowing in relationship to sales of equity securities might be of importance. If a company plans to raise external funds by the sale of both equities and bonds, the recommendation is generally made that the stock be sold first. The obvious reason for this timing is that the higher equity cushion would then provide an improved basis for selling bonds. Actually, many firms prefer to market the stock and bonds jointly, either as a package for each investor or for the advantage of having the entire transaction planned and underwritten as a unit.

44

Raising Capital to Finance the New Program[1]

Manley Howe Jones

Regardless of the size of the sum required and the sources of the funds, the executive must be in a position to demonstrate just what makes his company "tick"—how and why it has been able to compete in the past and, even more important, how and why it will be able to compete in the future. The underwriter requires detailed information which will provide him with the premises for deciding whether to float the issue, how much money should be (and can be) raised, and what kind of security would be most appropriate. His reputation among his clients and customers depends on how well his decisions stand up. This same kind of information, though perhaps less of it, will have to be prepared when the company intends to sell directly to

[1] From Manley Howe Jones, *Executive Decision Making* (Homewood, Ill., Richard D. Irwin, Inc., 1957), pp. 439–441. Used by permission.

individuals. Some of the more discriminating investors may want rather complete data, so that they can make their own decisions—they may want proof rather than some expert's recommendations which they must take on faith—so that they themselves can determine whether the investment is the best alternative for their purposes. . . .

The executives of the brokerage firm (and the individual investors?) first want a history of the company and copies of its operating statements, balance sheets, and the details of the surplus account for the past ten years or so. They will also ask about the background and the strong points and weaknesses of the company's executives, as well as the character and ability of the young management coming up. The young men are the ones on whom the investors will eventually have to depend for their returns.

But *most of all,* they will want a diagnosis of the company's departments—answers to most of those questions . . . which the company executives pondered when they were appraising the company and comparing it with its competitors. The premises derived from these are the ones that will be given greatest weight. Incidentally, the tendency of investment houses is to stress information that can be cast in numerical form.

Having secured information on the company's history and its executives, and on trends in the financial statements and the competitive position of the company's product development, sales, and manufacturing departments, the broker (and the investor?) next wants to examine the purpose of the new financing. What is desired here is a description of the niche the company is planning to fill, the premises underlying this choice, the executive's plan for improving the departments, and the expected costs of introducing the various changes versus the contributions these will make to overhead and profits.

Finally, it is necessary to show how the company expects to meet these obligations. A projection of earning power over the next few years provides the foundation for this—estimates of probable sales in units and dollars; the expected out-of-pocket costs of manufacturing as a percentage of selling price; the probable overhead in salaries and other fixed contractual obligations, including interest on the new loan, if any; and, out of this, an estimate of profits. They will also want to know what collateral the firm can offer as security if the loan is to be in the form of mortgage notes, and how the company plans to use the profits for paying off the loans. If stock is to be issued, estimates of the dollar earnings per share on the outstanding stock will be needed, even though the estimates of dividends must of necessity be conjectural; and they would hope for some inkling of when the dividends could be expected.

Not all the companies seeking investors will need to supply equally complete information on all the questions dealing with the company's competitive position. . . . Depending on the company, some of them can be covered in a sentence or two, while other facets will need to be discussed in considerable detail. The information described above would constitute the maximum demanded by a broker who is investigating a company with a view to issuing securities to the public. If the company is planning to raise the funds itself by offering securities directly to prospective investors, less elaborate information will ordinarily be required. But in such a case an attorney familiar with the issuance of securities should be consulted to ensure compliance with the rather complicated state and federal statutes and regulations relating to new security offerings.

Normally, a company will not require all the new money immediately, because the plan cannot be put into effect all at once. This is fortunate, for it takes time to sell securities such as these. If an underwriter is used, the executive's time schedule for introducing the changes in the departments provides a basis for scheduling the transfer of the new funds.

45

The Long-Term Budget Projection: A Case Study from Education[1]

Sidney G. Tickton

For many years, industrial firms, merchandising organizations, and government agencies have made long-range projections of income and expenditures on which to base their policy decisions on production planning, sales programs, new plant construction, new debt commitments, etc. The merchandising of a new product for nationwide consumption, for example, may span a decade from the time the laboratory research has been completed until the sales promotion has placed the product in millions of homes. Commitments of time, money, and resources can be allocated by responsible corporate officials to a long-term program only after the detailed plans have been worked out, plans that take into account all factors likely to be relevant. Sometimes two or more assumptions are used to allow for possible variations in timing, prices, costs, the extent of the market, the availability of finances, and the like.

The building of a new highway, bridge, airport, or public utility is likewise preceded by a detailed projection into the future of the operating accounts, giving full effect to possible changes in economic, social, and environmental factors that may impinge on the outlook for receipts and expenditures. If the financing involves the issuance of

[1] From *Financing Higher Education, 1960–70,* ed. Dexter M. Keezer. Copyright, 1959, McGraw-Hill Book Co., Inc. Used by permission.

securities, particularly revenue bonds, the projections are the work of appropriate specialists, are heavily documented, and may cover a time period of twenty to thirty years. They frequently become the entire basis upon which the project is organized, financed, and carried forth.

A less complicated example involving long-range projections of receipts and expenditures can be observed any day in the real estate field. Apartment houses, shopping centers, and office buildings are bought and sold on the basis of a probable income and expenditures analysis running from a few years to half a century ahead.

Although colleges and universities have long-range planning problems similar to those of industry and trade, it is unusual for them to engage in long-range fiscal planning. Recently, a few small liberal arts colleges decided to work out a long-range analysis technique built around their budgets. Their objective was to gain some financial perspective for the decade ahead, taking into account all their long-range commitments such as tenure, automatic-increase salary schedules, fringe-benefit arrangements with escalator clauses, and current maintenance on buildings to be constructed from funds provided by special gifts, campaigns, or borrowing, as well as rising prices and nationwide increases in the levels of faculty salaries.

These colleges recognized that institutions of higher education are not strictly business activities but that, on the financial side, their operations are certainly subject to business-type analysis. With the perspective provided by the projections, they were able to arrive at some new policy decisions on size of student body, faculty, building program and gift program, educational objectives of the college, and details of the curriculum, with the knowledge of what each individual decision meant to the operation of the college as a whole.

The purpose of this paper is to describe the process followed by one of these colleges, to indicate the types of data needed and the basis of the projections made, and to describe the results obtained. By using a technique similar to the one described, other colleges and universities can work out their own future pictures (in greater or lesser detail as their situations warrant) and can use organized data as a basis for new decisions on their future activities.

Another purpose of this paper is to indicate that the analysis process, although not difficult, requires considerable discipline; that is, the effect of every management decision on the budget, this year, next year, or for the entire period ahead, must be taken into account.

One decision may involve a number of additional decisions; for example, a projection of the size of the student body requires related projections on the size of the faculty, the size of classes, number of courses, and space requirements. Precision of projection is not as essential as is the reasonableness of the estimates and the following through of the process at all points where there are budgetary consequences.

As indicated elsewhere in this book, the management problems of colleges and universities will grow tremendously, both in size and in complexity, during the next few years. To meet these problems, top officials will need to sharpen old management tools and fashion new ones. The long-term budget projection is just such a new management tool.

We hasten to add, however, that the particular procedure described in this paper is only an example of an administrative technique which is in the early stages of development. Officials who prepare long-range projections for colleges and universities could be expected to improve the technique during the next few years and to incorporate for each college some amendments to reflect the needs of that particular institution. At some colleges and universities it might be necessary to set down a series of alternative assumptions and to run through the entire projection process a number of times before arriving at a series of figures which are both practical and desirable.

DESCRIPTION OF THE COLLEGE

For the purposes of this case study, we shall call the institution that we are describing Ashford College. It is a four-year liberal arts college located on a sixty-acre campus, in a town of 30,000 in the Midwest. Originally started in the 1830's and originally related to both Congregational and Presbyterian churches, the college is now a privately controlled institution accredited to the North Central Association. It offers B.A., B.Mus., and B.Mus.Ed. degrees.

There are 800 students, 64 per cent of whom are men. Ten per cent of the students are married. Of the students, 556 live on campus in college-owned properties, 150 live on campus in fraternity houses, and 94 are commuters and live at home. Seventy per cent of the students come from a radius of three hundred miles, nearly all from middle- and upper-middle-income families. Half of the students who enter Ashford do not stay for the entire four years. Dropouts include many women who marry and some men who transfer to five-year programs in engineering and business administration, as well as some students who transfer to the state university for preprofessional courses.

Ashford's campus is surrounded by the town and has been protected in recent years by the purchase of adjoining properties, some of which have been demolished and others of which have been turned into college offices and residences. It will be necessary to buy additional adjoining property in future years. The college plant consists of three classroom and office buildings, two gymnasiums, a music building, a library with 85,000 volumes, observatory, infirmary, chapel, athletic field, and dormitories. Laboratories, libraries, and classrooms are equipped primarily for the benefit of the student rather than for research.

Although a few of the buildings are relatively old, the plant is in first-class shape, and extraordinary maintenance is not a problem. The campus needs some new landscaping, and a new fine arts building is planned for 1962. Dormitories, dining halls, and student union facilities are used to capacity. An expansion of the college will require additional living quarters and recreation and eating facilities.

Classes meet five days a week, primarily between 9 A.M. and 4 P.M., and on Saturday morning. The school year runs from September 20 to June 5. Although there is no summer program, the college acts as host to a number of conferences during July and August, which permits it to employ its dormitory and dining hall staff on a year-round basis.

The college engages in intercollegiate athletics with neighboring institutions. There is a comprehensive intramural program; there is also an ROTC unit to which most of the men students belong.

THE FIRST STEP: BACKGROUND DATA

As the first step toward the preparation of a long-term budget, Ashford's president asked the business manager to assemble some data on the operations and activities of the college for the past ten years. The information submitted is shown in Table 1.

The business manager found that nearly all the information re-

TABLE 1
HISTORICAL DATA ON ASHFORD COLLEGE, 1949–59

Item	1948–49	1952–53	1957–58	1958–59
Data on students and faculty				
Number of students	834	775	759	800
Number of faculty	70	67	63	65
Student-faculty ratio	11.9:1	11.6:1	12:1	12.3:1
Average tuition per student	$ 470	$ 593	$ 806	$ 817
Total compensation of faculty:				
Salary	$ 262,374	$ 285,733	$ 355,111	$ 389,790
Fringe benefits	9,736	18,572	23,270	30,770
Average compensation of faculty:				
Salary	$ 3,748	$ 4,265	$ 5,637	$ 5,997
Fringe benefits	139	277	369	473
Data on endowment and gifts				
Amount of endowment (book value)	$2,914,300	$4,103,600	$4,472,800	$4,600,000
Total income from endowment	177,862	184,019	201,889	221,830
Rate of return (on book value)	6.10%	4.48%	4.51%	4.82%
Amount of gifts received:				
For endowment	$ 143,400	$ 57,200	$ 100,414	$ 100,000
For plant			30,000	40,000
For other uses	39,000	100,000	210,874	326,091
Data on educational plant and equipment				
Book value	$2,282,000	$3,295,000	$4,633,000	$4,650,000
Replacement value				4,150,000
Data on budget income				
Educational and general:				
Student fees	$ 390,790	$ 417,418	$ 611,678	$ 653,870
Endowment income	137,920	147,868	161,676	150,525
Gifts	31,057	58,643	120,667	197,652
Organized activities	19,928	21,121	23,430	27,559
Other items	4,437	4,730	25,873	56,040
Subtotal, educational, and general	$ 584,132	$ 649,780	$ 943,324	$1,085,646
Auxiliary enterprises:				
Residences	$ 71,370	$ 92,766	$ 170,349	$ 192,000
Dining halls	175,942	175,658	173,361	225,000
Student union		21,019	32,082	36,000
Other		35,957	58,965	56,000
Subtotal, auxiliary enterprises	$ 247,312	$ 325,400	$ 434,757	$ 509,000

(continued)

HISTORICAL DATA ON ASHFORD COLLEGE (CONTINUED)

Item	1948–49	1952–53	1957–58	1958–59
Student aid:				
Gifts and endowment	$ 23,174	$ 31,850	$ 122,420	$ 162,244
Other allocations to student aid	4,300	20,300	54,803	68,756
Subtotal, student aid	$ 27,474	$ 52,150	$ 177,223	$ 231,000
Total income	$ 858,918	$1,027,330	$1,555,304	$1,825,646
Data on budget expenditure				
Educational and general:				
General administration	$ 53,549	$ 63,487	$ 86,437	$ 91,557
Student services	41,771	73,210	81,199	92,121
Public services	29,574	37,031	74,040	70,980
General institutional expense	10,456	29,028	56,107	94,674
Instructional expense	271,988	322,731	440,826	520,364
Organized activities	37,443	30,652	31,239	35,991
Library	31,358	33,305	43,917	44,587
Plant operation and maintenance	115,289	136,777	163,682	190,631
Subtotal, educational and general	$ 591,428	$ 726,221	$ 977,447	$1,140,905
Auxiliary enterprises:				
Residences	$ 59,583	$ 95,767	$ 170,349	$ 192,000
Dining halls	148,968	151,302	173,361	225,000
Student union	1,786	21,017	32,082	36,000
Other		35,957	58,965	56,000
Subtotal, auxiliary enterprises	$ 210,337	$ 304,043	$ 434,757	$ 509,000
Student aid:				
Scholarships	$ 26,875	$ 53,743	$ 173,421	$ 228,533
Fellowships and prizes	440	759	3,802	2,467
Subtotal, student aid	$ 27,315	$ 54,502	$ 177,223	$ 231,000
Total expenditure	$ 829,080	$1,084,766	$1,589,427	$1,880,905

quested was readily available from the books and records of the college. In setting down the student and faculty figures, he used the full-time equivalents averaged for the year. Faculty included those on leave with pay, excluded those on leave without pay. Physical education instructors were included, but ROTC officers were excluded, inasmuch as their salaries are not paid by the college. Fringe benefits included the college's contribution to its pension plan, social security, major medical insurance, and group life and health insurance.

THE SECOND STEP: ASSUMPTIONS FOR THE FUTURE (UNITED STATES AS A WHOLE)

As a second step toward the preparation of a long-term budget for his college, Ashford's president, with the head of his economics department, worked out a number of basic assumptions about the character of the United States economy as a whole during the next ten years. Within this framework, he worked out with his dean some assumptions on the outlook for higher education. The objective was to improve the reliability of the calculations by allowing for changes likely to occur in the environment in which the college would operate. The assumptions for the years 1959–70 were as follows:

1. The United States will be blessed with a high-employment economy without a war or other national disaster.
2. Prices can be expected to increase during the period, say, about 1 per cent each year on the average.
3. The number of students going to colleges and universities can be expected to double by the end of the period.
4. State universities, city colleges, and community and junior colleges will provide for a large share of the increased college enrollment.
5. There will be a substantially larger number of applicants for admission to private liberal arts colleges. These colleges will be able to select students of better than average academic ability. Parents of the students (except scholarship students) will be able and willing to pay an increasing tuition charge.
6. The large number of applicants to private liberal arts colleges and their willingness to pay increasing tuition will be made possible by the high-employment condition of our national economy and by the feeling on the part of a sufficient number of parents that private liberal arts colleges will provide a superior education for their children.
7. Salaries of college faculty members will double, on the average, nationwide, during the next five to ten years as recommended by the President's Committee on Education Beyond the High School.
8. Although there will be a growing number of federal and state scholarships for college students, they will constitute a minor per-

centage of the total number of scholarships necessary for higher education. Continued solicitation by all private colleges and universities of private gifts for scholarship purposes will be necessary throughout the period.

9. Long-term loans to private colleges will be available from the federal government, state governments, or commercial sources for the construction of dormitories, dining halls, student unions, and other revenue-producing facilities. Private gifts will be required, however, to provide funds for the construction of classrooms, laboratories, libraries, and other facilities from which direct revenue is not ordinarily obtained.

THE THIRD STEP: ASSUMPTIONS FOR THE FUTURE (THE COLLEGE ITSELF)

As the third step toward the preparation of a long-term budget, Ashford's president, dean, and business manager worked out a number of basic assumptions that would be involved in a projection for ten years ahead. They were the following:

1. The purposes and objectives of the college will remain unchanged, that is, the college will continue to provide high-quality undergraduate education in the liberal arts for young men and women of better than average academic ability.

2. Teaching methods will remain essentially unchanged except for a greater emphasis on independent study and a larger number of student teaching assistants.

3. The college calendar will remain essentially unchanged.

4. Services to students will remain essentially unchanged.

5. The college will continue to be essentially residential in character. Increases in students over the present number will have to be accompanied by an expansion of dormitory or other living quarters.

6. Enrollment will grow approximately as follows:

1957–58	759	1960–61	975
1958–59	800	1961–62	1,100
1959–60	875	1962–63 and after	1,250

7. Enrollment by 1962–63 will consist of 60 per cent men, 40 per cent women, to be arrived at as follows:

	Men, per cent	*Women, per cent*
1958–59	64.3	35.7
1959–60	63.0	37.0
1960–61	62.0	38.0
1961–62	61.0	39.0
1962–63 and after	60.0	40.0

8. Upperclassmen (juniors and seniors) will constitute a growing proportion of the student body, increasing from 36.8 per cent in 1958–59 to 45.0 per cent by 1962–63. This will permit the filling up of the upperclass courses, which are now underpopulated. It will be achieved when necessary by working with a number of junior and community colleges, expanding scholarship grants to students at such colleges, etc.

9. The ROTC program will continue at the college, enrolling the same proportionate share of men students as heretofore.

10. The teaching faculty will grow approximately as follows:

1958–59	65	1961–62	78
1959–60	67	1962–63 and after	84
1960–61	73		

This growth takes into account the filling up of the upper classes, a trend away from small sections, and the expansion of independent study for average and above-average students. (The honors students already carry on a substantial volume of independent study but at a high faculty-student cost ratio.)

11. Faculty salaries will double, on the average, between 1958 and 1968. The averages arrived at for each year (after some adjusting of the scale to make the totals balance out) were as follows:

1957–58	$ 5,637	1963–64	$ 9,190
1958–59	5,997	1964–65	9,650
1959–60	6,900	1965–66	10,133
1960–61	7,390	1966–67	10,640
1961–62	8,055	1967–68	11,172
1962–63	8,753		

12. Fringe benefits for the faculty (which at Ashford include the TIAA—Teachers Insurance and Annuity Association—pension program, group life and health insurance, major medical insurance, and social security) will grow from 6.5 per cent of salaries in 1957–58 to

15¾ per cent of salaries by 1963–64 and will continue at that level.

13. Sabbatical leaves will be provided to the extent of 1½ per cent of the faculty salary budget in 1960–61; 1¾ per cent in 1961–62; 2 per cent in 1962–63; 2¼ per cent in 1963–64, and 2½ per cent in 1964–65 and thereafter.

14. In the future the budget for the college will be divided into four parts as follows: (a) educational and general, (b) auxiliary enterprises, (c) scholarship, and (d) plant.

Educational and General Budget

15. The educational and general budget will be balanced each year, without gifts, starting in 1962–63. It will include the following items: (a) general administration, (b) student services, (c) public service and information, (d) general institutional expense, (e) instruction, (f) organized activities related to educational departments, (g) library, (h) operation and maintenance of physical plant, (i) depreciation reserve on educational plant, and (j) contingency reserve.

16. The projection of general administration expense includes allowances for the addition of one secretary in the school year 1960 and one clerk in 1961. Student services include allowances for the addition of a full-time doctor in 1961, a dean of men in 1962, and one secretary in each of the years 1961, 1962, and 1963. Public service and information includes an additional person in each of the years 1960 and 1961. Library expenditures include the addition of one professional staff member in 1961.

17. The item for depreciation of educational plant will be based on estimated replacement value of buildings as listed in Table 2. These amounts will be transferred to a special fund to be used for repairs and remodeling of the plant and to repay the endowment funds for amounts invested in the plant.

18. The item for contingencies in the educational and general budget will amount to 3 per cent of expenditures for the fiscal year 1960–61 and 5 per cent of such expenditures thereafter.

19. The educational and general budget will be financed from the following sources of income: (a) tuition and fees, (b) endowment income (unrestricted), (c) income from organized activities, (d) miscellaneous income, (e) income from administration of auxiliary enterprises, and (f) gifts and grants as follows: $165,000 in 1959–60, $100,000 in 1960–61, $50,000 in 1961–62. No gift money will be allocated to this budget in 1962–63 and thereafter.

TABLE 2

Year	Estimated Replacement Value	Amount for Depreciation	Rate (per cent)
1959–60	$4,200,000	$ 22,500	0.535
1960–61	4,250,000	34,500	0.811
1961–62	4,300,000	43,000	1.00
1962–63	5,600,000	70,000	1.25
1963–64	5,650,000	84,000	1.49
1964–65	5,700,000	98,000	1.72
1965–66	5,800,000	140,000	2.41
1966–67	5,800,000	140,000	2.41
1967–68	5,800,000	140,000	2.41

20. Starting in 1962–63, the tuition will be computed by (a) estimating the total educational and general budget; (b) subtracting from this total the estimated unrestricted income from endowment, organized activities, and the miscellaneous sources shown above; and (c) dividing the remainder by the average number of students expected for the year.

AUXILIARY ENTERPRISES BUDGET

21. The auxiliary enterprises budget will cover income and expenditure of residence halls, dining halls, student union, and book store. It will be balanced in all years after: (a) transferring book store and student union profits to scholarship fund (NOTE: The book store and student union will aim to make a 5 per cent net profit on operations after payment of all costs); (b) including an administrative charge amounting to 5 per cent of total operating income to cover the supervisory time of the business manager and the record-keeping function of his office; and (c) including a charge for amortization of borrowed funds, interest, repairs, and remodeling amounting to:

5 per cent of estimated replacement value in 1959–60
6 per cent of estimated replacement value in 1960–61
7 per cent of estimated replacement value in 1961–62
7½ per cent of estimated replacement value in 1962–63 and thereafter

NOTE: An amount equivalent to this charge will be transferred each year to the Auxiliary Enterprises Reserve Fund, from which costs of amortization and other expenses will be paid in whatever year they occur. This procedure will serve to smooth out the financial effect of repairs and remodeling operations over the years.

22. Auxiliary-enterprise services will be essentially the same in the future as in 1957–58. Student living quarters will be operated as a single unit, and uniform charges will be made for all rooms. Charges will be estimated on the basis of 95 per cent occupancy.

23. Student living quarters will be expanded only as enrollment actually increases. When dormitories are financed by borrowing (either from endowment funds, government sources, or the commercial market), they will be amortized over fifty years with interest on the unpaid balance.

Scholarship Budget

24. The college's objective will be to provide a total of scholarships and wages paid to students for on-campus employment equal to 25 to 30 per cent of the college's annual income from student tuition and fees in order to assure the desired composition of the student body.

25. The scholarship budget will include amounts allowed by the college for tuition, room, and board. It will exclude compensation for student employment. This will be paid to the student out of funds appropriated to the function he performs. It will also exclude loan funds (which are created at Ashford in the first instance from gifts or from government sources). Loans are expected to be recovered ultimately by the college and to be used again on a revolving fund basis.

26. The scholarship budget will be self-balancing. It will be financed by current gifts and endowment income specifically earmarked for scholarships, state or federal scholarship funds, if any, and profits from the operation of the book store and student union. Inasmuch as the scholarship budget will not be financed from other sources, special efforts will be made to build up scholarship funds. Loan funds will be built up, also. An extended payment plan financed by bank credit will be worked out as soon as possible.

Plant Budget

27. The plant budget will consist of expenditures for land, buildings, and major equipment. Minor equipment will be included in the educational and general budget.

28. The plant budget will be financed entirely from endowment income earmarked for plant, current gifts for plant, special campaign gifts for plant, and long-term loans for plant, if any are desirable and available.

29. The college will raise $1.3 million for a fine arts building and construct it in 1962. This building will permit the college to expand art, music, and drama facilities, which are now inadequate. There will be no other classroom buildings constructed between 1959 and 1969.

30. Better utilization of space will make it possible to expand Ashford's enrollment from 800 to 1,250 without increasing the educational plant beyond the addition of the fine arts building. It may be necessary, however, to schedule more classes in the late afternoon and some in the evening and to put classes regularly on a forty-four- instead of a thirty-eight-hour week. (NOTE: Five evening classes were in operation in 1958–59 for the convenience of students who preferred more daytime hours for extracurricular activities and sports.)

ENDOWMENT FUNDS

31. Gifts and bequests to build up endowment funds will amount to $100,000 a year. The return on endowment investments will amount to approximately 4.8 per cent of book value per year throughout the period of the projection.

32. Four per cent interest will be paid on endowment funds invested in the educational plant.

THE FOURTH STEP: MAKING THE TEN-YEAR PROJECTION

In light of:

- The historical data about the college
- The assumptions for the future of the United States economy
- The assumptions for the future of higher education, generally
- The assumptions for the future of the college

which were now on hand, Ashford's president, dean, and business manager worked out the projection of the college budget for the decade ahead. At this point, the working time required for the preliminary calculations and discussion was just about two days.

The group found that the process involved making a number of initial guesses, following the trends indicated by historical figures, and then adjusting the projections subsequently in order to arrive at a proper balancing of the figures. The projections were worked out on both the income and expense side on four accounting work sheet schedules as follows:

A. Educational and general budget
B. Scholarship budget
C. Auxiliary enterprises budget
D. Plant budget

In some cases the details were not filled in; the broad picture was enough to work with. In other cases subsidiary tables were needed to assemble subtotals or additional working data. . . . Table 4 picks up the main figures for 1959, 1963, and 1968 from the work sheets and emphasizes the four parts of the budget, each of which is balanced within itself (see pp. 520–521).

A budget is a financial plan in which all the factors involved are interrelated to the extent that they involve money. Ashford's president found, in recapitulating the results, that changes in some of the critical factors in his college's future worked out as follows:

STUDENT-FACULTY RATIO

1958–59	12:1	1962–63	15:1
1960–61	13:1	1967–68	15:1

TUITION AND ROOM AND BOARD CHARGE PER STUDENT

	Tuition	*Room and Board*	*Total*
1958–59	$ 817	$ 755	$1,572
1960–61	1,208	825	2,033
1962–63	1,450	875	2,325
1967–68	1,841	1,032	2,873

FACULTY COMPENSATION

	Average Salary	*Including Fringe Benefits*
1958–59	$ 5,997	$ 6,470
1960–61	7,390	8,143
1962–63	8,753	10,038
1967–68	11,172	12,932

UTILIZATION OF SPACE

	Per Cent Used	*Basis, Hours per Week*
1958–59	40	38
1967–68	65	44

PERCENTAGE CHANGES 1959–68

Average tuition per student	+125%
Average compensation per faculty member, including benefits	+100%
Endowment income per student allocated to educational and general budget	– 13%
Gifts per student allocated to educational and general budget	–100%

Given these changes in critical factors, the necessary fund raising would be as shown in Table 3.

TABLE 3
FUND-RAISING REQUIRED
(thousands of dollars)

Year	Educational and General Budget	Scholarships	Endowments	Plant	Total
1958–59	$198	$128	$100	$ 40	$ 466
1960–61	100	285	100	40	525
1961–62	50	305	100	40	495
1962–63	0	375	100	1,300	1,775
1963–64	0	400	100	40	540
1967–68	0	470	100	40	610

Ashford's president found that the ten-year budget gave him a coordinated timetable. There was a detailed noting of actions to be taken for each segment of the college's life in each of a series of time periods. For example, the plan provided that for the school year 1962–1963 as compared to 1961–1962:

- The student body would increase by 150
- The faculty would increase by six
- The tuition and room and board would go up by $106, to $2,325

TABLE 4

TEN-YEAR BUDGET SUMMARY FOR ASHFORD COLLEGE

(thousands of dollars)

Expense items	1958–59	1962–63	1967–68	Income items	1958–59	1962–63	1967–68
Educational and general				*Educational and general*			
General administration	$ 92	$ 149	$ 168	Tuition and fees	$ 654	$1,813	$2,301
Student services	92	159	192	Endowment income	151	190	205
Public services	71	118	135	Gifts and grants	198	0	0
General institutional expense	95	102	112	Organized activities	28	34	35
Instructional expense	520	966	1,232	Miscellaneous income	56	29	32
Organized activities	36	45	48	Administration of auxiliary enterprises	0	45	60
Library	45	67	80	Operations deficit*	55	0	0
Operation and maintenance of educational plant	191	334	402				
Depreciation of reserve, educational plant	0	70	140				
Contingency	0	101	125				
Total, educational and general	$1,141	$2,111	$2,633	Total, educational and general	$1,141	$2,111	$2,633

Scholarships				*Scholarships*			
				Income earmarked for scholarships:			
				Book store and student union profits	$ 1	$ 9	$ 17
				Endowment	34	39	53
				Gifts	129	375	470
				Operating deficit*	67	0	0
Total, scholarships	$ 231	$ 423	$ 540	Total, scholarships	$ 231	$ 423	$ 540
Auxiliary enterprises				*Auxiliary enterprises*			
Residences and dining halls	$ 417	$ 743	$ 981	Room and board charges	$ 417	$ 743	$ 981
Book store and student union	92	152	184	Book store and student union	92	152	184
Total, auxiliary enterprises	$ 509	$ 895	$1,165	Total, auxiliary enterprises	$ 509	$ 895	$1,165
Plant				*Plant*			
Fine arts building	$ 0	$1,300	$ 0	Income earmarked for plant construction:			
Other buildings and grounds	50	10	50				
				Gifts	$ 40	$1,300	$ 40
				Endowment	10	10	10
Total, plant construction	$ 50	$1,310	$ 50	Total, plant construction	$ 50	$1,310	$ 50

* Covered by transfers from college's reserve funds.

• Faculty salary would go up by $698 to reach an average level of $8,753

• Top faculty pay would go to $18,000

• Fringe benefits would go up 2 per cent of pay to reach 14.7 per cent

This meant that every decision or action taken by the board, the administration, or the faculty in 1959, and in subsequent years too, would have to be weighed against the objectives of the long-range plan. Did it fit into the plan, did it amend the plan, was it premature, or was it out of line?

THE FIFTH STEP: WHAT THEY DID ABOUT IT

The ten-year budget projection set forth in summary fashion a preliminary and tentative plan for operating the college during the decade 1959–68. Although the possibilities of miscalculation were obvious, Ashford's president felt that he had, for the first time, a coordinated set of assumptions. From them he drew the following critical conclusions about the future of the college:

1. Ashford could balance its educational budget each year in the decade ahead.
2. Balancing the budget would mean that tuition would go up, but within the realm of possibility.
3. Budget balancing meant that the size of the college would grow, but not so large as to change the character of the college.
4. Budget balancing allowed for the doubling of faculty salaries, on the average, between 1958 and 1968.
5. Within this framework, Ashford could look forward to a top faculty salary of $18,000 to $20,000 within a few years, compared to $10,000 now.
6. The financial objectives could be achieved while maintaining first-class education objectives.
7. The student-teacher ratio would need to go no higher than 15:1.
8. If greater independent study were encouraged and some large lectures were introduced, the 15:1 ratio would allow adequate opportunity for all the necessary seminars and small discussion groups desired by the faculty, with a teaching load of no more than the present twelve hours per week.

In the light of these conclusions, Ashford's president submitted the ten-year budget to his trustees for discussion and study. At the succeeding annual meeting, the document was adopted as the basis of a program for action. It was clear to all, however, that the planning document would never be looked upon as a fixed, unchangeable blueprint for the next decade; it was, rather, a thoughtfully developed set of guide lines to be used in charting the course of the college's future.

One other point emerged from the meeting. The president and the trustees agreed that through the preparation and study of the long-range budget they had begun to realize for the first time how their college was really put together. They observed as they never had before:

> . . . how a decision on one aspect of the college's activities controlled important decisions on another;
> . . . how short-term commitments and expediency frequently determined the course of the college's long-run future;
> . . . how the failure to consider long-range implications of today's decisions (because projections of the distant future were thought to be too speculative) could, in itself, subject the college to a host of substantial but unintended risks;
> . . . how the mere postponing, for the time being, of a decision on a critical item could be of great and direct influence on future operating results.

They concluded that this dynamic technique could be of greatest use as a management tool only if the assumptions and figures were examined and constantly revised in the light of the social and economic changes occurring on the campus and in the country at large. They concluded also that long-range planning is a continuing job. The president put it this way:

> As our long-term objectives and our projections move toward us with time, they must be reassessed, readjusted, and reevaluated. Meantime, of course, we must also be ready to push our projections further into the future in order to keep the guideposts visible ten or fifteen years away.

46

Long-Range Planning in Industrial Relations[1]

James W. Oram

To keep pace with the sweeping changes that are taking place in our economy today, industrial relations executives are forced continually to chart new courses in management-union affairs. The decisions reached at the bargaining table concern every aspect of the management function from the financing of welfare benefits to the establishment of formulas for adapting wage structures to new machines and processes. Even more challenging is the fact that today's collective bargaining decisions are inevitably of a *long-run* character, with consequences that extend far into the future. And the margin for error is uncomfortably small—competitive survival in 1967 may well depend upon a company's foresight in current negotiations.

Negotiating a contract, then, is no longer a one-man job. No one can be expected to know the answers to all the questions that come up during a bargaining session. When a company sits down to talk to the union about wages, hours, and working conditions, it will need engineers and production men to advise on operating problems, legal specialists to make certain that the agreements are properly drawn up and in accord with existing laws, and most of all, informed opinions on the long-range prospects of business.

In short, collective bargaining must be considered as an integrated

[1] From *Personnel* (published by the American Management Association), July–August 1957, pp. 63–68. Used by permission.

management function. It calls for thorough preparation, intelligent planning, and bold and fluid execution. Though based on research in advance of negotiation, it must not be hamstrung by the narrow approach sometimes associated with research. From a solid platform of facts, the negotiators must venture into unexplored territory. Hence their judgment, while rooted in realistic common sense, must at the same time be positive, imaginative, and flexible.

THE HIDDEN PERIL

It goes without saying that executives must be thoroughly familiar with *all* the terms of the labor contract, not merely with a few of its more spectacular features. This is all the more important inasmuch as what a company pays out in dollars and cents to get a new contract may be a trivial expense compared to the ultimate cost of restrictive clauses in the agreement. These clauses may pass unnoticed when the contract is signed, but later on prove to be extremely costly in preventing management from utilizing its work force effectively.

On the other hand, such provisions as wage increases, insurance benefits, or vacations and holidays are often eye-catching and awe-inspiring but—like the above-water portion of an iceberg—not necessarily dangerous if a company's increased productivity and competitive position in its industry permit management to grant these benefits without damaging the price structure of its product. The peril is to be found in those parts of the agreement that are hidden beneath the surface. It is there that the ship comes to grief.

A Case in Point

Let me cite a typical example. This concerns the collective bargaining experience of a certain company in the Midwest not too many years ago. From 1946 to 1953, the demand for this firm's product, particularly by the automobile industry, was extremely heavy. Hence management was mainly concerned with keeping the plant running at all cost.

With regard to wages and employee benefits, the concessions that had been granted by the company were not too far out of line with those of other companies in the same industry and area. On the other hand, over the years management had permitted disastrous "mutual consent" clauses to creep into the contract. Its eyes were so firmly fixed on the visible costs of the operation that it did not think it worthwhile to make a fight over provisions affecting work assignments, certainly not to risk a strike over them.

But that was where the company made a serious mistake.

One clause in the contract stated that a furnace crew must consist of seven men. If one member was missing, the crew could not work at their regular jobs unless a substitute was available. Nothing wrong with that, you may say. However, management also agreed that, should an absence occur, it would obtain the union's permission to fill its crew from other qualified employees. There was the joker!

For some months before each contract expired, the union would see to it that, about three times a week, the furnace crew was short one man. It would then deny management the right to transfer a qualified employee to the job. These harassing tactics preliminary to bargaining wore the company down. By the time management was ready to talk contract, it was willing to make almost any concession just to keep in operation.

Eventually, of course, management was forced to take a long strike to remedy the situation. Having given away its right to manage, the company had to fight to get it back. If, on the other hand, the issues had been met head on when they were comparatively inconsequential, the crisis might have been avoided. But management had not looked far enough ahead.

THE LONG-RUN POINT OF VIEW

Such laxity carried smaller penalties in the past than it does today. Until 1950, contracts in most industries were for a year's duration. Any mistakes made in negotiation might be straightened out the next year before too much damage had been done. But all this changed when the automotive industry signed five-year agreements and the long-term contract took over in other major industries.

By and large, this is probably a step forward. Three-, four-, and five-year agreements tend to stabilize working conditions. They enable management to plan ahead with greater assurance, since basic wage costs are fixed and major strikes are less likely.

At the same time, however, mistakes made in negotiation are likely to be much more costly. If for no other reason than this, collective bargaining must be given thorough and continuous attention. We cannot afford to rely on random methods. We must calculate the effects of present decisions on events taking place not just next month or next year, but five or ten years from now.

Without either endorsing or criticizing the principle of supplemental unemployment benefits, it may be suggested that the strategy and tactics used by Ford in its 1955 negotiations provide a good illustration of the value of advance planning.

The company anticipated the demand for a guaranteed annual wage and began to study its own situation three years ahead of time. Long before negotiations started, it had decided what was the best thing to do from the standpoint of its own interests. Its approach to the problem was based on sound research, and the decisions taken in the 1955 bargaining sessions were in keeping with a positive philosophy of collective bargaining.

MANAGEMENT'S DUAL RESPONSIBILITY

In planning its industrial relations future, management is faced with what might be called a dual responsibility.

First, and above all, it must do what it considers best for its own company. Management today cannot afford to play follow-the-leader in union relations. Since conditions vary from industry to industry, even from company to company within a single industry, each management must plan its own course of action in labor relations as far as possible, always keeping in mind that its decisions must assure the competitive advancement of the company. It is reckless for any company to accept the results of other companies' negotiations without first making sure that its own future will not be imperiled.

Of course, companies that are involved in industry-wide or area bargaining must accept the results of such bargaining as long as they are tied in with it. Even so, a time may come when a particular company is compelled to decide whether to continue to share the safety of numbers or to withdraw and make its own fight for survival.

The second responsibility is one that might seem to be in conflict with the first. Actually, it is more in the nature of a restraining influence. This is the responsibility for avoiding—as much as possible—actions that will have an adverse effect on other managements.

While the overriding responsibility of any management is to protect and advance its own company, the fact is inescapable that labor relations have developed to the point where management can no longer enjoy the luxury of isolationism. Much as we should like to feel that we have complete freedom and self-determination, we are increasingly under an obligation to weigh the effect of our actions on other companies.

Union Strategy

This situation has been brought about by the union strategy of securing a gain in one negotiation and then attempting to force it on other companies. The technique is familiar enough. Once a concession is made, the unions go to work on other companies. It seems to make little difference whether the circumstances which justified the concession initially are the same in other cases—the pressure is on.

In large companies, particularly in those industries where the unions make a practice of moving on an industry-wide basis, management is acutely aware of "patterns."

Take my own industry for example. Once a railroad agrees to something, the unions take this as the floor and go to work on the other companies to jack it up. In consequence, any railroad management, even in handling individual matters on its own properties, has to give a great deal of thought to the effect its decisions may have on others. This has been something of a deterrent to free collective bargaining, unfortunately, but the unions have only themselves to blame.

The difference between industries where such conditions exist and those where bargaining has a more localized impact is only one of degree—and one that will narrow as the unions extend their pressure techniques. Even today, there are very few places where the problem does not exist to some extent. Certainly management cannot afford to be complacent and take the attitude that the little things it does from day to day are designed merely to meet its own situation and will have no wider effects.

These "little things" in fact are stepping stones—pieces of mosaic that the unions will try to fit together if they like the picture. Let me emphasize this point with an extreme example. A company on the Florida East Coast, say, agrees to make a substantial extra payment for operating a snow plow. Will this "pattern" find its way eventually to the Boston and Maine?

WHAT DOES LABOR WANT?

In planning our industrial relations future, the question that naturally arises is, "What will labor try to obtain?" We receive considerable help from labor itself in answering that question, since unions make no secret of what they expect to accomplish. Any industrial relations executive with access to a newspaper knew in 1945 that labor wanted paid holidays and vacations. In 1946, these benefits were granted.

Industry was likewise aware of the unions' desire for pension plans and insurance programs many years before these became an actuality.

In the auto industry, Walter Reuther began to talk about the productivity factor in 1948; in 1950, it was granted. The union leaders commenced to pound the drum for the guaranteed annual wage (GAW) in 1953. They did not get it—at least not in the form originally proposed—but they did secure a supplemental unemployment benefit plan in 1955 which, they say, embodies that principle.

Much of labor's recent activities has been centered on the problem of minimizing the impact of automation. The SUB plan is one approach to this problem, but there are others as well. For example, my railroad has been confronted with demands which would have the effect of fixing the minimum size of our work force over certain periods of time. Labor can be expected to continue its efforts in this direction in the future, as the recent convention of the United Automobile Workers made clear.

At this convention [1956], the union served notice that it intended to push for a shorter workweek with increased pay, improved supplementary unemployment benefits, and protection of employees in cases of plant or work transfer. All of these proposals are, of course, designed to provide job security either by spreading the work or by providing protection for employees adversely affected by changes in jobs.

In addition, of course, there will be the inevitable demands for wage increases—and they will not be modest. Labor itself anticipates that wages will rise about 50 per cent between now and 1966. Efforts to raise the minimum wage to $1.50 or $1.75 an hour may be expected as well as demands for longer vacations, more holidays, and longer week ends.

Certainly labor will want more in the way of welfare, and no doubt management will be asked to pay all the costs. Among other things, there will be pressure to reduce the retirement age from 65 to 60 years for men and to 55 for women and to increase pension payments from the present level to a range of $250 to $300 monthly.

THE ROLE OF MANAGEMENT

If all these demands are added up, the prospect is an awesome one. It must not be forgotten, however, that management's ingenuity and its dynamic approach to industrial problems have made labor's gains possible. It is only because industry has found ways to increase its production, to better the quality of its goods and services, and to sustain prosperity that labor has been able to achieve its ends.

The unions will continue to make demands because that is their business. But, regardless of the sound and fury over claims and counterclaims, labor's working conditions will improve only to the extent that industry's growth makes it possible.

We must continue to grow, not merely to make the predictions of union leaders look good, but to advance the interests of everyone in the country. It is the responsibility of industrial relations men to plan the future in such a way that management retains control over its own operations—while at the same time employees receive a fair share of the fruits of their efforts.

A LONG-RANGE STRATEGY

As to how to do this, there is no pat solution or ready-made formula. Every company has its own problems and its own opportunities for growth. However, if management is to contribute its share to the continuing development of the economy, it must plan wisely and on a long-term basis. Collective bargaining is an important part of such planning.

In devising a collective bargaining strategy for, say, the next ten years, the following suggestions may provide some general guidance:

1. Production time is a company's most important commodity. If management can secure maximum utilization of its work force, labor's gains will be limited only by the rapidity with which technological advances can be made and by the demands of the consumer, assum-

ing of course a fair return to the owners of the property. In negotiating contracts, therefore, the aim should be to secure full efficiency and flexibility of operation.

2. The exact cost of labor for every operation must be known in order to calculate the value of whatever changes in contracts may be necessary to compensate for restrictions on the use of labor.

3. Contracts should be negotiated on a competitive basis and with full knowledge of the wage rates and fringe benefit costs of other companies in the area and industry.

4. A positive and detailed program of management objectives should be developed, with employee relations treated as an integral part of the program.

5. Contracts should be drawn up in such a way as to permit management to take quick advantage of technological changes that will increase the efficiency of operations.

6. Negotiations should not be based solely on the union's demands. Collective bargaining is a two-way street, and management as well as union negotiators must know what they want.

7. Employee communications must be such as to establish a healthy climate for contract negotiations. Only if the employees understand contemplated changes will they recognize them as being to their advantage.

47

Forecasting Manpower Needs—A Tested Formula[1]

Wendel W. Burton

Industry has devoted a great deal of time, effort, and money to the study of economic influences: past, present, and future. Sales forecasts, budgets, and plant and equipment expansion, among many profit tools, are determined by these studies. Unfortunately, this same time and effort have not been expended to study manpower forecasting. Most employment departments and cost departments throughout the country have overlooked or neglected this field. Perhaps the "feast or famine" nature of our work has kept us on the run too much in recent years, but I am not convinced that our own lack of planning has not contributed to this general confusion.

Although we in industry try to anticipate our needs in plant expansion with long-range programs, we normally wait until the last minute before instituting a request for the specialized manpower needed to operate these plants. Under the pressures of immediate need, a compromise is frequently made in the selection of a person or people to direct a part of our operations; and as a result, some of the gains we should expect are not realized. "Lead time" to get desired personnel is needed.

Minnesota Mining and Manufacturing Company is a growth company with a history of yearly additions. We, too, were subjected to

[1] Based on a presentation to the American Management Association, 1957. Used by permission of the author.

the problems caused by war, postwar, Korea, and the pressures since then. We were not completely free from the influences of the "bulls" and "bears" of the employment market. With colleges and high schools releasing their graduates primarily in June, it was most important that we recruit large numbers early; otherwise, we would have to pull our applicants from other companies. This situation pointed up very clearly the need for accurate facts and figures.

About four years ago on a visit to General Motors, I had the opportunity to discuss these problems with Merle Hale, head of Salaried Personnel and, in turn, a chance to preview their "lead time" program for replacements. This discussion gave me the idea that an accurate forecast could be made of future needs by a careful analysis of the past. I determined on my return to take the General Motors replacement program and statistically relate it to economic forecasts.

The first step in this program was to discuss my idea with our director of personnel and secure his approval for such a study. He recommended that the first study be made of part of our management payroll so that this information could be utilized by the Personnel Development Committee.

A five-year statistical history of this management payroll was made, dividing the group into five classifications: sales, laboratory, engineering, administrative, and production. A tabulation was made of the number in each group at the start of the year, and additions and deletions for the year and the total at the end of the year. (Although a detailed analysis was made of the additions and deletions, nothing significant developed.) Turnover percentages were determined and the possible retirements within the next five years listed (see Figure 1).

Our company uses sales dollars as the basis for all forecasts and budgets. If a relationship could be established between manpower and sales dollars, then it would be possible to forecast manpower for as many years in the future as sales forecasts were available. With this in mind I tried relating the number of managers at the end of the year to parent company sales for the year. There was an excellent correlation on the first attempt. The average amount of sales per manager was quite consistent each year even in the various classifications. I then received a five-year sales forecast from our Economic Research Department. The total parent company sales forecast for each year was divided by the average sales per manager, and the re-

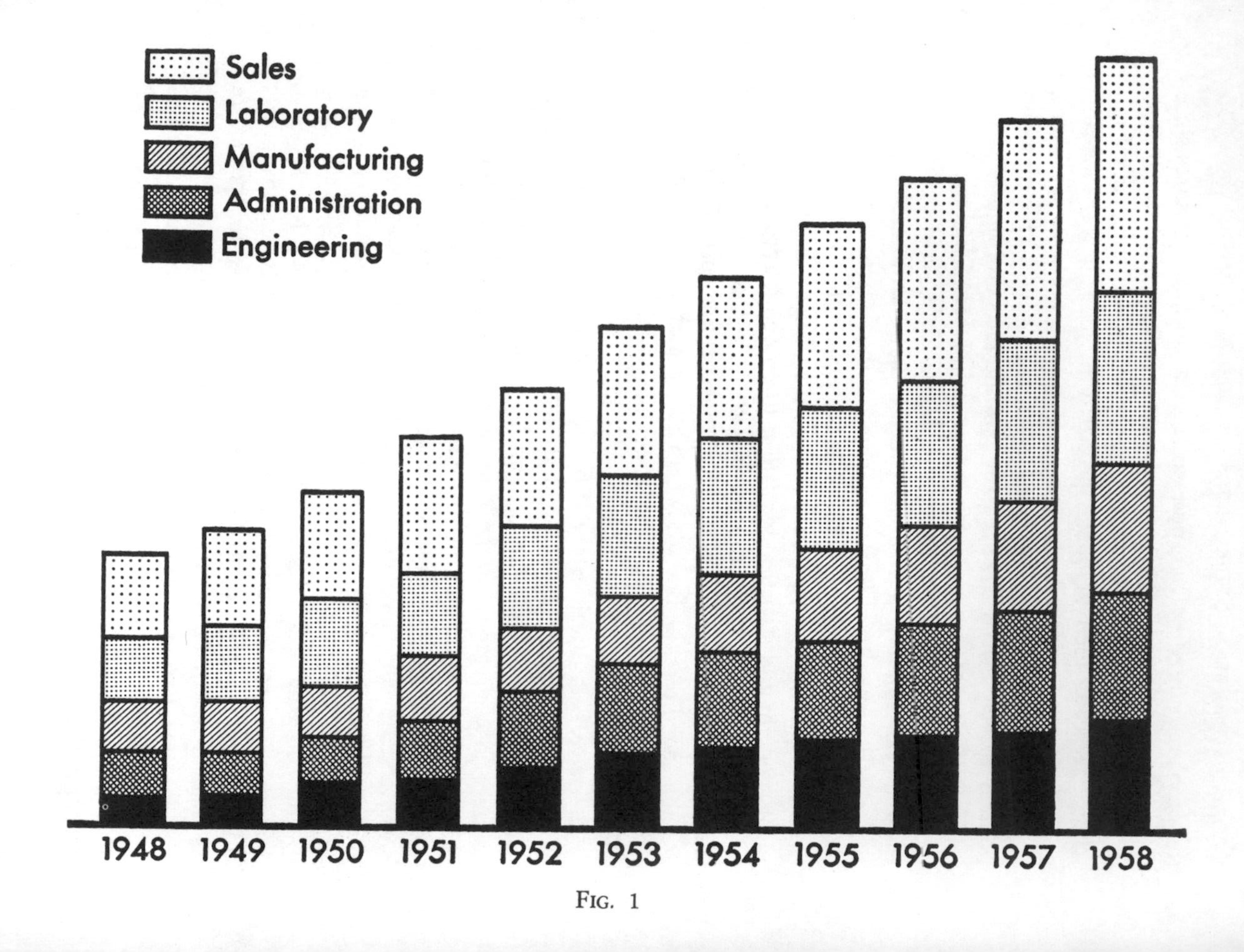
Sales
Laboratory
Manufacturing
Administration
Engineering
1948
1949
1950
1951
1952
1953
1954
1955
1956
1957
1958

FIG. 1

sult was a total of managers for each year of the next five years. By multiplying the total managers each year by the turnover ratios and adding the number of additional managers to be secured that year, we were able to determine the number necessary to develop (see Table 1 and Figure 2).

TABLE 1

Year	Salesmen End of Year (number)	Average During Year	Sales Per Man Col. 2 (000)	Per Cent of Turnover	1955 Sales Forecast + Or — (000)	Loss Through Turnover (number)	+ Or — Forecast
1950	72	70	$211	7			
1951	77	74.5	220	5	$1,387		
1952	87	82	219	11			
					Avg.		
1953	93	90	234	8	212		
1954	92	92.5	210	6		7	None
Avg.				7			

In view of the fact that we obtained a correlation on sales, it was not necessary to explore other areas such as units produced or sold, plant worth, and so forth.

Our charts were submitted to the Personnel Development Committee with a recommendation that a quarterly analysis be made to insure accuracy. The information resulting from this study gave them an accurate forecast on which to base their development plans. The question might well be asked, "How accurate has this forecast proven?" A check on December 31 of each year starting with 1954 has shown the following margin of error:

December 31, 1954—less than ½ of 1 per cent
December 31, 1955—less than ½ of 1 per cent
December 31, 1956—8/10 of 1 per cent

Today, three and one-half years from the date of the original forecast, we are still following our historical pattern. Should management make any policy or procedural decisions that would affect this pattern, our calculations could be adjusted accordingly.

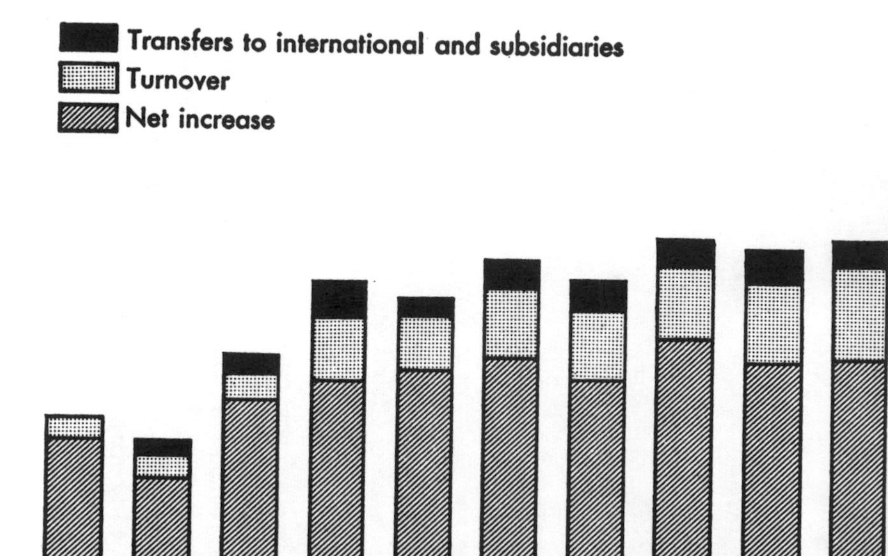

FIG. 2. Managerial Requirements

After the presentation to the Development Committee, I asked permission to study an operating division, and a member of the committee offered his division as a "guinea pig." An analysis of the management payroll in that division again gave us a fine correlation, and our forecasts were made in the same manner as in our first study.

In studying the division, I was particularly anxious to try this method on salesmen, for management had experienced difficulty in meeting its sales forecasts. Our study quickly pointed out the reason. It took about six to nine months for a new salesman to start pulling his own weight and, as a result, unless men were added well in advance they could not contribute. To meet the sales goals for any year it was necessary to have *x* men on the payroll at the start of the year for every million dollars of sales forecast. A suggested schedule for the addition of salesmen was prepared for the division. Periodic checks of the management forecast have shown about the same percentage of error as experienced in our first study.

These forecasting activities were a spare-time operation of the Employment Department, and as a result nothing further was attempted until the fall of 1954. At that time, we were notified by our sales executive that a combination of sales forces might release a large number of men for assignment to other divisions. The suggestion was made that it might be desirable to withhold hiring additional men until these men were properly transferred. Permission was asked and given us to make a study, analysis, and forecast of all sales divisions.

Working with the statistical department, we tabulated a five-year history of each sales force. In establishing the amount of sales per man, both the number of men at the end of the year and the average number of men during the year were tried. We found our best results with the average number of men during the year. Using the year's sales for that division and dividing by the average number of men involved, the sales per man were determined. The sales forecast for the coming year was then divided by the number of men on the force at that time.

This new figure was compared to the present figure and past history in order to determine if additional manpower would be needed. The turnover percentages were calculated for each year and a reasonable percentage used to determine turnover for the coming year. The total number of men needed because of turnover and additions was then calculated and the result compared with the total of those who might be available for transfer. It was very apparent that we could continue hiring salesmen on a modified scale and easily absorb those available for transfer (see Table 2).

TABLE 2

Year	Salesmen End of Year (number)	Average During Year (number)	Sales Per Man Col. 2 (000)	Per Cent of Turnover	1955 Sales Forecast + Or — (000)	Loss Through Turnover (number)	+ Or — Forecast (number)
1950	54	52	$ 96	18			
1951	54	54	103	26			
1952	72	63	118	28	$2,585		
1953	81	76.5	120	13			
1954	78	79.5	135	7	Avg. 155	13	18
Avg				17			

This information was presented to our top sales officer and all sales managers. Permission was given the Employment Department to recruit or transfer as we determined best. It was pointed out to each sales manager that the trend in sales per man could give him an excellent picture of the size of his force. If the amount per man was getting too high, additional men should be added; if too low, perhaps some should be removed or at least additions stopped. The information is now analyzed every six months, and, if considered advisable, presented to the sales manager.

The statistical department and I next tried a study and forecast of our laboratories. With a ten-year history of personnel readily available from the budgets prepared by our Controller's Department, we decided to double our normal five-year analysis. We first tried to compare total laboratory personnel with sales each year, but found a poor correlation. When we eliminated the nontechnical employees from our calculations, however, we found a very good correlation. Every time we increased company sales a million dollars, we added *y* number of technical employees. When we carried our calculations into the individual product laboratories and compared their technical manpower with the sales of that product division, however, we found wide differences. The correlation that we experienced for the combined laboratories would not hold true for them individually.

In our analysis of this situation, we did not attempt to tell who was right or which laboratory had the better balance. It appeared on the surface that one laboratory had nontechnical personnel engaged in technical activities and another probably was forcing its technical personnel to do some nontechnical supporting work. A meeting was held with several of our laboratory heads in the controller's office. The results of the study were discussed, and it was decided that some of the laboratories would try to experiment for a year or two and determine how much nontechnical help is required effectively to back up a technical man. It is quite possible that this study may affect our method of laboratory budgeting.

In the summer of 1955, our vice-president of engineering appointed a committee of engineers to analyze the manpower situation in the Engineering Division. They were concerned with a sudden shortage of manpower and wanted to do something about it. At our first meeting, as consultant, I acquainted the committee with the results of previous studies, and it was decided to approach this problem in a similar way. Members of the committee were assigned by the chairman the task of gathering certain statistics for the second meeting. We determined to analyze several factors, such as engineering costs, plant worth, total expenditures, and operating expenses in relationship to manpower. At the second meeting these comparisons were made, but again sales and technical personnel gave us our best correlation.

The committee presented this information to the vice-president of engineering with the suggestion that our hiring be brought back into balance with the sales curve. Approval was granted, and our hiring program was stepped up.

My goal in manpower forecasting has always been the accurate preparation and use of forecasts by our operating divisions. The Controller's Division has had the same goals; therefore, over a year ago they insisted on manpower forecasts as a part of each budget plan for the following year. When all manpower forecasts were received they were tabulated and then discussed with the Employment Department. With the ratios determined from our studies we jointly made some corrections on the technical requirements. The office requirements were not adjusted due to the fact that up to that time we had not made a five-year history of that division. The Employment Department then calculated the turnover figures for sales, technical, and salaried nontechnical. These figures were added to the increased manpower forecasts, and my department had an excellent picture of its recruiting responsibility. The factory and temporary estimates (not a problem) were included, and the forecast for 1956 was complete.

48

Control of Overseas Operations[1]

Willem Holst

One of several aspects of control—remote or otherwise—is the establishment of targets, or objectives, by the top management of a company. In overseas operations such targets may be arrived at in a number of ways—for example, on the basis of American experience, or by a comparative analysis of a number of overseas units, or by an individual analysis of conditions applying to a single operation in a particular country. Frequently a combination of these approaches is used. But whatever route is taken, whether past performance or some other criteria are employed, these two conditions must be met if the goals are to be set successfully and if subsequent control is to be maintained:

There must be a continuous flow of information between the field and the central office.

[1] By permission from *Management Guide to Overseas Operations,* ed. Dan H. Fenn, Jr. Copyright, 1957, McGraw-Hill Book Company, Inc.

The information must be consolidated and analyzed in reference to given standards of performance.

I will limit my discussion in the following pages to the longer-range aspects of remote control, concentrating on the planning and coordination of supply and demand for five to ten years ahead, and the associated financial problems. Long-range planning is just as dependent on a continuous flow of information between the fields and the central office as is short-range planning. But the type of information and the relationships between the overseas units and headquarters are likely to be somewhat different in short-range planning, where an appraisal of past performance is usually involved. Before describing Standard-Vacuum's control system in this context, however, I would like to digress briefly to describe the company's operations.

SCOPE OF ACTIVITY

From the 1890's to 1933, the Standard Oil Company (New Jersey) and the Socony Mobil Oil Company had been operating as separate firms in the Eastern Hemisphere. Jersey Standard had only producing and refining facilities there, while Socony Mobil was limited to a marketing organization. The two companies felt that they could achieve better service and greater operating efficiencies by combining operations. So in 1933 they formed the Standard-Vacuum Oil Company, which was to operate in the Asian and African countries east and southwest of the Persian Gulf. This portion of the world includes more than fifty separate political entities and has a population of almost 900 million, exclusive of the mainland of China.

Today, Standard-Vacuum operates as a fully integrated, separate oil company. It has its own officers and directors, and formulates and administers its own policies. It has just completed a new headquarters office in White Plains, New York, which houses the seven hundred employees who constitute the company's headquarters staff.

Overseas, Standard-Vacuum has 40,000 employees. About 95 per cent of them are nationals of the countries in which they work. The company has established twenty-one wholly owned subsidiaries and fourteen branches abroad; in addition, it has one affiliate in which it owns a majority interest, and seven in which its interest is less than

50 per cent. These operating units cover all phases of the oil industry —exploration, production, pipeline transportation, refining, marine transportation, and marketing. At present, the company's principal exploration activity is in Indonesia, India, Pakistan, Western New Guinea, Papua, British Somaliland, and the Philippines. Standard-Vacuum currently operates refineries in Indonesia, India, South Africa, Australia, and Japan. Marketing activity throughout the so-called "Stanvac Area" is conducted through twenty-two branches and subsidiaries. In addition to its own production, Stanvac is a purchaser of both crude oil and products in the Middle East, where its parent companies have a share in petroleum operations in Iran, Iraq, Saudi Arabia, and Qatar. For transporting the petroleum, the company owns and operates twenty-three vessels totaling about 340,000 dead-weight tons. In addition, it usually has another thirty to forty ships under period charter.

Stanvac's branch and subsidiary offices are located at points as far apart as Capetown, South Africa; and Yokohama, Japan; and Karachi, Pakistan; and Wellington, New Zealand. Some 10,000 miles separate these locations. Singapore, close to the center of the Stanvac area, is 180° both east and west of New York, where the company has its headquarters; hence the adjective "remote" is particularly applicable to Standard-Vacuum's operations.

The company's rapid postwar growth, combined with the vastness of distance and variety of activities it embraces, has made the problem of remote control an exceedingly complex one for us. Our volume of business increased from about 70,000 barrels per day in 1938 to 200,000 barrels per day in 1955. Consequently, the topic of this chapter represents an operating problem which demands our continuing attention.

PLANNING AGENCIES

Standard-Vacuum's long-range planning is done through the cooperation of several agencies in the central office, which consolidate field information and translate it into company-wide plans for the future:

The functional departments—exploration, producing, manufacturing, marketing, and marine transportation—act as technical liaison agents between their field counterparts and other central office control agencies.

The economic coordination department provides the supply-and-demand framework for the company's long-range logistical planning, evaluates possible alternatives of supply through the preparation of economic studies, and establishes the basis for a long-term capital investment program.

The treasurer's department translates the investment program into its financial implications. Included in its reports are a consolidated forecast of cash available from profit and depreciation, a breakdown by currencies, and a statement of sources for additional funds, if such are needed to arrive at a balance with the company's over-all capital requirements.

The coordination committee is responsible for reviewing all forward plans, associated budgets, and appropriation requests before recommending action by the board of directors.

THE CONTROL MECHANISMS

We can now look at Standard-Vacuum's machinery for long-range planning and control in somewhat greater detail. There are four main mechanisms:

1. The establishment of definite objectives with regard to areas of operation, degree of integration, product quality improvement, and similar matters
2. A forecast of petroleum consumption five to ten years ahead on an area-wide basis, with an estimate of the company's sales opportunities based on that probable consumption
3. The determination of an optimum supply-and-demand balance by individual years
4. The preparation of a cash and currency forecast, taking into account capital investment requirements, crude and product pricing, freight rates, and the profitability of each phase of the company's operations

The long-range objectives are established at two levels—the policy level, where the political stability and economic climate of particular regions determine their acceptability as areas of large-scale future investment; and the operational or budgetary level, where the long-range logistical and financial framework determines how much each phase should be expanded or contracted, or what degree of integration should be sought, taking into account parent company supplies of crude and product in the Persian Gulf.

The determination of the economic climate is accomplished in various ways. Many governments publish pamphlets describing incentives for foreign investment, and these are most helpful. Also, agencies of our own government prepare excellent material on foreign industrial opportunities through local embassies and consulates. Stanvac's own field offices periodically submit pertinent data to guide the central office in matters affecting both the economic and political climate. In addition, when a large new investment is contemplated, direct contact is established between directors of the company and high government officials to explore the economic conditions further and to discuss terms.

FORECASTING DEMAND

The second planning mechanism is one which I am sure is familiar to all readers: the forecasting of future business volume. Standard-Vacuum has continuously modified its forecasting techniques over the past ten years. In the process we have markedly changed the character of our relationships with the field, especially in this matter of appraising future outlook.

Prior to 1947 forecasting of demand was almost exclusively the responsibility of overseas marketing units and was confined to Stanvac sales as opposed to industry-wide prospects. The New York office did little reviewing or revising beyond the consolidation of individual field forecasts, which were largely based on local knoweldge of sales contracts for the near future, combined with an attempt at simple projection of past sales trends for individual petroleum products. While this method yielded reasonably good over-all results for the two or three years immediately ahead—with errors averaging only 2 per cent to 5 per cent for aggregate demand—estimates for five to ten years into the future were always far too low. For example, a projection made in 1946 for the year 1955 proved to be 40 per cent below the actual tenth, or terminal year, of the forecast period.

In order to improve such forecasts—particularly those for individual products—and to permit a more careful New York review, the field units were given new instructions. These programs suggested the preparation of forecasts by an "end-use" technique—that is, an estimate of the number of passenger cars, buses, trucks, and tractors that would be in operation and the average amount of petroleum each would consume. Such forecasts, prepared on an industry-wide basis for two to four years ahead, made possible a more careful New

York appraisal of field estimates and provided a good basis for a reasoned exchange of views when New York felt the estimates required revision. However, longer-range estimates for over four years continued to be made largely on the basis of the simple projection technique, a device with limitations which readily became apparent.

More recently, therefore, the New York staff has adopted a technique which is coming into ever more widespread use: the determination of long-range trends in petroleum demand by an analysis of the entire energy balance of an area. This means forecasting the *total* demand for all forms of energy from primary sources such as coal, hydropower, natural gas, petroleum, and, eventually, nuclear sources. Then an estimate is made of the part that petroleum is likely to play in meeting that total demand. This requires an appraisal of the probable rate of industrialization and economic development generally, of future balance-of-payments problems, and of the availability and rate of exploitation of competing energy sources. With New York's encouragement, a few of our major field units are beginning to adopt this technique; smaller units, however, simply do not have an adequate staff to carry through such a relatively sophisticated approach.

Japan provides an illustration of the operation of this energy-balance method of forecasting demand:

About five years ago, when we first tried this approach, we looked at the Japanese government's estimates of future coal production. Their figure was something like 55 million tons a year. As time went by, Japan's actual coal production dropped from a level of 48 million tons down to 43 million. At that point, of course, we became quite worried about our balances. We made a local survey and discovered that the coal situation seemed to be getting even worse, indicating that the government's higher coal production forecast was likely to be nowhere near correct. Consequently, we turned our plans around completely, basing them on the more realistic figure of 43 million tons of coal. The difference in consumption of fuel oil was enormous, and we had to make drastic changes in our expansion plans for the next five years.

BALANCING SUPPLY AND DEMAND

The determination of supply and demand is a complex problem, involving an infinite number of permutations and combinations. We have more than a dozen crude oils available, at least eight refinery sources of supply including the Persian Gulf, and over twenty marketing entities to satisfy with products covering a wide range of quality specifications.

Our third control mechanism, designed to balance supply and demand, is based generally on estimates of product output by overseas operational units, but any plan extending beyond three years can be modified if necessary by selection and construction of appropriate refinery equipment. The final determination of what may be regarded as an optimum over-all balance for the company as a whole is therefore essentially an economic problem, involving a comparison of major alternatives. By its very nature, this is a centralized New York office function. In large measure, the staff work is carried out by the economic coordination department, which works in close collaboration with the New York functional departments. Of course, some trial and error is involved in arriving at optimum solutions, but a new supply-and-demand balance must be prepared once every six months because of the ever-changing aspects of the petroleum industry as a whole.

The fourth and final mechanism of long-range planning is the translation of the supply-and-demand balance into financial terms, and the reappraisal of various major alternatives in the light of over-all financial feasibility. Costs, requirements for investment in fixed capital and working capital, and cash generation through profits, depreciation, self-insurance, and other reserves must be projected by major functions.

Standard-Vacuum's overseas units are responsible for the initial preparation of such cash forecasts for periods up to four years into the future. However, these estimates are subject to general guidance from the New York office, which determines the assumptions that should be used with regard to prices, freight rates, and so on. Some New York adjustments usually prove to be necessary. Generally, we have found that these modifications suggested by the central office and based on its comparative analysis of past field forecasts are helpful in improving future field accuracy.

The New York staff tends to assume primary responsibility for the preparation of longer-range financial forecasts—that is, forecasts extending beyond four years. Individual field units are not in a good position to determine the size and location of needed new refineries, or to judge the relative priorities to be assigned to various regions in terms of their comparative political stability or investment climate. As in the case of demand forecasting, however, it is hoped that the larger field units can make an increasing contribution to such longer-range financial projections.

In closing, I would like to make a few general observations, based on Stanvac's experience, about the relationships between field and central office with respect to long-range forward planning:

Standard-Vacuum's system of remote control is not static, but is subject to constant development, experimentation, and change.

What appears to be a highly centralized long-range planning control function belies the fact that in many other respects, and even in short-range planning, Standard-Vacuum encourages an ever-increasing degree of decentralization in order to free top management for major policy issues.

Because of the complexity of the company's operations, certain appraisals and decisions can be made only in New York; nevertheless, here too an attempt is made to keep information flowing in both directions between the field and the central office. A continuous interchange is essential for improving the accuracy of longer-range forecasting and for logistical coordination.

In planning a sound program for the future, Stanvac feels that the central office agencies should always have the courage to look as far into the future as is necessary to discern the major trends. Because it may well take up to five years to negotiate, plan, and build a new refinery from scratch—and even longer to develop a new producing field—Stanvac believes that forecasting and planning should extend up to ten years ahead.

CONCLUSION

I know we can reach our immediate goals without a great deal of reflective thinking. But I doubt that we can build vitality for tomorrow without a lot of it, for this is the way we get deeper understanding of our problems.

—Frederick R. Kappel

49

Knowledge for Long-Range Planning

David W. Ewing

In the preceding chapters we have looked at long-range planning as a philosophy, as a management concept, as a set of methods, as a solution to special company problems. We have assessed its importance. We have viewed it in relation to other business issues and requirements.

In this concluding chapter let us look at long-range planning in a different way. Let us analyze it in terms of knowledge. This is an appropriate way to close out a volume like this, because it allows us to see long-range planning in perspective, in its entirety, and to see where thc gaps and rough edges are. Long-range planning is not yet, we shall find, a completed concept or tool. It is unfinished business. Indeed, it is ironical but true that the kinds of knowledge in shortest supply are the most important; whereas the kinds in greatest supply are of secondary importance.

What types of knowledge are important to the long-range planner? What is their role in the planning effort of an organization? How adequate are they? I shall take these questions first, then speculate in a more general way on the future needs of planning.

KNOWLEDGE OF PLANNING METHODS

We bring this type of knowledge to bear in planning when the problem is already formulated and the assignment is to solve it. The problem may either be one thrust on us by trends and events—for instance, the need to double sales in five years because of rising costs or changes in the competitive picture—or it may arise out of our own previous thinking and analysis, as when we decide we *want* to achieve new goals to satisfy our ambitions. In any event, the job is relatively clear: find out *how* such-and-such an objective can be attained.

Suppose that a company finds itself losing more and more business to competitors; both production and sales costs have risen to dangerous levels. It is clear to everyone in management that either the company must regain its position in the market or find new markets to succeed in. If, as is more than likely, such a reversal cannot be accomplished in one or two years but requires a longer term, the need for a formal long-range planning effort may be apparent. If executives want to learn the ABC's of how to do that, they can pick up the knowledge from a variety of sources—magazine articles about how other companies have organized for long-range planning, chapters in books on organization and planning (either of these sources might, of course, be found right in this volume), papers read at business meetings, consultants, conversation with other businessmen. This information is an example of methods knowledge.

To illustrate again, suppose that an oil company wants to find the best combination of investment, production, transportation, refining, and sales operations for a five-year period. What program of yearly crude oil production targets, expansions in refining facilities, sales by product, and so forth will (given certain data or estimates) lead to the greatest profit figure? Here, too, the experience of other companies is available. The chapter by Rapoport and Drew in this book is a case in point; and in the literature of operations research and mathematical programing there is a wealth of detail on specialized aspects of the problem.

I do not mean to imply that managers in business, government, and education can readily procure *all* the information about planning methods that they need. There is a lack of good material on the techniques of revising long-range plans as they get out of date, on the special problems of planning in small business, on the qualities to look for in planners, and on other topics. Nevertheless there is, relatively speaking, a fairly good supply of information, and it has been growing at an encouraging rate in recent years. Some superb work has been done by experts in this area.

KNOWLEDGE OF CONDITIONS AND TRENDS AFFECTING PLANNING

Here we deal with present and future conditions, internal and external, that have a potential influence on the success of a long-range program. Sometimes this type of knowledge is closely related to methods knowledge and may seem to overlap it, yet it is distinct enough in character to demand different skills, judgments, and resources.

For example, *The Wall Street Journal* reported that the Martin Company, a division of Martin-Marietta Corporation, was planning to abandon missile production after a few years.[1] The reason was that management foresaw a leveling off of the missile business as a predicted East-West stalemate developed. This phase of the company's long-range planning rested on information gathered about probable developments in one large military market.

Again, when Northrop Company began long-range planning in the mid-1950's, its business was concentrated, according to reports, in about a dozen large contracts, all of them subject to cancellation. Management wanted this changed. After seven years of planning it succeeded in spreading out the company's business into some seventy contracts, most of them comparatively small. The company was less vulnerable to cancellations, had a much higher ratio of net income to sales, and 50 per cent higher earnings.[2] This remarkable progress was based in good part on knowledge about the business environment.

Internal trends and conditions enter in here, too. We all know that an organization's ability to expand, contract, or change depends crucially on such factors as personal talents, morale, financing, facilities, contractual commitments, and so on. Knowledge of the present and probable future state of such factors, with or without specific management efforts to alter them, obviously has (or should have) a great bearing on many long-range plans.

It is significant, I think, that this kind of information calls different skills into play than are required by methods knowledge (the type previously discussed). The subjective factor is greater. The manager must do a more discerning "intelligence" job, making experienced guesses not only about the probable cause-and-effect relation-

[1] October 25, 1961, p. 1.
[2] *The Wall Street Journal,* October 25, 1961, p. 10.

ships of different trends and developments, but also about the validity of the informational sources themselves. This may be why top executives are so likely to get in the act when this type of knowledge is used. They may delegate much of the fact-gathering task to subordinates, but when it comes to evaluating and applying the information, they are accustomed to taking over personally.

How adequate is this type of information? All in all, it seems to be in fairly good supply—never good *enough,* of course, yet satisfactory compared to other knowledge sources. The art of forecasting is well developed in many companies; the kinds of effort described earlier in this volume by Busch, Payne, Hunt, Tickton, and Burton, just to name a few, will strike most observers as impressive. Then, too, we have magazines like *Harvard Business Review, Fortune,* and *Business Week,* and newspapers like *The Wall Street Journal* and *The New York Times,* which regularly contain useful information about developing trends and likely future consequences. Business consultants have again and again done a superb briefing job for companies inquiring about conditions affecting their future. And excellent research has been done and will doubtless continue to be done by organizations like Stanford Research Institute, RAND Corporation, the American Management Association, and the National Industrial Conference Board.

These sources of knowledge have been used profitably in long-range planning. I know of no company, university, or public agency that does not wish it could take the guesswork out still further; yet its officers can generally be thankful that they have as much data to work with as they do. Equally encouraging, vigorous efforts are being made all over the country to improve the quality and reliability of environmental knowledge.

KNOWLEDGE OF DESIRABLE GOALS AND OBJECTIVES

This type of knowledge has to do with the goals that managers plan *for*—their choice of objectives, the end results sought, the conditions desired. This kind of knowledge is not limited to broad corporate goals. It may include activities close to the operations of individual groups—for example, an assumption about the quality and amount of management control that is desirable in a manufacturing division (and which may enter into a long-range manpower plan), or about the ways in which different departments should work together (and which may affect the planned steps and procedures for a marketing or research program).

As an illustration, some years ago a manufacturer of industrial equipment was plagued with law suits for damage to employees' health as a result of conditions in the foundries. The chief executive pondered these claims for a while and came to the conclusion that the company should seek to go far beyond the minimum standards of health and safety for workers. He made this decision during a period of lean profits, reaching it not because it was being forced on him but because he felt it was the "right" thing to do. The knowledge behind his decision, and behind the values that motivated him, is an example of goals knowledge. It is interesting to note that if this executive had used only knowledge of the types previously described —methods and conditions—he would not have made the same decision. Methods knowledge alone would have dictated a plan of legal action and defensive measures. Environmental knowledge would probably have indicated some kind of compromise plan—the advantage of improving working conditions to some extent, perhaps, but not of going to the limits envisaged by the chief executive.

Similarly, when a company plans its collective bargaining strategy in a certain way, or bases its manufacturing strategy on the achievement of certain steps in collective bargaining, it draws on knowledge about what is desirable in the way of labor relations. (Note how Oram does this in his chapter on "Long-Range Planning in Industrial Relations.") Or when a company decides to diversify in a different way, it draws on information about the kind of company it should be, the kinds of risks and protective measures that are desirable, the amount of return that should be assured the stockholders, and so on. Other examples are given in Part II of this book.

Admittedly, values often enter into such decisions as well as facts. But values themselves are likely to be based on information, at least in part. Take the case of the son who inherits a family business and goes on believing, as his father did, that the goal of the firm should be to make a certain textile. The son's image of the family business is obviously associated with a value; yet he will be able to justify that value by certain information learned over the years—e.g., the past goals of the company, advantages of a "shoemaker-stick-to-your-last-product" philosophy, first-hand observation of what is good for employees, etc. This information may be fragmentary and inadequate; yet it does enter into the son's long-range thinking.

How important is such information? It is the most important of the three types. Knowledge about the mechanics of planning can help make planning efficient, but what good is that if the plans are directed toward the wrong targets? At the same time, this type of knowledge is the least distinct of the three, since it is mixed in with values and feelings that may not be rationally arrived at. When a decision is based more on the nonrational elements than on the rational, one should not leap to conclusions and criticize the decision makers for lack of thought. Were they given ample opportunities to *consider* objective factual data?

Inadequate State

How adequate is goals knowledge today? I think it is generally in short supply. This answer may come as a surprise to those who equate long-range planning with forecasting, but as readers of this volume have already learned, there is a deep and important difference between the two. Forecasting may enter into the planning process, but at most it is only a part of it.

Evidence of the inadequacy of our knowledge about desirable goals and objectives is not hard to find. As one example, take the diversification fad. I am told on good authority that the reason for many failures of diversification moves to pay off as expected is that companies in an industry play follow-the-leader. They all rush in the same direction for new acquisitions because they accept the lead company's standard of what is desirable, while the lead company in turn has relied on the conventional notion that a company should diversify into fields that are technologically related to its original one. This notion is very common indeed in the literature. How often do we find a contrasting philosophy written up? Quite infrequently, in my experience. Yet we know that a great many companies have succeeded in using diversification patterns radically different from the "related business" one. Considerable knowledge that we *might* have on diversification standards seems never to have been communicated.

To take another example, earlier this year I attended some case discussions on publishing strategy. The publishers attending the meetings were debating what the "guinea-pig" company in the case should do—whether, for instance, it should base its strategy on doing what it had been doing in the past, only better, or whether it should branch out into a new publishing venture. During the course of the meetings a good deal of information was passed back and forth on what was and what was not wrong with the case-company's method of operations, but when it came to the question of whether or not a strategic change was desirable, the conversation thinned out into unsupported opinions. Little or no evidence was adduced as to why it would be desirable in such a situation to stand pat, or why it would be desirable to diversify into a new operation. The reason for this was simple: Such information did not exist in written form. No doubt the conferees could have produced many poignant memories about strategic moves that had or had not been found desirable, but the knowledge was personal and subjective.

Turning to a quite different kind of example, consider the question of managerial behavior. I am impressed by how many times close observers of executive action have found that a man delegates in this particular way or that, or makes his policy decisions in such-and-such a way, because he *is not aware that there are other acceptable ways*. When, as a consequence, the executive bases his planning on certain assumptions about organizational behavior, with no careful consideration of alternative assumptions that might be useful, we should not be surprised. Some careful, well-researched studies have been made of the long-term effects of contrasting leadership patterns,[3] and they are available to managers; but they have not circulated in management circles nearly as freely as have the more numerous books and articles describing techniques, conditions, and personal success credos.

All this is symptomatic of a fairly general state of affairs. In textbooks and professional journals on management one finds many more competent discussions of, say, forecasting or quality control than of policy making or case histories of policy making. In schools of business the emphasis (with some conspicuous exceptions) is more on conceptual methods and analytical approaches for solving problems than on the formulation of goals and problems. In company training programs one is far more likely to hear of a good session on selling than on departmental or business objectives. And in promotion practices there is considerably more stress on how well the man-

[3] See, for example, Rensis Likert, *New Patterns of Management* (New York, McGraw-Hill Book Company, Inc., 1961).

agerial candidate has carried out assignments than on how well he has selected and conceived them.

NEEDS FOR THE FUTURE

What are the implications of this state of knowledge for the future of long-range planning?

1. *We need more emphasis in the literature on desirable goals and strategies.* Business executives themselves could make a real contribution to this need by releasing more concrete cases and examples from their companies' experience; writers and editors could more aggressively seek out such experience. When a management group is debating whether or not to decentralize operations, branch into unrelated businesses, or set higher profit goals, it should not have to rely so much on guesswork. It should be able to draw on a fair sampling of experience just as it does when it ponders how to analyze a market trend or increase productivity. In the literature of politics and government there are many superb criticisms of various goals and policies, from free trade to a free press. Why should not the literature of management be just as rich in discussions of organizational goals?

It is true that in the literature of such professional groups as doctors, engineers, and lawyers (with whom the new "professional manager" is often compared), most of the space is devoted to problem solving, with comparatively little attention to long-range objectives; but then long-range planning does not occupy the crucial role in these professions that it does in business or education.

2. *The need is growing for broader, more penetrating kinds of research.* For instance, it seems probable that research in depth of markets will serve an increasingly important role. What kinds of products *would* the consumer like if they were made available? What kinds of needs and services *would* he buy if he could? With more access to and confidence in research that could handle such questions as these, management could generate some of the desired knowledge on its own initiative. I foresee the same increased potential for research on organizational behavior. Factual, empirical evidence on the desirable or undesirable effects of different organization patterns, for example, would surely have an impact on management thinking. Naturally, executives will not alter their values about leadership overnight, but at least they will not have to conduct their probings

and defenses in an informational vacuum. Such a vacuum exists in countless organizations today, not because no one has ever tried to fill it (some truly fine efforts have been made), but because not *enough* researchers have tried to fill it and not *enough* media people have helped in the task of persuasive communication.

3. *There needs to be more emphasis in managerial training and development on activities that stimulate thinking about aims and goals.* For instance, a company might make good use of cases that pose questions about what a department or division should be doing —and emphasize objective, open-minded, inquiring group discussion of such questions. In on-the-job coaching a boss might do well to hand out more free-wheeling assignments to subordinates—assignments that will force them to look into departmental needs and formulate them, rather than assignments that simply require subordinates to execute tasks defined by the boss. I know, too, that the long-range planning activity itself can be used profitably to this end. In at least one company with which I am familiar, one of the main jobs of the planning group, as they see it, is to seek out and define future problems and then present these findings in an arresting way to the rest of the company. Thus, operating executives' attention is continually drawn to the needs of the future, and they are continually confronted with opportunities to thrash out their views in informal "bull sessions."

4. *Organizations need better ways of identifying men who can think discerningly about goals as well as about problem solving.* Some men assimilate information and ideas about desirable objectives better than others do. Some men are better than others in seeing new implications in data. Some men succeed better than others in breaking away from operating problems and thinking about the future. Who are these men? How can they be identified relatively early in their careers so that they can be given opportunities to develop their talents? Must a company, federal agency, college, or military organization wait until it has promoted a man to the top to learn whether he is a first-rate strategist?

Unfortunately, our traditions in education and training are not altogether helpful here. In college courses students are generally graded on how well they work with assigned data, not on how well they think ahead with bits and pieces of information. The A student *may* have this ability, but if so, it is not usually implied by his grades.

It is significant, too, in my opinion, that our IQ and aptitude tests measure the capacity to assimilate, manipulate, apply, and feed back —not the capacity to see and organize for new needs and goals.

College grades, achievement tests, ability to carry out the boss's orders, "trouble-shooting" skills, and ability to solve operating problems—all these are therefore inadequate for measuring all-around long-range planning ability. Until better ways are found of assessing "thinking ahead"-type skills, the selection and promotion of good planners must continue to be on a wait-and-see basis.

The knowledge we need for better long-range planning will be forthcoming. It will come through businessmen, public officials, researchers, teachers, and journalists. It will be reported in magazines, books, speeches, cases, and films. It will be used in managerial operations and in the classroom. It will add excitement to administration. It will focus more attention on the aims of organizations, as opposed to the mechanics of operations. It will enhance the power and prestige of the manager. He will come to be seen more clearly in his role as creator, innovator, architect, and coordinator. He will more readily be seen as more than a merchant, if he is in business, and more than a politician, if he is in government.

Index